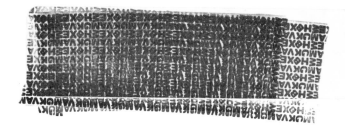

STANDARD CONVERSIONS

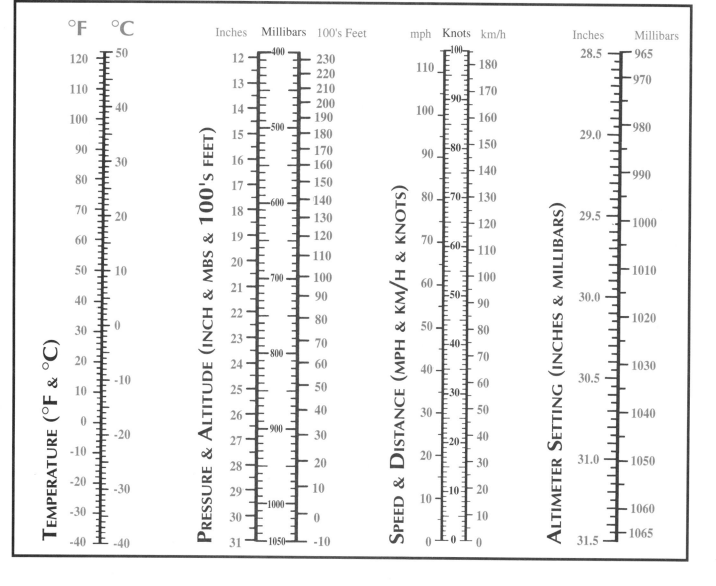

TEMPERATURE (°F & °C)

°F	°C
120	50
110	40
100	
90	30
80	
70	20
60	
50	10
40	
30	0
20	
10	-10
0	
-10	-20
-20	-30
-30	
-40	-40

PRESSURE & ALTITUDE (INCH & MBS & 100'S FEET)

Inches	Millibars	100's Feet
12	400	230
		220
13		210
14		200
	500	190
15		180
16		170
		160
17		150
18	600	140
19		130
		120
20		110
21	700	100
		90
22		80
23		70
24	800	60
25		50
26		40
27	900	30
28		20
29		10
30	1000	0
31	1050	-10

SPEED & DISTANCE (MPH & KM/H & KNOTS)

mph	Knots	km/h
110	100	180
		170
100	90	160
		150
90	80	140
80	70	130
		120
70	60	110
60		100
	50	90
50	40	80
		70
40	30	60
30	20	50
		40
20		30
	10	20
10		10
0	0	0

ALTIMETER SETTING (INCHES & MILLIBARS)

Inches	Millibars
28.5	965
	970
	980
29.0	
	990
29.5	1000
	1010
30.0	1020
30.5	1030
	1040
31.0	1050
	1060
31.5	1065

Nature's Tale: "The crab was the gull's supper"

THE ULTIMATE OUTDOORS BOOK

To contact the publisher address you correspondence
to: Paul Tawrell,
         Post Office 866,
         Shelburne, Vermont   05482
Please visit your local bookstore to buy your own
copy of this book. If they do not have it in stock,
please have them order it for you. If you find it
difficult obtaining a copy please order from:

In the United States

Telephone Orders: 1-800-356-9315

Fax Orders: 1-800-242-0036

E-mail: UpperAcces@aol.com

In Canada

Telephone Orders: 1-613-525-1313

Fax Orders: 1-613-525-5218

Telephone Orders: 1-514-671-3888

Fax Orders: 1-514-671-2121

In Europe

Telephone Orders: 33.1.43.54.49.02

Fax Orders: 33.1.43.54.39.12

CAMPING & WILDERNESS SURVIVAL

PAUL TAWRELL

THE ULTIMATE OUTDOORS BOOK

PAUL TAWRELL

SHELBURNE, VERMONT   GREEN VALLEY, ONTARIO

THE ULTIMATE OUTDOORS BOOK

Graphic Design
Ler Watt
Illustrations
Melita Fechner

Printed in Canada

Tawrell, Paul
        Camping & Wilderness Survival: the ultimate outdoors book

Includes bibliographical references and index.
ISBN 1-896713-00-9

        1. Camping. 2. Outdoor life. 3. Wilderness survival. I. Title. II. Title: Camping and wilderness survival.

GV200.5.T39 1996   796.54   C95-920807-0

Notice

The aim of this book is to entertain its readers, to alert readers to the potential dangers and emergencies that might occur in the wilderness and how to avoid them. This knowledge might help a person survive or avoid a difficult situation. Some of the activities and survival methods may be inappropriate for certain individuals due to their lack of forest and outdoor skills, material, physical condition, or other handicaps. Local laws and private property should be respected and the security of other outdoor travelers should always be kept in mind. *Some of the techniques outlined in this book can cause serious injury and the publisher and author disclaim any liability.*

Readers are advised to read and follow usage instructions included with camping and survival products that they buy. A First Aid course is a *must* for a well rounded knowledge of the outdoors and this book does not attempt to replace this course nor the techniques taught in a First Aid course.

PAUL TAWRELL
SHELBURNE, VERMONT   GREEN VALLEY, ONTARIO

CONTENTS

INTRODUCTION

This book has been written to help you acquire skills to enjoy the wilderness. It tells you how to travel, make a camp, understand your environment, and choose equipment.

In the case of an emergency it will help you find water, food, shelter from the weather, and care for yourself if you are sick or injured.

The information is treated in topics such as *Signals, Animals, and Weather,* and then applied specifically to such special activities as *Summer Hiking, Desert Travel, Water Travel, and Car Travel.*

Individual skills such as *Maps and Compass, First Aid*, and *Mountain Climbing,* provide a good foundation on which to build your knowledge of the outdoors. This information will help you enjoy the outdoors while at the same time alert you to the risks that you might encounter.

Survival topics such as *Woodcraft, Fire Making, Food and Water, Shelter,* and *Navigational Techniques* are covered in detail. The book gives you a wide overview of nature and your surroundings so as to help you improve your ability to improvise and respond to your immediate situation.

You can remain alive anywhere in the world if you keep your wits. Nature and the elements are neither your friend nor your enemy but it is your determination to live and your ability to make nature work for you that are the deciding factors. *Camping & Wilderness Survival* attempts to give you and your family a chance to enjoy the outdoors.

GETTING LOST CHAPTER 1

It is easy to get lost and this book is intended to give you an overview of the wilderness, an understanding of your environment, and how you can use the material available to survive.

Before entering a wilderness Area or abandoning your Car

•

Tell someone where you are going or leave a note indicating where you have gone, which path you are taking, and when you will be back.
Do it every time even if entering a familiar area for a short period. You can break a leg a few hundred feet from home as well as 10 miles (16 km) from camp.

•

Always carry survival tools as a hunting knife, compass, matches in a waterproof container, and a windbreaker or poncho.

•

For longer trips take a survival kit as listed in this book.

Knowledge

is the first step in overcoming fear.
Knowledge can be amplified by the confidence in your equipment, use of the equipment, group interaction, and survival techniques. The understanding of the smells, noises, physical characteristics of land, weather, and your relationship with them will also be of great help.

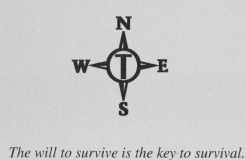

The will to survive is the key to survival.

AVOID GETTING LOST

When traveling make it a habit to:

• Check your approximate location on the map and try to compare its markings with your surroundings. Do this every 15 to 20 minutes.
• Direction of the wind.
• Watch where you cast a shadow to make sure you are not walking in circles and that you are not misreading the direction on your compass.
• How long have you traveled and estimate the distance covered.
• How do the contours of the land compare to the contours on the map?
• Major landmarks as large hills, rivers or large trees, that have been passed.
• If following a trail and somehow you lose your direction, do not just walk back but remember your "lost" position by looking for an identifiable landmark and head back. Leave markings as broken branches or blazes at "lost" position to find your way back. Make sure that you are following a blaze and not an abrasion on a tree caused by a falling branch or gnawed by an animal as a moose or bear. Man made blazes will usually have a mechanical feature as a straight cut, etc. See *Signal Chapter.*

Food Rationing

Immediately start rationing and do not eat any food on the first day. Limit the intake of water if it is not readily available . Eat food in small amounts at a time and eat slowly. Trap small animals, catch insects, and find edible plants to supplement your rations.

HYGIENE

Good physical health is essential to survival.

• The *Cooking, Fishing, and Trapping Chapters* outline methods of catching, cooking and storing food.
• The *First Aid Chapter* highlights insect stings, snake and animal bites, cleanliness, drowning, etc. The *First Aid Chapter* also outlines methods to prevent disease and treatment of injuries.
• *Injuries:* Even minor injuries are potentially serious as they can become infected. Carefully treat every cut, sprain, or bruise.
• *Bleeding:* Limit bleeding by the methods outlined in the *First Aid Chapter.*
• *Blisters:* Avoid blisters on your feet as they will restrict your movement. Never miss a chance to dry your socks by the fire.
• *Insects:* The ferocity, persistence and quantity of insects in the bush are always an insurmountable surprise. Small insects as black flies can be a major problem. Short exposure to them can make life unbearable.
• Follow the simple rules of personal hygiene to protect yourself against disease and injury.
• Brush your teeth using table salt or baking soda as a substitute for toothpaste. If you do not have a toothbrush chew a green twig to a pulpy consistency. Rinse your mouth after each meal.
• Use soap and water to keep clean. Special attention should be given to areas on your body that are susceptible to rash and fungus infection; between your toes, your crotch and scalp. If soap is not available use wood ash as a substitute. A daily shower with hot water and soap is ideal. If this is impossible, keep your hands as clean as possible and sponge *and* dry your face, armpits, crotch, and feet at least once a day.
• Keep your clothing, especially your underclothing and socks, as clean and dry as possible. If laundering is impossible shake out your clothing and expose them to the sun and air every day. Clothing should be kept clean as clean clothing does not wear out as fast and cleanliness will reduce your exposure to rashes and infections.
• Have up to date immunization before you travel.
• Guard against heat illness, cold, windchill, hypothermia and fatigue.
• *Sunburn and Windburn:* Severe sunburn can occur summer or winter. In the late winter months the sun can produce a severe burn in a short time. Wear a hat, sunglasses, long sleeved clothing and take advantage of the shade.

IF YOU GET LOST

If You Are Alone

- The shock of realizing that you are lost can be mentally crippling but you have to hope for the best and plan for the worst. Recall survival techniques or training and expect them to work as it will increase your chances for success by increasing your confidence in that you *can* survive.

- *Stay "Put"*. If you're not sure of the way out and people know you are missing. Remain calm. Usually it is best to stay where you are and build a shelter. This is especially true if you are lacking food or are injured. Staying will give you a chance to conserve your energy.

- Carefully study your surroundings. Find water, if possible an open area for a signal fire, a sheltered area for a camp, and wood. If the wood supply permits, keep a *small* fire going, at all times, for a signal fire.

- Build a simple safe comfortable shelter and fire as quickly as possible.

- Once well sheltered and warm form a plan. A survival plan will alleviate your fear. Your confidence and morale will increase.

- Be calm. Take it easy and think of how to implement your action plan. Establish where you are by identifying landmarks and compass directions.

- Take stock of your situation once your signal fire has been built, your campfire, and shelter is ready. Mentally list everything you have on you. Empty your pockets and use your imagination to discover how your belongings can be used. *This book gives many original survival ideas which are based upon common items in your pockets.*

- Any shiny object can be used to attract the attention of passing aircraft. See the *Signaling Chapter* for more details.

- Do not be too eager to find your way out until you have adapted to your environment and have the basic survival necessities of food, water, and shelter. Unnecessary risks will be taken if you are careless and impatient.

If in a Group

- A group should *chose* a leader and assign responsibilities to all individuals so that all have a responsibility for the rescue of the group. Always try to determine and use special skills offered by members of the group. *The leader can consult with the group but he has to make the decisions.* Above all, the leader must at all times avoid the appearance of indecision.

- Make sure that no member of the group is left on his own as he might be in a depression. *Negative ideas should be squashed as soon as possible.*

- Panic, confusion, and disorganization are minimized by good leadership.

- Problems usually occur in a group. These problems can be due to fatigue, hunger, close quarters, cold, and strategic decisions that have to be made.

- Develop a feeling of team work and stress that each man depends on the other individuals for survival. Teamwork fosters higher morale and unity as each member feels the support and strength of the group.

Intestinal Sickness

Common diarrhea, food poisoning, and other intestinal diseases are common if you are in the wilderness especially if you are trying to survive on a limited diet and primitive storage conditions. To guard against discomfort:

- Keep the body and hands clean. Keep fingers out of your mouth. Avoid handling food with your hands. Wash hands after handling wild foods.

- Avoid eating raw foods, especially those grown on or in the ground. Wash and peel fruit. See *Cooking Chapter* on how to store food. Eat food right after preparation especially meat and fish. Cook all food *well done*.

- Purify drinking water. *See Summer Hiking Chapter.*

- Sterilize eating utensils by boiling in water or heating over a flame.

- Keep insects and other vermin off your food and drink.

- Keep camping area clean and food away from camp.

- Human waste should be kept away from camp site and water supply.

If you develop vomiting or diarrhea rest and stop eating solid foods. Drink water in small amounts at frequent intervals. Maintain normal salt intake. See the *First Aid Chapter* for more information on salt requirements.

A marsh is a bad place to get lost.

FEAR AND PANIC

Panic can cause a person to act without thinking.

- To feel fear is normal and necessary. It is nature's way of giving you that extra shot of energy. A caveman would sleep and at the first unusual sound would bound up and get out of danger's way. This rapid response is due to an extra charge of adrenaline and it is released by the body because of fear.

- Undue fear is usually caused by the unknown. Look carefully at a situation to determine if your fear is justified. *Upon investigation you will usually find many of your fears are unreal.* The dangerous noise might be a squirrel dropping a nut falling from a tree and bouncing through the leaves.

- If you are injured pain might turn fear into panic. Panic can cause a person to act without thinking and go running off into the forest.

- Panic can be caused by loneliness which can lead to hopelessness, thoughts of suicide and carelessness.

- Keep your mind busy and plan for survival. Recognizing the signs of fear and panic will help you overcome their devastating effect. Develop a plan for the next few days. This will raise your morale. Make sure that your doorway faces east towards the rising sun. Get up as soon as it is light and get busy.

Self confidence can be established by the knowledge of survival techniques and understanding the wilderness. This knowledge serves to lessen fear and prevent panic and irrational panic decisions from being made.

Use your Imagination and Improvise

- Improvise to improve the situation. This will give you more control and raise your morale.

- Remember your goal is to get out alive. Raise your morale by "dreaming" of the time after you "get out alive" will help you value life now.

- Conserve your health and strength. Illness or injury will greatly reduce your chance of survival.

- Hunger, cold, and fatigue lower your efficiency, stamina, and *will make you careless.* You will realize that your low spirits are the result of your physical condition and not danger.

- Improvising includes eating insects and other unusual foods.

LIST OF LISTS CHAPTER 2

Basic Wilderness Emergency Kit

Brass wire
Brown sugar
Candle or lantern
Canteen
Compass
Emergency blanket (poncho)
Extra pair of prescription glasses
Fire starter
First aid kit
Fishing kit
Flashlight & batteries
Flare
GI can opener
Heavy knife or ax
High energy food
Poncho
Mess kit
Razor blades
Rope 12'-24' (4-8 cm)
Sewing kit
Signal mirror
Small pot
String
Tea bags, broth cubes
Tube tent
Water bottle
Waterproof matches
Waterproof match container
Water purifying tablets or filtration system
Whistle

Emergency Fishing Kit

35mm film container for storage and as a float.
Different sized hooks.
15' of monofilament line 10 lb test.
Rubber bands.
Sinkers.
Sewing needle.
Waterproof emery paper to sharpen hooks.

FIRST AID

See your physician for advice.

- First Aid kit
- Insect repellant
- Salt tablets
- Table salt
- Rubbing alcohol
- Bandages
- Aspirin
- Tweezers
- Feminine napkins
- Medical thermometer
- Snakebite kit
- Moleskin for sore feet
- Baking soda
- Distilled water
- Cotton applicators
- Petroleum jelly
- Mild antiseptic
- Thick blunt needle
- Scissors
- Aspirin
- Sterile gauze dressings, individually wrapped (2"x2" and 4"x4").
- Piece of clean folded old bed sheet
- Roll of 1/2" wide adhesive tape
- Oral antibiotics for infections
- Nausea or vomiting tablets
- Motion sickness tablets
- Diarrhea medication
- Pepto Bismol - for traveler's diarrhea (turista)
- Aromatic spirits of ammonia
- Mild antiseptic
- Steristrips for cuts (hold edges of cut together)
- Suturing kit (see your physician)

CHILD'S DAY PACK

- Whistle to use in case of an emergency.
- Water and snacks. Teach the child to keep some for an emergency.
- Child sun block.
- Quality sunglasses.
- Insect repellent not have a higher than 30% DEET.
- Flashlight: A model that is easy to use.
- Child's own first aid kit.
- Garbage bag for poncho. Be careful for suffocation.
- Simple sturdy compass.
- Watch.
- Map of the trail showing the route and the destination point. Major features highlighted.
- Tube tent.
- One time use camera.
- *See article on hiking with a child.*

Electrical Current While Traveling

The voltage, cycle, and electrical plug can vary from country to country and sometimes even within the country. Buy the required adaptor or adaptor kit before you leave on your trip.

Area	Voltage
North America	110V
Caribbean	110V-220V
Europe	220V
except Andorra	125V
Canary Is.	110V
Turkey	220V
Former Yugoslavia	220V
Former USSR	220V

Before Leaving Home

- Leave keys and itinerary with a friend.
- Obtain permits (fishing, camping, hunting) if required.
- Passport and visas.
- Fill prescriptions and have copies.
- Mail on hold at Post Office
- Stop newspaper delivery.
- Traveler's medical insurance.
- Vaccinations and/or inoculations.

Take With You

- Address book
- Binoculars
- Camera and film
- Credit cards
- Drivers license
- Electrical converter or adapter
- Flashlight
- Itinerary
- Maps
- Money belt
- Padlock
- Pen
- Short wave radio
- Soap
- Traveler's checks
- Walking shoes
- Wallet

Camping

- Air mattress
- Backpack
- Bottle opener
- Can opener
- Candle/lantern
- Compass
- Cookware and utensils
- Cutlery
- Day pack or small fanny pack.
- Disposable butane lighter
- Drinking cup
- First aid kit
- Flashlight/extra batteries
- Foam pad
- Knife
- Nylon cord
- Plastic bags for storage
- Plastic bags (re-sealable)
- Plastic containers
- Pot gripper
- Repair kits
- Scissors
- Sewing kit
- Signal mirror
- Sleeping bag
- Stove / fuel
- Tarpaulin, ground sheet, or poncho
- Tent
- Towel
- Washing liquids
- Water bottle
- Waterproof matches
- Waterproof pouch
- Water purifier or tablets
- Whistle

Summer Travel
- Cotton hat
- Light colored cotton shorts and shirt
- Insect repellent
- Light walking shoes
- Sunglasses
- Sun lotion
- Towels

Cold Weather Travel
- Balaklava
- Emergency blanket
- Outerwear (poncho)
- Scarf
- Survival candles
- Thermal underwear
- Warm hat
- Warm parka
- Warm waterproof boots
- Wool gloves
- Wool socks
- Wool sweater

Food
- Chocolate bars
- Freeze dried food
- Raisins & brown sugar
- Salt
- Tea & broth cubes
- Water treating tablets

Personal Items
- Aspirin
- Baking Soda
- Cold medication
- Dental floss
- Diarrhea medication
- Ear plugs
- Extra glasses
- Laxative
- Moleskin for feet
- Motion sickness medication
- Personal hygiene items
- Personal medications
- Prescription drugs
- Shampoo
- Shaving kit
- Biodegradable Soap
- Toiletries
- Toothbrush and paste
- Vitamins

Camping Gear
- Back Pack
- Citronella candle
- Compass and maps
- Cot or mat
- Emergency candles
- Fire starter
- Flashlight or lantern
- Pocket knife
- Sleeping bag & pad
- Shelter (tube tent)
- Stove & fuel
- Tent pegs

Cooking Gear
- Canteen & mess kit
- Knife
- GI can opener
- Plastic bags
- Utensil kit

Rock Climbing
- Helmet
- Rock hammer
- Hammer holster
- Pitons
- Carabiners
- Chocks and nuts
- Kletterschuhe
- Swami belt
- Rope

Ice & Snow Climbing
- Helmet
- Cagoule (Balaklava)
- Extra socks
- Gaiters
- Mittens, Fingerless mittens
- Slings, rappel anchors, runners, seats, etc.
- Rock pitons
- Tubular ice screws
- Rucksack
- Crampons
- Emergency shelter
- Boots
- Rope
- Carabiners
- Alpine hammer
- Hammer holster
- Ice ax
- Down jacket

DESERT SURVIVAL

PLANNING A DAY TRIP

Plan an Itinerary
Make a detailed plan as to where you are going and where you plan to stay. Leave a copy of the plan with someone and tell them when you will report back to them. If you do not report back on time they will report you as "lost" to the authorities. When traveling do not leave the road or track because you will find that cacti and rocks all look the same if you are lost. If you have any problems en route or change your plan inform your contact.

Food and Water
Bring at least two or three days of water. 4 quarts per person per day and use it sparingly.

Clothing
Wear the right clothing and be prepared for cold nights.

Accessories
Bring sunscreen (use at least SPF 30), hats, bandana, and sunglasses. For tent anchors use "Ziploc" bags filled with sand. Place them *inside* self standing tents to hold them down.

Car Supplies
Gasoline in a five gallon jerry can and make sure that the inside of the can is not rusted as the rust flakes might block your fuel system. Extra radiator fluid, fan belt, radiator hose, distilled water for the battery. Shovel with at least a three foot handle. A hydraulic jack, pulley and rope to disengage the car. If you are driving off the road you will encounter sand and you will require high-axles, wide tires and preferably a four wheel drive car.

Walking
Walking on sand is difficult as you have the tendency to slide back. The energy required for one mile on sand is equivalent to two miles on regular terrain. Wear boots and heavy socks as the sand is so hot that it can cause burns.

Desert Survival
Survival items for the desert:
- Mirror for signaling.
- Magnifying glass to a start fire.
- Water purification tablets.
- Brass wire for trapping.
- Collapsible water container.
- 4 quarts of water per person per day.
- Fishing line to construct shelter out of brush.
- Hat with a wide brim. Sunglasses.
- Loose fitting light colored clothing that will cover the body *and arms*. Clothing made of natural materials as cotton or wool. Wool blanket.
- Sturdy boots with wool socks.

CAMPING

CAR TRAVEL CHAPTER 3

Volkswagen Thing

Volkswagen Beetle

Jeep CJ 5

Jeep Commando

EMERGENCY CAR ACCESSORIES

- A quality car jack can have many uses.
- Chains for tires especially in sandy, muddy and snowy areas.
- Warm clothing and boots.
- Methyl hydrate added to water to make windshield washer.
- Tire pump, either electric or a quality foot pump.
- Flares, rectangular reflectors, and a flashlight.
- First aid kit which should be inside the car and not in the trunk.
- Fire extinguisher.
- Dried fruit and chocolates.
- Maps and car repair manual.
- First Aid Kit.
- Booster cables.
- Shovel made of metal which can be used as a shovel or for traction for a skidding tire.
- Set of wrenches, screwdrivers, tire repair kit, one inner tube.
- Oil for car and a jerry can of gasoline.
- Gas antifreeze or methyl hydrate in cold areas.
- CB radio with a quality antenna (Channel 9 for emergencies).

DRIVING AND SURVIVING

Drive slowly on back roads especially if your car is low as you might pierce your oil pan while going over boulders.

To drive over soft spots and to increased traction you might have to slightly deflate your tires. When you park cover your car with a blanket as this will reduce the heat inside the car. When sunlight goes through glass the wavelength changes and the heat waves from this light cannot leave the inside of the car. For this reason a cover should be placed on the outside of the glass to keep the inside cool. Do not leave animals in a car.

In general if your car breaks down on a traveled route stay with it as it:

- Contains your survival tools and water.
- Has items that can be used for survival.
- Side mirrors for signaling.
- Hubcaps to collect water and cooking.
- Spare tire to burn as a rescue signal because black smoke can be seen over a large distance.
- Seats can be used as a bed.
- Car provides shade.
- Battery can be used to light a fire with the cigarette lighter or two wires.
- If car still works or battery is strong headlights can be used for night time signaling.
- Battery can be used to magnetize a needle to use as a compass.

If you leave your car make sure of your route and where you will get your next drink of water. Scavenge your car before you leave but do not take too many heavy things.

Take:

- Mirrors for signaling.
- Seat covers to cover head or use as blanket.
- Leave a note in the car to indicate direction of travel and leave blazes on your route.
- Water.
- Fuel to help you start a fire during the desert's cold nights.

Do not leave during the heat of the day.

See the previous chapter and the Desert Travel Chapter for more information.

Estimating Distance While Driving

Objects look much closer than they actually are when:

- Looking up or down a hill.
- There is a bright light on the object being looked at.
- Looking across water, snow or flat sand.
- The air is clear.

Objects look much farther away than they actually are when:

- The light is poor.
- The color of the object blends with the background.
- The object is at the end of a long avenue or highway.
- You are looking over undulating ground.

Chemical Burns

While traveling the most probable cause of an acid burn would be from the car battery or from cleaning fluids. *See the First Aid Chapter for more information.*

Electrical Burns

Electrical burns do not look too serious but the tissue under the small skin wound can have been destroyed. *See the First Aid Chapter for more information.*

Did the driver make it?

DRIVING IN A SANDSTORM

- Pull off the road and out of the way of traffic.
- Turn off the engine as you will clog your air filter with sand.
- If possible cover your windshield because a violent sand storm can 'sand' the glass.
- Park your car so that the engine does not face into the wind as sand will infiltrate into all parts of the engine.

Driving in Remote Desert Country

Before leaving on a trip in the desert, check:
- Battery.
- Radiator and coolant quality and level.

Take:
- First Aid Kit.
- Flares.
- Extra radiator coolant.
- Cooling hoses.
- Spare tire(s), tubes, and repair kits.
- Air pump and small hydraulic jack.
- Spare fan belts.
- Fire extinguisher.
- Extra motor oil and check the manufacturers specifications as to SAE for hot weather.
- Extra air filters as you might want to change it every few hundred miles if it is dusty.
- Set of tools.
- Spot light for night repairs or signalling.

Special Equipment for Desert Travel

- Shovel and ax.
- Wool blanket.
- Sturdy car cover.
- Winch with a heavy rope.
- Wide tires.
- 4 quarts of water per person per day.
- Two planks to help in releasing the car from soft sand.

FALLEN POWER LINES

Power lines by themselves are not dangerous as long as the object touching them is not grounded. You can see birds sitting on power lines and not getting a shock. If someone touches a "hot" power line *and at the same time* is standing on wet ground or is 'grounded', they complete the circuit and the electricity flows through the person causing an electrical shock.

In a Car With a Fallen Power Line on the Car

If a power line has fallen across a car assume that the line is live. The rubber tires of the car form a satisfactory insulation between the fallen wire and the ground. The people in the car are safe as long as they *do not touch the metal frame of the car and the ground - at the same time*. This would bypass the insulation of the car's tires. The person should stay in the car if help is on its way. If the car is on fire, in a dangerous location, or no help is on the way then the occupants can jump clear of the car making sure that they are *not touching the car and the ground at the same time*.

WINTER DRIVING

Three things are important:
1. Get car started.
2. Keep it on the road.
3. Get it to stop.

Getting Car Started

Animals on the Road are Hard to See
When driving in the summer watch for large animals as deer and moose. They might wander across a road or highway especially at night. Hitting a moose at high speed will demolish your car and you might get killed. In some states and provinces the local authorities, especially in state parks, might charge you, per pound, for the dead animal and you do not get to keep it.

If the door lock is frozen, heat the keyhole with a match and insert the key but do not force. If it still does not work use a lock deicer. Make sure that the battery retains its charge, the fan belt is in good condition and tight enough to turn the alternator, the battery terminals are clean and covered with petroleum jelly. Make sure the spark plugs, rotor, distributor, and cables are in good condition.

- In very cold climates use 5W30 oil.
- Add gas line antifreeze to your gasoline.
- Test the antifreeze in the radiator.

Staying on the Road

- Do you have low mileage, four season tires or winter tires?
- Do not tailgate as you might require *more than* double the distance to slow down and stop.
- Do not pass the slowpoke in front of you - yes, he does own the road - if you try to pass you might drive onto a snow patch or black ice and end up in the ditch.
- On a slippery road do not give your steering wheel any quick twitches as it might send you out of control. Hold the steering wheel with both hands.
- Watch for frozen spots on bridges and below underpasses.
- When going into a skid, turn the wheels in the same direction as the back wheels are going. Do not react in any sudden fashion, *pump the brakes slowly* to avoid a skid. If you have to, you might want to go into a ditch which is better than hitting a car head on.
- Have a shovel that is long enough to reach under a car and strong enough to penetrate packed snow.
- Check your tire pressure. In very cold weather the tire will have a lower profile as the required pressure will have less volume.

In certain mountain areas you might want to or have to use chains.

Chains are classified as:

SAE class S for passenger and light truck vehicles.

SAE class U for vehicles with larger wheel wells and clearance.

SAE class W for larger clearance vehicles and trucks.

Make sure the chain size is for your car model. Chains on a car give better traction than four-wheel drive cars with the best snow tires.

Stopping the Car

If you have considered all the above cross your fingers. There is no guarantee that a small ice patch might not show up.

SUMMER HIKING CHAPTER 4

THE ART OF HIKING

- Plan your trip on a map and indicate rest points and your destination for the day. This destination should have shelter for the group. If not, you should plan to arrive early enough to pitch camp. The route should be chosen so that everyone can muster the require energy to have a pleasant trip. Make sure that all members of the group agree and have the physical stamina and experience to reach these objectives. Have an alternative plan in case of an emergency. Leave your itinerary with a responsible person and indicate when you will check back.

- Have a check list of all items required for the trip. These should include a first aid kit and other emergency material specific to the area, e.g. extra water in a dry area. Make sure that some individuals do not overpack.

- Start slowly so that your body gets warmed up, your feet get coordinated, your shoes are well adjusted, and your backpack is comfortable and well balanced.

- Wear comfortable and loose clothing. Have sufficient head cover. Make sure that you have the right clothing for the trip and upcoming weather.

- Pace your trip and do not rush.

- Stop periodically, remove your pack, stretch, swing your arms and check your progress on the map. If you see that you are falling behind on your trip because of difficulties in the terrain or a slow individual revise your destination for the day. Consider returning to the base camp if there are any critical problems or your ultimate destination cannot be reached in the required time. Remember if you are having difficulties at the start of a long trip things will probably get worse. A problem trip should be aborted if the moral of the group is not too positive.

- Walk in a zigzag up steep slopes. This will minimize your effort and you will be able to walk further and have less strained muscles the next day.

- When going uphill, check your footing, first place your right foot keeping your weight on your left foot. When the right foot is well and securely placed, transfer your weight to the right foot and move uphill.

- When going downhill, tighten the shoulder straps on your pack because if the pack shifts it might destabilize you. Check your boots making sure that the laces are tight enough so that your toes do not touch the front of the boot. If adjustment is difficult you might want to wear an extra pair of socks.

KNOW HOW TO FALL

When traveling assume that a problem lies ahead and prepare for any eventuality. When descending a hill or steep bank make sure that you are balanced so that you will fall backwards and into a position in which you can slide. Your fall might disengage loose rocks, earth or snow which you will have to ride downhill. Be prepared to jettison your backpack when traveling downhill.

Problems you can encounter are:

- Slippery, slimy, and moving stones while crossing a stream.
- Moss growth on rocks.
- The earth on or below a rock might give way.
- Morning dew can make rocks, logs, and grass slippery.
- Morning hoar frost can bring surprises the same as morning dew.
- Be careful when crossing a stream on a fallen log because the log might break, move, be slippery, or the rotten bark on a log slips off.
- You might sprain your ankle.

Ancient Greek Army Ration

Philon of Byzantium in 150 BC developed a ration pill for his soldiers. This pill was the size of an olive and consisted of: sesame seeds, honey, opium, poppy and squill (a root plant).
These pills provided protein (sesame), hydrocarbons (honey), alleviated pain from hunger and discomfort (opium), and a general tonic (squill). Most likely white squill which acts as an expectorant, diuretic and cough remedy (large doses of squill cause severe vomiting). Active soldiers were given two pills daily, one at 8 am and one at 4 pm.

Average Pace Per Mile

Average terrain	2112 paces per mile (1.6 km)
Rough terrain	2800 paces per mile (1.6 km)

People Can Hike

Level ground   2.5-4 miles (4-6.4 km) per hour

Method of Measuring Map Route

Bend a thin copper wire along the travel route. Straighten the wire and place it against the scale on the map.
This will probably be more accurate than adding all of those "little" numbers.

CRIME WHILE CAMPING OR HIKING

Trailhead Break-ins

Break-ins and car vandalism are a potential problem in the parking area at the head of a trail. Precautions for trailhead problems are:

- Check to see if the trailhead has a high break-in or vandalism problem. If so do not use the facilities in that area. This might motivate the local authorities to provide better protection.

- Park your car(s) in a safe spot such as a garage or ranger station and use one car (the oldest), shuttle service or taxi to deposit you at the trailhead.

- Check the parking area for evidence of vandalism and broken glass from car windows.

- If the trailhead has little traffic or is close to a main road the probability of a problems is relatively high.

- Park with the tail of the car facing the parking area. This will expose any potential tampering to other hikers who might be present.

- Remove all valuables, open the glove compartment and do not cover or seem to cover anything in the car.

- Do not hide objects in the car *when you have parked* as it would be obvious for anyone observing you from the woods. Do not hide car keys, wallets with credit cards, in the car.

- Plan your baggage, at home, so that everything can fit into your bags and leave nothing of value in your car.

HIKING WITH KIDS

FIRST TRIP WITH A CHILD

Plan a child's first hiking trip so that it is enjoyable.

- Make the trip short and within the physical abilities of the child. Have numerous stops and points of interest (e.g. pond with frogs).
- Show the child a map of the planned trip and the progress of the trip.
- Do not walk too fast. Give the child a chance to look around.
- If you fall behind on your trip do not push your child to go faster. An excursion should be well planned so that you can reach your destination point long before dusk.
- Keep safety in mind by explaining all your activities. For example, choice of a fire site, how to cross a stream, etc. Always explain the dangers involved in these activities without scaring the child.
- Develop games en route for the child. These games should help the child to appreciate nature. Some games as not walking on ants, roots; seeing wild animals, birds, and look for toads.
- Along the way give the child healthy snacks.
- Listen to the child and explain all noises and dark spots so that he is not afraid.
- Explain the hiking environment to the child and the positive ecological features.

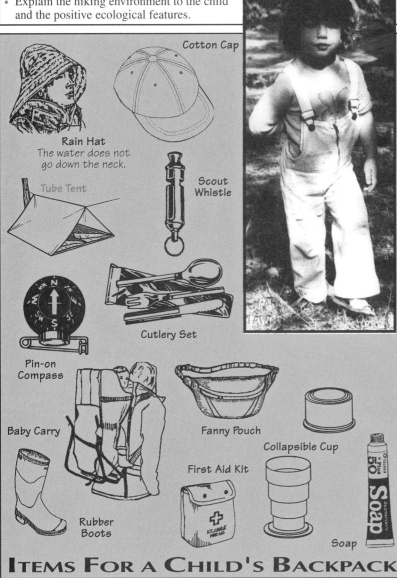

Cotton Cap

Rain Hat
The water does not go down the neck.

Tube Tent

Scout Whistle

Cutlery Set

Pin-on Compass

Baby Carry

Fanny Pouch

First Aid Kit

Collapsible Cup

Rubber Boots

Soap

ITEMS FOR A CHILD'S BACKPACK

EQUIPMENT FOR A CHILD

Clothing

Clothing should be layered so that the individual items can be gradually removed when it gets warm or applied if it gets cool. A waterproof, slightly oversize shell jacket is important as it will protect the child from the sun, rain, scratches, insects and abrasions.

A wide brimmed hat with a built in mosquito net. Rain gear is needed for rainy days. Have an extra pair of socks as one pair will certainly get wet. *The clothing should be bright colored so that the child can be easily seen on the track or in the woods.*

Footwear

Should be sturdy, well fitting, and broken in. The footwear should be lightweight, offer good support and be comfortable.

Backpacks

The day pack should fit the child. The weight the child carries should, in general, not exceed 20% of his weight. Give the child some responsibility and let him carry an important item.

KID'S BACKPACK

Day Pack

Rucksack

A child's pack should contain:

- Whistle to use in case of emergency.
- Water and snacks: Teach the child to keep some in for an emergency.
- Child sun block.
- Quality sunglasses.

Sun Glasses

- Insect repellent: Try to use a natural repellent. Make sure that any repellent does not have higher than 30% DEET content for children.
- Flashlight: A model that is easy to switch on and off.
- First Aid Kit: If a child gets scratched have him use his own kit. This will give the child a sense of pride and he will want to know how to use the items in *his* kit.
- Toilet paper and small garbage bags. The garbage bag can be used as a poncho if you encounter a sudden downpour. Make sure that the child does not suffocate in the bag.
- Simple sturdy compass.
- Watch: This will teach the adolescent the time factor in the trip and the need to get back before dusk.
- Map of the trail showing the route and the destination point. Identify the main features (bridges, streams, hills) on the map and show them to the child while traveling.
- Tube tent so the child can take a planned nap in his own tent.
- Disposable camera.

EMERGENCY KITS

BASIC EMERGENCY TRAVEL KIT

Survival Items
- Compass
- Poncho or emergency blanket
- Waterproof container of matches
- Penknife
- Fishing kit
- Brass wire
- Water bottle and purifying tablets

Tweezers + Magnifying Glass

Bandage
- A box of bandage
- Steristrips for cuts (To hold the edges of a cut together)
- Sterile gauze dressing (2"x2" & 4"x4") and a 2" wide roll
- Roll of 1/2 " wide adhesive tape
- Cotton applicators
- Suturing kit (see your physician)
- Moleskin for sore feet.

Medication (see your physician for advice)
- Oral antibiotics for infections
- Nausea or vomiting tablets
- Motion sickness tablets
- Diarrhea medication
- Pepto Bismol - for traveler's diarrhea (turista)
- Aromatic spirits of ammonia
- Aspirin
- Mild antiseptic
- Snakebite kit

General
- Petroleum jelly
- Rubbing alcohol
- Medical thermometer
- Tweezers
- Salt tablets
- GI can opener
- Insect repellent
- Baking soda
- Scissors & sewing kit
- Bottle of distilled water

Food
- Raisins in sealed packages
- Brown cane sugar in sealed packages

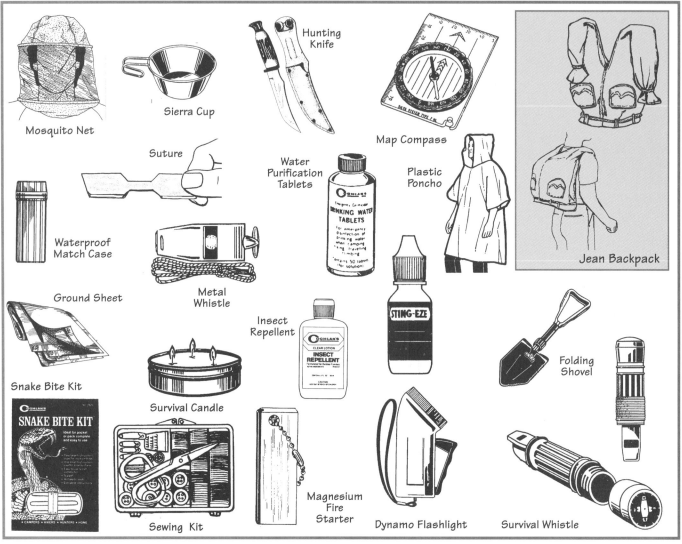

Mosquito Net

Sierra Cup

Hunting Knife

Map Compass

Suture

Water Purification Tablets

Plastic Poncho

Jean Backpack

Waterproof Match Case

Ground Sheet

Metal Whistle

Snake Bite Kit

Insect Repellent

STING-EZE

Folding Shovel

Survival Candle

SNAKE BITE KIT

Magnesium Fire Starter

Dynamo Flashlight

Survival Whistle

Sewing Kit

EMERGENCY KITS

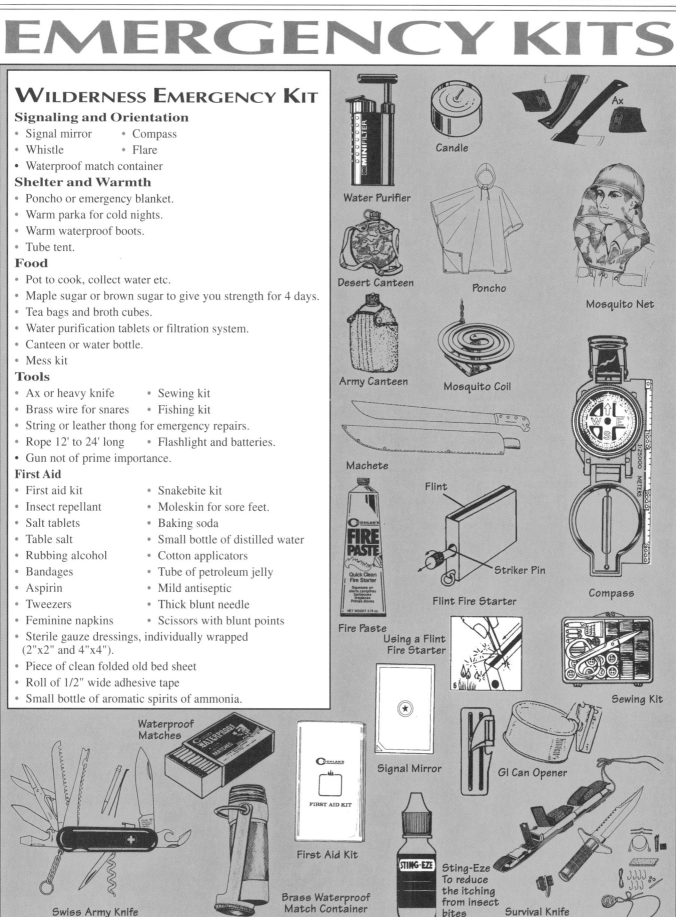

WILDERNESS EMERGENCY KIT

Signaling and Orientation
- Signal mirror
- Compass
- Whistle
- Flare
- Waterproof match container

Shelter and Warmth
- Poncho or emergency blanket.
- Warm parka for cold nights.
- Warm waterproof boots.
- Tube tent.

Food
- Pot to cook, collect water etc.
- Maple sugar or brown sugar to give you strength for 4 days.
- Tea bags and broth cubes.
- Water purification tablets or filtration system.
- Canteen or water bottle.
- Mess kit

Tools
- Ax or heavy knife
- Sewing kit
- Brass wire for snares
- Fishing kit
- String or leather thong for emergency repairs.
- Rope 12' to 24' long
- Flashlight and batteries.
- Gun not of prime importance.

First Aid
- First aid kit
- Snakebite kit
- Insect repellant
- Moleskin for sore feet.
- Salt tablets
- Baking soda
- Table salt
- Small bottle of distilled water
- Rubbing alcohol
- Cotton applicators
- Bandages
- Tube of petroleum jelly
- Aspirin
- Mild antiseptic
- Tweezers
- Thick blunt needle
- Feminine napkins
- Scissors with blunt points
- Sterile gauze dressings, individually wrapped (2"x2" and 4"x4").
- Piece of clean folded old bed sheet
- Roll of 1/2" wide adhesive tape
- Small bottle of aromatic spirits of ammonia.

Water Purifier

Candle

Ax

Desert Canteen

Poncho

Mosquito Net

Army Canteen

Mosquito Coil

Machete

Flint

Compass

Fire Paste

Flint Fire Starter

Striker Pin

Using a Flint Fire Starter

Sewing Kit

Waterproof Matches

Signal Mirror

GI Can Opener

Swiss Army Knife

Brass Waterproof Match Container

First Aid Kit

Sting-Eze To reduce the itching from insect bites

Survival Knife

Emergency Fishing Kit

- 35mm film container for storage and use as a float.
- Different sized hooks.
- 15' of monofilament line of at least 10 pound test.
- Rubber bands.
- Round sinkers.
- A sewing needle (to use monofilament to do any emergency repairs).
- Piece of waterproof emery paper to sharpen hooks.

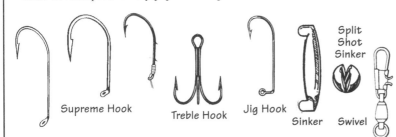

Fishing Line

Supreme Hook   Treble Hook   Jig Hook   Sinker   Swivel   Split Shot Sinker

Baking Soda

This is a standby of a camper and hiker. Major uses are:

- Foot powder.
- Toothpaste.
- **Antacid**: 1/2 teaspoon in cup of water.
- **Insect Bites**: Mix baking soda with a small quantity of water to make a paste. Apply the paste to the bite. Do not apply too much as when it dries it will fall off. A light coating will only crack.
- **Eliminate Odor**: Use on the body as deodorizer or on coolers or other food containers. Wash hands with soda after cleaning animals or fish to remove any lingering odor. To avoid having a stale odor in canteens, sprinkle some baking soda in them before storing.

Chapped Lips

To avoid having your lips chap use:

- Butter
- Edible oil
- Vaseline
- Thick catsup

Folding a Poncho

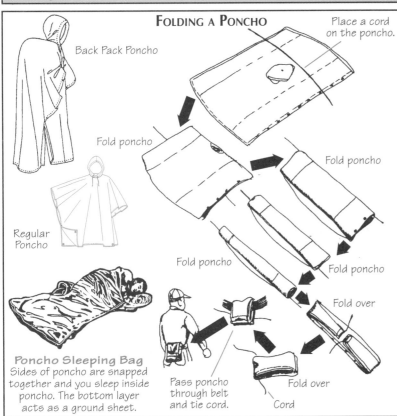

Back Pack Poncho

Regular Poncho

Place a cord on the poncho.

Fold poncho

Fold poncho

Fold poncho

Fold poncho

Fold poncho

Fold over

Fold over

Pass poncho through belt and tie cord.

Cord

Poncho Sleeping Bag
Sides of poncho are snapped together and you sleep inside poncho. The bottom layer acts as a ground sheet.

California Cyclist Beats Off Cougar

Los Angeles, California

The 27 year old cyclist, Scott Fike, said of the attack: "It was very much a shock. 'Don't think it can't happen' is what you should probably tell people."

Mr. Fike was alone and riding on a trail in the Angeles National Forest when a cougar loped up alongside. He stopped and tried to use the mountain bike as a shield but the mountain lion chewed on the bike tire, clawed the spokes and maneuvered around the cycle. Mr. Fike fell but managed to beat off the cougar with rocks, gaining enough time to get away. Mr. Fike was bitten and cut but not seriously injured and declined hospital treatment.

"It ended up with a few wounds itself," Mr. Fike said of the cougar.

Hunters are trying to find the animal. If found, animals that attack humans in the wild are usually killed.

INSECTS & ANIMALS

RABID ANIMAL ATTACK

When you are attacked by a suspected rabid animal such as a raccoon, wolf, coyote, wild dog, bat, or fox, do not run as you will expose your back, the back of your legs, and your ankles.

Grab a stick or use a clenched fist to hit the animal across its snout. This is very painful and the animal might fall to the ground in a stupor or beat a fast retreat.

ANIMAL REPELLENT

Spray ammonia on your trash. This will keep curious animals away.

PORCUPINE REPELLENT

Use moth balls to keep porcupines away from camp areas and the cottage. Porcupines are always looking for salt and will eat through treated wood and leather.

LICE REPELLENT

Camphor, carried in your pocket, can be used against body lice.

ANT STOPPER

Use a piece of white chalk to mark lines on the table legs or eating area. This should keep most non-flying insects away.

BEAR ATTACK

To Avoid Bear Attack

- Keep all food away from the sleeping area.
- Wash all utensils and preferably do not store them near the tent.
- If you have caught a fish, do not get the fishy smell on your clothing and body. Bears love fish no matter what size. Wash your hands and clothing. Store your clothing, to dry, some distance from the camp.
- Do not eat and cook adjacent to the camp.

In Bear Country

As a bear has a very acute sense of smell there are a few things you should avoid in a camp:

- The cooking area should be separated from the shelter area. The cooking area should be downwind and 300 feet (100 meters) away.
- Make sure that you do not get the odor of food on your clothing, towels or blankets. It is preferable to wear separate cooking clothing that will be left at the cook site.
- All food scraps and even empty tin cans should be thrown into the fire so that all traces of food will be burnt. Remember to remove the burnt cans and take them to a disposal area.
- Avoid foods like sardines, bacon or other "smelly" meat products.

MOSQUITOES

Some of the latest studies on mosquitoes show the following:

- Mosquitoes seem to be attracted to taller people and ones that are fidgety. Tall and fidgety people exhale more carbon dioxide which attracts mosquitoes. If you are swatting at the mosquitoes and moving all the time you will attract more mosquitoes.
- Mosquitoes do not die after biting but can bite up to six times.
- Only female mosquitoes feed on humans and they will lay 200 eggs after biting.
- Mosquitoes live two weeks and some females up to 5 months.
- Upon biting the mosquito injects saliva into the body to help extract the blood. This saliva causes the itching.
- Mosquitoes can detect humans from as far away as 20 feet (six meters). They are attracted by heat, moisture and carbon dioxide. All of these factors are increased if you are moving a lot on a warm day.
- The movement of the wings causes the mosquito to produce the high pitched whine.
- One million malaria deaths are caused by mosquitoes each year.

BEST MOSQUITO REPELLENT

The best repellents contain "N.N-diet-m-toluamide" known as DEET. This is the most effective long term repellent. *See page 13 for children.* A natural repellent which is nearly as effective contains oil of citronella.

Mosquito Repellent

Citronella Candle

HOME REMEDIES

Insect Repellent

The pioneers used "Nessmuk Juice" made of:

- 3 oz. (90 ml) pine tar.
- 2 oz. (60 ml) castor oil.
- 1 oz. (30 ml) pennyroyal oil.

Slowly simmer over a low fire until it becomes a pasty substance and smear it on your body. Have your friends do the same or you will have no friends.

Mosquito Repellent

Add 10 drops of oil of thyme and 20 drops of pennyroyal to olive oil, lard or add to your favorite sun block.

To Keep Bugs Away

Pour some sweet sticky syrup or molasses some 20 feet (6 m) upwind from your shelter and most bugs will converge on this spot and not in your living and cooking area.

Sting Stopper

To neutralize the stinging sensation of a mosquito bite wet the area with some saliva or water and pass a bar of soap over the spot. This will usually stop the stinging and itching sensation.

FIRST AID CHAPTER

FOR MORE INFORMATION ON INSECT, SNAKE, AND ANIMAL BITES

TICK CHECK

Check for ticks and tick bits every day or after walking through grassy areas.

If you find one, cover it with petroleum jelly or oil to kill the tick. Apply hydrogen peroxide to kill any germs at the entry point. If the head remains stuck, see a doctor. *See the article on Lyme Disease in the First Aid Chapter.*

WATER PURIFICATION

WATER FILTER

With the "advance" of civilization even the most remote water source has a high probability of being contaminated. The latest in water purification methods are filters that strain the water and remove microscopic contaminants.

The purity of the water depends upon the size of the pores in the filter. It takes a pore size of 0.4 microns to eliminate bacteria. Because of the large variety and similarity of products on the market only the Penta Oasis is described here.

This water purifier is self contained. You fill the bottle with water, you squeeze the bottle, and the treated water comes out through the spout. This bottle can be placed in the bottle attachment of your bicycle. There are no tubes attached. One filter is good for approximately 100 gallons. With use the filter clogs and it becomes more difficult to draw water. In some models you can clean the filter. In the case of the Oasis you change the three-stage purification cartridge.

Three Stage Purification

Stage One: Removes the sediment and stops pathogenic cysts with a filter.

Stage Two: Using iodinated resin this stage kills and disables water borne microorganisms, including E. coli and Vibrio cholera bacteria, polio, hepatitis and other harmful viruses.

Stage Three: Is a coconut based carbon which captures much of the water's unwanted flavors, odors and residual iodine (These flavors come from stage two).

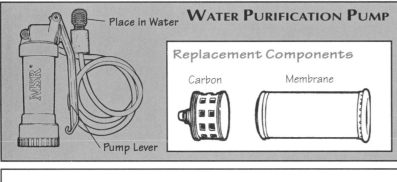

WATER PURIFICATION PUMP

Place in Water

Pump Lever

Replacement Components

Carbon   Membrane

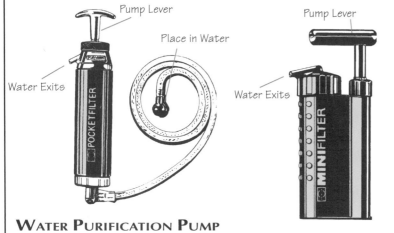

Pump Lever

Place in Water

Pump Lever

Water Exits

Water Exits

POCKETFILTER

MINIFILTER

WATER PURIFICATION PUMP

TRAVEL CUP

The Travel Cup features:

Phase 1: Gravity filter.

Phase 2: Iodine resin.

Phase 3: Carbon filtration.

It provides microbiologically pure water from any water source. The carbon component removes unwanted chemicals and excess iodine from the treated water. The cup will treat a total of 100 gallons at 1/2 pint per minute. Weighs: 6 oz (170 g).

Drinking Water Tablets

Three Level Water Filter

This survival water filtering method is described in the *Finding Water Chapter*.

WATER TREATMENT

Organism	Illness
Parasitic microorganism *(protozoa)*	Giardia cysts Lamblia "Beaver Fever"
Bacteria	Typhoid, diarrhea, etc.
Virus	Polio, hepatitis, etc.

METHODS TO TREAT WATER

Boiling: Kills nearly everything but is impractical as it requires time and much fuel.

Chemical Disinfectant: Is lightweight, inexpensive and effective. Iodine based tablets are usually used but the water they produce is not tasty.

Filtration: Removes contaminants by passing the liquid through a fine filter.

Purification: Uses a filtration method combined with the chemical method.

PUR SCOUT

Compact weighing 12 ounces (340 g). Will process 1/2 quart (0.625 L) of water per minute and purify approximately 200 gallons (1000 L) of water.

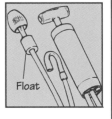

Float

Filler Cup

PUR TRAVELER

Fills from the top and will process 100 gallons (500 L) of water.

TRANSPORTING WATER

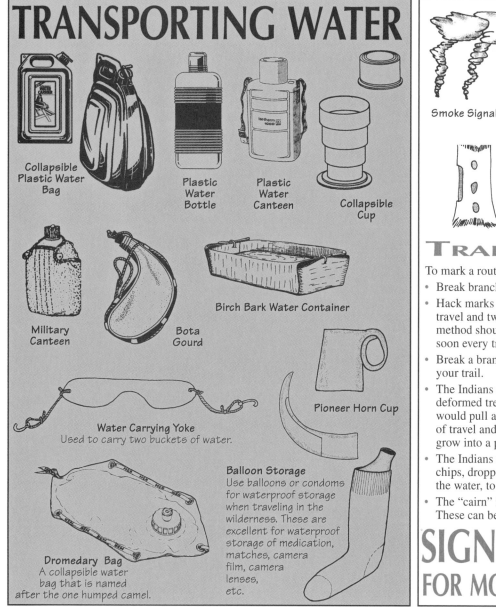

Collapsible Plastic Water Bag

Plastic Water Bottle

Plastic Water Canteen

Collapsible Cup

Military Canteen

Bota Gourd

Birch Bark Water Container

Pioneer Horn Cup

Water Carrying Yoke
Used to carry two buckets of water.

Balloon Storage
Use balloons or condoms for waterproof storage when traveling in the wilderness. These are excellent for waterproof storage of medication, matches, camera film, camera lenses, etc.

Dromedary Bag
A collapsible water bag that is named after the one humped camel.

Smoke Signal

Broken Branch

Tied Grass

Tree Slashes

Rock Cairn

TRAILBLAZING

To mark a route in the forest you can:

- Break branches in the direction you are taking.
- Hack marks on trees - one gash in the direction of travel and two gashes on the return side. This method should not be overused otherwise fairly soon every tree will have blazes.
- Break a branch in the direction of the turn in your trail.
- The Indians of the Eastern United States deformed trees in the direction of travel. They would pull a branch of a sapling in the direction of travel and tie it down with vines and this would grow into a permanent marker.
- The Indians of British Columbia used cedar chips, dropped from the back of their boat into the water, to mark their route in the fog.
- The "cairn" is currently used on many trails. These can be made of snow, ice, rocks, and wood.

SIGNAL CHAPTER
FOR MORE INFORMATION

SUNGLASSES

Feature	Type/Color	Notes
Protection from sunlight	99% UV elimination/any color	A required feature.
To drive		Sunglasses that are not too dark.
High contrast	Yellow, amber, rose	Increase perception of details, for hunting, skiing, mountain biking.
See through water surface	Polaroid	Eliminate reflections. For fishing.
Shadow and sunlight	Photochromics/variable density	Hiking, general use.
Bright snow and sun	Slit glasses (Eskimo). Dark top and bottom, light centre.	For skiing, winter hiking.
Limited color distortion	Gray or green	Photography, painting, seeing nature.
Plastic lenses	Will not shatter	Easily get scratched.
Frames	Quality plastic	Stand up better than thin metal frames.
Lens size	Get largest possible	Wider angle of vision.
Glass lenses	Better quality	High optical standard grinding, distortion free and scratch resistant.

Eye Glass Cords
If you wear glasses, this is a required item in the wilds. You will know that your glasses are around your neck and will not be mislaid or sat on. The cord will prevent you from losing your glasses while climbing or fishing.

WALKING IN CIRCLES!

WHY DO WE HAVE A TENDENCY TO WALK IN CIRCLES?

Every human is lopsided usually caused by a difference in leg length. This "deformation" will cause the person to veer if he is walking normally.

The Imperial German Army did research on the deviation factor of individual soldiers to help him correct his deviation in direction at certain intervals. The deviation is greater at a faster pace and is increased when the head is bent forward as when carrying a back pack. The full circle march time can vary from one to six hours.

Other causes of deviation from a straight line are:

- We all have a *dominant eye*. If you point at something, at a distance, with both eyes open, you will see that the finger has been aligned with only one eye.
- Wrong balance of items in a backpack or pack incorrectly adjusted on the back.
- Hikers tend to "edge away" from an obstacle such as the wind, rain, slope of a hill, snow, dust storm and strong sun in the face.
- Hikers approaching an obstacle might tend to always pass on the "right" side and gradually veer off course. This has been shown to be the case in Swiss Army studies on mountain travel.

HOW TO WALK IN A STRAIGHT LINE

"The shortest distance is between two points"

In open, treeless country pick a distant landmark and walk towards it or orient yourself by it.

- Find two landmarks ahead of you and line them up or find two prominent points behind you and line them up. Look back ever so often to make sure that you are still on course.
- If only one landmark is available *place* a second landmark (e.g. a flag on a stick which is lined up with a distant hill and walk forward). Make small fires along your path to help maintain your direction day or night. This would be useful on a flat surface as a plain or desert.
- **Indian file:** A group of hikers in a landmarkless area can become landmarks themselves. The hikers are spaced so that the last individual is far enough back that he can watch the leader and the line. He lines up the leader with the people in the line. When he sees the leader deviate he can signal him to fall in line. This method can be used during snow storms (the group should be rope-linked). A dog team and sled which has a length of 50 feet (15 m) can be aligned to a distant landmark or with a definite angle to the direction of the snowdrifts (the drifts are formed by the predominant winds).
- In the dark or fog, shouts or a penetrating whistle can be used to keep direction.
- A distant noise can be chosen as the destination. To verify your direction cup your ears and rotate your head horizontally to get the direction of the highest sound intensity.

ESTIMATING DISTANCE

50 yds	46m	Mouth and eyes can be clearly distinguished.
100 yds	91m	Eyes are dots.
200 yds	183m	General details of clothing can be distinguished.
300 yds	274m	Faces can be seen.
500 yds	457m	Colors of clothing can be distinguished.
800 yds	732m	Man looks like a post.
1 mi.	1.6km	Trunks of large trees can be seen.
2.5 mi.	4km	Chimneys and windows can be distinguished.
6 mi.	10km	Large houses, silos and towers can be recognized.
9 mi.	14km	Average height church steeple can be seen.

ESTIMATING DISTANCE

Being able to judge distance is important in survival situations as it will help you maintain your bearings, judge height, and calculate time relative to the speed of walking.

Counting Paces *(a step being a pace)*

- An average person has a pace of 30" (76 cm) and will walk at three miles an hour over flat ground. You might want to calculate your average pace.
- To help you count your pace, *count your right foot pace only* and multiply by two when you reach 100 paces.
- To keep track of your counted paces put pebbles or nuts in one pocket and transfer one to the other pocket at each 100 paces.

Objects look much nearer when:

- Looking up or down a hill.
- There is a bright light on the object.
- Looking across water, snow or flat sand.
- The air is clear.

Objects look much farther when:

- The light is poor.
- The object is at the end of a long avenue.
- You are looking over undulating ground.
- The color of the object blends with the background.

Distance is underestimated when starting a trip and overestimated at the end of a trip

FINGER METHOD OF JUDGING DISTANCE

This method is based upon the principle that the distance between the eyes is about 1/10 of the distance from the eye to the extended finger.

When you know the width or height of a distant object:

- Extend your right arm and hold your forefinger upright and align it with one eye at the end of the object. *See note on dominent eye above.*
- Do not move the finger and observe where it is when looking with the other eye.
- Estimate the displacement in feet along the length of the object.
- The distance in feet from the object will be 10 times the displacement of the finger.

This can also be done *vertically* but hold the head sideways. This method might give you a more exact estimate if you want to judge the distance from a building as we know the height of each floor is between 10 to 12 feet (3-4 m) high.

To determine distance with your binoculars measure the distance between the center of the eyepieces, when adjusted for your eyes, and multiply this distance by 10.

Traveling Along a Ridge
River Photograph Showing Highlands

TRAVELING ALONG A RIVER BASIN DIVIDE

On ridges or divides, between two major river watersheds, the footing is usually better, vegetation is thinner, fallen trees are smaller, there is no mud or bog, and there is a better view of the surrounding area to help find your direction.

Divide or Ridge Line

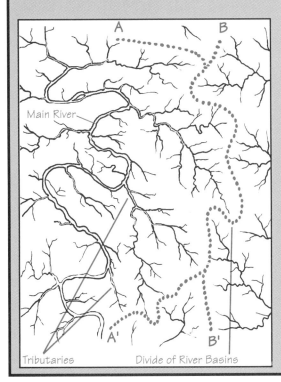

A
B

Main River

A'
B'

Tributaries   Divide of River Basins

RIVER DIVIDE TRAILS IN CROSS COUNTRY TRAVEL

A river is still considered as being man's natural highway. This is true where you have great rivers such as the Mississippi, Hudson, and St. Lawrence. Water travel is the only form of travel in the muskeg swamp country in Northern Canada in the summer as land travel is impractical until everything freezes up.

In general the Indians did not use small rivers and streams but traveled along the ridges between streams or divides between two river basins. An exception to this was in the fur trade when heavy loads were carried by large canoes. These trading routes transported beaver pelts and merchandise along the river systems.

The advantage of a route traveled on a divide can be seen on the map. To travel from A or A' to B or B' it is easier to follow the divide and avoid fording all the rivers and streams. If the travelers had followed the bank of the river they would have had to ford streams and rivers, go through marshes, swamps, dense thickets and also have to face the 'friendly' mosquitoes and blood suckers.

On ridges or divides, between two major river watersheds, the footing is usually better, vegetation is thinner, fallen trees are smaller, there is no mud or bog, and a better view of the surrounding area to help find your direction. In windblown areas there will hardly be any mosquitoes. If following a divide plan your trip, or take frequent sightings (climb a high tree), so that you do not end up in a dead end from which you have to descend to the lowlands.

TRAVELING ON HILLS

Avoid barriers (mountains, rivers, cliffs, etc.) and plan a route at the same elevation so that you avoid going up and down hills.

Breathing

If you find that you are breathing too fast, or gasping for breath, this means that you are traveling too fast.

Rest

Rest 5 to 10 minutes every hour. But not too long because your muscles will cool and stiffen.

Feet

Your feet have many nerves in them and when they hurt travel can be very painful. When you stop to rest change your socks and cool your feet. Never travel without bandages, change of socks, and other first aid items for your feet. Make sure that your new boots have been broken in *before* you leave on a major trip.

Traveling Uphill

Do not walk straight up a slope but zigzags up the hill. You will find that on a long slope, by zigzagging, you will arrive at the top at more or less the same time but you will be less tired.

When walking always plant each foot fully on the ground. Do not walk uphill on your toes. If the footing is not too secure gradually transfer your weight onto the advancing foot to see if the location is stable. See the *Mountain Travel Chapter* for more details.

Steep Slopes

You will have a tendency to "hug" the slope but this is not advisable as the angle at which your foot stands on the ground will be very flat and your footing might slip. Your hands can be used for balance but keep your body at least at arm's length from the slope. Test each hand hold and footing for each step before transferring your body's weight.

Use the *three secure point system* to hold your body at dangerous spots on the slope, e.g. two handholds and one foot well placed before slowly shifting the second foot. When this foot is secure then you can shift one hand.

Climbing Down Steep Hills

This is more difficult than climbing uphill as your ankles, knees and legs tire faster as they have to absorb the weight for thousands of steps.

Keep your backpack well attached, balance your weight, keep your knees bent to cushion your weight while shifting from leg to leg. Do not go too fast as you will have too much momentum and might sprain your ankle or fall because of insecure footing.

Safety on Slopes

The hiker on the upper part of the slope should be careful not to dislodge rocks that might fall on the column below. The column should advance at a slight angle up the slope so that any loose debris will fall without hurting anyone below. The lead climber can dislodge, with advance warning, any loose rocks that might affect his group.

If you encounter areas of loose rocks or talus the group on the lower part of the hill can seek shelter behind a tree or boulder until the lead climbers pass the dangerous area.

VISIBILITY WHILE TRAVELING

A sudden dust storm, squall, sleet or fog bank might envelope you. If you are not sure of your trail or are in hilly terrain it might be best to make a shelter and wait out the storm as to proceed might be very dangerous.

Upon laying down and covering yourself it is best to indicate your direction of travel with a line of stones or a stick. When the storm is over you might not recognize the surroundings and not know in which direction you were heading.

Ocean and Sea Shores

Oceans are large bodies of water that are affected by tides and winds. If you are following the shore be careful of incoming waves. If an unexpected big wave arrives hold your footing, do not attempt to run. You will not be sure of your footing or the depth of the water. You might be caught in an undertow and be swept into deep water and drown. In general it is quite easy to follow the sea shore as there is usually a beach that has been created by the incoming waves and tides. Difficulties might be encountered when you are in an area where a river flows into the sea as it might be swampy with many islands. *See Rafting.*

River and Lake Shores

The tributaries of rivers that run *through a wide bottomland* are likely to be deep or run over fathomless mud, sometimes quicksand and require long detours or be crossed with a raft or boat. The vegetation, in these areas, up to the very bank of the river can be exceedingly thick, a wretched tangle of bushes, vines, briers, tall grass, and fallen trees. In periods of heavy rain the river might rise out of its banks and maroon you on a high piece of land.

Rivers in *mountain areas* are swift and usually in gorges or steep valleys which would lead to numerous impassable dead ends. Each bend in the river will be a surprise and for this reason it would be best to cross the area on the divide. *See the article about traveling along a divide.*

TRAVELING ALONG THE SHORELINE

MOUNTAIN CLIMBING
SEE CHAPTER FOR MORE DETAILS
Hiking and Climbing

Hikers in good condition can climb 1000 feet (300 meters) per hour. This varies with the type of terrain. On level ground the speed would be 2.5 to 4 miles per hour (4 to 7 km).

QUICKSAND

The sign of quicksand is the presence of water oozing upwards. This water keeps the sand and muck in suspension. There might be a thin crust on the surface.

If you step into quicksand or mire:

- *Do not struggle.*
- Trying to lift one foot makes the second foot sink deeper as all the weight is on one foot.
- Drop to your hands and knees and try to crawl slowly. The surface of your hands, knees and legs will distribute your weight over a wider area.
- If the mire is too soft and you feel that you are still sinking, lie flat on your stomach and move only one part of your body at a time. Try to float out of the quicksand by using snake like movements.

CROSSING A STREAM

PREPARING TO CROSS A STREAM

- Meandering streams usually flow slowly and can easily be crossed.
- When two streams meet, cross above the meeting point as the current usually is slower due to a lower volume of water.
- Ford a stream further up its course where it is smaller. If you have a choice follow a land divide or ridge while traveling.
- In a forest area trees will have fallen on a stream. These can be used as a bridge.

On a Trip

- Watch the weather. Sudden rains or thaws can change placid streams into roaring torrents.
- Distant mountain thunderstorms can dramatically raise the level of the water especially in narrow valleys.
- If the stream is fed by melting snow cross in the morning before the sun melts more snow.

Study the Stream

- Before crossing a stream look for potential rescue points.
- Watch for debris in rapidly flowing water.
- The shallowest water is usually where the stream is the widest or the current is the fastest as a certain volume of water has to pass a certain point on the river at a certain time.
- Study the flow of the water for the location of eddies. Eddies are a spiral or circular movement of water and can be relatively calm. A strong eddy can become a whirlpool. These areas are usually behind rocks or where a stream passes into a wider area.
- Place clothing and sleeping bag in a waterproof bag. Make sure that the contents of your bag are well balanced and firmly attached so that the contents will not shift.
- It is safer to wade through water than the risk of jumping between slippery logs or stepping stones and chance spraining your ankle.
- Watch for bubbly areas behind rocks as the water-air mixture will not have the buoyancy to hold up your body and if you enter this area of turbulence your body might be held down against the rocks. *See Canoeing Article.*
- If the stream has a strong current chose an entry point where, if you lose your footing, you will be swept to a calm shallow spot or an eddy near the opposite side. Do not cross in areas of cliffs, logs, brush or rapids.
- When crossing wear old running shoes for traction and to help you avoid any sharp objects. The running shoes will also keep your feet warm and you will not wet your hiking boots.

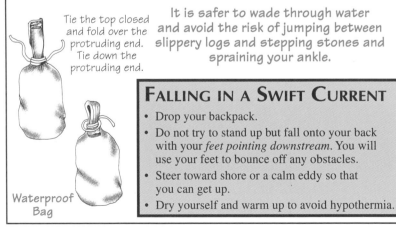

Tie the top closed and fold over the protruding end. Tie down the protruding end.

Waterproof Bag

It is safer to wade through water and avoid the risk of jumping between slippery logs and stepping stones and spraining your ankle.

FALLING IN A SWIFT CURRENT

- Drop your backpack.
- Do not try to stand up but fall onto your back with your *feet pointing downstream*. You will use your feet to bounce off any obstacles.
- Steer toward shore or a calm eddy so that you can get up.
- Dry yourself and warm up to avoid hypothermia.

WADING ACROSS

- Find a shallow crossing point where the riverbed looks stable and clear.
- If the water is cloudy with silt or debris use a walking stick to probe in front of you.
- Use a pole to probe your advance. Do not put your weight on it, until it is well placed, as it might slip and destabilize you. Only move one of the three contact points at a time.
- Keep your pack lightly attached so that it can be jettisoned if necessary.
- Wade across fast streams into the flow of the water. Deep slow streams are crossed while going downstream as the current will help you angle across.
- Do not tie a rope to a person crossing a stream as the current might make him fall and the secured rope will pull him *under the water*. The first person, the strongest, wading across should carry the rope loosely in his hand, so that it can be released in case of an emergency. Once he has waded across it can be attached so that the rest of the group can cross while holding on to it on the downside of the current's flow.
- Mountain streams can be very cold and by crossing and getting wet you might expose yourself to hypothermia even on warm days.
- You might consider using a flotation device to float your backpack and to grab if you loose your balance.
- Legs should be dragged through the water, not lifted, so that the force of the current will not throw the you off balance.

Crossing on Rocks or Logs

- Make sure that they are well anchored and dry. Sprinkle sand on a wet log before stepping on it.
- Use a walking stick for additional stability.

MOUNTAIN STREAM CROSSING
SEE THE MOUNTAIN TRAVEL CHAPTER

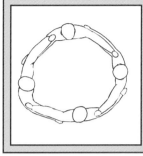

THE PIVOT CROSSING

This method can be used by three or more people. Hold clothing or backpack straps on each others shoulders and cross the stream in a wheel-like way. One person moves at a time while the others stabilize him. The ideal number of people is three. If the group gets too large it will be difficult to resist the current. The danger of the pivot method is that if one person slips the whole structure could collapse.

LEAPING

When leaping the point of departure and the landing spot have to be considered. The point of departure because you will be exerting additional pressure on the ground below you. If it is a river bank it might slide and collapse. The landing point has to be stable enough to take your weight, the additional pressure of your landing (which might be double your weight) and the fact that you are landing at an angle. This might cause a rock or trunk to roll.

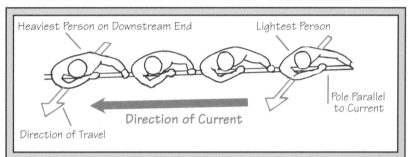

Heaviest Person on Downstream End   Lightest Person

Pole Parallel to Current

Direction of Current

Direction of Travel

POLE ASSISTED CROSSING

A pole 5 inches (13 cm) in diameter and about 8 feet (2.4 m) long can be used as a group anchor point to cross a swift stream. When a group is traversing keep the pole parallel to the current and the direction of travel is gradually downstream.

FLOTATION SYSTEMS

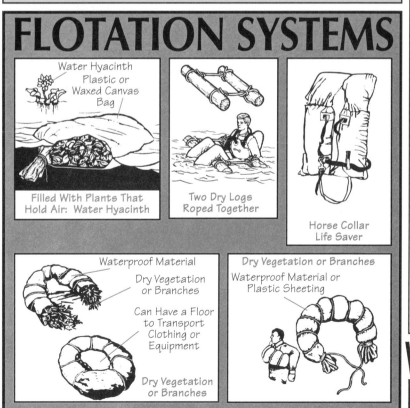

Water Hyacinth Plastic or Waxed Canvas Bag

Filled With Plants That Hold Air: Water Hyacinth

Two Dry Logs Roped Together

Horse Collar Life Saver

Waterproof Material

Dry Vegetation or Branches

Can Have a Floor to Transport Clothing or Equipment

Dry Vegetation or Branches

Dry Vegetation or Branches

Waterproof Material or Plastic Sheeting

FORDING A RIVER

Inspect the River

Inspect the river, potential crossing areas, current, eddies, obstacles, and footing under the water.

- Look for possible natural bridges.
- Look for an area where the current is not as strong. If you are in a canyon or gorge go towards a widening in the river.
- Study the river bed and any potential stepping stones. The bed and stones might be slimy with moss and the stones with a coating of ice.

Prepare for Crossing

Plan a strategy:

- Which shoes will you wear? Preferably have a pair of canvas running shoes with well notched soles. These shoes will be removed after the fording and carried, to dry, hanging from your backpack.
- How should you cross the river?

  You might consider fording straight across. This is the shortest distance but you will have to resist the current.

  You might cross at a diagonal in the direction of the current. This will give you potentially better footing because your forward step will be pushed by the current.

- There is a current/body weight strength ratio which, if it is exceeded, will lead to you being pushed over by the current. This fall ratio depends upon how strong you are, how tall, do you have a walking stick support or are you wearing baggy pants that will add to the resistance to the current. *A basic rule of thumb is that if the water is up to your knees and the water starts to churn and boil you will not be up for very long.* If the water is cold, even cool, you might even suffer muscle cramps.
- The safest might be to build a log raft or other flotation device and float across at a point where the current is deflected to the other side or enters a calm area on the other side.

WATER TRAVEL CHAPTER FOR FLOTATION DEVICES

CHOOSING A GOOD POCKETKNIFE

HOW TO RECOGNIZE A QUALITY POCKETKNIFE

Body

A well made back spring keeps the blade of the knife either open or closed. A low quality spring can only handle two blades, one on each side of the spring, never parallel.

Spacers of Brass

The spacers *between the blades* prevent the blades from sticking to each other.

Side Plates

The side plates sandwich the blades and spring together. The knife and side plates are held together by a pair of end rivets which also act as the pivots for the blades. To protect the pivots, good knives have two solid metal bolsters, one on each side of the knife. The bolsters reinforce the pivot action of a pocket knife and hold the decorative plates in place. A quality knife should have well fitted parts and the blades should have a solid sounding return when released.

Blades

The blades should feel comfortable in your hands and should have a rest area when half opened *to avoid snapping closed on your fingers*. Blades should be easy to open. With blades open, check the alignment of all moving parts and the body. The blades should move parallel to the body. Blades should not feel loose and move side to side when open.

Carbon Steel or Stainless Steel Blades?

Carbon Steel: Carbon steel will accept a very fine edge but is subject to rust and staining. Quality carbon steel is very brittle and should not be used as a screw driver.

Stainless Steel: As it says it does not "stain" or rust. It cannot be honed as well as carton steel.

Stainless or Carbon Steel? Use carbon steel if you will require a continuous sharp blade as for cutting wood, leather, etc. Use stainless steel if you don't like the "stain" on carbon blades. Use a stainless blade in saltwater, for fishing or basic outdoor activities.

Hardness of Steel

The standard of measuring hardness is the *Rockwell Hardness Test* and for a knife the hardness should be from 20-68 and most blades specify 55-65. The Rockwell hardness of 65 is not necessarily the ideal as it is too hard to sharpen and the blade might be brittle. A quality knife blade will be tested for temper and hardness. You can see the test point as a small pock mark on the side of a quality blade.

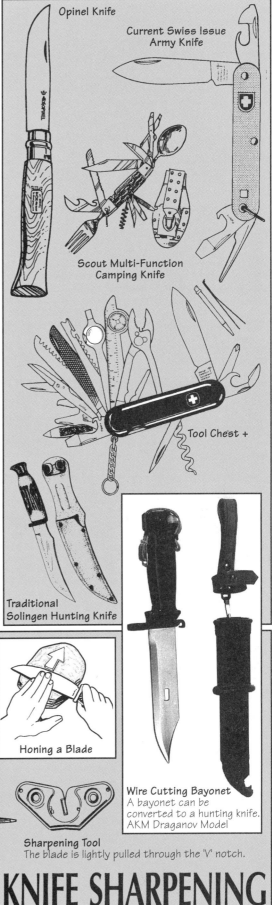

Opinel Knife

Current Swiss Issue Army Knife

Scout Multi-Function Camping Knife

Tool Chest +

Traditional Solingen Hunting Knife

Wire Cutting Bayonet
A bayonet can be converted to a hunting knife. AKM Draganov Model

Honing a Fine Edge

Buy a quality sharpening stone and apply a lubricant as specified for the stone. Immerse the stone in oil for a day before using. The oil prevents the grit from clogging the holes in the stone. Sharpen the knife as soon as you feel it's getting dull. For minor touch ups, place the blade on the stone and pull it toward you with the cutting edge at a 10° angle on your side. Repeat this on both sides an *equal* number of times. First pull the blade over the coarse side of the stone and then hone with the fine stone.

Honing a Blade

Angle Between the Blade and Stone

Type of Edge	Angle	
Very sharp edge	10° or less	Very sharp
General purpose	15°	General work
Tough edge	20°	Rugged work

Two Sided Honing Stone

Sharpening Steel

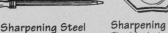

Sharpening Tool
The blade is lightly pulled through the 'V' notch.

Using a Steel

A steel is used to maintain a fine edge, not to produce one. The same angle should be used on the steel but the blade should be *pulled* from the cutting edge and not as in the case of the stone where it is *pushed towards* the edge.

KNIFE SHARPENING

POCKET TOOLS

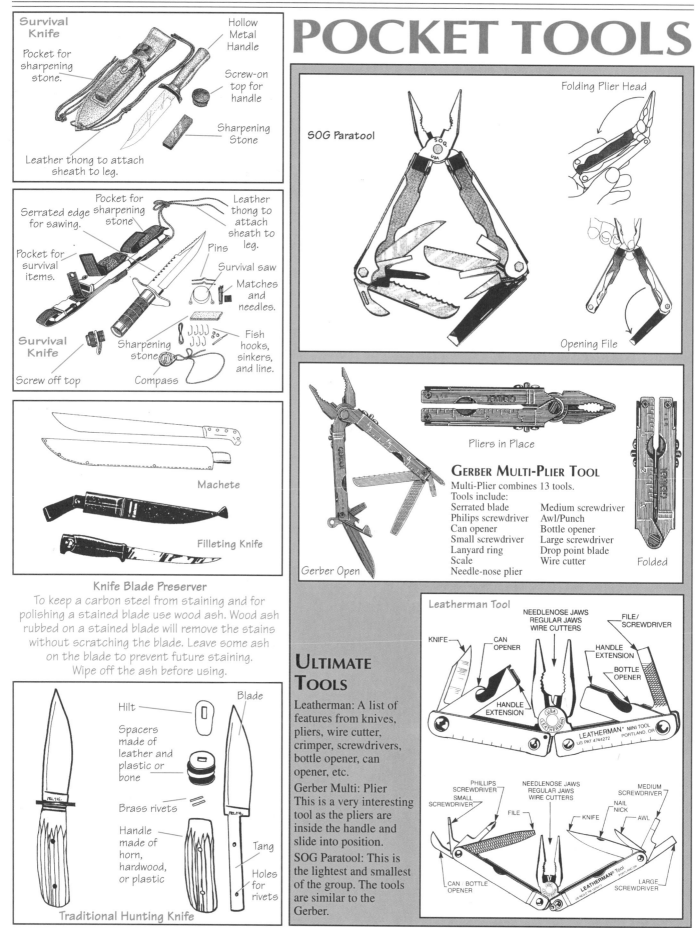

Survival Knife

- Pocket for sharpening stone.
- Hollow Metal Handle
- Screw-on top for handle
- Sharpening Stone
- Leather thong to attach sheath to leg.

Survival Knife

- Serrated edge for sawing.
- Pocket for sharpening stone.
- Leather thong to attach sheath to leg.
- Pocket for survival items.
- Pins
- Survival saw
- Matches and needles.
- Screw off top
- Sharpening stone
- Compass
- Fish hooks, sinkers, and line.

Machete

Filleting Knife

Knife Blade Preserver

To keep a carbon steel from staining and for polishing a stained blade use wood ash. Wood ash rubbed on a stained blade will remove the stains without scratching the blade. Leave some ash on the blade to prevent future staining. Wipe off the ash before using.

Traditional Hunting Knife

- Hilt
- Spacers made of leather and plastic or bone
- Brass rivets
- Handle made of horn, hardwood, or plastic
- Blade
- Tang
- Holes for rivets

SOG Paratool

Folding Plier Head

Opening File

Pliers in Place

GERBER MULTI-PLIER TOOL

Multi-Plier combines 13 tools.
Tools include:

Serrated blade	Medium screwdriver
Philips screwdriver	Awl/Punch
Can opener	Bottle opener
Small screwdriver	Large screwdriver
Lanyard ring	Drop point blade
Scale	Wire cutter
Needle-nose plier	

Gerber Open

Folded

ULTIMATE TOOLS

Leatherman: A list of features from knives, pliers, wire cutter, crimper, screwdrivers, bottle opener, can opener, etc.

Gerber Multi: Plier This is a very interesting tool as the pliers are inside the handle and slide into position.

SOG Paratool: This is the lightest and smallest of the group. The tools are similar to the Gerber.

Leatherman Tool

- KNIFE
- CAN OPENER
- NEEDLENOSE JAWS REGULAR JAWS WIRE CUTTERS
- FILE/SCREWDRIVER
- HANDLE EXTENSION
- BOTTLE OPENER
- HANDLE EXTENSION
- LEATHERMAN® MINI TOOL US PAT 4744272 PORTLAND, OR

- PHILLIPS SCREWDRIVER
- SMALL SCREWDRIVER
- NEEDLENOSE JAWS REGULAR JAWS WIRE CUTTERS
- FILE
- MEDIUM SCREWDRIVER
- NAIL NICK
- KNIFE
- AWL
- CAN BOTTLE OPENER
- LARGE SCREWDRIVER
- LEATHERMAN® Tool

SWISS ARMY KNIFE

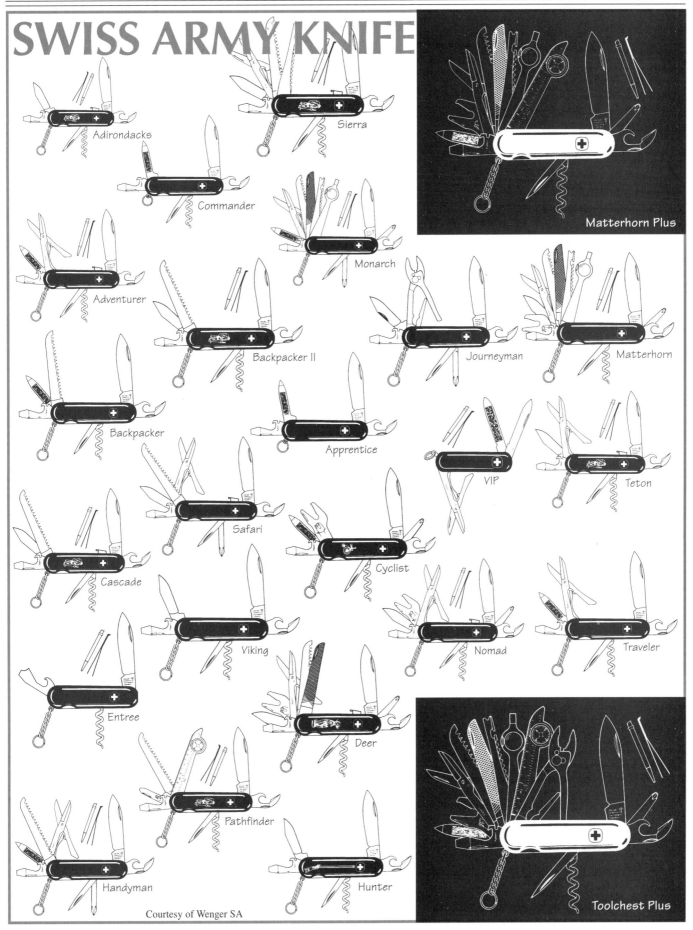

Adirondacks

Sierra

Commander

Monarch

Matterhorn Plus

Adventurer

Backpacker II

Journeyman

Matterhorn

Backpacker

Apprentice

VIP

Teton

Cascade

Safari

Cyclist

Viking

Nomad

Traveler

Entree

Deer

Handyman

Pathfinder

Hunter

Toolchest Plus

Courtesy of Wenger SA

FLASHLIGHTS

Over the last few years lighting systems have gone through a major revolution. Bulbs have gone from the Edison type to Halogen, Xenon-gas, and Krypton. Each bulb has a certain use and advantage.

Bulb Type	Light	Notes
Edison type	yellowish	inexpensive
Halogen (H)	white-bright	more power than Edison
Xenon (X)	more white bright light	
Krypton	less white bright light	less expensive less power than (H+X)

The most popular modern flashlight is the Mini Mag which has 2AA batteries. The Mini Mag can work up to 5 hours on 2 AA's. The flashlight is quite flexible as it has water resistant '0' rings, is made out of aluminum, and the lens can zoom to change the angle of projection. There is an extra light bulb in the base.

A modern head lamp is in the series offered by the French company Petzl. One model, the Petzl Zoom, sits on your forehead, freeing your hands, and the batteries are attached to the head band on the back of your head. The batteries it can use are 3 AA's (8 hours), 1 4.5 volt (17 hours) or a Ni-cad kit (7 hours).

RED FILTER FOR NIGHT READING

Red light does not affect your eye's adaptation to night vision. A white light will cause your eyes to contract and it will take several minutes for your eyes to readapt to the dark.

This is especially useful when reading a map. Military flashlights have three extra lenses stored in the base of the lamp. These filters are a red, green and a Fresnel lens to help focus the light rays.

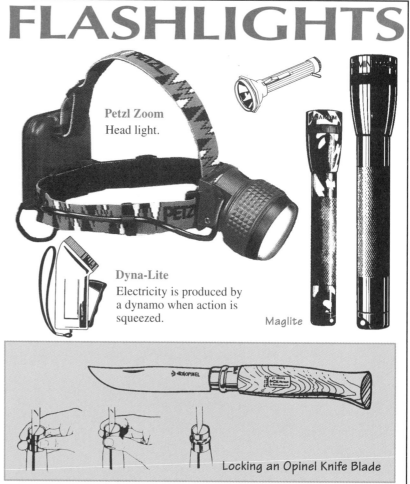

FLASHLIGHTS

Petzl Zoom
Head light.

Dyna-Lite
Electricity is produced by a dynamo when action is squeezed.

Maglite

Locking an Opinel Knife Blade

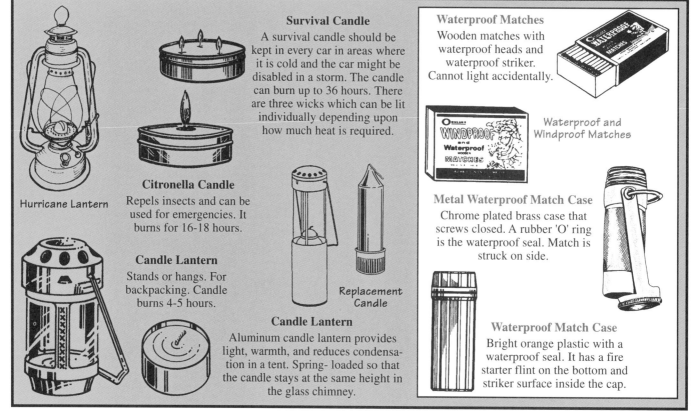

Hurricane Lantern

Survival Candle

A survival candle should be kept in every car in areas where it is cold and the car might be disabled in a storm. The candle can burn up to 36 hours. There are three wicks which can be lit individually depending upon how much heat is required.

Citronella Candle

Repels insects and can be used for emergencies. It burns for 16-18 hours.

Candle Lantern

Stands or hangs. For backpacking. Candle burns 4-5 hours.

Replacement Candle

Candle Lantern

Aluminum candle lantern provides light, warmth, and reduces condensation in a tent. Spring- loaded so that the candle stays at the same height in the glass chimney.

Waterproof Matches

Wooden matches with waterproof heads and waterproof striker. Cannot light accidentally.

Waterproof and Windproof Matches

Metal Waterproof Match Case

Chrome plated brass case that screws closed. A rubber 'O' ring is the waterproof seal. Match is struck on side.

Waterproof Match Case

Bright orange plastic with a waterproof seal. It has a fire starter flint on the bottom and striker surface inside the cap.

FOOT GEAR

Well rounded top so that it does not cut into the calf.

Tongue

Quality Laces
Laces that tie easily and do not slip.

Leather Inner Lining

Leather Uppers
With a minimum of seams.

Heel
Well formed to offer good support.

Steel Shank

Oil Resistant Sole

Traction Ribs on Soles

CHOICE OF FOOT GEAR

Your feet are extremely sensitive, especially when walking. Frequently the shoes are the problem.

- Size of shoe: If too small it will restrict the movement of your bones and muscles. Poor circulation of the blood will cause your feet to be cold. If too large or too wide the heel will move, up and down or laterally, and you will not be sure of your footing.
- When wearing boots try to buy socks for your foot size.
- Sole material: Leather can be very slippery in the woods. A better choice is a well indented rubber composite sole.
- Upper of shoe or boot: Avoid rubber boat shoes or hunting boots that have a high rubber foot. Rubber does not breath and humidity will build up in the boot. It will be too hot and you will literally cook your feet or in cooler weather, with the accumulation of humidity, you will have cold and clammy feet.
- Shoelace: The Canadian Army uses a loose woven round nylon shoelace that stretches and contracts depending upon the fit of the boot. The lace does not undo as it is always under tension. The stretching also helps when the foot is swelling.
- The best choice for the top of a boot is leather or a modern breathable synthetic material.
- Waterproofing: Sole should be fused onto the upper of the shoe. Avoid too many stitches on the upper part of the boot. They can leak or break open.
- The boot should have a steel shank to give you long term support at the arch.

REDUCE PAIN BY CORRECT LACING

Lacing Hiking Boots: The way you lace your hiking boot changes the pressure points in your boot and changes the feel of your boot.

Pressure Point that Hurts: Bypass the eyelets that are near that spot.

High Arch: Tie the laces so that the lower layer does not cross from side to side but goes up on the side.

Pressure on the Toe: Run one side of the lace back and forth and the second lace goes up diagonally. This method is frequently used for army boots.

To Improve the Fit of the Heal: To remove the pressure from the heal lace the boot but do not lace the last top hole or holes.

When buying boots or shoes remember that your feet will swell while traveling. If too large or too wide the heel will move, up and down or laterally, and you will not be sure of your footing.

BOOT LINERS

Remove the felt liners from winter boots when not in use as this will let them dry out. The best type of felt liners are those that are made of woven wool which are then cooked in boiling water which mats the wool and it looks like felt. Boots having this type of lining are used by the Canadian Army and are rated to -58°F (-50°C).

CARE OF YOUR LEATHER WALKING BOOTS

- Break in your boots on leisurely walks.
- Do not apply too much oil that will decompose the leather. Do not over wax your boots.
- Do not walk on machine oil as this will deteriorate your soles.
- Wash salt and perspiration stains off your boots with warm water. Let boots dry for a few days before applying Neat's foot oil.
- Do not leave your boots in the sun.
- Store your boots on a shoe tree.
- Do not store boots in plastic bags as they have to breath.
- Vary the tension of the lacing on your boots. At the top of the boot and in the shoe area it should be tight. Around the ankle it should be loose.
- When on a trip, always turn your boots upside down and shake them to remove any visitors before putting them on. The visitors can be scorpions.
- To avoid having the boot laces untie roll your socks over the knots of your laces.

TREATING LEATHER BOOTS AND CLOTHING

If leather gets wet do not place it too close to heat as it will get hard and brittle. After the leather is dry, wipe it with Neat's foot oil (or any oil that you can render from the hoofs and feet of moose, antelope, cow). Do not apply too much oil as you will fill the air pores in the leather and the garment or shoes will not retain heat.

NEAT'S FOOT OIL

This oil, which is derived from boiling the feet and shinbone of cows and other hoofed animals, is used to nourish and soften leather. Using it on straps, leather jackets, or boots will prolong their useful life.

HUMID BOOTS

Have a few pair of socks and change your socks at regular intervals during the day. The socks will accumulate unwanted humidity and your boots will stay fairly dry. Do not store your socks in your boots overnight as the boots cannot dry.

Shake your boots before putting them on, especially in the desert or dry areas, as insects might be sheltered in the humid boots. Humid boots are a likely refuge for scorpions and spiders.

SOCKS

Wear wool or cotton socks, they will absorb perspiration. Buy quality socks because a loosely wound yarn will wear out. Do not store your socks in your boots overnight as the socks and boots will not be able to dry. Have a second pair of socks and change them every few hours. Tie your humid socks to your backpack so that they can dry.

Extending the Life of Your Socks

If your socks have given up and your soles are getting thin, make a new insole with several sheets of birch bark. To replace or add to the soles of the socks you can use some soft grass, the fluff from milkweed seeds, or the fluff from cattails in the fall and winter. Milkweed seeds and cattail fluff are excellent insulators which should be replaced at regular intervals.

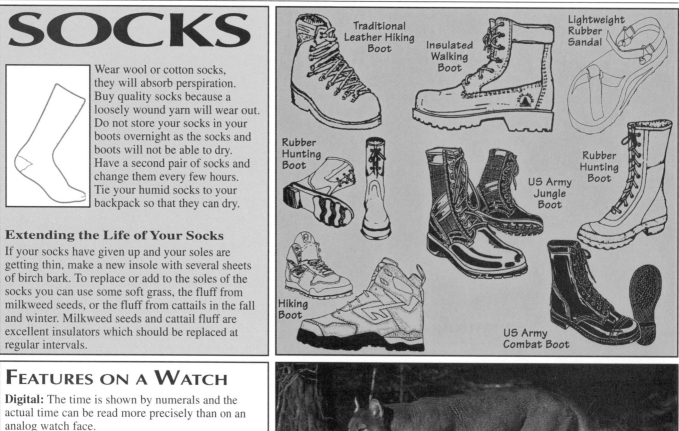

Traditional Leather Hiking Boot

Insulated Walking Boot

Lightweight Rubber Sandal

Rubber Hunting Boot

US Army Jungle Boot

Rubber Hunting Boot

Hiking Boot

US Army Combat Boot

FEATURES ON A WATCH

Digital: The time is shown by numerals and the actual time can be read more precisely than on an analog watch face.

Analog: This watch face is the old fashioned watch with hands indicating the time. With use the analog is easier to read because at a glance it will "show" the time and it does not have to be read.

- Depth in meters and waterproof to 600 feet (183 m).
- Time of high tide in your area.
- Sailing race icons indicating red and blue.
- Alarm: wake up and appointments.
- Calendar and face that lights up.
- Thermometer °C or °F.
- Stainless steel or plastic.
- Altimeters and barometers.
- Magnetic compass.
- Shock proof.

Minimize the choice of features. They all take electrical power from your watch's battery.

Puttees

Are gaiters used by armies all over the world for many centuries. They were used by the British, Canadian, and American forces up to the First World War and partially in the Second World War. The French Foreign Legion still uses them in Africa. Puttees were made of wool or cotton ribbons that were wound around the legs to cover the top of the boots and in some cases to below the knee.
Wool puttees were used in the winter and the cotton ones in the summer and in desert areas.

Increased Cougar Attacks In California

The population of cougars in California has reached between 4000 and 6000 and the number of encounters with humans are dramatically increasing from year to year. Game wardens are enrolled in a new 'Mountain Lion Boot Camp' so as to appreciate the power of a cougar.

Cougars have killed two people in 1994. These super hunters have wounded and menaced others. Luckily these people have managed to escape.

Man's increased encroachment on their territory, with the renewed interest in wildlife activities, has probably led to some of the wild cats losing their fear or respect of man.

California has a ban on cougar hunting since the 1960's but, because of more human contact, pressure is mounting to control the population.

At the boot camp, in the Tahoe National Forest, game wardens are taught the Old West tracking skills to recognize the age, sex, weight, and pace pattern of the cougar being followed. They also learn to measure the bite pattern of individual cougars to recognize their sex, age, and how to relate these marks to the injuries on the victims. The lessons include treeing a cougar with hounds and observing its reaction. The cougar is then released. The freed cougar will also have learned a lesson on how humans act.

The typical attack of a cougar is from behind biting into the jugular vein in the neck and shaking the victim to break the neck or using a front leg to twist and break the neck.

These attacks are very disconcerting as there were no cougar attacks on humans in the state from 1910 to 1986. Since 1990 eight attacks have occurred two of which were fatal. These two fatalities occurred during leisure activities, a woman walking and a man jogging in two different state parks.

SLEEPING BAG

TEMPERATURE RATING

This is the lowest temperature at which the bag will keep you warm. The rating is established by the manufacturer.

SIZE

The size of a bag should match the size of your body but also depends upon your other requirements. Ideally you want a bag as small as possible as it is easier to heat with your body.

WEIGHT

The ideal is the minimum weight with the least bulk when backpacking. The bag should still meet your temperature rating and size requirements. If you are traveling in a car you can buy a cheaper bulkier bag. The weight of a bag depends upon the temperature rating, size, insulation material, design, weight of material used in the construction, and the fixture such as zippers.

BULK

The bulk of a bag depends upon the temperature rating and the heat retention factor of the insulation. A quality insulation has the least weight and the least bulk while being transported and the highest loft for maximum retained heat. The insulation that has these best qualities is white goose down.

CONSTRUCTION

The construction of a sleeping bag includes:

Baffles: The baffling keeps the insulation material well distributed inside the bag. Well designed baffling reduces cold spots.

Different types of baffling:

Down filled bags have slant box baffles. *See the adjacent article.*

Synthetic Bags

- Shingle construction (louvered) is the most efficient.
- Double quilt sandwich is used in cheaper bags.
- Sewn through quilting is used in cheaper bags.

Cut of Material: The *standard cut* is called the space filler cut and it's advantage is that the inner shell falls onto the body and reduces the airspace. In the standard cut the inside liner is the same size as the outer shell.

The inside liner can be cut smaller than the outside shell. This is called a *differential cut*. This cut stops the elbow or other body parts from touching the outer shell which reduces the loft.

Shell: The shell should not be waterproof as it should breath to reduce moisture accumulation inside the bag. If moisture accumulates the sleeper becomes damp and cold. The material should allow 1 1/2 pints of water to escape in 8 hours. A sleeping bag should be well aired after and before use.

INSULATION MATERIAL

White Goose Down Filled

It retains the most warmth for the least weight. A down bag can be packed tighter than a synthetic bag and takes less space. A disadvantage of down is that it does not retain its loft if wet and it takes a long time to dry. Sleeping bags are usually used in tents so rarely get wet. The best down is white goose down as it has the highest heat retention to weight ratio. The main difference between duck down and goose down is the fact that the down in geese has a hard spin which helps in maintaining a high loft. Duck down has a soft spine so requires more down (more weight) for the same loft. Some other exotic products are used for insulation - silk cocoons, Asian camel hair, Tibetan goat hair.

Synthetic Fill

All better quality synthetics are nearly the same. There is a whole array of man-made insulation material available. They usually are easy to maintain and dry.

SELECTING A SLEEPING BAG

A sleeping bag does not warm you but it retains the heat that your body generates. The heat is retained by the air trapped inside the insulation of the bag. The more loft in the bag the more air space and the warmer the bag. A quality bag, for its weight, lets the minimum heat leave the body area. Sleeping bags are chosen with a temperature rating. The rating you choose should be the temperature at which you will camp. You can buy a summer bag, three season bag, winter bag, or a multilayer four season bag.

Features of a sleeping bag are:

- Temperature rating.
- Size.
- Weight.
- Design or Shape.
- Bulk.
- Type of construction.
- Insulation material.

BAFFLES

Quilt
- Polyester or down.
- Cold at stitching.

Double Quilt
- Polyester or down.
- More material than filling by weight.

Box
- Good for heat retention.

Slant and Off Set Construction
- Down only.
- Better than Box construction.

V-Tube Construction or Overlapping Tube
- Down only.
- Excellent for cold weather.

You can check the baffle type by moving the outside shell and inner shell up and down to feel the construction.

Verify:
- The foot baffle and space for your feet.
- Stitches should be double sewn at stress points.
- Avoid length wise baffles as the down accumulates in the feet.

SLEEPING BAG DESIGN

The design of a bag should match your needs.

Shape of a Bag

There are a wide range of shapes from a tight mummy bag up to a rectangular bag.

Rectangular Bag: The rectangular bag is the least efficient but it has many uses. It is a good family bag as it can be used by a child or adult or as a bed cover. Two rectangular bags can be zippered together to have a "family format". To increase the efficiency of a rectangular bag use a cotton flannel sleeping sack inside the bag to reduce the air cavities. A rectangular bag weighs an extra pound because of its shape. A rectangular bag has no hood so air will circulate over the head and shoulders. The bag is bulkier and cannot easily be compressed. Usually weighs much more than a mummy bag. Cold air comes in by way of the long zipper.

Semi-Rectangular: Slightly tapered but not as much as a semi-mummy bag.

Semi-Mummy Bag: A regular mummy bag is not too comfortable as it restricts the movement of the body. A semi-mummy bag is the choice if you need more room.

Mummy Bag: The mummy bag is the most efficient as there is limited airspace to heat. A well insulated tight mummy bag, with a short well covered zipper, a hood with a drawstring is very warm. You can get cramps as you will not be able to move your body in a tight mummy bag. It is difficult to enter the bag because of the tight fit and short zipper.

Hood

A hood covers your head and shoulder area. At least 85% of your body heat can be lost by this area. Hoods come with different fits, tight or loose. A tightly formed hood is very efficient but can be too warm for a summer bag. You will have to become used to a tight shoulder area. A hood is required if the tent has draft or convection currents (which occur in large tents) or you are sleeping outdoors.

Zipper

They must be strong, have pull tabs inside and outside, two way if possible, not jam easily, and be easy to maintain. The zipper opening should be covered by at least one wind baffle. Ideally there should be two or three baffles that can be buttoned down.

A two way zipper on a bag can zip up from the bottom to cool the feet without exposing the chest. A half-length zipper on an efficient mummy bag can leave the feet too hot.

Two rectangular bags can be zipped together to make a large bag. To do this you need a right hand and left hand zipper to mate two bags together.

SLEEPING BAG LINER

A cotton liner for your sleeping bag will eliminate the clamminess in a nylon blend sleeping bag. The liner will hug the body and reduce the heating energy required to keep you warm.

SLEEPING BAG COVER

Improves the insulating characteristic of the bag when camping with no tent. The bottom of the bag is waterproof material, the top of the bag can be cotton or other breathable material.

STORAGE AND MAINTENANCE

Hang a bag or roll it loosely but never store it in its stuff sack. Hand wash the bag in a large tub with mild soap and water. Rinse to remove all soap. Do not lift a wet bag by one end but lift it altogether as the wet weight of the bag might tear some of the baffling. Let the bag dry on a board inclined at an angle.

Mountaineers

Mountaineers might choose a quality child's bag instead of an adult bag. A child's bag is lighter to carry, has less bulk and is only required to cover the legs and thighs of the traveler. The mountaineer's heavy winter parka with its hood covers the upper part of the body.

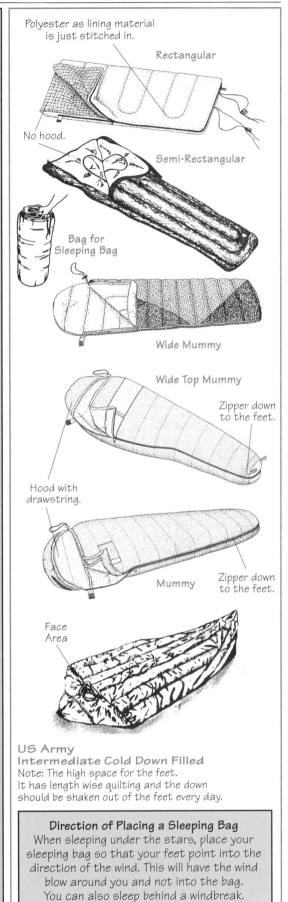

Polyester as lining material is just stitched in.

Rectangular

No hood.

Semi-Rectangular

Bag for Sleeping Bag

Wide Mummy

Wide Top Mummy

Zipper down to the feet.

Hood with drawstring.

Mummy

Zipper down to the feet.

Face Area

US Army
Intermediate Cold Down Filled
Note: The high space for the feet. It has length wise quilting and the down should be shaken out of the feet every day.

Direction of Placing a Sleeping Bag

When sleeping under the stars, place your sleeping bag so that your feet point into the direction of the wind. This will have the wind blow around you and not into the bag. You can also sleep behind a windbreak.

Sleeping Bag Pad
Self inflating.

Sleeping Bag Pad
Closed cell foam.

Pneumatic Sleeping Pad
Comfortable but heavy and can leak.

SLEEPING BAG PADS

These are an excellent investment as they will let you sleep more comfortably and they will reduce the transmission of humidity and cold from the ground. A quality foam pad will have closed air cells that will retain their spring and not let water pass through like a sponge.

Body Heat Loss
Radiation
Heat from the face that is not totally covered.
Respiration
Inhaling cold air and exhaling warm air.
Evaporation
Body cooling system releases
1 1/2 pt (1 L) of water in 8 hours.
Convection
From movement of air over
exposed parts of the body.
Transmission
Heat that is lost through contact
with the cold ground.

D. T. ABERCROMBIE SLEEPING BAG

This is the ultra light weight sleeping bag and weather protection made for D. T. Abercrombie for the ultimate camper-hiker of the 1890's. At that time a camping-hiking-mountain climbing-nature craze swept North America and Europe. Wealthy people bought quality equipment that had the lowest weight and left for long excursions in the woods and mountains. Abercrombie was a high end supplier who had exotic products such as Egyptian cotton tents, British Hardy fly rods, rucksacks, etc. These quality products have hardly been matched and are in high demand by collectors.

D. T. Abercrombie Sleeping Bag

TENTS 1860's - 1920's
PRODUCTS FOR FOREST CRUISERS

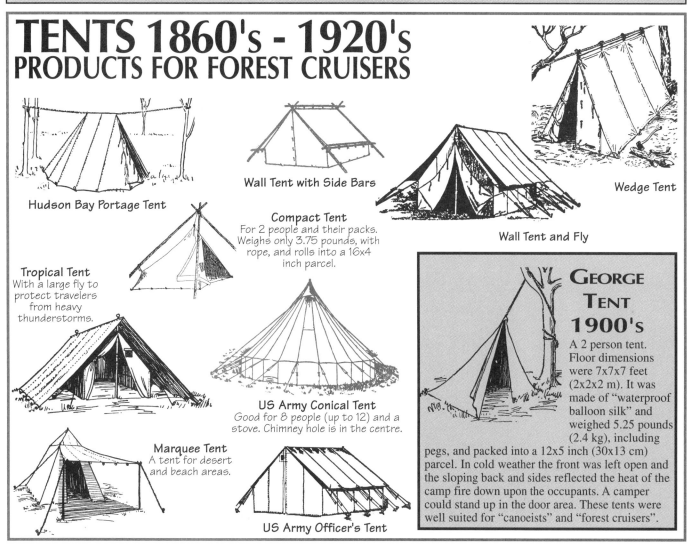

Hudson Bay Portage Tent

Wall Tent with Side Bars

Wedge Tent

Compact Tent
For 2 people and their packs. Weighs only 3.75 pounds, with rope, and rolls into a 16x4 inch parcel.

Wall Tent and Fly

Tropical Tent
With a large fly to protect travelers from heavy thunderstorms.

US Army Conical Tent
Good for 8 people (up to 12) and a stove. Chimney hole is in the centre.

Marquee Tent
A tent for desert and beach areas.

US Army Officer's Tent

GEORGE TENT 1900's
A 2 person tent. Floor dimensions were 7x7x7 feet (2x2x2 m). It was made of "waterproof balloon silk" and weighed 5.25 pounds (2.4 kg), including pegs, and packed into a 12x5 inch (30x13 cm) parcel. In cold weather the front was left open and the sloping back and sides reflected the heat of the camp fire down upon the occupants. A camper could stand up in the door area. These tents were well suited for "canoeists" and "forest cruisers".

BACKPACKS

Quick Snap Metal Clips
Allows adjustment of both the load-lifter and shoulder straps to a range of height and width setting.

Load-Lifter Straps
Controls pack sway and the distance between the pack and the suspension.

Kelty External Frame Back Pack

TYPES OF BACKPACKS

- Day packs
- Rucksacks
- External frame
- Internal frame
- Convertible luggage
- Pack board

Rucksack

Fashion Day Pack

Day Pack

Pack Board

Day Pack and Rucksack

For day trips and rock climbing. It is small and choose one that is well balanced. It should be easy to load with some external pockets, some lash points for extra items, padded shoulders and a waist strap for stability.

External Frame

Is made to carry heavy loads on long excursions. Most of the weight is carried on the hips. As the frame keeps the bag off your back you will be more comfortable on a hot day (*see First Aid on prickly heat*). Additional items can be attached to the framing and the frame can include a head strap to help balance a heavy load.

Internal Frame

Rides closer to the back giving you a better balance and is usually slimmer and so is easier to maneuver on tight trails. If you are in difficult terrain, biking, skiing or mountain climbing, an internal frame has a tighter fit and a lower center of gravity which will have less tendency to shift. When carrying a smaller load, at the end of the trip, the bag can be easily adjusted in accordance to the load.

Convertible Luggage

These bags can be either a backpack or a suitcase. The harness can be covered with a zippered cloth panel. It is useful when the bag is checked as airplane luggage because the harness will not get jammed on the conveyer belts.

Pack Board

It is used to carry very heavy objects such as boat motors or batteries. It is very flexible because anything can be lashed onto it. *See US Army Pack Board.*

BACKPACKS FOR WOMEN

Women have to choose a backpack to fit their physique. Some companies manufacture women's models.

Torso Length or Drop

Women usually have shorter torsos than men so that a man's backpack and hip straps will ride too low and the women's shoulders will have to carry most of the load.

Shoulder Harness

Women usually have narrower shoulders and regular shoulder straps will slip off especially when going up or down hills.

Harness Pads

Unisex pads are usually too wide, and lack the required curvature. They cause chafing at the armpits. This is because the up and down movement of the arms. Wide pads will also restrict the breasts.

Hip Belts

Men's hip belts do not accommodate a woman's profile. The bottom of the pad digs into the woman's hip.

TO CHOOSE A BAG

A good bag should distribute the weight of the cargo over your shoulders and hips. Meet your travel needs and be large enough. *See article for women.*

Factors to consider:

Volume: To determine the size of bag required assemble everything that you will take for the trip. Place these items in a large garbage bag and measure, in inches or centimeters, the height, width and length of the filled bag. Multiply these numbers and you will have the number of cubic inches or centimeters of volume you require for your bag. Buy a bag with this volume.

Torso Length: Every person has a different "drop". The "drop" is the length from the bottom of your neck to the hollow in your back (waist). The bag should have adjustments on the back panel to accommodate your torso length.

Width of Back: Your bag should be narrow enough for your elbows, while hiking, to swing back and forth with limited interference.

Adjustments: There should be a range of adjustments on the harness to adapt the bag to fit comfortably to your body.

Harness: Select a well padded harness.

Hip Belt: The hip belt should be cushioned and have adjustment straps ("trim straps") on the sides. These will let you adjust the belt to hug your waist without pressing your stomach. The hip belt should support 2/3 of the bag's weight.

Pockets: Check that pockets, strap attachments, add-on pouches are what you require.

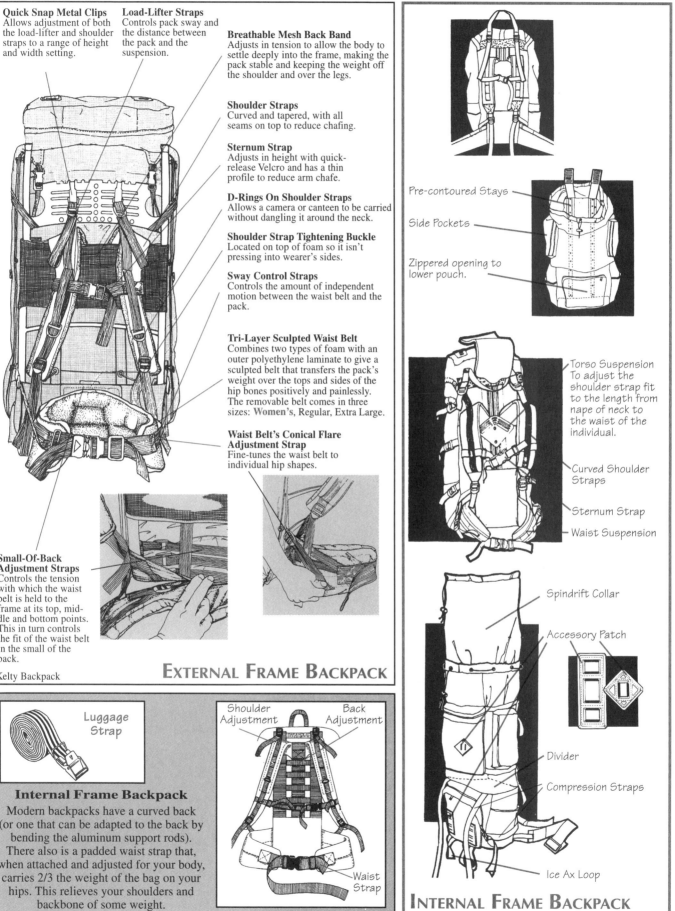

Quick Snap Metal Clips
Allows adjustment of both the load-lifter and shoulder straps to a range of height and width setting.

Load-Lifter Straps
Controls pack sway and the distance between the pack and the suspension.

Breathable Mesh Back Band
Adjusts in tension to allow the body to settle deeply into the frame, making the pack stable and keeping the weight off the shoulder and over the legs.

Shoulder Straps
Curved and tapered, with all seams on top to reduce chafing.

Sternum Strap
Adjusts in height with quick-release Velcro and has a thin profile to reduce arm chafe.

D-Rings On Shoulder Straps
Allows a camera or canteen to be carried without dangling it around the neck.

Shoulder Strap Tightening Buckle
Located on top of foam so it isn't pressing into wearer's sides.

Sway Control Straps
Controls the amount of independent motion between the waist belt and the pack.

Tri-Layer Sculpted Waist Belt
Combines two types of foam with an outer polyethylene laminate to give a sculpted belt that transfers the pack's weight over the tops and sides of the hip bones positively and painlessly. The removable belt comes in three sizes: **Women's**, Regular, Extra Large.

Waist Belt's Conical Flare Adjustment Strap
Fine-tunes the waist belt to individual hip shapes.

Small-Of-Back Adjustment Straps
Controls the tension with which the waist belt is held to the frame at its top, middle and bottom points. This in turn controls the fit of the waist belt in the small of the back.

Kelty Backpack

EXTERNAL FRAME BACKPACK

Pre-contoured Stays

Side Pockets

Zippered opening to lower pouch.

Torso Suspension
To adjust the shoulder strap fit to the length from nape of neck to the waist of the individual.

Curved Shoulder Straps

Sternum Strap

Waist Suspension

Spindrift Collar

Accessory Patch

Divider

Compression Straps

Ice Ax Loop

Luggage Strap

Internal Frame Backpack

Modern backpacks have a curved back (or one that can be adapted to the back by bending the aluminum support rods). There also is a padded waist strap that, when attached and adjusted for your body, carries 2/3 the weight of the bag on your hips. This relieves your shoulders and backbone of some weight.

Shoulder Adjustment

Back Adjustment

Waist Strap

INTERNAL FRAME BACKPACK

PACKING BACKPACKS

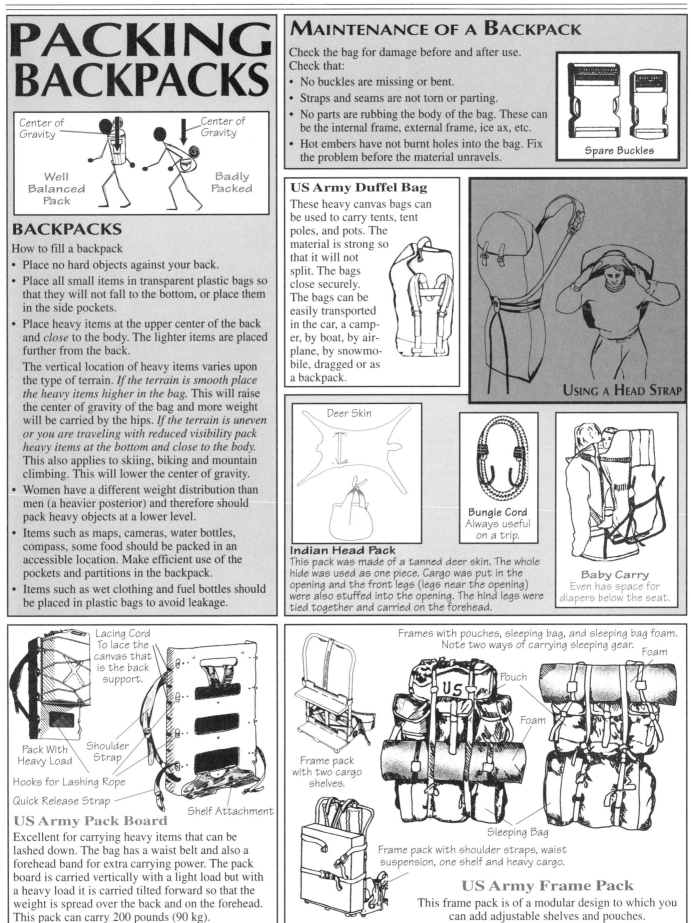

Center of Gravity

Center of Gravity

Well Balanced Pack

Badly Packed

BACKPACKS

How to fill a backpack

• Place no hard objects against your back.

• Place all small items in transparent plastic bags so that they will not fall to the bottom, or place them in the side pockets.

• Place heavy items at the upper center of the back and *close* to the body. The lighter items are placed further from the back.

  The vertical location of heavy items varies upon the type of terrain. *If the terrain is smooth place the heavy items higher in the bag.* This will raise the center of gravity of the bag and more weight will be carried by the hips. *If the terrain is uneven or you are traveling with reduced visibility pack heavy items at the bottom and close to the body.* This also applies to skiing, biking and mountain climbing. This will lower the center of gravity.

• Women have a different weight distribution than men (a heavier posterior) and therefore should pack heavy objects at a lower level.

• Items such as maps, cameras, water bottles, compass, some food should be packed in an accessible location. Make efficient use of the pockets and partitions in the backpack.

• Items such as wet clothing and fuel bottles should be placed in plastic bags to avoid leakage.

MAINTENANCE OF A BACKPACK

Check the bag for damage before and after use. Check that:

• No buckles are missing or bent.

• Straps and seams are not torn or parting.

• No parts are rubbing the body of the bag. These can be the internal frame, external frame, ice ax, etc.

• Hot embers have not burnt holes into the bag. Fix the problem before the material unravels.

Spare Buckles

US Army Duffel Bag

These heavy canvas bags can be used to carry tents, tent poles, and pots. The material is strong so that it will not split. The bags close securely. The bags can be easily transported in the car, a camper, by boat, by airplane, by snowmobile, dragged or as a backpack.

USING A HEAD STRAP

Deer Skin

Bungie Cord
Always useful on a trip.

Indian Head Pack

This pack was made of a tanned deer skin. The whole hide was used as one piece. Cargo was put in the opening and the front legs (legs near the opening) were also stuffed into the opening. The hind legs were tied together and carried on the forehead.

Baby Carry
Even has space for diapers below the seat.

Lacing Cord
To lace the canvas that is the back support.

Pack With Heavy Load

Shoulder Strap

Hooks for Lashing Rope

Quick Release Strap

Shelf Attachment

US Army Pack Board

Excellent for carrying heavy items that can be lashed down. The bag has a waist belt and also a forehead band for extra carrying power. The pack board is carried vertically with a light load but with a heavy load it is carried tilted forward so that the weight is spread over the back and on the forehead. This pack can carry 200 pounds (90 kg).

Frames with pouches, sleeping bag, and sleeping bag foam. Note two ways of carrying sleeping gear.

Foam

US

Pouch

Foam

Frame pack with two cargo shelves.

Sleeping Bag

Frame pack with shoulder straps, waist suspension, one shelf and heavy cargo.

US Army Frame Pack

This frame pack is of a modular design to which you can add adjustable shelves and pouches.

TENTS

TO CHOOSE A TENT

A tent should keep you dry, cool in the summer (summer tent), warm in the winter (winter tent), be a reasonable weight and easy to setup.

- Functional design and easy setup.
- High quality material and design.
- The stitching should be sturdy, well placed, and possibly waterproofed. The adjacent material can have some form of secure overlapping.
- No-seeum mesh in the windows and doors to protect you from insects.
- Tub style waterproof floors to raise the floor seams above the ground to prevent leaking. In better quality tents the floor seams are fully taped for extra protection against moisture.
- Each individual, including children, need approximately 3x8 feet (1x2 m) or 24 square feet (2 m²).
- Two or three windows that have zip closed flaps and bug netting to let the air circulate.
- A high doorway for easy access. The door can also have an awning cover for inclement weather and protection against the sun.
- Mesh side storage pockets.
- Quick attaching rainfly with sealed seams.
- Vestibule for extra gear storage.
- Tempered aluminum shock-corded poles. Spun aluminum with no welding seams.
- Correct pegs for the camping site.

Snap-on Clip System

This is the ideal system to attach the tent material to the self supporting poles.

It is very convenient as you do not have to feed the poles through the long tubes as on regular tents.

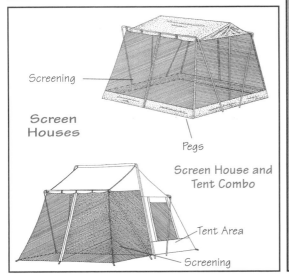

Screening

Screen Houses

Pegs

Screen House and Tent Combo

Tent Area

Screening

TENT DESIGNS

'A' FRAME TENT

This is the traditional tent design with two poles on the inside (one partially blocking the doorway) and guy cords. The biggest disadvantage is the lack of headroom and the difficulty to stand up. To improve upon the headroom larger models have vertical walls on the sides and the roof had a flatter pitch.

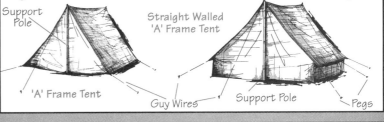

Support Pole

Straight Walled 'A' Frame Tent

'A' Frame Tent

Guy Wires

Support Pole

Pegs

DOME TENT

A dome tent has straight walls and more usable interior space. Most models are self supporting and have easy access. As the tent is freestanding it can be installed on hard ground and weigh it down with some heavy rocks on the inside. Its weight/sleeping area ratio is much less than the "A" Frame. A vestibule which is part of the rain fly can be added to a dome tent to enlarge the storage area.

With Medium Fly

Clip-on Attachments

A World Famous Free Standing Dome Tent With Clip-on attachments

Pegs

Small Fly

Full Fly

Pegs

Three Season Tent With Vestibule

Sleeping Capacity and Size

Standing Position

Pictograms
These illustrations give the size of a Eureka tent, the sleeping capacity, and the standing position at the centre of the tent.

Tunnel Hoop Tent

This tent is like a spider covered with material. It is arch walled but tapers at the feet. It sleeps one or two but is very tight. It is very light and excellent for cycling.

Hoop

Door

Screen

A fly is put over the tent.

Tapered at Feet

USING A TENT

Ground Preparation

Make sure the ground is free of sharp twigs and rocks.

Ground Sheet

A ground sheet placed under the floor of the tent will prolong the life of the tent. Make sure that the footprint, of the tarpaulin, is *smaller* than the tent's to avoid water collecting below the tent. A ground sheet can also be placed in the tent to reduce the humidity that wicks through the floor. Never wear shoes in a tent as they will apply too much pressure on the soft flooring and pierce holes.

Drainage Trench

Dig a small trench around the tent, especially on the up slope side of the tent.

Trowel
A trowel is used to dig a trench around a tent.

Pegs

Always use pegs or rock weights even with a self supporting tent as it might be blown into the lake or fire.

Fly

This is the outer protective shell of the tent. It should not touch your tent's surface but offer sufficient space for currents of air to keep your tent cool. It is usually made of nylon taffeta or rip stop nylon that is made waterproof with a polyurethane coating. Always use your rainfly to protect your tent against ultra violet rays. A nylon tent left erect for a long time in the sun can be damaged by UV rays. If camping in one spot for a long time pick a shaded campsite. Always have the possibility of lightning on your mind.

Cooking Fires and the Tent

Do not cook with open flames inside or near your tent. Never store flammables or refuel any appliance in your tent. All campfires should be built at a distance from the tent and downwind to avoid embers from blowing onto the tent. Tents are fire retardant but not fireproof and the retardant loses its effect over time.

Oils, Insect Repellent, etc.

Do not put any oils, insect repellent or other liquids on the surface of your tent or fly.

INSECTS IN FIRST AID CHAPTER

FEATURES OF A TENT

Size

Take a tent one person larger than you expect in the tent. You will appreciate the extra room.

Season

The season category of the tent you choose depends upon in which season you will travel *and at what altitude*. It can be very cold at night. For cold regions get a sturdy (to carry some snow) tight fitting tent. In warm areas you need ventilation and insect screens.

Poles

Aircraft aluminum poles are sturdy, light and will not corrode. Metal tipped fiberglass is more economical. Most poles have shock cords.

Pegs

Some tents are free standing but they should be pegged down as they might blow away. The type of pegs you choose depends upon the type of ground. Special pegs exist for snow and loose sand.

Tent Models

Many different models of tents are available each one for a specific market.

Tent Materials

A tent is usually made of nylon or rip stop nylon. A three season tent has nylon mesh doors and windows to keep the tent cool, improve ventilation and keep out the insects. Tents have waterproof floors which sometimes rise up the sides. This tub style floor keeps out the water from a downpour but makes the tent more difficult to pack. Tents can also have flat floors with waterproofed and taped edge seams.

TREATING AND MAINTAINING A NEW TENT

Seal the Seams

Use a seam sealer to seal the needle holes that can wick water through the seams of a tent. Reapply the sealer as necessary. Most leakage will usually occur along a stitched seam. Apply sealer on both the outside and inside seams of the tent.

Waterproofing

Exposure to heat, cold, UV radiation, stress on the seams, folding during storage, and bad storage conditions can all affect the material and waterproofing of a tent.

USE OF TENT

Accessories

Aluminum and fiberglass poles and pegs should be kept clean and dry. Poles with shock cords are fragile especially at the interlocking edges between the pole sections. They can be bent, stepped on, or damaged by the shock card. Lubricate the ends of the pole sections with soap or wax to reduce any resistance when assembling them. Do not snap fiberglass poles together as the ends can be easily damaged.

Zippers

Lubricate the zippers with a mild soap or paraffin wax. Do not use oil as it will attract grit and make the nylon deteriorate. Never force a zipper as it can damage the slider or teeth. Keep sand off the zipper.

Repairs

Small holes can be closed by using seam sealer or nail polish. Ripstop repair tape can repair small tears.

Cleaning the Tent

Erect your tent before hand washing it. Wash it with a sponge and a mild soap. Do not use detergent, machine wash or dry clean. Do not fold your tent, for storage, when wet or on very humid days. Store it in a cool dry spot (not in the sunlight near the window). Nylon can be damaged when in the proximity of acids and caustic solutions. Avoid car batteries, acidic fruit juices, insect repellents, and hair sprays.

Storage

Make sure that your tent is clean and dry before storing. If your tent was taken down on a humid or rainy day re-erect at your house, wipe it down and let it dry. Store the tent in a cool, dark and dry spot. Do not store on a concrete floor as moisture and released chemicals from the cement can damage nylon. If stored in a damp environment there might be color transfer from the dark to light areas.

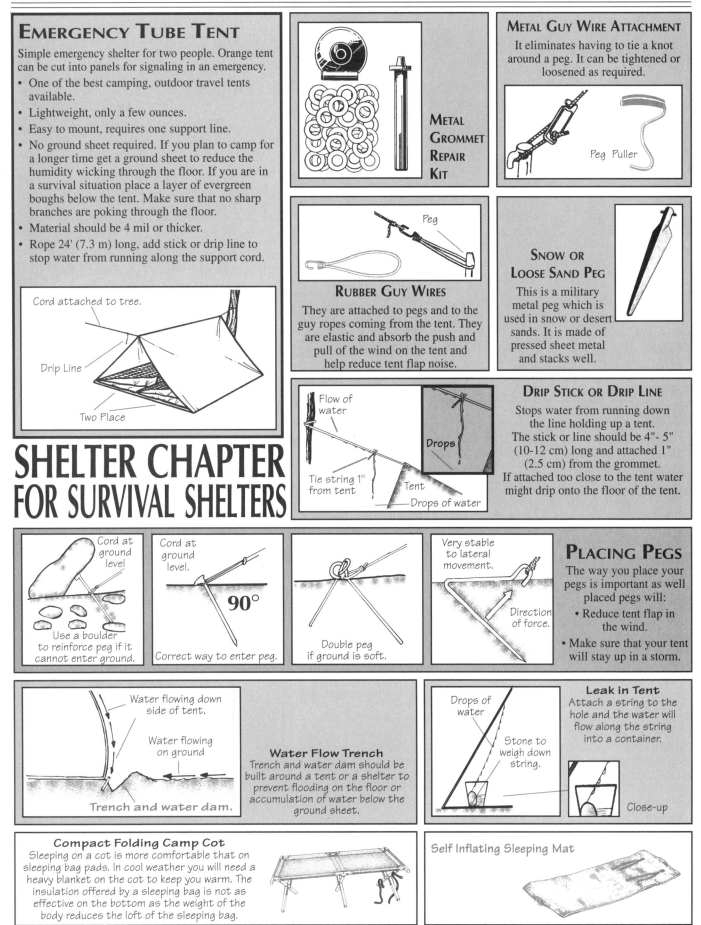

EMERGENCY TUBE TENT

Simple emergency shelter for two people. Orange tent can be cut into panels for signaling in an emergency.

- One of the best camping, outdoor travel tents available.
- Lightweight, only a few ounces.
- Easy to mount, requires one support line.
- No ground sheet required. If you plan to camp for a longer time get a ground sheet to reduce the humidity wicking through the floor. If you are in a survival situation place a layer of evergreen boughs below the tent. Make sure that no sharp branches are poking through the floor.
- Material should be 4 mil or thicker.
- Rope 24' (7.3 m) long, add stick or drip line to stop water from running along the support cord.

Cord attached to tree.

Drip Line

Two Place

SHELTER CHAPTER FOR SURVIVAL SHELTERS

METAL GROMMET REPAIR KIT

RUBBER GUY WIRES

They are attached to pegs and to the guy ropes coming from the tent. They are elastic and absorb the push and pull of the wind on the tent and help reduce tent flap noise.

Peg

Flow of water

Tie string 1" from tent

Tent

Drops of water

Drops

METAL GUY WIRE ATTACHMENT

It eliminates having to tie a knot around a peg. It can be tightened or loosened as required.

Peg Puller

SNOW OR LOOSE SAND PEG

This is a military metal peg which is used in snow or desert sands. It is made of pressed sheet metal and stacks well.

DRIP STICK OR DRIP LINE

Stops water from running down the line holding up a tent. The stick or line should be 4"- 5" (10-12 cm) long and attached 1" (2.5 cm) from the grommet. If attached too close to the tent water might drip onto the floor of the tent.

Cord at ground level

Use a boulder to reinforce peg if it cannot enter ground.

Cord at ground level.

90°

Correct way to enter peg.

Double peg if ground is soft.

Very stable to lateral movement.

Direction of force.

PLACING PEGS

The way you place your pegs is important as well placed pegs will:
- Reduce tent flap in the wind.
- Make sure that your tent will stay up in a storm.

Water flowing down side of tent.

Water flowing on ground

Trench and water dam.

Water Flow Trench
Trench and water dam should be built around a tent or a shelter to prevent flooding on the floor or accumulation of water below the ground sheet.

Drops of water

Stone to weigh down string.

Leak in Tent
Attach a string to the hole and the water will flow along the string into a container.

Close-up

Compact Folding Camp Cot
Sleeping on a cot is more comfortable that on sleeping bag pads. In cool weather you will need a heavy blanket on the cot to keep you warm. The insulation offered by a sleeping bag is not as effective on the bottom as the weight of the body reduces the loft of the sleeping bag.

Self Inflating Sleeping Mat

CAMPING STOVES

Find a reliable stove, one that has easily available fuel, works in all weather conditions and at high and low altitudes.

WHITE GAS

This is the best fuel for avid campers, hikers and mountaineers. The flame blows like a pressurized blow torch and because of this it is quite wind proof. It is efficient at all temperatures and cooks fast but sometimes it is difficult to have a low enough setting to "simmer". The fuel is easy to find.

Maintenance

A white gas stove requires attention.

* The air pressure pump has to be pumped to pressurize the fuel. When lighting the stove there might be a temporary flare-up (light it from the side). The stove has to be kept clean, *especially the jet assembly*.

* Keep it clean, oil the pump. Replace the gasket rings if the pump leaks. If a replacement gasket is not available cut one out of a piece of leather. Oil the leather and this will serve as a temporary gasket.

* Disassemble the jet section (it is simple) if your stove sputters. It is time to soak it in white gas and wipe it clean with a soft tissue.

* Do not use old fuel (one which has been opened or is in the stove) as the fuel decomposes after a few months, and forms soot in the jet system.

GASOLINE OR KEROSENE

If traveling to remote a area or overseas buy a "dual fuel" stove that can use white gas, gasoline or kerosene. When using gasoline or kerosene clean your stove at frequent intervals. These fuels being dirty will deposit carbon soot on your stove an reduce its heating capacity.

ALCOHOL

Alcohol burns at low temperatures therefor take longer to heat your meal. Stoves using alcohol require minimal maintenance. The fuel is easy to find. You can use denatured alcohol, methyl alcohol (wood alcohol) or isopropyl alcohol (rubbing alcohol). In general alcohol stoves are simple to operate.

BUTANE OR BUTANE-PROPANE MIXTURE

These stoves are easy to operate and require minimal maintenance. Butane comes in small (usually blue) replaceable canisters. These canisters *cannot* be refilled but are usually easy to find.

Their major drawback is that pure butane will not vaporize (go from liquid state to a gas state) below 32°F (0°C). For lower temperatures: at 20°F (-7°C) you will need a mixture of *butane-propane* and at 10°F (-12°C) you will need *ISO butane*. If the canister is not well mounted it might leak gas when not in use.

A butane tank is filled with liquid gas topped off with a layer of lighter vaporized gas. *Do not shake the tank before using* as some of the liquid gas might come out with the vaporized gas when you light the stove.

Maintenance

Liquid butane to vaporize into gas requires heat to make the transition from a liquid to a gas state. This heat partially comes from the surroundings of the butane tank and from the remaining liquid butane. (This is similar to the workings of a refrigerator or when sweat on your forehead dries (becomes a gas) and cools your forehead). If the outdoor temperature is cold water will condense on the outside of the butane tank and the liquid gas, inside, has also become colder. This reduces the liquid butane conversion to gas and the flame pressure will decrease. Keep a spare tank in a warm place and change tanks or warm your cold tank *in your hands. Do not place a canister in hot water or over a fire as it might explode.*

SEE COOKING CHAPTER

STOVE FUELS

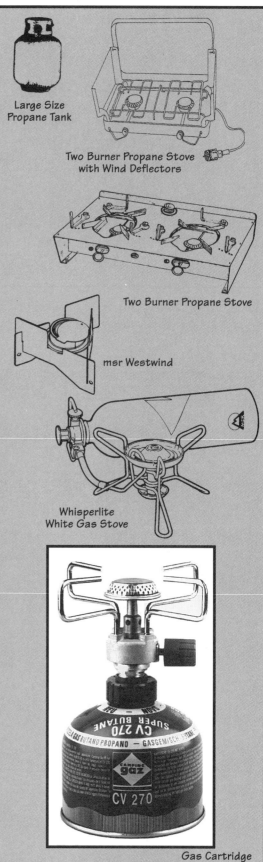

Large Size Propane Tank

Two Burner Propane Stove with Wind Deflectors

Two Burner Propane Stove

msr Westwind

Whisperlite White Gas Stove

Gas Cartridge

COOKING & CAMPING ACCESSORIES

Insect Repellent

Supreme Hook

Fish Line

Whistle

Sinker

First Aid Kit

Match Case

Snelled Hook

Survival Mirror

Jig Hook

Water Purification Tablets

Map Compass

Plastic Egg Carrier

Folding Grill

Heat Reflector for Camping Stove

Plastic Water Bottle

Family Mess Kit

GI Can Opener

Flint Fire Starter

Camping Cutlery Kit

Dual Burner Propane

Dual Burner Propane With Wind Deflector

X/GX Multifuel

Rapid Fire ISO Butane

Whisperlite International White Gas + Kerosene

FIRE CHAPTER
HOW TO COOK & MAKE A FIRE

SEWING KIT
Repairing buttons, torn seams, torn garments or buckles on your backpack. A must on any trip.

Stitching Canvas

COOKING & CAMPING ACCESSORIES

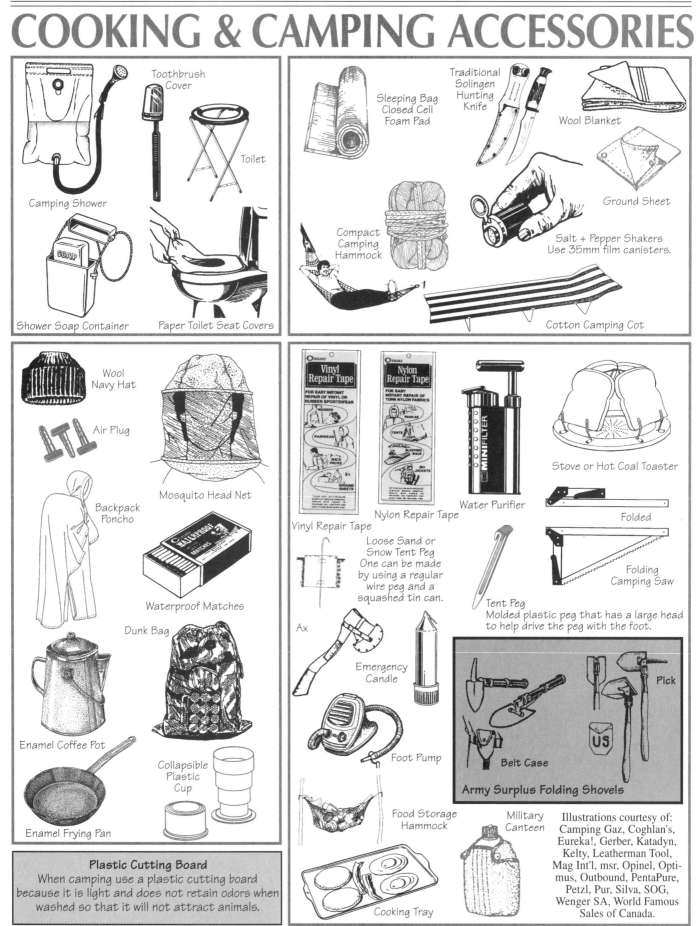

Toothbrush Cover

Toilet

Camping Shower

Shower Soap Container

Paper Toilet Seat Covers

Sleeping Bag Closed Cell Foam Pad

Traditional Solingen Hunting Knife

Wool Blanket

Ground Sheet

Compact Camping Hammock

Salt + Pepper Shakers Use 35mm film canisters.

Cotton Camping Cot

Wool Navy Hat

Air Plug

Mosquito Head Net

Backpack Poncho

Waterproof Matches

Dunk Bag

Enamel Coffee Pot

Collapsible Plastic Cup

Enamel Frying Pan

Vinyl Repair Tape

Nylon Repair Tape

Water Purifier

Stove or Hot Coal Toaster

Folded

Folding Camping Saw

Loose Sand or Snow Tent Peg One can be made by using a regular wire peg and a squashed tin can.

Tent Peg
Molded plastic peg that has a large head to help drive the peg with the foot.

Ax

Emergency Candle

Foot Pump

Pick

Belt Case

US

Army Surplus Folding Shovels

Food Storage Hammock

Military Canteen

Cooking Tray

Illustrations courtesy of: Camping Gaz, Coghlan's, Eureka!, Gerber, Katadyn, Kelty, Leatherman Tool, Mag Int'l, msr, Opinel, Optimus, Outbound, PentaPure, Petzl, Pur, Silva, SOG, Wenger SA, World Famous Sales of Canada.

Plastic Cutting Board
When camping use a plastic cutting board because it is light and does not retain odors when washed so that it will not attract animals.

DESERT TRAVEL CHAPTER 5

Deserts cover 20% of the land surface of the world. It is an arid and barren region which does not support normal life due to the lack of water. Temperatures range from over 136°F (58°C) in Mexico to the extreme cold of the Gobi desert (-50°F, -45°C) in Asia. Day to night time temperature fluctuations can range 72°F (39°) in the inland Sinai.

Some species of animals and plants have adapted to this rigorous environment even though annual rainfall can vary from zero inches to ten inches (0-25.4 cm). Desert terrain can vary but the common factor is the lack of water. Deserts can be divided into three categories:
Mountain, rocky plateau, and sandy or dune deserts.

Mirage of Water on Road

MIRAGE

Heat Wave Mirage
Image in black is the actual horizon. The color shows the horizon through the diffraction of the rising heat waves. Your mind might project this image as being palm trees. What you think you are seeing (the palm trees) is a mirage.

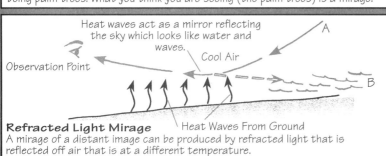

Heat waves act as a mirror reflecting the sky which looks like water and waves.
Cool Air
A
B
Observation Point
Heat Waves From Ground

Refracted Light Mirage
A mirage of a distant image can be produced by refracted light that is reflected off air that is at a different temperature.
In the above case the air is cool, and dense, below the arrows shows air that is hot coming from the sun heated ground. The distant image coming from A (can be clouds, mountains etc.) will be reflected by the unequal densities of the air and can appear as 'water' at B. You can see this effect on highways that have a shimmering wet look on hot sunny days. *See above photograph.*

SUNLIGHT LIGHTING TRICKS

Atmospheric conditions and sunlight can cause tricks with your vision and interpretation of images that you see.

- A strong sun with low cloud density can combine to produce *bright glaring light* conditions during the day.
- Sometimes light allows *unlimited visibility* and your normal perception of distance can be totally distorted. In this case you will have a tendency to grossly underestimate distance. This is important if you are aiming at a target because you will shoot short.
- Visibility can be degraded by rising heat waves which cause *mirages*. This heat shimmer distortion is strongest when you look into the sun or through binoculars. Observation is best from a high point at dusk or dawn or on moonlit nights.

CLIMATE AND WEATHER

Temperature Extremes in the Desert

Highest Temperature	136.4°F (58°C)	**Mexico**
Coldest Temperature	-50°F (-45°C)	**Gobi Desert**

- Low temperatures can be aggravated by a high windchill factor.
- The sun in the cloudless sky will heat the desert but at night the desert will cool to near freezing.

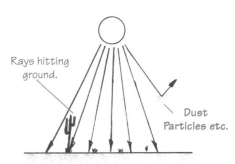

Rays hitting ground.

Dust Particles etc.

Daytime: As the desert sky is clear with no clouds, humidity or vegetation cover 90% of the solar rays hit and heat the ground. Only 10% of the rays are deflected by dust particles etc. in the sky. This is why desert areas are so hot in the day.

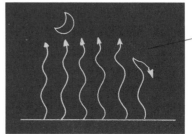

Dust Particles

Nighttime: As there is no insulating cover 90% of heat is lost by the ground and only 10% is reflected back by dust particles. This loss of heat causes the sharp temperature drop at night. This is why clothing should not be discarded in the day and you should travel in the early morning, evening or moonlit nights if there are no obstacles.

DESERT CAUSED BY A MOUNTAIN OBSTRUCTION

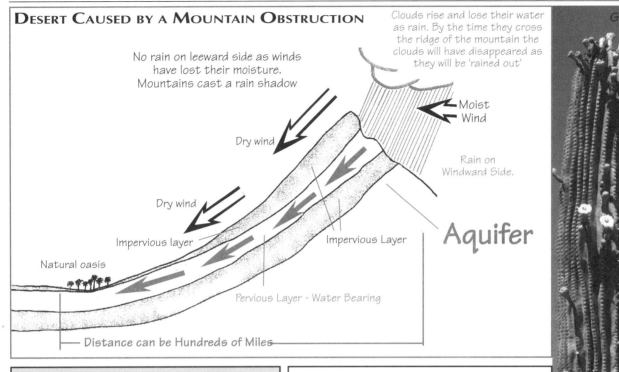

No rain on leeward side as winds have lost their moisture. Mountains cast a rain shadow

Clouds rise and lose their water as rain. By the time they cross the ridge of the mountain the clouds will have disappeared as they will be 'rained out'

Giant Saguaro Cactus

Dry wind

Moist Wind

Rain on Windward Side.

Dry wind

Aquifer

Impervious layer

Impervious Layer

Natural oasis

Pervious Layer - Water Bearing

Distance can be Hundreds of Miles

THE ELEMENTS IN THE DESERT

RAIN

There is a lack of water in all deserts. When it rains it might be as a single rainstorm, including hail, which will rapidly run off. Rain falling several hundred miles away can cause flash flooding in the local dry stream beds. This can be extremely hazardous so be alert to any sudden changes in the surrounding noise.

WATER

All life on the desert is based upon the availability of water. Permanent rivers do exist, e.g. Colorado, but they are fed by the drainage basin in wet areas outside of the desert area. Ground water in oasis or near surface wells comes from aquifers that might originate hundreds of miles away and the water might have fallen as rain 2000 years ago.

Water in the desert should be given the highest respect and a natural source should never be disturbed or contaminated as it might take years for it to be potable again.

WINDS

Desert winds can reach hurricane force and the blown sand can feel as if it is emerging from a sand blaster. The winds in Iran can blow up to 75 miles per hour for up to 120 days. Rapid temperature changes will follow strong winds.

VEGETATION

The indigenous vegetation has physiologically adapted itself to desert conditions. Some plants have large horizontal root systems to take advantage of any rain that might fall. Other plants have vertical root systems so that they can reach the water table or subsurface water.

- Palm trees indicate water within two to three feet (1 m) from the surface.
- Salt Grass implies water within six feet (2 m).
- Cottonwood and willow trees imply water within 10 - 12 feet (3-4 m).

Other plants, e.g.. cacti, have no relationship to the water table because they store their water. Some drought resistant seeds lie dormant for years and only grow for a brief period after a rainstorm.

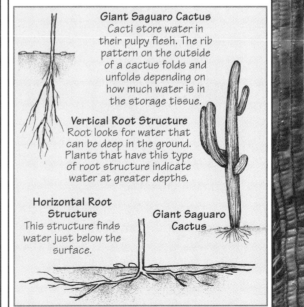

Giant Saguaro Cactus Cacti store water in their pulpy flesh. The rib pattern on the outside of a cactus folds and unfolds depending on how much water is in the storage tissue.

Vertical Root Structure Root looks for water that can be deep in the ground. Plants that have this type of root structure indicate water at greater depths.

Horizontal Root Structure This structure finds water just below the surface.

Giant Saguaro Cactus

The Large Deserts of North America

Desert	Location
Sonoran Desert	Arizona extends south into Mexico.
Colorado Desert	California and Arizona.
Chihuahuan Desert	Mexico and north into Texas and New Mexico.
Mojave Desert	California, extends into Nevada and Arizona.
Great Basin Desert	Utah and Nevada

TYPES OF DESERTS

DIFFERENT DESERT ZONES IN NORTH AMERICA

Life Zone	Inches of rain per year	Location	Elevation above sea level (feet)	Plants	Animals
Arctic-Alpine	30-35	Above the timber line	Above 12,000	Lichens, grasses	Mountain goat
Hudsonian	30 -35	High mountains	9,500-12000	Spruce, Alpine fir	Golden eagle, Bighorn sheep
Canadian	25 - 30	Mountains	8,000-10,000	White & Douglas fir	Black bear, grouse
Transition	19 -25	Plateau	7,000-8,000	Ponderosa pine	Mountain lion, Chipmunk
Upper Sonoran*	12 - 20	Mesas, foothills, Great Basin Desert	3,5000-7,000	Sage brush, Pinyon juniper	Prairie dog, Black-tailed jack rabbit
Lower Sonoran*	3 - 15	Sonoran, Mojave & Chihuahuan deserts	500-4000	Ocotillo, Creosote bush, Salt bush	Collared lizard, Kangaroo rat
Dry Tropical*	1 - 6	along Colorado River	below 500	Senita cactus, Organ pipe cactus	Gila monster, Sidewinder rattlesnake

* Considered as traditional deserts.

MOUNTAIN DESERT

Mountain deserts are areas of barren hills or mountains separated by flat and dry basins. The high ground can rise to the height of several thousand feet (300+ m) above sea level.

Rainfall occurring at high altitudes runs off in flash floods which erode deep gullies and ravines and deposit sand and rocks at their mouths. The water might give life to temporary vegetation, but rapidly evaporates. The land returns to its barren state until the next rainfall. If all the water does not evaporate it might remain in a basin creating a shallow lake like Great Salt Lake or the Dead Sea, both known for their high salt content.

ROCKY MOUNTAIN PLATEAUS

These plateaus have slight relief interspersed by extensive flat areas with quantities of solid or broken rock at or near the surface. The area might be cut by dry steep walled canyons. Very narrow canyons being very dangerous because of possible flash floods.

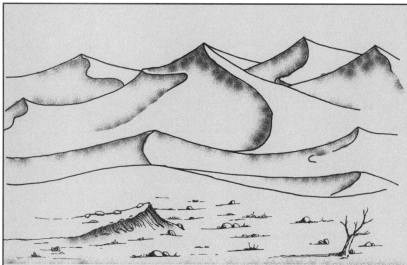

North American Sand Dunes

State	Sand Dune Park
Colorado	Great Sand Dunes
New Mexico	White Sands
California	Imperial Dunes
Utah	Coral Pink Sands
Idaho	St. Anthony Dunes
Idaho	Bruneau Sand Dunes
Oregon	Oregon Dunes
Michigan	Sleeping Bear Dunes
Indiana	Indiana Dunes
Wyoming	Killpecker Dunes

SANDY OR DUNE DESERTS

These deserts are extensive relatively flat areas covered by sand or gravel which can be ancient deposits or modern wind erosion. In some cases the dunes can rise to over 1000 feet (300 m) and be 10 - 15 miles (16-24 km) long. The plant life is scrub that reaches six feet (2 m) high. Examples of this type of desert can be seen in parts of California and Mexico.

DUNES

Sand dunes cover less than one percent of the deserts in North America.

Sand dunes can move from less than one foot (0.3 m) to up to 80 feet (24 m) per year. This movement depends upon the strength of the wind (in a constant direction), the size of the dune, the shape of the dune, and the amount and height of the surrounding vegetation.

Alaska dunes are perched on the frozen ground.

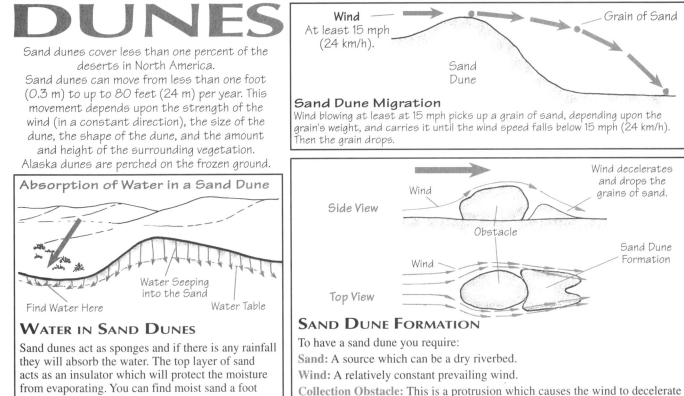

Wind
At least 15 mph (24 km/h).

Grain of Sand

Sand Dune

Sand Dune Migration

Wind blowing at least at 15 mph picks up a grain of sand, depending upon the grain's weight, and carries it until the wind speed falls below 15 mph (24 km/h). Then the grain drops.

Absorption of Water in a Sand Dune

Find Water Here

Water Seeping into the Sand

Water Table

WATER IN SAND DUNES

Sand dunes act as sponges and if there is any rainfall they will absorb the water. The top layer of sand acts as an insulator which will protect the moisture from evaporating. You can find moist sand a foot below the surface. Plants do not grow on this potentially ideal water source because the sand is continually shifting. Plants can be buried by the sand or their roots can be exposed by the shifting sand. The sand in the dunes do not provide the nutrients for plant growth.

Desert areas with no dunes will usually lose any water from a rainstorm by runoff.

Snow in the Sonoran Desert

Wind decelerates and drops the grains of sand.

Side View

Wind

Obstacle

Wind

Top View

Sand Dune Formation

SAND DUNE FORMATION

To have a sand dune you require:

Sand: A source which can be a dry riverbed.

Wind: A relatively constant prevailing wind.

Collection Obstacle: This is a protrusion which causes the wind to decelerate and it will drop the sand which will then build up. On a small scale this can be observed in a sandy area where there is a sand accumulation on the leeward side of a blade of grass protruding through the sand. In the winter you see snow drifts in sand dune type formations.

TRAVERSE DUNE

A variant of the crescent dune but it is more straight and usually found in the center of a dune field. They occur in areas of large quantities of sand and wind blowing from one constant direction.

LONGITUDINAL DUNE

They are parallel and form in the direction of the wind. They form where there is limited sand.

STAR DUNE

These are formed by winds blowing equally strong from different directions during the year. They occur in areas of much sand. Major examples of this type of dune are in the Sahara and Arabian deserts.

PARABOLIC DUNE

These usually are stable dunes which are anchored by vegetation where the leeward tip can be creeping very slowly.

CRESCENT SHAPED DUNE (BARCHAN)

This is an active dune which moves up to eighty feet per year. The winds will usually blow from one direction all year and their tips point leeward. As this dune is always moving vegetation will not have time to establish a foot hold. These dunes usually are on the outside fringes of a dune field. They form in areas of limited sand.

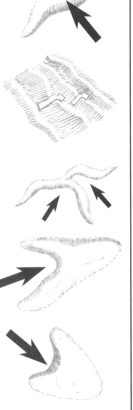

ANIMALS OF THE DESERT

INVERTEBRATES

Invertebrates such as spiders, scorpions and centipedes as well as insects of almost every type are found in the desert. Lice, mites, and flies are attracted by food or moisture or the presence of humans. These invertebrates are unpleasant and can carry diseases such as scrub typhus and dysentery. Scorpion stings, centipede and spider bites can be very painful but seldom fatal. Death can be caused by certain species of scorpion, black widow or recluse spiders. *For more information on poisonous animals see the First Aid & Insect Chapters.*

Scorpions

Their daytime dwelling is given away by a flat tunnel entrance that has been dug into the earth. The dirt entrails at the opening of the tunnel give away the location. Most are harmless and the sting being as bad as a bee or wasp sting.
A small (2", 5 cm) scorpion found in Northern Mexico and the adjacent area in Arizona has a poisonous injection. Symptoms are: restlessness and increased flow of saliva. See First Aid.

Millipedes
Small worms with a '1000' legs. They are harmless.

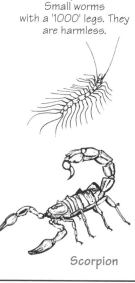

Scorpion

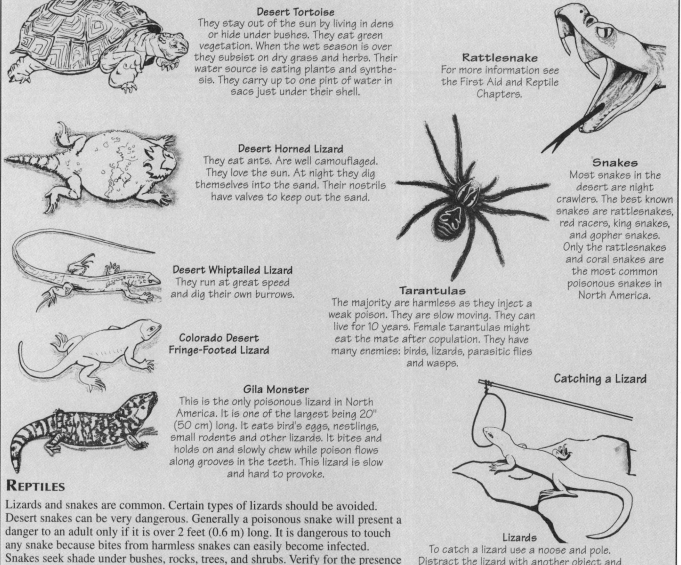

Desert Tortoise
They stay out of the sun by living in dens or hide under bushes. They eat green vegetation. When the wet season is over they subsist on dry grass and herbs. Their water source is eating plants and synthesis. They carry up to one pint of water in sacs just under their shell.

Rattlesnake
For more information see the First Aid and Reptile Chapters.

Desert Horned Lizard
They eat ants. Are well camouflaged. They love the sun. At night they dig themselves into the sand. Their nostrils have valves to keep out the sand.

Snakes
Most snakes in the desert are night crawlers. The best known snakes are rattlesnakes, red racers, king snakes, and gopher snakes. Only the rattlesnakes and coral snakes are the most common poisonous snakes in North America.

Desert Whiptailed Lizard
They run at great speed and dig their own burrows.

Tarantulas
The majority are harmless as they inject a weak poison. They are slow moving. They can live for 10 years. Female tarantulas might eat the mate after copulation. They have many enemies: birds, lizards, parasitic flies and wasps.

Colorado Desert Fringe-Footed Lizard

Catching a Lizard

Gila Monster
This is the only poisonous lizard in North America. It is one of the largest being 20" (50 cm) long. It eats bird's eggs, nestlings, small rodents and other lizards. It bites and holds on and slowly chew while poison flows along grooves in the teeth. This lizard is slow and hard to provoke.

REPTILES

Lizards and snakes are common. Certain types of lizards should be avoided. Desert snakes can be very dangerous. Generally a poisonous snake will present a danger to an adult only if it is over 2 feet (0.6 m) long. It is dangerous to touch any snake because bites from harmless snakes can easily become infected. Snakes seek shade under bushes, rocks, trees, and shrubs. Verify for the presence of snakes, scorpions, etc. before putting on your boots or clothing. *See First Aid and Reptile Chapters.*

Lizards
To catch a lizard use a noose and pole. Distract the lizard with another object and gently slip the noose over its head. Lizards have a diet of insects, fruits, and eggs.

MAMMALS

The mammals that live in the desert have adapted to their environment. An example being small mammals such as rodents conserve their moisture by burrowing underground and only come out during the night.

The kangaroo rat does not require much water as its body synthesizes water from the elements of starchy foods or slow oxidation of fats and from the oxygen in the air.

Peccary

Small wild pig 3' (1 m) long and 15" (40 cm) high. The only native American wild pig. It has a black and white banding which has a salt and pepper grey color effect. This pig can eject an odorous liquid for protection or as a trail marker. It is found in roving bands. It lives in the wild brush country of low mountains. It can get aggressive if cornered. It has nocturnal feeding habits. Drinks water when necessary but the pulp of cacti will suffice.
Enemies: mountain lions, jaguars and man.

Kangaroo Rat

These are 2" (5 cm) high rodents that have affinity with the squirrel and chipmunk families. Their colors vary from pale to reddish. They have a habit of storing food. They eat plant stems, seeds, and fleshy fungi. Pouches in cheeks to transport food. They do not require much water as their bodies synthesize water from the elements of starchy foods or slow oxidation of fats and from the oxygen in the air. When surprised it will leap a foot or two into the air on its elongated hind feet and escape at 17 feet (5 m) per second. The tail acts as a rudder. It can make a 90° turn while in flight. They are nocturnal. Predators: coyotes who will dig into their dens, Desert fox and Kit fox also will hunt them on the ground. Snakes and hawks eat them to derive water from their flesh.

Mountain Lion

Vulture

They hunt in the daytime looking for carrion. They use their excellent eyesight to find carcasses of animals which will usually are covered with sarcophagid flies.

Cactus Wren

Largest of all wrens. Body 8" (20 cm) long. Nests are in the spines of the cholla cactus.
Food: spiders, insects, larvae.
Enemies are small owls, wood rats, wild mice, and ground squirrels eat their eggs and young.

California Roadrunner

It runs very fast and rarely flies.
Food: lizards, grasshoppers, horned toad, mice, centipedes, spiders, baby rats and newborn rabbits.

White Tailed Ground Squirrel

Has stripes on the sides of the body.
Food: seeds, succulent herbs, grasshoppers, crickets, flies.

Desert Hare

Also called the desert jack rabbit.
Enemies: lynx, car accidents, large birds of prey, large snakes (gopher, bull snake, rattlesnake).
They are nocturnal.
Food: variety of green stuffs and twigs.

Sage Sparrow

They live in sagebrush in the valleys of high deserts.

Desert Bighorn

They live at higher elevation in a rocky habitat.
Male: 5' long from nose to tail. 3 1/2' (1 m) high. Weight 250-300 pounds (113-136 kg).
Food: thistles, grass, annual flowers, leafy bushes. Will break open barrel cacti with their horns and eat the pulp inside.

Ringed Tail Cat

An excellent hunter of mice. Member of the raccoon family.
They are nocturnal.
Food: fruits, grasshoppers, insects, small mammals.

Desert Kit Fox

Nose to tail 20" (51 cm) long.
Its large ears serve as radiators by which the fox stays cool.
Color: grizzled white with yellowish buff and black tipped over hair. It hunts at night.
Food: kangaroo rats, lizards, insects.

Desert Bat

There are different species of bats in the desert. They live in caves, crevasses, and mine tunnels all day. They leave to feed just before and after sunset. They fly in a zigzag pattern.
Food: insects.

DESERT SURVIVAL

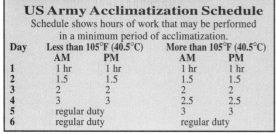

US Army Acclimatization Schedule

Schedule shows hours of work that may be performed in a minimum period of acclimatization.

Day	Less than 105°F (40.5°C)		More than 105°F (40.5°C)	
	AM	PM	AM	PM
1	1 hr	1 hr	1 hr	1 hr
2	1.5	1.5	1.5	1.5
3	2	2	2	2
4	3	3	2.5	2.5
5	regular duty		3	3
6	regular duty		regular duty	

Sources of Heat in the Desert
A - Reflected from ground.
B - Hot winds which might include sand.
C - Direct from sun.
D - Radiant heat from sand and rocks.

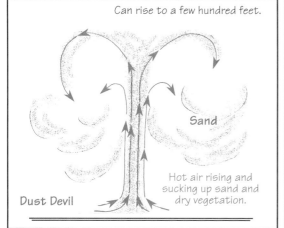

Can rise to a few hundred feet.

Sand

Dust Devil

Hot air rising and sucking up sand and dry vegetation.

THE DESERT AND MAN

Humans and the desert are compatible as long as humans know what to expect, what to do and have the required equipment. Desert tribes and cultures have survived for centuries in the most difficult circumstances.

The desert is physically and emotionally fatiguing. Discipline and attention to detail are required. If you are not in an emergency situation you should have the luxury of approximately two weeks to acclimatize yourself in progressive degrees to both the heat and physical exertion in a hot area. Initially heavy labor should be limited to cooler times of the day with frequent rests.

Shelter is lacking as there is minimal or no vegetation. This can cause *agoraphobia* (fear of open spaces) to some soldiers on active duty because they require cover for their security. This phobia normally disappears with acclimatization.

SUN'S RAYS AND HEAT

The sun's rays and heat come from four directions:
• Directly from the sun.
• Sun reflected from the earth.
• Heat gain from the sand and rocks (radiant heat).
• Hot winds which might be sand laden.

The sun's rays, either direct or reflected, can cause eyestrain and temporary impaired vision. Too much exposure or lack of protection can cause sunburn especially to light-complexioned people. Do not expose skin for more than 5 minutes on the first day. Exposure can be increased by 5 minutes per day. Loose garments covering the body should be worn at all times following the example of the tribes of the desert. You should never forget the high risk of getting skin cancer at a later stage of your life.

Cloudy days are as dangerous as sunny days. Sun tan lotion is not made to protect you against excessive exposure. Sleeping in the sun or too much sunbathing can be fatal.

Climactic stress can be caused by the heat's effect on the body, humidity, wind, and radiant heat. Consider the factors of lack of acclimatization, overweight, alcohol, lack of sleep, old age and poor health.

THE BODY

The human body has an internal thermometer that regulates the body heat at 98.6°F (37°C). This temperature is maintained by the body radiating heat, conduction, convection, and evaporation (sweat). Sweat is the most important, especially when the humidity is very low, because the evaporation of water from the skin causes the skin and body to cool. This is why dogs breath through wide open mouths with their tongue hanging out on hot days. If the relative humidity is very high this system of body air conditioning will not work.

WIND

Wind and sand can cause irritation of the mucous membrane, chapped exposed skin and chapped lips. Your eyes can get irritative conjunctivitis from fine dust particles entering them. Use skin and eye ointments (and goggles) when you have to expose yourself to these extreme conditions.

SANDSTORMS

These storms of windblown sand are common in deserts.

Wind blown sand is like sandblasting and is painful to the unprotected skin. Always be fully clothed in the desert. During a sandstorm do not leave your group or shelter without being attached to a guide rope. During a storm always keep your nose covered and protect your eyes.

DUST DEVIL

This is a whirlwind of sand that rises out of the desert caused by the formation of convection currents above the hot surface. Sand and other debris will rise in this hot turbulence of air which can reach a few hundred feet. This type of sandstorm only lasts for a few minutes.

DESERT CLOTHING

Pants

US Army combat pants are ideal desert pants as they are 100% cotton and have a dense weave to make them wind proof. They are baggy, have numerous sealed pockets, and have an ankle drawstring to tighten around boots. Some models even have a lined seat and knees.

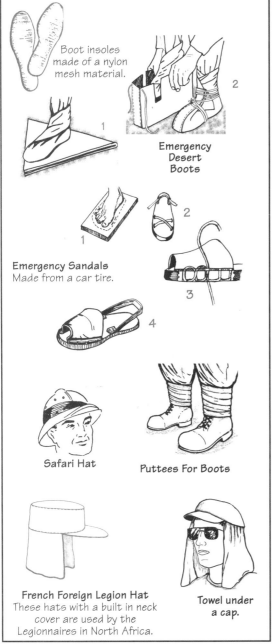

Boot insoles made of a nylon mesh material.

Emergency Desert Boots

Emergency Sandals
Made from a car tire.

Safari Hat

Puttees For Boots

French Foreign Legion Hat
These hats with a built in neck cover are used by the Legionnaires in North Africa.

Towel under a cap.

CLOTHING

In the desert the main purpose of clothing is to protect the body against the sun, the heat, insects, reptiles, and to regulate excessive sweat production.

Follow the example of desert dwellers, cover the whole body, wear layers of light-colored clothing made of natural breathable materials such as cotton. This clothing should be loose fitting and in many layers so that it can gradually be discarded during the day and reapplied in the evening.

A large woolen scarf can be draped to offer protection during the cold nights.

A bandana can be worn loosely around the neck to protect it from the sun and to prevent sand from blowing down the collar. This bandana covers the face during a sand storm.

Wash clothing if possible; if not, air it in the sun to kill bacteria or fungi growth.

Do not expose your skin unless you are in the shade and even then reflected radiation can give you a sunburn.

FOOTWEAR

Your feet are the most sensitive part of the body. When they hurt or are injured they will impede travel.

The desert is very hard on boots. Leather should be treated with saddle soap or it will dry out and crack. Boots should be worn with heavy socks, to keep out the radiant heat of the ground. They should be well laced to keep out the sand. Sand will sift into the breather holes of military jungle boots.

Boots will protect against snake and scorpion bites and help weak ankles. If the soles get worn reinforce them with a piece of cloth or other padding.

While resting in the shade remove your boots and socks. Be careful because your feet might swell. Before putting your boots back on always check for insects, snakes, and scorpions.

If your calves need covering make some puttees. Puttees were used by armies before high boots were commonly used. They are wound, above ankle boots, around the ankle up to below the knees. They are made from a stretchy (knit) strip of cloth 3 - 4 inches wide 4 feet long. They are wrapped in an overlapping spiral by starting at the knee to the ankle. They will keep out the sand and reduce the effect of the heat radiated from the sand.

- The sidewall of an old tire can be used to make the soles of a pair of sandals.
- Protect the tops of your feet from the sun because a sunburn in this location is extremely painful and you will not be able to wear boots.
- Do not walk barefoot because hot sand will blister your feet. If crossing barefoot on salt flats or mire you will receive alkali burns.

HAT

Protecting the head and eyes is of prime importance. The hat should be of a two layer construction with a layer of air that can circulate between the head and the top outside layer. The old colonial pith helmets are ideal as they are not heavy and have a broad brim to cover the eyes and neck. The original helmets were called 'pith' helmets as the layer of material below the cloth was made of the white pulp from below the outside cover of an orange or other citrus fruit. Modern helmets usually have a Styrofoam core. This core is more fragile as it can be chemically unstable and can disintegrate in contact with petroleum products. You can chose a French Legionnaire style hat with a neck cover.

SUNGLASSES

Avoid scratching them with sand particles. If you have no glasses you can wear your scarf so that your eyes peer through a slit to reduce the reflected sunlight. A pair of Eskimo slit sunglasses can be cut from a piece of wood, leather, plastic, or heavy cloth.

Eskimo Slit Sunglasses
These eye protectors can be made from a piece of cloth, whittled from wood, etc. The narrow slits reduce the amount of reflected light that reaches the eyes.

T-Shirt Used for Head Protection

SHELTER IN THE DESERT

Shelter from sun, heat, wind and possible sandstorms (with access to water) is the most important factor for surviving in the desert.

- Material generally is not available to easily build a shelter.
- Covering your body with sand provides some basic protection from the heat and will reduce water loss from the skin.
- In sandy areas, dig a shallow depression or find a natural hollow and cover it with tarpaulin or parachute material. The edges can be anchored with sand.
- In rocky desert areas pile some stones to form a support for a parachute cover.
- Drape parachute material over desert growth and anchor with rocks and sand.
- Use natural desert features for shade or shelter: a tree, bushes, a rock pile, cave, slope of a sand dune, wall of dry stream bed (watch and listen for any signs of a flash flood which might be the result of a cloudburst many miles away).
- Use shelters that have been made by previous travelers.

DESERT SHELTER

Indian Pueblo

Cover
Two layers of tarpaulin or parachute material. The layers should be at least 10" (25 cm) apart and will act as an insulation from the heat of the sun.

Top View

Desert Shelter

Side View

Trench
The trench should be 2' to 3' (0.6-0.9 m) deep and the entrance is oriented towards the north. Cover the ground in the trench to reduce any ground humidity.

Entrance
Make the entrance very small or long so that the sun's rays do not reflect into the shelter.

Sandstorm Protection

Wind

Covered Person

Boulder or Vegetation

DESERT SURVIVAL

Water is key to desert survival. Take all you can. If you have to leave some items behind keep things that provide shade help reduce heat or water consumption. *See the First Aid Chapter regarding Heat Illnesses.*

- Travel only in the early morning or late evening. During the hot part of the day find shade or a low hollow and cover it with a piece of cloth and rest. *Avoid expending energy and water in building a more elaborate shelter.*
- Attempt to establish a direction towards a traveled route, water, or an inhabited area.
- Take the route that requires the least physical exertion. Do not attempt to take short cuts over dunes or across loose sand or rugged terrain. Follow trails, the crests of sand dunes, or the low inter-dune area.
- Desert streams should not be followed, as they usually lead towards a temporary salty lake basin. In coastal areas desert streams and large rivers can lead to larger bodies of water.
- Dress properly to protect yourself against direct sunlight and excessive evaporation of sweat. Clothing is necessary for warmth in the desert because cool nights are common
- If you do not have sunglasses, make slit goggles.
- Care for your feet. Boots are needed for desert travel. You can cross sand dunes barefooted in cool weather, but during the summer the sand will burn your feet.
- Maps of desert regions are usually inaccurate. Check maps for accuracy by identifying obvious physical features.
- Take shelter, on the lee side of a dune, before a sandstorm arrives. It can be very disorienting so indicate the direction of travel before settling in, by scratching, placing a line of stones, position a stick, or clothing. Avoid traveling when visibility is bad. Cover your face, lie with your back to the wind. The blowing sand will not bury you.
- Due to the absence of distinctive features, your estimation of distances should be multiplied threefold.

DESERT TRAVEL

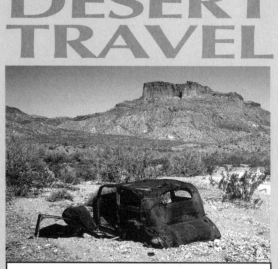

DANGERS OF SUN EXPOSURE
Types of Ultraviolet Radiation

Type	Effect	Long Term Effects
UVA	No pain	Penetrates the deepest layers of the skin. Linked to skin cancer and photoaging. *UV exposure is cumulative during your life.*
UVB	Burns skin	The body protects itself by producing pigment melanin which produces a tan. Over exposure produces a burn which shows that the defence mechanism has been overwhelmed.
UVC		Filtered out by the ozone layer.

If you want to camp in the desert. Have one twenty-four hour trial to see if you like it. It might not be fun. Animals in the desert only run around at night. The whole trial can be a great experience as you will be in direct exposure to the one thing that is hard to escape - *HEAT*. The extreme climate and environment of the desert can be a challenge as:

- The sunlight's effect on the landscape always changes and you might see mirages.
- The heat and intensity of the sun will affect your water intake and your diet.
- You will be adapting your daily schedule around the cooler hours.
- Build shelter against the heat of the sun, dust storms and the cold nights.

If you like the 24 hour trip then you might be ready for an extended camping trip and have a unique experience.

There are two types of deserts in North America. The low latitude sand deserts and the high altitude rocky, rugged, hilly terrain which has sand, stones and sometimes snow. Prepare yourself for the type of desert that you will visit.

DAY TRIP

The first day trip should be well-planned and possibly use a guide:

Plan an Itinerary

Make a detailed plan as to where you are going and where you plan to stay. Leave a copy of the plan with someone and tell them when you will report back. If you do not report back in time they will report you "lost" to the authorities. When traveling *do not leave the road or track* because you will find that cacti and rocks all look the same if you are lost. If you have any problems en route or change your plan inform your contact.

Food and Water

Have sufficient food with you as it is difficult to find food in the desert. Bring at least two or three days of water with 4 quarts per person per day and use the water sparingly. Use containers that help water keep its natural flavor. Get some hot weather water canteens. They are covered with canvas and you wet the canvas with water which gradually evaporates and cools the water in the container.

Clothing

Wear the right clothing and be prepared for cool nights.

Accessories

Bring sunscreen (use at least SPF 30), hats, bandana, and sunglasses. For tent anchors use "Ziploc" bags filled with sand. Place them *inside* self standing tents to hold them down. Pack your tent and retreat to the car during sand storms.

Car Supplies

Take extra gasoline in a five gallon jerry can making sure that the inside of the can is not rusted as the rust flakes might block your fuel system.

Extra radiator fluid, fan belt, radiator hose, distilled water for the battery. Shovel with at least a three foot handle.

If you are driving off the road you will encounter sand and you will require high-axles, wide tires and preferably a four wheel drive

Walking

Walking on sand is difficult as you have a tendency to slide back. The energy required for one mile on sand is equivalent to two miles on regular terrain. Wear boots and heavy socks as the sand is so hot that it can cause burns.

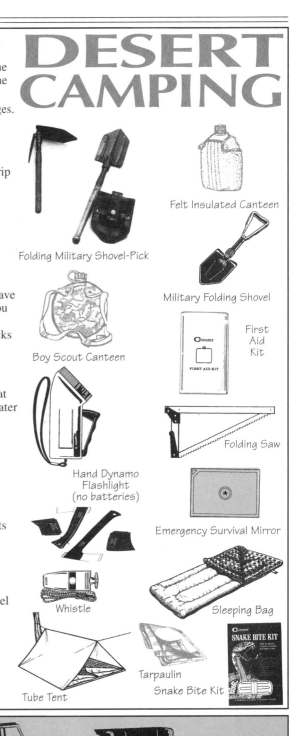

DESERT CAMPING

Folding Military Shovel-Pick

Felt Insulated Canteen

Military Folding Shovel

Boy Scout Canteen

First Aid Kit

Folding Saw

Hand Dynamo Flashlight (no batteries)

Emergency Survival Mirror

Whistle

Sleeping Bag

SNAKE BITE KIT

Tube Tent

Tarpaulin

Snake Bite Kit

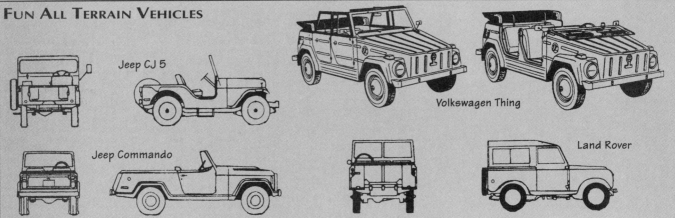

FUN ALL TERRAIN VEHICLES

Jeep CJ 5

Jeep Commando

Volkswagen Thing

Land Rover

FOOD

SOURCE OF FOOD

Food is hard to find in the desert. Food can be rationed as it is secondary to water. If a problem occurs *start rationing immediately by stopping to eat immediately for twenty four hours* to help you establish a new biorhythm.

NATURAL SOURCES

Animals are rare and hard to find in the desert. They are usually nocturnal and stay in cool areas, holes, shade, and your clothing! Rodents (mice, rats, prairie dogs, rabbits) and lizards caught near a water hole may be your only diet. Antelope or deer are hard to catch or kill without a gun. Other creatures that can be found are snakes, insects, snails, and birds.

Birds such as bustard, pelicans, and grouse are found on the desert. Attract them by making a plucking sound by sucking the back of your hand. *See Trapping Chapter on how to trap birds.*

Insects can be found in cool areas under rocks. *While looking watch for snakes and scorpions.*

Plants usually are found near a water source. These plants might look dry and unappetizing but they usually have soft parts that are edible. There might be fruits, seeds, young shoots and bark. These seeds or fruit can be beans that grow on bushes, the prickly pear of the cactus etc. Nearly all grass is edible. *See Edible Plants Chapter.*

COOKING AND FIRE

Palm leaves and other growth near an oasis can be used as fuel. In the desert use any fuel you can find or build a solar stove.

See Fire and Cooking Chapters for more information.
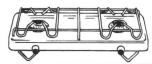

- The more you sweat the more salt you lose.
- Too much salt will cause thirst, a sick feeling, and can be dangerous.
- Extra salt should be taken in proportion to the water available.
- Salt tablets should be dissolved before use.
- Water must be tested before adding salt as it might have a natural saline content that is sufficient for your needs.
- *See the First Aid Chapter on Heat Illness.*

US ARMY SALT REQUIREMENT GUIDELINES

Addition of table salt to produce 0.1% salt solution

Table Salt	Amount of Water
1/4 spoon (3.7 ml)	1 quart canteen (625 ml)
1 1/3 level mess kit spoons	5 gallon can (19 L)
9 level mess kit spoons (3/10 lb)	36 gallon bag (136 L)
1 LB (450 g)	100 gallon tank (379 L)
1 level canteen cup	250 gallons (946 L)

SALT REQUIREMENTS

DESERT FOOD

Desert Hare

Prickly Pear Cactus

SEE EDIBLE PLANT CHAPTER

Collared Lizard

DESERT SICKNESS

HEAT ILLNESS

The temperature of the body is auto-regulated within very narrow limits. Attention should be paid to anything that will possibly destabilize the system.

- Lack of salt may lead to heat cramps.
- Lack of salt and insufficient water may lead to heat exhaustion.
- General collapse of the body's cooling mechanism will lead to heat stroke which can be fatal.

If you expend more calories than you absorb you will become more prone to heat illness. You might lose your appetite due to the heat but you should eat your required ration with the major meal being during a cool period. Work in groups and learn to quickly recognize heat stress symptoms. When a person is suffering from heat stroke the tendency is for the victim to creep away from the group and attempt to hide in a shady and secluded spot. If he is not found and treated he will die.

DISEASE

Diseases found in the desert include: plague, typhus, malaria, dengue fever, dysentery, cholera, and typhoid. Some of these can be prevented with vaccines or prophylactic measures. High levels of field hygiene and sanitation should be observed at all times.

FUNGUS INFECTION AND PRICKLY HEAT

Excessive sweating can aggravate prickly heat and some forms of fungus infections of the skin. The higher the humidity and if clothing is not cleaned or aired in the sun the greater the possibility of this happening.

RESPIRATORY DISEASE AND COLD WEATHER INJURIES

The desert can be very hot during the day and cool to cold at night. You should gradually remove covering clothing in the morning and reapply the clothing in the evening. Never completely expose your skin. If traveling in the day do not discard clothing along the route as you will need it in the evening.

POLLUTED WATER INFECTION

Untested water should not be drunk or even used to wash your clothing, as it might cause skin diseases. Polluted water can be used for the vehicle cooling systems.

US ARMY HEAT ILLNESS GUIDELINE

An individual who has already had a heat stroke or severe case of heat exhaustion is more likely to fall sick again than one who has not suffered from these illnesses. An individual who has already been affected should be subsequently exposed to *potential heat stress with caution.*

Symptoms to Distinguish Between Salt Depletion and Water Depletion

Symptoms	Salt Depletion	Water Depletion
Duration of symptoms	3-5 days	1 day
Thirst	seldom	prominent
Fatigue	prominent	seldom
Cramps	prominent	none
Vomiting	prominent	none
Weakness	progressive	acute

DEHYDRATION

The customs of the tribal people of the Sahara should not be forgotten.

- Keep completely clothed as this will keep the sweat on the skin surface longer and improve the cooling process.
- A resting person can lose as much as a pint of water an hour by sweating. At low relative humidity the skin might always be dry because of rapid evaporation.

Dehydration is difficult to determine but a very dark urine is a warning sign. Other signs could be hallucinations, fatigue, listlessness, lack of clear judgement and surliness of voice, difficulty in focusing the eyes. You should increase your water intake at this point as there might be a shortage of 1 to 2 quarts of water in your system. Reestablish your water level by drinking in slow sips - do not guzzle.

See First Aid Chapter for more information.

Centipede
See First Aid Chapter
on poisonous insects

To Reduce the Chance of
Desert Illness You Must be:
Physically fit
Thoroughly acclimatized
Drink sufficient water with the necessary salt.

HEAT ILLNESSES *Consult the First Aid Chapter for more information.*

Illness	Cause	Symptoms	First Aid
Heat Exhaustion	Excessive loss of water and salt.	*Cool moist skin, profuse sweating.* Headache, dizziness, vomiting, weakness, rapid pulse and breathing. May be slight rise in temperature.	Heat cramps are relieved by replacing the salt lost from body. Place individual in cool outer clothing. Give all water slowly in the form of 0.1% saline solution. *If cramps are very severe individual should be sent to a hospital.*
Heat Cramps	Excessive loss of salt from body.	Severe cramps in limbs, back and/or abdomen, following exposure to heat. Body temperature remains normal.	Move patient to cool shaded place. Remove outer clothing. Elevate feet or message legs above the cramp area. Give all water that can be drunk in form of 0.1% saline solution. *Get medical attention.*
Heat Stroke	Collapse of body cooling mechanism.	*Hot dry skin.* Headache, mental confusion, and bizarre behavior, dizziness, weakness and rapid breathing and pulse. High temperature (106°F 41°C or more). May be unconscious.	*Medical emergency. Seek medical aid immediately.* The lowering of the patient's body temperature as rapidly as possible is the most important objective in the treatment of heat stroke. Move individual to shaded area. Remove clothing. Sprinkle or bathe patient with cool water and fan to increase cooling effect. Massage trunk, arms, and legs. *If evacuating to a hospital continue treatment on way.*

TRAVELING IN MOUNTAIN AREAS

Where there are no roads or trails, it is particularly important to have a full knowledge of the terrain to choose the most feasible route for cross-country movement. You should check all available data as topographic or photo maps, weather data, size, location and characteristics of land forms, drainage, nature and types of rock and soil, and the amount and distribution of vegetation.

CLIMATE ·

Mountain climate has a very definite effect on the physiology and pathology of the individual because the human body is sensitive to weather changes, differing climates, and altitude.

AIR

Mountain air is relatively pure. The higher the elevation, the more nearly pure it becomes. Above 15,000 feet (4,500 m) it is practically germ free. The physical composition of the atmospheric air is considerably different at high altitudes from that found at sea level. Forests, especially those with coniferous trees, purify the air by lowering the percentage of carbon dioxide in the air. Falling snow purifies the air by capturing and holding many of the impurities remaining in the air.

High mountain air is dry, especially in the winter when the humidity in the air condenses into ice. The amount of water vapor in the air decreases as the altitude increases.

Atmospheric pressure drops as the altitude increases. The temperature drops and the air becomes more rarefied with altitude.

The sun's rays are either absorbed or reflected by the atmospheric haze which fills the air above low country, especially over cities. The rarefied dry air of the higher altitudes allows all the visible rays of the solar spectrum to pass. In pure atmosphere, the proportion of ultraviolet rays remains constant, regardless of the altitude. These conditions increase the possibility of sunburn especially when combined with the existing snow cover.

ROUTE SELECTION

Plan an ascent or descent by noting each rock obstacle, the best approach, height, angle, type of rock, difficulty, distance between belay positions, amount of equipment, skill, condition, and number of individuals involved, the weather that might be encountered, and potential rock slides. Identify primary and alternate routes for ascents and descents. *At least two vantage points should be used*, so that a three dimensional understanding of the climb can be attained. Use of early morning or late afternoon light, with its longer shadows could be helpful.

DANGER

- On long trips change in weather is an important consideration. Wet or icy rock can make an otherwise easy route almost impassable, cold may reduce climbing efficiency, and snow may cover holds. Obtain weather forecasts if possible.
- Smooth rock slabs are treacherous, especially when wet or iced after a freezing rain. Ledges should be sought.
- Rocks overgrown with moss, lichens, or grass become treacherous when wet. Cleated boots will then be far better than composition soles.
- Tufts of grass and small bushes that appear firm may be growing on loosely packed and unanchored soil, all of which may give way if the grass or bush is pulled upon. Grass and bushes should be used only for balance by touch or as push holds, never as pull holds. *See Holds at end of this chapter.*
- Gently inclined but smooth slopes of rock may be covered with pebbles that will treacherously roll underfoot.
- Ridges may be free of loose rock, but may be topped with unstable blocks.
- Gullies provide the best defilade and often the easiest routes. Watch for flash floods and rocks.
- Climbing slopes of talus, moraine, or other loose rock is not only tiring to the individual but dangerous because of the hazard of rolling rocks on others in the party. Climbers should close up intervals when climbing.
- Lightning can endanger the climber on peaks, ridges, pinnacles, and lone trees should be avoided.

ROCK FALLS

Rock falls are the most common mountaineering danger.

The most frequent causes of rock falls are:
- Other climbers.
- Great changes of temperature in high mountains that produce splitting action by intermittent freezing and thawing.
- Heavy rain.
- Grazing animals.

Warning of a rock fall is the cry "ROCK", a whistling sound, a grating, a thunderous crashing, or bright sparks where the rocks strike each other when they fall at night.

A rock fall can be a single rock or a large rock slide covering a relatively large area. Rock falls occur on all steep slopes, particularly in gullies and chutes. Areas of frequent rock falls may be indicated by:
- Abundant fresh scars on the rock walls.
- Fine dust on the talus piles.
- Lines and grooves along the cliff.
- Rock strewn areas on snow beneath cliffs.
- Lack of trees or large vegetation along the slope.

Immediate action during a rock fall is to seek cover. If there is not enough time to avoid the rock fall, the climber should lean into the slope to minimize his exposure. Rock fall danger is minimized by careful climbing and by judgment in choice of route.

CHAPTER 6
MOUNTAIN TRAVEL

WIND IN MOUNTAIN AREAS

In high mountains the ridges and passes are seldom calm; however, strong winds in protected valleys are rare. Normally, wind speed increases with altitude, since the earth's frictional drag is strongest near the ground, and this effect is accentuated by mountainous terrain. Winds are accelerated when they are forced over ridges and peaks or when they converge through mountain passes and canyons. Because of these funneling effects, wind may blast with great force on an exposed mountain side or summit. In most cases, the local wind direction is controlled by the area's topography and not the continental masses.

The force exerted by wind quadruples each time the wind speed doubles. Wind blowing at 40 knots pushes four times harder than does a 20 knot wind. With increasing wind strength, gusts become more important and may be 50% higher than the average wind speed. When wind strength increases to a hurricane force of 64 knots or more, *you should hug the ground during gusts and push ahead during lulls*. If a hurricane force wind blows where there is sand or snow, dense clouds fill the air, and rocky debris or chunks of snow crust are hurled along near the surface. Position yourself behind an obstruction.

In general, the speed of the winds accompanying local storms is less than that of winds with traveling storms. There are two winds which result from the daily cycle of solar heating. During calm clear days in valleys that are subject to intense solar radiation, the heated air rises and flows gently up the valleys producing a wind called the *valley* or *up-valley breeze*. On clear nights the mountain sides lose heat rapidly and cool the surrounding air which settles down slope to produce the *mountain* or *down-valley breeze*. The down-valley breeze, by pouring cold air into a valley, aids in the creation of a temperature inversion.

During the winter season or at extremely high altitudes, always be aware of the *Windchill Factor (See First Aid)* and associated frostbite. Frostbite is a constant hazard when traveling at freezing temperatures, especially when the wind is strong.

During all seasons, exposed areas of the body are subject to windburn or extreme chapping. Although windburn is uncomfortable, it is seldom incapacitating.

MOUNTAIN WEATHER

Barometer / Altimeter
For mountain climbing
see Page 65 for details.

Weather Forecasting

The use of the portable aneroid barometer, thermometer, and hygrometer can be of great assistance in making local weather forecasts. Reports from other localities and from any weather service are also of great value.

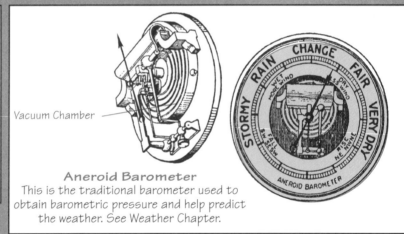

Vacuum Chamber

Aneroid Barometer
This is the traditional barometer used to obtain barometric pressure and help predict the weather. See Weather Chapter.

SEE WEATHER CHAPTER

MOUNTAIN WEATHER

Mountain weather is highly changeable and every effort must be made to anticipate the weather.

The safety or danger in almost all high mountain regions, especially in winter, depends upon *a change of a few degrees of temperature above or below the freezing point*. Ease and speed of travel are largely dependent on weather. Terrain that can be crossed swiftly and safely one day may become impassable or highly dangerous the next because of snowfall, rainfall, or a rise in temperature. The reverse can happen just as quickly. There is always a danger of avalanche or rockfalls.

CHARACTERISTICS OF WEATHER IN MOUNTAINS

Mountain weather is erratic. Hurricane force winds and gentle breezes may occur just short distances apart. The weather in exposed places contrast sharply with the weather in sheltered areas. Weather changes in a single day can be so variable that in the same locality one may experience hot sun and cool shade, high winds and calm, gusts of rain or snow, and then perhaps intense sunlight again. This variability results from the life cycle of a local storm or from the movement of traveling storms. In addition, the effects of storms are modified by the local influences:

- Variation in altitude.
- Differences in exposure to the sun and to prevailing winds.
- Distortion of storm movements and normal winds by irregular mountain topography. These local influences dominate summer storms.
- Local storms in the form of thunderstorms with or without showers.
- Traveling storms which may be accompanied by radical and severe weather changes over a broad area. Usually, each type of storm may be identified by the clouds associated with it. *See Weather Chapter for cloud formations.*
- Seasonal moisture-bearing winds of the monsoon type which bring consistently bad weather to some mountain ranges for weeks at a time.

LOCAL WEATHER

Indications of local thunderstorm showers, or squally weather:

- An increase in size and rapid thickening of scattered cumulus clouds during the afternoon.
- The approach of a line of large cumulus or cumulonimbus clouds with an advance guard of altocumulus clouds. At night, increasing lightning windward of the prevailing wind gives the same warning.
- Massive cumulus clouds hanging over a ridge or summit at night or in the daytime.

Fair Weather is Associated with:

- A cloudless sky and shallow fog or layers of smoke or haze at valley bottoms in the early morning; or from a vantage point of high elevation, a cloudless sky that is quite blue down to the horizon or down to where a level haze layer forms a secondary horizon.
- Conditions under which small cumulus clouds appearing in the forenoon do not increase, but *decrease or vanish* during the day.
- Clear skies, except for a low cloud deck which does not rise or thicken during the day.

Strong Winds

Indications of strong winds seen at a distance may be:

- Plumes of blowing snow from the crests of ridges and peaks or ragged shreds of cloud moving rapidly.
- Persistent lens-shaped clouds, or a band of clouds, over high peaks and ridges or downwind from them.
- A turbulent and ragged banner cloud which hangs to the lee of a peak.

During Precipitation

When there is precipitation and the sky cannot be seen:

- Very small snowflakes or ice crystals indicate that the clouds above are thin and there is fair weather at high altitudes.
- A steady fall of snowflakes or raindrops indicates that the precipitation has begun at high levels and that bad weather is likely to be encountered on ridges and peaks.

LOCAL WEATHER

CLOUDINESS AND PRECIPITATION IN MOUNTAIN AREAS

Cloudiness and precipitation increase with height until a zone of maximum precipitation is reached; above this zone they decrease. Maximum cloudiness and precipitation occur near 6000 feet (1800 m) elevation in middle latitudes and at lower levels as the poles are approached. Usually a dense forest marks the zone of maximum rainfall.

Slopes facing the prevailing wind are cloudier, foggier, and receive heavier precipitation than those protected from the wind, especially when large bodies of water lie to the windward side. However, at night and in winter, valleys are likely to be colder and foggier than higher slopes. Heads of valleys often have more clouds and precipitation than adjacent ridges and the valley floor.

MOUNTAIN TEMPERATURES

Temperature Inversion: Normally, a temperature fall off from 2°-5° F (1°- 3°C) per 1000 feet (300 m) rise in altitude will be encountered. Frequently, on cold, clear, calm mornings when climbing is started from a valley, higher temperatures may be encountered as you rise in altitude. This reversal of the normal situation is called temperature inversion. This condition occurs when air cooled by ice, snow, and heat loss by radiation settles into valleys and low areas. The inversion will continue until the sun warms the surface of the earth or a moderate wind causes a mixing of the warm and cold air layers. Temperature inversions are very common in the mountainous regions of the Arctic and sub-Arctic.

SOLAR HEATING

At high altitudes, solar heating is responsible for the greatest temperature contrasts. More sunshine and solar heat is received above than below the clouds. The important effect of altitude is that the sun's rays pass through less of the atmosphere and so more direct heat is received than at lower levels where solar radiation is absorbed and reflected by dust and water vapor.

There may be differences of 40°-50°F (22°-27°C) between the temperature in the sun and that in the shade. Special care must be taken to avoid sunburn and snow blindness which result from the combined action of intense sunlight and the reflected rays from snow fields or clouds.

Besides permitting rapid heating, the clear air at high altitudes also favors rapid cooling at night. The temperature rises very fast after sunrise and drops quickly after sunset. Much of the chilled air drops downward, because of convention currents, so that the differences between day and night temperatures are greater in valleys than on slopes or higher elevations.

FOG IN MOUNTAINS

On windward slopes, persistent fog, as well as cloudiness and precipitation, frequently can last for days. They are caused by the local barrier effect of the mountain on prevailing winds. Any cloud bank appears as a fog from within. Fog limits visibility and causes whiteout conditions. If fog is accompanied by precipitation protection against the uncomfortable combination of cold and wetness is required. When traveling without landmarks it will be necessary to use a compass, altimeter and a topographic map to maintain direction.

TRAVELING STORM INDICATORS

If a traveling storm is encountered in an alpine zone during winter, all your equipment and skill will be pitted against low temperatures, high winds, and blinding snow.

Rapidly changing weather conditions often create glaze, a coating of ice which forms on all exposed objects.

The approach of a traveling storm is indicated when:

- A thin veil of cirrus clouds spreads over the sky, thickening and lowering until altostratus clouds are formed. The same trend is shown at night when a halo forms around the moon and then darkens until only the glow of the moon is visible. When there is no moon, cirrus clouds only dim the stars while altostratus clouds hide them completely.
- Low clouds which have been persistent on lower slopes begin to rise at the time upper clouds appear.
- Various layers of clouds move in at different heights and become more abundant.
- Lens-shaped clouds accompanying strong winds lose their streamlined shape and other cloud types appear in increasing amounts.
- A change in the direction of the wind is accompanied by a rapid rise in temperature not caused by solar radiation. This may also indicate a warm damp period.
- A light green haze is observed shortly after sunrise in mountain regions above the timberline.

TRAVELING STORMS

Various layers of clouds move in at different heights and become more abundant.

The most severe storms involve strong winds and heavy precipitation and are the result of widespread atmospheric disturbances which generally travel in an *easterly direction*. If a traveling storm is encountered in an alpine zone during winter, all your equipment and skill will be pitted against low temperatures, high winds, and blinding snow.

Traveling storms result from the interaction of cold and warm air. The center of the storm is a moving low pressure area where cyclonic winds are generally the strongest. Extending from this storm center is a warm front which marks the advancing thrust of warm air, and the cold front which precedes the onrushing cold and gusty winds. The sequence of weather events, with the approach and passing of a traveling storm depends on the state of the storm's development, and whether the location of its path is to the north or south of a given mountain area. Generally, scattered cirrus clouds merge into a continuous sheet which thickens and lowers gradually until it becomes altostratus. At high levels, this cloud layer appears to settle. Lower down, a stratus deck may form overhead. A storm passing to the north may bring warm temperatures with southerly winds and partial clearing for a while before colder air with thundershowers or squally conditions moves in from the northwest. However, local cloudiness often obscures frontal passages in the mountains.

A Traveling Storm in Mountains

The storm may go so far to the north that only the cold front phenomena of heavy clouds, squalls, thundershowers, and colder weather are experienced. The same storm passing to the south would be accompanied by a gradual wind shift from northeasterly to northwesterly, with a steady temperature fall and continuous precipitation. After colder weather moves in, the clearing at high altitudes is usually slower than the onset of cloudiness, and storm conditions may last several days longer than in the lowlands. *See Weather Chapter.*

Rapidly changing weather conditions often create glaze, a coating of ice which forms on exposed objects. Glaze occurs under special storm conditions when light rain or drizzle falls through air below 32°F (0°C), and strikes a surface that also is below 32°F, freezing to the surface in the form of glaze. Glaze usually forms near the warm front of a storm and only persists if colder weather follows.

Weather Effect on Trees in the Mountains

VALLEY BREEZE

In hilly areas the air flows up the slope in the daytime and down slopes at night. This happens because in the day the tops of the hills become warmer causing the air in the valley to rise. Hills cool off faster than the surrounding area at night and heavy cold air flows into the valleys.

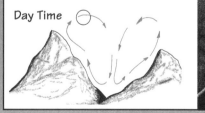

Day Time

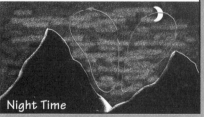

Night Time

LIGHTNING & THUNDERSTORMS

This person in a very shallow cave or ledge is an excellent conductor of electricity as he forms a conduit for the current.

Person in a small dry cave should not touch the walls but sit or lie, on a dry mat. This is to maximize the distance between the head and top of the cave.

This individual sitting on a wide ledge has a low probability of being hit especially if he is sitting on a dry insulator. He should not be wearing a backpack.

Body positioned in the direction of flow of the current is at high risk.

Backpack with a metal frame makes a good electrical conduit. Do not keep the backpack close to the body.

Body is perpendicular to current flow so it will not be a conductor. The backpack should be placed at a distance from the body especially if it has a metal frame. The climber should lie on a dry location on a rubber pad or dry clothing to minimize electric activity.

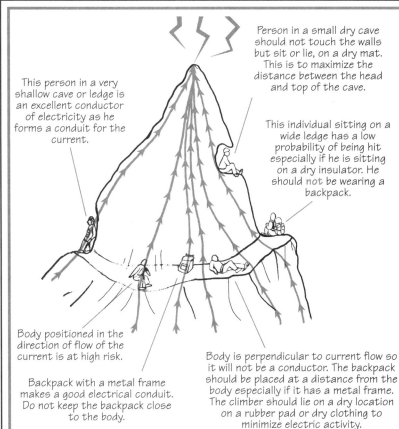

Equipotential electric fields during a storm

Metal on frame might attract lightning.

High probability of being hit as the head is the high point.

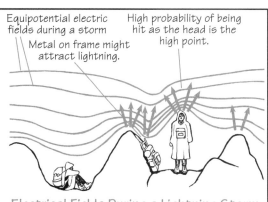

Electrical Fields During a Lightning Storm

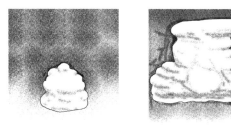

Scattered fair weather clouds (cumulus) often appear harmless, but upon growing larger and reaching a vertical depth of several thousand meters they may rapidly turn into thunderstorms.

LIGHTNING

Although statistics show that lightning is not one of the major hazards of mountaineering, enough casualties and near casualties are reported to make it a matter of concern. Mountain climbers often find themselves on prominent peaks and exposed ridges, which are particularly subject to lightning.

- Ridges help produce the vertical updrafts and the rain cloud conditions which generate lightning.
- Prominences serve to trigger lightning strokes.

There are, however, precautionary measures that can be taken by the climber.

- Avoid being on exposed peaks or ridges, or in an unprotected flat area during an electrical storm.
- Do not climb if a storm is predicted. *Lightning can strike in front of a storm.*
- Avoid being under prominent or isolated trees.
- If caught in an exposed place, and you have some time before the storm reaches you, you should get as far down the mountain and away from exposed ridges as you can. Especially avoid ridges that dominate the skyline. If stuck the middle of a ridge is preferable to the edge of a ridge.
- If lightning seems imminent or is striking nearby, at once seek a place that will protect you from direct strokes and from ground currents. A flat shelf, a slope, or a slightly raised place dominated by a nearby high point would give protection from lightning.
- If there is any choice select a spot on dry, clean rock in preference to damp or lichen covered rock. A scree slope would be very good.
- Tie yourself in if you are where a severe shock might cause you to fall.

The main thing to remember when caught in an electrical storm is to quickly take precautions.

THUNDERSTORMS

Although individual thunderstorms are normally local in nature and usually are of short duration, they can be part of a large weather system. In the alpine zone above timberline, thunderstorms may be accompanied by freezing precipitation and sudden squally winds. Ridges and peaks become focal points of concentrated electrical activity which is very dangerous. Thunderstorms occurring at night or in the early morning are associated with major changes in the weather conditions, which often results in a long period of foul weather before clearing on high summits. Thunderstorms occurring at these times may also be part of a general storm front and are followed by a prolonged period of cool, clear, and dry weather.

Local Thunderstorms

Local thunderstorms develop from rising air columns resulting from the intense heating by the sun of a relatively small area. They occur most frequently in the *middle or late afternoon.* Scattered fair weather clouds (cumulus) often appear harmless, but when they continue to grow larger and reach a vertical depth of several thousand meters they may rapidly turn into thunderstorms.

WEATHER CHAPTER
FOR LIGHTNING & THUNDERSTORMS

MOUNTAIN STREAM CROSSING

Sudden rains or thaws can change placid streams into roaring torrents.

- The best time for crossing is in the early morning when the water is low. As glaciers, snow, or ice melt during the day, the rivers rise, reaching their maximum height between mid-afternoon and late evening, depending on the distance from the source.

- A crossing point should be chosen, if possible at the widest point of the stream where the water is normally not as swift and usually not as deep or where it branches into several smaller streams. Wherever possible, select a point where there are few, if any, large stones on the river bed. Large stones increase the difficulty of maintaining an easy footing.

- Shoes should be worn to prevent foot injuries, but socks and insoles should be removed and kept dry.

- A shallow stream with a moderate current can be forded without the use of ropes or logs.

Water is normally turbulent over large stones, while it flows smoothly over small stones.

SUMMER HIKING CHAPTER
FOR MORE INFORMATION

- The river should be crossed at an upstream angle facing upstream.

- Feet should be set wide apart, kept flat with the bed of the stream, and should always be set down on the upper side of any obstruction in the stream bed.

- Legs should be dragged through the water, not lifted, so that the force of the current will not throw the individual off balance and drag him under.

DIFFICULT CROSSINGS SHOULD BE AVOIDED

- **Swift current:** To cross using the ring method, the group forms in a ring, locking hands with each other and placing the arms behind their backs. The body is bent well forward.

- **Swift current:** In the chain crossing, group forms in line, lock arms with each other, and then cross their own arms and lock their hands in front to give added support. The line then moves across diagonally downstream.

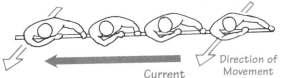

Direction of Movement

Current

- If the current is moderate and the water *less than knee deep*, a staff or a walking stick may be used and worked ahead of the individual on the downstream side.

- Where the current is fast, the water is more than knee deep, or when it has a shifting bottom crossing is facilitated by using a rope or balance pole that is at least head high. The balance pole is worked ahead of the individual, always on the upstream side. The weight of the body must be evenly distributed between the pole and the feet to maintain the necessary points of support.
The pole is first moved forward and planted, and the feet are then moved ahead.

- When jumping from boulder to boulder, jump from a crouching position pushing off simultaneously with both feet, and landing with both feet flat on the rock. Make sure that the rock is not wet, slimy or unstable.

- When crossing with a rope, each individual stays on the *downstream side* of the rope, as the current has a tendency to pull one under the rope.

- If equipment is being carried always be ready to jettison it in case of an emergency. Not to lose the equipment attach it with a snaplink to the crossing rope before you start crossing.

MOUNTAIN SURVIVAL

HIGH ELEVATION DIFFICULTIES

- High altitude air is colder.
- Air is thinner so there is less oxygen.
- Weather is more severe and can change rapidly.
- Above 14000 feet (4100 meters) the metabolism has problems due to the lack of oxygen to process and use fatty foods. Climbers will get bloated because they cannot digest fatty food.
- Diets have to be changed to more carbohydrates (sugar, rice, wheat) and proteins (meat and dairy products).
- Air is dry and sweating and deep breathing will rapidly dehydrate the body.

Medical Problems of Mountain Climbing

At 7000-8000 feet (2000-2350 meters) mountain sickness can develop in some travelers. At 12000+ feet (3500+ meters) *everyone* can develop mountain sickness.

Symptoms of Mountain Sickness

- General sense of weakness and lack of energy.
- Tiredness.
- Nausea and headaches.

Symptoms of Lack of Oxygen

- Lips and fingertips have a bluish color.
- Face has a lack of color.

If Mountain Sickness Symptoms are Present

- Do not eat heavily as your system will require more oxygen to digest the food.
- Do not smoke.
- Do not drink alcohol.

Acclimatization to Higher Elevations

Acclimatization requires the body to change by increasing the blood's capacity to absorb oxygen and the lungs to become more efficient. People have different acclimatization rates from 10 days to 5 or 6 weeks.

HIGH ALTITUDE PULMONARY EDEMA

High Altitude Pulmonary Edema

Symptoms are similar as those of pneumonia. It is the accumulation of fluids in the lungs that reduces the lungs' breathing capacity and death can result from suffocation or heart failure.

Pulmonary edema usually occurs above 9,000 feet (2,700 meters) but it varies from person to person. It depends upon the individuals capacity to acclimatize to the elevation.

Symptoms of Pulmonary Edema

If you are susceptible, the symptoms occur 12 to 36 hours *after your arrival at a high elevation*. This is one of the reasons mountain climbers travel to a base camp and stay there for a while and move up in stages.

The first indications are:

- weakness
- shortness of breath
- nausea
- constricted feeling around the chest
- loss of appetite

Second stage:

A cough develops becoming more frequent and deeper.

Third stage:

- The cough brings up a frothy sputum which might include blood.
- The blood pulse and respiration may increase and become rapid.
- Lack of oxygen will be indicated by the lips and fingertips turning blue.

Final stage:

- Victim feels that they are drowning (which they are as their lungs are filling with liquid).
- A bubbling sound occurs in the chest as the lung fluids gurgle with each breath.

Treatment

While the victim is still mobile he should be brought to a lower elevation. Even a descent of 2000 feet (600 meters) might restore normal breathing.

Hypothermia at High Elevations
High elevations have all the ingredients for hypothermia. Cold, wet, winds, and low energy reserves due to the exertion involved in climbing and the probability of not eating properly. See section on Hypothermia: First Aid Chapter.

Pulmonary Edema
Usually occurs above 9,000 feet (2,700 meters) but it varies from person to person.

High Altitude Pulmonary Edema
Is the accumulation of fluids in the lungs that reduces the lungs' breathing capacity and death can result from suffocation or heart failure.

Women at High Altitudes
Women have a different physiology than men so that at higher altitudes they will have different reactions. Less suffering from pulmonary edema. Women can experience swelling of the extremities in their premenstrual stage.

EMERGENCY SUNGLASSES

Slit sunglasses can be made from some birch bark, a piece of wood, strapping, rubber, etc.

FILLING WATER BOTTLES

When using pliable water bottles, fill them and them squeeze out the remaining air. This will keep the bottle pliable, the vacuum will keep the top on, and the bottle can expand when you travel to higher altitudes or the bottle freezes.

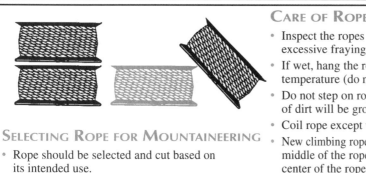

Selecting Rope for Mountaineering

- Rope should be selected and cut based on its intended use.
- Nylon rope is most commonly used in climbing. The rope is 1.1 cm in diameter and is issued in 36 1/2 meter lengths. The actual breaking strength when dry averages 3,840 pounds (+ 5%). The breaking strength is reduced by 18% when the rope is wet.
- Nylon sling rope is commonly used in 4 meter lengths. It is the same diameter as the nylon climbing rope.
- Manila rope 1.9 cm in diameter and larger is used in the construction of various types of installations as suspension and rope bridges because it has less of a stretch factor and are not affected by UV rays.
- All ropes when they are bent sharply, as around a snaplink, lose some of their strength at the bend.
- *Impact force* (the jerk on a climber caused by a fall) should be low.
- *Elasticity* (stretch) should be considered (dynamic vs. static ropes for ascending and descending).
- Weight of rope should be considered (rope length and diameter).
- Versatile and multiuse ropes should be selected.
- Know the *tensile strengths* and characteristics and capabilities of the rope you select.

Care of Ropes Used in Mountaineering

- Inspect the ropes thoroughly before, during, and after use for cuts, excessive fraying, abrasions, mildew, soft and worn spots.
- If wet, hang the rope to drip dry on a rounded peg, at room temperature (do not apply heat).
- Do not step on rope or unnecessarily drag it on the ground Small particles of dirt will be ground into the strands and will slowly cut them.
- Coil rope except when in use. *See Rope & Knots Chapter.*
- New climbing rope should be marked, by whipping, in the middle. A mark at the middle of the rope, so that the exact center of the rope can quickly be found.
- New sling rope as well as any other rope that has been cut from a long piece should be whipped at the ends.
- New rope is stiff and should be worked.
- Keep the rope dry as much as possible. Dry it as soon as possible
- Climbing rope should never be spliced, since it will be hard to manage at the splice.
- Avoid running rope over sharp or rough edges (pad if necessary) especially if it is under tension.
- Keep the rope away from oil, acids, and other corrosive substances.
- Avoid rubbing ropes together under tension (nylon to nylon friction will harm the rope).
- Do not leave rope knotted or tightly stretched longer than necessary.
- Clean in cool water, loosely coil and hang to dry (out of direct sunlight, since ultraviolet light rays will harm synthetic fibers). Store in a cool, dry, shaded area on a round wooden pegs.

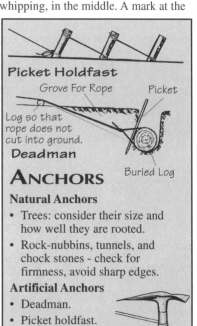

Picket Holdfast

Grove For Rope Picket

Log so that rope does not cut into ground.

Deadman

Buried Log

Anchors

Natural Anchors
- Trees: consider their size and how well they are rooted.
- Rock-nubbins, tunnels, and chock stones - check for firmness, avoid sharp edges.

Artificial Anchors
- Deadman.
- Picket holdfast.
- Three or four piton anchor.
- Bolts with carriers.
- Well placed chocks.

ROPES AND CLIMBING

Ropes are intended to provide security for climbers and equipment when there are steep ascents and descents. They are also used for establishing rope installations and hauling equipment.

Coiling a Rope

There are two methods of coiling a rope:

- One end of the rope is taken in the left hand; the right hand is run along the rope until both arms are outstretched. The hands are then brought together forming a loop which is laid in the left hand. This is repeated forming uniform loops until the rope is completely coiled. If there is any tendency for the rope to twist or form figure eights, give it a slight twist with the right hand. The rope should always be coiled in a clockwise direction.
- The rope is coiled around the left foot and knee while in the kneeling position with the left foreleg being vertical. In coiling on the leg, start from the inside, bring the rope over the knee to the outside around the foot to the inside, and continue in this manner until the rope is coiled using the same technique as in the hand coil method.

See Rope & Knot Chapter

Tying a Coiled Rope

In tying the coil, a 30 cm long bend is made in the starting end of the rope and laid along the top of the coil. Uncoil the last loop and take the length of rope formed and wrap it around the coil and the bend. The first wrap is made at the open end of the bend in such a manner as to lock itself. Then continue wrapping toward the closed end until just enough rope remains to insert through the bight. Pull the running end of the bend to secure the wrapped rope. A rope properly coiled has from six to eight wraps. The coil can be carried either on the backpack by forming a figure eight and doubling it, and placing the coil under the flap of the backpack, or by placing it over one shoulder and under the opposite arm.

ROPE THROWING

Carefully coil the rope before throwing. In throwing the full rope, grasp the coil in the right hand and take the end of the rope nearest the fingertips and anchor it. Take five or six loops from the anchored end of the coil and hold it in the left hand while holding the remaining coil, which will be thrown first, in the right hand. A few preliminary swings will ensure a smooth throw with the arm nearly extended. The coil should be thrown out and up. A slight twist of the wrist so that the palm of the hand comes up as the rope is thrown will cause the coil to turn, the loops to spread, and the running end to fall free and away from the thrower. A smooth follow-through is essential. As soon as the coil is thrown and spreading, the loops held in the left hand should be tossed out. Where possible, the rope should be thrown with the wind so that the running end is to the leeward side. As soon as the rope starts to leave the hand, the thrower shouts the warning "ROPE" to alert anyone below his position.

Divide rope coil in half. Throw first half and feed second half while the first half is in the air.

A stone or stick can be attached if throwing a short heavy rope into the wind or over a branch. A light guide rope, which is thrown, can be attached to a heavier rope which is then pulled over by the guide rope.

KNOTS

Knots used by a climber are grouped into four functions.

- Knots to tie the ends of two ropes together.
- Anchor knots.
- Middle rope knots.
- Special use knots.

TYING ENDS OF TWO ROPES TOGETHER

Square Knot

The square knot is used to tie the ends of two ropes of equal diameter together and must be secured by a half hitch on each side of the knot.

Double Sheet Bend

The double sheet bend is used to tie together the ends of two ropes of equal or unequal diameter. It can also be used to tie the ends of several ropes to the end of one rope. When a single rope is tied to a multiple of ropes, the bend is formed with the multiple of ropes.

ANCHOR KNOTS

Anchor knots are used to tie the end of a rope to any object. An anchor knot is easy to tie and untie. Care must be used in selecting an anchor knot that will not work itself loose when alternate tension and slack are put on the rope. *The round turn with two half hitches and the clove hitch may work loose under these conditions; but not the bowline.*

Bowline

Used to tie the end man into a climbing rope and to tie a fixed loop in the end of a rope.

Round Turn

The round turn is tied with two half hitches.

Clove Hitch

Tension must be maintained to prevent slipping.

MIDDLE ROPE KNOTS

They form a fixed loop or loops in the middle of a rope without using the ends. The butterfly knot is used for the middle man in a rope party and for tightening installation ropes.

Butterfly Knot will form a single loop.

Bowline on a bight forms a double loop.

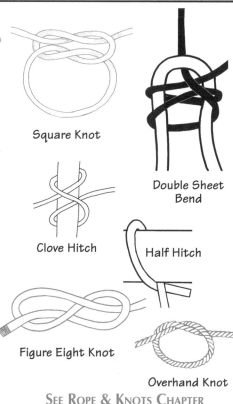

Square Knot

Double Sheet Bend

Clove Hitch

Half Hitch

Figure Eight Knot

Overhand Knot

SEE ROPE & KNOTS CHAPTER FOR MORE INFORMATION

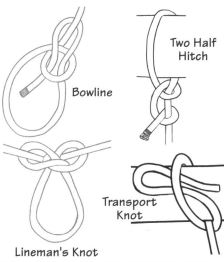

Bowline

Two Half Hitch

Transport Knot

Lineman's Knot

Prusik Knot

SPECIAL USE KNOTS

Prusik Knot

The prusik knot is tied with a short rope around a longer rope. For example, a sling rope around a climbing rope, in such a manner that the short rope will slide on the climbing rope if there is no tension applied and will hold if tension is applied on the short rope. It is tied with a bend of rope or end of rope. When tied with an end of rope the knot is finished off with a bowline. The prusik knot is used to anchor a fixed rope to various anchors and in crevasse rescue techniques.

Overhand Knot

The overhand knot is used to make a knotted rope for a hand-line, to make the carrying rope for a suspension traverse, and stirrups in tension climbing. It is also used to temporarily whip the end of a rope.

Bowline on a Coil

The bowline on a coil can be used by the first and last man on a climbing rope to take up extra and unnecessary slack. A half hitch must be employed behind the knot.

Three Loop Bowline

The three loop bowline will provide three bights, two of which can be adjusted against the other one. It is used mainly for a 4 piton anchor and in evacuation procedures.

Figure-of-Eight Slip Knot

The figure-of-eight slip knot is used as an anchor knot on fixed ropes.

Transport Knot

The transport knot is used to secure the tightening arrangement on rope installations and consists of a slip knot and half hitch.

PITONS, SNAPLINK, CHOCK AND PITON HAMMER

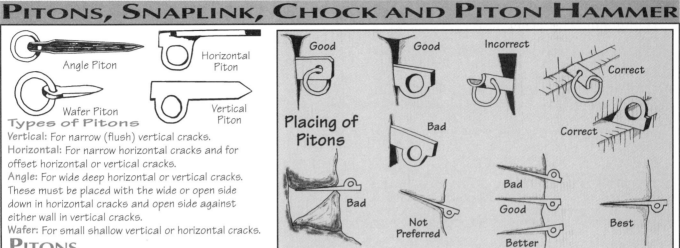

Types of Pitons

Angle Piton

Wafer Piton

Horizontal Piton

Vertical Piton

Vertical: For narrow (flush) vertical cracks.
Horizontal: For narrow horizontal cracks and for offset horizontal or vertical cracks.
Angle: For wide deep horizontal or vertical cracks. These must be placed with the wide or open side down in horizontal cracks and open side against either wall in vertical cracks.
Wafer: For small shallow vertical or horizontal cracks.

PITONS

Pitons are driven into cracks in the rock to increase the climber's safety. If well placed and tested they will limit his fall to twice the distance he is above the piton, plus the stretch factor of the rope. A well placed piton can withstand a force of several hundred pounds (wafer) to more than 2,000 pounds (900 kg) (angle). The advantage over chocks is that pitons provide support for an omnidirectional pull, and are well suited for anchors and rope installations. Pitons provide a secure point on the cliff to which the rope may be attached by means of a snaplink. If the leading climber falls he may be held, pulley-wise, by a man below him. It will also hold each following man. Successive pitons are driven as the climber moves upward this will secure points along the course of a fixed rope. The placement of pitons can be extended by attaching runners (utility ropes or nylon webbing). You can insert a snaplink through the eye of the piton.

In placing pitons the climber should *study the rock*. See that driving of a piton will not split or weaken it. *Test rock for soundness* by tapping with the hammer. In hard, solid rock select a crack which is wide enough to admit 1/3 to 1/2 of the piton shaft *before* driving the piton in. The driving of pitons in soft or rotten rock is not always practical. When this type of rock must be used, loose rock from the crack should be *removed before* driving the piton. In this type of rock it is not necessary to be able to insert the piton into the crack as far as in solid rock. *Select the right piton;* the one that the rock will support best and that the snaplink can be hooked into after the piton is driven in.

Placing of Pitons — Good, Good, Incorrect, Correct, Bad, Correct, Bad, Not Preferred, Bad, Good, Better, Best

Driving the pitons. While driving watch the rock to see that it is not being weakened by further cracking. The piton should go in smoothly and notice if the point hits a dead end. Listen to the piton's sound at each blow; good verticals and horizontals usually go in with a *rising pitch*, wafer and angle pitons will have *no noticeable pitch* as long as the ring is swinging free. Drive the piton with slow moderate strokes. The piton should always be attached to the hammer thong or to the sling rope by a snaplink. If the piton is knocked out of the crack while it is being driven it will not be lost. The greater the resistance overcome in driving the piton, the firmer it will be. An appropriately placed and well-driven piton into rock of average strength will withstand a force of from several hundred pounds (wafer) to more than 2,000 pounds (900 kg) (angle) exerted in the direction of pull.

Testing of pitons. Pull up approximately one meter of slack on the climbing rope, or use sling rope or the piton hammer thong; snap rope into a snaplink; grasp rope at least 1/2 meter from the snaplink. Make sure that you have secure footing, jerk vigorously outward, downward, and to each side, meanwhile observing the piton. Repeat if the test is questionable. Tap the piton. If the pitch *has changed much*, drive the piton in as far as possible; if the sound regains its original pitch the piton is good. If not, drive another piton into new location.

To remove pitons. The climber should knock the piton back and forth in the crack with the piton hammer, and when they are loosened, pull them out with a bight of the climbing rope or sling rope, or hammer thong, which has been hooked into a snaplink. Be well braced when pulling out pitons, as they sometimes tend to suddenly come out. Make sure that no one will be struck by the extracted piton.

Second-Hand Pitons
Pitons that have been used, removed, bent, and straightened should be discarded. Pitons already in place should not be trusted, as they can be loosened by weathering. They should be tested and redrive until the climber is certain of their safety.

PITON HAMMER

Always secure your piton hammer with a lanyard before starting the climb.

Piton hammers are used for:

- Driving and removing pitons. Do not use the point.
- Testing rock (avoid hollow or rotten rock).
- Cleaning out cracks of dirt and debris.
- Chipping rock or ice.

NYLON WEBBING

Used for making runners, etriers (stirrups) and other general purpose slings. Flat or tubular nylon webbing is either 9/16 inch (1.43 cm) or 1 inch (2.5 cm) wide.

Care of Nylon Webbing

- Cut with a hot knife to fuse the ends to prevent fraying.
- Keep away from oil, acids and other corrosive substances.
- Inspect before, during and after use for fraying, cuts and excess dirt.
- Clean in cool water, air dry, and store in a cool dry area out of direct sunlight. Do not store on cement floors.
- Do not store in closed plastic bags.

CLIMBING LIST

ROCK CLIMBING

- Helmet
- Piton hammer
- Hammer holster
- Pitons
- Carabiners
- Chocks and nuts
- Kletterschuhe (rock climbing shoes)
- Swami belt
- Rope (check each time before using)

ICE AND SNOW CLIMBING

- Helmet
- Cagoule (Balaklava)
- Extra socks
- Gaiters
- Mittens, Fingerless mittens
- Slings, rappel anchors, runners, seats, etc.
- Rock pitons
- Tubular ice screws
- Backpack
- Crampons
- Emergency shelter
- Boots
- Rope
- Carabiners
- Alpine Hammer
- Hammer holster
- Ice ax
- Down jacket

SNAPLINKS OR CARABINERS (BINERS)

Snaplinks are metal devices used to attach a climbing rope to anchor points, conducting rappels, and erecting rope installations in mountainous terrain. The snaplink will hold a load of 2,000 pounds (900 kg) when the gate is closed.

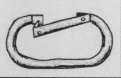

- Know characteristics and use of the type of snaplink selected. They might be: steel, aluminum, chrome molybdenum, or steel alloys; oval, D-shape, modified D-shape, pear shape. Locking and non-locking gate snaplinks.
- Check gate for safety and proper locking. Check the threads and locking nut on locking snaplinks.

- Correctly position snaplink to prevent accidental opening of the gate. Consider single versus multiple snaplink employment.
- Inspect snaplinks before, during, and after use for cracks, burrs, grooves, and defects. Remove all rust with steel wool. Use dry graphite, as lubricant, on hinges and moving parts. Store in a dry area when not in use. Do not store in plastic bags.

THE USE OF CHOCKS

Chocks are angled metal stoppers which are used to provide artificial protection when climbing, rappeling, erecting rope installations and emplacment security. A well placed chock is quicker and easier to place than pitons.

Chocks provide protection for a *single direction of pull*. Placing chocks in opposition gives additional security. Insert a proper size chock into the crack and rotate it so that at least two sides are wedged into the crack. Test by pulling up, down, sideways and out with increasing weight. Retrieve by pushing in and turning side to side or up and down. Well wedged chocks may require tapping out with a piton hammer.

Types of Chocks

Hexagonal: Six sides in a selection of sizes for a wide variety of small to immediate sized crack structures.

Wired Stoppers: These are the smallest chocks and are tapered at the ends to wedge into small cracks. They come in a variety of sizes.

Cammed Chocks: Half moon shaped, wired and looped chocks come in a variety of sizes and are well suited for small to intermediate placements. Mechanical spring activated camming devices can be easily emplaced with one hand, and are easy to retrieve.

HYPOXIA

Hypoxia occurs when there is a lack of a oxygen which is the case at high elevations. Individuals who are not in good physical shape are more susceptible to be affected by hypoxia.

Symptoms are:

- Breathing rate increases.
- Dizziness.
- Warm sweating sensation.
- Sleepiness.
- Skin, fingernails, and lips turning blue.
- Reduced field of vision.
- Problems of judgment and behavior.
- Loss of consciousness

Night Vision Problems

At 5000 feet vision might become blurred, angle of vision reduced, and night vision might be reduced. At 8000 feet night vision might be reduced by 25%. This would not occur during the day time.

With increased elevation and reduced oxygen the other symptoms will occur.

Treatment

Increase the supply of oxygen.

ALTIMETER

Walk at a constant elevation to find the pass.

Couloir

Altimeter

An altimeter is a barometer calibrated in feet or meters. When taking a reading hold it level and look directly down. Tap the meter lightly before each reading and average several readings. Check the reading when you reach a known elevation.

- Can help you establish your speed of climb. Usually you can travel 750-1000 feet (250-300 m) per hour.
- Help you find your location on a topographic map.
- Can help you find a couloir or passage through the mountains.

Accuracy of an altimeter is affected by:

- Wind and temperature. When the temperature is high the warmer air is lighter and the altimeter will read high.
- High or low atmospheric pressure. There is a lower elevation reading when there is low atmospheric pressure.
- Keep the temperature of the altimeter constant.
- An altimeter calibrated in a 20 foot scale can have an error of +/- 30 feet.

MOUNTAIN WALKING

MOUNTAIN WALKING

Mountain walking is divided into four techniques dependent upon the general characteristics of the terrain;

- Walking on hard ground.
- Grassy slopes.
- Scree slopes.
- Talus slopes.

WALKING ON HARD GROUND

Hard ground is firmly packed dirt that does not give way or crumble under the weight of your step.

Ascending on Hard Ground

- Steep slopes are traversed at an angle rather than walked straight up.
- In traversing, the full sole (boot) principle is accomplished by rolling the ankle away from the hill on each step.
- For small stretches, the herring bone step may be used when ascending straight up with the toes pointed out. This can be very tiring.

Descending on Hard Ground

- Walk straight down the slope without traversing.
- Keep the back straight and the knees bent.
- Keep the backpack securely attached, to keep it stable, but be ready to jettison.

GRASSY SLOPES

Grassy slopes are usually composed of small tufts of growth rather than continuous vegetation.

Ascending on a Grassy Slopes

The upper side of each tuft is stepped on where the ground is more level.

Descending on a Grassy Slope

It is best to traverse because of the uneven nature of the ground and the difficulty of aiming your foot onto the tuft of grass. If traversing, the uphill foot points in the direction of travel. The downhill foot points in the direction of travel or for more stability, especially with a heavy load, the downhill foot points about 45° downhill off the direction of travel.

Rockfall

Rockfall is the most common mountaineering hazard. The mountain walking techniques discussed are designed to reduce the likelihood of rockfall. Whenever rock, debris, or equipment falls, the warning "Rock" or "Equipment" is shouted. People below should immediately lean into the cliff to reduce their exposure, cover their heads, and do not look up.

PROPER WALKING TECHNIQUE

These apply to all mountain travel.

- Weight centered over feet at all times.
- Maintain as much boot sole-to-ground surface contact as possible.
- Straighten the trail knee after each step to rest the leg muscles.
- Keep a slow rhythmic pace, maintaining good balance taking small steps.
- Use all available hand and footholds.
- Normal progression as the slope steepens would be from walking straight up the slope, to a herring bone step (toes point out), and then to a traverse (zig- zag pattern) on the steeper areas.
- On steep or slippery slopes, climbers should use a roped party climb to increase mutual safety.

Rock Slope

Scree Slope

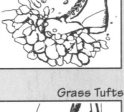

Grass Tufts

Talus Slope

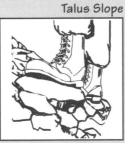

SCREE SLOPES

Scree slopes consist of small rocks and gravel that vary in size from grains of sand to that the size of a fist. It may occur as a mixture of all sizes, but usually scree slopes consist of the same size particles. These particles tend to slide downhill and do not offer very stable support.

Ascending a Scree Slope

- Ascending scree slopes is difficult, most tiring, and should be avoided whenever possible.
- Kick in with the toe of the upper foot so that a step is formed in the scree.
- Gradually transfer your weight from the lower to the upper foot, and repeat the process.
- Be careful not to dislodge any debris on members of your group that are below you. If possible it is best to ascend in a traverse as any debris would roll freely down the hill.

Descending a Scree Slope

- Descend scree slopes by going straight down using a short shuffling step with the knees bent, back straight and feet pointed downhill.
- When several climbers descend a scree slope, together, they should be as close together as possible, one behind the other, to prevent injury from a dislodged rock.
- Avoid running down a scree slope as you might lose control.
- Use caution when the bottom of the route cannot be seen as there might be a cliff.

TALUS SLOPES

Talus slopes are formed by the accumulation of rock debris which is larger than a man's fist. When ascending or descending, *always step on the top and on the uphill side of the rock*. This prevents the rocks from tilting and rolling downhill. The rock is partially embedded and will distribute your weight to the rocks below it. Avoid dislodging rocks which may cause a rock slide. Climbers must stay in close columns while traversing.

ROCK CLIMBING

Three Points of Contact

Three points of contact with the rock (i.e., 2 hands and 1 foot, or 2 feet and 1 hand).

BALANCED CLIMBING TECHNIQUE

Balanced climbing is the type of movement used to climb rock faces. It is a combination of the balanced movement of a tightrope walker and the unbalanced climbing of a man ascending a tree or ladder. In balance and party climbing, the climber must study the route he is to travel in order to make sure he has selected the best route and has the necessary equipment. During the process of route selection, he should mentally climb the route so he will know what to expect. Climbers should not wear gloves when balance climbing. They should, however, wear gloves for all types of rappels to protect the palms from rope burns.

- Weight of body is centered over the feet.
- Feet and legs carry weight.
- Hands mainly for balance.
- As much boot sole as possible in contact with the rock.
- Keep handholds low, between waist and shoulder height. This helps keep the desired upright and balanced position while providing the maximum rest for the arms.
- Keep the body out and away from the rock surface. This will help you keep the weight and center of gravity on your feet. This posture will usually maximize the sole/ground contact.
- Three points of contact with the rock (i.e., 2 hands and 1 foot, or 2 feet and 1 hand).
- Use relaxed slow, rhythmic and deliberate motions.
- Be observant and plan your route two or three moves ahead.
- Use all available hand and footholds. Avoid over stretching and ending in a spread eagle position.

In Ascent:

Facing sideways: climbing will be easy to difficult.
Facing inward: climbing will be more difficult.

In Descent:

Facing out: climbing will be very easy when hill is not too steep.
Facing sideways: climbing will be easy to difficult.
Facing inward: climbing will be more difficult when hill is very steep.

PRECAUTIONS WHILE CLIMBING

- Margin of safety. Stay within individual abilities.
- Use roped party climbs as the slope steepens and the difficulty increases.
- Plan entire route this will prevent the group from getting "stuck".
- Avoid overstretching, i.e., "spread eagle" position.
- Avoid "hugging" the rock.
- Test loose rock before placing weight on it.
- Avoid using knees, elbows, and buttocks.
- Do not dislodge rocks intentionally. Yell "Rock" when causing rock to fall.
- Never climb alone.
- Do not jump or lunge to reach a hold.
- Avoid wet moss covered rock.
- Clean boot sole (cleats) before climbing.
- Do not use vegetation as foot or hand holds.
- Do not use snaplinks as hand holds.
- Avoid wearing gloves when climbing.
- Remove jewelry from the hands before climbing.
- When a climber falls, shout the warning "Falling" to signal the belay man and to warn climbers below.

Right   Wrong

FOOTHOLDS

- **Step**
- **Friction**
- **Jam**
- **Cross Pressure**

FOOTHOLDS

On steep slopes the body should be kept vertical, with use being made of small irregularities in the slope to aid friction. Footholds less than one inch (1.5 cm wide) can be sufficient for intermediate holds, even when they slope out.

Push Hold

Push holds are pushed down upon a secure rock surface. This hold helps the climber keep his arms low, but they are more difficult to hold onto in case of a slip. A push hold is often used in combination with a pull hold.

Pull Holds

A pull hold is a hold that is pulled down upon. These the easiest holds to use. They are also the most likely to slip or break out.

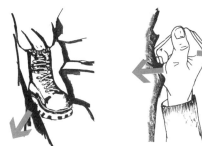

Jam Holds

Jam holds involve jamming any part of the body or extremity into a crack. This can be done by putting the hand into the crack and clenching it into a fist or by putting the arm into the crack and twisting the elbow against one side and the hand against the other side. When the foot is in a jam hold care must be taken to ensure that the boot is not jammed into the crack in such a way that it cannot be easily removed when climbing is continued.

Pinch Hold

Pinch a protruding part between the thumb and fingers. Pulling outward or pressing inward with the arms.

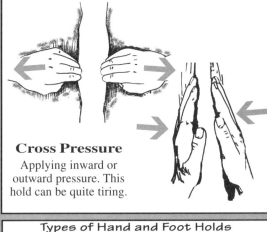

Cross Pressure

Applying inward or outward pressure. This hold can be quite tiring.

Types of Hand and Foot Holds

Holds need not be large to be safe. Plan each move in advance, knowing exactly where the hands and feet are going to be placed. All hand and foot holds should be tested before they are used by gradually applying weight.

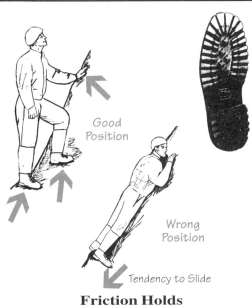

Good Position

Wrong Position

Tendency to Slide

Friction Holds

Friction holds are those dependent solely on the friction of hands or feet against a relatively smooth surface with a very shallow hold. They are difficult to use because they give a feeling of insecurity which the inexperienced climber tries to correct by leaning too close to the rock, thereby increasing his insecurity. They often serve well as intermediate holds, some of which will give needed support while the climber moves over them, but would not hold him were he to stop.

USE OF HOLDS AND MOVEMENT

A hold need not be large to be good. The climber must not try to skip or jump from one to another. It is, however, often desirable while traversing to use the hop step in which the climber changes feet on a hold so that he can move sideways more easily. A slight upward hop followed by *precise footwork* will accomplish this useful step. All hand holds and foot holds are tested by applying weight gradually before they are used.

Chimney Hold

Where cross pressure is exerted between the back and the feet or hands or knees.

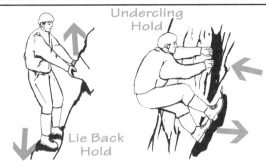

Undercling Hold

Lie Back Hold

ADDITIONAL HOLDS AND MOVEMENTS

Combination Holds

These are combinations and variations of the hand and foot holds.

- **Lie Back**

  Lie back is done by leaning to one side of an offset crack with the hands pulling and the feet pushing against the offset side.

- **Inverted Pull or Push**

  This method uses the undercling hold in which you pull from under a ledge towards yourself.

- **Manteling**

  Changing step, transferring body weight only when necessary using a hop-skip movement.

Crab Walk

A crab walk is facing away from the slope squatting over feet and hands when ascending, traversing, or descending slopes. The weight is evenly balanced over the hands and feet. This technique relies mainly on friction.

Shoulder Stand

The shoulder stand or human ladder, is used to overcome a holdless lower section of a pitch in order to reach for easier climbing above. The lower man is anchored to the rock and belays the leader who uses his body as a ladder to overcome the difficult pitch.

Movement on Slabs

A slab is a relatively smooth portion of rock lying at an angle. When traversing, the lower foot is pointed slightly downhill to increase your balance and friction of the foot. All irregularities in the slope should be utilized for additional friction. On steep slabs it may be necessary to squat with the body weight well over the feet and hands for added friction. This position may be used for ascending, traversing, or descending. A slip will result if you lean back or let the buttocks drag. *Wet, icy, mossy, or scree covered slabs are dangerous.*

Moving on a Slab

On a smooth portion of rock, lie at an angle.

- Full sole-to-surface contact to increase balance and friction of the foot.
- Use all irregularities in the rock surface.
- Point lower foot downhill in traversing.
- Upper foot pointed in the direction of movement.
- Stand erect, maintain balance and control.
- Keep moving at a rhythmic pace.

HIGH-ALTITUDE COOKING

High-altitude cooking requires special consideration:

- Low atmospheric pressure at high altitudes causes water to boil at:

201°F at 5281 feet	**93.8°C** at 1600 m
194°F at 10,000 feet	**90°C** at 3000 m
212°F at sea level	**100°C** at sea level

- The lower boiling point of water, at high altitudes, means that it cannot get as hot before steaming and this cooler water will prolong cooking and baking time. At 6000 feet (1800 m) 3 minute eggs will take five minutes. Water steams off (evaporates) more rapidly, at 6000 feet (1800 m) twice as much water should be used in a cookie recipe.

- Add water to boiling water as it will rapidly boil away.

- A two pound (0.9 kg) fish that takes 15 minutes at sea level will take 20 minutes at 6000 feet (1800 m).

- Dehydrated foods should be soaked for a longer time and cooked at a low temperature.

BELAYING

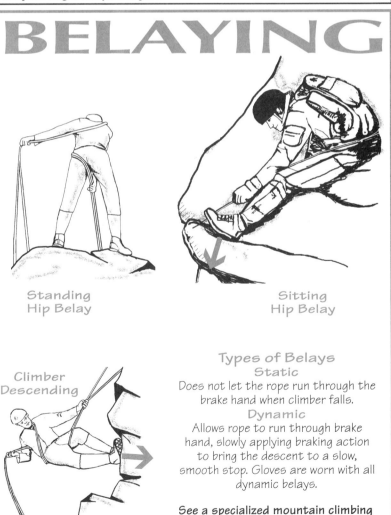

Standing Hip Belay

Sitting Hip Belay

Climber Descending

Types of Belays

Static

Does not let the rope run through the brake hand when climber falls.

Dynamic

Allows rope to run through brake hand, slowly applying braking action to bring the descent to a slow, smooth stop. Gloves are worn with all dynamic belays.

See a specialized mountain climbing book for more information.

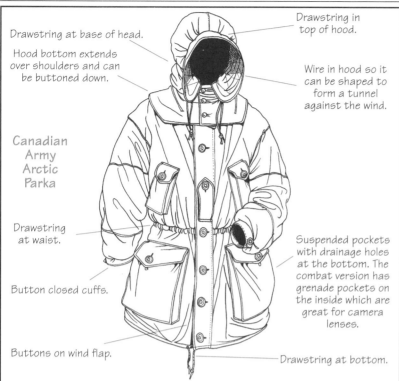

Drawstring at base of head.

Hood bottom extends over shoulders and can be buttoned down.

Drawstring in top of hood.

Wire in hood so it can be shaped to form a tunnel against the wind.

Canadian Army Arctic Parka

Drawstring at waist.

Button closed cuffs.

Suspended pockets with drainage holes at the bottom. The combat version has grenade pockets on the inside which are great for camera lenses.

Buttons on wind flap.

Drawstring at bottom.

CANADIAN ARMY ARCTIC PARKA

This parka is designed for the Canadian Arctic which extends to the North Pole. It has many unique features that are made for cold weather survival.

Removable Lining: The lining can be removed to dry while you can still wear the shell. The filling is a suspended polyester which is like a web loft. There are drainage holes, for water, at the bottom of the lining to rapidly expel water.

Pockets: All pockets are suspended at the upper edges from the cover flaps so that if they are unbuttoned they will not fall open.

Buttons: Buttons are attached by pieces of ribbon. The buttons ride on these ribbons which do not wear out as fast as thread. *Certain versions of the parka are made with survival buttons. These buttons are made of a protein plastic material that can be cooked in water to provide emergency food.*

Hood: The hood, which can be unbuttoned and unzipped, is made with a wide bottom overlay that is buttoned onto the parka. This overlay protects from wind blowing into the zipper. The hood has a wire near the brim so that it can be shaped to make a tunnel for the face if there is a strong side wind. The hood has two drawstrings, one over the front of the face and the second over the scalp. This cups the head and does not let the hood fall over the eyes when the front cord is drawn.

Front Closure: The front zipper is made from heavy brass which is lubricated with wax or soap. To keep out the wind there are three overlapping wind flaps. The outside wind flap is buttoned down.

NORTHERN WINTER TRAVEL

If you weigh the odds of surviving in the Canadian north or in Alaska, in the summer or winter, winter might give you a better chance.

- In the winter there are no insects to drive you crazy.

- Frozen rivers and streams are excellent routes for travel. They are devoid of most obstacles except fallen trees and ice piles (on the shores of larger bodies of water). *Do not camp in the shelter of the ice piles.* They are formed by the contraction and expansion of ice which occurs with the change of temperature. The ice expands, upon getting warmer, it needs more space and might explode and buckle onto the shoreline. This might injure you if you are camping in the area.

- *Water has a special characteristic when it freezes. Upon cooling it contracts (as most materials) but when it starts to become ice it expands. Once it is ice and gets colder the ice starts contracting again and fissures in ice will occur. These fissures are filled with water that freezes. Now when the ice warms up and starts to expand it will not have enough space, and explode upwards causing the buckles in the ice that are seen near the shoreline on lakes and rivers.*

- Snowshoes on deep snow cover can help you pass over brush and swamp which can be impenetrable in summer. This will let you shorten your travel time by many days.

- The dry cold air lets you see further and hear better. When it is very cold you might hear noise from an encampment 5 miles away. To determine the direction of the sound stand away from any obstructions (to avoid echoes), close your eyes, cup your ears and slowly rotate your head.

- If you have no snowshoes travel where loose snow is the thinnest, which would be on the windblown areas along stream beds, and in heavy evergreen groves.

WINTER TRAVEL CHAPTER 7

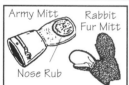

Army Mitt

Rabbit Fur Mitt

Nose Rub

Winter Gloves
They have a high cuff to protect against snow. The palm is made of soft leather that will not get stiff when it is -30°F (-34.4°C). The army mitt has a nose wipe cushion on top of the hand to remove condensation from the nose.

Gaiter to keep snow and ice off the boot and sock.

Cotton face mask and throat protector

PROTECTING THE FACE IN COLD WEATHER

Vaseline should be applied on the face in cold weather. This coating provides protection again the biting wind. Wear a hat as most of the body heat is lost through the head. In very cold weather wear face protection.

Cagoule or Balaklava

WINTER DIRECTION INDICATORS

DIRECTION OF THE WIND

Winds are named for the directions from which they come, i.e. North wind from the North

Each area has a predominant wind that dominates a season or all seasons. The dominant wind is nearly always the same as the prevailing wind which blows longer or more violently from a *given* direction. The dominant wind will affect the growth of trees, direction of snow drifts, direction of tall grass, etc. In northern snow covered areas the prevailing wind is usually from the northwest. To establish the direction find an open spot, where local landmarks do not deflect the wind, and look at wind features as snow drifts, windpacked or wind polished snow. Wind polished snow can be very hard and slippery.

In the polar regions, the wind temperature, if warmer than the surroundings, indicates the direction of water. A sudden drop in temperature, without a change in the direction of the wind, might indicate the presence of an iceberg.

The sun and wind can leave signs which help in finding your direction.

- Erosion by frost is more evident on southern slopes of hills because there is a much larger temperature change from heating by day and cooling at night.
- On southern slopes, heat of the sun will leave "melted shadows" of trees, shrubs and stones in the accumulated snow. This is evident in the spring. There is less snow on the side of a hill facing south.
- The direction of the wind should be observed as a warm strong wind can melt snow *faster* than the sun. This might affect direction indicators.

Candle Lantern
Lightweight Aluminum candle lantern provides light, warmth, and reduces condensation in a tent.

Crampons to Walk on Ice
These are attachments, with spikes, that are strapped onto boots and help you walk on ice.

REFLECTIONS IN THE SKY

Clouds can reflect certain surface features.

- On land, off an ice covered sea, clouds can reflect open water as there is less light reflected off dark open water than a white frozen snow area. This reflection is a dark spot on the underside of clouds. The dark spot does not indicate the size of the open water because a small area can affect a large area of cloud. This happens when open water in the Arctic gives off vapor which affects the reflected light around the open area and increases the dark spot area. This is known as a "water sky".
- An ice flow or iceberg can be seen as an "ice blink" which is a patch of brightness in a gray sky. A small area of ice can show a large "ice blink".
- In the arctic or snow mountain country, the whole anatomy of the land surface can be reflected on a high overcast sky. You will be able to see snow fields, open water areas, naked rock areas, new ice (which is blue green and will show as gray patches), patches of vegetation or the plants called "pink snow" will reflect pinkish. These contrasting areas will reflect on the lower sides of the clouds.
- In vegetation-covered areas, ice patches and small snow fields will reflect steel-blue on the under surface of the clouds.

JUDGING DISTANCE ON SNOW SURFACES

Distance is underestimated when starting and overestimated at the end of the trip. An error in overestimation can also occur when a trip or route is difficult.

Objects look *much nearer* than they actually are when:

- Looking up or down hill.
- There is bright sunlight on the snow.
- Looking across water, or snow covered areas.
- The air is clear which is common in the winter.

Objects look *much farther* away than they actually are when:

- The light is poor during the latter part of a short winter day.
- The color of the destination blends in with the background as during a snowfall or blowing snow.
- The object is at the end of a long narrow area as a valley in the mountains.
- You are looking over undulating ground as snow drifts.

MELTED HALF CIRCLES INDICATING "SOUTH"

When a small, vertical, dark object (branch, leaf, etc.) is on the surface of the snow, on a sunny day, the object will absorb heat and melt a hole into the snow. The sun will continue shining into the hole and the sun's rays will raise the temperature melting the snow to create a hole up to a foot deep. The depth of the hole decreases when closer to the North Pole. The hole that is formed is in the shape of a half circle adjacent to the dark object. In the northern hemisphere, the straight side of the half (the diameter) is aligned *east-west*. The arc of the half circle is the *south*.

This action of the sun can also be seen in animal tracks in the snow .

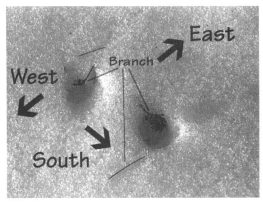

North of the Arctic Circle, this method does not work because during the summer months the sun never sets but goes around the horizon and a practically round circle is formed.

Ski Sled

This is a sled made of old skis. Two pairs of skis are used to make both the runners and the seat supports.

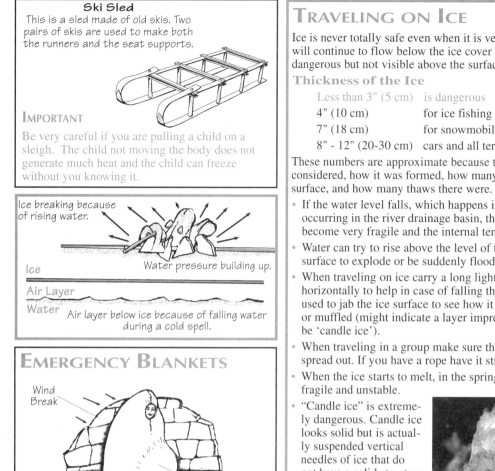

IMPORTANT

Be very careful if you are pulling a child on a sleigh. The child not moving the body does not generate much heat and the child can freeze without you knowing it.

Ice breaking because of rising water.

Water pressure building up.

Ice

Air Layer

Water   Air layer below ice because of falling water during a cold spell.

EMERGENCY BLANKETS

Wind Break

Emergency Bag

Emergency Bag

Similar to the emergency blanket but is in the shape of a body bag. It can be used as an emergency sleeping bag or over a regular sleeping bag. If used with a sleeping bag air the sleeping bag the next day as the emergency bag does not let the humidity pass through.

Emergency Blanket

Thermal blanket weighing 2 oz. (57 g) but retains over 80% of radiated body heat to provide protection in cold or a crisis situation. Silver reflecting sides can be seen at a distance.

All-Weather Blanket

This reflective blanket retains over 80% of radiated body heat, even in subzero temperatures. Waterproof, windproof, light weight, and grommets on corners. In silver or orange.

SEA ICE

Ice Type	Old Sea Ice	New Sea Ice
Color	bluish or blackish	milky or gray
Brittleness	shatters easily	doesn't break easily
Features	rounded corners	sharp corners
Taste	relatively salt free	tastes extremely salty

TRAVELING ON ICE

Ice is never totally safe even when it is very cold. In rivers a swift current will continue to flow below the ice cover and these areas can be thin and dangerous but not visible above the surface.

Thickness of the Ice

Less than 3" (5 cm)	is dangerous
4" (10 cm)	for ice fishing and skating.
7" (18 cm)	for snowmobiles.
8" - 12" (20-30 cm)	cars and all terrain vehicles.

These numbers are approximate because the type of ice has to be considered, how it was formed, how many snow layers are on the surface, and how many thaws there were.

- If the water level falls, which happens if it is very cold and no melting is occurring in the river drainage basin, the ice can be suspended in the air and become very fragile and the internal tension of the ice might not be stable.
- Water can try to rise above the level of the ice and cause the ice surface to explode or be suddenly flooded.
- When traveling on ice carry a long light pole. This pole should be carried horizontally to help in case of falling through the ice. The pole can also be used to jab the ice surface to see how it rings. It might sound hollow, heavy, or muffled (might indicate a layer impregnated with air or water which might be 'candle ice').
- When traveling in a group make sure that you are in single file and well spread out. If you have a rope have it strung between you - *but not tied to you.*
- When the ice starts to melt, in the spring, it is dangerous because it is very fragile and unstable.
- "Candle ice" is extremely dangerous. Candle ice looks solid but is actually suspended vertical needles of ice that do not have a solid structure because they are not attached laterally. Stepping on candle ice is like stepping on slush. This ice is very dangerous because there is no solid rim to grab if you fall through it.

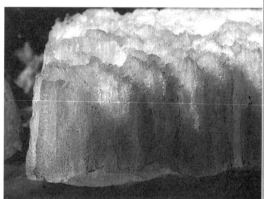

Candle Ice

FALLING INTO WATER THROUGH THE ICE

When traveling over water watch for areas of strong currents under the ice which can produce thin spots through which you can fall.

Hypothermia might result in a few minutes after falling through ice.

- If you fall through ice, break off as much thin ice in the direction of escape as possible. When you are near ice that can support your weight, squirm up onto the surface. Slide and roll along the surface so that your weight is distributed and you do not break through a second time. Move towards shore, dry and warm up as soon as possible. Dry by rolling in the snow. Your weight will blot the water out of the clothing and the snow will absorb the water. The remaining water will freeze and make a shell around you. The ice will add additional weight and make you very uncomfortable. Your clothing will also lose most of its insulation capacity. Change your clothing and warm up as soon as possible or you might expose yourself to hypothermia. *See First Aid.*
- Another method is, while falling, to immediately stretch your arms so that they might find ice strong enough to support your weight. Keep your arms spread out and try to slide your legs onto the ice edge to crawl out.
- A sheath knife can help you crawl out of icy water. Upon falling in the water plunge your knife into the solid ice and roll yourself onto the solid surface.

WINTER SURVIVAL

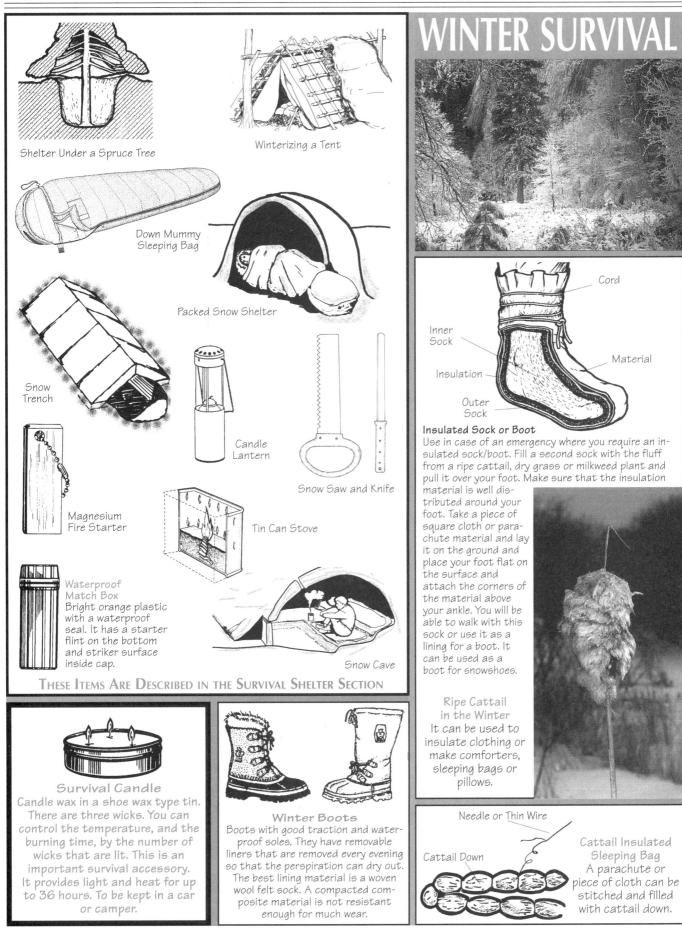

Shelter Under a Spruce Tree

Winterizing a Tent

Down Mummy Sleeping Bag

Packed Snow Shelter

Snow Trench

Candle Lantern

Snow Saw and Knife

Magnesium Fire Starter

Tin Can Stove

Waterproof Match Box
Bright orange plastic with a waterproof seal. It has a starter flint on the bottom and striker surface inside cap.

Snow Cave

THESE ITEMS ARE DESCRIBED IN THE SURVIVAL SHELTER SECTION

Survival Candle
Candle wax in a shoe wax type tin. There are three wicks. You can control the temperature, and the burning time, by the number of wicks that are lit. This is an important survival accessory. It provides light and heat for up to 36 hours. To be kept in a car or camper.

Winter Boots
Boots with good traction and water-proof soles. They have removable liners that are removed every evening so that the perspiration can dry out. The best lining material is a woven wool felt sock. A compacted composite material is not resistant enough for much wear.

Cord
Inner Sock
Material
Insulation
Outer Sock

Insulated Sock or Boot
Use in case of an emergency where you require an insulated sock/boot. Fill a second sock with the fluff from a ripe cattail, dry grass or milkweed plant and pull it over your foot. Make sure that the insulation material is well distributed around your foot. Take a piece of square cloth or parachute material and lay it on the ground and place your foot flat on the surface and attach the corners of the material above your ankle. You will be able to walk with this sock or use it as a lining for a boot. It can be used as a boot for snowshoes.

Ripe Cattail in the Winter
It can be used to insulate clothing or make comforters, sleeping bags or pillows.

Needle or Thin Wire

Cattail Down

Cattail Insulated Sleeping Bag
A parachute or piece of cloth can be stitched and filled with cattail down.

SNOW TYPES

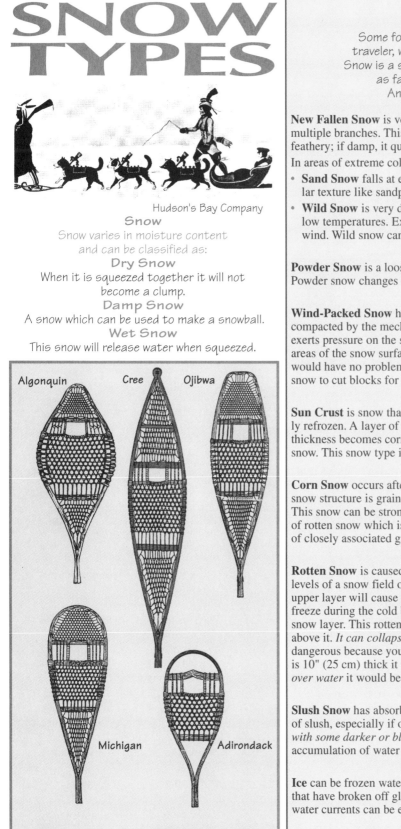

Hudson's Bay Company

Snow
Snow varies in moisture content
and can be classified as:

Dry Snow
When it is squeezed together it will not
become a clump.

Damp Snow
A snow which can be used to make a snowball.

Wet Snow
This snow will release water when squeezed.

Algonquin   Cree   Ojibwa

Michigan   Adirondack

Eskimo Sled

Snow Types
Some forms of snow are of benefit to the winter
traveler, while others are a source of great danger.
Snow is a substance that follows a life cycle starting
as falling snow and terminating as water.
An in between step might even be ice.

New Fallen Snow is very loose and light and the snow flakes still have their multiple branches. This snow is an excellent insulation. If new snow is dry, it is feathery; if damp, it quickly consolidates into a stage of settled snow.

In areas of extreme cold and at high altitudes, new snow is in two forms:

• **Sand Snow** falls at extremely low temperatures. It has a sandy sharp granular texture like sandpaper. Skiing, sledding, and walking is difficult.

• **Wild Snow** is very dry new snow which falls during calm periods and at low temperatures. Extremely light and feathery and is easily blown by the wind. Wild snow can create dangerous whiteouts.

•

Powder Snow is a loose snow but the flakes have lost their branches. Powder snow changes to some form of settling or settled snow.

•

Wind-Packed Snow has been windblown, usually from one direction, and is compacted by the mechanical force of the wind. The blowing of the wind exerts pressure on the snow and causes a form of cold-heat hardening. In some areas of the snow surface it will be strong enough to carry your weight and you would have no problem staying on the surface with snowshoes. This is good snow to cut blocks for igloos or other snow structures.

•

Sun Crust is snow that has had the upper layer melted by heat and subsequently refrozen. A layer of snow that is sun crusted and weathered throughout its thickness becomes corn snow. Sun crust commonly is a layer over powder snow. This snow type is not be very stable on a slope and can be dangerous.

•

Corn Snow occurs after a period of thaw and a refreezing of the snow. The snow structure is grainy snow ice crystals. This usually occurs in the spring. This snow can be strong enough to carry weight but might indicate the presence of rotten snow which is very dangerous. Advanced corn snow or *neve* consists of closely associated grains of ice, separated by air spaces.

•

Rotten Snow is caused by repeated melting and freezing and is found at lower levels of a snow field or on south sides of hills. The melting and freezing of the upper layer will cause water to seep to the lower layers. This water does not freeze during the cold because it is insulated from the weather by the covering snow layer. This rotten snow is strong enough to support the layers of snow above it. *It can collapse if a heavy weight is placed on it.* This snow type is dangerous because you might fall through it while walking on the surface. If it is 10" (25 cm) thick it would not be too dangerous but at 5 feet (2 m) thick *and over water* it would be serious. *See article on page 72 regarding Candle Ice.*

•

Slush Snow has absorbed water from melting snow or rain. To recognize areas of slush, especially if on a river or lake, you will *see a depression in the snow with some darker or bluish snow areas.* These areas show holes in the ice or an accumulation of water on the surface of the ice.

•

Ice can be frozen water or cold heat packed snow as in glaciers and icebergs that have broken off glaciers. If traveling on a snowmobile avoid river ice as the water currents can be eroding the ice from below.

•

Glacier Ice is composed of crystals of advanced corn snow cemented by a film of ice. There is no air space between the grains and any air spaces present are within the grains themselves.

Lake Ice for snowmobile travel requires at least 7"(18 cm) and for walking *at least* 3" (5 cm). Ice strength depends under what conditions it was formed.

Aluminum Snowshoes
Modern snowshoe frames are made of high quality lightweight aluminum tubing. The frame is covered with a stretch resistant plastic compound. The shoe is attached with a harness that pivots on the balance cross bar. Some models have a crampon grip that pivots at the toe area which helps in crossing icy areas.

Winter Trigger Mitt
This mitt is useful because you can tie a heavy cord, use a rifle or camera, fasten snowshoes, and perform other basic functions without removing it.

Deerskin Snowshoe Moccasin

SNOWSHOE STRIDE

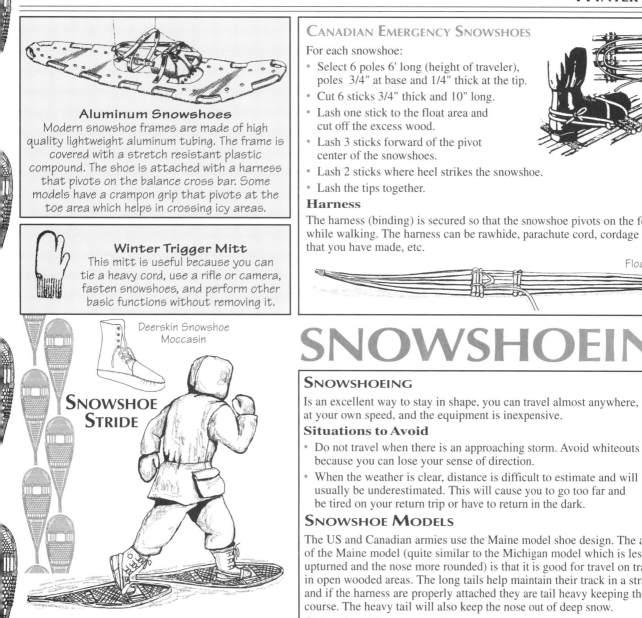

HOW TO TRAVEL WITH SNOWSHOES

To Turn: Use the kick turn by taking one leg and turning it 180° and firmly placing it and then moving the second foot 180°. Poles might help you maintain your balance especially if you are carrying a heavy backpack.

Stepping: On soft snow or semi compacted snow step forward firmly and let snowshoe sink into the snow to form a firm base for the next step. At each step give your body a slight lurch so that the snowshoe will get a firmer stand for the following step.

Downhill Travel: Make sure that your binding is tight enough or your toes will slide under the crosspiece and you will fall forward. Study the hill to find the best path of decent. If it is steep you can descend in a zigzag or if snow is firm you can place one shoe behind the other and sit on the rear snowshoe to slide down the hill.

Climbing Hills: Use a pole to help you climb a steep hill. Poles are useful if you have to back out of an area in heavy snow or between trees.

CANADIAN EMERGENCY SNOWSHOES
For each snowshoe:
- Select 6 poles 6' long (height of traveler), poles 3/4" at base and 1/4" thick at the tip.
- Cut 6 sticks 3/4" thick and 10" long.
- Lash one stick to the float area and cut off the excess wood.
- Lash 3 sticks forward of the pivot center of the snowshoes.
- Lash 2 sticks where heel strikes the snowshoe.
- Lash the tips together.

Harness

The harness (binding) is secured so that the snowshoe pivots on the foot while walking. The harness can be rawhide, parachute cord, cordage that you have made, etc.

Float Area

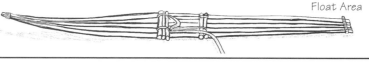

SNOWSHOEING

SNOWSHOEING
Is an excellent way to stay in shape, you can travel almost anywhere, at your own speed, and the equipment is inexpensive.

Situations to Avoid
- Do not travel when there is an approaching storm. Avoid whiteouts because you can lose your sense of direction.
- When the weather is clear, distance is difficult to estimate and will usually be underestimated. This will cause you to go too far and be tired on your return trip or have to return in the dark.

SNOWSHOE MODELS
The US and Canadian armies use the Maine model shoe design. The advantage of the Maine model (quite similar to the Michigan model which is less upturned and the nose more rounded) is that it is good for travel on trails and in open wooded areas. The long tails help maintain their track in a straight line and if the harness are properly attached they are tail heavy keeping them on course. The heavy tail will also keep the nose out of deep snow.

Selection Factors to Consider
Size of Toe Hole: Front of boot should be able to move in and out of toe hole without rubbing the sides or the front crossbar.
Weight: Aim for the lightest snowshoe and harness. Do not buy an oversized snowshoe as it will be larger, weigh more and affect the width of your walk. One pound of weight on your foot is equal to five pounds on your back.

Storage and Care
- Wooden frames, when dry, should be touched up with spar varnish when scratched. The finish waterproofs the snowshoes and keeps out the humidity.
- The rawhide webbing should be coated with spar varnish, when dry, before use and ideally after every trip to stop stretching and rotting.
- Aluminum snowshoes with neoprene or sheet webbing require no maintenance.
- Nylon webbing requires a heavy coating of finishing resin to keep it from wearing and breaking.
- Store snowshoes in a cool, dark, dry place especially if your snowshoes are laced with rawhide.

Snowshoe Harness
The type of harness depends upon the type of terrain on which the snowshoes will travel. The most popular traditional combination harness used in eastern Canada and the eastern United States are made of thick leather that can easily be, replaced or repaired at home. Current harnesses are in nylon.

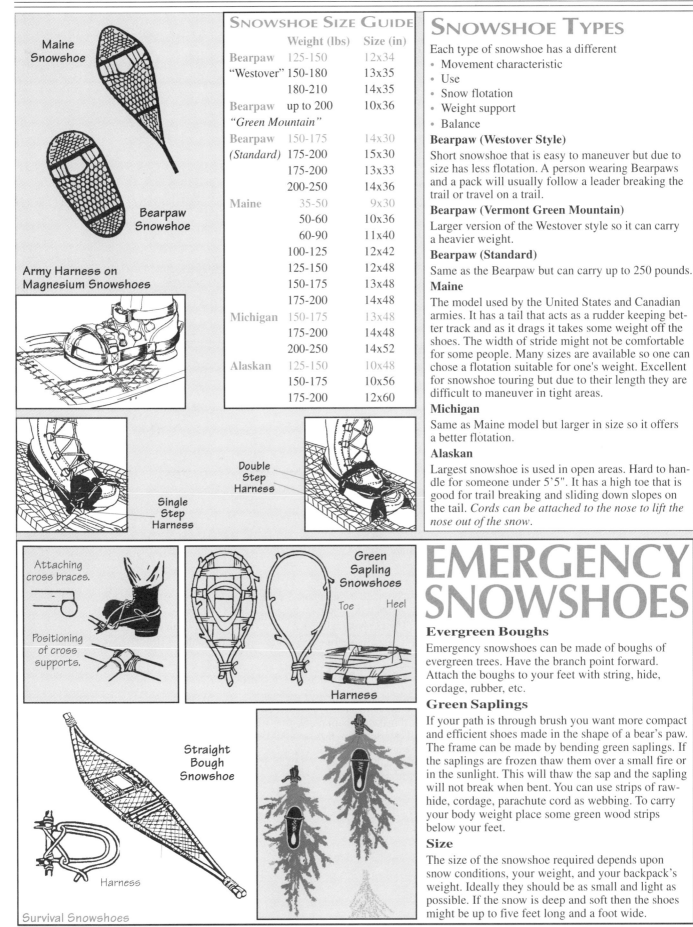

Maine Snowshoe

Bearpaw Snowshoe

Army Harness on Magnesium Snowshoes

Single Step Harness

Double Step Harness

SNOWSHOE SIZE GUIDE

	Weight (lbs)	Size (in)
Bearpaw "Westover"	125-150	12x34
	150-180	13x35
	180-210	14x35
Bearpaw "Green Mountain"	up to 200	10x36
Bearpaw (Standard)	150-175	14x30
	175-200	15x30
	175-200	13x33
	200-250	14x36
Maine	35-50	9x30
	50-60	10x36
	60-90	11x40
	100-125	12x42
	125-150	12x48
	150-175	13x48
	175-200	14x48
Michigan	150-175	13x48
	175-200	14x48
	200-250	14x52
Alaskan	125-150	10x48
	150-175	10x56
	175-200	12x60

SNOWSHOE TYPES

Each type of snowshoe has a different
- Movement characteristic
- Use
- Snow flotation
- Weight support
- Balance

Bearpaw (Westover Style)

Short snowshoe that is easy to maneuver but due to size has less flotation. A person wearing Bearpaws and a pack will usually follow a leader breaking the trail or travel on a trail.

Bearpaw (Vermont Green Mountain)

Larger version of the Westover style so it can carry a heavier weight.

Bearpaw (Standard)

Same as the Bearpaw but can carry up to 250 pounds.

Maine

The model used by the United States and Canadian armies. It has a tail that acts as a rudder keeping better track and as it drags it takes some weight off the shoes. The width of stride might not be comfortable for some people. Many sizes are available so one can chose a flotation suitable for one's weight. Excellent for snowshoe touring but due to their length they are difficult to maneuver in tight areas.

Michigan

Same as Maine model but larger in size so it offers a better flotation.

Alaskan

Largest snowshoe is used in open areas. Hard to handle for someone under 5'5". It has a high toe that is good for trail breaking and sliding down slopes on the tail. *Cords can be attached to the nose to lift the nose out of the snow.*

Attaching cross braces.

Positioning of cross supports.

Green Sapling Snowshoes

Toe   Heel

Harness

Straight Bough Snowshoe

Harness

Survival Snowshoes

EMERGENCY SNOWSHOES

Evergreen Boughs

Emergency snowshoes can be made of boughs of evergreen trees. Have the branch point forward. Attach the boughs to your feet with string, hide, cordage, rubber, etc.

Green Saplings

If your path is through brush you want more compact and efficient shoes made in the shape of a bear's paw. The frame can be made by bending green saplings. If the saplings are frozen thaw them over a small fire or in the sunlight. This will thaw the sap and the sapling will not break when bent. You can use strips of rawhide, cordage, parachute cord as webbing. To carry your body weight place some green wood strips below your feet.

Size

The size of the snowshoe required depends upon snow conditions, your weight, and your backpack's weight. Ideally they should be as small and light as possible. If the snow is deep and soft then the shoes might be up to five feet long and a foot wide.

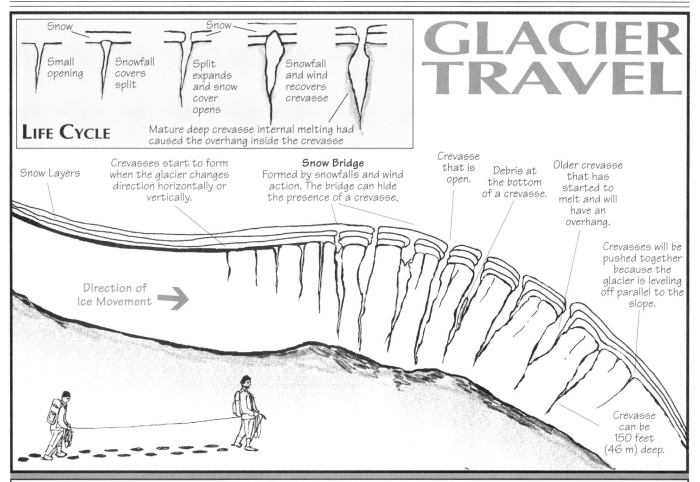

GLACIER TRAVEL

LIFE CYCLE

Snow — Small opening — Snowfall covers split — Snow — Split expands and snow cover opens — Snowfall and wind recovers crevasse — Mature deep crevasse internal melting had caused the overhang inside the crevasse

Snow Layers

Crevasses start to form when the glacier changes direction horizontally or vertically.

Snow Bridge
Formed by snowfalls and wind action. The bridge can hide the presence of a crevasse,

Crevasse that is open.

Debris at the bottom of a crevasse.

Older crevasse that has started to melt and will have an overhang.

Crevasses will be pushed together because the glacier is leveling off parallel to the slope.

Direction of Ice Movement →

Crevasse can be 150 feet (46 m) deep.

DANGER ON GLACIERS

DANGERS IN GLACIAL AREAS

Crevasses, icefalls, and ice avalanches are the principal dangers to movement in glacial areas. Snow-covered crevasses make movement on a glacier very treacherous. In winter, with poor visibility and snow cover, the difficulty of recognizing them is increased. Toward the end of the summer, crevasses are at their widest and are covered by the least amount of snow. Snow bridges constitute the biggest potential danger in movement over glaciers.

CREVASSES

When ice flows over an irregularity (a steep slope, a cliff) crevasses can appear on the down slope of the glacier. If the cliff is high the ice will break into ice blocks and towers which will be crisscrossed with crevasses. This jumbled cliff is known as an icefall. Icefalls present a major obstacle for safe movement on glaciers. Ice avalanches are common in the vicinity of icefalls. The safest time to move through an icefall is early in the morning *before* sunrise.

FALLS ON SLOPES

Unforeseen falls are always a possibility when moving over ice or snow covered slopes. If the party is roped together, the person falling can usually be arrested by other members of the group.

Unroped Fall Down a Slope
- If you are traveling unroped and you fall, immediately roll onto your stomach in the direction of the head of the ice ax.
- The ax should always be secured to the hand with the wrist strap.
- If you are wearing crampons, your legs should be spread apart and bent at the knee with the feet up in the air.

GLACIAL SUNBURN

Light and heat rays reflected from ice, snow, water, and rocks irritates and rapidly burns the skin. Sunburn can even occur on cloudy days. A strong wind will make the burn more severe. Sunburn cream should be applied frequently on all exposed skin. It is particularly dangerous to expose parts of the body which are not accustomed to the sun's rays. As soon as any part of the body becomes burned, it should be protected from further exposure. Bad cases of sunburn can lead to fever and possibly reduced muscle activity. It might take several days to recover.

SNOW BLINDNESS

Snow blindness occurs when strong sunlight shines on an expanse of snow. The injury is due to the reflection of ultraviolet rays. It is likely to occur after a new snowfall and even when the rays of the sun are partially obscured by a light mist or fog. In most cases, snow blindness is due to negligence or failure to use goggles.

Symptoms of snow blindness are a sensation of grit in the eyes, pain in and over the eyes, watering, redness, headache and an avoidance of light. First aid includes blindfolding the eyes for a few days until the pain is gone.

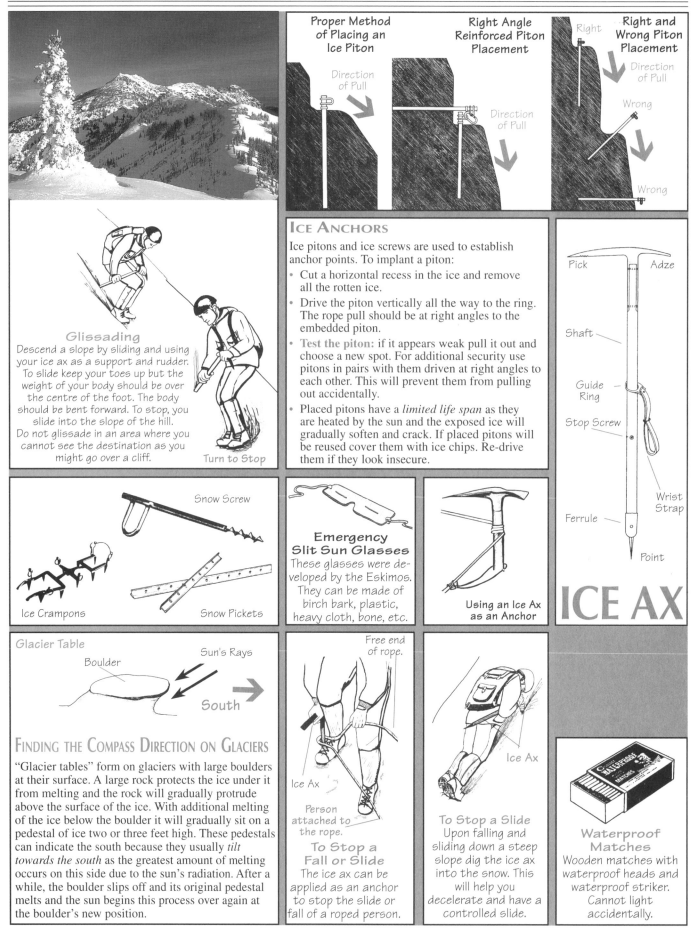

Proper Method of Placing an Ice Piton

Direction of Pull

Right Angle Reinforced Piton Placement

Direction of Pull

Right and Wrong Piton Placement

Right

Direction of Pull

Wrong

Wrong

Glissading

Descend a slope by sliding and using your ice ax as a support and rudder. To slide keep your toes up but the weight of your body should be over the centre of the foot. The body should be bent forward. To stop, you slide into the slope of the hill. Do not glissade in an area where you cannot see the destination as you might go over a cliff.

Turn to Stop

ICE ANCHORS

Ice pitons and ice screws are used to establish anchor points. To implant a piton:

- Cut a horizontal recess in the ice and remove all the rotten ice.
- Drive the piton vertically all the way to the ring. The rope pull should be at right angles to the embedded piton.
- **Test the piton:** if it appears weak pull it out and choose a new spot. For additional security use pitons in pairs with them driven at right angles to each other. This will prevent them from pulling out accidentally.
- Placed pitons have a *limited life span* as they are heated by the sun and the exposed ice will gradually soften and crack. If placed pitons will be reused cover them with ice chips. Re-drive them if they look insecure.

Pick — Adze

Shaft

Guide Ring

Stop Screw

Wrist Strap

Ferrule —

Point

ICE AX

Snow Screw

Ice Crampons

Snow Pickets

Emergency Slit Sun Glasses

These glasses were developed by the Eskimos. They can be made of birch bark, plastic, heavy cloth, bone, etc.

Using an Ice Ax as an Anchor

Glacier Table

Boulder

Sun's Rays

South

FINDING THE COMPASS DIRECTION ON GLACIERS

"Glacier tables" form on glaciers with large boulders at their surface. A large rock protects the ice under it from melting and the rock will gradually protrude above the surface of the ice. With additional melting of the ice below the boulder it will gradually sit on a pedestal of ice two or three feet high. These pedestals can indicate the south because they usually *tilt towards the south* as the greatest amount of melting occurs on this side due to the sun's radiation. After a while, the boulder slips off and its original pedestal melts and the sun begins this process over again at the boulder's new position.

Free end of rope.

Ice Ax

Person attached to the rope.

To Stop a Fall or Slide

The ice ax can be applied as an anchor to stop the slide or fall of a roped person.

Ice Ax

To Stop a Slide

Upon falling and sliding down a steep slope dig the ice ax into the snow. This will help you decelerate and have a controlled slide.

Waterproof Matches

Wooden matches with waterproof heads and waterproof striker. Cannot light accidentally.

CUTTING STEPS IN ICE

Steps are made with the pick end of an ice ax. Black ice is harder to cut and requires more blows. The blows should be made as close to right angle to the ice face as possible. This will reduce the danger of flaking off the outside layers. The step should slope inwards and downwards.

In climbing, steps may be cut straight up or at a diagonal to the line of ascent. In descending, it is only practical to cut steps in a diagonal.

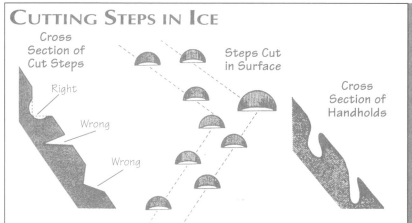

AVALANCHE

CONDITIONS CAUSING AVALANCHES

Mechanical and weather properties of snow that might cause avalanche are:

Terrain: a grade of 20° or steeper.

Old Snow Depth: enough to cover ground obstructions which would retain the snow.

Surface Crusted: normally only new snow will slide.

Surface Loose: good cohesion between layers and both old and new snow may slide.

New Snow Depth: 10 inches (25 cm) or more.

Snowfall Intensity: 1" (2.5 cm) per hour or more is not uncommon. This can be assumed when snowfall is heavy enough to restrict visibility to 300-600 ft (100-200 m).

Precipitation Intensity: 0.01" (0.25 cm) or more per hour of water plus strong winds. This can be assumed if snowfall intensity is 1" (2.5 cm) per hour and snow is damp or noticeably heavy. Dry snow by comparison is of granular or pellet form. Rainfall may fall on the snow in coastal zones creating avalanche conditions.

Settlement: noticeably low. Watch the snow collars around the trees or posts.

Wind: an average of 15 knots or higher. This can be assumed if snow is blown parallel or almost parallel to the ground. Wind action during storms, in the mountains, is generally strong and its influence on snow is an important contributory factor for avalanches. It transports snow from one exposed area to another during storms and fair weather, this increases overloads on certain slopes. It also modifies the size and shape of snow particles.

Temperature: sudden changes up or down can cause avalanches, for example, a thawing temperature day and night for 36 hours and no overnight freezing. Temperature greatly affects the cohesion of snow; a rise in temperature slows settlement of the snow mass and increases the brittleness and tension of slab formation. Temperature fluctuates widely and rapidly in the mountains. Prolonged spells of extremely low temperatures occur and there might be occasional intrusions of warm air masses, usually in connection with a new storm.

Depth Hoar: must be assumed on any avalanche slope in the high alpine zone.

TERRAIN AND AVALANCHES

- There is a low avalanche probability if the ground surface is a broken, serrated, or boulder-strewn that provides an anchor for a snowpack. Snow slides, breaking off at ground level, are unlikely.
- Smooth, even slopes of bare earth, solid rock, or shale favor massive ground level avalanches, typical of the high alpine zone.
- Contours of a mountain influence the avalanche. Terraces, talus, basins, and outcrops are effective barriers. They either divert the moving snow or give it room to spread out and lose its momentum.
- Gullies collect and channel the descending snow, making powerful slide paths which must be avoided.
- Ridges lying parallel to the slide path are relatively secure.
- A *convex slope* is more likely to have avalanches because the snow layers are under tension. Avalanches usually fracture at the sharpest point on the curve, get up to full speed instantly, and pulverize rapidly. The steepest part of a convex slope is generally near the bottom, leading to a sudden transition and poor anchorage at the toe of the snow layer.

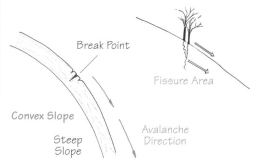

- On a *concave surface*, snow is under compression. The steepest part of the slope is generally near the top; the transition is more gradual and the anchorage at the toe is better than for a convex slope.
- The dimensions of the slope (length and width), are factors that determine the size of the snow slide and the possible destruction caused by it.
- The *most important factor*, of the terrain features, is the *grade of the slope*. The steeper the slope, the more likely it will cause a slide regardless of any other conditions. The minimum angle favorable to avalanches is 25°. Slopes from 25° to 35° may avalanche especially if disturbed by the cutting action of a skier or some other factor. The critical zone lies above 35°. From 35° to the angle where snow can no longer cling to the slope, except by wind packing, some form of snowslide is likely to occur with **every storm**.
- *Vegetation* of any kind, except grass, has a restraining effect on avalanches. The existence of heavy forest cover is an indication that slides in the location are rare or of minor importance. It is a mistake, however, to consider all forested areas as safe. Scattered timber is not a good deterrent. Slopes where the timber has been destroyed by fire or clear-cut has a good potential for slides.
- Slopes facing the sun favor avalanches produced by thawing.
- Loose snow avalanches are more common on slopes opposite the sun; the north side of hills.
- *Cornices* habitually form along ridges and crests lying at right angles to the prevailing wind.
- *Lee slopes* are the most probable locations for overloads of wind-driven snow and formation of a slab. Snow is blown from wind-beaten slopes and the remaining snow is packed and stabilized.

FORECASTING AN AVALANCHE

Forecasting an Avalanche

The accurate prediction of an avalanche is impossible. The actual occurrence is governed by a set of variable factors which cannot be reduced to a simple factor. An experienced mountaineer can usually recognize the development of a hazardous situation in sufficient time to avoid the danger area.

Military Avalanche Disasters

Large military disasters occurred during World War I when at least 40,000 men died in avalanches in the Tyrol and South Tyrol. It has been estimated that during fighting on the Austro-Italian front in 1916, as many as 9,000 to 10,000 troops were killed in a single avalanche period of two days duration.

AVALANCHE TRIGGERS

Every avalanche must have a "trigger."

A loose-snow slide usually occurs during or immediately after a storm or some other weather that creates instability. A slab avalanche may come as a delayed action. There has to be some final nudge, some force or combination of forces, to account for the release of masses of snow at a particular time and place.

Four Avalanche Triggers

- Overloading
- Shearing
- Temperature
- Vibration

Overloading

Weight is probably the most frequent cause of an avalanche. New snow piles up until it overcomes cohesion and the structure collapses of its own weight and begins to slide.

Shearing

This can be applied in various ways: the slicing action of a pair of skis, a wad of snow falling out of trees or over a cliff, or any exterior force that cuts the bond. The vibration of a slide in motion has a shearing effect on the snow beneath.

Temperature

Temperature triggers avalanches by its effect on the cohesion of snow. A rise in temperature weakens the bonds, while a fall in temperature retards settlement of the snow mass and increases the brittleness and tension of a slab.

Vibration

This factor is related to shearing, but it is treated separately. Unlike the other triggers, it can operate at long range. Avalanches may be released by thunder and other loud or sharp sounds, shock waves from high speed aircraft, explosions, earthquakes, and by vibrations transmitted through the earth and snow by the movement of bulldozers, or heavy machinery. They can also be triggered by the primary or reflected blast waves resulting from the detonation of a cannon.

Depth and Condition of the Base

A 24" (60 cm) depth is generally sufficient to cover ground obstructions and provide a smooth sliding base. Greater depths will obliterate such major natural barriers as terraces, gullies, outcrops, and clumps of small trees. If the bottom snow layer consists of granular snow (depth hoar), the slope is dangerous because the snowpack has no anchorage at its underside. This can be compared to the snow sitting on ball bearings. Depth hoar is usually at the bottom of the snowpack, and can be detected by reversed ski-poles probes, or digging vertical trenches.

Old Snow Surface

A loose snow surface helps for good cohesion with a fresh fall but allows for a deeper avalanche if it starts. A crusted or wind packed surface means poor cohesion with the new snow, but restricts the avalanche to the new layer making for a shallower slide.

Depth of New Snow

10" (25 cm) of new snow is regarded as the minimum requirement to produce, by itself, an avalanche of dangerous proportions.

Types of new snow based upon free moisture content:

Very dry snow has low cohesion qualities and will readily avalanche so that it seldom builds up to a dangerous volume except under true blizzard conditions.

The moisture in *damp snow* acts as a cement and improves cohesion.

Wet snow is saturated with water that "lubricates" rather than cements

Transition snow (on the dividing line between dry and damp) is especially susceptible to the formation of a slab under wind action. This is caused by the wind chill freezing the surface snow.

Average Density and Water Content

The *average density* (water content per centimeter of snow) of dry snow varies from 0.06 -0.1" (0.15 - 0.25 cm) of water per 1" (2.5 cm) of new snow. *Very dry snow*, typical of the high alpine zones but found occasionally in other areas is much lighter with densities as low as 0.04" (0.10 cm). *Damp and wet snow*, in contrast, have a density as high as 0.14" (0.35 cm). These are normal densities and have little significance. When *dry snow density* exceeds 10%, its weight may be increasing faster than its cohesion strength and a slide may occur.

Snowfall Intensity

When the snow piles up at the rate of 1" (2.5 cm) or more per hour, the pack is growing faster than stabilizing forces, such as settlement, can take care of it. This sudden increase in load may fracture a lower slab and result in a slide.

Precipitation Intensity

Based upon experience, a continuous precipitation intensity of 0.1" (0.25 cm) of water or more per hour with sufficient wind action, will cause the avalanche hazard to become critical when the total water precipitation reaches 1" (2.54 cm).

Settlement of Snow

Snow settlement is continuous and with one exception it is always a stabilizing factor. The exception is shrinkage of a lower loose snow layer detaching it from a slab thus depriving it of support. In new snow a settlement ratio less than 15% indicates that little consolidation is taking place; above 30%, stabilization is proceeding rapidly. Over a long period ordinary snow layers shrink up to 90%, but slab layers may shrink no more than 60%. Abnormally low shrinkage in a layer indicates that a slab is forming.

Wind Action

Wind action is an important factor contributing to avalanches. It overloads certain slopes at the expense of others, it grinds snow crystals to simpler and less cohesive forms, it forms stable crusts and fragile slabs, often side by side. Warm wind ("Chinook" of North America and the "Foehn" of Europe) is an effective thawing agent, even more than sunlight. By sudden changes in direction and velocity, wind can act as a shearing trigger on a layer of snow it has just deposited. An average velocity of 15 knots is the minimum effective level for wind's action in building avalanche hazards.

Temperatures

Temperature directly influences the type of snow. Dry snow normally falls at 25°F (4°C) and below. Temperatures above 28° F (-2.2°C) promote rapid settlement and the metamorphosis of the snow is sometimes too rapid. A sudden rise of temperature causes a loss of cohesion fast enough to trigger an avalanche. A sudden drop increases tension particularly in a slab. Gradual warming in spring leads to cumulative deterioration of the snow and to heavy wet avalanches.

PROTECTIVE MEASURES

Areas which are considered hazardous may be placed "off limits". This may affect only a few narrow avalanche paths, or an entire valley, or several valleys depending upon the terrain and weather conditions.

Stabilization of Potential Avalanche Areas

Skiing

Constant use of the hazardous slide path area prevents the snow from building up into avalanche conditions. The work is done by teams of expert skiers (2 and 3 on each team). Great care, coordination between teams, and supervision must be exercised because of the dangerous nature of the work.

Explosives

Under extremely dangerous conditions it may be safer to stabilize the snow by using hand placed charges. Huge cornices are blasted by digging charges into the snow along the probable fracture line. Individuals digging holes and placing charges must be belayed (supported with rope) while working.

Artillery, Rockets, and Infantry Weapons

Artillery pieces can be used to trigger an avalanche. Due to the difficulty of moving artillery pieces off the road or over secondary mountain trails, recoilless rifles can be used.

Aircraft

The pilot selects suitable slopes and makes the snow slide by using guns, rockets or a sonic boom.

Use of Barriers

Lines of communication and fixed installations, under avalanche threat, can be protected by the construction of avalanche barriers. Barriers can be formed by adding rocks and earth, concrete, or other similar materials to natural obstacles.

TYPES OF AVALANCHES

Avalanches may be classified according to the type of snow, the manner of release, or the size.
- Loose snow avalanches.
- Packed snow avalanches.

A Wet or Dry Snow Avalanche

Break point

Avalanche

The avalanche is triggered and can slide on a heavy crust layer.

Heavy crust

Sheet Avalanche

A snow mantle with a hard, frozen coating can be covered with a layer of snow that is composed of snow crystals, ice droplets, layers of refrozen snow. The layers and weather changes can cause loose cohesion and the top layer(s) of snow can slide off.

LOOSE SNOW AVALANCHES

An avalanche of loose snow always starts on the surface from a point or a narrow sector. From this starting point it grows fanwise, expanding in width and depth. The speed and nature of its development depends on whether the snow is dry, damp, or wet.

Dry Loose Snow Avalanches

These are composed of loose snow, possibly drifted but not wind packed. They normally start at a point of origin and travel at high speed on a gradually widening path, increasing in size as they descend creating an enormous cloud of snow dust. A dry loose snow avalanche is always shallow at the start and depends on the snow it can pick up during its run for volume. A dry snow avalanche of dangerous size can only occur on a long slide path, or from a large accumulation zone which funnels into a constricted outrun. Occasionally, heavy snowfall at low temperatures produces the phenomenon of the "Wild Snow" avalanche. This is a formless mass pouring down the mountain side. These are actually avalanches of air and snow mixed together. The wind blast, a side effect of very large, high speed avalanches, is powerful enough to damage structures and endanger life outside the actual avalanche path. The danger from loose snow avalanches passes very fast.

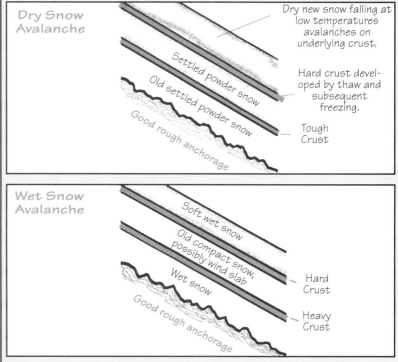

Dry Snow Avalanche

Dry new snow falling at low temperatures avalanches on underlying crust.

Settled powder snow

Old settled powder snow

Good rough anchorage

Hard crust developed by thaw and subsequent freezing.

Tough Crust

Wet Snow Avalanche

Soft wet snow

Old compact snow, possibly wind slab

Wet snow

Good rough anchorage

Hard Crust

Heavy Crust

DAMP AND WET SNOW AVALANCHES

These resemble dry snow avalanches with the same arrowhead point of origin, gradually becoming wider. Their mass is much greater than that of a dry avalanche and they are much more destructive. They are heavier and stickier and so they develop more friction and travel at a slower pace. The principal hazard of damp and wet snow avalanches is to fixed installations. Their comparatively low speed causes them to stop rather suddenly when they lose momentum and to pile up in towering masses. This is in contrast to the dry slide which tends to spread out like the splash of a wave.

Damp and wet avalanches solidify immediately upon release from the pressure of motion. This adds to the difficulty of rescue or clearing operations. Wet slides have the distinctive characteristic of channelling. The moving snow constructs its own banks and flows between them like a river of slush, often in unexpected directions as it does not always choose the most direct downhill route. The damp snowslides of midwinter are generally shallow. But the wet avalanches of spring, caused by deep thawing either from rain or prolonged temperatures above freezing, often involve enormous masses of snow and debris and have tremendous destructive power.

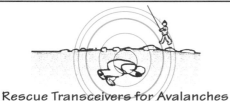

Rescue Transceivers for Avalanches

This is a signaling device used in avalanche areas. A person traversing an avalanche zone carries a transmitter which has a range of approximately 6000 meters and 350 hours of transmission on 2 AA batteries.

The rescuer has a receiver with a speaker and a jack for earphones. It can also have a LED display that indicates the distance and direction to the victim's transmitter.

IF CAUGHT IN AN AVALANCHE

What to do if You are Caught in an Avalanche

There are certain actions that can be taken which will greatly increase your chance of survival and recovery.

Most important, DON'T PANIC. Maintain self-control and attempt to stay on the surface and get out of the main slide path.

Execute "swimming" motions to combat the tendency of the sliding, rolling snow to pull you under. Grab any object to assist the fight to the surface. Remove skis if possible. If you are completely covered by the snow mass, hold both arms in front of the face and push against the covering snow in an attempt to provide an airspace before the slide hardens.

PACKED SNOW AVALANCHES

Windslab

Wind packed snow, called windslab or snowslab is unquestionably the worst killer of all and equal to the wet spring avalanche as a destroyer of property.

Hard slab is usually the result of wind action on snow picked up from the surface.

Soft slab is usually the result of wind action on falling snow.

A windslab avalanche behaves in an altogether different manner from loose snow. It has the ability to retain its unstable character for days, weeks, and even months; this leads to the unexpected release of delayed-action avalanches, often triggered by minor causes such as the addition of a small amount of new snow, a skier cutting across a hillside, sun action, or even a minor vibration.

The windslab avalanche combines great mass with high speed to produce enormous energy. It may originate either at the surface or through the collapse of a stratum deep within the snowpack. It starts on a wide front with deep penetration. The entire slab top, sides, and bottom release almost simultaneously. The place where the slab has broken away from the snow pack is always marked by *an angular fracture line instead of a point*, roughly following the contour. It usually breaks at the sharpest part of the curve on a convex slope

In a packed-snow avalanche the main body of the slide reaches its maximum speed within seconds. Speeds of 63 miles (100 km) per hour are not uncommon. It exerts its full destructive power from the place where it starts while a loose snow avalanche does not attain its greatest momentum until near the end of its run.

Due to the delayed release action, the slab avalanche *is the most dangerous of all types*. A series of slab avalanches may stabilize local conditions but leave an adjacent slab very lethal. *If the unstable part is near the surface the windslab has a dull, chalky, non-reflecting appearance and has a hollow sound underfoot.* If the slab is hard, it often settles with a *crunching sound* which an experienced mountaineer recognizes as a danger signal. The only way to insure that movement across the slab formation is safe, is to break the slab by one of the stabilization methods described in the stabilization article.

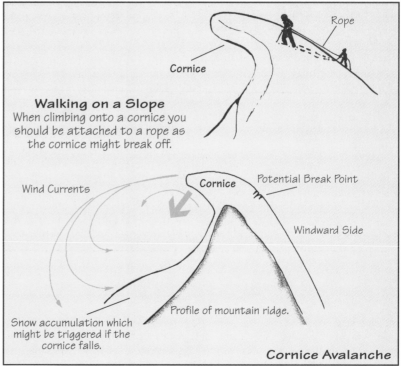

Walking on a Slope
When climbing onto a cornice you should be attached to a rope as the cornice might break off.

Rope

Cornice

Wind Currents

Cornice

Potential Break Point

Windward Side

Profile of mountain ridge.

Snow accumulation which might be triggered if the cornice falls.

Cornice Avalanche

Cornice

A cornice is a snow formation similar to the slab. It builds up on the lee side of crests and ridges which lie at or near right angle to the wind. Occasionally it is straight-walled, but the characteristic shape is that of a breaking wave. The obvious hazard from cornices is due to the fractures of the overhang from overloading, weakening due to temperature, rain, or sun erosion. These falling blocks are generally large enough to be dangerous by themselves. They may also release avalanches on the slopes below.

Combination Avalanche

Combination avalanches are composed of both loose and packed snow layers making it more difficult to determine which part of the combination acted as the trigger and which is the main charge of the avalanche.

Climax Avalanche

The climax avalanche is a special combination. The distinguishing characteristic of this type of avalanche is that it contains a large proportion of old snow and is caused by conditions which have developed over a considerable period of time; at least a month and possibly an entire season. Climax avalanches occur infrequently because they require an unusual combination of favorable factors. Whenever they occur, *the penetration of a climax fracture is always in great depth*, usually to the ground. They travel farther and spread out wider than ordinary avalanches on the same slide path.

SAFETY RULES

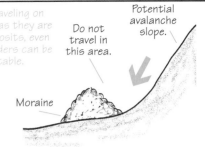

Narrow valley can have simultaneous avalanches from both sides.

Avoid traveling on moraines as they are loose deposits, even large boulders can be unstable.

Do not travel in this area.

Potential avalanche slope.

Moraine

Many of the hazards peculiar to avalanche areas can be avoided or their danger greatly reduced by knowing and practicing a few simple, common sense rules.

Adjusting Equipment

To insure the freedom of legs and arms, the ice ax safety strap is removed from the wrist. When using skis, the bindings are loosened to facilitate their removal and ski pole straps are removed from the wrists. Skis tend to get tangled, restrict movement, and get dragged under the sliding snow. When snow conditions permit, dangerous zones can be negotiated more safely on foot. Carry the skis. While skiing, all movements are executed with caution. Backpacks are either removed or loosened.

Selection of a Route

Learn the avalanche paths and whenever possible, detour around the hazardous slopes. The crest of a ridge can be a safe route but never move on the overhang of a cornice. Avoid moving along the bottoms of narrow, V-shaped valleys where a disturbance can cause a double-sided avalanche that almost instantaneously fills a narrow valley floor with masses of snow. Moving along the middle of wide, U shaped valleys is less dangerous; if an avalanche occurred its force would tend to be expended on a wide valley floor. Do not move above natural barriers, such as moraines located on the valley floor, since a slide could have you collide with the barrier.

Weather

Obtain the latest weather forecast before traveling. Be alert to any sudden changes especially a change in the direction of the wind.

Ascent and Descent

When on potential avalanche slopes climb as straight up or as straight down as possible, preferably along a line of protruding rocks, ledge, and trees where the snow cover is less likely to slide. Avoid traversing back and forth as you will cross many potential avalanche trigger areas. Avoid ravines, gullies, and low terrain features which are locations of snow deposits.

Observation and Testing

The area to be traversed must be constantly observed for signs of danger. Test the snow if possible. Windslab formations should be avoided, since they give a false impression of solidity. Watch shadows because when *they point at a slope* the sun action is at its maximum. Seek the protection of heavy timber, windblown slopes, and terrain barriers.

Proper Timing

When moving over areas of avalanche danger increase the distance between the members of the party. The least possible number of people should be exposed to danger at a time.

Use of an Avalanche Cord

In avalanche areas and especially when testing, one end of a brightly colored cord (50 - 66 feet (15 - 20 m) in length) is tied around the body and trailed behind the individual. The cord, being light, tends to remain on or near the surface if a slide occurs.

AVALANCHE RESCUE

If an individual is caught by an avalanche, prompt and organized rescue operations offer the only hope of getting the victim out alive. There are records of people who lived as long as 72 hours while buried. Ordinarily, the victims are either killed instantly by crushing, or die within a short period from exposure, shock, and suffocation. *One hour is the average survival time.*

If any indication of the location of the victim is found, random probing starts in that vicinity. If no indications are found, the random probing starts in likely locations such as obstructions in the slide path caused by trees, boulders, or transitions. The tip and edges of the slide are also searched. A human body is bulky and all being equal, is apt to be thrown toward the surface or the sides. *Avalanche victims who are rescued alive must be evacuated under the care of medical personnel by the most expeditious means available.*

Methods of Locating Avalanche Victim

The concept of probability is important to the design of search operations. The object is to optimize the victim's chance for survival. There is a double requirement for success. *The victim must be found, and the victim must be found alive.* A slow and thorough search could be organized which would almost guarantee finding the victim, but the chances of finding him alive would be remote.

Establish from witnesses where the victim was just prior to the avalanche, then determine the point where the victim disappeared - the "last seen" point. Making use of this and any other information, establish a probable victim trajectory line leading to high priority search areas. Make a rapid but systematic check of the avalanche debris surface and mark all clues. At signs of equipment, clothing or an avalanche cord, make an initial random probe of the high priority areas. If no clues, make a coarse probe of all likely areas of burial. Repeat the coarse probe as long as a live rescue remains possible.

Avalanche Victim's Chance of Survival
The survival clock shows the probability of survival with the minutes of submersion.

The concept of probability is important to the design of search operations. The victim must be found, and the victim must be found alive.

Ordinarily, the victim is either killed instantly by crushing, or die within a short period from exposure, shock, and suffocation. One hour is the average survival time.

Avalanche victims who are rescued alive must be evacuated under the care of medical personnel by the most expeditious means available.

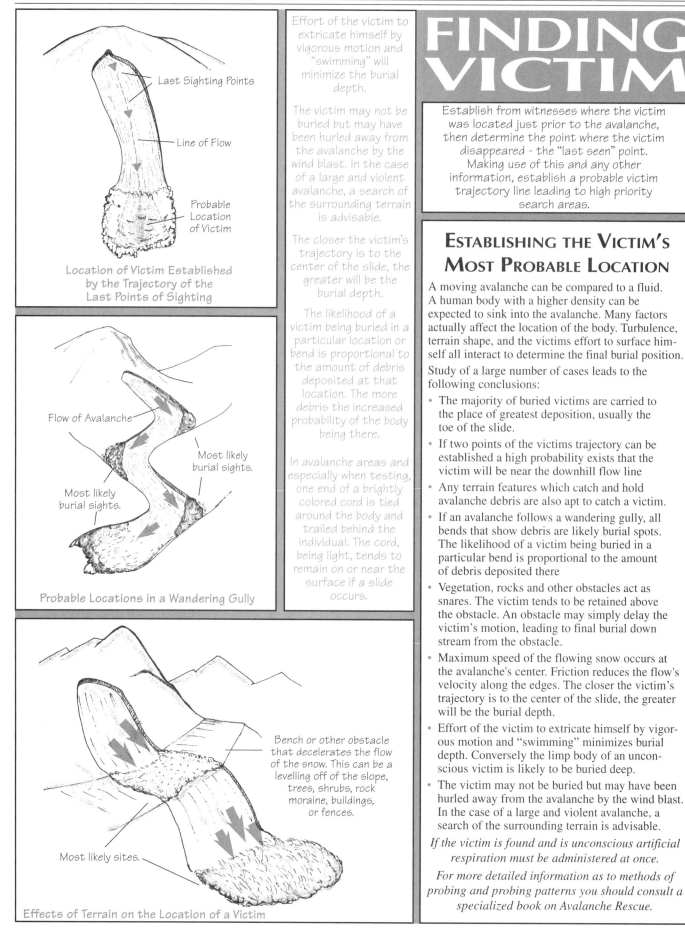

Location of Victim Established
by the Trajectory of the
Last Points of Sighting

Last Sighting Points

Line of Flow

Probable Location of Victim

Flow of Avalanche

Most likely burial sights.

Most likely burial sights.

Probable Locations in a Wandering Gully

Bench or other obstacle that decelerates the flow of the snow. This can be a levelling off of the slope, trees, shrubs, rock moraine, buildings, or fences.

Most likely sites.

Effects of Terrain on the Location of a Victim

Effort of the victim to extricate himself by vigorous motion and "swimming" will minimize the burial depth.

The victim may not be buried but may have been hurled away from the avalanche by the wind blast. In the case of a large and violent avalanche, a search of the surrounding terrain is advisable.

The closer the victim's trajectory is to the center of the slide, the greater will be the burial depth.

The likelihood of a victim being buried in a particular location or bend is proportional to the amount of debris deposited at that location. The more debris the increased probability of the body being there.

In avalanche areas and especially when testing, one end of a brightly colored cord is tied around the body and trailed behind the individual. The cord, being light, tends to remain on or near the surface if a slide occurs.

FINDING VICTIM

Establish from witnesses where the victim was located just prior to the avalanche, then determine the point where the victim disappeared - the "last seen" point. Making use of this and any other information, establish a probable victim trajectory line leading to high priority search areas.

ESTABLISHING THE VICTIM'S MOST PROBABLE LOCATION

A moving avalanche can be compared to a fluid. A human body with a higher density can be expected to sink into the avalanche. Many factors actually affect the location of the body. Turbulence, terrain shape, and the victims effort to surface himself all interact to determine the final burial position.

Study of a large number of cases leads to the following conclusions:

- The majority of buried victims are carried to the place of greatest deposition, usually the toe of the slide.
- If two points of the victims trajectory can be established a high probability exists that the victim will be near the downhill flow line
- Any terrain features which catch and hold avalanche debris are also apt to catch a victim.
- If an avalanche follows a wandering gully, all bends that show debris are likely burial spots. The likelihood of a victim being buried in a particular bend is proportional to the amount of debris deposited there
- Vegetation, rocks and other obstacles act as snares. The victim tends to be retained above the obstacle. An obstacle may simply delay the victim's motion, leading to final burial down stream from the obstacle.
- Maximum speed of the flowing snow occurs at the avalanche's center. Friction reduces the flow's velocity along the edges. The closer the victim's trajectory is to the center of the slide, the greater will be the burial depth.
- Effort of the victim to extricate himself by vigorous motion and "swimming" minimizes burial depth. Conversely the limp body of an unconscious victim is likely to be buried deep.
- The victim may not be buried but may have been hurled away from the avalanche by the wind blast. In the case of a large and violent avalanche, a search of the surrounding terrain is advisable.

If the victim is found and is unconscious artificial respiration must be administered at once.

For more detailed information as to methods of probing and probing patterns you should consult a specialized book on Avalanche Rescue.

ESTIMATING LATITUDE BY POLARIS

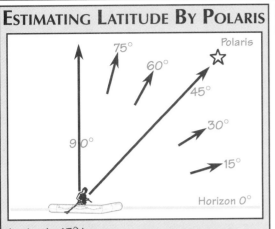

Latitude 45°N — *The number of degrees that Polaris is **above** the horizon is your Latitude.*

Polaris 30° above the horizon means that you are at latitude 30°N. To estimate the angular distance that Polaris is above the horizon that recall that directly overhead (the zenith) is 90°. Halfway to the horizon is 45°. Half of 45° would be 22.5°. If you do not have an instrument (sextant) to give you an exact reading the approximation of latitude is not too useful as a 1° error means that you are off by 60 miles (96 km) and a 10° error *is* 600 miles (960 km).

COMPASS CHAPTER
ASTRONOMY CHAPTER
FOR MORE METHODS TO FIND POSITION

TYPES OF OCEAN CURRENTS

The currents are like rivers in the ocean. They are immense flows of water much larger than any river on land.

Surface Currents: The surface current is quite constant varying only with the seasons. The surface current is described by the *set*, the direction in which it flows, and the *drift*, the velocity at which it flows. These are indicated on nautical charts. You should know the surface currents in your path of travel.

Tidal Currents: These currents should be given consideration when approaching coastal waters. This current is caused by the rise and fall of the tide. *Tidal currents do not exactly follow the rise and fall of the tide but depend upon the coastal features.* Tidal currents are shown on Tidal Current Tables. There are four maximum currents for every tidal day period of 24 hours and 50 minutes.

Wind Driven Currents: Strong continuous winds can slightly affect the surface currents. The direction of the wind-driven currents is slightly to the right of the direction in which the wind is blowing in the northern hemisphere and slightly to the left in the southern hemisphere.

Deep Ocean Currents: Deep ocean currents do not affect boaters but they are involved with the overall movement of the oceans.

ABANDONING SHIP

Ventilation Sock & Rainwater Collector

Have an escape plan when using a boat, discuss the function of each member of the crew, and have frequent drills.
Prior to abandoning a boat establish the geographic position and activate any locating device that is on board. Take the locating device with you.

- Prepare yourself for possibly abandoning the boat by:
  - Packing in a canvas duffel bag: emergency flares, compass, emergency radio beacon, map of the area, water, and survival food. Tie the duffel bag with a rope to the raft or lifeboat.
  - Remain fully clothed and put on a life jacket. Clothing should include a wool sweaters, heavy socks, and tie down hat.
  - Each person should attach a waterproof light or flare, knife, and whistle to his life jacket.
- Do not launch the life raft *unless* there is imminent danger of sinking. Do not inflate the life raft on the boat as it might get entangled with the deck gear or rigging. When the life raft is launched keep it tethered to the boat and climb into it. *Do not jump.* The first person in the raft should keep it away from the boat. *Cut the tether only when everyone is aboard.*
- If no life raft is available enter the water on the windward side of the boat. The untended boat can drift leeward and endanger people in the water.
- Minimize movement in the water to keep body heat and assume the fetal position. *See First Aid Chapter:Drowning &Hypothermia.*

EMOTIONAL EFFECT

The panic reaction of members of the crew to abandoning ship can be totally unexpected and not in the character of the individual.

- A person may freeze, weep, scream for help, or fight for a place on the raft. He may become agitated, pale, tense, freeze up, or may stutter. Keep everyone busy and performing a function to avoid any irrational behavior.

Once on the Raft

- A person may become delirious or behave dangerously to himself and others and might even suddenly attack other members in the party.
- He might want to dive off the raft or *"To go below for a cup of coffee."*
- He might drink sea water or eat the rations on the raft. This person must be closely watched, talked to in a positive way or held in restraint if necessary. *See Getting Lost Chapter on Group Leadership.*
- This initial reaction, to the stress, is a strained emotional attitude and speculation as to chances of survival. This pronlem can worsen into an intense preoccupation, moroseness, and withdrawal from the rest of the group with ideas of food and drink dominating thinking and dreaming.

HOPELESSNESS IS DANGEROUS

It is important that the group help each other to maintain hope and a good group morale.

Hopeless once started, grows rapidly worse and harder to overcome. Treat any danger signs **immediately by cheering up the group**. Good humor can do much to lighten the tense grim moments which are certain to arise. Good morale reduces quarreling and potential pilferage of food and water. The group should have a leader, who is respected, as then they can follow orders.

WATER TRAVEL
CHAPTER 8

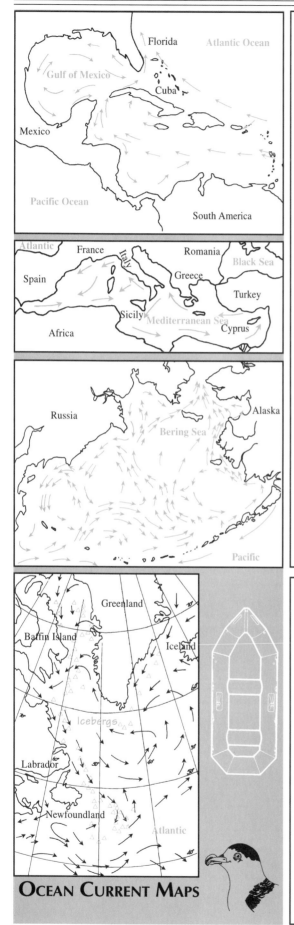

OCEAN CURRENT MAPS

ADRIFT AT SEA

Survival on a Life Raft

- Secure gear as any equipment not lashed down is liable to be lost.
- Dry clothing as soon as possible. If feet swell, remove your shoes but keep feet covered. A sunburn on top of the feet is very painful and can be infected.
- Rig a sail or covering against the sun's rays. Minimize direct exposure to the sun. Sunlight will reflect from the water during the day.
- Take inventory of provisions and store them where they will be safe. Keep the food cool if required. Immediately ration food and water. Avoid eating and minimize drinking during the first 24 hours.
- All movements should be slow and deliberate to conserve energy and to avoid perspiring.
- Save all clothing as the nights might be cold and to stay warm if soaked.
- Prepare to signal any airplane or passing boat by having easy access to signal mirrors, marking dyes, flares, and smoke signals.

Adrift for a Short Time

Survivors adrift in lifeboats or rafts need warmth, cover from the sun and ocean spray, dry clothing, water, and some food.

Upon rescue survivors who had been immersed for a short time in relatively warm water should be given a warm bath and dry clothing.

Adrift for Many Days

Upon rescue if survivors experienced a shortage of food and water, they will be weak, demoralized, and at some stage of hypothermia. Treat for hypothermia if required (*see First Aid Chapter*). Give them warm drinks which they should not drink too fast as they might vomit. Food in the form of soup and bread should be given sparingly and should be easy to digest.

Oil Fuel Contamination

External contact usually is of no special medical harm except that there might be vomiting and coughing from oil and water in the stomach and lungs. Eyes might be sore from the oil and salt water mixture. These problems will clear up.

To clean the skin take a bath using a mild soap. To treat the eyes apply some soft wax to the eyelids. Drink some warm milk with honey or sweet tea to help soothe the stomach. *See a doctor.*

WIND & OCEAN CURRENTS

When using a raft you have to decide whether you should favor the wind or current while navigating.

You should know: your approximate position, the direction you wish to go, and the direction of the wind and current.

- The direction of the movement of a raft without a sail will be governed by prevailing winds and currents. They should be used to help in navigation.
- The wind and current does not necessarily move in the same direction in a given area. One of these elements may be favorable, the other unfavorable.
- The lower the raft rides in the water and the lower its occupants remain, the greater will be the *effect of the current*. The effect of the current can be increased by the use of a sea anchor or drag. This is important if the current will guide you to a shipping route or land.
- To *favor the wind* the raft should be lightened as much as possible. Passengers should sit erect to maximize wind resistance and any sort of sail should be raised.
- The most difficult situation would be to be afloat in a rubber life raft and having no way to rig a sail. If this happens start saving rations to maintain life as long as possible.

RAFT EMERGENCY KIT

Items to be placed in a duffel bag which should be attached to the raft:

- First aid kit.
- Compass with cord.
- Waterproof matches in match case.
- Needle and thread and safety pins, razor blades.
- Cord (10 - 20 feet), fishing line hooks.
- Flares. Whistle with cord.
- Knife with cord.
- Signal mirror with cord or sheet of shiny metal.
- Tube tent for shelter, sail and catching water.
- High energy food. Tea bags, broth cubes.
- Purifying tablets and water filter.
- Water bottle.
- Waterproof plastic bags.
- Small pot to catch water and drinking.
- Small stove.
- Emergency blanket (poncho).

First Aid Kit

Metal Mirror

Waterproof Match Case

Whistle

Fish Hook

Sinker

Waterproof Bag Showing tying method.

Rubber Foot Air Pump

Fishing Monofilament

Tie a rope and swim to the far side. Stand on raft to right it. Take care not to get trapped below raft.

RIGHTING RAFT

RAFTING

Water Flow

Sea Anchor Closed
When closed it will pull raft in the direction of the current.

Water Flow

Sea Anchor Open
When open the raft will remain stationary.

Crest   Trough   Crest

Sea Anchor

Do not deploy a sea anchor when traveling through coral or near the coast.

OPEN SEA TRAVEL

Make Use of the Ocean Currents

- Deploy a sea anchor as in illustration.
- Sit low in the raft to minimize the effect of the wind.
- Keep the raft at low pressure to lower its profile in the water.

To Use the Winds

- Pull in the sea anchor.
- Inflate the raft so that it floats higher in the water.
- Sit up in the raft so your body catches more wind.
- Mount a sail or other item which will catch a breeze.

RAFTING ASHORE

- Carefully select a landing site especially if you are landing into the setting sun as it will reflect on the water and you will not see submerged objects.
- Try to find a landing spot on the lee side (downwind) of an island or point of land.
- Head for gaps in the surf line as you will land with a minimum of force. If you have to go through surf, take down a mast, adjust and fasten any loose items. *Put on some clothing and shoes* to avoid abrasions when landing. Use your paddle to maintain control and deploy your sea anchor. Do not use the sea anchor when traveling through coral. Be ready to cut or release your sea anchor if it gets caught.
- Avoid areas where waves explode upon rocks. If you must land on rocks choose a spot where the waves rush up onto the rocks.
- When a landing site is selected, face forward and sit with your feet planted firmly to absorb any shock from hitting submerged objects.

SWIMMING ASHORE

- Try to use a flotation aid.
- Wear foot gear and one layer of clothing as there might be sharp objects near the shore.
- Use the side or breast stroke to conserve energy.

If the surf is moderate:

- Swim forward on the back of a wave.
- Make a shallow dive just before the wave breaks.

If the surf is high:

- Swim ashore in a trough between waves.
- When the seaward wave approaches face it and submerge. After it passes work your way toward the shore in the next trough.

If caught in an undertow of a large wave:

- Push off the bottom or swim towards the surface, *stay as close to the surface as possible* and swim ashore.

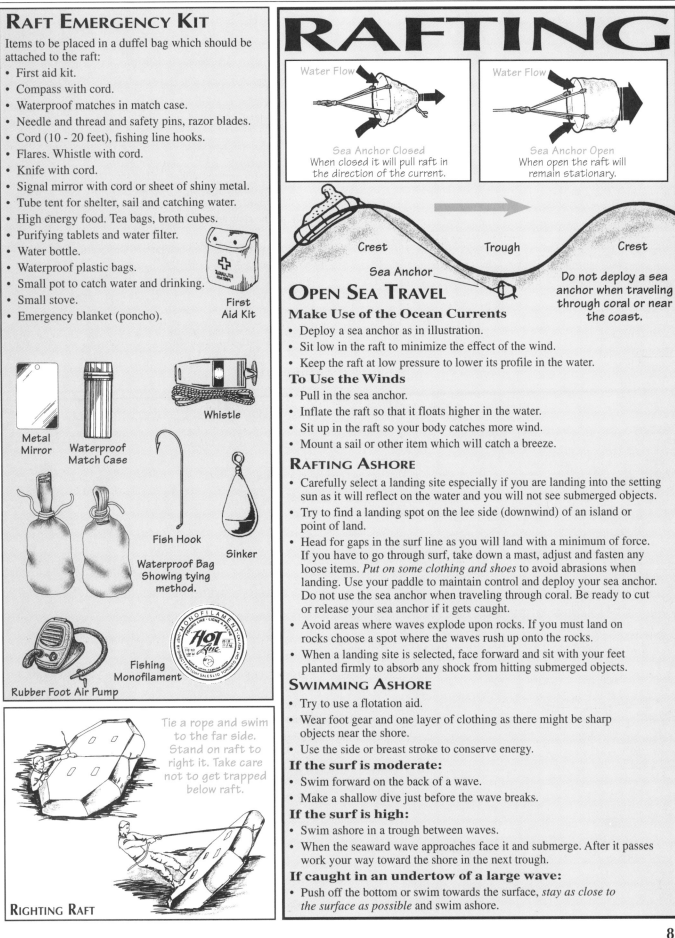

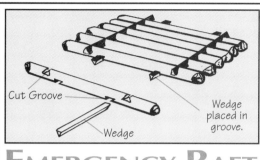

Cut Groove

Wedge

Wedge placed in groove.

EMERGENCY RAFT

If you are lost consider rafting downstream.

Shape of a Raft

Build a *long* raft with three or four logs as it is easier to guide than a square raft which will have a tendency to spin. Build a raft of sound dry wood (spruce is the best) and if possible of dead trees that are still standing. Use roots, vines, handmade cordage or cut grooves to fasten the logs together. rope is not to stable if the current is swift, use the groove system for better results.

Making a Raft

Assemble a raft by using three or four logs parallel to each other and put two or three cross pieces on top of the parallel logs. Mark where these logs cross and cut a dovetailed groove with an ax, knife, sharp rock, or burn with a burning stick. Place or wedge the three cross pieces into the grooves. Soak the assembled raft in the water to obtain a tight fit.

Inflatable Raft

SAFE RAFTING

• Scout ahead by climbing a large tree or hill and look downstream. This is will give you an overview of the surrounding land.

• Have a rudder to steer the raft when descending a river. Carry a long pole or paddle to maneuver around tight spots and to push the raft out of still water or off sand bars.

• *Listen for any sounds of rushing water* which might indicate rapids or waterfalls. Bad water does not always reveal itself until you are on top of it.

• Guide the raft with ropes from the shore over turbulent waters. If this is not possible let the raft find its own course, down the rapids or over small falls, and attempt to retrieve it.

• On a raft, pack provisions in a waterproof bag and *include* a piece of light dry wood. This wood will give the bag buoyancy if it is lost overboard. Tie down everything securely to the raft.

• For steering down a slow moving river attach a pail or water logged piece of wood to a short cord to the bottom of the raft. This cord is attached below the raft in the *middle but forward of the longitudinal center* of the raft. With this "sea anchor" your raft will automatically *follow the main channel* of the river and no steering is requited. Throw some sawdust on the water to find the outlet of a slow flowing river (there will be many islands and much growth).

BOATING

Embarking and Debarking Procedures for a Crew

• When launching, the crew should maintain a firm grip on the boat until they have embarked.

• When debarking, they should hold on to the boat until it is completely out of the water.

• Loading and unloading is done using the bow as the entrance and exit point.

• Keep a low center of gravity when entering and exiting the boat to avoid capsizing. Maintain 3 points of contact at all times. Two feet and one hand, or two hands and one foot.

• Beaching the boat is a method of debarking the entire crew at once into shallow water allowing the boat to be quickly carried out of the water.

CAPSIZE

Inform all members of the crew of a potential capsize by crying "Prepare to capsize". This will alert the crew to raise their paddles above their heads, with the blades pointed outward. All loose articles should be stowed if possible.

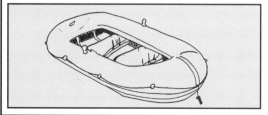

BOATING ON A RIVER

River Boating Terminology

Know the local conditions prior to embarking on a river.

• A *bend* is a turn in the river course.

• A *reach* is a straight portion of river between two bends.

• A *slough* is a dead end branch from a river. They are normally quite deep and can be distinguished from the true river by their lack of current.

• *Dead water* is a part of the river, due to erosion and changes in the river course, has no current. Dead water is characterized by excessive snags and debris.

• An *island* is usually a pear-shaped mass of land in the main current of the river. Avoid the upstream portions of islands as they usually catch debris.

• The current in a narrow part of a reach is *normally greater* than in a wide portion.

• The current is *greatest on the outside of a bend* in the river; sandbars and shallow water are found on the inside of the bend.

• *Sandbars* are located at points where a tributary feeds into the main body of a river or stream. The main course of a river usually flows slower than the water in the tributary. This slower flow of the water lets suspended sediments drop onto the riverbed forming sandbars.

• Choose a member of the crew to watch the water for obstacles and overhanging vegetation and projections (tree trunks etc.) from the bank. If alone be very observant for any telltale signs, as unusual waves, that might indicate obstacles.

NAVIGATION

An individual in the group is designated to verify the progress on a river. Ideally have an aerial photograph, or a topographic map. A compass is helpful to corroborate the assumed position on the map. When navigating in a flat land area there might be many similar looking branches and tributaries which can easily confuse a navigator, especially if there are no prominent landmarks.

SURVIVAL AT SEA

In the Water

- Water temperatures below 68°F (20°C) can cause hypothermia if the body is not protected. Hypothermia will occur after 4 hours with limited clothing. It will occur in 8 hours if clothed. At 57°F (15°C) unclothed survival time is approximately 2 hours. *See the Hypothermia article in First Aid.*

- If water is cold keep head out of the water and stay immobile to conserve heat. Drown proofing is dangerous in cold water. Drown proofing has a 50% higher cooling rate than treading water so drown proofing shortens survival time.

- Protect neck, sides of chest, and groin with insulation or wool clothing. These areas have high heat loss. Raise knees and wrap arms across the chest.

Drinking Water

- Drinking sea water reduces survival time.

- The lack of drinking water causes dehydration which results in lassitude, loss of appetite (digestion requires water), drowsiness, nausea, and delirium. The senses as hearing and sight are affected. A 25% loss of body fluids usually causes death. At a 15% loss of body fluids the victim will break down and drink salt water.

DIRECTION INDICATIONS FROM WAVES AND SWELLS

A sea swell is formed by the prevailing wind. It takes a major wind to redirect a swell. Normally, the momentum of the swell does not change no matter what the weather.

Swells are not waves. The surface waves will assume the direction of the wind. The undulating swell will follow its normal direction.

- Waves can sometimes indicate the presence of land as the wind might be deflected off the land mass. On the leeward side (wind shadow) of land the swell and waves will be smaller and if the wind is the prevailing wind the swells will also be reduced.

- The Polynesians understood the movements of swells and waves. The Micronesians developed charts of the anatomy and topography of local water surfaces. These charts indicated the meeting points of the dominant swells around the islands. The charts were made of ribs of the coconut palms and tied together with coconut fiber. They showed the islands and used a *sailing time scale not a distance scale.*

- These charts showed: the directional swells throughout the group of islands, the distance from land at which coconuts palms can be seen. Position and distance from the island of the meeting of the waters of the oncoming swell and the ebbing tide from an island or lagoon. These meeting places can be beyond the sight of land.

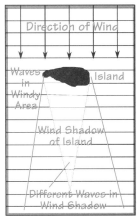

VISIBILITY OVER WATER

The daytime range that an unaided eye can see an unlighted object. On the water the distance of sight is affected by the amount of water vapor or water particles in the air. This can be fog, snow, or water mist.

International
Visibility

Code	Description	Range
0 - 2	Dense - moderate fog	0-500 yds (457 m)
3, 4	Light to thin fog	500 yds-1 mi(1.67 km)
5	Haze	1-2 mi (3.2 km)
6	Light haze	2-5.5 mi (8.9 km)
7	Clear	5.5-11 mi (18 km)
8	Very clear	11-27 mi (43 km)
9	Exceptionally clear	over 27 mi (43 km)

SEA SURVIVAL
MORE DETAILS IN FIRST AID CHAPTER

CAPTIVE BIRD OCEAN NAVIGATION

Sailors of antiquity would set sail with captive land birds. When looking for land a bird would be released. If the bird saw land it would fly in that direction. If not, it would return to the ship. This method was used by the ancient Babylonians, the Hindi of 500 BC, the Polynesians, the Vikings, Arabians in the Indian Ocean, etc.

USING THE WIND TO FIND THE DIRECTION

Winds are named for the direction from which they come, i.e. North wind from the North.

Dominant Wind

Each area has a predominant wind that dominates a season or all seasons.

In general, in regions of temperate climate, the wind usually blows from the west (both in the Northern and Southern hemispheres). In the tropics, the winds are between northeast and southeast. On the equator, usually from the east.

If you have no compass in the Northern hemisphere, a northerly wind is usually colder than a southerly wind.

- Winds from the desert are dry and carry dust.

- Winds from the ocean are moisture laden and might bring rain.

- The prevailing wind in all regions has its own personality of velocity, temperature, and humidity which varies with the seasons.

- On the ocean, the prevailing wind has its own characteristics and also its own accompaniment of clouds.

- In polar regions, the wind temperature, if warmer than the surroundings, will indicate the direction of water. A sudden drop in temperature, without change in direction, might indicate the presence of an iceberg.

- Wet your finger or throw ashes in the air to detect a light breeze.

OCEAN NAVIGATION

USING ECHOES AND SOUND TO FIND DIRECTION

- The Eskimos of Greenland use the sound of the male Snow Bunting's nesting area as a guide in the fog. Each male bird has a distinctive song and the Eskimos know the song of the Snow Bunting at the head of *their* fjord. During a fog they will turn upon hearing the distinctive song and head home.
- When traveling rotate your head to "scan" for sounds. You will hear your environment. You might hear a heavy surf, nesting birds, boats, etc. When the sound of the breakers disappear, that indicates the presence of an inlet or harbor.
- In fog or at night a shout or whistle will echo from any promontory. If you hear an echo recall that sound takes 5 seconds to travel a mile so you can approximate the distance. This method is used on ships during a fog. They use bells, gunshots, siren blasts or shouting. Each second between blast and echo means a distance of about 560 feet from the reflecting surface.

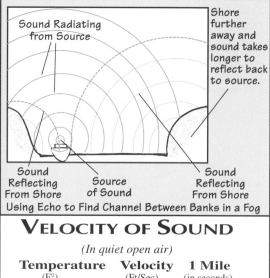

Using Echo to Find Channel Between Banks in a Fog

VELOCITY OF SOUND

(In quiet open air)

Temperature (F°)	Velocity (Ft/Sec)	1 Mile (in seconds)
32°	1092	4.83
40°	1100	4.80
50°	1110	4.78
60°	1120	4.73
70°	1130	4.68
80°	1140	4.63
90°	1150	4.59
100°	1160	4.55
110°	1170	4.51
120°	1180	4.47

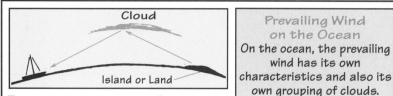

Prevailing Wind on the Ocean

On the ocean, the prevailing wind has its own characteristics and also its own grouping of clouds.

REFLECTIONS IN THE SKY

Clouds can reflect features of the surface below.

- On land off an ice covered sea the clouds can reflect open water as there is less light reflected off dark water that the white frozen area. This reflection is a dark spot on the underside of the clouds. The dark spot would not indicate the size of the open water because a small area can affect a large area of cloud. This happens as open water in the Arctic gives off a vapor and this will affect the reflected light around the open area and increase the dark spot area. This is known as a "water sky".
- An ice flow or iceberg can be seen as an "ice blink" which is seen as a noticeable patch of brightness in a gray sky. A small area of ice can show a large "ice blink".
- Islands and other vegetation-covered areas, ice patches and small snow fields will reflect steel-blue on the under surface of the clouds.

SENSE OF SMELL TO FIND LAND

The sense of smell is important, especially at sea.

- The Polynesians carried pigs on their 100 foot (30 m) catamarans because pigs have a highly developed sense of smell and would get excited upon smelling land.
- The direction of the sea breeze and the smell gives the direction of land.
- New smells are easier to distinguish at sea than on land as the smell of salt is more constant.

SEA ICE

Ice Type	Old Sea Ice	New Sea Ice
Color	Bluish or blackish	Milky or gray
Brittleness	Shatters easily	Does not break easily
Features	Rounded corners	Sharp corners
Taste	Relatively salt free	Tastes extremely salty

SEA ICE AND NAVIGATION

- Bay ice, is smooth, low, and flat can give you an indication as to the distance from a bay.
- Pieces of ice close together like a jigsaw puzzle indicate that land is near.
- The edges of the ice being sharp and fresh will indicate a closeness to shore. If the edges are rounded and the pieces far apart will indicate that the shore is at some distance.
- To get fresh water in an ice flow area, cut a piece of ice from the upper part of an older larger flow. The salt will have leached out.
- In polar regions, the wind temperature, if warmer than surroundings, will indicate the direction of water. A sudden drop in temperature, without a change in direction, might indicate the presence of an iceberg.

FINDING YOUR WAY IN THE POLAR REGIONS

Use the following to confirm magnetic compass readings due to the proximity of the Magnetic North Pole. *See the Compass Chapter for the magnetic declinations etc.*

- Reflections in the sky.
- Direction of prevailing wind.
- Movement of clouds.
- Direction of sun and shadows.

LANDING ON ICE OR ICE FLOWS

Try to land on large stable ice slabs. If landing on small flows, icebergs and disintegrating flows, you might encounter serious problems:

- Ice can cut the raft. Use the paddle to keep it away from sharp edges.
- Store raft away from the ice's edge, keep it inflated and ready for use, and weigh it down as it might be blown away by the wind.

POLAR NAVIGATION

ESTIMATING DISTANCE ON THE WATER

Objects look much nearer than they actually are when:
- The sun is shining, from behind you.
- Looking across water.
- Air is clear.

Objects look much farther away than they actually are when:
- The light is poor and there is low contrast or a fog.
- Looking over larger regular waves especially when the waves are perpendicular to the observer.

Table to judge distance:

50 yds	Mouth and eyes can be clearly distinguished.
100 yds	Eyes appear as dots.
200 yds	General details of clothing can be distinguished.
300 yds	Faces can be seen.
500 yds	Colors of clothing can be distinguished.
800 yds	Man looks like a post.
1 mi	Trunks of large trees can be seen.
2 1/2 mi	Chimneys and windows can be distinguished.
6 mi	Large houses, silos, and towers can be recognized.
9 mi	Average church steeple can be seen.

FINGER METHOD OF JUDGING DISTANCE

This method is based upon the principle that the distance between the eyes is about 1/10 of the distance from the eye to the extended finger.

When you know the width or height of a distant object e.g., the height of a person or building.

a) Extend your right arm and hold your forefinger upright and align it with one eye at the end of the object.

b) Do not move the finger and observe where it is when looking with the other eye. We actually look with one eye and judge depth with the second.

c) Estimate the displacement in feet along the length of the object.

d) The distance in feet of the object will be 10 times the displacement of the fingers.

This can also be done vertically but hold the head sideways. This might be easier because if you want to judge the distance of a building as we know the height of each floor is between 10 to 12 feet high.

You can do this with your binoculars but measure the distance between the center of the *eyepieces*, when adjusted for your eyes, and multiply this distance by 10.

Marking Water Trail
During calm weather the Indians of British Columbia used cedar chips, dropped from the back of their dugout boats into the water, to mark their route in the fog.

DISTANCE AT SEA

Due to the curvature of the earth, the higher you are above sea level the further you can see.

To Determine the Distance of the Horizon:

Take the square root of the height in feet of the observer's eye, *above see level*, and multiply by 1.15. This will give you the distance of the horizon in miles.

e.g. Eye height above sea level 16 ft.

square root of 16 ft. = 4

Multiply by 1.15   4 x 1.15 = 4.6 miles

This tells you that any low object on the horizon will be approximately 4 1/2 miles away.

Object Between You and the Horizon

Estimate the proportionate distance between you and the object, object and horizon to give you the approximation of the distance.

Object Below the Horizon (partially visible)

If you can see a mast above the horizon but not the ship. From the mast you can recognize the type of ship and you can estimate the height of the ship *above* the waterline.

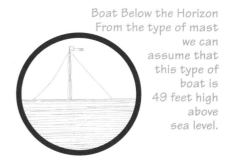

Boat Below the Horizon
From the type of mast
we can
assume that
this type of
boat is
49 feet high
above
sea level.

e.g. Part of mast of a sailboat above the horizon. Assume a sailboat 49 ft. above the waterline.

Square root of 49 = 7.

Square root of height of observer 16 = 4.

Add 7 + 4 = 11 x 1.15 = approx.. 12 2/3 miles.

This means the sailboat is 12 2/3 miles away.

The same method can be used on objects where the height is known as a headland, church steeple, average tree height, palm tree.

STANDING CLOUDS IN FINDING LAND

Standing clouds give the impression of staying in *one spot* while the surrounding clouds keep on moving. A cloud can even be the only one in the sky.

Standing clouds occur above islands. The island or hills on the island and cause humid air to rise and *continuously* form clouds which appear to be standing (staying) in one spot. The cloud is continually dissipating once the air has passed over the island. Due to their height, these clouds can be seen from many miles over the horizon. These clouds often have a woollier appearance than the normal trade-wind clouds.

In the tropics islands even produce distinctive reflections upon these clouds.

Coral islands though flat and low can produce standing clouds as the atoll reflects more heat than the surrounding water causing a temperature gradient along which clouds will form. These clouds usually are on the lee side of the island. They will reflect the bright turquoise lagoon of the atoll.

Clouds might even hover over dangerous shoals below the water.

Lightning at Sea & Finding Land
Lightning from one direction in the early hours of the morning (before sunrise) is usually a sign of land in the tropics.

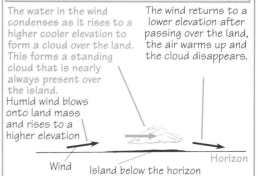

The water in the wind condenses as it rises to a higher cooler elevation to form a cloud over the land. This forms a standing cloud that is nearly always present over the island. Humid wind blows onto land mass and rises to a higher elevation

The wind returns to a lower elevation after passing over the land, the air warms up and the cloud disappears.

Wind   Island below the horizon   Horizon

SEA BIRDS INDICATING THE PROXIMITY OF LAND

Bird	Time of Year	# at one time	Distance From Land
Albatross	Any month Breeding season	Any number. 12+	May be far from land. Within 100 miles of breeding spot.
Petrel	Breeding season Other months Increasing numbers Direction of flight at dawn and dusk shows direction of land.	6+ 6 or less far from land. Show proximity to land.	Within 75 miles of breeding spot.
Shearwater	Breeding Season Direction of flight at dawn and dusk gives direction of land. April-October	6 + Any number	Within 100 miles of breeding spots. May be far from land.
Fulmar	Increasing numbers	Show proximity to land.	
Black Skimmer	Any month	1 +	Within 25 miles.
White Tern	Any month	1 +	Within 40 miles.
Atlantic Gannet	Any month	3 +	Up to 100 miles.
Brown Booby	Any month	3 + 6 or more	75 miles Usually within 30 miles.
Tropic-Bird	Any month	1 or 2 3 +	May be far from land. 60-80 miles
Frigate-Bird	Any month The direction of flight of even 1 bird at dusk usually points to land. Do not sleep on the water.	3 or more 6 or more	100 miles Within 75 miles.
Cormorants	Any month	Any number	25 mile limit.
Pelicans	Any month	More than one Increasing numbers.	25 mile limit; usually much less. Show approach to land.
Great Skua	Summer months Winter months	Increasing numbers Any number	Show proximity to land. May be far from land.
Gulls	Any month	3 or more Increasing numbers	50 miles (or within the 100 fathom line off coasts). Show approach to land.
Common Guillemot	Any month	Increasing numbers.	Show proximity to land.

See Bird Chapter for Details on Water Birds

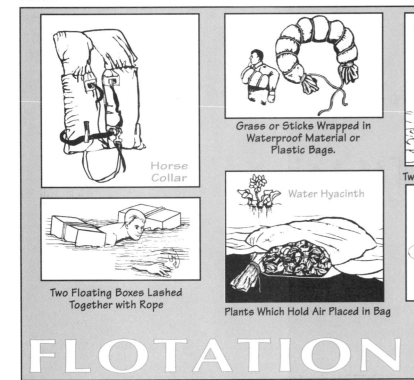

Plastic Segmented Air Pockets

Grass or Sticks Wrapped in Waterproof Material or Plastic Bags.

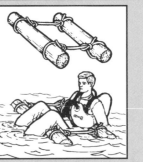

Water Hyacinth

Plants Which Hold Air Placed in Bag

Horse Collar

Two Logs Attached by Ropes

Two Floating Boxes Lashed Together with Rope

Wet Pant Legs

Closed Cell Foam Flotation

FLOTATION DEVICES

COLOR OF THE SEA

Zebra Fish

The sea has two colors:

Green: When the quantity of particles and organisms are high and when there is low salinity.

Blue: Organisms or particles low and salinity content high.

The intensity of coloration (green or blue) depends upon the amount of sunlight and the depth of the water, the deeper the darker.

The different salt and organism content of the currents (Gulf and Labrador in the North Atlantic) are visible in the changing colors of the ocean.

• One could navigate by the knowledge of the coloration of the sea.

• In the tropics, coral reefs can be avoided by watching the change of color of the water (over coral it is usually yellowish).

• These colors cannot be accurately distinguished when the sun is low or if the weather is bad.

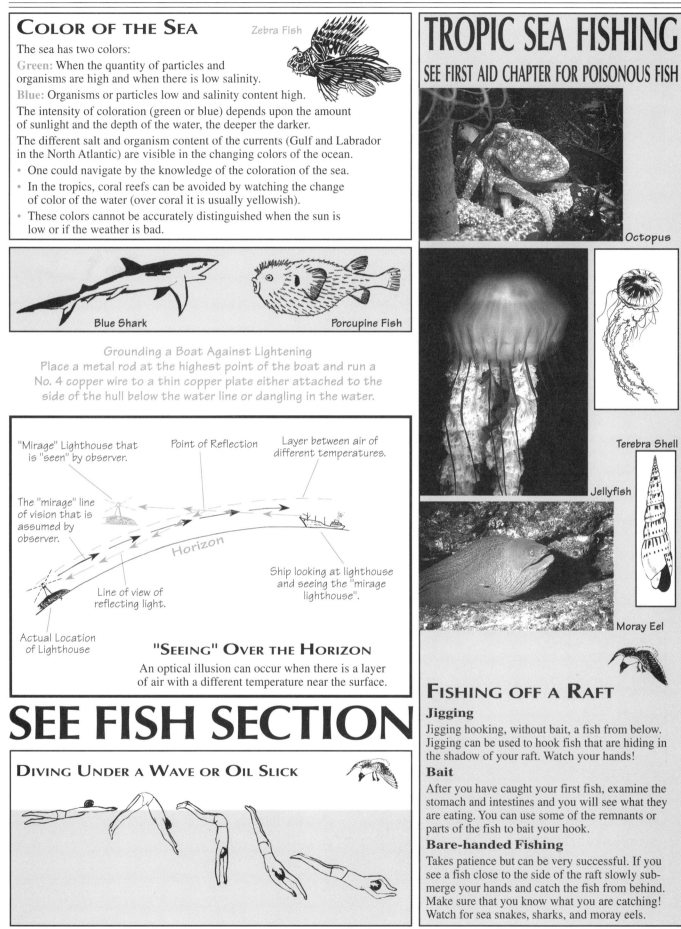

Blue Shark

Porcupine Fish

Grounding a Boat Against Lightening
Place a metal rod at the highest point of the boat and run a No. 4 copper wire to a thin copper plate either attached to the side of the hull below the water line or dangling in the water.

"Mirage" Lighthouse that is "seen" by observer.

Point of Reflection

Layer between air of different temperatures.

The "mirage" line of vision that is assumed by observer.

Horizon

Line of view of reflecting light.

Ship looking at lighthouse and seeing the "mirage lighthouse".

Actual Location of Lighthouse

"SEEING" OVER THE HORIZON

An optical illusion can occur when there is a layer of air with a different temperature near the surface.

SEE FISH SECTION

DIVING UNDER A WAVE OR OIL SLICK

TROPIC SEA FISHING

SEE FIRST AID CHAPTER FOR POISONOUS FISH

Octopus

Terebra Shell

Jellyfish

Moray Eel

FISHING OFF A RAFT

Jigging

Jigging hooking, without bait, a fish from below. Jigging can be used to hook fish that are hiding in the shadow of your raft. Watch your hands!

Bait

After you have caught your first fish, examine the stomach and intestines and you will see what they are eating. You can use some of the remnants or parts of the fish to bait your hook.

Bare-handed Fishing

Takes patience but can be very successful. If you see a fish close to the side of the raft slowly submerge your hands and catch the fish from behind. Make sure that you know what you are catching! Watch for sea snakes, sharks, and moray eels.

CANOES & KAYAKS

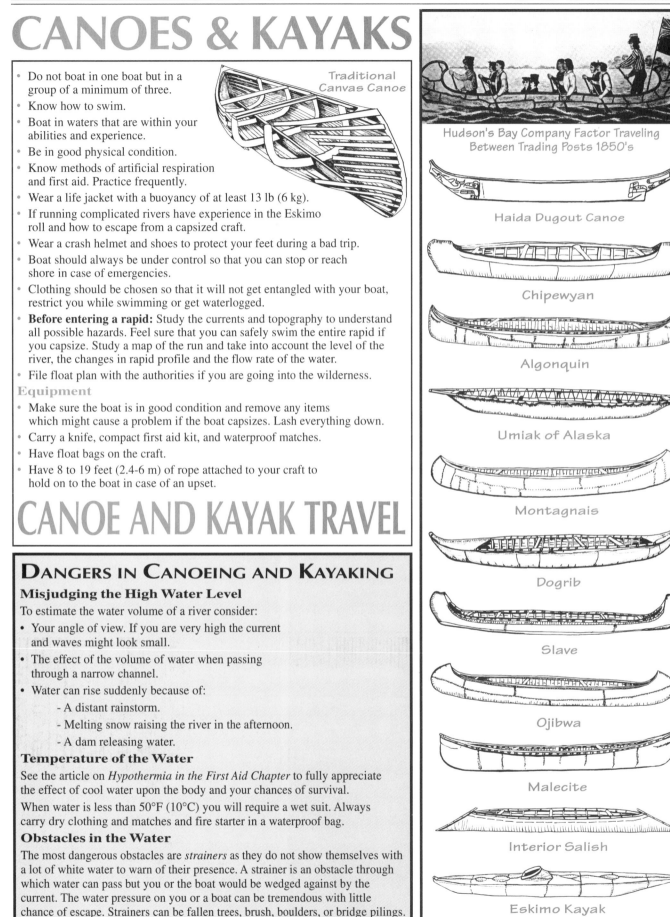

- Do not boat in one boat but in a group of a minimum of three.
- Know how to swim.
- Boat in waters that are within your abilities and experience.
- Be in good physical condition.
- Know methods of artificial respiration and first aid. Practice frequently.
- Wear a life jacket with a buoyancy of at least 13 lb (6 kg).
- If running complicated rivers have experience in the Eskimo roll and how to escape from a capsized craft.
- Wear a crash helmet and shoes to protect your feet during a bad trip.
- Boat should always be under control so that you can stop or reach shore in case of emergencies.
- Clothing should be chosen so that it will not get entangled with your boat, restrict you while swimming or get waterlogged.
- **Before entering a rapid:** Study the currents and topography to understand all possible hazards. Feel sure that you can safely swim the entire rapid if you capsize. Study a map of the run and take into account the level of the river, the changes in rapid profile and the flow rate of the water.
- File float plan with the authorities if you are going into the wilderness.

Equipment

- Make sure the boat is in good condition and remove any items which might cause a problem if the boat capsizes. Lash everything down.
- Carry a knife, compact first aid kit, and waterproof matches.
- Have float bags on the craft.
- Have 8 to 19 feet (2.4-6 m) of rope attached to your craft to hold on to the boat in case of an upset.

CANOE AND KAYAK TRAVEL

Traditional Canvas Canoe

Hudson's Bay Company Factor Traveling Between Trading Posts 1850's

Haida Dugout Canoe

Chipewyan

Algonquin

Umiak of Alaska

Montagnais

Dogrib

Slave

Ojibwa

Malecite

Interior Salish

Eskimo Kayak

DANGERS IN CANOEING AND KAYAKING

Misjudging the High Water Level

To estimate the water volume of a river consider:

- Your angle of view. If you are very high the current and waves might look small.
- The effect of the volume of water when passing through a narrow channel.
- Water can rise suddenly because of:
    - A distant rainstorm.
    - Melting snow raising the river in the afternoon.
    - A dam releasing water.

Temperature of the Water

See the article on *Hypothermia in the First Aid Chapter* to fully appreciate the effect of cool water upon the body and your chances of survival.

When water is less than 50°F (10°C) you will require a wet suit. Always carry dry clothing and matches and fire starter in a waterproof bag.

Obstacles in the Water

The most dangerous obstacles are *strainers* as they do not show themselves with a lot of white water to warn of their presence. A strainer is an obstacle through which water can pass but you or the boat would be wedged against by the current. The water pressure on you or a boat can be tremendous with little chance of escape. Strainers can be fallen trees, brush, boulders, or bridge pilings.

Bow Stroke
In coordination with the stern paddler will keep the canoe in a straight line.

Push Over Stroke
Moves the canoe away from the paddle side.

Backward Stroke
To slow or halt the canoe or to move it backward.

Draw Stroke
To pull the paddler's end of the boat toward the side of his paddle.

Sweep Stroke
Used to turn the canoe.

J Stroke
To turn the canoe toward the side of the paddle. The basic steering stroke.

All Clear
All clear in the direction that the paddle points. Never use the paddle to point as someone might misread the instructions.

Emergency - Help
Can also use a 3 blasts on a whistle to attract attention.

EQUIPMENT FOR A CANOE OR KAYAKING TRIP

- First aid kit.
- 50' - 100' (15-30 m) of throwing rope.
- Life jackets and helmets.
- Boat flotation devices.
- Tube tents.
- Waterproof bags and pouches.
- Repair kits for the boats.
- Extra paddles.
- High energy food.
- Water purification kit and other survival supplies.
- *See the Emergency Boating List for more items.*

Stop
Following boats should not proceed until the 'Clear' signal is given.

Gulls off Shore

REACTION TO EMERGENCIES

- Evacuate the boat *immediately* if you feel that you are entering a strainer. A strainer is an obstacle through which water can pass but you or the boat would be wedged against by the current. Strainers can be fallen trees, brush, boulders, and bridge pilings.
- If you capsize recover by using the Eskimo roll.
- If you are swimming hold on to your boat as it is visible and has flotation. You might have to release your boat to reduce your risk if you are entering more difficult rapids of the water is very cold. You might have to swim to the nearest shore.

See article on Hypothermia in the First Aid Chapter.

- Stay on the *upstream* side of a capsized boat. This will prevent the craft from crushing you against an obstacle.
- When being washed along float with your *feet downstream* to push off rocks.
- Avoid getting caught in strainers, against rock cliffs or fissures, weirs, souse holes or water reversals.
- To escape watch for eddies and slack spots which you should try to enter while gradually moving towards the shore.
- Always rescue boaters before considering the salvage of the equipment.
- The equipment should only be salvaged if it can be done with a minimum of risk.

Flotation Bag

Flotation Bag

Packing a Kayak

Seal on Ice Floe

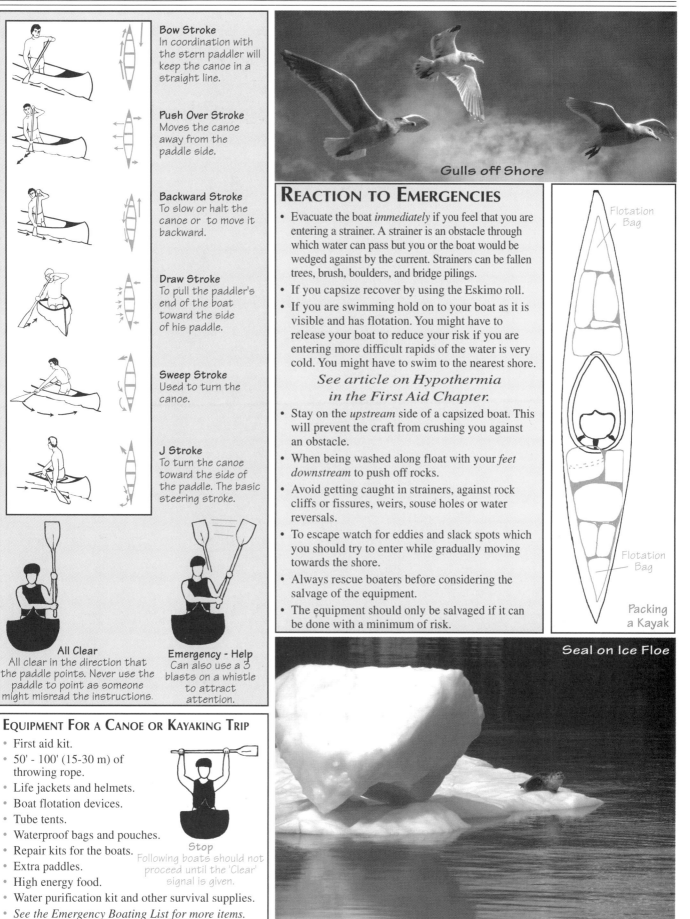

WHY YOU NEED A SHELTER

If you are lost in the wilderness and have decided to stay put, at least for the night, your priority is to find or make a shelter.

Shelter is needed to:

Help to give you a more positive morale and a good night's sleep.

Cool you off: A cooling shelter can be built in the sand on a beach or desert or be provided by a tree.

Keep you warm: To get you out of the wind and rain. A shelter will help you retain your body heat, reduce the effect of wind and air currents and should be easy to heat. Body heat is not lost as fast by the body in still air.

Retard thirst: A shelter will reduce your need of water.

Protect from sun: This will reduce the water consumption and reduce the risk of heat illnesses.

Protect from rain or snow: Being wet will make you feel cold and can lead to hypothermia and feeling depressed.

Protect from animals: Even though animals normally are not dangerous you do not want them walking over you during your sleep.

Protect from insects: Mosquitoes and black flies, in large quantities, might drive you crazy.

MAKING A SHELTER

The first consideration in building a shelter is how much time is left till nightfall and how much time do you expect to stay at this spot. If there are less than two hours before sunset it is best to build a simple shelter for the first night. Examples are the *Bough Shelter, Tree Bark Shelter, Root Shelter, or Poncho Shelter.*

Study your surroundings to chose a spot to stay the night or for a longer term. The area you are in will determine the type of shelter you can build by the choice of building materials available. In the summer your preoccupation is rain, sun, and insects which would usually require a simple shelter. Retaining heat is the principal factor for a shelter in the winter and this would need a more complex structure as an igloo, snow cave, or snow trench. Winter shelters should be small, snug and windproof but with sufficient ventilation to avoid asphyxiation. A winter shelter should be easy to build not requiring too much energy to build.

Tarpaulin or Poncho Tent
Takes five minutes to mount.

SURVIVAL SHELTER
CHAPTER 9

The type of survival shelter to build depends upon the equipment and material available, the season of the year, and the length of the stay. By the proper use of available material some sort of shelter can be built during any season and under any conditions.

Your comfort and ability to build a shelter will depend upon your initiative and skill at improvising a structure with the available materials. This chapter outlines a wide range of shelters, with different levels of required skill, for any season of the year. Special emphasis has been made to show Indian and Eskimo shelters used in different areas of North America.

WHERE TO BUILD

The ideal location is near water, building materials, and fuel.

Land Features

- Site large enough and flat for comfortable bedding.
- Site elevated and well drained.
- Sheltered from wind. Choose south or east sides of hills, forests or other obstacles as the wind is usually from the west in the northern hemisphere.
- Use natural windbreaks as cliffs, trees, fallen trees, caves, rock ledges, and sand dunes to minimize the building effort.
- If traveling in mountainous areas look for caves, crevices or rock ledges.
- If near large bodies of water avoid areas below the high water mark.
- Stay out of dry river gullies as a distant storm might flood the shelter.

Water

- Is water available?
  Build a shelter at least 30 yards (27 m) from and down stream from your water source. This is to avoid polluting your water source.
- Do not build too close to stagnant or slow flowing water as there might be many insects.

Building Material

- Choose a location with building material and fuel.

Insects and Animals

- Choose a breezy ridge or where there is an onshore breeze to reduce the number of insects.
- Sites in forest near fast flowing streams are desirable as these streams do not breed mosquitoes.
- Avoid animal trails or watering holes.
- Watch for areas infested with ants.
- Check for bee and hornet nests.

Other Factors

- Visible to signal for rescue if necessary.
- Make a small shelter as it requires less energy needs less heating, and usually has a less complicated roof structure.
- Consider for how long you will need the shelter and how long it will take to build.
- How much energy should you expend in building a shelter.
- In a temperate climate build with a southern exposure. The sun will give the longest and maximum heat and dry the shelter.
- The entrance should, if possible face east so that you will catch the first rays of sun. This will give you both a warm feeling and raise your morale.
- You might want to sleep in a hidden area to avoid any potential problems. A tent is be more visible than using a natural shelter. Sleeping in a tent reduces your sensitivity to the environmental signals of danger (as abnormally chattering squirrels).
- The military requires concealment from enemy observation, good observation positions, and have a few camouflaged routes that can be used for escape.

AVOID IN BUILDING A SHELTER

- Dry gullies or river beds as there might be a flash flood from a distant storm.
- Building in thick woods as these shelters will be hard to dry due to the lack of wind and sun.
- Pebbly ground, it will be hard to sleep, dig or enter stakes.
- Areas with strong wind currents, as in the opening of a valley.
- Areas where branches or large pine cones might fall.
- Areas under high trees during a thunderstorm.
- Areas that might be a bear run or den.
- Ant nests, poisonous plants, bees, hornet dwellings and other pests.
- Dead trees or trees that might fall during a storm.
- Slow flowing woody river edges as they are humid and shelter mosquitoes.
- Slopes as it might be difficult to build. If you have no choice dig or scrape a drainage channel around the high part of shelter.
- Low valley areas where cold air pockets might be frosty at night.
- Avalanche areas; rock slides in the summer and snow avalanches in the winter. Summer avalanches or mud slides might be caused by a heavy rainfall. Summer avalanche areas can be recognized by the lack of vegetation on the slope.
- In the winter avoid snow cornices or ledges.

Natural Shelters

Think of what type of shelters animals use: caves, ledges, hollow logs, boughs of trees, rock overhangs, crevasses, natural terraces.

Watch an animal cross an open space in the winter. You will see it weave back and forth avoiding cold air currents that are invisible and undetectable to us. It is obvious that they are very sensitive to the environment and in the wilds we should learn from them.

A natural shelter can be improved by adding a bedding of leaves, protective branches and other covering to retain heat or keep out moisture.

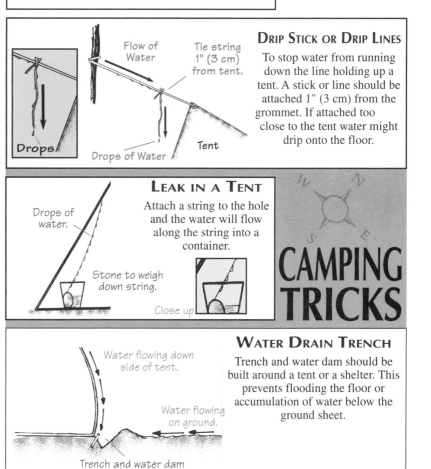

DRIP STICK OR DRIP LINES

To stop water from running down the line holding up a tent. A stick or line should be attached 1" (3 cm) from the grommet. If attached too close to the tent water might drip onto the floor.

Flow of Water

Tie string 1" (3 cm) from tent.

Drops

Drops of Water

Tent

LEAK IN A TENT

Attach a string to the hole and the water will flow along the string into a container.

Drops of water.

Stone to weigh down string.

Close up

CAMPING TRICKS

WATER DRAIN TRENCH

Trench and water dam should be built around a tent or a shelter. This prevents flooding the floor or accumulation of water below the ground sheet.

Water flowing down side of tent.

Water flowing on ground.

Trench and water dam

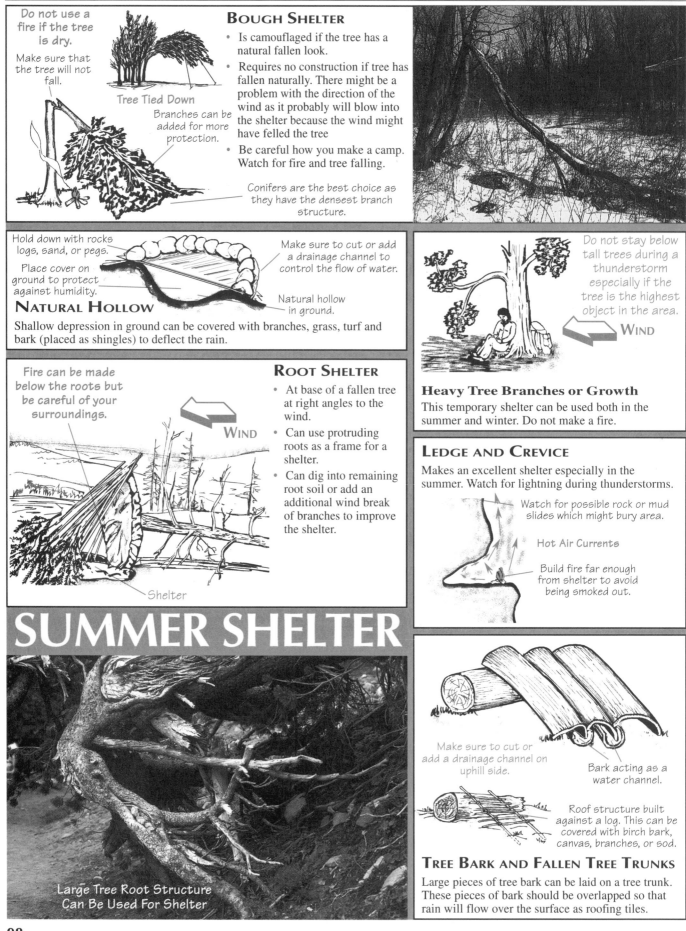

Do not use a fire if the tree is dry.

Make sure that the tree will not fall.

Tree Tied Down

Branches can be added for more protection.

BOUGH SHELTER

- Is camouflaged if the tree has a natural fallen look.
- Requires no construction if tree has fallen naturally. There might be a problem with the direction of the wind as it probably will blow into the shelter because the wind might have felled the tree
- Be careful how you make a camp. Watch for fire and tree falling.

Conifers are the best choice as they have the densest branch structure.

Hold down with rocks logs, sand, or pegs.

Place cover on ground to protect against humidity.

Make sure to cut or add a drainage channel to control the flow of water.

Natural hollow in ground.

NATURAL HOLLOW

Shallow depression in ground can be covered with branches, grass, turf and bark (placed as shingles) to deflect the rain.

Do not stay below tall trees during a thunderstorm especially if the tree is the highest object in the area.

WIND

Heavy Tree Branches or Growth

This temporary shelter can be used both in the summer and winter. Do not make a fire.

Fire can be made below the roots but be careful of your surroundings.

WIND

ROOT SHELTER

- At base of a fallen tree at right angles to the wind.
- Can use protruding roots as a frame for a shelter.
- Can dig into remaining root soil or add an additional wind break of branches to improve the shelter.

Shelter

LEDGE AND CREVICE

Makes an excellent shelter especially in the summer. Watch for lightning during thunderstorms.

Watch for possible rock or mud slides which might bury area.

Hot Air Currents

Build fire far enough from shelter to avoid being smoked out.

SUMMER SHELTER

Large Tree Root Structure Can Be Used For Shelter

Make sure to cut or add a drainage channel on uphill side.

Bark acting as a water channel.

Roof structure built against a log. This can be covered with birch bark, canvas, branches, or sod.

TREE BARK AND FALLEN TREE TRUNKS

Large pieces of tree bark can be laid on a tree trunk. These pieces of bark should be overlapped so that rain will flow over the surface as roofing tiles.

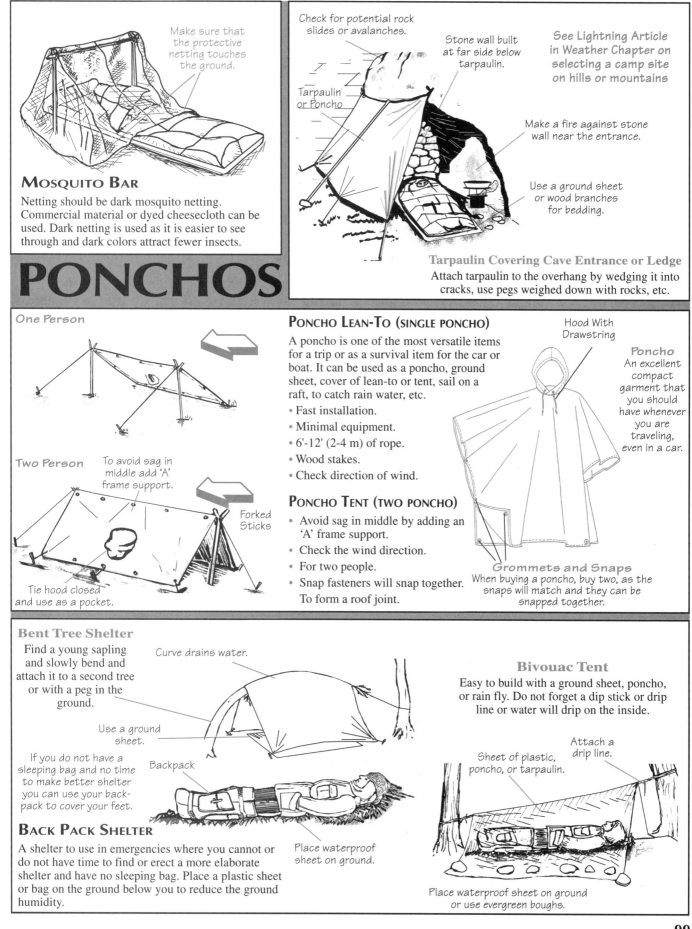

MOSQUITO BAR

Make sure that the protective netting touches the ground.

Netting should be dark mosquito netting. Commercial material or dyed cheesecloth can be used. Dark netting is used as it is easier to see through and dark colors attract fewer insects.

PONCHOS

Check for potential rock slides or avalanches.

Stone wall built at far side below tarpaulin.

See Lightning Article in Weather Chapter on selecting a camp site on hills or mountains

Tarpaulin or Poncho

Make a fire against stone wall near the entrance.

Use a ground sheet or wood branches for bedding.

Tarpaulin Covering Cave Entrance or Ledge

Attach tarpaulin to the overhang by wedging it into cracks, use pegs weighed down with rocks, etc.

One Person

Two Person

To avoid sag in middle add 'A' frame support.

Forked Sticks

Tie hood closed and use as a pocket.

PONCHO LEAN-TO (SINGLE PONCHO)

A poncho is one of the most versatile items for a trip or as a survival item for the car or boat. It can be used as a poncho, ground sheet, cover of lean-to or tent, sail on a raft, to catch rain water, etc.

- Fast installation.
- Minimal equipment.
- 6'-12' (2-4 m) of rope.
- Wood stakes.
- Check direction of wind.

PONCHO TENT (TWO PONCHO)

- Avoid sag in middle by adding an 'A' frame support.
- Check the wind direction.
- For two people.
- Snap fasteners will snap together. To form a roof joint.

Hood With Drawstring

Poncho
An excellent compact garment that you should have whenever you are traveling, even in a car.

Grommets and Snaps
When buying a poncho, buy two, as the snaps will match and they can be snapped together.

Bent Tree Shelter

Find a young sapling and slowly bend and attach it to a second tree or with a peg in the ground.

Curve drains water.

Use a ground sheet.

If you do not have a sleeping bag and no time to make better shelter you can use your backpack to cover your feet.

Backpack

BACK PACK SHELTER

A shelter to use in emergencies where you cannot or do not have time to find or erect a more elaborate shelter and have no sleeping bag. Place a plastic sheet or bag on the ground below you to reduce the ground humidity.

Place waterproof sheet on ground.

Bivouac Tent

Easy to build with a ground sheet, poncho, or rain fly. Do not forget a dip stick or drip line or water will drip on the inside.

Attach a drip line.

Sheet of plastic, poncho, or tarpaulin.

Place waterproof sheet on ground or use evergreen boughs.

The secret of survival is to observe your surroundings and nature.

Tarpaulin and Woven Polyethylene

A tarpaulin is a very versatile camping and survival accessory. The original tarpaulins were made of heavy 8 oz. (227 g) cotton canvas that was impregnated with oils or wax. These are very resistant, long lasting and are hardly affected by the sun. They should be well dried, to avoid mildew, before being folded for storage. Modern 'tarpaulins' are made of woven ripstop polyethylene. This material is much cheaper and weighs less. It is affected by UV rays of the sun, can get worn by continuous wind movement, can not be folded as well as canvas tarpaulins and is very noisy.

Folded Polyethylene Tarpaulin

Tarpaulin Sizes for Shelters
2 person	9' x 12'
4 person	11' x 14'

GROUND SHEET

Ground sheets should be smaller than the tent floor and never extend beyond the tent floor as it will accumulate water during a rainstorm.

GROUND SHEET

Lightning

When building a summer shelter below trees you are at the risk of being hit by lightning. When choosing a shelter support tree make sure that it is not the tallest in the area nor the only one. In summer a storm can blow up very fast and lightning can even strike in front of a storm. For more information see the Weather Chapter.

CAMOUFLAGE TARPAULIN

Metal Grommet

Tarpaulins can be used as covers. As they gather wind make sure that they are fastened down. If you are covering a light object weigh it down or it might fly away.

COVER

LEAN-TO

If you have a wide tarpaulin you can fold the bottom part to form a ground sheet. Attach it well because a shift in the wind's direction can cause your lean-to to balloon. Your ground sheet fold will not let the wind escape below the shelter.

Make sure that you do not build a shelter over a depression in the ground which might become flooded during a rain storm.

Dig a rain trench at the edge of the shelter.

Center Pull

Wind

TARPAULIN BETWEEN TREES   **STICK FRAME**   **PONCHO ON TREE**

TARPAULIN

Smooth stone, ball, large button, coin, etc.

Place object below surface making sure that there are no sharp edges that might damage the material.

Tie cord tightly below the object and this will act as a grommet.

Tarpaulin or Rain Fly Garter

If tarp lacks sufficient grommets or ties then the garter system can be used. It is simple, economical and can be used in many situations. To act as a retainer a coin, pebble or ball can be used. Make sure that the retainer is not sharp as the material could be damaged.

WEAVING STRAW AND GRASS

Build a frame of poles, as in the illustration, and attach cord (A) between opposite poles. Attach a second set of cords from one set of poles to a horizontal stick (B). Raise the horizontal stick (B) and place a bundle of straw or rushes horizontally across the cord (A) and lower the stick (B) below the level of the cords (A). The first bundle of straw (X) will now have been attached. Continue ...

Woven straw that can be used as roofing, clothing, floor matting, or sail for a raft.

Malay Hitch

Use straw, long grass, or bulrushes.

As twine use : cordage, raw hide, rope, etc.,

Weaving Using a Malay Hitch

This hitch is used in simple weaving. The strength and flexibility of the resulting matting, wall structure, poncho, depends upon the size, weight, and spacing of the material and binding cord that has been used. This is a very economical structure because upon leaving the campsite only the rope is taken with you and you can weave new matting at the next camping site.

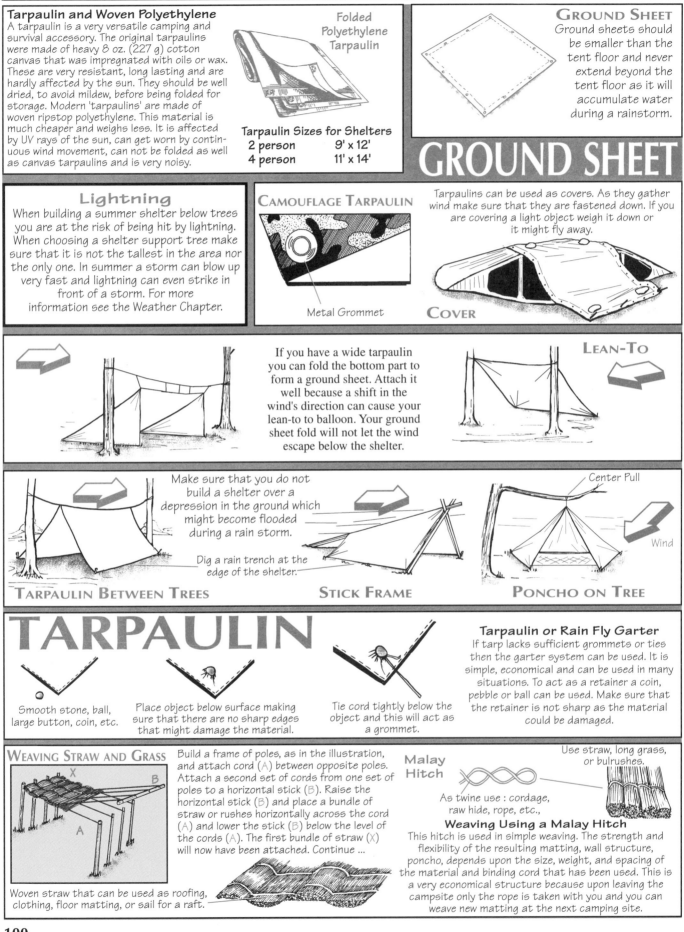

LEAN-TO WITH A REFLECTOR

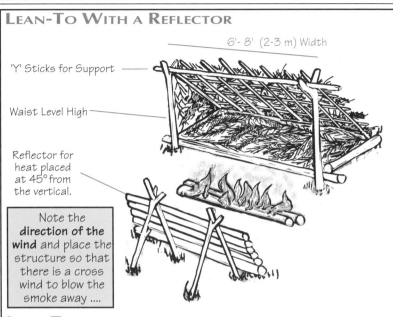

6'- 8' (2-3 m) Width

'Y' Sticks for Support

Waist Level High

Reflector for heat placed at 45° from the vertical.

Note the **direction of the wind** and place the structure so that there is a cross wind to blow the smoke away ....

LEAN-TO

An easy to assemble shelter that can be built by using a support structure of two trees and some poles. The lean-to is one of the most practical and multipurpose shelters. It can be used as a temporary refuge on a travel circuit. This structure was called a *Matchejin* by the Indians. All that is required is a wooded area, a knife and some time. There are many variants and different materials can be used.

LEAN -TO CONSTRUCTION

Reflector to Retain the Heat

Reflector

Fire

REFLECTORS AGAINST THE WIND

LEAN-TO BETWEEN TREES

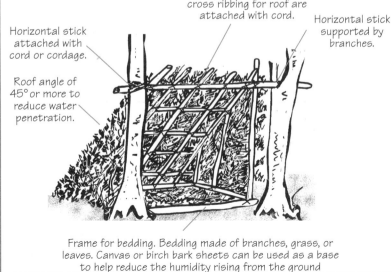

Support sticks and cross ribbing for roof are attached with cord.

Horizontal stick supported by branches.

Horizontal stick attached with cord or cordage.

Roof angle of 45° or more to reduce water penetration.

Frame for bedding. Bedding made of branches, grass, or leaves. Canvas or birch bark sheets can be used as a base to help reduce the humidity rising from the ground

BUILDING A LEAN-TO

Two Vertical Supports 6' to 8' (2-3 m) apart.

These supports can be trees with branches, at approximately waist height, to hold the horizontal bar. The bar can be attached with a cord.

The vertical supports can be a tripod of sticks (attached by rope or vines) or forked sticks which are stuck into the ground.

Covering of Roof and Sides

The covering can be logs that are cut to measure (if one requires a strong roof to support snow)

- Rotten log castings which can be placed, in an over lapping fashion e.g., Spanish roof tiles.
- Tree boughs on a grid structure of branches.
- Grass sod on a grid structure of branches.
- Large leaves, palm branches on a matrix.
- Sheets of birch bark.

To place the layers of roofing:
Start as the bottom and the additional layers should overlap for waterproofing.

- Tarpaulin, airplane insulation panels, wing covers, parachute material, can also be used for the roof and sides.

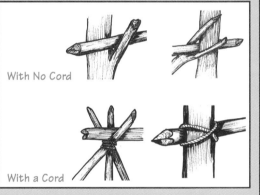

With No Cord

With a Cord

WEAVING WITH A PALING HITCH

The Indians used this system to form wall shelters, fences, etc. The best binding that can be used is wet rawhide. As it shrinks upon drying thereby producing a very tight binding.

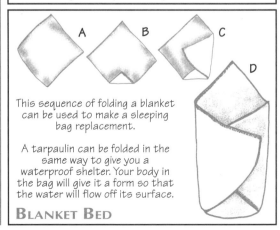

A

B

C

D

This sequence of folding a blanket can be used to make a sleeping bag replacement.

A tarpaulin can be folded in the same way to give you a waterproof shelter. Your body in the bag will give it a form so that the water will flow off its surface.

BLANKET BED

The secret of survival is to observe your surroundings and nature.

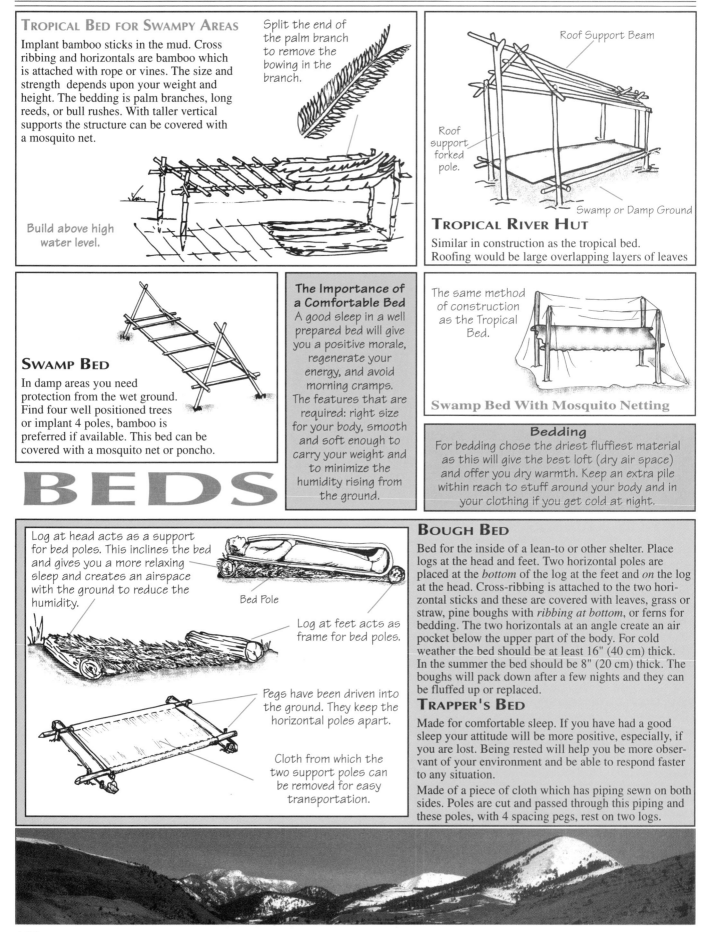

TROPICAL BED FOR SWAMPY AREAS

Implant bamboo sticks in the mud. Cross ribbing and horizontals are bamboo which is attached with rope or vines. The size and strength depends upon your weight and height. The bedding is palm branches, long reeds, or bull rushes. With taller vertical supports the structure can be covered with a mosquito net.

Split the end of the palm branch to remove the bowing in the branch.

Build above high water level.

Roof Support Beam

Roof support forked pole.

Swamp or Damp Ground

TROPICAL RIVER HUT

Similar in construction as the tropical bed. Roofing would be large overlapping layers of leaves

SWAMP BED

In damp areas you need protection from the wet ground. Find four well positioned trees or implant 4 poles, bamboo is preferred if available. This bed can be covered with a mosquito net or poncho.

The Importance of a Comfortable Bed

A good sleep in a well prepared bed will give you a positive morale, regenerate your energy, and avoid morning cramps. The features that are required: right size for your body, smooth and soft enough to carry your weight and to minimize the humidity rising from the ground.

The same method of construction as the Tropical Bed.

Swamp Bed With Mosquito Netting

Bedding

For bedding chose the driest fluffiest material as this will give the best loft (dry air space) and offer you dry warmth. Keep an extra pile within reach to stuff around your body and in your clothing if you get cold at night.

BEDS

Log at head acts as a support for bed poles. This inclines the bed and gives you a more relaxing sleep and creates an airspace with the ground to reduce the humidity.

Bed Pole

Log at feet acts as frame for bed poles.

Pegs have been driven into the ground. They keep the horizontal poles apart.

Cloth from which the two support poles can be removed for easy transportation.

BOUGH BED

Bed for the inside of a lean-to or other shelter. Place logs at the head and feet. Two horizontal poles are placed at the *bottom* of the log at the feet and *on* the log at the head. Cross-ribbing is attached to the two horizontal sticks and these are covered with leaves, grass or straw, pine boughs with *ribbing at bottom*, or ferns for bedding. The two horizontals at an angle create an air pocket below the upper part of the body. For cold weather the bed should be at least 16" (40 cm) thick. In the summer the bed should be 8" (20 cm) thick. The boughs will pack down after a few nights and they can be fluffed up or replaced.

TRAPPER'S BED

Made for comfortable sleep. If you have had a good sleep your attitude will be more positive, especially, if you are lost. Being rested will help you be more observant of your environment and be able to respond faster to any situation.

Made of a piece of cloth which has piping sewn on both sides. Poles are cut and passed through this piping and these poles, with 4 spacing pegs, rest on two logs.

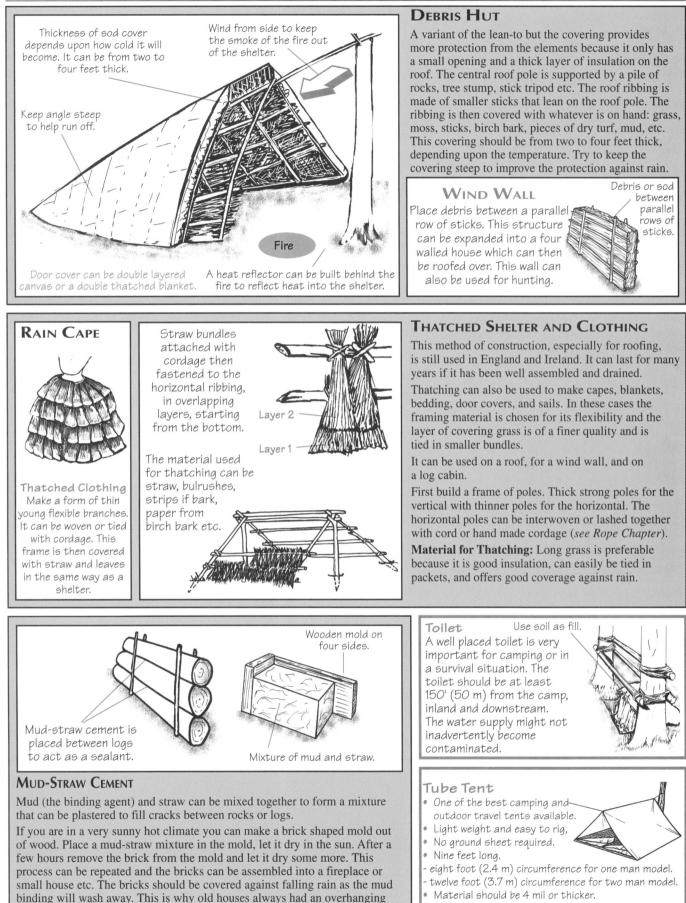

Thickness of sod cover depends upon how cold it will become. It can be from two to four feet thick.

Wind from side to keep the smoke of the fire out of the shelter.

Keep angle steep to help run off.

Fire

Door cover can be double layered canvas or a double thatched blanket.

A heat reflector can be built behind the fire to reflect heat into the shelter.

DEBRIS HUT

A variant of the lean-to but the covering provides more protection from the elements because it only has a small opening and a thick layer of insulation on the roof. The central roof pole is supported by a pile of rocks, tree stump, stick tripod etc. The roof ribbing is made of smaller sticks that lean on the roof pole. The ribbing is then covered with whatever is on hand: grass, moss, sticks, birch bark, pieces of dry turf, mud, etc. This covering should be from two to four feet thick, depending upon the temperature. Try to keep the covering steep to improve the protection against rain.

WIND WALL

Place debris between a parallel row of sticks. This structure can be expanded into a four walled house which can then be roofed over. This wall can also be used for hunting.

Debris or sod between parallel rows of sticks.

RAIN CAPE

Thatched Clothing
Make a form of thin young flexible branches. It can be woven or tied with cordage. This frame is then covered with straw and leaves in the same way as a shelter.

Straw bundles attached with cordage then fastened to the horizontal ribbing, in overlapping layers, starting from the bottom.

Layer 2

Layer 1

The material used for thatching can be straw, bulrushes, strips if bark, paper from birch bark etc.

THATCHED SHELTER AND CLOTHING

This method of construction, especially for roofing, is still used in England and Ireland. It can last for many years if it has been well assembled and drained.

Thatching can also be used to make capes, blankets, bedding, door covers, and sails. In these cases the framing material is chosen for its flexibility and the layer of covering grass is of a finer quality and is tied in smaller bundles.

It can be used on a roof, for a wind wall, and on a log cabin.

First build a frame of poles. Thick strong poles for the vertical with thinner poles for the horizontal. The horizontal poles can be interwoven or lashed together with cord or hand made cordage (*see Rope Chapter*).

Material for Thatching: Long grass is preferable because it is good insulation, can easily be tied in packets, and offers good coverage against rain.

Wooden mold on four sides.

Mud-straw cement is placed between logs to act as a sealant.

Mixture of mud and straw.

MUD-STRAW CEMENT

Mud (the binding agent) and straw can be mixed together to form a mixture that can be plastered to fill cracks between rocks or logs.

If you are in a very sunny hot climate you can make a brick shaped mold out of wood. Place a mud-straw mixture in the mold, let it dry in the sun. After a few hours remove the brick from the mold and let it dry some more. This process can be repeated and the bricks can be assembled into a fireplace or small house etc. The bricks should be covered against falling rain as the mud binding will wash away. This is why old houses always had an overhanging roof in the direction of the falling rain.

Toilet
Use soil as fill.

A well placed toilet is very important for camping or in a survival situation. The toilet should be at least 150' (50 m) from the camp, inland and downstream. The water supply might not inadvertently become contaminated.

Tube Tent
- One of the best camping and outdoor travel tents available.
- Light weight and easy to rig,
- No ground sheet required.
- Nine feet long.
- eight foot (2.4 m) circumference for one man model.
- twelve foot (3.7 m) circumference for two man model.
- Material should be 4 mil or thicker.
- Rope 24' (8 m) long.

Sewing two pieces of heavy cloth together

Back Stitch

Sapling Shelter

If you are in an area of young tree growth you can select two rows and cut the saplings that are in between. The chosen saplings are stripped of their branches and lashed together to form a dome. This dome is covered with material or it can be thatched.

Saplings are tied together.

Tied saplings are covered.

Poles are lashed together.

CAMP SHOWER

Built with a teepee like frame. It is a luxury but it might make you feel at home.

Shower Head With Valve

Water in Bucket

PLASTIC SHEET SHELTER

Stones

Stones Underneath

For areas lacking wood, stones can be piled to form a U and the roof can be made of drift wood, or tarpaulin.

Cover

CAMP CHAIR

PONCHO COVERED HAMMOCK

Use an extra rope to support the poncho.

Attach a piece of cord or wood to prevent water from running down the rope into the sleeping area. This should be done on both sides.

BIRCH BARK

Ideal covering material that has been used for thousands of years. It can be used for shelter, canoes, clothing, parchment, fire starter, torches, and water containers. To remove it from the tree incise the bark in two horizontal lines that are 18" (50 cm) apart. Make a vertical cut between these lines and peel off a layer of bark. *Do not cut too deeply as you do not want to injure or kill the tree.*

SEE SUMMER HIKING CHAPTER

WICKIUP

Used by the plains Indians, in areas where building material was scarce.

- Use three strong poles and lash them at the top using rope, if it is not available weave a braided rope out of straw or long grass. Lean some additional poles on the top.

- Fill in the sides with branches and cover with sagebrush, bush, or dry cacti. For additional protection and to keep out the rain add denser roofing material such as sod, leather, or woven thatching, make sure that the pitch of the roof is quite high so that rainwater can run off.

- The entrance to the house faces east so that you can catch the heat and light of the rising sun.

Face East

YURT OF MONGOLIA

The yurt is the four season dwelling of the inhabitants of central Asia. Wood is very scarce in the area. The inhabitants migrate with their herds so they need a simple roomy lightweight structure that is easy to assemble and transport. The structure is made of poles that are lashed together. The covering is animal skins. The doorway would be a carpet or skins.

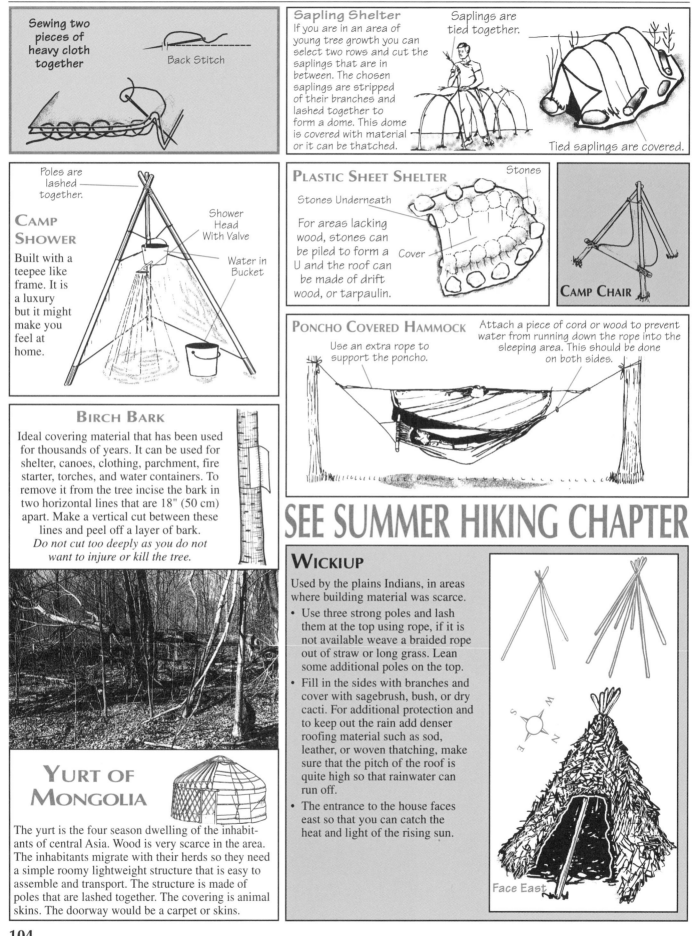

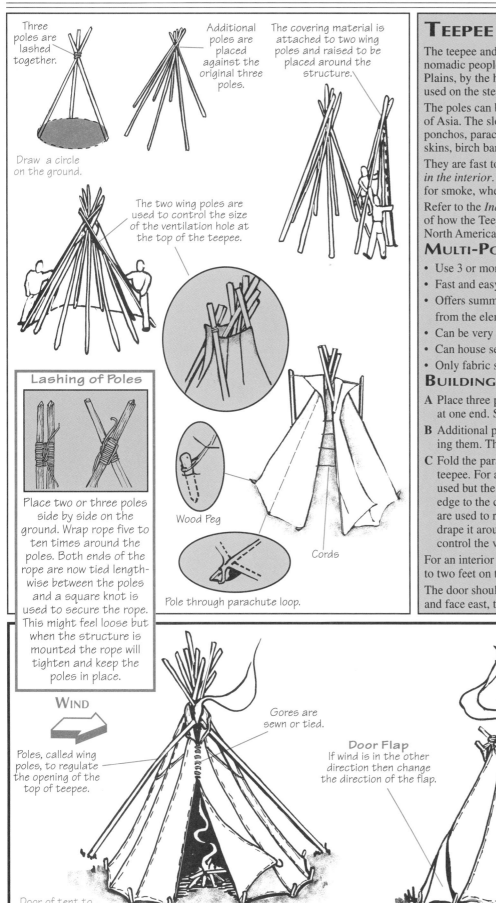

Three poles are lashed together.

Draw a circle on the ground.

Additional poles are placed against the original three poles.

The covering material is attached to two wing poles and raised to be placed around the structure.

The two wing poles are used to control the size of the ventilation hole at the top of the teepee.

Lashing of Poles

Place two or three poles side by side on the ground. Wrap rope five to ten times around the poles. Both ends of the rope are now tied lengthwise between the poles and a square knot is used to secure the rope. This might feel loose but when the structure is mounted the rope will tighten and keep the poles in place.

Wood Peg

Cords

Pole through parachute loop.

TEEPEE OR WIGWAM

The teepee and its variants were developed by nomadic peoples. They were used on the American Plains, by the hordes of Genghis Khan and are still used on the steppes of Asia.

The poles can be straight or curved as the yurts of Asia. The sloping poles can be covered with ponchos, parachute, woven material, branches, skins, birch bark, or modern materials.

They are fast to assemble and *can have an open fire in the interior*. There is a ventilation hole at the top, for smoke, where the poles merge.

Refer to the *Indian Shelter Section* to see examples of how the Teepee was used and in what areas of North America.

MULTI-POLE PARACHUTE TEEPEE

- Use 3 or more poles 10'-15' (3-5 m) long.
- Fast and easy to assemble.
- Offers summer and winter protection from the elements.
- Can be very visible for rescue.
- Can house several people and equipment.
- Only fabric shelter that can have an open fire.

BUILDING A PARACHUTE TEEPEE

A Place three poles on the ground and lash them at one end. Stand up the poles as a tripod.

B Additional poles can then be added without lashing them. They are propped up against the tripod.

C Fold the parachute in half (or cut) for a small teepee. For a large teepee the whole surface is used but the parachute is cut from the outside edge to the center. Two extra poles, wing poles, are used to raise the parachute material and to drape it around the tripod. The wing poles control the ventilation hole

For an interior open fire leave an opening of one to two feet on the top.

The door should be 90° from the prevailing wind and face east, to the rising sun, if possible.

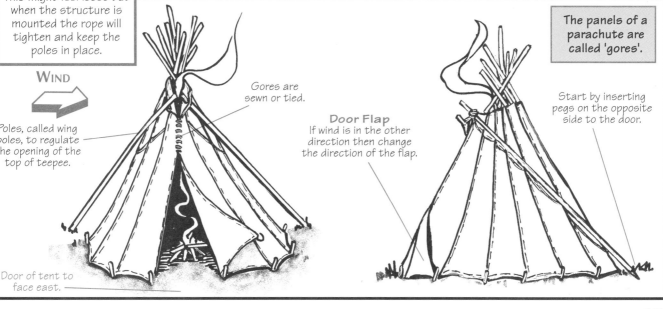

WIND

Poles, called wing poles, to regulate the opening of the top of teepee.

Door of tent to face east.

Gores are sewn or tied.

Door Flap
If wind is in the other direction then change the direction of the flap.

The panels of a parachute are called 'gores'.

Start by inserting pegs on the opposite side to the door.

PARACHUTE HAMMOCK BED TENT

When you are on humid ground and have a parachute and some parachute cord. A piece of parachute is draped over the rope attached between two sturdy trees. The bottom of the shelter is attached to four poles driven into the ground and to the horizontal sticks. A hammock is made from the remaining material by attaching it to the two trees. Part of the material of the hammock can cover your body as protection against insects.

Hammock on the inside of the tent.

PARACHUTE-HAMMOCK TENT

This is a one-man tent-hammock. It is suspended between two trees. There is a horizontal bar across the entrance which gives the shelter its shape. This shelter is off the ground, keeps out the insects and can be heated with a small survival candle. This structure could not support a snow fall.

The roof can be built with additional layers for better insulation against the elements.

Cross-Section

Profile of the shelter showing the layers of parachute folded on the floor.

Folded Parachute

Rig lines from the parachute that are braided together to attach to the tree.

A stick is placed between A-B to brace the tent.

SIOUX TEEPEE

A typical teepee is a sloped cone. This is due to the location of the ventilation hole and the door overlap area.

Cone

Door

An Indian teepee pattern is shown in the adjacent illustration. The Plains Indians were nomads following the buffalo herds. They needed a transportable shelter that could comfortably accommodate a family and be strong enough to resist winter winds. The material used were buffalo hides that were stitched together to form a pattern as in the adjacent illustration. The Teepee was lined with buffalo hides in the winter. The Sioux even had an altar in their Teepees. All Teepees had inside fires. The outside walls of the Teepees were decorated with records of war, bird and animal figures from visions.

Holes for lacing the tent together.

Overlap flap for the front of the teepee.

Center Point

Typical Pattern of a Teepee Cover

TRAPPER TARPAULIN CABIN

This can almost be considered as a permanent structure. It is hard work to build and difficult to displace if the wrong location is chosen. A location near water would be ideal. A ridge or promontory is an excellent choice as with wind there will be less insects and the elevation less risk of flooding. A double layered (air-spaced) roof of canvas would improve the insulation and waterproofing.
Requires straight logs of 4"-8" (10-20 cm) diameter.

Winter Roof

Overlapping layers of birch bark.

Layer of sod.

Overlapping layer of birch bark.

Frame and cross ribbing.

SINGLE POLE PARACHUTE TEEPEE

The pole is supported by a stable part of a tree.

To make these tents you can use one half of a parachute. You can cut it in half or make a double wall. When staking start at the side opposite to the door. Place the door in a direction perpendicular to the wind and facing east if possible.

TEEPEE SUPPORTED FROM A TREE

The rig lines are attached to a branch of a tree.

Log Frame

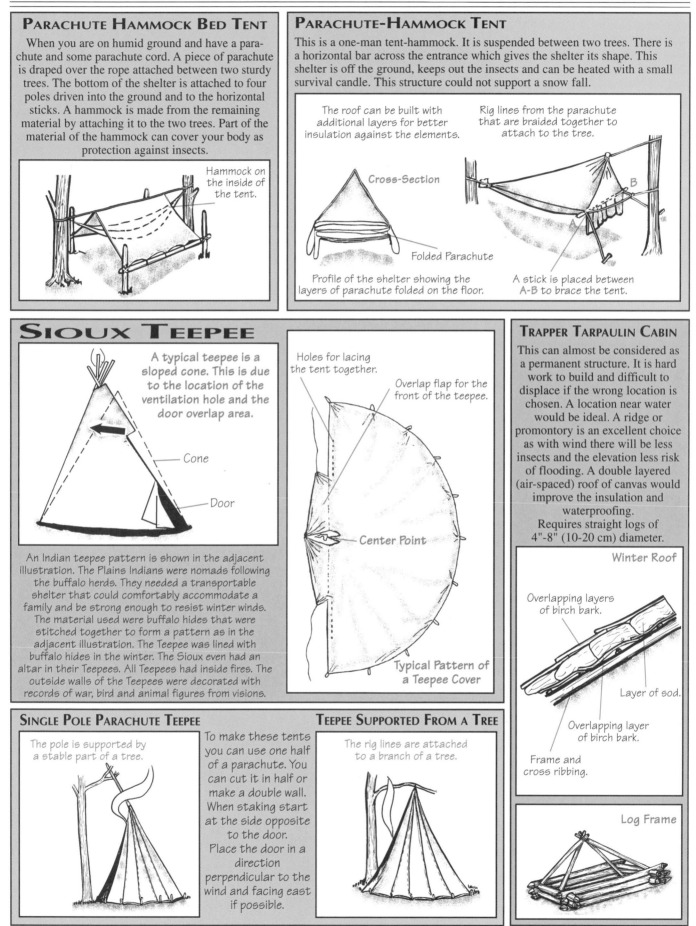

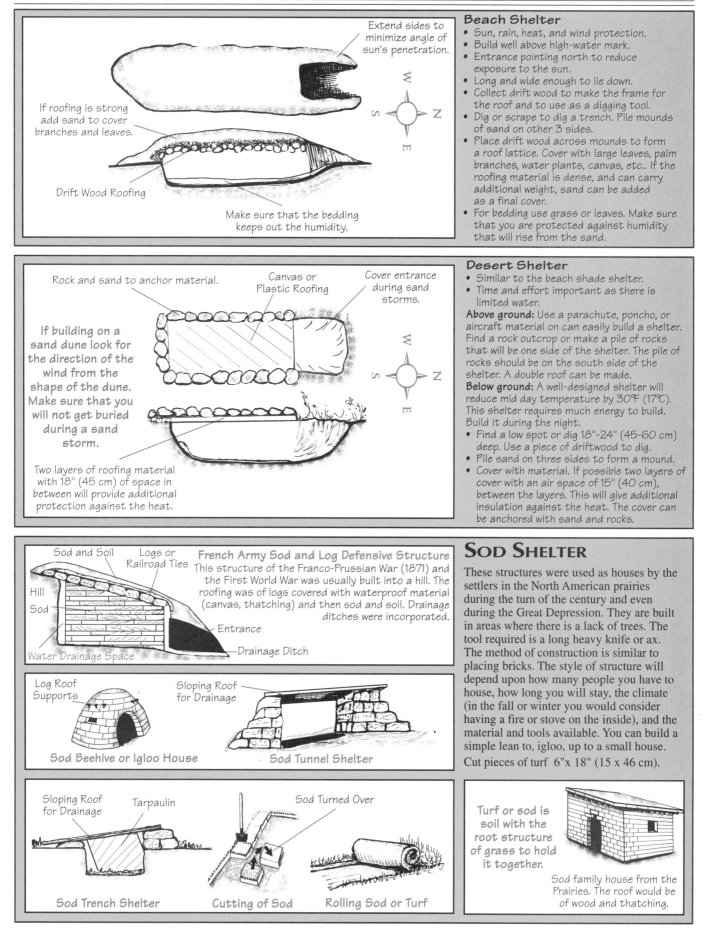

Beach Shelter

- Sun, rain, heat, and wind protection.
- Build well above high-water mark.
- Entrance pointing north to reduce exposure to the sun.
- Long and wide enough to lie down.
- Collect drift wood to make the frame for the roof and to use as a digging tool.
- Dig or scrape to dig a trench. Pile mounds of sand on other 3 sides.
- Place drift wood across mounds to form a roof lattice. Cover with large leaves, palm branches, water plants, canvas, etc.. If the roofing material is dense, and can carry additional weight, sand can be added as a final cover.
- For bedding use grass or leaves. Make sure that you are protected against humidity that will rise from the sand.

Extend sides to minimize angle of sun's penetration.

If roofing is strong add sand to cover branches and leaves.

Drift Wood Roofing

Make sure that the bedding keeps out the humidity.

Desert Shelter

- Similar to the beach shade shelter.
- Time and effort important as there is limited water.

Above ground: Use a parachute, poncho, or aircraft material on can easily build a shelter. Find a rock outcrop or make a pile of rocks that will be one side of the shelter. The pile of rocks should be on the south side of the shelter. A double roof can be made.

Below ground: A well-designed shelter will reduce mid day temperature by 30℉ (17℃). This shelter requires much energy to build. Build it during the night.

- Find a low spot or dig 18"-24" (45-60 cm) deep. Use a piece of driftwood to dig.
- Pile sand on three sides to form a mound.
- Cover with material. If possible two layers of cover with an air space of 15" (40 cm), between the layers. This will give additional insulation against the heat. The cover can be anchored with sand and rocks.

Rock and sand to anchor material.

Canvas or Plastic Roofing

Cover entrance during sand storms.

If building on a sand dune look for the direction of the wind from the shape of the dune. Make sure that you will not get buried during a sand storm.

Two layers of roofing material with 18" (45 cm) of space in between will provide additional protection against the heat.

SOD SHELTER

These structures were used as houses by the settlers in the North American prairies during the turn of the century and even during the Great Depression. They are built in areas where there is a lack of trees. The tool required is a long heavy knife or ax. The method of construction is similar to placing bricks. The style of structure will depend upon how many people you have to house, how long you will stay, the climate (in the fall or winter you would consider having a fire or stove on the inside), and the material and tools available. You can build a simple lean to, igloo, up to a small house.

Cut pieces of turf 6"x 18" (15 x 46 cm).

Sod and Soil

Logs or Railroad Ties

French Army Sod and Log Defensive Structure
This structure of the Franco-Prussian War (1871) and the First World War was usually built into a hill. The roofing was of logs covered with waterproof material (canvas, thatching) and then sod and soil. Drainage ditches were incorporated.

Hill

Sod

Water Drainage Space

Entrance

Drainage Ditch

Log Roof Supports

Sloping Roof for Drainage

Sod Beehive or Igloo House

Sod Tunnel Shelter

Sloping Roof for Drainage

Tarpaulin

Sod Turned Over

Sod Trench Shelter

Cutting of Sod

Rolling Sod or Turf

Turf or sod is soil with the root structure of grass to hold it together.

Sod family house from the Prairies. The roof would be of wood and thatching.

The secret of survival is to observe your surroundings and nature.

PLACING PEGS

The way you place your pegs is important because a well placed peg will: Reduce tent flap in the wind and make sure that your tent will stay up in a storm.

Angle Peg
Direction of force.
Very stable to lateral movement

Double Peg
Ground is soft.

Cord at ground level.
90°
Correct Way to Enter Peg

Cord at ground level.
Use a boulder to re-enforce peg if it cannot enter ground.

Line Tighteners
Used to adjust tent support lines. Can be either of aluminum or plastic.

COMMERCIAL PEGS

Plated Steel Pegs

A quality plastic stake peg. It is molded with a reinforcing rib and a foot push.

Iron Peg Used by army.

Steel Skewer Pegs For pebbly ground.

Nail Pegs

Plastic Stake Pegs

Aluminum Pegs High strength aluminum. For weight conscious backpackers.

Sand Peg Can be made by using a steel skewer and a flattened tin can.

Tent Peg Puller Removes all types of tent pegs. Hardened steel construction. Soft rubber handle.

Home Made Pegs Cut in the direction of the grain.

LOG CABIN

These shelters are built by forest dwellers in temperate climates from the Americas to Russia. Logs provide solid stable structures that are well insulated from the elements. Logs are placed as shown in the illustrations and mud/straw cement is placed between them as insulation. The design of the roof is important as it should extend over the wall that is exposed to the rain to prevent the rain from washing away the mud cement.

Saddle Notch

Log trimmed on one side only.

Log trimmed on two sides.
Placing insulation between logs.
Double Notch

Reduce wind flap.
Elastic cord.

Guy Line Adapter
Canopies, shelters and tents always stay firm. Prevents stress on grommets and material.

Guy Line Hitch
Rope can be adjusted by sliding lower knot up and down.

In hole on ice or hard snow. Fill with water to freeze.

Under rocks.

In water that will freeze.
Ice
Water

Buried in soft sand or snow.

Winter Deadman
If no pegs are available, ground is frozen or will not retain pegs.

COLD WEATHER TENT SUPPORT

During cold weather you have to plan the most efficient way to mount a tent. The taut-line and clove hitch are useful as they can be adjusted without being detached. The illustration also shows a deadman ground attachment. This deadman is made of a pole covered with boughs with snow being placed on the boughs to weigh them down.

Taut-Line Hitch: Permits variable adjustment of the ridge rope without having to untie it to adjust its length.
Clove Hitch: Permits variable adjustment as it can be raised or lowered and the pole can be moved in or out to remove wrinkles from the tent.

Deadman Branch buried in snow.

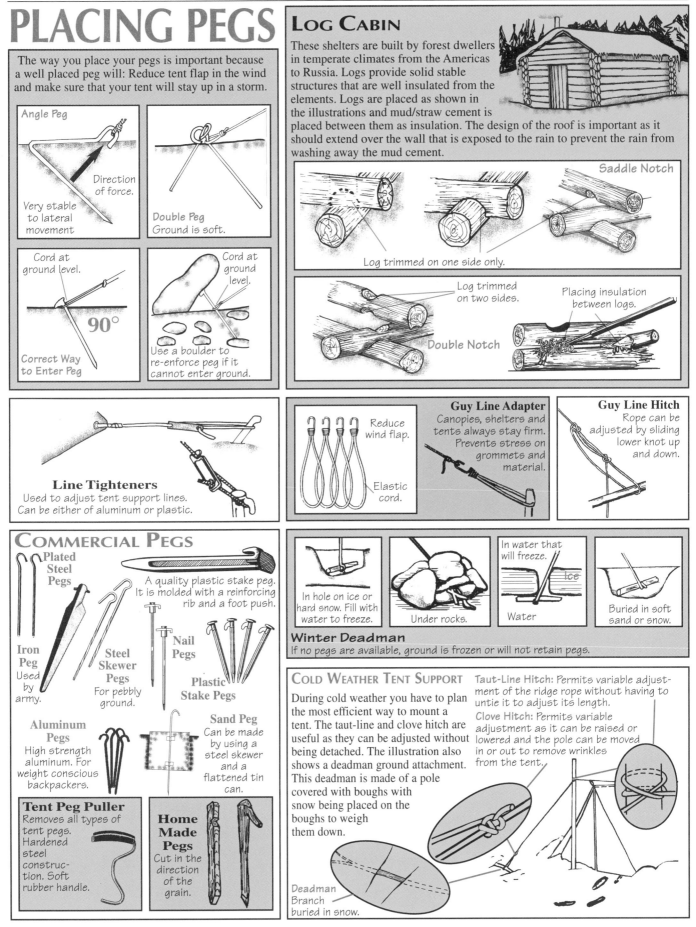

INDIAN SHELTERS

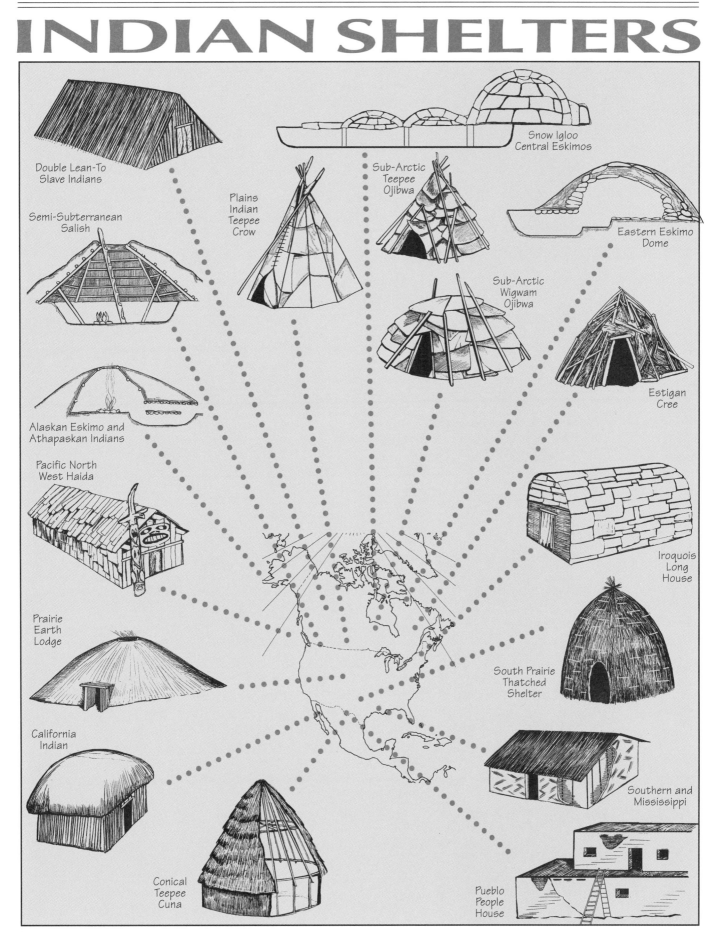

Double Lean-To
Slave Indians

Snow Igloo
Central Eskimos

Sub-Arctic
Teepee
Ojibwa

Eastern Eskimo
Dome

Semi-Subterranean
Salish

Plains
Indian
Teepee
Crow

Sub-Arctic
Wigwam
Ojibwa

Estigan
Cree

Alaskan Eskimo and
Athapaskan Indians

Pacific North
West Haida

Iroquois
Long
House

Prairie
Earth
Lodge

South Prairie
Thatched
Shelter

California
Indian

Southern and
Mississippi

Conical
Teepee
Cuna

Pueblo
People
House

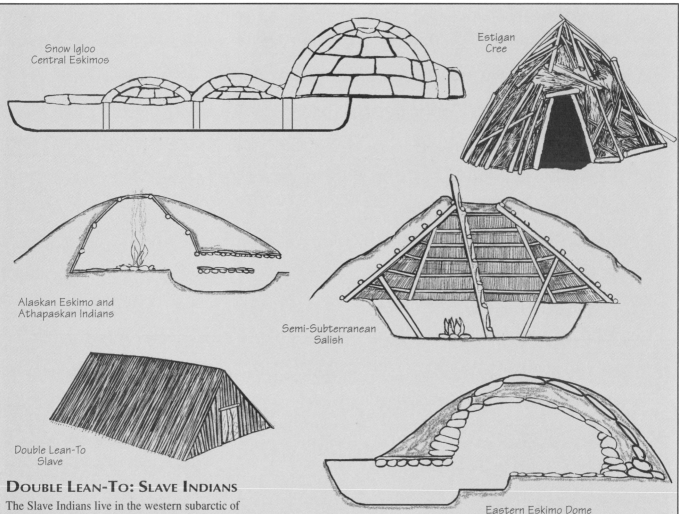

Snow Igloo
Central Eskimos

Estigan
Cree

Alaskan Eskimo and
Athapaskan Indians

Semi-Subterranean
Salish

Double Lean-To
Slave

Eastern Eskimo Dome

DOUBLE LEAN-TO: SLAVE INDIANS

The Slave Indians live in the western subarctic of North America. Double lean-tos are of similar construction as the survival lean-to, but larger. They have a wood frame and are covered with bark, hides, sod, and brush. The roof is low and the occupants crawl through the doorway. Usually made for a single family. A small fire can be made inside as the smoke goes through the overlapping material on the roof.

SEMI-SUBTERRANEAN: SALISH

The house was built over a pit dug two to three feet into the ground. The center pillar or pillars supported the roof. Teepee type rafters were placed on the pillars and they were covered with small sticks which were then thatched with bark, sod, and covered with earth. The ventilation hole in the middle of the roof also served as a door. In the winter the hole was partially covered with a skin.

ALASKAN ESKIMO & ATHAPASKAN INDIANS

This structure was built by the Alaskan Eskimos and the adjacent Indian tribes. Built of a framework of horizontal logs. The roof was of a rectangular pitched structure of logs. There was a center hole for smoke and lighting. The frame was covered with several feet of branches, earth, and sod. The doorway was the lower passage. The area above the passage was for storage. During cold weather the door was covered with layers of skin. The construction is similar to an igloo. The floor was covered with boughs and furs. The structure was usually large and occupied by a few families.

SNOW BLOCK IGLOO: CENTRAL ESKIMO

Used by the central Eskimos the igloo was made to be a permanent winter residence and was used by one extended family. The feature of a permanent igloo is the extended entrance which was negotiated on hands and knees. This tunnel was a wind break, used for cold storage, and helped to keep heat in the igloo. Outer layer clothing made of untanned fur was stored in the cold tunnel. A double door of hide was suspended at the main lodging area. During severe cold and wind more hides could be hung along the tunnel.

EASTERN ESKIMO DOME

Eastern Eskimos used an off-round structure whose arched roof was made with whale ribs, drift wood or stone slabs. The frame was covered with sod or stone up to five feet (1.5 m) high. The entrance was a low-level vaulted tunnel similar to the igloos. This structure was reused every winter. The structure was common property and belonged to the first occupant of the season.

ESKIGAN: CREE

Used by the Cree Indians who live in the James Bay area south of Hudson's Bay. The Cree live just south of the Eskimos and the Eskigan they build can be inhabited all year round even in the freezing winter of -55°F (-48°C) with the wind chill factor. As there are trees in this semi tundra area, logs are used to build a semi conical structure similar to a teepee. Logs are placed side by side and the cracks are filled with mud, moss and pieces of bark. The door usually is a blanket or animal hide. In the cold of winter there might be two or three hides for better insulation. These might even be a vestibule. The fire is built in the middle of the floor with a small opening in the center of the roof. This is not a smoke hole but the logs are not sealed in the top. The floor is covered with spruce boughs covered with a blanket or hide.

Sub-Arctic Teepee: Ojibwa

Sub-Arctic Indian Teepee and Wigwam: Ojibwa

Sub-Arctic Teepee Ojibwa

Prairie Earth Lodge

Sub-Arctic Wigwam Ojibwa

Iroquois Long House

Plains Indian Teepee: Crow

Fir and Rush Teepee: Prairie

Plains Indian Teepee: Crow

SUB-ARCTIC INDIAN TEEPEE: OJIBWA

The Ojibwas built a teepee and covered it with bark and pieces of hide (not sewn together). This covering was held in place by additional outside poles. Smoke escaped through a smoke hole at the top.

WIGWAM OJIBWA SUB-ARCTIC

These were used near the Western Great Lakes and called "Wigwam" in the Algonquin language. Similar in construction to the Sub-Artic teepee except that the poles were bent and tied together. The advantage over a teepee is that there is a lower wind profile and the more vertical walls give more headroom. They were covered by bark, hides, sewn or woven mats.

PRAIRIE EARTH LODGE

The frame was made of posts covered with smaller horizontal logs. These logs were covered with brush, sod, and then covered with earth. The floor, one to two feet below ground level, were covered with split logs. The inside of these multifamily lodges were up to 40 feet (13 m) in diameter.

PLAINS TEEPEE: CROW

The teepee is an ideal home, on the prairies, as it was easy to transport. The cover was a sewn buffalo hide, or by the 1890's denim, as most of the buffalo herds had disappeared. The cover was tailored for their poles. In winter, the floor was covered with buffalo hide which ran up the side to prevent drafts. Dogs dragged the poles with the buffalo hide when the settlement was following the buffalo herds. The poles were reused as the plains are treeless.

IROQUOIS LONG HOUSE

The Iroquois Indians lived in long houses that were up to 80 feet (24 m) long. Poles were set in the ground and supported by horizontal poles along the walls. The roof was made by bending a series of poles. The frame was covered by bark that was sewn in place and layered as shingles. Light poles were attached on the outside to hold down the shingles during a wind storm. Smoke from the cooking and heating fires passed through the losely attached bark covering. Separate families occupied booths on both sides of a central hallway. The booths had a wood platform on the ground and platforms for sleeping. Fires were in the central hallway and shared by the two facing families.

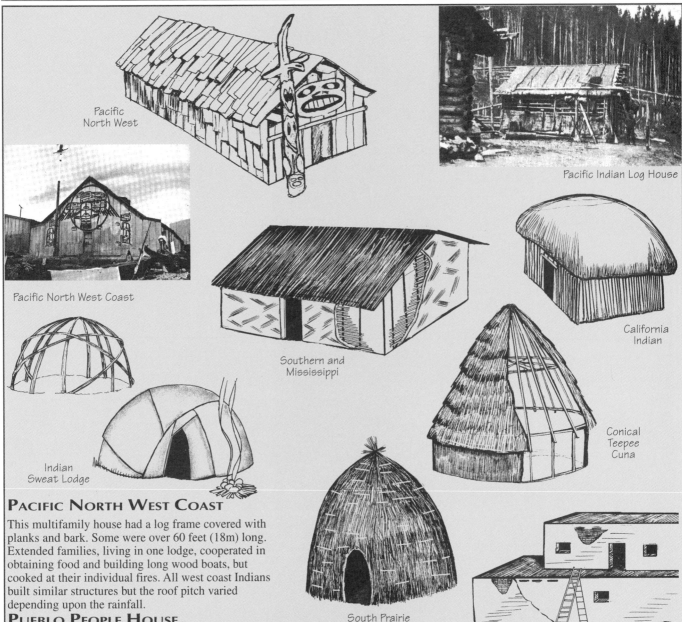

Pacific North West

Pacific Indian Log House

Pacific North West Coast

Southern and Mississippi

California Indian

Indian Sweat Lodge

Conical Teepee Cuna

South Prairie Thatched Shelter

Pueblo People House

PACIFIC NORTH WEST COAST

This multifamily house had a log frame covered with planks and bark. Some were over 60 feet (18m) long. Extended families, living in one lodge, cooperated in obtaining food and building long wood boats, but cooked at their individual fires. All west coast Indians built similar structures but the roof pitch varied depending upon the rainfall.

PUEBLO PEOPLE HOUSE

The Anasazi built large apartment structures that could house hundreds of people. The rectangular flat roof were supported by logs covered with mud and stones. The structures were multilevel, up to five stories, and accessible by ladders. Western Pueblo Indians built houses of stone which were covered with clay. The Indians of the Rio Grande built houses of clay mixed with grass.

CONICAL TEEPEES: CUNA

Conical teepees were covered with bark, brush, and wood. Sand was piled around the structure as a wind-break. This structure had many variants as per: height of roof, domed roof, flat roof, rectangular, and different pitches depending upon the climate.

CALIFORNIA INDIAN

They built houses that had a thatched roof and walls. Sometimes the walls were covered with mud which dried and became a stucco like surface. The roofs were domed or conical and sometimes covered with bark or thatched.

SOUTHERN MISSISSIPPI & CENTRAL PLAIN

Houses similar to those of the Iroquois except the roof was sloping instead of round. The walls were woven sticks (like wicker) and covered with mud or thatched. The roof was covered with bark or thatched in layers to repel the rain. The fire was in the middle with the smoke passing through the roofing. Winter houses were semi-subterranean similar to the earth lodge of the Prairies. Towns of up to 30,000 inhabitants were built.

SOUTH PRAIRIE THATCHED SHELTER

These southern Prairie houses similar to the teepee except that the framing poles were bent to join at the center. Horizontal poles were attached at intervals and covered with grass. The grass was kept in place by outside pole binders. A fire was made in the middle with the smoke passing through the thatching.

INDIAN SWEAT LODGE

A sweat lodge is a small domed structure of bent poles covered with hides, blankets and branches. A fire heats stones and the hot stones are carried into the lodge and water is poured over them. A hot dense cloud of steam is formed. Sweet grass and sage are placed on the rocks to perfume the steam. The bathers stay in the lodge as long as they can and then plunge into the river outside.

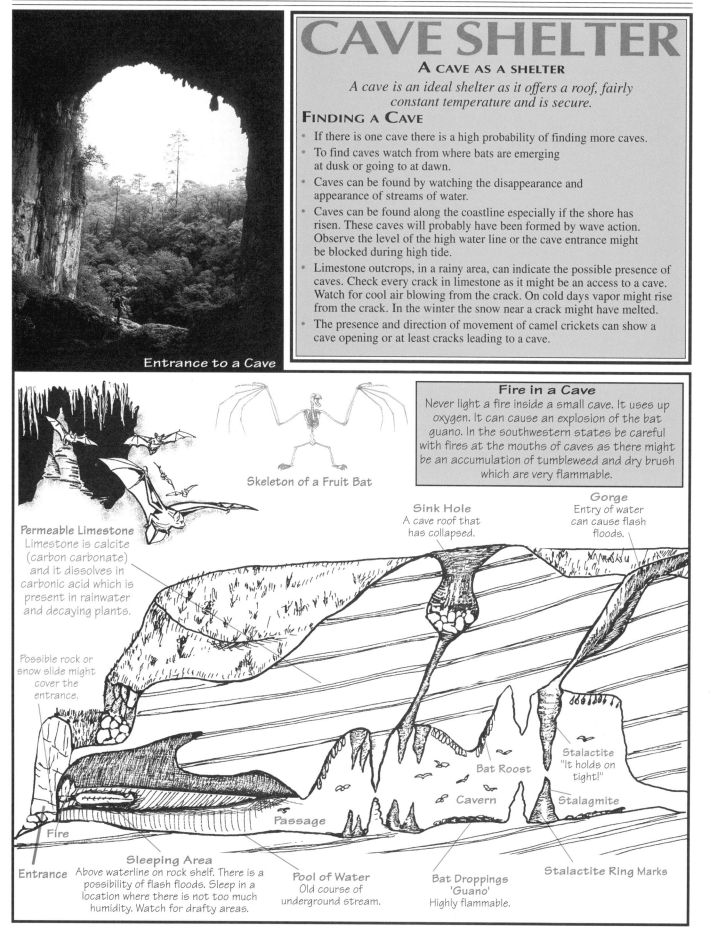

Entrance to a Cave

CAVE SHELTER

A CAVE AS A SHELTER

A cave is an ideal shelter as it offers a roof, fairly constant temperature and is secure.

FINDING A CAVE

- If there is one cave there is a high probability of finding more caves.
- To find caves watch from where bats are emerging at dusk or going to at dawn.
- Caves can be found by watching the disappearance and appearance of streams of water.
- Caves can be found along the coastline especially if the shore has risen. These caves will probably have been formed by wave action. Observe the level of the high water line or the cave entrance might be blocked during high tide.
- Limestone outcrops, in a rainy area, can indicate the possible presence of caves. Check every crack in limestone as it might be an access to a cave. Watch for cool air blowing from the crack. On cold days vapor might rise from the crack. In the winter the snow near a crack might have melted.
- The presence and direction of movement of camel crickets can show a cave opening or at least cracks leading to a cave.

Fire in a Cave

Never light a fire inside a small cave. It uses up oxygen. It can cause an explosion of the bat guano. In the southwestern states be careful with fires at the mouths of caves as there might be an accumulation of tumbleweed and dry brush which are very flammable.

Skeleton of a Fruit Bat

Permeable Limestone
Limestone is calcite (carbon carbonate) and it dissolves in carbonic acid which is present in rainwater and decaying plants.

Sink Hole
A cave roof that has collapsed.

Gorge
Entry of water can cause flash floods.

Possible rock or snow slide might cover the entrance.

Bat Roost

Stalactite
"It holds on tight!"

Cavern

Stalagmite

Passage

Fire

Stalactite Ring Marks

Entrance

Sleeping Area
Above waterline on rock shelf. There is a possibility of flash floods. Sleep in a location where there is not too much humidity. Watch for drafty areas.

Pool of Water
Old course of underground stream.

Bat Droppings
'Guano'
Highly flammable.

DANGERS

DANGERS IN A CAVE

- Beware of other occupants: rattle snakes, bats.
- Do not venture too far into a cave as there might be crevasses, slippery slopes, rock falls, etc.
- Build a fire just outside entrance far enough not to be smoked out or use up the oxygen.
- Place leaves, grass and branches on ground for a bed. Try to make a thick branch base or waterproof sheeting as it will be less humid.
- Avoid air currents in cave.
- Watch for water as cave might be a water funnel and water can rush through after a distant rain storm.

CAVE FLOODING

If there has been a recent rain storm in the area be on the lookout of a potential flash flood in the cave. It is possible that the cave system serves as a drainage funnel and there could be flooding.

Be alert to: changes in air movement, rising water level, unusual noise from the stream's flow or increasing debris or mud in the water. If you notice any changes *immediately* leave the cave or climb to a higher level.

CAVE AIR

- If you are short of breath and do not know why leave the cave immediately. You might have entered a pocket of bad air. This air might have been contaminated by rotting vegetation, and landfill seepage.
- Judging the quality of the air by the fact that there has been no effect on the flame of a carbide lamp is not a good standard. The human body has a lower danger point than a carbide flame.

Do Not Enter Old Mines
Danger of falling timber, bad air, vertical mine shafts, and collapsing passages.

CAVE DWELLERS

CAVES HAVE TWO ZONES

Twilight: Area used by rats, raccoons, porcupine, bears, skunks, and insects during part of the year. They use the twilight zone for protection from predators or the weather.

Total Darkness: Supports very specialized fauna. These consist of two categories: A group that only lives in caves (blind cave fish, cave salamander, shrimp, and snails) these commonly have no pigment and small eyes or no eyes at all. A group that can live in a cave or outside of the cave (salamanders, spiders, gnats, mosquitoes).

BATS

The most famous residents of caves are bats. They are the only flying mammals. There are two types of bats divided by the what they eat: insects or fruit.

Insect Eaters: Live in all temperate areas of in North America.

Fruit Eaters: Live in tropic climates, these are larger than the insect eaters. These are eaten as a delicacy on the Caribbean islands.

There might be two to a million bats in one cave. In the confined quarters of a cave bats do not usually attack humans but might bump into you in a tight passage in a cave. If bitten immediately wash the wound with hot soapy water for 15 minutes. *See a doctor as soon as possible.* Do not touch bats flapping on the ground as they might be sick. Bat droppings "guano" might fill the area below a large bat roost. *Guano is highly flammable and explosive in large quantities.* Do not disturb bats as they are part of the ecological system and eat large quantities of insects.

VAMPIRE BAT

The most famous bat of them all are vampire bats. They have been made famous or infamous by the legends of the sucking of blood of humans. These bats are not monsters that fly in front of a full moon. Vampire bats are part of the insect eater family. They are smaller than fruit eaters and larger than insect eaters. These bats drink the blood of animals especially cattle and midsize animals. They have *very sharp hollow teeth* through which they can suck blood. The saliva forms an anti coagulant preventing the teeth from clogging up.

Humans are not necessarily their favorite meal. If they bite a sleeping human they usually bite the uncovered feet. The human will usually feel nothing as the teeth are very sharp. The only indication that you have been bitten are small holes in the skin. *They are not dangerous but could be rabid.*

They live in South America and in the United States near the border of Mexico.

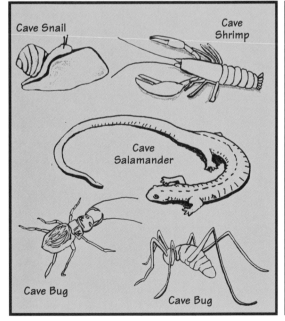

Cave Snail

Cave Shrimp

Cave Salamander

Cave Bug

Cave Bug

VISITING CAVES

- Watch for CO_2 as this shows an area lacking oxygen. To identify these areas watch a flame of a lantern or candle. If it starts to dim and seems to be trying to catch its breath leave the area immediately as there is a lack of oxygen.
- Wear a hard hat. You never know when you might bump your head or fall.
- A good lamp for caves is a carbide lamp. This is a lamp fueled by water drops dropping at regular intervals on calcium carbide this gives off acetylene gas which can be lit. Old cars had this system of lighting.
- A sudden downpour outside could cause a flash flood in the cave. Watch for indications of recent water flows in the cave. Make sure that entrance is not below high tide or waterline as your exit might become blocked.
- Do not venture too far into a cave as it might be dangerous. If an expedition is organized there should *never be less than 3 people*. If one gets injured then the other two can carry him out.

CAVE CONSERVATION RULES

- Do not leave anything behind.
- Do not take anything. Do not collect any plants or animals. Do not disturb the geological formations. Caves took thousands of years to form and can be destroyed in a few minutes.

WHAT YOU SHOULD KNOW ABOUT SNOW SHELTERS

Remember cold weather construction takes much energy.

Consider ...

•

How long will you stay?

•

How many people in the group?

•

How much energy can you use up?

•

Make the shelter as small as possible to make it easy to heat but still have enough space for your group and space to scrape snow and ice off clothing.

A snow shelter is an excellent way to stay warm and secure but the following should be observed:

• Watch for snow erosion on the outside walls. Blowing snow can be as abrasive as sandpaper and a whiteout can cause major damage. An inspection has to be made *after every storm* and additional snow should be piled up. If you are in a very windy area consider building a snow wall a few feet from the shelter.

• Remove some clothing, to reduce sweating, when doing physical work. Make sure your clothing is always dry as it should retain heat and also help avoid hypothermia.

• Clear snow accumulation from the entrance right after every storm. Build a snow wall if there is a problem of drifting.

• Do not overheat as the shelter will ice up and lose its insulation and breathing qualities. Overheating might also cause the roof to weaken and it might even collapse which could suffocate the occupants.

• Before entering, frost, ice, snow must be brushed off your clothing.

• All gasoline stoves and lanterns must be filled outside. On the inside they must be placed in a location where they will not be knocked over.

• A smaller shelter is easier to heat.

• Drips can be stopped by placing snow on their source.

• Keep a digging tool in the shelter as you might have to dig yourself out.

• Check the ventilation holes frequently as they might be blocked with snow and the carbon monoxide and humidity cannot escape. At least two holes are required, one at the top, to let air escape, and one near the ground to let in fresh air.

• Make sure that you always have a supply of fuel and food, *stored at a low and cold level*, in the shelter as unexpected bad weather might set in and last for days.

• Clearly mark the entrance and remember the physical characteristics of your surroundings. This will help you find your shelter if a storm suddenly arrises.

• Staying in a snow shelter can be boring. If there is a group every person should be assigned a task that can be rotated. Tasks can be divided into: tending the fire *at all times*, gathering fuel, preparing food, gathering food, hunting in pairs, checking vent holes, checking structure, and watching for the possibility of signaling to a search party in a survival situation. These tasks should be viewed as entertainment especially when morale has to be raised.

• In the inside of a well built snow shelter the temperature will always be above 32°F (0°C). A survival candle will easily raise the temperature by 10°F (4°C). *See article on Eskimo Koolik.*

WINTER SHELTER

Winter Camp
The best location for a camp is in a thick forest, in a hollow, or a protected valley and out of the wind. Use as much natural insulation as possible. Dig into the snow, build wind breaks, and cover the shelter with boughs.

Snow Cornice

Do not build below a snow cornice as it might collapse or cause an avalanche

Evergreens, with their large low branches, make an temporary shelter or hunting position.

TREE SNOW SHELTER

Branches can be cut away from underside or you can tunnel into the snow drift below a large evergreen tree. The door should be at right angle to the wind. For insulation place a pile of evergreen boughs on the ground.

Snow is an excellent insulating material that keeps you warm, safe, and dry.

TREE-PIT

Select a large tree with thick lower branches and surrounded with deep snow. Below the tree you will find a pit with less snow. This area can be enlarged and you can dig deeper, even to ground level. As insulation you can collect tree branches from other trees and cover the bottom and walls. As roofing you can use a poncho or other material covered with snow. Position the entrance out of the wind's way. Make a small pit shelter to retain as much heat as possible.

The secret of survival is to observe your surroundings and nature.

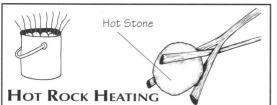

HOT ROCK HEATING

If you have a fire burning you can add some large rocks and let them heat for an hour. Dig a hole in the ground to the depth of your stones. The glowing hot stones are then picked up with sticks and dropped in the hole. Cover with some earth and place your sleeping bag over this warm spot.

No combustible material should be near the hot rocks as a fire could start up or you can be smoked out of your shelter.

HEATING

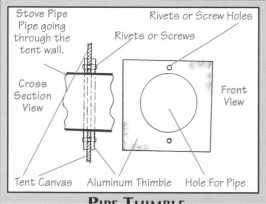

PIPE THIMBLE

If you install a stove with a chimney in a tent you need a pipe thimble. The thimble creates a barrier between the tent material and the hot pipe. This thimble is made of two sheets of aluminum riveted together.

Only use a stove in an approved tent.

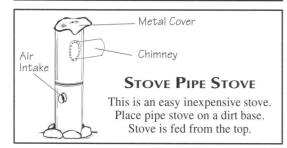

STOVE PIPE STOVE

This is an easy inexpensive stove. Place pipe stove on a dirt base. Stove is fed from the top.

USING HOT ROCKS TO HEAT BED

To keep warm while sleeping on the ground place large dry flat stones on the burning wood in the fire pit. Before going to sleep scrap the remaining burning wood to one side, removing all burning particles. Leave the hot stones in the pit and cover this warm area with a layer of sand. Place your ground cloth and sleeping bag over this spot and have a warm night.

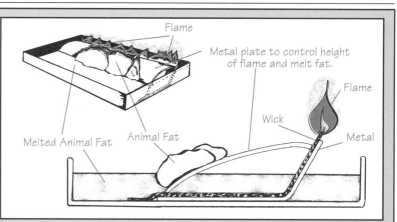

KOOLIK

The Eskimos have used the koolik for thousands of years. The Eskimo koolik is carved from soapstone but it can be made out of any flat metal container.

A piece of cloth, absorbent cotton, or dense moss can be used as a wick. The heat can be controlled by changing the length of the wick and by the metal or stone damper covering the wick . To avoid smoke animal fats are used as fuel, in the case of the Eskimos, seal oil or caribou fat. Lubricating oil can be burned but the wick will have to be frequently trimmed so that the flame will not smoke. Gasoline cannot be used as it is very explosive. Two or three drops of gasoline can be put on the wick to start the fire.

The koolik is used for heating, light and cooking. It is seated on sticks that have been pushed into the snow shelf. The cooking pot would be suspended from hooks pierced into the snow wall.

TIN CAN STOVE

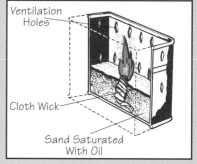

This stove can be made with any large tin can. For ventilation pierce holes on the sides of the can. Partially fill the can with fine sand while holding a cloth wick in place. Saturate the sand with aircraft fuel or oil. Do not pour too much fuel and *do not add fuel until the stove and sand are cold*. This stove can be used for heating and cooking. Make sure that there is sufficient ventilation.

Bulrush Sleeping Bag

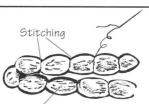

Use bulrushes (cattail) as insulation to make an emergency sleeping bag. Collect the hair from ripe bulrushes, fluff it up, place it between two layers of material, and stitch the insulation in place. Ripe bulrushes can be found in humid areas or drainage ditches all winter.

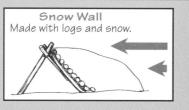

SNOW WALL

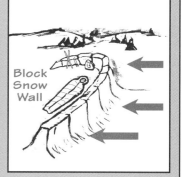

In open areas a snow wall can be built as protection against strong winds and blowing snow. Make sure that you do not get covered by drifting snow on the lee side of the wall.

SNOW CAVE

Ventilation Hole

Smoke

Ground Sheet or Evergreen Boughs

Heating

Bedding

Backpack in Entrance

Entrance

Living Platform

LOCATION FOR A SNOW CAVE

- Dig into a hard snow drift, or a slope with a firm crust. This is usually found on the lee side (the opposite side from which the wind is blowing) of a steep ridge or river bank. The snow drift should be at least 9' (3 m) deep. Snow that is newly fallen, powdery, or loose should be avoided.
- Before digging test the depth of the snow and also its consistency by probing with sticks, ski pole, or skis.
- The entrance should be 45° downwind so that the wind will keep it free of snow.
- Make sure that the drift is not below a cornice or in an avalanche area.

BUILDING A SNOW CAVE

- The shelter should be as small as possible so that minimum heating is required. A lit candle can raise the temperature to 40°F (4°C). It is better to build one large cave for numerous occupants than many small ones. It uses less fuel to heat and less energy to build. When a large cave is built it can be made to suit the physical constraints of the terrain and short side tunnels can be built for sleeping quarters, latrine, storage space, and kitchen.
- A small tunnel is burrowed, at the lowest level of the chamber, for one yard (one meter).
- A chamber is now dug at right angles to the tunnel entrance.
- The chamber should be high enough to provide comfortable sitting space.
- The sleeping and sitting platform should be *above* the level of the entrance. This will be the warmest area of the cave.
- The roof should be well arched, without sharp gauges, to provide the maximum support. Gauges would be week spots as there would be a shearing in the packed snow. The arching would also prevent water from dripping on the floor as it would flow along the slope and ice up.
- The roof should be at least 18" (30 cm) thick.
- There should be a roof ventilation hole to allow carbon monoxide gases and smoke to escape and to asphyxiation. There should also be a ventilation hole in the door to allow fresh air to enter. These should be checked every two to three hours.

LIVING IN A SNOW CAVE

- Heating with gas stove or candles. These should be extinguished when occupants are asleep. If weather is very cold one person will have to stay awake to watch the fire and the ventilation holes.
- The entrance should be small and can be blocked with a hard piece of snow or backpacks but leave a small crack, near the floor, for fresh air to enter.
- Ponchos, cardboard, and tree branches can be used for ground blankets.
- When you are cooking you might consider leaving the door open.
- Do not walk on the roof as it might collapse.
- Chores can be assigned to different individuals to assure that everything is taken care off, to avoid any conflicts in a confined area and to reduce boredom.

Carbon monoxide gas is colorless, tasteless and odorless.

Carbon monoxide gas is the highest risk of death in a well insulated environment.

It is produced by incomplete combustion when there is a lack of oxygen to turn the burnt product into carbon dioxide (CO_2). Hemoglobin in the blood will absorb carbon monoxide two hundred times faster than oxygen. It breaks down the hemoglobin's ability to absorb oxygen and the body will starve of oxygen. Carbon monoxide *is cumulative* and can accumulate over a number of days.

You will *not* know that you are lacking oxygen as you will *not* be short of breath *nor* have a bluish discoloration of the fingernails, lips or the skin.

The first signs of carbon monoxide poisoning are fainting and collapsing. Further effects are nausea, frontal headaches, and decreased mental capacity. The brain requires a large supply of oxygen to function.

To eliminate carbon monoxide from the system one requires four hours of fresh air to reduce the carbon monoxide by one half.

VENTILATION

Cross-ventilation is required to have a sufficient change of air in restricted quarters, especially when using interior oil, gas, or charcoal heaters. *In cold regions carbon monoxide is a common cause of death because shelters are well insulated.* Ventilation and awareness of potential carbon monoxide problems are extremely important in building a shelter.

CARBON MONOXIDE (CO)

SNOW CAVE SURVIVAL

- It is important to have an air vent 3 to 4 inches (7-10 cm) in diameter.
- Try to dig to ground level as the exposed ground has its own built-in heat supply.
- If there is a frosty coating on the ceiling after a cold night this indicates that the roof is too thin, add more snow on the roof.
- After a few days the ceiling can ice. Scrape the ceiling because the roof should "breathe" to prevent the air from being stuffy and risking a buildup of carbon monoxide.
- If ceiling arches there should be no problem with the ceiling collapsing.
- If the roof sags, scrape the inside to raise the ceiling's height. If possible cook outside.
- The snow cave is most comfortable during extreme cold. It will be humid and drippy when there is too much heat or it is warm outside.
- Take all your equipment into the snow cave as a snowstorm can bury everything.
- Sleeping bags should be turned inside out. Beat out the frost and fluff them up.
- Do not let candles or a stove burn all night as this might deplete the oxygen.
- Mark the entrance of the cave so that you will find it in the white wilderness. This is especially true if there are potential whiteouts or the land has no distinguishing features.

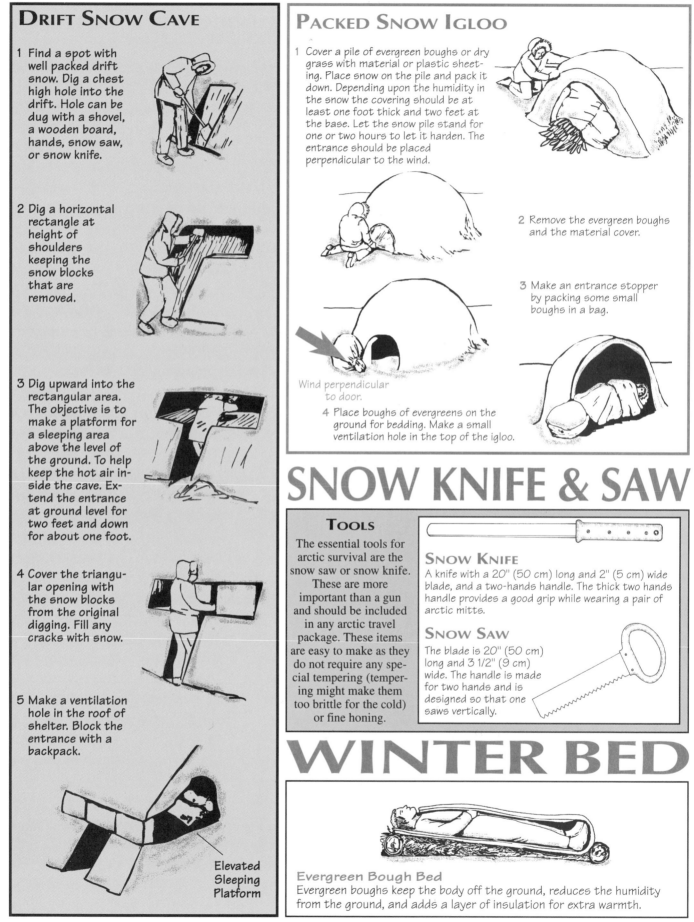

DRIFT SNOW CAVE

1. Find a spot with well packed drift snow. Dig a chest high hole into the drift. Hole can be dug with a shovel, a wooden board, hands, snow saw, or snow knife.

2. Dig a horizontal rectangle at height of shoulders keeping the snow blocks that are removed.

3. Dig upward into the rectangular area. The objective is to make a platform for a sleeping area above the level of the ground. To help keep the hot air inside the cave. Extend the entrance at ground level for two feet and down for about one foot.

4. Cover the triangular opening with the snow blocks from the original digging. Fill any cracks with snow.

5. Make a ventilation hole in the roof of shelter. Block the entrance with a backpack.

Elevated Sleeping Platform

PACKED SNOW IGLOO

1. Cover a pile of evergreen boughs or dry grass with material or plastic sheeting. Place snow on the pile and pack it down. Depending upon the humidity in the snow the covering should be at least one foot thick and two feet at the base. Let the snow pile stand for one or two hours to let it harden. The entrance should be placed perpendicular to the wind.

2. Remove the evergreen boughs and the material cover.

3. Make an entrance stopper by packing some small boughs in a bag.

Wind perpendicular to door.

4. Place boughs of evergreens on the ground for bedding. Make a small ventilation hole in the top of the igloo.

SNOW KNIFE & SAW

TOOLS

The essential tools for arctic survival are the snow saw or snow knife. These are more important than a gun and should be included in any arctic travel package. These items are easy to make as they do not require any special tempering (tempering might make them too brittle for the cold) or fine honing.

SNOW KNIFE

A knife with a 20" (50 cm) long and 2" (5 cm) wide blade, and a two-hands handle. The thick two hands handle provides a good grip while wearing a pair of arctic mitts.

SNOW SAW

The blade is 20" (50 cm) long and 3 1/2" (9 cm) wide. The handle is made for two hands and is designed so that one saws vertically.

WINTER BED

Evergreen Bough Bed

Evergreen boughs keep the body off the ground, reduces the humidity from the ground, and adds a layer of insulation for extra warmth.

MILITARY FIGHTER TRENCH

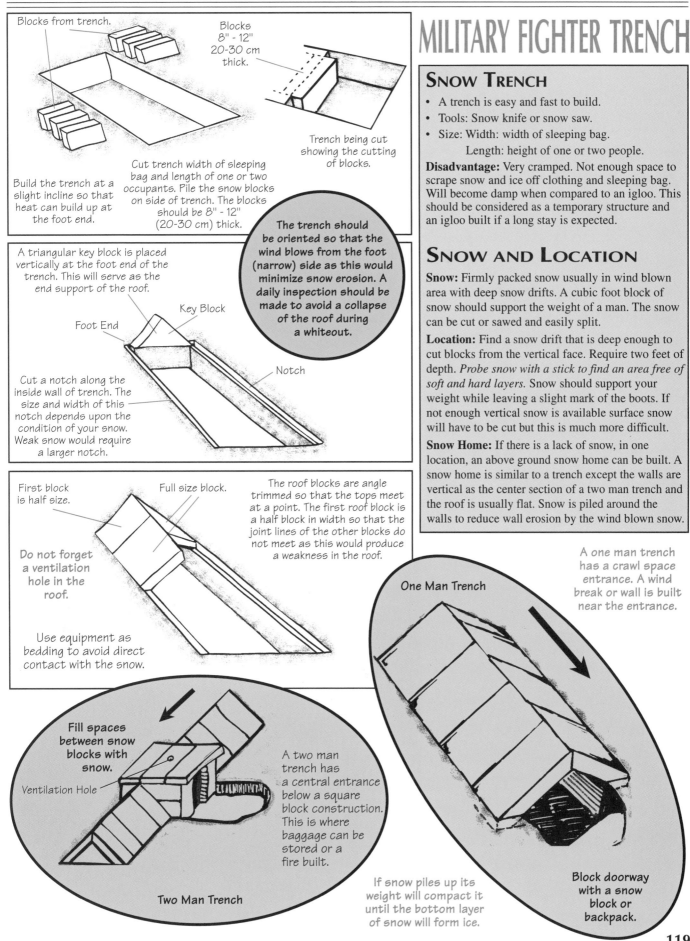

Blocks from trench.

Blocks 8" - 12" 20-30 cm thick.

Trench being cut showing the cutting of blocks.

Build the trench at a slight incline so that heat can build up at the foot end.

Cut trench width of sleeping bag and length of one or two occupants. Pile the snow blocks on side of trench. The blocks should be 8" - 12" (20-30 cm) thick.

The trench should be oriented so that the wind blows from the foot (narrow) side as this would minimize snow erosion. A daily inspection should be made to avoid a collapse of the roof during a whiteout.

A triangular key block is placed vertically at the foot end of the trench. This will serve as the end support of the roof.

Key Block

Foot End

Cut a notch along the inside wall of trench. The size and width of this notch depends upon the condition of your snow. Weak snow would require a larger notch.

Notch

First block is half size.

Full size block.

The roof blocks are angle trimmed so that the tops meet at a point. The first roof block is a half block in width so that the joint lines of the other blocks do not meet as this would produce a weakness in the roof.

Do not forget a ventilation hole in the roof.

Use equipment as bedding to avoid direct contact with the snow.

SNOW TRENCH

- A trench is easy and fast to build.
- Tools: Snow knife or snow saw.
- Size: Width: width of sleeping bag.
  Length: height of one or two people.

Disadvantage: Very cramped. Not enough space to scrape snow and ice off clothing and sleeping bag. Will become damp when compared to an igloo. This should be considered as a temporary structure and an igloo built if a long stay is expected.

SNOW AND LOCATION

Snow: Firmly packed snow usually in wind blown area with deep snow drifts. A cubic foot block of snow should support the weight of a man. The snow can be cut or sawed and easily split.

Location: Find a snow drift that is deep enough to cut blocks from the vertical face. Require two feet of depth. *Probe snow with a stick to find an area free of soft and hard layers.* Snow should support your weight while leaving a slight mark of the boots. If not enough vertical snow is available surface snow will have to be cut but this is much more difficult.

Snow Home: If there is a lack of snow, in one location, an above ground snow home can be built. A snow home is similar to a trench except the walls are vertical as the center section of a two man trench and the roof is usually flat. Snow is piled around the walls to reduce wall erosion by the wind blown snow.

A one man trench has a crawl space entrance. A wind break or wall is built near the entrance.

One Man Trench

Fill spaces between snow blocks with snow.

Ventilation Hole

A two man trench has a central entrance below a square block construction. This is where baggage can be stored or a fire built.

Two Man Trench

If snow piles up its weight will compact it until the bottom layer of snow will form ice.

Block doorway with a snow block or backpack.

The secret of survival is to observe your surroundings and nature.

ESKIMO IGLOO

Eskimos say that in the barren north you need a large knife or you need a miracle to survive.

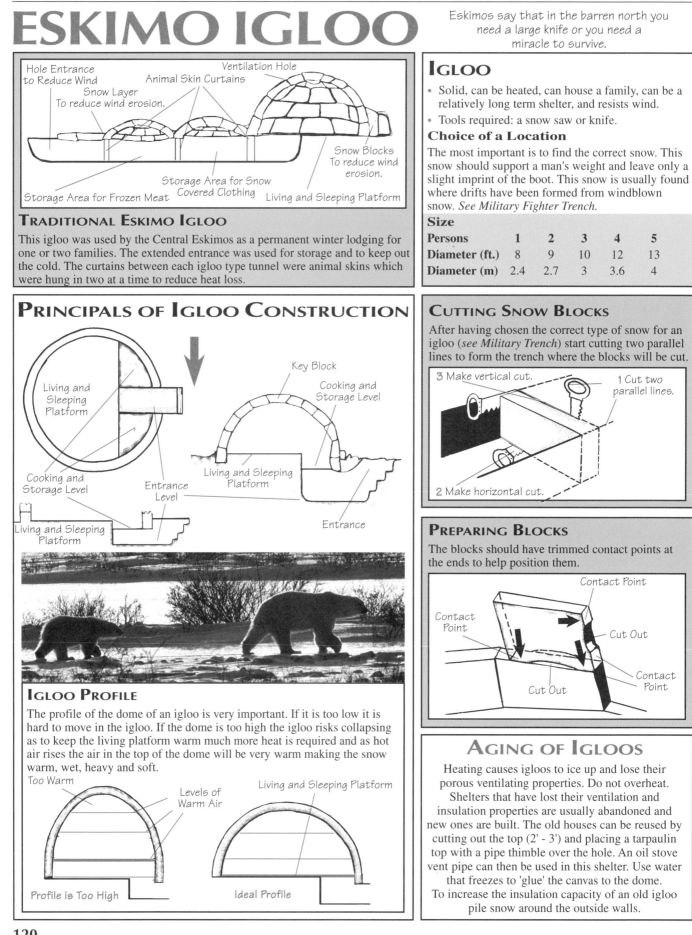

TRADITIONAL ESKIMO IGLOO

This igloo was used by the Central Eskimos as a permanent winter lodging for one or two families. The extended entrance was used for storage and to keep out the cold. The curtains between each igloo type tunnel were animal skins which were hung in two at a time to reduce heat loss.

IGLOO

- Solid, can be heated, can house a family, can be a relatively long term shelter, and resists wind.
- Tools required: a snow saw or knife.

Choice of a Location

The most important is to find the correct snow. This snow should support a man's weight and leave only a slight imprint of the boot. This snow is usually found where drifts have been formed from windblown snow. *See Military Fighter Trench.*

Size

Persons	1	2	3	4	5
Diameter (ft.)	8	9	10	12	13
Diameter (m)	2.4	2.7	3	3.6	4

PRINCIPALS OF IGLOO CONSTRUCTION

CUTTING SNOW BLOCKS

After having chosen the correct type of snow for an igloo (*see Military Trench*) start cutting two parallel lines to form the trench where the blocks will be cut.

PREPARING BLOCKS

The blocks should have trimmed contact points at the ends to help position them.

IGLOO PROFILE

The profile of the dome of an igloo is very important. If it is too low it is hard to move in the igloo. If the dome is too high the igloo risks collapsing as to keep the living platform warm much more heat is required and as hot air rises the air in the top of the dome will be very warm making the snow warm, wet, heavy and soft.

AGING OF IGLOOS

Heating causes igloos to ice up and lose their porous ventilating properties. Do not overheat. Shelters that have lost their ventilation and insulation properties are usually abandoned and new ones are built. The old houses can be reused by cutting out the top (2' - 3') and placing a tarpaulin top with a pipe thimble over the hole. An oil stove vent pipe can then be used in this shelter. Use water that freezes to 'glue' the canvas to the dome.
To increase the insulation capacity of an old igloo pile snow around the outside walls.

IGLOO CONSTRUCTION

TWO TYPES OF IGLOOS

Flat Tier Model: Blocks are placed horizontally in layers as bricks.

Spiral Model: Blocks are inclined and gradually slope to the top. This method is easier for a beginner as the successive rows tie in better reducing the chance of collapse. *Below is a description of the spiral method.*

Spiral Model
Layout of Floor

In an area where the snow is at least two feet deep draw a circle with a diameter as per the occupant chart on the surface of the snow. This will be the *inside* diameter of the igloo. Layout the circle with the direction of the door perpendicular to the wind.

Lay a line A-B perpendicular to the door approximately 1/3 the diameter from the door. This moon shaped floor area will produce some blocks and become the storage, cooking, and exit area.

Blocks Cut From Part of Floor Area

Blocks 40 x 40 x 80 cm (15 x 15 x 30 inches) are cut from the floor inside of the circle and placed outside of the circle. These blocks will then be split. *See adjacent article.*

Starting First Layer of Blocks

To start the first layer place a full-sized block on the *outside* of the circle. Adjacent to it place a block with a slope cut into it. This will give the igloo its spiral form. The third and fourth blocks will also have a slope then full blocks are used.

Second Layer and Other Layers

The blocks will start to tilt inwards and be trimmed for the contact points mentioned on the previous page.

To lay the layers of snow blocks the person stays inside the igloo and then will dig himself out.

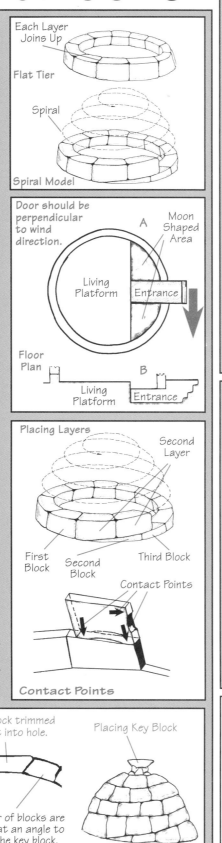

Each Layer Joins Up

Flat Tier

Spiral

Spiral Model

Door should be perpendicular to wind direction.

A

Moon Shaped Area

Living Platform

Entrance

Floor Plan

B

Living Platform

Entrance

Placing Layers

Second Layer

First Block

Second Block

Third Block

Contact Points

Contact Points

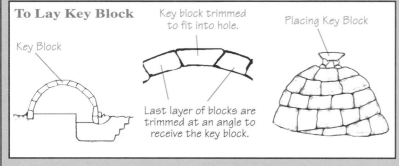

To Lay Key Block

Key Block

Key block trimmed to fit into hole.

Placing Key Block

Last layer of blocks are trimmed at an angle to receive the key block.

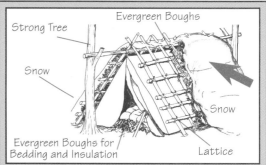

Curtain
Double layer if possible.

Entrance

Ski Pole

Snow Shoe

Snow Blocks

Sleeping Platform

Tarpaulin Cover

SNOW TRENCH

Material Required: Ski poles, snow shoes, or skis; a 5' x 7' (1.5 x 2) tarpaulin, waterproof nylon sheet, or tube tent.

Construction: Choose a spot where the snow is deep and relatively soft. Stamp down the snow *with* snowshoes or skis. The size of the depression should be a bit larger than your body. Complete stamping without snowshoes. Collect some evergreen boughs and lay the boughs in the stamped area. Place the ski poles, snow shoes, or skis across the depression and cover them with the tarpaulin. Weigh the tarpaulin down with blocks of snow. Place a curtain across the doorway.

Strong Tree

Evergreen Boughs

Snow

Snow

Evergreen Boughs for Bedding and Insulation

Lattice

INSULATING A TENT

The tent should be erected perpendicular to the prevailing wind to avoid snow accumulation in front of the entrance. Place a lattice frame over the tent and cover it with evergreen boughs. Slip branches of the boughs through the lattice to attach them. Throw a layer of snow over the boughs and add to the layer every few days as it will melt and get eroded by blowing snow. Powder snow is a good insulation as there are many air pockets.

Splitting Igloo Blocks

Cut Groove

The blocks from the floor area are split on the large flat side. To split cut a groove, with your saw, two inches wide at each *end* of the block six inches (15 cm) from the face. Then score a groove along the length of the block parallel to the surface joining the cut grooves. Cut with a saw between the two inch groves and the block will break apart. If using a snow knife deepen the groove by continuous scoring and then with a firm stroke the block will separate.

Score Groove

FIRE AND SURVIVAL

Fire has a strong positive psychological impact upon an individual in a survival situation.

Fire is the most important survival tool after your personal wilderness knowledge, maintenance of calm and a positive attitude.

- Fire provides warmth which helps your mind have a positive approach.
- Fire makes you feel protected from all "those wild animals out there in the shadows".
- Fire lets you cook meals and use many edible plants that would otherwise be hard to prepare.
- Wet clothing can be dried in a fire. This can help you to avoid hypothermia.
- Water can be boiled for purification.
- Fire can be used to send smoke signals.
- Fire can be used to burn the end of a stick to make a pointed spear.
- Fire and smoke can repel insects.
- Fire can be used to burn trunks or large sticks so that they are more manageable to be used for construction of a shelter.
- Smoke can be used to smoke out wild bees to access their honey.
- Fire can be used to smoke small animals out of their burrows into traps.
- Fire torches, at night, can be used to blind fish in shallow streams making them easier to capture.

Building a fire, when needed, will increase your ability to survive in the wilderness. Build a fire as soon as you have a basic shelter. You can improve on your shelter, once you have a fire going, in the dark.

You should appreciate the importance of fire and know the different methods of starting a fire, transporting fire, and building a fire to fill your needs. Always keep a case of waterproof matches on you body.

FIRE MAKING CHAPTER 10

Build a small fire as it requires less energy, burns wood at a slower rate, and is easier to control. To maximize heat build a series of small fires, in a circle, around your encampment.

SITE FOR A FIRE

- Avoid windy areas as the fire can flare up and burn out of control. If required build a reflector or windbreak out of green wood, rocks, or dig a pit. The advantage of a reflector is that it concentrates the heat in the desired direction.
- Clear the camp ground of *all inflammable material* before starting a fire. Rake towards centre where you will burn all the dead leaves, pine needles, and other debris then clear a perimeter outwards from the fire area.
- Do not build a fire against an old log or tree trunk as it may smolder for days and burst into flame when fanned by a breeze.
- Do not build a fire below the boughs of a tree as they will be dried by the heat and might catch fire.
- Before decamping make sure that all sparks of the fire have been put out by thoroughly drenching or smothering it completely with wet earth or sand.
- If the ground is wet or snow covered build a platform of green or wet logs or stones. Do not use wet or large humid rocks as they might explode when they are heated.

MATCHES

Matches are the easiest way to make a fire. Always carry matches on you. Carry matches in a waterproof container in you backpack, in your pant pockets *and* your jacket. Make sure the matches will not fall out of your pockets even when you fall out of a boat.

LIGHTING A MATCH IN THE WIND

Strike the tip of the match on a dry surface to light the match.

To light a match in the wind:

- Face the wind.
- Cup your hands against the wind.
- Hold the match with its head pointing down and towards the wind.
- Strike the match with the right hand and rapidly resume the former cupped position.
- Because of the wind the flame will run up the match stick having something to feed on.

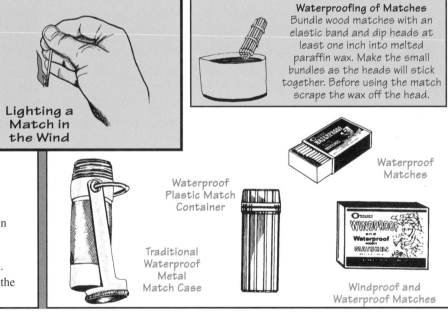

Lighting a Match in the Wind

Waterproofing of Matches
Bundle wood matches with an elastic band and dip heads at least one inch into melted paraffin wax. Make the small bundles as the heads will stick together. Before using the match scrape the wax off the head.

Waterproof Matches

Waterproof Plastic Match Container

Traditional Waterproof Metal Match Case

WINDPROOF and Waterproof MATCHES

Windproof and Waterproof Matches

Types of Wood

Hardwood

In general hardwoods make good, slow burning fires that yield long lasting coals.
These trees have broad leaves which most of them loose in the fall (deciduous).
Hardwoods are not necessarily always harder than softwoods.

•

Softwood

Softwoods make a hot fast fire that is short-lived.
These trees have needles (flat needles: cedars, round needles: pine) and cones. This is why they are called conifers.
Most are evergreen (do not loss their needles) excepting larch, cypress, and tamarack.

•

Wood for a Fire

You have to know:
• The relative heating value of different woods.
• How well each wood burns in the green state.
• Which wood makes long lasting coals and which on dies down to ashes.
• Which wood pops when burning and casts embers that may burn holes in bedding, cloths, tents, and possibly cause a forest fire.
• Difficulty in splitting.
• Ease of lighting.

SEASONING OF WOOD

When a live tree is cut into logs the wood is said to be "green" as there is sap in the cells of the wood. When the wood is dried it is called *seasoned* wood which usually produces a better fire.

Seasoning time depends upon the size of log, its age when cut (older trees have less sap), season of cutting, and climate.

Medium sized logs of apple, oak, hickory will season in one year and if exposed to the summer sun in only a few months.

Green Wood
This wood has not been dried out or seasoned. All woods do not have to be seasoned to be used for fuel. Green wood can be used as reflectors for a fire and as a support for pots.

Seasoned Wood
Contraction cracks radiating from the center of logs. This does not necessarily mean that it is easier to split as it depends upon the characteristic of each wood.

WHY DOES WOOD BURN? ... PYROLYSIS!

The correct amount of oxygen, in the presence of a high enough temperature to ignite the different compounds in the wood, are required. If one of these elements is missing wood will not burn. The oxygen and temperature required varies with the type of the wood.

Pyrolysis is produced inside wood, in the absence of oxygen, by high temperatures that chemically breaks up the wood and releases gases that burn further heating the wood thus releasing more gases...

Logs added to the fire, before burning, are heated to above 540°F (282°C), undergoing pyrolysis, giving off gases and burning. Gases need enough oxygen and a temperature of 1000°F (537°C) to burn. A flame ignites the gases.

PEAT MOSS

Peat moss is an accumulation of plant deposits that have collected in swamps and bogs over thousands of years. The plant debris did not decompose as it lacked oxygen. The peat moss is removed by slicing it like blocks of snow. On harvesting it is dried before use. Peat is found in different areas of the United States and Canada. It can be used to make peat fires and was used during the colonist times.

CHOOSE THE CORRECT WOOD

FEATURES OF DIFFERENT TREES TO CONSIDER IN CHOOSING FIREWOOD

Feature Softwoods	Example	Special Characteristics
SOFTWOODS		*Only when seasoned; good for kindling, quick cooking fire, split easily, shave readily, catch fire easily. Wood growing along streams is usually softwood so driftwood is usually a bad choice of fuel unless available in large quantities.*
	Balsam fir, basswood, white pines	Quick fires soon spent.
	Gray (Labrador), pine (jack pine)	*Considered good fuel in the north where hardwoods are scarce.*
	Tamarack	When seasoned is good.
	Spruce	Poor fuel, being resinous it kindles easily and makes a good blaze for building up a fire.
	Pitch pine	*Most flammable of all woods when dry ('fat' with much resin). Will hardly burn in green state.*
	Yellow pine	Burns well as its sap is resinous instead of being watery as soft pines.
	Red cedar	Hard to ignite and start with small pieces.

FEATURES OF DIFFERENT TREES TO CONSIDER IN CHOOSING FIREWOOD

HARDWOODS

Feature	Example	Special characteristics
Best fuel Hardwoods	Northern: hickory, green or dry South: oak and holly chestnut oak, overcup, white, blackjack, post and basket oaks, pecan, ironwood, Magnolia, tulip, catalpa, willow	*Hot fire, lasts a long time, bed of hard coals that heats for hours.* Poor fuels.
	Dogwood, applewood	Burns to a characteristic white ash.
	Black birch birch: in order of black, yellow, red, paper, white	Oil in the birch assists in combustion.
	Seasoned chestnut and yellow poplar	Hot fire, crackle, no coals.
	Sugar maple (a favorite)	Ignites easily, clear steady flame, leaves good coals.
	Locust, mulberry (excellent night wood)	Lasting fuel, easy to cut, splits well when green, thick bark takes fire readily, wood burns slowly, leaves good coals.
	White ash (best of green woods)	Easy to cut and split, lighter to carry than most hardwoods, and is normally so dry that even green wood easily catches fire. Burns with a clear flame, and lasts.
	Sycamore, buckeye	Good fuel when seasoned, will not split.
	Northern poplar (large toothed aspen)	*Dry: gives off intense heat with nearly no smoke, lasts well, does not blacken utensils. Favorite cooking fire.*
	Alder	Burns easily but does not last long.
Bad fuels Hardwood	Scarlet and willow oaks	Poorest of hardwoods for fuel.
	White elm, slippery elm	Poor.

SPACING OF WOOD FOR AN EFFICIENT FIRE

Wood Too Close
Lacks sufficient air to sustain a fire, the temperature drops, and it will go out. Blowing air into the cavity would keep the fire burning. If the pieces of wood were resting on green wood or a metal grate leaving an air space below the burning pieces there might be an updraft to help the wood burn.

Correct Distance
Good balance of air and heat to let the fire burn. While the wood will burn very well the fact that it is burning will enlarge the spacing and you should stoke the fire so that the remaining wood will be pushed closer together or additional fuel added.

Splitting Wood
Split wood is better for a fire as it catches fire easier and burns more evenly.

Too Far Apart
The heat is lost and the temperature is not high enough to sustain a fire. The fire will gradually go out.

CHARCOAL

Earth

Wood

Charcoal makes a very hot fire, is smokeless, and has the least weight for a fuel. Wood burnt with much air burns completely, if air is restricted wood gives of gases and becomes *charcoal*. To produce charcoal stack wood tightly together, cover it with earth, ignite in several places, and maintain a slow burn by *admitting limited amounts of air*. At 500°F (260°C) a chemical reaction occurs making the burning wood very hot which consumes the air and turns the wood into carbon (charcoal). The process can take a few days depending upon the quantity being produced. The charcoal should be left in the covered pit until it cools off or it will burst into flame when exposed to the air. The quality of charcoal depends upon the wood used.

COAL OR WOOD?

Advantage of Wood
Easier to start a fire.
Easier and cleaner to handle.
Wood has a more pleasant and romantic odor.

Advantage of Coal
Per heat value coal requires less space to store.
A give quantity burns for a longer time.
Gives off less heat so it is more comfortable for mild temperatures.

MISCELLANEOUS CHARACTERISTICS OF WOOD (SPLITTING, EMBERS, GREEN WOOD)

Feature	Example	Special characteristics
Inflammable wood in green state (1)	Basswood, black ash, balsam, box elder, buckeye, cucumber, black or pitch pine, white pine, poplar, aspen, yellow poplar, tulip, sassafras, sour wood, sycamore, tamarack, sour gum, water oak	Will scarcely burn in the green state. (1) These woods are good for backlogs, hand sticks, side logs on a cooking fire, pot supports.
	Butternut, chestnut, red oak, red maple, persimmon	Burns very slowly in the green state.
Flammable when green	Yellow ash, white ash	Burns better green than seasoned.
Dead logs only	Pine	Should be split, if not the outer shell catches fire but it chars and the fire goes out unless in proximity of tinder.
Green wood		*Burns best in autumn and winter when the sap is low. Trees growing beside water is very hard to burn. Trees that grow on high, dry ground burn better than those of the same species that stand in moist soil.*
	Chestnut	Cut at the summits of the Appalachians burns well even when green
Spitfire wood (Cause flying embers)	White cedar, chestnut box elder, red cedar, hemlock, sassafras, tulip, balsam, tamarack, spruce	Burns to dead coals that do not give off flame. Prone to pop great crackling and snapping.
	Soft pines	Prone to pop.
	Sugar maple, beech, white oak, some hickory	Watch for embers a time after the fire is started as they shoot out are long lived so more dangerous that those of softwoods. Excellent fuel.
Stubborn wood (Hard to split)	Blue ash, box elder, buckeye, cherry, white elm, sugar maple, sycamore, winged elm, sour gum, hemlock (generally),	Hard to split.
	Hickory, beech, dogwood, sugar maple, birch, slippery elm	Easy to split when green.

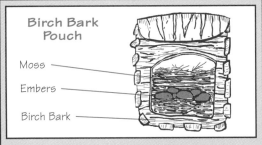

Birch Bark Pouch

Moss

Embers

Birch Bark

CARRYING EMBERS

It is easier to carry smoldering embers than to start a new fire with no matches. Containers that can be used: tin can, animal horn, birch bark pouch, hardwood box.

Fill the bottom of the container with dry moss, place the embers on the moss and cover with moss. Check the embers from time to time and blow on them if they seem to be losing strength. Embers, if well taken care of, can be transported for a few days. The moss limits the air reaching the embers and retards their burning but *sufficient* air has to reach the embers or they will go out.

Eskimo Koolik Uses blubber from seals. See the Winter Shelter Section.

Animal Fat — Flame — Oil

UNUSUAL FUELS

Any concentration of carbon, hydrogen, and methane can be used to make a fire. This can be dry peat moss, dry seaweed, animal dung in desert areas, bat droppings (use outdoors in small quantities as it is very flammable even explosive), animal oils, dry leaves, coal, or oil that seeps to the surface or saturated as tar sands.

On polar ice, or in areas where other fuels are unavailable, blubber or animal fat is a source of fuel.

If near the wreckage of an aircraft or a disabled snowmobile or car, use a *mixture* of gasoline and oil as fuel. Be careful as to how you ignite and feed the gasoline mixture.

You can use almost any plant for firewood, but do not burn the wood, leaves or branches of any plant *that can poison on contact.*

Rotting Wood

Rotting wood decreases the potential energy in the wood. Dried rotten wood is flammable and will burn very fast but giving off limited heat. Rotten wood chips can be used as tinder. Rotting is caused by fungi that require oxygen, humidity and temperatures between 60°F and 90°F. Wood in houses usually does not rot as it is too dry.

Fire Making

Steps in Making a Fire

- Clean the surrounding area of any flammable material and watch for overhanging trees.
- A source of a flame, a spark, or other heat source. Start with a material that is easy to burn as grass, twigs, and other materials listed under tinder and kindling.
- Build a fire step by step taking all the factors listed below into account and you will succeed on your first try. Do not build a fire that is too large as it will be too hot to use for cooking and consume much fuel.

1 Tinder
Used to start a fire when no flame or matches are available.

Tinder

2 Kindling
Small sticks and leaves that will catch fire from the tinder or a match are placed in a teepee fashion. Leave one side open for the tinder and/or match.

Kindling stacked in the form of a teepee

Match and/or tinder at the opening

3 Wood Fuel
Wood is gradually added not too much to smother the fire. The first pieces should be finger thin and then when the fire is hot enough add larger pieces.

4 Fire Burning to Coals and Ashes
Once the fire is at the coal stage it can be used for cooking as the heat will be fairly constant. Two stones or greenwood supports can be added to each side of the fire to support a frying pan.

5 Heavy Log Star Fire
If the cooking fire is to be used as a heating fire for the night large logs can be butted together as a star. The log tips are gradually pushed into the fire. The advantage of this is that the logs do not have to be cut. A long heavy log can be placed across the fire and be burnt in half. Green wood can be used selectively to retard the burning.

Advance logs to increase size of fire.

Star Shaped Fire for Heating

Tinder

Prepare some extremely dry tinder before attempting to start a fire without matches. Once prepared, shelter this tinder from wind and dampness.

Some tinder is:

- Birch bark, resin shavings, and pitch or fat from coniferous trees (described below). They burn even when wet.
- Punk (the dry insides of rotten trunks of trees), lint from cloth, rope or twine, dead palm frond, finely shredded dry bark, dry moss, powdered dry bat droppings, dry powdered wood, bird nests, shelf mushrooms growing on tree trunks, wooly material from plants (pussy willow, cat tail), dry grass, dry crushed leaves, and wood dust produced by insects and often found under the bark of dead trees.
- These can be saturated with light oil, gasoline, or alcohol based insect repellants.

To prepare the tinder for use break it, roll it in your hands, or cut it into small powdery pieces to minimize the surface area that the sparks or hot wood have to heat to ignite and smoke.

To save tinder for future use, store it in a waterproof container.

Kindling

Kindling is material that also is used to start a fire. It is a step up from tinder, which is used to start a fire in very difficult situations i.e. having no matches or starter fire.

- Kindling can be small strips of dry wood, pine knots, bark, twigs, palm leaves, pine needles, dead upright grass, ground lichens, ferns, plant and bird down, and the dry, spongy threads of the giant puffball, which by the way are edible.
- Cut your dry wood into shaving before attempting to set it on fire.
- One of the best and most commonly found kindling material is punk as described under tinder. Dry punk can be found even in wet weather by knocking away the soggy outer portions with a knife, stick, or even your hands.
- Paper or gasoline may be used as tinder.
- Even when wet the resinous pitch (fat) in pine knots or dried stumps readily ignites. *See article below.*
- Loose bark of the birch tree also contains a resinous oil which ignites well.
- Arrange the kindling in a wigwam or log cabin pile to maximize the air flow.

Pitch, Fat, or "Pine-Gum"
Is the resinous deposit found in old coniferous tree stumps or butt cuts on pine trees especially trees that died on the stump. The resin will have flowed down and collected at the bottom part of the tree. Old-timers and Indians swear by its use in fire making. A few shavings of pitch can start a fire at the touch of a match. Whenever you see some collect a few pieces for future use. Find pitch in the debris of rotting logs. It is yellowish in color and looks like a resin wood lamination on old stumps. Watch for old stumps that look yellowish as they might contain pitch. If the stump is gray it probably is rotten, old and soggy and contains no pitch.

Pine Needle Tinder

Cutting a Fuzz Stick

Placing Fuzz Sticks

Fuzz Sticks
Cut a dry soft wood stick making sure that the shavings do not fall off the stick. These sticks can be piled, into a teepee shape on some curls of birch bark. Light the fuzz and you will have a good blaze in a few minutes. Have heavier wood ready to add to the fire.

Birch Bark Kindling
Bark of all species of birch, especially the Paper Birch, is excellent for kindling and torches. It is full of resinous oil which blazes up and will burn in the wind.

BOW & DRILL FIRE

BOW AND DRILL ACTION

Make a bow strung with a shoelace, string or leather thong. Use the bow to spin a dry, soft drill stick pushed by a small bearing block of hardwood which is cupped in your left hand. The rotation and pressure of the drill, grinding on the base board, heats the wood which ignites and a hot black powder falls through the grove-hole onto the tinder. The tinder gradually starts to smolder and smoke. When there is much smoke remove the base board and gently blow on the tinder which will burst into flame. Add tinder or some light kindling to get a larger flame.

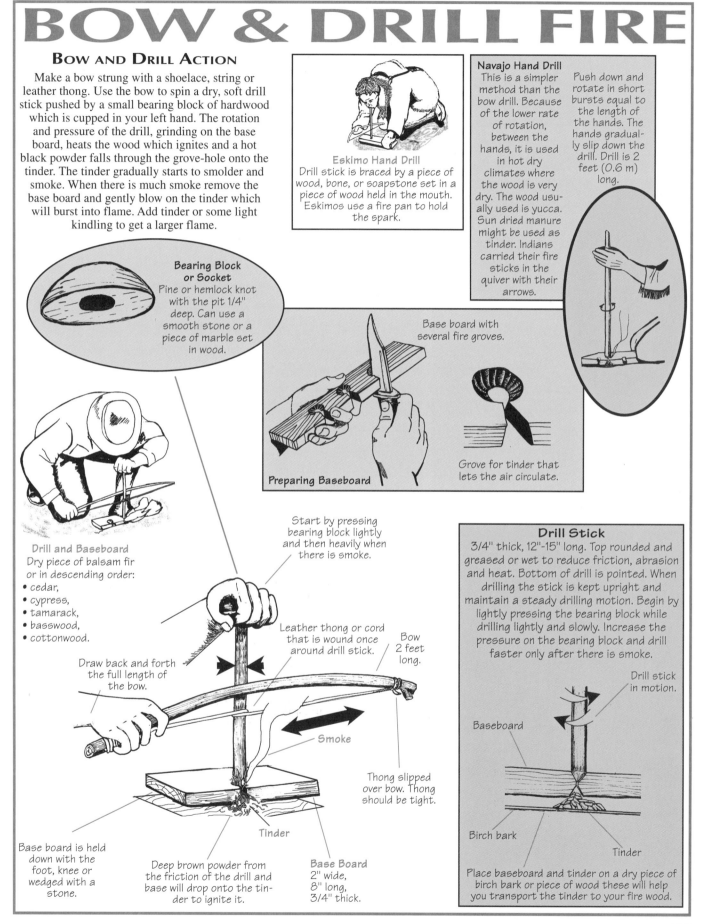

Eskimo Hand Drill
Drill stick is braced by a piece of wood, bone, or soapstone set in a piece of wood held in the mouth. Eskimos use a fire pan to hold the spark.

Navajo Hand Drill
This is a simpler method than the bow drill. Because of the lower rate of rotation, between the hands, it is used in hot dry climates where the wood is very dry. The wood usually used is yucca. Sun dried manure might be used as tinder. Indians carried their fire sticks in the quiver with their arrows.

Push down and rotate in short bursts equal to the length of the hands. The hands gradually slip down the drill. Drill is 2 feet (0.6 m) long.

Bearing Block or Socket
Pine or hemlock knot with the pit 1/4" deep. Can use a smooth stone or a piece of marble set in wood.

Base board with several fire groves.

Preparing Baseboard

Grove for tinder that lets the air circulate.

Drill and Baseboard
Dry piece of balsam fir or in descending order:
- cedar,
- cypress,
- tamarack,
- basswood,
- cottonwood.

Draw back and forth the full length of the bow.

Start by pressing bearing block lightly and then heavily when there is smoke.

Leather thong or cord that is wound once around drill stick.

Bow 2 feet long.

Smoke

Thong slipped over bow. Thong should be tight.

Base board is held down with the foot, knee or wedged with a stone.

Tinder

Deep brown powder from the friction of the drill and base will drop onto the tinder to ignite it.

Base Board
2" wide, 8" long, 3/4" thick.

Drill Stick
3/4" thick, 12"-15" long. Top rounded and greased or wet to reduce friction, abrasion and heat. Bottom of drill is pointed. When drilling the stick is kept upright and maintain a steady drilling motion. Begin by lightly pressing the bearing block while drilling lightly and slowly. Increase the pressure on the bearing block and drill faster only after there is smoke.

Drill stick in motion.

Baseboard

Birch bark

Tinder

Place baseboard and tinder on a dry piece of birch bark or piece of wood these will help you transport the tinder to your fire wood.

PROBLEMS IN STARTING A FIRE WITH A FIRE DRILL OR FIRE PUMP

Problem	Reason or Action
Kindling gets covered with dark drilled powder.	Dust off the tinder.
Light brown	*Wood is not under enough pressure or you are not drilling fast enough.*
Black	Pushing too hard so that the powder burns before it lands on the tinder.
Spindle jumps out of bearing block	*Hole in block not deep enough or too small for size of the drill stick.*
Thong slips on drill stick	Thong loose, drill stick too smooth, too much pressure on bearing block.
Thong runs up and down drill stick	*Thong should be in middle of drill stick and bow should be perpendicular to drill stick.*
Bearing block smokes	Pushing too hard, wood too soft when compared to hardness of the drill stick add some lubrication (water, oil, grease).

MAKING A FIRE IN THE RAIN

Find a fat pine log and split it open and light a fire from underneath. Dry fuel can be found under rock shelves, in a core of an old stump, the underside of a large fallen log, or look for a dead softwood tree that leans to the south as the wood and bark on the underside will be dry. If the rain is falling from a constant direction a tarpaulin can be used to protect the fire. The tarpaulin has to be placed far enough to accommodate the growing flames.

Trench

FIRE SAW

The fire saw consists of two pieces of dry wood one of which is rubbed vigorously against the other in a sawing motion.

This method of starting fires is commonly used in the jungle. Use a split half piece of bamboo as the fireboard and soft wood as a rub stick. A good tinder is the fluffy brown covering of the apiang palm and the dry material found at the base of the coconut leaves.

Preparing the Bamboo

On the inside of the fireboard pick and splinter some of the stringy fibers. On the outside opposite the fibers cut a narrow grove in which the sawing will be done.

Rub Stick
Grove
Fireboard

Sawing Motion

Tinder

SOUTH SEAS FIRE MAKER

This fire making method was developed by natives of the South Seas. The plunger is hit repeatedly with the palm of the hand. The air inside is so highly compressed that heat is generated igniting the tinder.

Bamboo Tube
Inside of cylinder is greased.
Plunger wrapped with fiber to make plunger tight fitting.
Dried moss is fastened by fibers to the end of the plunger.

Hard Wood Plunger

Bamboo Joint

FIRE THONG

Use a strip of dry rattan, preferably about 1/4 inch (0.6 cm) in diameter and about two feet long; and a dry stick. Prop this stick off the ground by using a rock. Split the end of the stick. Hold it open with a small wedge. Place a small wad of tinder in the split, leaving enough room to insert the thong behind it. Secure the stick with your foot or knees, and work the thong back and forth.

Thong

PUMP FIRE DRILL

The Iroquois Indians had a fire drill that used the principal of the flywheel. The fly wheel was of hardwood with a hole at the centre through which the drill stick is forced and attached. The crossbar of hardwood is attached by a cord or leather thong and slides freely on the drill stick. The drill stick and fireboard use the same woods, dimensions, carved holes, and tinder as the fire drill.

The pump fire drill works by first winding up the flywheel which pulls up the cross bar. The cross bar is then pushed down and its momentum rewinds it in the opposite direction. The process is repeated until there is black powder and smoke.

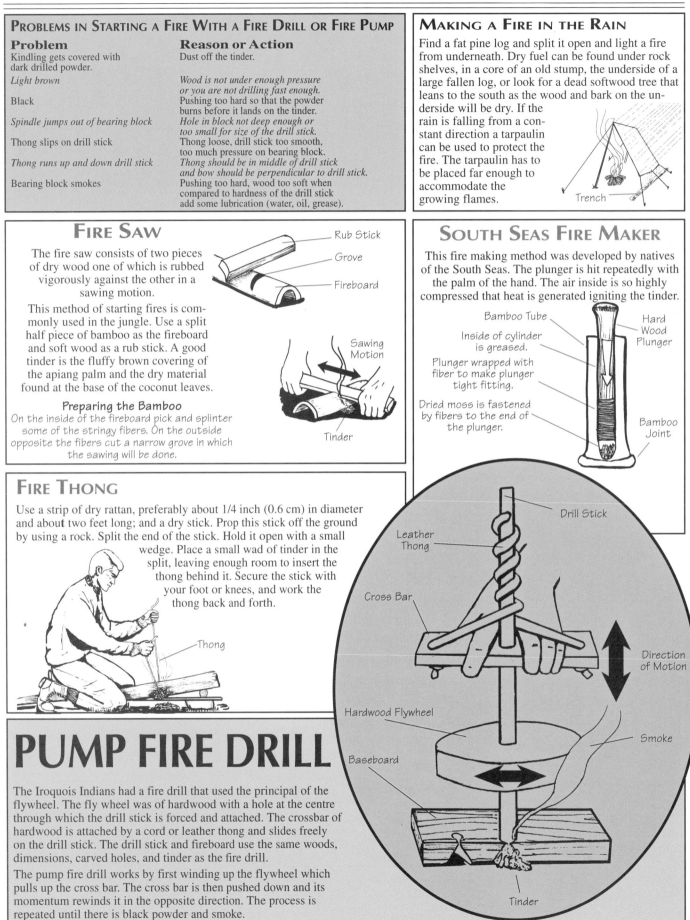

Drill Stick
Leather Thong
Cross Bar
Direction of Motion
Hardwood Flywheel
Baseboard
Smoke
Tinder

MAGNESIUM FIRE BLOCK

This block can be bought in sporting goods stores or your favorite Army Navy store. The block is in aluminium which contains magnesium. You cut or scratch, with a knife, shavings off the block which are ignited by striking the blade on the flint rod embedded on the edge of the block.

Striking Flint

Cut Shavings

STARTING FIRE WITHOUT MATCHES

CANDLE FIRE STARTER

Place a lit candle below a teepee of kindling and it will start a fire. Remove and extinguish the candle for future use.

TIN CAN HEATERS

Heat stones in a fire and place the hot stones into a tin can and put a few cans into your tent. This will provide excellent, safe, smokeless heat for your tent.

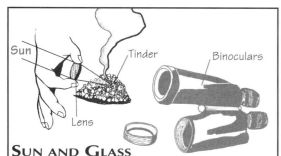

Sun   Tinder   Binoculars

Lens

SUN AND GLASS

A camera lens, a convex lens (a *convex* lens is one that the centre bulges out and one that slopes *in* is *concave*) from a binocular, a lens from a telescopic sight, the bottom of an old pop bottle, a magnifying glass on a compass may be used to concentrate the rays of the sun on your tinder.

Concave mirrors can also be used to make a fire but this method is difficult as a large reflector is required. This mirror can be from a shaving mirror, or car headlight.

BATTERY

Remove the battery from vehicle or boat. Attach two wires one to the positive and one to the negative terminal. Place some tinder in a pile and touch both wires, *for a second*, over or in the tinder the spark should start the smoldering of the tinder. Proceed as usual to start the fire. Note: This can damage or discharge your battery if done too frequently. *Be careful of not causing an engine fire if the battery is not removed from the car.* This can also be tried with two large flashlight batteries. The car's cigarette lighter can be used with some facial tissue, paper or cloth.

Battery   Terminals

Wires

Tinder

FINDING FLINT AND QUARTZ

Flint: Is jet black, very hard, and because of weathering will look pitted and dull. Upon finding a rock split it open by pounding it against another rock. If it is flint it will crack as easily as glass and will have a smooth black sheen on the inside surface. Flint can be found on a river bed or on a hillside with loose rock deposits.

Quartz: Is white and looks like dull window glass but can be with or colored by other minerals. River beds, rocky slopes, and ridges are usually strewn with chunks of quartz. Mountain formations are streaked with white glassy quartz.

Indians and Eskimos used iron pyrites, instead of iron or steel, before the white man came to America. Indians carried the pyrites and flint in a pouch on the belt.

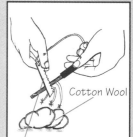

Steel or iron knife struck against any glassy stone as quartz, agate, jasper or flint will produce a spark that ignites the tinder. Blow on tinder when it starts to smoke.

STEEL & FLINT

This is the best method to light tinder if you do not have matches. Use the flint at the bottom of your waterproof match case. *Hold the flint as near the tinder as possible and strike it with the back of knife blade or a small piece of steel.* Strike downward so that the sparks will hit in the center of the tinder. When the tinder begins to smolder, fan or blow it gently into a flame. These sparks are formed by tiny bits of metal from the steel that are superheated to the igniting point of the tinder. Gradually add kindling to your tinder, or transfer the burning tinder to the base of your fire wood.

Cotton Wool

Magnesium flint alloy with a steel saw blade produces a large spark.

Flint on Waterproof Match Case

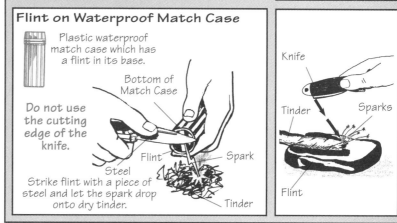

Plastic waterproof match case which has a flint in its base.

Do not use the cutting edge of the knife.

Bottom of Match Case

Flint   Spark

Steel

Strike flint with a piece of steel and let the spark drop onto dry tinder.

Tinder

Knife

Tinder   Sparks

Flint

POTASSIUM PERMANGANATE

Pour a teaspoon of crystals of potassium permanganate (a mild antiseptic), from your first aid kit, on a piece of paper, dry leaf, or piece of cloth. Add a *few drops (too much fluid will retard heat production)* of antifreeze from your radiator and *tightly (to retain heat produced and raise temperature to 450°F (232°C) - average paper's flash point)* roll the paper into a ball. Instantaneous combustion will cause the bundle to burst into flame in a few minutes. *If for some reason this method is not successful do not put the paper bundle in any flammable area as it might start burning at any time.* Unwrap the package and bury any unsuccessful attempts in sand and pour water on the spot.

FIRE FROM FIREARMS

Use a firearm with a large bore.

- Prepare tinder and kindling.
- Remove lead bullet or shot pellets from shell.
- Sprinkle 2/3 of powder on a piece of dry frayed cloth.
- Push the frayed cloth into the muzzle.
- Fire the firearm straight up in the air or into a solid object a few feet away. The flaming or smoldering cloth will only fly for a few feet.
- Pick it up (have stick ready to pick up the flaming cloth) and place it under the prepared tinder and kindling. If required blow and fan to produce a flame.

Do not use this method if there are highly flammable materials in the area.

FIRE STARTER

Stuff lint from your dryer or shredded cloth into the compartments of a paper egg carton. Melt candle wax and pour a thin layer over the lint or cloth and let it set. To use break up the carton and light a section. The fire will burn from 5 to 15 minutes depending on the mixture of lint and wax.

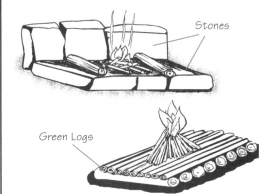

Stones

Green Logs

PLATFORM FIRE

A platform of logs or rocks can be used to raise the level of fire above wet ground, snow, or mud.

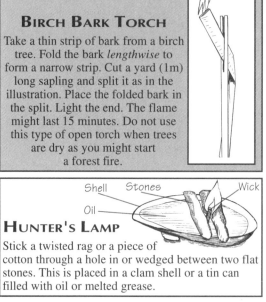

TIN CAN LANTERN

Useful if it is windy or you want to project the light in a specific direction. In a small tin the candle will burn slower as there is less air.

BIRCH BARK TORCH

Take a thin strip of bark from a birch tree. Fold the bark *lengthwise* to form a narrow strip. Cut a yard (1m) long sapling and split it as in the illustration. Place the folded bark in the split. Light the end. The flame might last 15 minutes. Do not use this type of open torch when trees are dry as you might start a forest fire.

Shell   Stones   Wick

Oil

HUNTER'S LAMP

Stick a twisted rag or a piece of cotton through a hole in or wedged between two flat stones. This is placed in a clam shell or a tin can filled with oil or melted grease.

Powder tinder collects at end of grove.

FIRE PLOUGH

Method used by Iroquois Indians. A grove is cut in a soft baseboard. A hardwood shaft is pushed, under heavy pressure, up and down the grove more and more rapidly. This friction produces tinder which ignites.

Wind

CATERPILLAR FIRE

This type of fire should only be built when the wind direction is steady, the ground has been well cleaned and there are no overhanging trees.

The logs are placed as in the illustration beginning the pile in the *direction of the wind*. The supports are in green wood. If there is little wind make the pile shorter by increasing the overlap of the pieces.

Cattail Torch

A cattail dipped in oil or animal fat can be used as a torch. The fuzz from a ripe cattail can be used as tinder to start a fire.

Tin Can Stove

Pour hot wax onto a wick in a tin can. The tin can should be notched or have holes near the top for air. Place the tin can on a flat surface before using. This tin can can be reused by adding wax. Animal blubber can also be used.

Can Stove Using Gasoline and Sand

HUNTER'S FIRE

This is a fire for the colder part of the year. It can be a cooking fire and a heating fire.

Cut two hardwood bed logs a foot thick and your height. Place *the logs on level ground* as an air draft, caused by the slope, will make the logs burn too fast. Place in a 'V' shaped position.

Place green sticks across both logs and place a crisscrossed pile of dry wood on the sticks and light. The burning wood will burn to coals and fall between the logs which will start to slowly burn on the inner sides. The narrow part of the 'V' of the logs can be used for cooking.

For an all night fire place thick *green logs* across the bed logs and put night wood on them. The night wood will fall into the fire when the green logs are burnt. A more sophisticated fire construction is a caterpillar fire. *See previous page.*

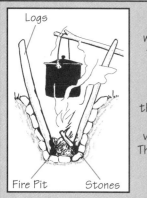

Logs

Fire Pit   **Stones**

Automatic Fire
Dig a pit and line it with rocks. Make sure the rocks are dry as humid rocks can explode if heated. Start a small fire in the pit and place some semi-green logs vertically into the pit. These logs will gradually dry, burn, and slide down into the pit to dry and burn.

Green Wood Structure

Small Fire

Signal Fire
A signal fire can be built as in the illustration. A small fire can be kept burning below the structure of green logs. When you want to signal add dry wood to the fire and place green branches, rubber, plastic, or heavy oil on the structure. This will produce heavy black smoke.

After a Forest Fire

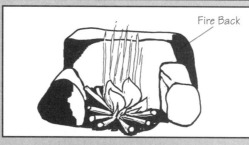

Fire Back

Winter Fire With Stone Back or Back Log

A fire-back reflects the heat into a lean-to or tent. The fire-back serves as a windbreak. A fire-back can be big flat faced rocks, green logs, or a ledge with the fire between the tent front and the fire-back. For better heating fill the space between the logs with mud. The face of the back logs should not be more than 5' (1.5 m) from the front of the tent. A well tended small fire should not be over 4' (1.2 m) away. Choose wood that does not crack and send off to many embers.

INDIAN FIRE

Indians traditionally did not have good cutting tools so they developed efficient heating methods that can be used today to conserve fuel and save the forests. Cut hardwood saplings with a small hatchet. With tinder build a hot fire and place saplings in a star shaped form radiating from the fire. While the fire is burning gradually advance the butts towards the centre and replenish with additional saplings as required. This fire saves much chopping, can be easily controlled, and economizes fuel. Build a windbreak behind you and lie close to the fire.

Maintaining a Fire

Bank your fire properly. Use green logs to keep your fire burning slowly. Keep the embers out of the wind. Cover them with ashes and put a thin layer of soil over them. Remember it takes less work to keep your fire going than to build another one.

Fire Buffalo Chips

Trees are sparse on the western plains. The Indians used dried buffalo dung for firewood. The smell was not too pleasant but it worked.

Hot Sand Bags

When you have no hot water bottle, heat sand in a frying pan. Pour sand into cloth bags and place these hot bags into your sleeping bag.

Ember Heaters

Punch holes into a large tin can. Scoop up embers and put them into the can and place the can on a few rocks in your tent. Note that the embers are still burning so *you require ventilation*.

Wood Storage

Place cut wood on two skid logs to keep it off the damp ground. Pile it neatly between two vertical supports. If wood is split, keep the bark side up. Cover the wood pile with long strips of bark or a piece of waterproof canvas.

Glass Bottle Lantern
Heat a clear glass bottle in a fire then dip the bottom in cold water this causes the bottom to crack and fall off. Place a candle inside the neck of the bottle and the neck is stuck in the ground.

Wood Ash
Can be used as a fertilizer because of its potassium content. In wet regions ashes can decrease the acidity of the soil. Potassium carbonate can be extracted from ash to make soap.

3 Fire Types
• A **hot little fire** that will quickly boil water and then burn down to embers that are good for frying.

• A fire that produces a **bed of long lived coals** that are smokeless and can produce heat for roasting, baking, and broiling.

• A fire that is made of **big logs** that will throw its heat forward on the ground towards a lean-to. This fire will last for a few hours without replenishing.

FOREST FIRES CHAPTER 11

HOW FIRES START IN NATURE

Lightning: During a single lightning storm there might be thousands of strikes of which 1% might start fires. The percentage can be higher and depends upon drought conditions, availability of fuel, and the quantity of rain during the storm.

Humans: Deliberately setting a fire or by simple carelessness.

Spontaneous Combustion: This is when rags, paper or other flammable material has been soaked in a solvent, paint or other petrochemical product, reaches a temperature in the presence of oxygen, at which it starts burning on its own.

SPEED OF THE SPREADING OF A FIRE

Depends upon the wind, the humidity of the fuel, the topography and actual size of the fire:

- *Grass fires* will advance at 2 to 4 miles an hour. This fire can easily be out-walked.
- *Crown fires* can spread at over 5 miles per hour. A strong wind can cause the fire to spread much more rapidly but then the fire front will only burn the crowns of the trees. The remaining forest will burn more slowly.
- A *ground fire* can smolder for months.

THE LIFE CYCLE OF A FIRE

A fire starts in a location that has all the required conditions for a fire (*fuel, oxygen, and heat*).
For fire to spread:

- It heats the potential adjacent fuel and dries it out.
- The heat then chemically breaks down the potential fuel so that it gives off flammable gases which ignite causing it to burn and spread.
- To stop the fire you have to remove one of the three ingredients of a fire (fuel, oxygen or heat).

Fire Tent

This tent, which is similar to a pup tent in construction but is aluminized, is used by fire fighters in emergencies when the fire is overtaking them. They crawl into the tent and hold onto the flaps. The tent protects them from burns and from hot air and smoke.

Fire Smoke

The deposits of fire smoke lines the lungs in a similar fashion as cigarette smoke. The smoke is made up of different chemicals that come from the burning resins and oils of the trees and particles of charcoal and ash.

PSYCHOLOGY OF A FOREST FIRE

Each fire has its own personality and as in a human it is not totally predictable. The factors that affect a forest fire are:

Humidity: How wet is the fuel and the ground.

Fuel to burn: Ground deposits (deadwood), type of trees, grass, etc.

Spread of the fire: Height of trees and winds for a crown fire to be high enough so that embers can be blown over natural firebreaks or roads to start a fire on the other side.

Weather: If it is raining, humid, or very dry.

Wind: Feeds oxygen to a fire and spreads the embers.

Topography: What are the features on the land.

Topographic Features that Affect Fires

Slopes: Fires travel uphill faster than downhill because the hot air currents rise and dry out and preheat the fuel on the uphill side of a fire. The hot air currents help a fire move up the slope. The slope on the south and west sides has more sun so is dryer, has a tendency to have more, larger and hotter fires.

Barriers: As roads, rivers, previously burned areas, fire trenches, etc. will slow down or stop a fire.

FIRE FIGHTING AND THE HEIGHT OF THE FLAMES

- *Under 4 feet* (1.2 m) can be fought with traditional hand tools to remove fuel or oxygen supply. To remove the oxygen, to fight a small fire, use wet brush, burlap bags, sand, or blankets. Remove branches and other flammable objects from the direction of travel of the fire and it might burn out. This method can be supplemented by digging a fire trench. This is usually successful if there is no strong wind. Fight a small fire *from* the direction it is moving in.

- *Above 4 feet* (1.2 m) it is more difficult because the heat the fire radiates and it is hard to approach it without insulated clothing. Fight these fires from the *sides* of their direction of travel. Pay close attention to any possible changes in the direction or intensity of the wind. Use water, wet sand, drop water-soaked burlap bags along the edge of the fire. Try to guide the front of the fire towards a natural break such as a road, stream, or lake. Never set a back fire unless you have experienced fire fighters present because they can easily get out of hand.

- *Above 12 feet* (3.3 m) a fire is considered as being a *crown fire* and it can travel very fast, if driven by strong winds, across large areas. Never be in front of a crown fire but stay on its flank. Watch for shifts of wind which can change the direction of the fire.

HOW FIRES SPREAD

A fire starts at a point and gradually spreads out from the point, ideally in a circle. In real life there is wind, the slope of the land, and obstacles that will misshape the circle, usually into an eclipse. The center, being the source of the fire, will be burnt out and the factor for misshaping the circle (wind, slope) will cause the fire to burn in a certain direction. The direction of travel is called the **head**, the sides are the **flank**, and the end is the **tail**.

- The wind affects the fire by blowing the heat (which dries the adjacent fuel) and flames in a certain direction causing that part of the circle to expand more rapidly. This misshaped circle usually has the form of an ellipse.
- The slope affects a fire by the fact that the heat of the fire rises up the slope. This dries the fuel higher up so that it can ignite more easily. Even if there is no wind the fire is pulled uphill by the rising heat (**updraft**) which causes wind in the form of convection currents.
- The fire soon breaks out of this ideal circle structure and adapts to the wind, updraft, and topography of the land. The fire advances in a **line** or **front**.

TEMPERATURES AT STAGES OF A FIRE

400°-700°F	200°-370°C	Wood glows
800°F	426°C	Burst into flames.
2300°F	1230°C	Temperature of a fire.

Direction of the Wind
Fire Head
Tail of Fire
Flank of Fire
Origin of Fire

FIRE TERMINOLOGY

Conflagration

These are crown fires that are spreading quickly, are very large, and have a tendency to throw their embers over long distances ahead of the fire (because of the wind) that start spot fires. These spot fires can occur two to three miles *ahead* of the fire.

Convection Winds & Fire Storm

- A large fire produces much heat. Hot air rises as it is lighter than the surrounding cooler air. This upward moving column, *convection column or updraft,* of air carries smoke and embers.
- As the column of hot air rises it pulls cool air into the fire which brings in additional oxygen to increase the size of the fire which can become a *whirlwind*. These winds can carry the flames and embers up to 300 feet (90 m).
- The extreme form of a convection column is a *fire storm*. A fire storm throws a shower of embers onto the surrounding area.
- A small twisting variant of the fire storm is a *fire whirl* which acts more like a small tornado.

COTTAGE PROTECTION

If you live in a potential forest fire area plan for a forest fire before it occurs. Keep the area (at least 30 feet (9 m)) around the house clear of trees, logs, fuel and fuel storage tanks. You can install a sprinkler system for the roof. If you have an electric pump use a hand pump or a protected generator for the pump as the power lines might be down. The roof should not be made of regular wood shingles but fire-resistant material. The location of your house is also important.

- Avoid the top of that picturesque valley.
- Use a level area away from wilderness growth.
- What kind of firebreaks do you have in your area - a river, highway, or field. These firebreaks should be at least 200 feet (60 m) wide.
- Does your community have a fireproof shelter?

If There is a Fire

- Place all inflammable objects outside, far from the house not indoors. Do not put the propane tank of your BBQ in the house.
- Close and cover all windows; close all inside doors to avoid drafts.
- Fill pails with water, wet mats, blankets and mops. You could use these to put out small fires that might start.
- Attach all your lawn sprinklers and water down the house. Place a sprinkler on your roof and water it down.

FIRE AND SURVIVAL

Fire has a strong positive psychological impact upon an individual who is lost:

Fire and warmth is the most important survival tool after your personal wilderness knowledge, maintenance of calm and a positive attitude.

- Fire provides warmth which helps your mind think logically.
- Fire makes you feel protected from all "those wild animals out there in the shadows".
- Fire can be used to send smoke signals for rescue.
- Fire can be used to burn the end of a stick to make a pointed spear.
- Fire and smoke can repel insects.
- Fire can be used to burn trunks or large sticks so that they are more manageable to be used for construction of a shelter.
- Smoke can be used to smoke out wild bees to access their honey.
- Fire can be used to smoke small animals out of their burrows into trap.
- Fire torches, at night, can be used to blind fish in shallow streams making them easier to capture.

Matches

Matches are the easiest way to make a fire.

Always carry matches on you. Carry matches in a waterproof container in you backpack, in your pant pockets and your jacket. Make sure the matches will not fall out of your pockets even when you fall out of a boat.

TYPES OF OUTDOOR FIRES

Surface: These fires burn the shrubs, grass, ground debris and small trees.

- **Marsh Fires**

  These occur in the spring or fall when the vegetation of reeds and cattails are dry. Never have the wind blowing towards you when you are fighting a fire as it can easily flare up.

- **Grass Fires**

  These fires which are used to burn dry grass can get out of control and cause extensive damage.

Ground Fire: After much sun and periods of drought the layers of debris of rotten dry leaves, needles, peat moss, and other vegetation can easily catch fire. The fire can be easily started by lightning. A ground fire burns the organic deposits *below* the surface. This fire does not burn with a flame, as there is a lack of oxygen, but glows. A fire can start and smolder for many days betrayed by only a few wisps of smoke. If more oxygen becomes available the fuel can burst into flame. This can happen if you remove the covering soil. This fire is bad for wildlife because it kills the root structure of the plants deep in the ground. It is difficult to fight this fire because it is hard to reach. A heavy downpour would be of great help in controlling this type of fire. Ground fires can occur in coal mines and they can burn for a hundred years.

Forest Floor Fires

These burn swiftly through the underbrush and kill the seedlings and young growth, scar the trunks of larger trees and damage their roots. This fire burns the humus that nourishes the forest.

Crown Fires: These spread rapidly and burn only the tops (crowns) of trees and shrubs. These fires are usually carried by high winds. This is the most dangerous of fires because these can travel at high speeds when blown by the wind and can rapidly engulf complete mountain-sides.

ESCAPING A FOREST FIRE

HOW TO ESCAPE A FOREST FIRE

- Stay calm.
- Fires usually look *closer* than they are because there is much smoke, fire and movement. The fact that we rarely encounter forest fires or have a clear view of the size of the trees that are burning does not let us make a proportionate projection of the distance.
- Prepare to leave the area as soon as you detect a fire, even at a distance, because if it is a crown fire, with a wind, it can be upon you in no time.
- A fire can outrun you.
- Plan an escape route and a backup route if you are cut off.
- *Travel downhill if the fire is close.* Remember that fire travels four or five times faster uphill than downhill.
- Do not climb a canyon wall or steep slope because they are excellent chimneys in the spread of a fire.
- Keep your body covered with natural materials such as cotton or wool. Do not use synthetics which will melt in the heat and stick to your body and possibly burn. This occurred during the Falkland War when the British sailors wore modern synthetic uniforms which started to burn and stuck to their bodies when their ship was hit by the Argentinians.
- *Do not wet your clothing, because the water will scald your skin when heated.*
- Use **DRY** sand to cover your skin.
- Do not wear a backpack made of synthetic material because it might melt or burn and stick to your back.
- Discard any stove fuel that you might be carrying because it might explode in the heat of a fire.
- Lie with your face to the ground.
- If the fire front is low consider jumping into the burnt area but make sure that your skin and hair are covered.
- In a smoky fire area do not take deep breaths. Breathe through a piece of dry cloth. **If the cloth is wet the hot air from the fire will produce steam and you will damage your lungs.**
- Remember a large fire can consume all the oxygen for the duration of a few minutes. Be prepared for this possibility and *do not panic*.
- Do not hide in caves or airtight enclosed areas because the fire will use up the oxygen and you might suffocate.

CHOOSE A PROTECTIVE AREA

- Stay on dry ground, on rocks, in a depressed area, in a pond or stream. Make sure there is no fuel that can burn.
- The middle of a slope has the highest potential for a hot fire. The lower areas of a slope are usually more humid and the middle area would be dryer and probably has a more dense growth than the top of the hill. The middle of the hill could be dangerous because of an updraft.
- The southern sides of hills are dryer and have a higher potential for quick-burning fires.
- Find a depression in the ground. Clear the ground of any possible fuel. Do not remove your clothing. Bury your face in the earth. If the soil is loose and DRY, push some sand over yourself. Cover yourself with a heavy *non-synthetic* blanket. This is to avoid the searing heat of the fire. The fire will sweep over you in a few minutes.
- If you cannot find a secure area consider entering a burnt out area in which you can find protection from a larger fire.

IN A CAR AND FIRE IS APPROACHING

- Choose the area where you will ride out the fire. Consider an open area that does not have much fuel so that the fire will pass by very rapidly.
- Avoid wooded areas because burning trees might fall on you.
- Do not park in a depressed area, such as a narrow valley, because forest fires have a higher concentrated heat intensity in confined areas.
- Close all openings in a car such as windows and air intakes.
- Turn off the engine and put on the lights so that other vehicles can see you.
- Lie down on the floor of the car and cover yourself with a non-synthetic blanket or clothing.
- You might even *remove* the back seat to provide more space. The seat coverings are synthetic.
- As mentioned in the fire types section it might be very windy. The car might rock and it can be very noisy but do not panic. Exit the car as soon as the fire has passed. The odds are that the gas tank will not explode but do not stay near the car after the fire.

FOREST FIRE PROTECTION

Dryness Test: This test uses the fact that dry pine needles absorb and lose humidity very rapidly. Take a dry pine needle, two inches long, and place it lengthwise between your thumb and forefinger and slowly press them together.

- *If the needle breaks,* after bending a quarter of a circle, the needle is very dry and *the fire hazard is very high*.
- *If the needle bends more than half a circle,* without breaking, the humidity is high which indicates a *low probability for a forest fire*.

Factors to Consider

- In choosing a camp site look for a meadow or rocky area if you are expecting a lightning storm.
- If you are entering a wilderness or camping area ask a warden, police patrol or listen to your radio to obtain information as to the weather forecast or information on potential fires.

FOREST FIRES AND NATURE

Forest fires are a natural occurrence which might be considered a part of the ecosystem.

- Certain plants need open sunny spaces to grow. These plants are food for deer and other animals.
- A fire increases the amount of forest edge that will change the mix of animals that will inhabit the forest. The deer population might triple.
- A completely grown forest does not provide a suitable environment for many plants and animals.
- Some plants such as the Aspen need a fire to produce a large quantity of seeds.
- In the case of the Lodgepole Pine some of their seeds remain unopened up to 25 years and if there is no forest fire they will never open.
- Fires produce ash which acts as a fertilizer which in turn helps accelerate plant grown.

California Condors

With less small forest fires and less open spaces the California Condor is approaching extinction. Fires create open feeding space for rabbits, the prime food for condors. The lack of rabbits has reduced the calcium intake of condors leading to a calcium deficiency. Eggs and the bone structure require calcium for strength.
Condors being heavy birds require a running start to attain flight. Condor, after feeding, can hardly lift off in a dense growth area.

KEYHOLE FIRE

This dual purpose fire layout is ideal for both heating and cooking. First build a teepee style fire in the round part of the keyhole. When the fire has burnt down to coals scrape them into the narrow part of the keyhole and place a grill of green branches across the stones and you can cook. The main fire will continue burning and you can replenish the stove with additional coals when required.

BAMBOO COOKING POT

Water or soups can be cooked in a bamboo pot. You can place a piece of metal from a tin can or aluminum foil on the bottom of the bamboo to dissipate the heat and to protect your "pot" from the flame.

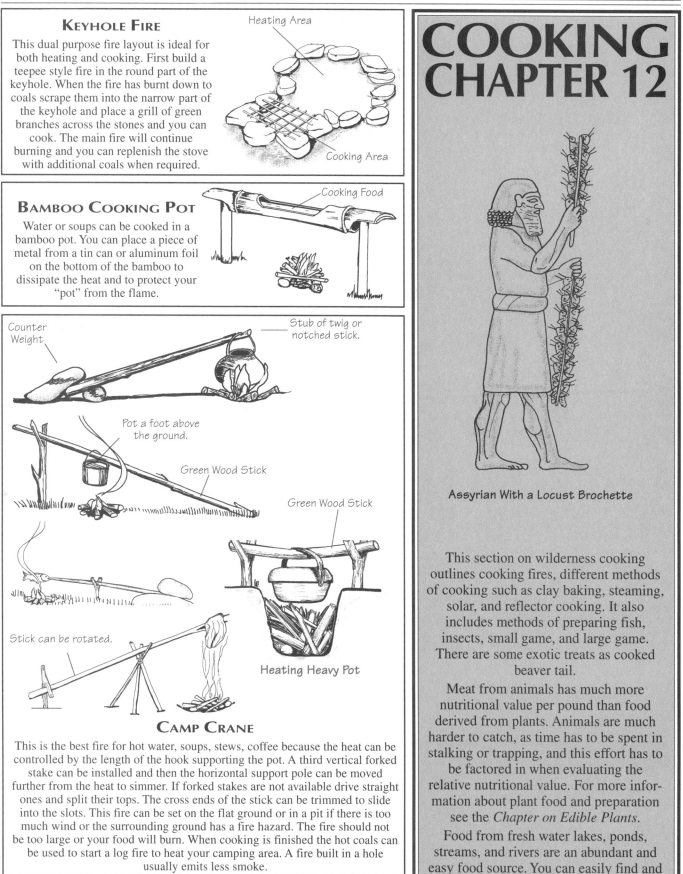

CAMP CRANE

This is the best fire for hot water, soups, stews, coffee because the heat can be controlled by the length of the hook supporting the pot. A third vertical forked stake can be installed and then the horizontal support pole can be moved further from the heat to simmer. If forked stakes are not available drive straight ones and split their tops. The cross ends of the stick can be trimmed to slide into the slots. This fire can be set on the flat ground or in a pit if there is too much wind or the surrounding ground has a fire hazard. The fire should not be too large or your food will burn. When cooking is finished the hot coals can be used to start a log fire to heat your camping area. A fire built in a hole usually emits less smoke.

COOKING FIRES

COOKING CHAPTER 12

Assyrian With a Locust Brochette

This section on wilderness cooking outlines cooking fires, different methods of cooking such as clay baking, steaming, solar, and reflector cooking. It also includes methods of preparing fish, insects, small game, and large game. There are some exotic treats as cooked beaver tail.

Meat from animals has much more nutritional value per pound than food derived from plants. Animals are much harder to catch, as time has to be spent in stalking or trapping, and this effort has to be factored in when evaluating the relative nutritional value. For more information about plant food and preparation see the *Chapter on Edible Plants*.

Food from fresh water lakes, ponds, streams, and rivers are an abundant and easy food source. You can easily find and catch water animals such as fish, frogs, snails, and crabs.

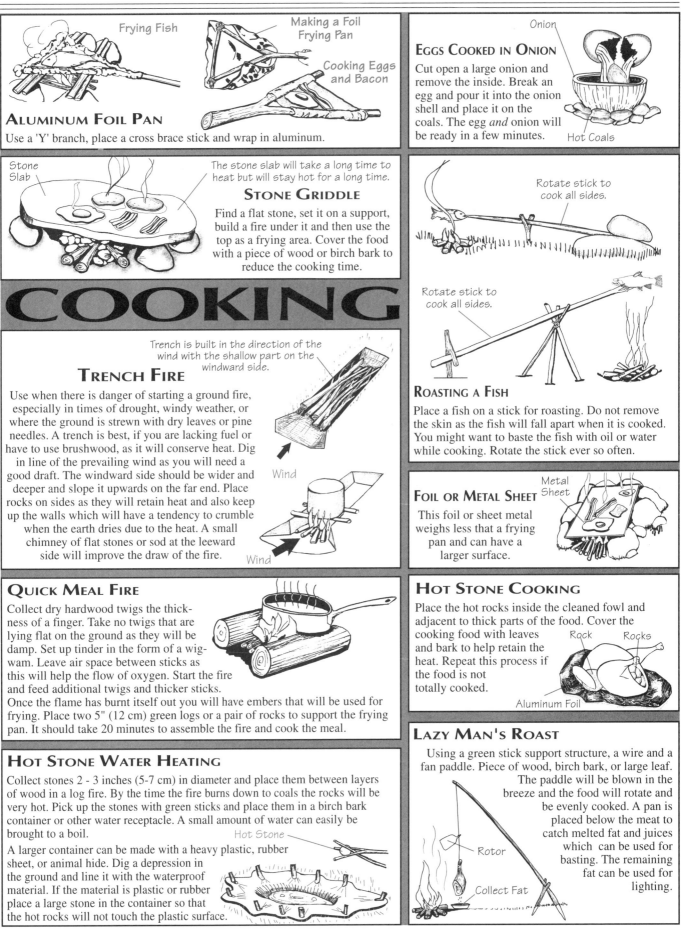

ALUMINUM FOIL PAN

Frying Fish

Making a Foil Frying Pan

Cooking Eggs and Bacon

Use a 'Y' branch, place a cross brace stick and wrap in aluminum.

EGGS COOKED IN ONION

Onion

Cut open a large onion and remove the inside. Break an egg and pour it into the onion shell and place it on the coals. The egg *and* onion will be ready in a few minutes.

Hot Coals

STONE GRIDDLE

Stone Slab

The stone slab will take a long time to heat but will stay hot for a long time.

Find a flat stone, set it on a support, build a fire under it and then use the top as a frying area. Cover the food with a piece of wood or birch bark to reduce the cooking time.

COOKING

TRENCH FIRE

Trench is built in the direction of the wind with the shallow part on the windward side.

Use when there is danger of starting a ground fire, especially in times of drought, windy weather, or where the ground is strewn with dry leaves or pine needles. A trench is best, if you are lacking fuel or have to use brushwood, as it will conserve heat. Dig in line of the prevailing wind as you will need a good draft. The windward side should be wider and deeper and slope it upwards on the far end. Place rocks on sides as they will retain heat and also keep up the walls which will have a tendency to crumble when the earth dries due to the heat. A small chimney of flat stones or sod at the leeward side will improve the draw of the fire.

Wind

Wind

Rotate stick to cook all sides.

Rotate stick to cook all sides.

ROASTING A FISH

Place a fish on a stick for roasting. Do not remove the skin as the fish will fall apart when it is cooked. You might want to baste the fish with oil or water while cooking. Rotate the stick ever so often.

FOIL OR METAL SHEET

Metal Sheet

This foil or sheet metal weighs less that a frying pan and can have a larger surface.

QUICK MEAL FIRE

Collect dry hardwood twigs the thickness of a finger. Take no twigs that are lying flat on the ground as they will be damp. Set up tinder in the form of a wigwam. Leave air space between sticks as this will help the flow of oxygen. Start the fire and feed additional twigs and thicker sticks.
Once the flame has burnt itself out you will have embers that will be used for frying. Place two 5" (12 cm) green logs or a pair of rocks to support the frying pan. It should take 20 minutes to assemble the fire and cook the meal.

HOT STONE COOKING

Place the hot rocks inside the cleaned fowl and adjacent to thick parts of the food. Cover the cooking food with leaves and bark to help retain the heat. Repeat this process if the food is not totally cooked.

Rock

Rocks

Aluminum Foil

HOT STONE WATER HEATING

Collect stones 2 - 3 inches (5-7 cm) in diameter and place them between layers of wood in a log fire. By the time the fire burns down to coals the rocks will be very hot. Pick up the stones with green sticks and place them in a birch bark container or other water receptacle. A small amount of water can easily be brought to a boil.

Hot Stone

A larger container can be made with a heavy plastic, rubber sheet, or animal hide. Dig a depression in the ground and line it with the waterproof material. If the material is plastic or rubber place a large stone in the container so that the hot rocks will not touch the plastic surface.

LAZY MAN'S ROAST

Using a green stick support structure, a wire and a fan paddle. Piece of wood, birch bark, or large leaf. The paddle will be blown in the breeze and the food will rotate and be evenly cooked. A pan is placed below the meat to catch melted fat and juices which can be used for basting. The remaining fat can be used for lighting.

Rotor

Collect Fat

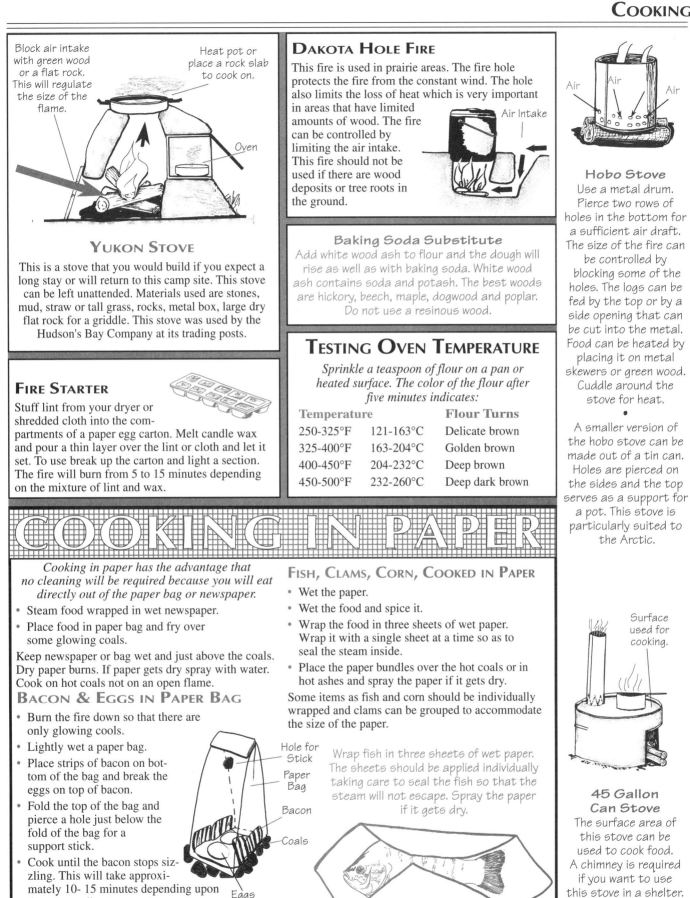

Block air intake with green wood or a flat rock. This will regulate the size of the flame.

Heat pot or place a rock slab to cook on.

Oven

YUKON STOVE

This is a stove that you would build if you expect a long stay or will return to this camp site. This stove can be left unattended. Materials used are stones, mud, straw or tall grass, rocks, metal box, large dry flat rock for a griddle. This stove was used by the Hudson's Bay Company at its trading posts.

FIRE STARTER

Stuff lint from your dryer or shredded cloth into the compartments of a paper egg carton. Melt candle wax and pour a thin layer over the lint or cloth and let it set. To use break up the carton and light a section. The fire will burn from 5 to 15 minutes depending on the mixture of lint and wax.

DAKOTA HOLE FIRE

This fire is used in prairie areas. The fire hole protects the fire from the constant wind. The hole also limits the loss of heat which is very important in areas that have limited amounts of wood. The fire can be controlled by limiting the air intake. This fire should not be used if there are wood deposits or tree roots in the ground.

Air Intake

Baking Soda Substitute

Add white wood ash to flour and the dough will rise as well as with baking soda. White wood ash contains soda and potash. The best woods are hickory, beech, maple, dogwood and poplar. Do not use a resinous wood.

TESTING OVEN TEMPERATURE

Sprinkle a teaspoon of flour on a pan or heated surface. The color of the flour after five minutes indicates:

Temperature		Flour Turns
250-325°F	121-163°C	Delicate brown
325-400°F	163-204°C	Golden brown
400-450°F	204-232°C	Deep brown
450-500°F	232-260°C	Deep dark brown

Air   Air   Air

Hobo Stove

Use a metal drum. Pierce two rows of holes in the bottom for a sufficient air draft. The size of the fire can be controlled by blocking some of the holes. The logs can be fed by the top or by a side opening that can be cut into the metal. Food can be heated by placing it on metal skewers or green wood. Cuddle around the stove for heat.

•

A smaller version of the hobo stove can be made out of a tin can. Holes are pierced on the sides and the top serves as a support for a pot. This stove is particularly suited to the Arctic.

COOKING IN PAPER

Cooking in paper has the advantage that no cleaning will be required because you will eat directly out of the paper bag or newspaper.

- Steam food wrapped in wet newspaper.
- Place food in paper bag and fry over some glowing coals.

Keep newspaper or bag wet and just above the coals. Dry paper burns. If paper gets dry spray with water. Cook on hot coals not on an open flame.

BACON & EGGS IN PAPER BAG

- Burn the fire down so that there are only glowing cools.
- Lightly wet a paper bag.
- Place strips of bacon on bottom of the bag and break the eggs on top of bacon.
- Fold the top of the bag and pierce a hole just below the fold of the bag for a support stick.
- Cook until the bacon stops sizzling. This will take approximately 10- 15 minutes depending upon the surrounding temperature.
- If egg is not done to your taste keep on cooking.
- Wet down the bag if it starts to burn.

Hole for Stick

Paper Bag

Bacon

Coals

Eggs

FISH, CLAMS, CORN, COOKED IN PAPER

- Wet the paper.
- Wet the food and spice it.
- Wrap the food in three sheets of wet paper. Wrap it with a single sheet at a time so as to seal the steam inside.
- Place the paper bundles over the hot coals or in hot ashes and spray the paper if it gets dry.

Some items as fish and corn should be individually wrapped and clams can be grouped to accommodate the size of the paper.

Wrap fish in three sheets of wet paper. The sheets should be applied individually taking care to seal the fish so that the steam will not escape. Spray the paper if it gets dry.

Fish in Wet Paper

Surface used for cooking.

45 Gallon Can Stove

The surface area of this stove can be used to cook food. A chimney is required if you want to use this stove in a shelter. A door cover helps regulate the size of the flame.

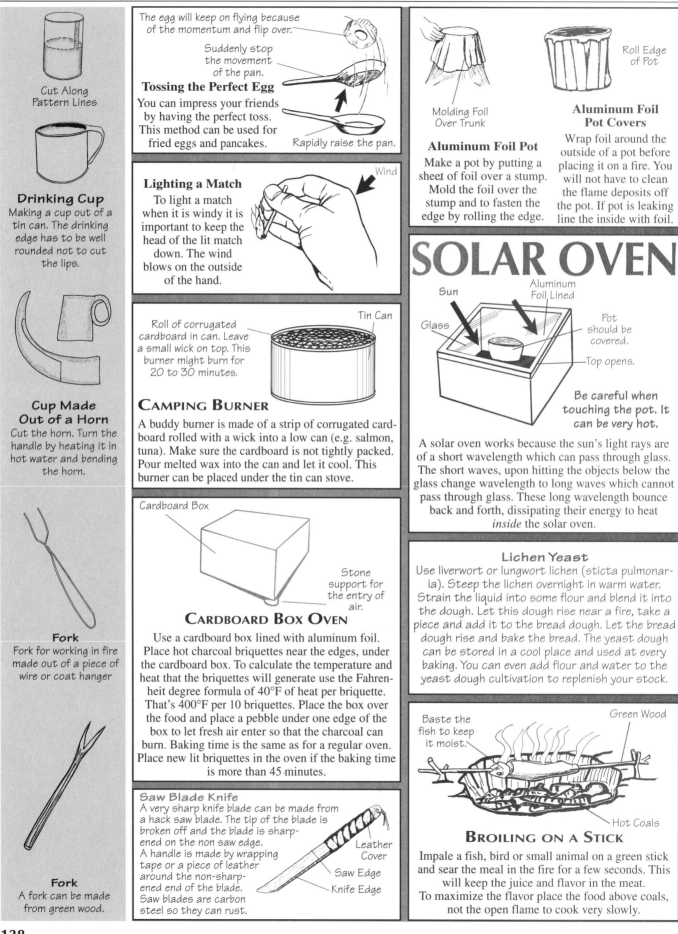

Drinking Cup
Making a cup out of a tin can. The drinking edge has to be well rounded not to cut the lips.

Cut Along Pattern Lines

Cup Made Out of a Horn
Cut the horn. Turn the handle by heating it in hot water and bending the horn.

Fork
Fork for working in fire made out of a piece of wire or coat hanger

Fork
A fork can be made from green wood.

Tossing the Perfect Egg
You can impress your friends by having the perfect toss. This method can be used for fried eggs and pancakes.

The egg will keep on flying because of the momentum and flip over.

Suddenly stop the movement of the pan.

Rapidly raise the pan.

Lighting a Match
To light a match when it is windy it is important to keep the head of the lit match down. The wind blows on the outside of the hand.

Wind

Roll of corrugated cardboard in can. Leave a small wick on top. This burner might burn for 20 to 30 minutes.

Tin Can

CAMPING BURNER
A buddy burner is made of a strip of corrugated cardboard rolled with a wick into a low can (e.g. salmon, tuna). Make sure the cardboard is not tightly packed. Pour melted wax into the can and let it cool. This burner can be placed under the tin can stove.

Cardboard Box

Stone support for the entry of air.

CARDBOARD BOX OVEN
Use a cardboard box lined with aluminum foil. Place hot charcoal briquettes near the edges, under the cardboard box. To calculate the temperature and heat that the briquettes will generate use the Fahrenheit degree formula of 40°F of heat per briquette. That's 400°F per 10 briquettes. Place the box over the food and place a pebble under one edge of the box to let fresh air enter so that the charcoal can burn. Baking time is the same as for a regular oven. Place new lit briquettes in the oven if the baking time is more than 45 minutes.

Saw Blade Knife
A very sharp knife blade can be made from a hack saw blade. The tip of the blade is broken off and the blade is sharpened on the non saw edge. A handle is made by wrapping tape or a piece of leather around the non-sharpened end of the blade. Saw blades are carbon steel so they can rust.

Leather Cover
Saw Edge
Knife Edge

Molding Foil Over Trunk

Roll Edge of Pot

Aluminum Foil Pot
Make a pot by putting a sheet of foil over a stump. Mold the foil over the stump and to fasten the edge by rolling the edge.

Aluminum Foil Pot Covers
Wrap foil around the outside of a pot before placing it on a fire. You will not have to clean the flame deposits off the pot. If pot is leaking line the inside with foil.

SOLAR OVEN

Sun

Aluminum Foil Lined

Glass

Pot should be covered.

Top opens.

Be careful when touching the pot. It can be very hot.

A solar oven works because the sun's light rays are of a short wavelength which can pass through glass. The short waves, upon hitting the objects below the glass change wavelength to long waves which cannot pass through glass. These long wavelength bounce back and forth, dissipating their energy to heat *inside* the solar oven.

Lichen Yeast
Use liverwort or lungwort lichen (sticta pulmonaria). Steep the lichen overnight in warm water. Strain the liquid into some flour and blend it into the dough. Let this dough rise near a fire, take a piece and add it to the bread dough. Let the bread dough rise and bake the bread. The yeast dough can be stored in a cool place and used at every baking. You can even add flour and water to the yeast dough cultivation to replenish your stock.

Baste the fish to keep it moist.

Green Wood

Hot Coals

BROILING ON A STICK
Impale a fish, bird or small animal on a green stick and sear the meal in the fire for a few seconds. This will keep the juice and flavor in the meat. To maximize the flavor place the food above coals, not the open flame to cook very slowly.

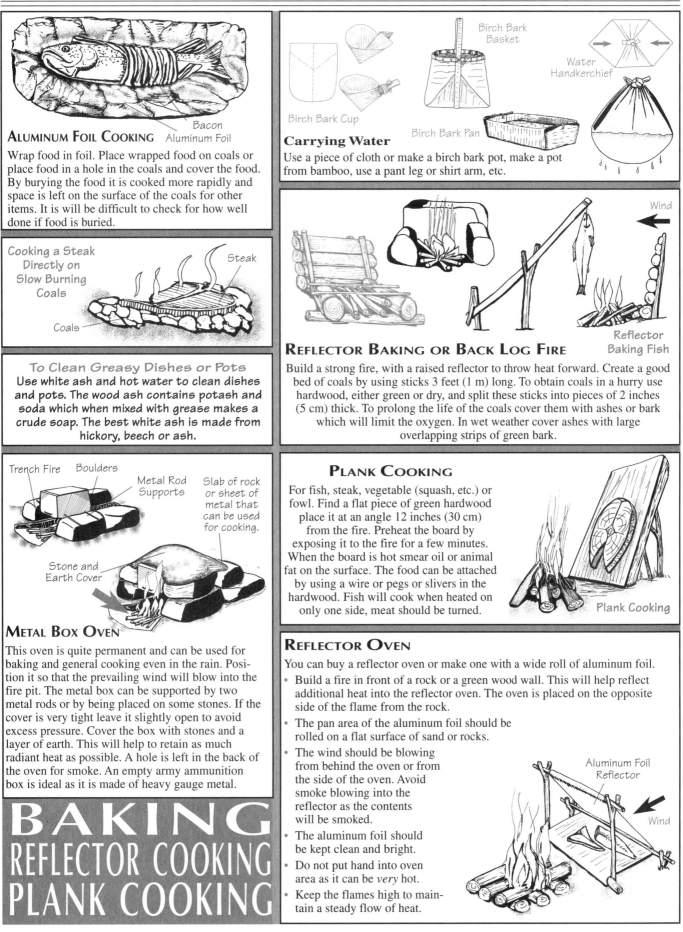

ALUMINUM FOIL COOKING

Wrap food in foil. Place wrapped food on coals or place food in a hole in the coals and cover the food. By burying the food it is cooked more rapidly and space is left on the surface of the coals for other items. It is will be difficult to check for how well done if food is buried.

Bacon
Aluminum Foil

Cooking a Steak Directly on Slow Burning Coals

Steak

Coals

To Clean Greasy Dishes or Pots

Use white ash and hot water to clean dishes and pots. The wood ash contains potash and soda which when mixed with grease makes a crude soap. The best white ash is made from hickory, beech or ash.

Trench Fire *Boulders*

Metal Rod Supports

Slab of rock or sheet of metal that can be used for cooking.

Stone and Earth Cover

METAL BOX OVEN

This oven is quite permanent and can be used for baking and general cooking even in the rain. Position it so that the prevailing wind will blow into the fire pit. The metal box can be supported by two metal rods or by being placed on some stones. If the cover is very tight leave it slightly open to avoid excess pressure. Cover the box with stones and a layer of earth. This will help to retain as much radiant heat as possible. A hole is left in the back of the oven for smoke. An empty army ammunition box is ideal as it is made of heavy gauge metal.

BAKING
REFLECTOR COOKING
PLANK COOKING

Carrying Water

Use a piece of cloth or make a birch bark pot, make a pot from bamboo, use a pant leg or shirt arm, etc.

Birch Bark Cup

Birch Bark Basket

Water Handkerchief

Birch Bark Pan

Wind

Reflector Baking Fish

REFLECTOR BAKING OR BACK LOG FIRE

Build a strong fire, with a raised reflector to throw heat forward. Create a good bed of coals by using sticks 3 feet (1 m) long. To obtain coals in a hurry use hardwood, either green or dry, and split these sticks into pieces of 2 inches (5 cm) thick. To prolong the life of the coals cover them with ashes or bark which will limit the oxygen. In wet weather cover ashes with large overlapping strips of green bark.

PLANK COOKING

For fish, steak, vegetable (squash, etc.) or fowl. Find a flat piece of green hardwood place it at an angle 12 inches (30 cm) from the fire. Preheat the board by exposing it to the fire for a few minutes. When the board is hot smear oil or animal fat on the surface. The food can be attached by using a wire or pegs or slivers in the hardwood. Fish will cook when heated on only one side, meat should be turned.

Plank Cooking

REFLECTOR OVEN

You can buy a reflector oven or make one with a wide roll of aluminum foil.

- Build a fire in front of a rock or a green wood wall. This will help reflect additional heat into the reflector oven. The oven is placed on the opposite side of the flame from the rock.

- The pan area of the aluminum foil should be rolled on a flat surface of sand or rocks.

- The wind should be blowing from behind the oven or from the side of the oven. Avoid smoke blowing into the reflector as the contents will be smoked.

- The aluminum foil should be kept clean and bright.

- Do not put hand into oven area as it can be *very* hot.

- Keep the flames high to maintain a steady flow of heat.

Aluminum Foil Reflector

Wind

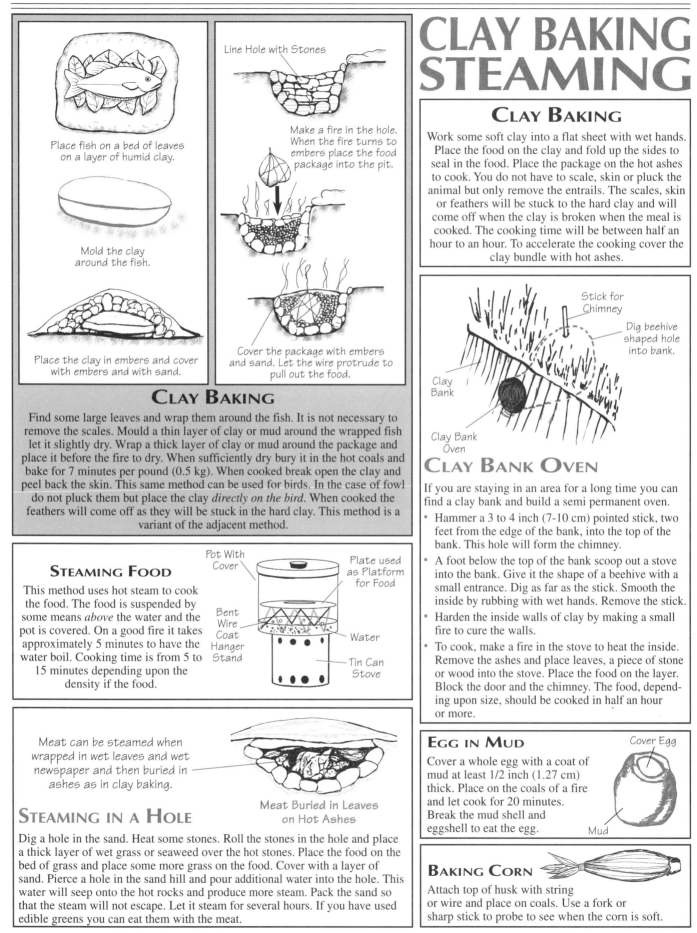

CLAY BAKING STEAMING

CLAY BAKING

Work some soft clay into a flat sheet with wet hands. Place the food on the clay and fold up the sides to seal in the food. Place the package on the hot ashes to cook. You do not have to scale, skin or pluck the animal but only remove the entrails. The scales, skin or feathers will be stuck to the hard clay and will come off when the clay is broken when the meal is cooked. The cooking time will be between half an hour to an hour. To accelerate the cooking cover the clay bundle with hot ashes.

Clay Baking (illustration panel)

Place fish on a bed of leaves on a layer of humid clay.

Mold the clay around the fish.

Place the clay in embers and cover with embers and with sand.

Line Hole with Stones

Make a fire in the hole. When the fire turns to embers place the food package into the pit.

Cover the package with embers and sand. Let the wire protrude to pull out the food.

CLAY BAKING

Find some large leaves and wrap them around the fish. It is not necessary to remove the scales. Mould a thin layer of clay or mud around the wrapped fish let it slightly dry. Wrap a thick layer of clay or mud around the package and place it before the fire to dry. When sufficiently dry bury it in the hot coals and bake for 7 minutes per pound (0.5 kg). When cooked break open the clay and peel back the skin. This same method can be used for birds. In the case of fowl do not pluck them but place the clay *directly on the bird*. When cooked the feathers will come off as they will be stuck in the hard clay. This method is a variant of the adjacent method.

Stick for Chimney / Dig beehive shaped hole into bank. / Clay Bank / Clay Bank Oven

CLAY BANK OVEN

If you are staying in an area for a long time you can find a clay bank and build a semi permanent oven.

- Hammer a 3 to 4 inch (7-10 cm) pointed stick, two feet from the edge of the bank, into the top of the bank. This hole will form the chimney.
- A foot below the top of the bank scoop out a stove into the bank. Give it the shape of a beehive with a small entrance. Dig as far as the stick. Smooth the inside by rubbing with wet hands. Remove the stick.
- Harden the inside walls of clay by making a small fire to cure the walls.
- To cook, make a fire in the stove to heat the inside. Remove the ashes and place leaves, a piece of stone or wood into the stove. Place the food on the layer. Block the door and the chimney. The food, depending upon size, should be cooked in half an hour or more.

STEAMING FOOD

This method uses hot steam to cook the food. The food is suspended by some means *above* the water and the pot is covered. On a good fire it takes approximately 5 minutes to have the water boil. Cooking time is from 5 to 15 minutes depending upon the density if the food.

Pot With Cover / Plate used as Platform for Food / Bent Wire Coat Hanger Stand / Water / Tin Can Stove

EGG IN MUD

Cover a whole egg with a coat of mud at least 1/2 inch (1.27 cm) thick. Place on the coals of a fire and let cook for 20 minutes. Break the mud shell and eggshell to eat the egg.

Cover Egg / Mud

Meat can be steamed when wrapped in wet leaves and wet newspaper and then buried in ashes as in clay baking.

Meat Buried in Leaves on Hot Ashes

STEAMING IN A HOLE

Dig a hole in the sand. Heat some stones. Roll the stones in the hole and place a thick layer of wet grass or seaweed over the hot stones. Place the food on the bed of grass and place some more grass on the food. Cover with a layer of sand. Pierce a hole in the sand hill and pour additional water into the hole. This water will seep onto the hot rocks and produce more steam. Pack the sand so that the steam will not escape. Let it steam for several hours. If you have used edible greens you can eat them with the meat.

BAKING CORN

Attach top of husk with string or wire and place on coals. Use a fork or sharp stick to probe to see when the corn is soft.

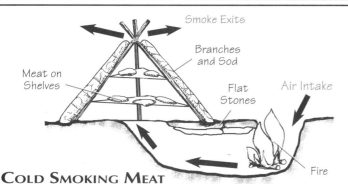

COLD SMOKING MEAT

Smoking is the best way to conserve meat and fish. Choose a location with soft earth and dig a trench about 1 1/2' (0.45m) wide and 7' (2 m) long. Cover the trench with flat stones and earth. Place a teepee covered with branches and sod at the higher end of the trench. Leave an opening for smoke to escape. Shelves for thin slices of meat made of green wood are suspended in the teepee. Start a small intense fire 5 feet (1.5 m) up the tunnel to heat the walls to creat an updraft. Build, at the end of the tunnel, and feed a small fire for about 10 hours. Store the smoked meat in a dry, well aired, and shady area.

DRYING FOOD

JERKY

Drying Meat

Jerky is a staple for wilderness living and if well prepared can be kept for years without refrigeration. Once prepared jerky can be eaten by slowly chewing it or using it as a base for a soup, meat drink, stew, or to make pemmican.

Making Jerky

Cut red domestic or wild meat into 1"x2"x8" (2.5x5 x20 cm) strips *removing any* fat, tendons, and gristle. Prepare seasoning of equal amounts of salt, pepper, chili pepper.

Pound the meat and season heavily at the same time.

Place the strips on a grill near coals and let cook until all the moisture has been removed. This will take approximately 6 hours. The finished jerky should be like dry leather and bend a little without breaking.

PEMMICAN

This is a high energy food developed by the North American Indian. Pemmican is a meal in a ball and it was the food used by the voyageurs to cross North America in canoes.

Making Pemmican

- Pound a pound (450 g) of dry jerky into a powder with a hammer or a clean stone.
- Melt small chunks of raw animal fat in a pan over a slow fire. Do not let it boil up and burn. When the fat has rendered remove the tissue and pour liquid fat over the powdered jerky.
- Add *dried* chopped fruit (serviceberry, apples, nuts, raisins etc.).
- Mix the ingredients until it has the consistency of porridge and the fat will act as a bonding agent. Before the mixture cools shape it into golf ball sized balls. Store in a *porous* bag to reduce the humidity.

It does not keep as well as jerky because the fat will sour in warm weather. It keeps for approximately one month in cool weather. It is excellent for fall hunting, camping or hiking. It can be chewed on or used in soups or stews. The Indians used dried serviceberries (*amelanchier*) as the fruit ingredient. Supplement your diet with sources of Vitamin C. *See Edible Plant Chapter.*

SMOKING

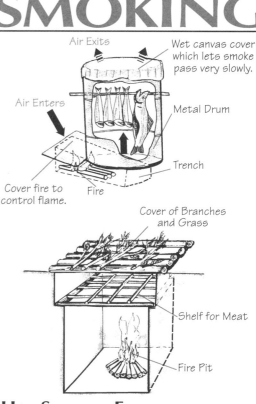

HOT SMOKING FOOD

Smoking gives a unique flavor to the food. This flavor depends upon the type of wood or bushes being burnt.

- Do not use wood from coniferous trees as the smoked food will have a tarry flavor. Use hardwood chips such as hickory, ash, apple, cherry, maple, aspen, and oak. If dry wood chips are used soak them in water for up to one hour.
- Build a fire in your smoke pit and let it burn down to coals. Drop your stock of soaked smoking chips on the coals, place food on grill above coals, and cover food and fire with smoker.
- Fish takes 15 minutes per side. A two inch (5 cm) thick slice of meat takes 1/2 hour per side.

Protection From Blow Flies

To protect meat from egg laying blow flies keep the meat in a dark cool dry location. Hang it 12 feet (3.6 m) above the ground. Keep it away from leaves. Suspend fresh meat above a small fire to smoke and sear the surface with a protrective hardened dry covering around the meat.

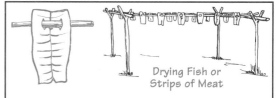

Drying Fish or
Strips of Meat

Eskimo Dry Meat (moose, caribou, muskrats)
Cut up the meat in slices 1 inch (2.5 cm) thick and hang over a pole. Be sure that the two halves do not touch. Keep turning it every day and keep a smoky fire burning to keep flies away.

Food placed in canvas bags 12 feet (3.6 m) above the ground.

FOOD CACHE

To protect food from animals you can hang the food from a pole suspended between two trees. The height of the bags depends upon which visitors you are expecting. You will require 12 feet (3.6 m) for a bear. This storage area should be downwind from the camp as you do not want animals trudging through your camp on the way to your storage area. Place it at least 50 feet (15 m) from your shelter.

FOOD STORAGE

In choosing a food storage method consider:

Animals: They will be attracted by the smells of your food especially when they prowl around during the night.

Insects: Odors of food will attract unwelcome insect attention.

Spoilage: Foods that require a cool environment will rapidly spoil if they are too warm.

Suspend Food: Store food in plastic bags inserted into sturdy canvas bags and suspend them from trees. This will keep the food out of reach of animals. *Suspend the food* some distance from the camp and downwind if possible. You do not want an animal to stumble through your campsite while investigating those strange odors.

Cooling Food: Keep food cool by using plastic containers and placing these in a *cool mountain stream*. Do not forget to weigh the containers down with rocks or they might float away during a rainstorm. Make sure that the containers are well sealed.

High Altitude Storage: Food can be stored, in late spring or all year at high altitudes, in snow patches.

Cooling by Evaporation: Your forehead cools with the evaporation of sweat. This same principle can be used while camping or where you are surviving in the woods. Place the food in plastic bags into a cotton canvas bag which you suspend in a breezy shaded area. Keep the bag moist by dousing it with water. Evaporation of the water from the surface of the bag will keep the contents cool.

COOLING FOOD

Food can be stored in plastic jars or bags and placed in cool mountain brooks. Place boulders and stones as a retaining wall so that the food does not float away. Cover the containers with rocks to protect against animals.

Boulders

Direction of Flow

STORAGE OF EGGS

To store eggs for several months, coat them with a thin layer of lukewarm mineral oil, drain well and place them in a cool place.

Eggs Stored in Jars Filled with Limewater

To prepare the limewater: Scald 2 pounds (0.9 kg) of hydrated lime in a little water and stir with 5 gallons (19 L) of previously boiled water. Allow to cool. Let settle and use the clear liquid. Place clean, fresh eggs in a clean jar and pour the liquid 2 inches (5 cm) above the eggs. Cover the jar and keep it in a cool dry place. To test eggs for freshness, put them in a bowl of cold water. If they are fresh *they will sink* to the bottom.

STORING FOOD

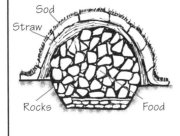

Sod
Straw
Rocks   Food

Ground Storage

FOOD SILO

Corn, carrots, apples etc. can be stored in a silo. Choose a dry spot and dig a hole into the ground. Line the hole with rocks making sure that you leave breathing space between the rocks. Place the vegetables to be stored into the hole. Place some dry straw, twigs, grass, and flat stones over the food. Place a layer of sod on top. This silo will protect the food from animals, from drying too fast, and from frost.

GROUND STORAGE

Dig a hole and line it with large stones. Cover with heavy logs and rocks to protect food from animals.

REVIVING STORED FOOD

- Fresh eggs will keep longer if dipped in a thin warmed mineral oil. Drain and store in a cool spot.
- Fresh potatoes can be frozen to be used all winter. Choose firm, clean potatoes and keep them frozen until ready to use. Put frozen potatoes in boiling salted water without peeling and cook until tender, then peel. Or defrost and cook in a microwave oven.
- Pour boiling water over stale walnuts.
- Break sprouts off stored potatoes, as soon as they appear, to prevent the potatoes from becoming soft.
- Freshen dried onion, red and green pepper or parsley flakes by soaking for 20 minutes in warm water. Drain and use as fresh vegetables.
- If cheese has started to mold, trim the mold, and wrap store it in a cloth dipped in vinegar.
- Bake stale peanuts at 275°F (135°C) in an oven for one hour.
- To preserve butter store in a sealed pot in a cool dark place.
- Frozen fish can be cut with a saw or axe. Peel off the skin and cut into pieces Eat with salt and blubber. The blubber is to give you some fat to help you resist the cold as fish usually is quite lean, especially trout.
- Brown sugar can be kept soft by storing it in an airtight container with a slice of fresh bread.

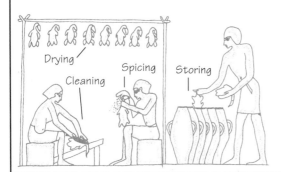

Drying
Cleaning
Spicing
Storing

Egyptians Storing Geese

The Egyptians cleaned the geese and then salted and spiced them and hung them up to partially dry. They were then placed in urns which were sealed with wax.

INSECT EATING

Insects are excellent food as they are mainly protein and can provide more emergency energy than fish or meat. You can eat moths, mayflies and other insects. Attract them with a small light at night. If it's too cold for flying, look under rotten logs and stones. Ants can be a problem as they contain formic acid and have a bitter taste. Grasshoppers, termites, locusts and crickets can be eaten when the hard parts, such as wings and legs, are removed. An old method of catching insects and small animals was by setting fire to large tracts of grassland. Once the fire had passed the roasted insects and animals can be collected. This method should *not be used* even in a survival situation as it is very destructive and the fire can get out of hand.

People in different parts of the world consider grasshoppers, hairless caterpillars, wood boring beetle larvae and pupae, spider bodies, and termites as delicacies. Insects might actually be their only source of protein. There are different recipes in cooking, methods of finding, and raising insects. If you want to try eating insects or have to do so to survive, you will find them much more palatable if you cook them until they are dry or in a stew.

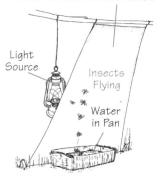

Insects hitting cloth while trying to approach light at night. Some will fall into the water.

Light Source

Insects Flying

Water in Pan

Grasshoppers: remove legs and wings and fry or cook over fire.

Red ants and night butterflies are edible.

Find white larvae "white worm" under rotten tree trunks.

Opening an Oyster

Enter the blade of a dull knife or an oyster knife near the oyster's muscle. This muscle is found at the thick more pointed end of the oyster. Twist the blade and the shell will open.

Eating Fish

Do not eat fish if:
- Eyes look milky.
- Does not look fresh.
- Finger pressure points leave indentations.
- It does not look like a fish; it inflates, snout like mouth, box shaped, or stone. These are fish but usually are not good to eat and should not be touched.
- Never eat offal of a fish.

While frog is watching wiggling fingers gradually approach this hand to catch the frog. Make sure that this hand does not cast a shadow on or near the frog.

Leopard Frog

Wiggle fingers to attract the attention of the frog. Do not advance this hand.

Eating Frogs

Skin frogs before eating as the skin of some frogs secrete an irritating and possibly poisonous liquid. Do not eat frogs with bright yellow or red marks.

CATCHING FROGS

Use a piece of cloth on a string. Let the cloth float on the water and yank the string when the frog takes the cloth into its mouth. Frogs can be speared. Frogs can be caught at night by holding a torch above the water. The frogs will watch the light and you can net them or even catch them from behind with your hands. The best part to eat is the hind legs, which can be cooked over hot coals.

SEAFOOD

Trout as Food

One pound (0.5 kg) of rainbow trout has 200 calories. 5000 calories per day are required to survive in the wilderness which would need over 25 trout per day.

Salmon and other fatty fish are a better meal as they provide, on the average, four times the calories per pound (0.5 kg). If you do not supplement your diet with plants and animals you will gradually starve.

Fish should be gutted and washed when caught. The guts can be used as bait or else bury them in the ground as their odor will attract insects and scavengers. Keep the fish cool and cook as soon as possible.

Seal

Seal meat is excellent nourishing food but highly flavored. Do not eat the liver of the bearded seal as it has a high concentration of vitamin A.

Seaweed

All seaweed is edible. Raw, simmered to make a soup, boiled with meat stew, or dry to store. The *Edible Plant Chapter* outlines some sea weeds.

Salt Water Clams

Discard the dark portion of the meat between the end of April to the end of October. *During this period there are possible dangerous concentrations of toxins.*

Crabs & Lobsters

Cook them before eating. Salt water crabs can be eaten raw but do not take any risks.

Sea Cucumbers

These look like cucumbers but are actually animals. Remove its insides and scrape the slimy outside skin keeping the fine long muscles. These muscles can be eaten boiled, fried, in a stew, or even raw.

Sea Urchin

The insides are edible especially in temperate and arctic waters of North America. Collect sea urchins at low tide when they can be picked off rocks.

Abalone

The abalone is a mollusk that clings to rocks along the northern Pacific coast and is exposed during low tide. Use a knife or sharp stick to pry it loose. Pry with a sudden jerk or the abalone has time to attach itself more securely. Slice the white of the meat. Pound it with a rock so that it becomes tender. Cook as a chowder or fried and boiled over an open fire. *Be careful when detaching them as they might suddenly close and catch your hand or piece of garment. You will drown if you cannot release yourself before the next tide. See Fish Chapter.*

Turtles

Turtles are very nutritious, especially the clear savory oil that can be rendered at very low heat. A turtle can be killed by striking or removing its head. Scald the turtle in hot water, for a few minutes, and then quarter the underside and remove the entrails. The turtle is then turned upside down and simmered in its shell.

To find turtle eggs you can back track its trail on a beach to where it has buried them. *Turtles are rare so avoid disturbing them.*

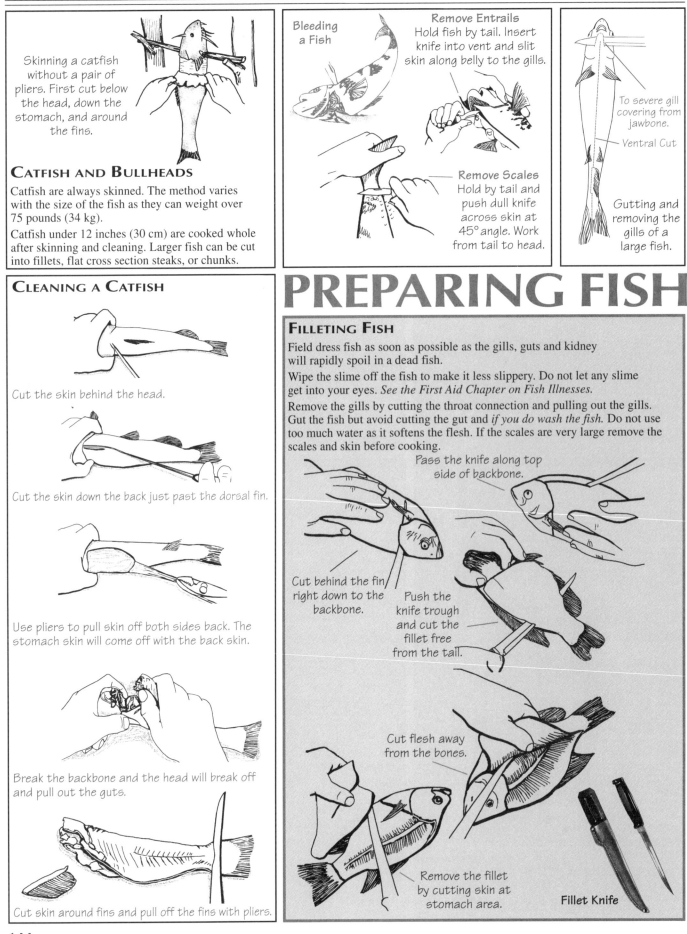

Skinning a catfish without a pair of pliers. First cut below the head, down the stomach, and around the fins.

CATFISH AND BULLHEADS

Catfish are always skinned. The method varies with the size of the fish as they can weight over 75 pounds (34 kg).

Catfish under 12 inches (30 cm) are cooked whole after skinning and cleaning. Larger fish can be cut into fillets, flat cross section steaks, or chunks.

CLEANING A CATFISH

Cut the skin behind the head.

Cut the skin down the back just past the dorsal fin.

Use pliers to pull skin off both sides back. The stomach skin will come off with the back skin.

Break the backbone and the head will break off and pull out the guts.

Cut skin around fins and pull off the fins with pliers.

Bleeding a Fish

Remove Entrails Hold fish by tail. Insert knife into vent and slit skin along belly to the gills.

Remove Scales Hold by tail and push dull knife across skin at 45° angle. Work from tail to head.

To severe gill covering from jawbone.

Ventral Cut

Gutting and removing the gills of a large fish.

PREPARING FISH

FILLETING FISH

Field dress fish as soon as possible as the gills, guts and kidney will rapidly spoil in a dead fish.

Wipe the slime off the fish to make it less slippery. Do not let any slime get into your eyes. *See the First Aid Chapter on Fish Illnesses.*

Remove the gills by cutting the throat connection and pulling out the gills. Gut the fish but avoid cutting the gut and *if you do wash the fish.* Do not use too much water as it softens the flesh. If the scales are very large remove the scales and skin before cooking.

Pass the knife along top side of backbone.

Cut behind the fin right down to the backbone.

Push the knife trough and cut the fillet free from the tail.

Cut flesh away from the bones.

Remove the fillet by cutting skin at stomach area.

Fillet Knife

INDIAN SURVIVAL FOOD

- Indians ate the contents of the stomachs of herbivorous (grass-eating) mammals, such as caribou, moose, and deer. The content consists of leaves, small branches, and water plants mixed in digestive acids. These acids have a sour taste as salad dressing.

Animal Blood

For additional iron take four tablespoons of animal blood which is equal to ten eggs.

Eating Rawhide

Rawhide, if it has not been treated with varnish, can be boiled or chewed raw.

Bone Marrow

Cook large bones to suck out the bone marrow.

REMOVING THE "WILD FLAVOR"

The wild flavor is mainly stored in animal fat. Trim most of the animal fat off the carcase and use oil, or water for cooking. The animal fat can be cooked separately and used for lantern oil and heating.

Animal Hair

All animal hair should be removed and kept *off* the meat as the musk oil on the hair will add unwanted musk flavor to the meat.

Musk Gland

Wild animals have some type of musk glands which should be removed as soon as it is killed.

Fishy Taste From Wild Duck

Wild ducks feeding on fish and fishgrass will have a fishy taste. The smell will be noticed when cleaning wild aquatic fowl. This taste and odor gives a unique flavor and aroma to the meat. To reduce the smell and camouflage the taste use strips of orange, grapefruit, lime, or lemon peels. Poke holes deep into the breast and insert the peels. Cover the fowl with peels and some citric fruit juice. Remove the peels for the last 30 minutes of cooking to let the skin brown.

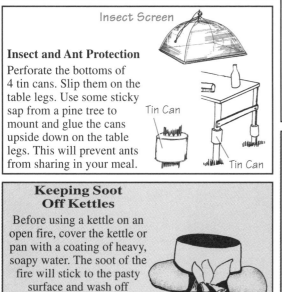

Insect Screen

Insect and Ant Protection

Perforate the bottoms of 4 tin cans. Slip them on the table legs. Use some sticky sap from a pine tree to mount and glue the cans upside down on the table legs. This will prevent ants from sharing in your meal.

Tin Can

Tin Can

Keeping Soot Off Kettles

Before using a kettle on an open fire, cover the kettle or pan with a coating of heavy, soapy water. The soot of the fire will stick to the pasty surface and wash off with hot water.

WINGED GAME

Butchering Birds Without a Knife

Remove feathers from a warm bird as it is more difficult if it is cold. The body can be pulled apart by hand. The entrails can be removed by pulling apart the skin on the stomach.

Scalding Birds

Place the bird head first in a small bucket. Pour hot water over the bird. Move the bird in the hot water by holding its legs. Scald until all the feathers become loose. After scalding remove the bird from the water and pluck the feathers in small tufts. Singe the remaining pinfeathers on a flame.

Gutting Duck

Plucking Feathers

DUCK

Clean duck and cut up to fry in deep grease with onions, salt and pepper. Ducks can be roasted on a stick or clay baked.

QUAIL

Clean them like chicken. Remove the gall bladder without breaking. This bird can be cooked in many ways but for camping or survival can be cooked over coals or rolled in leaves and clay baked the same way as fish. Quail are small so three or four are needed for a meal. To keep them moist wrap them in bacon or wet paper.

PTARMIGAN & GROUSE

Approach them very casually as if strolling by. When they stop moving throw a stone or stick at them. If you miss they will only fly for a short distance and you can try the same trick again. Cook as quail.

PTARMIGAN & GROUSE SOUP

Clean and cut up two birds. Put them into a pot with cold water and cover bring to a boil. Add onions, sliced tomato, one cup of rice, salt, and pepper.

Pouring Hot Water

AGE OF A BIRD

- The breastbone of a young bird is soft.
- The skin of a young bird has a light color.
- Young birds have tiny, pointed pin feathers at the tip of their wings. They are lost after the first year.
- Young pheasants have soft tails and old birds have rigid tails.
- Old birds have hard beaks.

Animal	Food Animal Eats	Taste
Bear	Berries, fruit, honey, vegetables.	Rich and savory.
Rabbit	Plants.	Wild, more gamey like chicken.
Muskrat	Plants.	Excellent
Wild Duck	Wild rice, marsh grains. Fish eating ducks wash with a damp cloth soaked in vinegar. Remove oil sacks in tail.	Excellent
Pheasant	Berries and fruit.	Hang 4-6 days for flavor.
Partridge	Berries and fruit.	Hang 4 days.
Quail	Berries and fruit.	Very dry. Wrap in bacon. Eat as soon as possible

SMALL GAME

PREPARING SMALL GAME

The example is a rabbit but the same procedure applies to other small fur bearing animals. *Read the article on Rabbit Fever below.*

- Remove the urine by holding the animal's forelegs and gradually squeezing down on the body from the chest to the bowels.
- Cut a hole into the belly area.
- Pull the skin apart at the hole and insert the first fingers from each hand. Pull the skin apart exposing the guts. Remove the guts.
- Cut the skin around the front and hind paws and between the hind legs. *See the illustration.*
- Hang the rabbit as in the illustration and pull off the skin.
- The last step in removing the skin is by pulling it over the head and cutting off the head.
- Dismember in the same way as a chicken.

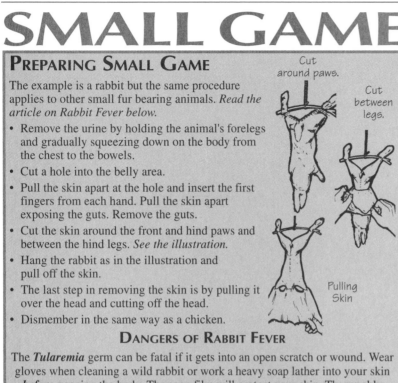

Cut around paws.

Cut between legs.

Pulling Skin

DANGERS OF RABBIT FEVER

The *Tularemia* germ can be fatal if it gets into an open scratch or wound. Wear gloves when cleaning a wild rabbit or work a heavy soap lather into your skin *before* opening the body. The soap film will protect your skin. Thoroughly wash your hands when finished. Do not hunt slow sluggish rabbits. Wait 2 or 3 weeks *after a heavy frost* before hunting for rabbit. *Cook all rabbits until well done.* The rabbit fever germ can be destroyed by intensive heat. Be careful when trapping as you will not know the health of the rabbit.

Rabbit "Starvation"

A diet of lean meat, with no other fatty food, can lead to starvation. Too much lean meat causes diarrhea. Rabbit meat is very lean. Having continuous diarrhea will make you very hungry and you will eat more and more rabbit. *This will cause starvation in a few days if you do not* **add fatty food to your diet.**

Boiled Rabbit Soup

Skin the rabbit, cut it up and put in a pot of cold salted water. Bring to a boil. Add rice and vegetables to make a broth. Add potatoes, rice or dumplings.

Roasted Rabbit

Cut up the rabbit and put in a pan *with grease* and some water. Add salt, carrots, onions and potatoes. Roast for an hour or until done. Mix a little flour with salt, pepper and enough water to make a thin mixture for gravy. Pour over the rabbit and mix. Roast a little longer until flour is cooked and water has partially evaporated.

DIFFERENCE BETWEEN HARE AND RABBIT

- Hare meat is dark. Rabbit meat is white.
- Hare are born open eyed and furred.
- Rabbits are born close eyed and naked.

Age of a Hare

Best hare are young. Judge the age by the teeth. Old teeth are dark and dull from use. Young teeth are sharp, white and short.

European Hare

HARE & RABBIT

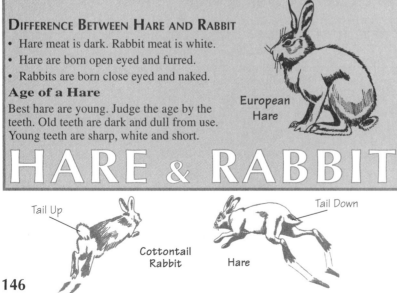

Tail Up

Tail Down

Cottontail Rabbit

Hare

Removing Skin

- Clean squirrel the same way as rabbit.
- Cut the skin around the paws.
- Cut through the skin on the back and pull the skin off.

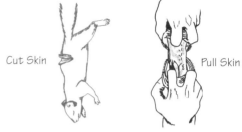

Cut Skin

Pull Skin

SQUIRREL

Flesh medium-red in color, is tender and delicious.
Remove: Small scent glands inside forelegs.

Squirrel

Squirrels can be fried, roasted on a spit over a campfire, broiled, or made into a stew.

Skin, clean and let them soak in salt water for an hour. Dry the pieces and prepare a savory meal. As some squirrels are small, once you remove the skin, you might chose to cook a stew with carrots, potatoes and some lard. If you catch a fox squirrel you are in for a royal meal!

Grey & Fox Squirrels

Grey squirrel is excellent. The flesh is light red or pink. Requires of half a squirrel per person.

OPOSSUM

Remove Hair: Dip for a minute in hot but not boiling water. Scrape off hair with a dull knife or flat stick. Avoid damaging skin. Do not skin an opossum.

Musk Glands: Remove musk glands from the small of the back and inside the forelegs.

Cut Open: Starting at throat and go to the anus. Remove entrails and cut off the tail and head.

Wash inside and out with hot water and remove all exposed fat. Let stand overnight in cold salt water.

To Roast

Cooking: Wash with hot water. Fill body cavity with stuffing of raisins, moist bread etc. and cook 20 minutes per pound (0.45kg). Baste every 15 minutes.

Cook on a Coals

Skin animal, Cut away any excess fat.
Rotate on skewer over coals until brown.

BEAVER

Beaver meat is dark red, fine grained and tastes like pork.

Remove: Musk glands from inside of legs and castor gland from under the belly near the tail.

Boiled Smoked Beaver

Smoke the beaver for a day or so. Then cut up the meat and boil in salted water until it is done.

Beaver Tail

Remove the scale like hide by hanging the tail near a fire (not too hot). The black hide will shrivel and puff and be freed from the oily gelatinous white flesh. Add meat to a stew of potatoes, carrots, etc.

Vegetation

Boiled Roots
Wash roots and boil until soft. Add to a pot of stew and eat with fatty meat or fish.

•

Inner Bark of Pine
The Lodge Pole Pine and other pines have an edible inner bark that can be eaten fresh or dried.

•

Pinon Nuts
Nuts from southern pines. They are soft and a delicacy. They can be eaten raw, roasted or used as a flour for bread.

•

Acorn Soup
Break shells of ripe acorns. Remove and crush the nuts. Pour warm water over the crushed nuts *three or four times* to remove the bitter taste. Indians buried acorns in swampy soil for a year to remove bitterness. Cook the acorn meal in hot water.

•

Birch Tree Spaghetti
The inner bark of the birch can be removed, cut into strips and added to soup or stew. The twigs and leaves can be cooked to make a tea.

•

Palmetto Cabbage
The Seminoles of Florida would cut off the new top of the palmetto and eat it raw or bake it.

•

Mushrooms
Avoid eating mushrooms as they have little food value and the risk of choosing the wrong one is very high. *See Mushroom Chapter.*

Lizard Catching Loop
Make the loop of light wire and sway it slowly in front of the lizard. Gradually bring the loop closer and closer and then lasso the lizard. Skin the lizard and fry it. It tastes like chicken.

Lizards
Lizards are excellent to eat. The only poisonous lizards are the Gila monster of the Southwest and the beaded lizard of Mexico.

PORCUPINE

A porcupine is an excellent survival food because it can be killed without a weapon.

Skin: Cut open and skin from the quill-less belly. Quills can also be burned off in a fire.

Scent Glands: Remove scent glands from the inside of the forelegs.

Remove fat surrounding the body cavity.

Boiled Porcupine

Cut into pieces and soak in salt water for 2 hours. Remove from the salt water.

Place in pot and cover with cold water, bring to a boil and simmer for 30 minutes. Remove and dry the pieces.

Brush cooked pieces with seasoned (salt, paprika, pepper) butter or oil and broil until brown, usually 25 minutes. Serve 2 to 4 people.

Porcupine Quills

If porcupine quills get stuck in your flesh remove them immediately as their barbed tips will work their way deeper into your flesh. *See the First Aid Chapter for more information.*

BAKED SKUNK

Clean (do not forget to remove glands!), skin, wash. Bake in oven with salt and pepper. Tastes like rabbit. Keep the melted skunk fat to cure whooping cough.

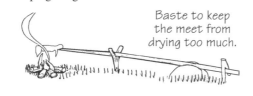

Baste to keep the meet from drying too much.

Small Rodent Cooking
Place animal on a stick and slowly turn while roasting on a fire.

SOUP HOLE

After catching a large animal cut off a piece of fresh hide and push it into a cavity in the ground. Add water and some wild onions or other greens. Throw a few hot stones into the liquid and let them do the cooking.

Arctic Vegetation
Arctic vegetation is nearly all edible except for some mushrooms. The best known food is rock tripe. It looks like a leathery dark lettuce leaf up to three inches wide attached to rocky surfaces. Rock tripe grows from the Arctic to the southern states. It can be eaten raw or in a soup or stew.

MUSKRAT

Muskrat meat is similar to rabbit.

Remove musk glands from inside of legs.

Cooking Muskrat

Strong spices are needed to hide the gamey taste. Muskrats are done when they are soft and the meat easily falls apart.

Boiled Muskrat

Cover with cold water and add salt. Boil until soft. Eat with a steak sauce to hide gamey flavor.

Smoked Muskrat

Place cleaned muskrat directly on the charcoals of an open fire for a few minutes. Then place them in a pot and boil. This gives the rats a smoked taste.

Roast Muskrat

Clean and wash the muskrat with salt. Put it in a roasting pan with a little water. Cook one hour.

Fried Muskrat

Cut up and dip in a bowl with flour, salt, pepper and a little water. Fry in a deep grease until done.

Muskrat Tail

Cut off the tail and dip in boiling water to remove the fur. Can be boiled or deep fried.

Stuffed Muskrat

Put cleaned muskrat into a roaster. Moist bread should be placed on the muskrat and roast until it is soft.

Dried Muskrats Pieces

Peel the flesh from the bones and cut it into small cubes. Place the pieces of meat in a smoker or on a rack near a fire to dry them. Store the dried meat in a cool dry spot. It should keep for a few months.

Muskrat Soup

Cover with cold water, add salt and bring to a boil. Add onions and wild rice and continue boiling until it is soft.

Steamed Muskrat Legs

Put flour, salt, pepper and other seasoning in a bag. Place the legs in the bag and shake. Put into a greased frying pan and cover tightly. Cook at low heat until tender.

Muskrat

Half a muskrat is served per person.

LYNX

Meat is white and very tender. Best seasons for hunting is the late fall and early winter. The rest of the year lynx is too lean.

Oven Roasted Lynx

Wash and clean the hind legs of the lynx and roast in a roaster with lard and a little water. Baste the meat to keep it from drying.

Boiled Lynx

Cut up the lynx and boil it until it is soft and well cooked.

BIG GAME

DRESSING DEER

Remove Metatarsal Glands

Bleeding

- Place animal, with head downward, on a slope.
- Plunge a 5" (12.7 cm) knife blade into the animal at the top of the breastbone. While tilting the blade downward toward the backbone.
- Withdraw the knife while maintaining a sawing motion. This will cut the carotid artery.
- Let the blood drain while raising the rear portion of the animal.

Field Dressing

- Remove musk glands on the hind legs. There are two on each leg and can be identified by the *up-raised hair* growing in oval patches around them. Remove them carefully and do not touch them as this will taint your meat when it is being handled.
- Avoid cutting into the paunch and intestines by holding them away from the knife with your free hand while guiding the knife with your other hand.
- Cut the area around anus with a small knife so that the anus will come out with the intestines. Do not cut or break the bladder.
- Cut edge of diaphragm which separates the chest and stomach cavities. Cut windpipe and gullet.
- Pull lungs and heart from the chest cavity. Save the heart.
- Drain excess blood by turning carcass face down.

Removing Skin

- Hang the animal by the antlers.
- Cut the skin around the neck.
- Cut along the inside of each leg from the cavity.
- Cut along leg.
- Pull the hide down from the carcass.
- Tack the skin, with flesh side out, to dry. Do not stretch the hide. Rub hide with table salt.

Hanging the Animal

Only cut up the animal after the carcass has aged (chilled) for 5 to 7 days in a well ventilated area. The temperature should be between 33°F (0.5°C).

Cutting

Hind and fore shank: Good for soups, stews and ground meat.

Round: Used for steak, if too small use for a roast, or ground meat.

Loin and rib: Cut into sirloin, porterhouse, T-bone, and rib steaks.

Shoulder: Pot roast, ground meat, corning.

Rump: Pot roast

Neck, flank, brisket: Stew or ground meat.

REINDEER & CARIBOU

Boiled Reindeer or Caribou Hoofs

Put the hoofs with skin in a large pot. Cover with hot water and boil for a couple of hours. When the skin easily peels off the muscles will be soft and ready to eat. The toe nails will be soft and sweet meat is be found inside them.

Boiled Reindeer Head

Skin and wash the head. Chop it in quarters with an axe. Cover the pieces with cold water and boil until soft. The head can also be roasted in an open pan in an oven.

Boiled Reindeer Tongues

Put tongues in boiling water and boil until thoroughly cooked.

BUFFALO

Young buffalo meat, under 3 years old, is tender and similar to top grade beef. Cook the same way as beef.

BEAR

Brown bear, grizzly and polar bear are tender and delicious if under 3 years old. Older meat should be placed in a marinade for 24 hours. Trim the fat to eliminate the gamey flavor. Cook until well done.

Boiled Bear Meat

Cut up the brisket and boil in a large pot with salt and water until soft.

Grizzly Bear Steaks

Cut up meat and fry in deep grease in a frying pan.

WILD BOAR

Right hind leg is more tender then the left. Boar rests on its right side and scratches itself with the left hind leg. The scratching exercise toughens the meat.

Animal Blood
Four tablespoons of animal blood is equivalent to 10 eggs in vitamins, iron, and mineral content.

•

Animal Bones
Can be chewed for nutrition and splinters can be used as needles.

•

Animal Liver
Animal liver is a source of vitamin A. Do not eat polar bear or seal liver as it contains too much vitamin A.

•

Untanned Animal Hide
Untanned and dried hide or leather shoe laces, if not varnished, can be boiled to make a soup.

WILD MEAT HINTS

- To **render animal fat**, cut the suet and surface fat into cubes, heat slowly in a heavy covered pot, then strain. Bring the liquid fat to a boil, reduce the heat and let it simmer for 10 minutes to sterilize it. Pour fat into hot, sterilized containers, seal and store in a cool place. Rendered bear fat makes excellent pastry.
- Lard large game as it is very dry. Push salt pork or bacon strips into the grain of the meat. Wrap small game as quail with thin slices of pork covering the breast.
- Mold on ham or bacon can be wiped off with a cloth dampened with vinegar.
- Meat from big game animals should be chilled before use. Chill animals for one week at 33°F (0.5°C). Liver and heart should be used at once, and the tenderloin can be used after 24 hours.
- For long term storage, wrap cut meat in moisture-proof paper and freeze.
- In cold weather, game birds can be frozen in a loaf pan of water. When frozen solid, remove the ice block from the pan and store in a freezer. The bird should be completely covered with water before freezing.
- Soak salty bacon slices in cold water for 5 minutes to reduce salt. Drain and dry before frying.
- **Indian Meat Stew**: Fry cubed meat in a frying pan. Add onions, salt and pepper. When almost done mix flour in with meat until meat is coated. Fill a pan with cold water. Keep steaming until gravy is well cooked. Eat with potatoes and vegetables.
- **Boiled Bone Grease:** Boil bones that are left after the meat has been removed. Boil in a big pot for two hours. Let the liquid cool and the grease solidify and remove it. Put the grease in a pot and store it in a cool dark place. Eat with dry meat or add to pounded dry meat.

POTABLE WATER IS THE NUMBER ONE CONCERN IN A DESERT

- Drinking water should be kept in distinctive containers that should not be contaminated by non potable water.

- Drinking water should only be taken from a secure disease free location.

- Sufficient water to last until the next water hole is reached should always be on hand. Be prepared to back track if you cannot find your next source.

- Look for water before your supply is exhausted.

- Water canteens should be transported in such a way that they cannot be damaged or the seams split.

- To keep the water cool keep the containers in the shade or in a windy location.

Bird Sipping Water

- You can drink 3.5 pints (2.1 L) of water at a time. The body sweats this amount in two hours.

- To maximize your water intake *drink slowly and in sips*. Drink as much as you can, rest and slowly drink again. Repeat this a few times until your body is saturated.

- Do not eat fats or proteins if you lack water. Food requires water for digestion especially for proteins and fats. Your tissues will supply the water if it is not otherwise available.

- We require a minimum of four quarts of water per day. Several gallons are required if you are doing strenuous activities on a hot day.

- To conserve water, do not travel in the heat of the day but only in the early morning, late evening or on a moonlit night. Set up a sheltered rest area for the day. A well built rest area might be 40°F cooler in the shade.

- The optimum drinking water temperature is between 50°-60°F (10°-15.5°C). To cool water it can be wrapped in a wet cloth which will cause cooling when the water evaporates. The tribes people use animal stomachs as gourds. These gradually breathe water which evaporates and cools the gourd.

You cannot be trained to adjust permanently to a reduced water supply. If rations are insufficient then movement should be reduced to the cool times of the day or night. In very hot areas it is better to take smaller quantities more frequently. This will reduce the water lost by excessive sweating.

Smoking increases the desire for water. Alcohol reduces the resistance to heat due to increased dehydration.

POTABLE WATER

- Never drink water from a source that contains dead animals or animal remains. The animals might have died as the water has a high concentration, due to evaporation, of minerals that have been leached from the bed rock. These minerals might be chlorine, sulphur or arsenic.

- Animals and birds drinking the water does not mean that it is safe because water can have a bacterial or parasite content that cannot be neutralized by the human digestive track.

US Army Water Requirement Guidelines

Activity	Typical Duties	Quarts per person per day	
		less than 105°F (40.5°C)	more than 105°F (40.5°C)
Light	Desk work, Radio operating, Guard duty	6	10
Moderate	Route march on level ground	7	11
Heavy	Forced marches, Route march with heavy loads, Digging in.	9	13

Water is the key to survival especially in the desert. The body is 75% water, by weight. The water lost by sweat, evaporation or body functions will have to be replaced. Water helps to maintain the body temperature. It is required to help in the digestion of the food. Control sweating by wearing layers of cotton clothing and traveling in cool mornings, evenings and moonlit nights. You can travel 20 miles (32 km) with a gallon (5 L) of water but if you travel during the day you can only cover half the distance.

A 2 quart (2.5 L) loss of body fluid (2.5% of body weight) reduces the body's efficiency by 25%. A fluid loss of 25% of body weight usually is fatal.

FINDING WATER CHAPTER 13

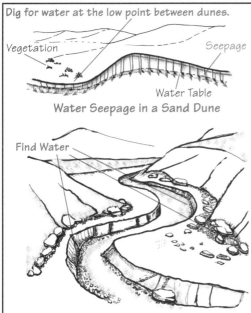

Dig for water at the low point between dunes.

Vegetation

Seepage

Water Table

Water Seepage in a Sand Dune

Find Water

WATER

Water in a Dry River Bed

You will require at least 4 quarts of water per day. To get this amount you should have access to a stable constant source. This source can be a well, high water table, or pool of water. You will usually see paths leading towards water sources, as they would have been used for centuries. Watch for markers which could be rocks placed in a row, a pile of rocks, or pieces of wood. These can be markers leading to water or covering a water source.

- Along sandy beaches or salty desert lakes, dig a hole in a sand depression 100 feet from the shore or in the first depression behind the first sand dune. Rain water from local showers will collect between the dunes. When digging near a salt lake stop digging upon hitting the humid sand and let water seep into this hollow. If you dig lower you might get seepage from the salty water.
- Dig a shallow well when you see damp sand or find plant growth.
- Dry meandering stream beds might have water deposits just below the surface at outside bends. Dig in these bends for water.
- Dew and condensation settle on cold surfaces. These surfaces can be pieces of metal, grass, smooth rocks. You can lick the grass or metal surfaces. Dew will evaporate at sunrise.
- Find natural deposits or accumulations in pools of water. These deposits can be found in gullies, behind large rocks, or under cliffs. These pools keep their water deposits because they are found on nonporous bedrock, on clay soil and are protected or partially protected from the sun.
- Watch the flight of birds, particularly at sunset and dawn. Birds circle water holes in desert areas.
- The large barrel cactus of American deserts contains considerable moisture which can be squeezed out of the pulp. This is a difficult task and your best bet is a well or other source.
- Purify all your water. This is especially true in native villages and around civilization. *See Summer Hiking Chapter for purification methods.*

FINDING WATER

SURFACE CHARACTERISTICS

- Follow a dry river bed and because of the rock structure or composition a stream might emerge. Dig a pit if the soil is moist.
- Follow the riverbed to the source. There might still be a trickle of water or humid soil.
- Find water at the leeward base (the steep side of the dune opposite the direction of the wind) of large dunes or at a very low spot between dunes.
- Watch for damp spots on the ground. This can be caused by a high water table.
- Old mines, ore dumps, and mining tailings might indicate the presence of water. Do not enter a mine because there is a danger of a mine collapsing. Water might be tainted by minerals that have been leached from the mining by-products.
- Water can be collected from dew accumulation.

PLANTS

- Look for green leaf growth of plants and trees that require much water. These plants might be cattails, bulrush, elderberries, and reeds. Trees are cottonwood, poplars, greasewood, and willows. This growth indicates a high water table and might be located on a dry river bed. To get at the water dig into the ground for one to two feet. After a while water will accumulate in this pit. It will most likely be cloudy but will slowly settle; if it does not, it can be filtered through a tightly woven piece of cloth.
- At base of cliffs where there is vegetation.
- The pulp of some cacti (not the giant Saquarro) can be crushed to a watery mash. To do this burn off the needles or spines in a fire and peel the pieces of cacti. The pulp can be sucked to release a sweet jellylike liquid.

ANIMAL INDICATORS

- Animals are the best indicators to desert water.
- Watch insects (bees, hornets), birds and animals.
- Insects require water and live within flying range of water. You can watch the direction of their flight.
- Grazing animals will go towards water every morning and evening. Watch for animal trails which will usually be well-worn because animals will have followed these trails for many years.
- Doves have a habit of perching in trees or shrubs near desert water holes, especially in the evening.
- Birds will fly to and from water, they might circle water or congregate in large flocks. Birds of prey use their victims as a source of fluids and do not go to water as frequently. The Bedouins of the Sahara desert, in North Africa, have a belief that birds flying *to* water fly low and directly to the water whereas birds flying *from* water are heavier and will have to rest frequently. A bird coming from water will be heavier and flaps louder.

Churning the Inside of a Cactus for Water

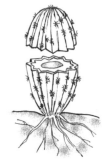

Cutting Open a Cactus

Water Pump Filter Kit
See Summer Hiking Chapter.

Condom in Sock
Place a condom in a sock and use it to transport water.
The sock acts as a retainer and gives the container its shape.

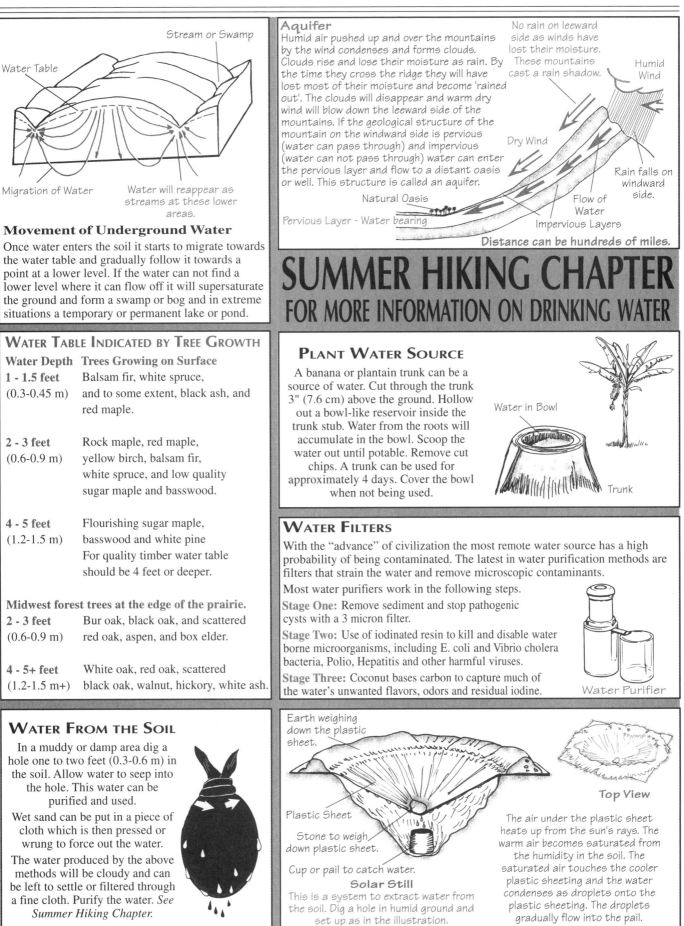

Movement of Underground Water

Once water enters the soil it starts to migrate towards the water table and gradually follow it towards a point at a lower level. If the water can not find a lower level where it can flow off it will supersaturate the ground and form a swamp or bog and in extreme situations a temporary or permanent lake or pond.

Water Table — Stream or Swamp — **Migration of Water** — Water will reappear as streams at these lower areas.

Aquifer

Humid air pushed up and over the mountains by the wind condenses and forms clouds. Clouds rise and lose their moisture as rain. By the time they cross the ridge they will have lost most of their moisture and become 'rained out'. The clouds will disappear and warm dry wind will blow down the leeward side of the mountains. If the geological structure of the mountain on the windward side is pervious (water can pass through) and impervious (water can not pass through) water can enter the pervious layer and flow to a distant oasis or well. This structure is called an aquifer.

No rain on leeward side as winds have lost their moisture. These mountains cast a rain shadow. — Humid Wind — Dry Wind — Rain falls on windward side. — Natural Oasis — Pervious Layer - Water bearing — Flow of Water — Impervious Layers

Distance can be hundreds of miles.

SUMMER HIKING CHAPTER
FOR MORE INFORMATION ON DRINKING WATER

WATER TABLE INDICATED BY TREE GROWTH

Water Depth	Trees Growing on Surface
1 - 1.5 feet (0.3-0.45 m)	Balsam fir, white spruce, and to some extent, black ash, and red maple.
2 - 3 feet (0.6-0.9 m)	Rock maple, red maple, yellow birch, balsam fir, white spruce, and low quality sugar maple and basswood.
4 - 5 feet (1.2-1.5 m)	Flourishing sugar maple, basswood and white pine For quality timber water table should be 4 feet or deeper.

Midwest forest trees at the edge of the prairie.

2 - 3 feet (0.6-0.9 m)	Bur oak, black oak, and scattered red oak, aspen, and box elder.
4 - 5+ feet (1.2-1.5 m+)	White oak, red oak, scattered black oak, walnut, hickory, white ash.

PLANT WATER SOURCE

A banana or plantain trunk can be a source of water. Cut through the trunk 3" (7.6 cm) above the ground. Hollow out a bowl-like reservoir inside the trunk stub. Water from the roots will accumulate in the bowl. Scoop the water out until potable. Remove cut chips. A trunk can be used for approximately 4 days. Cover the bowl when not being used.

Water in Bowl — Trunk

WATER FILTERS

With the "advance" of civilization the most remote water source has a high probability of being contaminated. The latest in water purification methods are filters that strain the water and remove microscopic contaminants.

Most water purifiers work in the following steps.

Stage One: Remove sediment and stop pathogenic cysts with a 3 micron filter.

Stage Two: Use of iodinated resin to kill and disable water borne microorganisms, including E. coli and Vibrio cholera bacteria, Polio, Hepatitis and other harmful viruses.

Stage Three: Coconut bases carbon to capture much of the water's unwanted flavors, odors and residual iodine.

Water Purifier

WATER FROM THE SOIL

In a muddy or damp area dig a hole one to two feet (0.3-0.6 m) in the soil. Allow water to seep into the hole. This water can be purified and used.

Wet sand can be put in a piece of cloth which is then pressed or wrung to force out the water.

The water produced by the above methods will be cloudy and can be left to settle or filtered through a fine cloth. Purify the water. *See Summer Hiking Chapter.*

Earth weighing down the plastic sheet. — Plastic Sheet — Stone to weigh down plastic sheet. — Cup or pail to catch water.

Top View

Solar Still
This is a system to extract water from the soil. Dig a hole in humid ground and set up as in the illustration.

The air under the plastic sheet heats up from the sun's rays. The warm air becomes saturated from the humidity in the soil. The saturated air touches the cooler plastic sheeting and the water condenses as droplets onto the plastic sheeting. The droplets gradually flow into the pail.

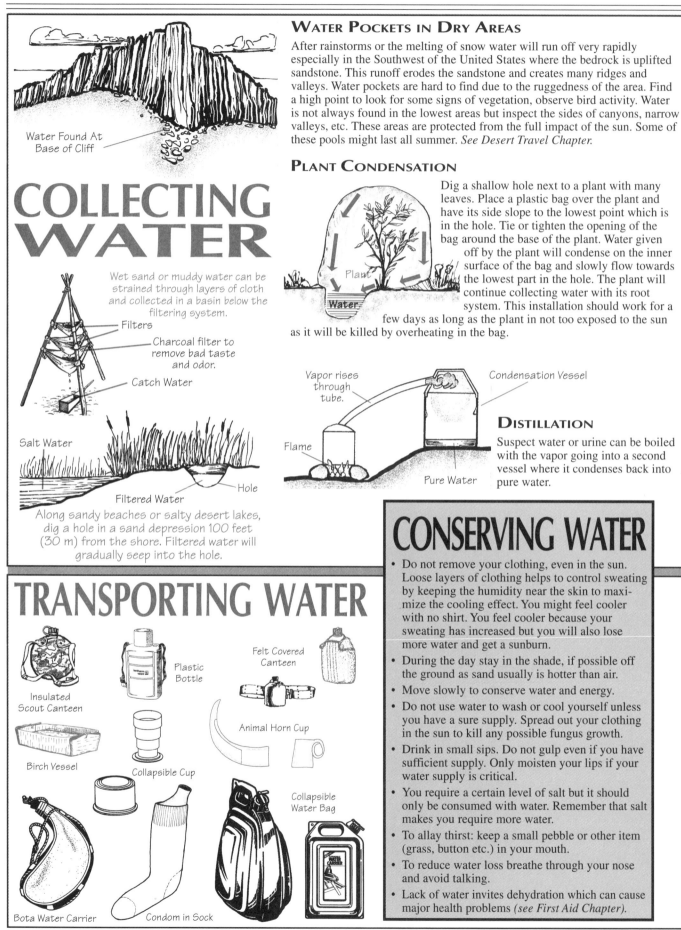

WATER POCKETS IN DRY AREAS

After rainstorms or the melting of snow water will run off very rapidly especially in the Southwest of the United States where the bedrock is uplifted sandstone. This runoff erodes the sandstone and creates many ridges and valleys. Water pockets are hard to find due to the ruggedness of the area. Find a high point to look for some signs of vegetation, observe bird activity. Water is not always found in the lowest areas but inspect the sides of canyons, narrow valleys, etc. These areas are protected from the full impact of the sun. Some of these pools might last all summer. *See Desert Travel Chapter.*

PLANT CONDENSATION

Dig a shallow hole next to a plant with many leaves. Place a plastic bag over the plant and have its side slope to the lowest point which is in the hole. Tie or tighten the opening of the bag around the base of the plant. Water given off by the plant will condense on the inner surface of the bag and slowly flow towards the lowest part in the hole. The plant will continue collecting water with its root system. This installation should work for a few days as long as the plant in not too exposed to the sun as it will be killed by overheating in the bag.

DISTILLATION

Suspect water or urine can be boiled with the vapor going into a second vessel where it condenses back into pure water.

Plant

Water

Vapor rises through tube.

Condensation Vessel

Flame

Pure Water

COLLECTING WATER

Wet sand or muddy water can be strained through layers of cloth and collected in a basin below the filtering system.

Filters

Charcoal filter to remove bad taste and odor.

Catch Water

Salt Water

Hole

Filtered Water

Along sandy beaches or salty desert lakes, dig a hole in a sand depression 100 feet (30 m) from the shore. Filtered water will gradually seep into the hole.

TRANSPORTING WATER

Insulated Scout Canteen

Plastic Bottle

Felt Covered Canteen

Animal Horn Cup

Birch Vessel

Collapsible Cup

Collapsible Water Bag

Bota Water Carrier

Condom in Sock

CONSERVING WATER

- Do not remove your clothing, even in the sun. Loose layers of clothing helps to control sweating by keeping the humidity near the skin to maximize the cooling effect. You might feel cooler with no shirt. You feel cooler because your sweating has increased but you will also lose more water and get a sunburn.
- During the day stay in the shade, if possible off the ground as sand usually is hotter than air.
- Move slowly to conserve water and energy.
- Do not use water to wash or cool yourself unless you have a sure supply. Spread out your clothing in the sun to kill any possible fungus growth.
- Drink in small sips. Do not gulp even if you have sufficient supply. Only moisten your lips if your water supply is critical.
- You require a certain level of salt but it should only be consumed with water. Remember that salt makes you require more water.
- To allay thirst: keep a small pebble or other item (grass, button etc.) in your mouth.
- To reduce water loss breathe through your nose and avoid talking.
- Lack of water invites dehydration which can cause major health problems (*see First Aid Chapter*).

MOOSE CALLING MEGAPHONE

Use canoe birch bark removed without injuring the tree. The horn can be the length of the forearm, the horn opening the width of the hand, and the mouth opening two fingers wide.

This horn is only useful in the rutting season (end of September to October). The moose mating season.

The sounds that should be made are the love calls of the cow moose. The use of the moose call during the rutting season may attract a bull. Remember that he is cantankerous and dangerous.

Traditional Moose Calling Megaphone

The cow moose song is sung at three or four o'clock in the morning. The first call is for 1/2 minute. The megaphone is blown in a circle towards the ground. If a bull answers, the caller makes a second call and remains very still (remember the bull moose can move through the forest in total silence). Just before daybreak, make another call towards the forest terminating with the megaphone pointed towards the ground. At daybreak give a sequel but with the horn a foot from the ground. At this point, if you are lucky, you will hear a trampling of the undergrowth and a slashing of the antlers. If you imitate this sound the bull will get very mad and think that there is a second bull nearby. Make another cow call and then shuffle your feet through the leaves. The bull will think that another bull is on his way towards the cow.

Deer Call

It is made from a piece of rhododendron leaf inserted into the split end of a twig. The sounds that you make can be varied by the amount of air pressure, by change in the angle of the lips upon the stick, and by cupping of the hands.

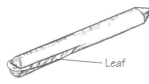

Leaf

Deer Call

Crow Caller

Study how crows call. The best way to attract them is to use the call they use when one of them has found a hawk or owl. Crows like to crowd one of these enemies and with the right call you will gather all the crows in the neighborhood.

Duck Hunting Blinds

Stick brush into the mud to form a dense screen. The inside of the screen should provide enough space for one or two hunters. The blind should shelter the hunters from high flying fowl. Decoys are planted in front of the blind.

ANIMALS ARE CURIOUS

Animals are curious especially when there is something new in their environment. Place a brightly colored handkerchief such as a flag on a stick. The flattering cloth will attract antelopes or deer who will walk right up to you. Make sure that the wind is blowing into your face. Small vermin are attracted to new noises as whistling or blowing on a blade of grass between the thumbs. They will come out of their burrows to see what's up.

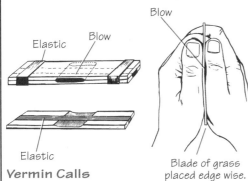

Blow

Blow

Elastic

Elastic

Vermin Calls

Blade of grass placed edge wise.

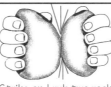

Strike and rub two rocks together at an angle to attract squirrels.

Squirrel Scolding

A squirrel scolds when someone invades its territory. If you are quiet and a squirrel starts to scold you know that someone or something has entered their territory. This lets you know that an animal or human is approaching. Jays, crows, hawks, beavers, etc. have the same territorial characteristics.

HUNTING & TRAPPING CHAPTER 14

HISTORY OF TRAPS

The use of traps is as old as human history. Traps serve the function of augmenting the food provider's ability to catch game while occupied somewhere else.

With ingenuity and understanding of an animal's habits the hunter was able to devise a mechanical system to catch animals and fish. Systems were developed by which the trapped animal would be transported out of reach of other predators. Hunters might have watched other predators, insect eating plants and their use of lures and liquid to drown the victim. The spider wove a net. The ermine going down rodent holes for their meals. Our ancestors also saw natural physical features as cliffs, quicksand, and depressions as areas to drive larger animals.

"Modern" traps are all based on models of antiquity. A person who is attempting to survive in the wilderness will see many natural examples of traps and will also be able to choose from the examples of traps that are shown in this book.

It is important to remember that placing a trap is dangerous to animals and people. Traps should never be used in inhabited areas. Before setting any traps check the laws and regulations of the state or municipality.

Steel Traps

Steel traps are not described in this book. If used, you should follow the instructions enclosed with the trap. The basic theory, of placing and baiting is the same as for the "primitive" traps discussed in this book.

INDIANS OF NORTH AMERICA

The Indians of North America used traps as:

- Deadfall traps made from logs and boulders.
- Snares made from horsehair (after the Europeans had imported the horse), from rawhide, and cordage made from plants.
- Pitfall traps for birds and animals.
- Woven baskets to catch fish and rodents.
- Toxic plants to paralyze fish so that they would float to the surface.
- Throwing sticks and bolas for birds.
- Animal drives: Indians were adept in erecting channeling barriers and then driving buffalo over cliffs. Indians would camouflage themselves in hides, stampede a herd, and guide them with beaters (Indians standing, waving and shouting) over a cliff or into a dead end valley.

BOW & ARROW

Courtesy National Museum of Canada

A bow and arrow is easy to make and does not require any specialized equipment:

Bow: Use a willow shaft or any straight flexible freshly cut sapling. No shaping will be required if the sapling is well chosen. The notches for the bowstring can be cut with a knife or by rubbing on a sharp rock. Eskimos made some of their bows with whale bones, they were riveted together.

Bowstring: A shoelace, dried sinew can be used, or cordage can be made from plants. The bowstring will carry the arrow around 15-20 yards (15-20 m) to hunt for small game and birds.

Arrows: Arrows have to be straight and a thin willow branch is a good choice. Peel off the bark, let the shaft dry while lying horizontally on a flat surface. Scrape the shaft if it has any small bumps. Arrow shafts can be made from reed with a hard wood insert as an arrowhead and string notch plug.

Fletching: Tie a feather to the shaft to give the arrow better stability. A piece of leaf or wing from a maple tree seed can be used.

Arrowhead: An arrow with a blunt point can be effective in stunning an animal. Use a small smooth rock attached to the arrowhead with a piece of cloth or some sticky pitch from a pine tree. Pieces of metal from a tin can can be wrapped around the tip of the arrow to make a sharp arrowhead. Make a selection of arrows with different heads for different game.

To Shot a Bow

- Stand relaxed with feet pointed apart.
- The shoulder of the hand holding the bow should be forward towards the target.
- Firmly hold the bow but be relaxed.
- Place the arrow on with the notch on the string.
- Grasp the string with the first 3 fingers with the end of the arrow being between the first and second finger. Hold the arrow lightly when you pull the string. An alternate method of holding the arrow is to hold it between the thumb and first finger. The arrow can slip when using this hold.
- When the arrow points at the target smoothly release the 3 fingers holding the string.

Safety Rules When Using a Bow

- Never point your set bow at anyone.
- Never shoot an arrow straight up into the air.
- Make sure that you will not injure anyone *behind your target.*
- If target practicing shoot into a target that has a hill behind it. You will not injure anyone behind your target nor lose your arrows.

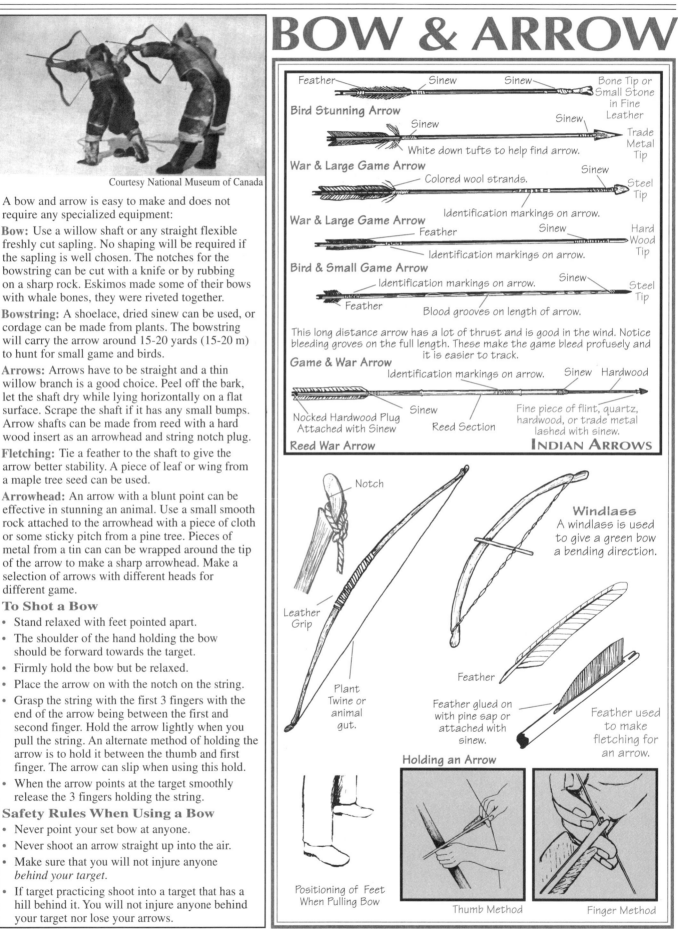

Feather — Sinew — Sinew — Bone Tip or Small Stone in Fine Leather
Bird Stunning Arrow

Sinew — Sinew — Trade Metal Tip
White down tufts to help find arrow.
War & Large Game Arrow

Colored wool strands. — Sinew — Steel Tip
Identification markings on arrow.
War & Large Game Arrow

Feather — Sinew — Hard Wood Tip
Identification markings on arrow.
Bird & Small Game Arrow

Identification markings on arrow. — Sinew — Steel Tip
Feather — Blood grooves on length of arrow.

This long distance arrow has a lot of thrust and is good in the wind. Notice bleeding groves on the full length. These make the game bleed profusely and it is easier to track.
Game & War Arrow

Identification markings on arrow. — Sinew Hardwood
Nocked Hardwood Plug Attached with Sinew — Sinew — Reed Section — Fine piece of flint, quartz, hardwood, or trade metal lashed with sinew.
Reed War Arrow

INDIAN ARROWS

Notch

Leather Grip

Plant Twine or animal gut.

Windlass
A windlass is used to give a green bow a bending direction.

Feather

Feather glued on with pine sap or attached with sinew.

Feather used to make fletching for an arrow.

Holding an Arrow

Positioning of Feet When Pulling Bow

Thumb Method

Finger Method

CAMOUFLAGE IN THE WOODS

Camouflage is an art. There are no application rules because it depends upon the environment, material available, and experience. Some ideas on camouflage:

- Do not disturb or stand out from the environment but blend into it.
- Avoid any rapid movement.
- Apply camouflage but not too much.
- Take advantage of your environment, the bush, the shadows, the weather, the silence.
- Avoid being profiled against the skyline.
- Do not expose shiny objects to the sun.
- Break up the natural outline of the body.
- Apply local vegetation and their colors.
- Odors: do not use scented soaps or shampoos, insect repellent, tobacco, gum or candy.
- Camouflage patterns for:

Leafy woods	blotch method
Desert areas	blotch method
Barren snow	blotch method
Evergreens	broad slash method
Jungle	broad slash method
Grass	slash method

Slash Camouflage Pattern

Blotch Camouflage Pattern

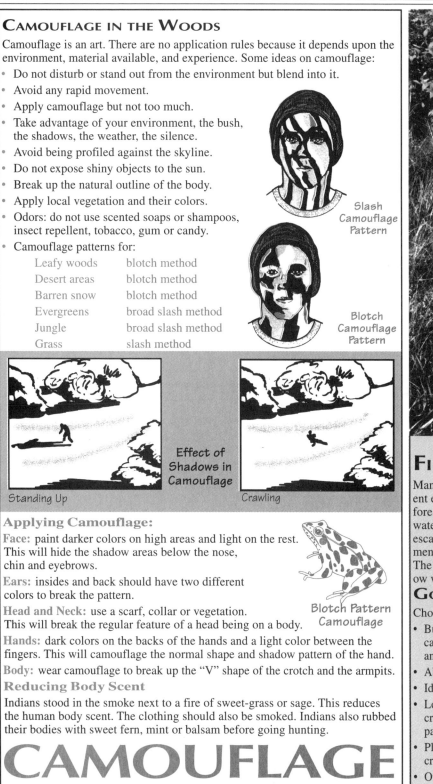

Effect of Shadows in Camouflage

Standing Up

Crawling

Applying Camouflage:

Face: paint darker colors on high areas and light on the rest. This will hide the shadow areas below the nose, chin and eyebrows.

Ears: insides and back should have two different colors to break the pattern.

Head and Neck: use a scarf, collar or vegetation. This will break the regular feature of a head being on a body.

Blotch Pattern Camouflage

Hands: dark colors on the backs of the hands and a light color between the fingers. This will camouflage the normal shape and shadow pattern of the hand.

Body: wear camouflage to break up the "V" shape of the crotch and the armpits.

Reducing Body Scent

Indians stood in the smoke next to a fire of sweet-grass or sage. This reduces the human body scent. The clothing should also be smoked. Indians also rubbed their bodies with sweet fern, mint or balsam before going hunting.

CAMOUFLAGE

Animal Path Into the Woods

FINDING ANIMALS

Many animals live at the meeting point of two different ecological areas. An example being between the forest and meadow (forest to hide, meadow to eat), water and land (land to eat or rest and water to escape). Find pathways that intersect these environments and these areas are prime areas for hunting. The photograph shows the forest meeting the meadow with an animal "highway" crossing the barrier.

GOOD TRAPPING AREAS

Chose your terrain and cover:

- Bushy woods bordering lakes, streams, hills, rocky canyons, springs, thickets, swamps, hollow logs, and arched roots.
- Abundance of food for animals.
- Identify dens, animal signs, tracks, trails, runways.
- Look for areas that are well drained by little, crooked, bush fringed streams that come down partly wooded hills.
- Places in thickets where a number of game trails cross.
- Overhang on river bank or stream is good for muskrat.

Snake and Reptile Hunting

They can be hunted with a forked stick at least 6 feet long. Rattlesnake heads should be cut off and buried as their fangs will remain poisonous even when detached. They can be roasted or smoked and are an excellent source of protein.

Snakes can also be caught in basket traps baited with eggs or the shells of eggs. Live rodents can also be used. Keeping them in small cages to protect them from the snake.

This method will attract numerous snakes.

Fence Traps

Used by the Indians all over North America. These traps were fences made of twine and sticks and animals would be driven into them. The animal drive could be a string of noisy Indians or a small field fire which would stampede the animals.

ANIMAL BAIT AND LURES

ANIMAL BAIT AND LURES

- Animals have a strong reliance on scent in their daily lives. For this reason we use a scented bait for the specific animal and make sure that human scent does not contaminate the site.
- An ideal bait should contain an odor that is volatile (odor giving) and at the same time has a long time volatility. These are the same specifications as for a lady's perfume. The odors produced activate the saliva glands, or territorial instincts, in animal and make them think "food or an intruder". To avoid drying the bait or having it rot too fast, traps should be set in the shade. The required odor of the bait will vary from animal to animal.
- Some animals and birds having a keen sense of sight will require movement to be attracted to bait. That means you have to provide live bait which you would have to catch in some form of tilt platform pitfall trap.

ODORS THAT REPEL ANIMALS

- The most negative scent, to animals, is the human scent. Never handle traps with your bare hands or store them around the house.
- Any new smell that animals might encounter (even human if they have never smelled a human before). But a new scent might also attract their curiosity.
- Use smoke from a dry grass fire to remove human sent that might be present at a trap site or on a trap.
- Certain animals will avoid areas where they can smell the odor of their deadly enemies. Field mice will avoid areas where there is an ermine scent. Ermines are so audacious that they will enter into mouse holes, eat the occupants, and in cold climates line the former mouse den with the fur of their victims and move in.

CURIOSITY

Hang a piece of tin, aluminum, tinfoil in shape of a small fish one foot above the trap.

SCENTS

Use the scent of glands of beavers, muskrat, mink, fox, raccoon, or weasel. These scents can be blended in a fish oil base or used unblended. It is a complicated procedure to get the right mix without experience. Animal droppings and urine can be used but the secretions should be from the same kind of animal one is trapping. Fish oil makes an excellent lure for fish-eating animals.

Three Categories of Scents

- *Unusual and new scents*, will be approached with caution.
- A scent that *means food*. This scent is usually given off by the usual food of the animal.
- *Territorial odors* which are secreted by the animal and rubbed or urinated at the limits of its territory. This scent, depending upon the season, has sexual connotations. Using a scent of this type, in the right season, will cause the animal to lose many of its cautious ways. They will act in an aggressive manner which will help in trapping. The adjacent list of scents that when added to bait will produce the desired effect.

  These scents might be of interest to wildlife photographers as they can mount their cameras and place the scented bait on a remote electronic shutter release.

FOOD THAT ATTRACTS ANIMALS

Chose an animal's favorite food:

Muskrat: Carrots, parsnips, fish, flagroot, mussel meat.

Raccoon: Wild grapes, pokeberries, fish, small birds, frogs, mussel meat and persimmons.

Fox: Mice, rabbits, small birds, poultry, eggs, burnt cracklings, decayed fish.

Mink: Fish, small birds, muskrat, meat, poultry.

Skunk: Grubs, birds, roots, berries, and bird's eggs.

Weasel: Likes to kill its food, so you should use live rabbits, birds, poultry.

Use scent in small amounts as too much will arouse suspicion rather than attract the animal.

ARTIFICIAL LURES FOR TRAPPING OR ANIMAL PHOTOGRAPHY

Do not confuse scents with bait. Bait is food that an animal likes to eat. Scents are lures appealing to the animal's sense of smell. These smells arouse the curiosity of the animal or its sexual impulse. The more wary the animal the less scent should be used. Scents will not mask human odor.

- Scents should be made in advance of the trapping season since, as a rule, they improve with time.
- To test the scent find a trail of the animal and put three drops ten feet from several trees or stumps. Check the next day to see if the animal's track deviates to inspect the scent. If it has the scent works.

Some Basic Ingredients

Fish Oil: For animals as raccoon, fox, wildcat, and coyote. Use any fish, trout, carp, and suckers are the most popular. Cut fish into small pieces and put them a glass jar which is stored in a warm spot. Do not seal the bottle but cover it to keep out insects. The oil from the fish will rise to the top. Fish oil can be used alone or mixed with other lures.

Fox Lures

- Chop one pound of muskrat meat and let it decompose as for the fish oil. Add some fox urine.
- Eel oil, 4 ozs; beaver castor, 1 oz; muskrat musk, 1 oz; skunk scent, 2 drops; tincture of asafetida, 4 drops. Age in a cool dark spot for 6 weeks.

Coyote Lures

- Trout oil, 4 ozs; beaver castor, 1 oz; asafetida, 1/4 oz; muskrat musk, 3 ozs; skunk scent, 5 drops. Age 2 months on a dark cool place.
- Coyote urine, 2 ozs; sun-rendered fish oil, 4 ozs; tincture of tonquin musk, 1 oz; valerian, 8 drops; beaver castor, 1/2 oz; skunk scent, 2 drops.

Mink Lures

- Sun-rendered trout oil, 4 ozs; tincture of muskrat musk, 1 oz; mink musk, 1/2 oz; beaver castor, 1/2 oz; oil of anise, 10 drops. Age 2 months.
- Commercial or homemade fish oil, 2 ozs; muskrat musk, 1/2 oz; tincture of tonquin musk, 8 drops; mink musk, 1 oz. A fairly efficient mixture.

Muskrat Lures

- Muskrat musk, 1 oz; mink musk, 1/2 oz; glycerin, 1/2 oz; oil of anise, 10 drops. Age 6 weeks.

Opossum Lures

- Fish oil, 4 ozs.; tincture of asafetida, 1 oz.; oil of lovage, 1/2 oz.; liquid camphor, 6 drops.

Raccoon Lures

- Honey, 4 ozs; beaver castor, 1/2 oz; muskrat musk, 1/2 oz; oil of anise, 20 drops.
- Fish oil, 1/2 pint; anise oil 12 drops; strained honey 1 oz. Age for 2 months in a dark cool place.
- Anise oil alone.

Skunk Lures

- Oil of skunk flesh, 4 ozs.; fish oil, 2 ozs.; muskrat musk, 2 ozs.; tincture of asafetida, 1/2 oz.

Weasel Lures

- Fish oil, 4 ozs; weasel musk, 2 ozs; beaver castor, 1/2 oz; rabbit blood, 2 ozs; oil of anise, 6 drops. Age in a cool dark spot for 6 weeks.

STALKING

Stalking

Study the wind and air currents as they can carry your scent to the animal's keen nose. *Always stalk against the wind.* When stalking in the mountains, early in the morning, remember that *air currents rise* in the morning because of the heat from the sun's rays. Always stalk from above. Animals' eyesight is usually not good but wear clothing that blends into the background. To confuse the animal, push a branch screen in front of you. Eskimos usually push a white cloth screen fastened to runners. Turkey hunters in the south drape themselves with Spanish Moss.

Stalking Caribou

Walk towards the animal in a bent over position using a stick or rifle to simulate the front legs. Stop every so often as if browsing. If the wind is in your favor you should be able to approach the animal quite easily.

Two-Man Stalk

Both hunters bend over. The second hunter rests his head on the front man's back holding on to his belt. Move forward like a four-legged animal. Make sure that the wind is blowing towards you.

Deer Stalking

Make sure the wind is towards you. Watch the deer while it is feeding. You will notice that the deer will feed with its head down and raise its head periodically to glance around. The white tail will twitch *just before it raises its head*. At this point you should freeze. The deer looks up and then lowers its head to feed again. At this point you can advance. With this method and some luck you can approach within ten feet the animal. Notice that the wind direction might be different close to the deer. To approach a branch screen might helpful.

Movement of Deer

- Deer move down to the water at dusk and before the sunrise. Air currents move uphill from the water at night. The deer will move into the night breeze.
- Deer move uphill when daylight comes. At the same time the wind shifts downhill towards the water. The deer are moving uphill into the morning breeze.
- Move into the breeze when approaching deer as they cannot smell your odor.

Tricks to Help You Approach Deer

- Avoid light colored clothing, as it is more easily seen when you move. This is especially true where there are dark forests in the background.
- Camouflage your skin by growing a beard or using fire coals to mark your face.
- Remain motionless at a good location.
- Avoid scented soap, hair tonic, or body lotions as these odors might give you away.
- Rub old clothes with cedar oil or stand in fire smoke to camouflage your human scent.

Eskimo Snares to Catch Birds

Eskimos would place snares in shallow lakes to catch diving birds. These snares would be on lines over 20 feet long with each line having 50 to 60 snares.

Duck and Snare

Bola

The Eskimos use a bola to hunt flying birds and running animals. These bolas are made with cord or strips of hide approximately a yard (1m) long. The weights are carried inside leather pouches. The bola is thrown by holding the center and twirling it above the head. When flying the bola opens up while rotating towards the game. With practice it can be used very efficiently. A bola is used in South America where it is used on large animals to entangle their front feet.

Bola

Sea Gulls

To catch sea gulls tie a hook, sharp nail, wedge of wood, or sharpened bone to a string or fish line. Place some bait, piece of decomposing fish or meat, on the hook and tie the string to a sturdy branch or post. The sea gull will swallow the food and be caught.

Bait

Mexican Gourd Trick

Float some empty plastic bottles or brush covered logs among a flock of geese or ducks on a pond. Once the flock is accustomed to their presence, place a plastic bottle over your head, leaving a slit for your eyes. Gradually swim towards the flock. When you reach a duck grab it by its feet and pull it under the water, twist its neck, and put it into a bag. If a plastic bottle is not available use some logs with weeds on them.

Plastic Bottle

Throwing Stick

This stick should be well balanced for your hand and approximately 2 feet (60 cm) long. Practice throwing it overhand and underhand as targets at different heights. It is very effective at stunning animals or temporarily incapacitating them.

Throwing Stick

Trapping an Animal in its Burrow

To force an animal to leave its burrow one can place some burning leaves into the entrance or pour water down the hole. Traps would be set up at the exit holes.

Rodent Skewer

This method was used by some Indians to catch small furry game in its burrow. Use a flexible branch from a willow tree with a fork at the end. If you see a rabbit or groundhog run down its burrow (there are a few burrows) flex the stick down the hole and upon feeling the softness of the animal quickly twist the fork of the stick into its fur. This will "tie" the animal to the stick which you will slowly withdraw form the hole. If you feel that you are losing your "grip" give the animal a few gentle stabs while twisting.

Entrance to burrow.

Skewer

ENTRY BIRD TRAPS

PHEASANT AND PARTRIDGE TRAPS

These are ground birds which usually hide by running through the undergrowth. Bait can be grain, berries, beans or peas. It is easy to trap these birds because they have stiff feathers that lay back in one direction and the feathers are difficult to bend.

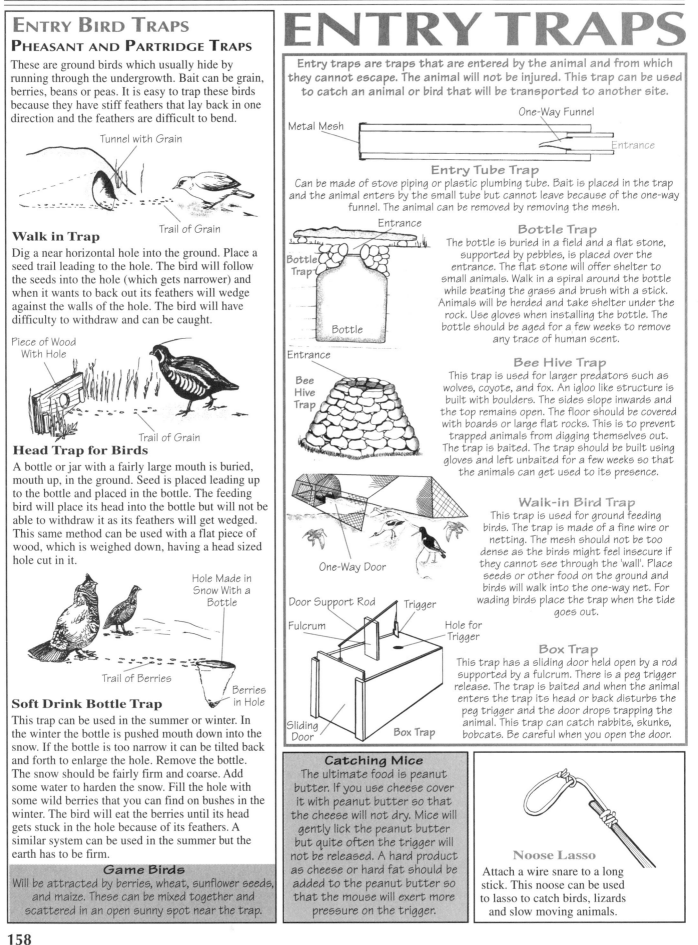

Tunnel with Grain

Trail of Grain

Walk in Trap

Dig a near horizontal hole into the ground. Place a seed trail leading to the hole. The bird will follow the seeds into the hole (which gets narrower) and when it wants to back out its feathers will wedge against the walls of the hole. The bird will have difficulty to withdraw and can be caught.

Piece of Wood With Hole

Trail of Grain

Head Trap for Birds

A bottle or jar with a fairly large mouth is buried, mouth up, in the ground. Seed is placed leading up to the bottle and placed in the bottle. The feeding bird will place its head into the bottle but will not be able to withdraw it as its feathers will get wedged. This same method can be used with a flat piece of wood, which is weighed down, having a head sized hole cut in it.

Hole Made in Snow With a Bottle

Trail of Berries

Berries in Hole

Soft Drink Bottle Trap

This trap can be used in the summer or winter. In the winter the bottle is pushed mouth down into the snow. If the bottle is too narrow it can be tilted back and forth to enlarge the hole. Remove the bottle. The snow should be fairly firm and coarse. Add some water to harden the snow. Fill the hole with some wild berries that you can find on bushes in the winter. The bird will eat the berries until its head gets stuck in the hole because of its feathers. A similar system can be used in the summer but the earth has to be firm.

Game Birds

Will be attracted by berries, wheat, sunflower seeds, and maize. These can be mixed together and scattered in an open sunny spot near the trap.

ENTRY TRAPS

Entry traps are traps that are entered by the animal and from which they cannot escape. The animal will not be injured. This trap can be used to catch an animal or bird that will be transported to another site.

Metal Mesh

One-Way Funnel

Entrance

Entry Tube Trap

Can be made of stove piping or plastic plumbing tube. Bait is placed in the trap and the animal enters by the small tube but cannot leave because of the one-way funnel. The animal can be removed by removing the mesh.

Entrance

Bottle Trap

Bottle

Bottle Trap

The bottle is buried in a field and a flat stone, supported by pebbles, is placed over the entrance. The flat stone will offer shelter to small animals. Walk in a spiral around the bottle while beating the grass and brush with a stick. Animals will be herded and take shelter under the rock. Use gloves when installing the bottle. The bottle should be aged for a few weeks to remove any trace of human scent.

Entrance

Bee Hive Trap

Bee Hive Trap

This trap is used for larger predators such as wolves, coyote, and fox. An igloo like structure is built with boulders. The sides slope inwards and the top remains open. The floor should be covered with boards or large flat rocks. This is to prevent trapped animals from digging themselves out. The trap is baited. The trap should be built using gloves and left unbaited for a few weeks so that the animals can get used to its presence.

One-Way Door

Walk-in Bird Trap

This trap is used for ground feeding birds. The trap is made of a fine wire or netting. The mesh should not be too dense as the birds might feel insecure if they cannot see through the 'wall'. Place seeds or other food on the ground and birds will walk into the one-way net. For wading birds place the trap when the tide goes out.

Door Support Rod

Trigger

Fulcrum

Hole for Trigger

Sliding Door

Box Trap

Box Trap

This trap has a sliding door held open by a rod supported by a fulcrum. There is a peg trigger release. The trap is baited and when the animal enters the trap its head or back disturbs the peg trigger and the door drops trapping the animal. This trap can catch rabbits, skunks, bobcats. Be careful when you open the door.

Catching Mice

The ultimate food is peanut butter. If you use cheese cover it with peanut butter so that the cheese will not dry. Mice will gently lick the peanut butter but quite often the trigger will not be released. A hard product as cheese or hard fat should be added to the peanut butter so that the mouse will exert more pressure on the trigger.

Noose Lasso

Attach a wire snare to a long stick. This noose can be used to lasso to catch birds, lizards and slow moving animals.

PITFALL TRAPS

Pitfall Traps

The trap requires:

• The right depth and size for the animal.

• Camouflage to hide the presence of the trap.

• A retaining device.

This probably is the most primitive trap still being used. Humans must have gotten the idea for this trap after falling into a hole. Natural pitfall traps would be sinkholes that are formed in a limestone area were you would also find caves. It can be used to catch any animal except one living permanently in the water. A pitfall trap is made by digging a hole and camouflaging it. This trap relies upon surprise as it is built on the pathway of an animal. The second feature that is required is a way to retain the animal in the trap. This can be done by making the trap deep, lining its walls so that the animal can not climb out or burrowing animals cannot dig their way out. Sharp upright stakes can be embedded in the floor of the trap and the animal killed when it falls on the spikes. The pit could be lined with clay or other impervious material and filled with water so that the animal can drown.

Modern pitfall traps can be used to catch live animals. In this case a revolving balanced lid (tilt trap) is placed on the trap and bait is put on the sensitive part of the lid. The predator jumps on the food and the lid rotates. The animal falls into the hole and the rotated lid levels off not letting it escape.

Pitfall traps can be baited or unbaited. By choosing the bait one could partially predetermine what animal one will catch.

Platform Pitfall

The Eskimos use a tilting platform trap to catch Arctic Fox. This trap is dug in the snow and has steep walls. The top is covered with blocks of ice with an opening of 1 1/2 feet in diameter. Bait is *attached* to a tilting platform a foot below the entrance. The tilting platform is designed so that it will right itself with the bait always returning to the top. This trap can catch a few fox without being opened.

A similar trap can be used for rodents but the walls should be sheet metal or they will dig or gnaw their way out. A buried barrel could be used as the pitfall trap.

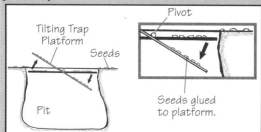

Tilting Trap Platform

Seeds

Pit

Pivot

Seeds glued to platform.

Tilt Platform Trap

This trap is built over a box or basket. The bait is placed (glued or attached) on a board that is balanced over a central pivot. A bird landing on the board or walking on it will tilt the lid and fall into the box below. This type of trap can be used on the ground or in trees.

TRAPPING BIRDS

Using a Sticky Substance

This method catches birds by sticking them to the branch of a tree. The glue is made by boiling evergreen tree bark to extract the sap. This sap, when boiled, becomes a sticky gum that can be smeared on a branch on which a bird will alight. To help in attracting birds one adds seeds of grain or rice to the gum.

Deadfall Traps for Birds

These traps, which are similar to animal traps, are smaller and have a more sensitive triggering device. *See the Figure 4 Deadfall trap as an example.*

Animals usually approach a trap because of the smell of the bait. Grain eating birds approach by seeing the bait so a *trail of grain* is required.

As birds are not as strong as animals the weight of a dead fall trap can be less than that for an animal. A brick or flat pieces of wood can be used.

If you want a live trap you can used a wire mesh cage instead of a weight. The birds that you will attract will be ground feeders as pheasant, quail, pigeons, partridges.

All birds are edible and are easy to catch with snares, baited hooks, noose at the end of a pole, deadfalls, and one way tunnels.

Grain Eating Birds

Large grain eating birds usually are ground birds. The grain can be laid down in a trail leading to a trigger. Some grain is placed below the trigger which is then disturbed by the bird, when it raises its head, and the trap falls. *See the Figure 4 Deadfall trap as an example.*

Carrion Eating Birds

Birds that eat carrion (crows, vultures, ravens) will be attracted by using meat as bait. The meat has to smell as they will be attracted by the odor, the same way as animals. If the weather is hot and dry the meat should be covered with fur or feathers as otherwise it will dry and lose its odor. Other bait can be killed animals (roadkill), eggs, porridge, etc.

Birds of Prey

Are attracted by live rabbits, birds or mice. If meat is used it has to be very fresh.

Noose and Snare Traps

These, as in the case of animals, are placed on trails used by ground running birds. Possible locations can be gaps in a fence, beside boulders Birds and animals will pass close to them so that they will not be seen.

Snares close to boulder in a field.

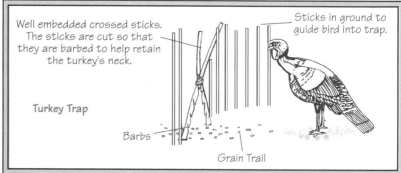

Well embedded crossed sticks. The sticks are cut so that they are barbed to help retain the turkey's neck.

Sticks in ground to guide bird into trap.

Turkey Trap

Barbs

Grain Trail

Quail: Use an inward spiraling stick fence in which you have dropped a path of seeds going to the center.

Geese: Lace a trail of wild grain that leads into a ditch or depression at least four feet deep. Rush the geese as they cannot escape because of the limited running range to start flying. They have difficulty spreading their wings.

Turkeys: Place a trail of seeds leading to a structure like a picket fence. The turkey will follow the bait below the picket and then will raise its head which will become trapped because of the direction of the feathers. Rush the turkey before it has time to untangle itself.

SNARE

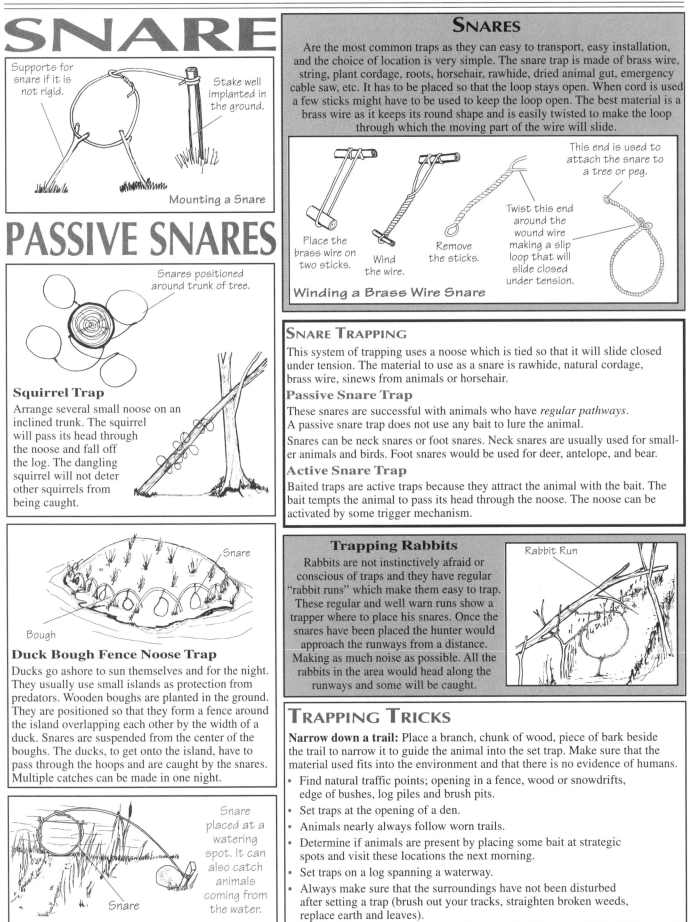

Supports for snare if it is not rigid.

Stake well implanted in the ground.

Mounting a Snare

PASSIVE SNARES

Snares positioned around trunk of tree.

Squirrel Trap

Arrange several small noose on an inclined trunk. The squirrel will pass its head through the noose and fall off the log. The dangling squirrel will not deter other squirrels from being caught.

Snare

Bough

Duck Bough Fence Noose Trap

Ducks go ashore to sun themselves and for the night. They usually use small islands as protection from predators. Wooden boughs are planted in the ground. They are positioned so that they form a fence around the island overlapping each other by the width of a duck. Snares are suspended from the center of the boughs. The ducks, to get onto the island, have to pass through the hoops and are caught by the snares. Multiple catches can be made in one night.

Snare placed at a watering spot. It can also catch animals coming from the water.

Snare

SNARES

Are the most common traps as they can easy to transport, easy installation, and the choice of location is very simple. The snare trap is made of brass wire, string, plant cordage, roots, horsehair, rawhide, dried animal gut, emergency cable saw, etc. It has to be placed so that the loop stays open. When cord is used a few sticks might have to be used to keep the loop open. The best material is a brass wire as it keeps its round shape and is easily twisted to make the loop through which the moving part of the wire will slide.

This end is used to attach the snare to a tree or peg.

Place the brass wire on two sticks.

Wind the wire.

Remove the sticks.

Twist this end around the wound wire making a slip loop that will slide closed under tension.

Winding a Brass Wire Snare

SNARE TRAPPING

This system of trapping uses a noose which is tied so that it will slide closed under tension. The material to use as a snare is rawhide, natural cordage, brass wire, sinews from animals or horsehair.

Passive Snare Trap

These snares are successful with animals who have *regular pathways*. A passive snare trap does not use any bait to lure the animal.

Snares can be neck snares or foot snares. Neck snares are usually used for smaller animals and birds. Foot snares would be used for deer, antelope, and bear.

Active Snare Trap

Baited traps are active traps because they attract the animal with the bait. The bait tempts the animal to pass its head through the noose. The noose can be activated by some trigger mechanism.

Trapping Rabbits

Rabbits are not instinctively afraid or conscious of traps and they have regular "rabbit runs" which make them easy to trap. These regular and well warn runs show a trapper where to place his snares. Once the snares have been placed the hunter would approach the runways from a distance. Making as much noise as possible. All the rabbits in the area would head along the runways and some will be caught.

Rabbit Run

TRAPPING TRICKS

Narrow down a trail: Place a branch, chunk of wood, piece of bark beside the trail to narrow it to guide the animal into the set trap. Make sure that the material used fits into the environment and that there is no evidence of humans.

- Find natural traffic points; opening in a fence, wood or snowdrifts, edge of bushes, log piles and brush pits.
- Set traps at the opening of a den.
- Animals nearly always follow worn trails.
- Determine if animals are present by placing some bait at strategic spots and visit these locations the next morning.
- Set traps on a log spanning a waterway.
- Always make sure that the surroundings have not been disturbed after setting a trap (brush out your tracks, straighten broken weeds, replace earth and leaves).

SNARE

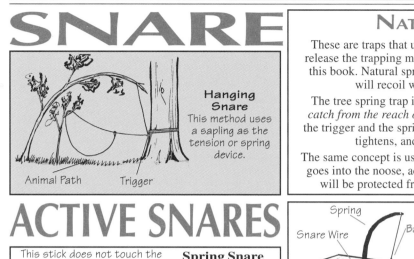

Hanging Snare
This method uses a sapling as the tension or spring device.

Animal Path   Trigger

NATURAL SPRING TRAPS

These are traps that use a spring. Either a flat spring or a coiled spring to release the trapping mechanism. Metal spring traps will not be discussed in this book. Natural springs can be made of young trees which are bent and will recoil when the triggering mechanism is activated.

The tree spring trap is used, with a snare, when you want to *remove your catch from the reach of predators*. The quarry enters the snare, disengages the trigger and the spring (bent tree) flings the animal into the air, the noose tightens, and the quarry is out of reach of any predator.

The same concept is used in an enclosure or box where the quarry enters and goes into the noose, activates the trigger and releases the spring. The catch will be protected from larger predators because it remains in the box.

ACTIVE SNARES

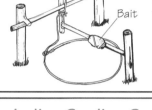

This stick does not touch the ground but is wedged by the bait stick.

Bait

Spring Snare
This snare can catch the foot or head. The bait stick is off the ground so that it will not be disturbed by small animals. The stick to which the cord is attached does *not touch* the ground.

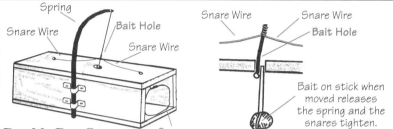

Spring   Bait Hole
Snare Wire   Snare Wire
Snare Wire

Snare Wire   Snare Wire
Bait Hole

Bait on stick when moved releases the spring and the snares tighten.

Snare

Double Box Snare
This box can be transported and used on trees (for squirrels) and on the ground. The bait is placed at the center so that the animal can approach from either side. The pulling on the bait will release the trigger which tightens the snare. As the animal will be caught in the box it will be protected from predators.

Indian Sapling Spring Noose
This method used by the Indians and early settlers consisted of a sapling tied down to the ground with a salted rawhide string. The animal, attracted to the salt, eats the rawhide while standing on the snare. The eaten trigger (rawhide) releases the sapling and the snare catches the animal.

Lemmings 'Wild Fast Food'
Lemmings are like mice and are easy to catch by placing fine wire snares along their paths. Find them under flat rocks or in the winter look for their paths and see where they enter into a snow drift. Dig down at a slight angle and you will easily catch one.

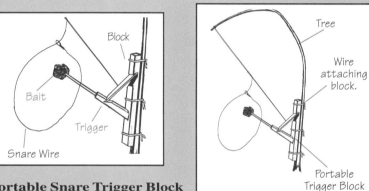

Block
Bait
Trigger
Snare Wire

Tree
Wire attaching block.
Portable Trigger Block

Portable Snare Trigger Block
The snare trigger block is transportable and can be assembled in any location. It is very handy, especially in survival situations, as a well made sensitive block can be used while traveling. A trapper will not have to spend time looking for the material at each stop to make a trigger.

Raccoon Tracks
Tracks found in a dry stream bed.

Wolf Pack

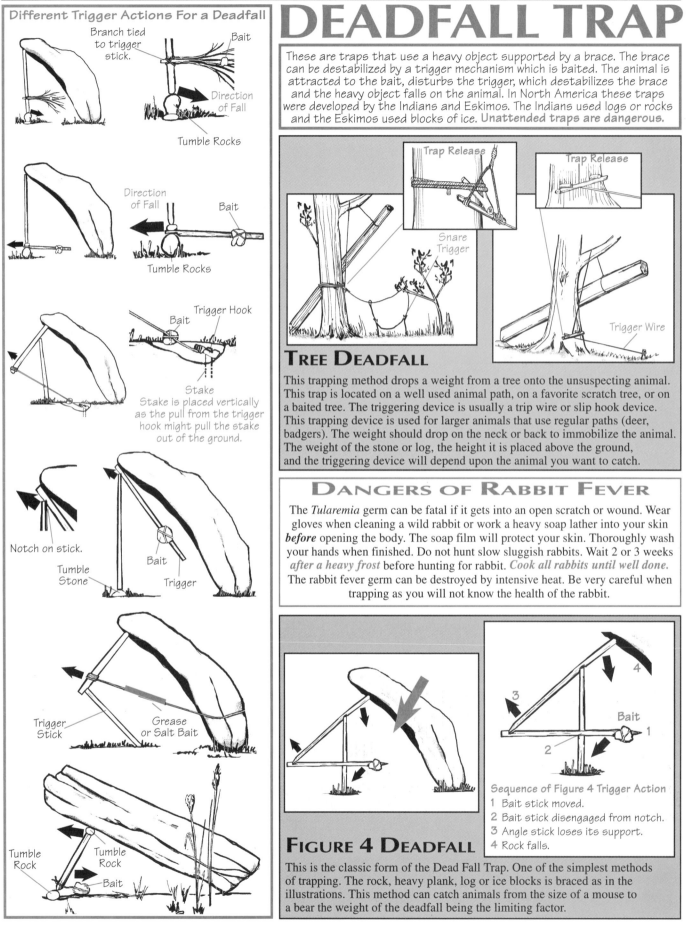

Different Trigger Actions For a Deadfall

Branch tied to trigger stick.

Bait

Direction of Fall

Tumble Rocks

Direction of Fall

Bait

Tumble Rocks

Trigger Hook

Bait

Stake
Stake is placed vertically as the pull from the trigger hook might pull the stake out of the ground.

Notch on stick.

Tumble Stone

Bait

Trigger

Trigger Stick

Grease or Salt Bait

Tumble Rock

Tumble Rock

Bait

DEADFALL TRAP

These are traps that use a heavy object supported by a brace. The brace can be destabilized by a trigger mechanism which is baited. The animal is attracted to the bait, disturbs the trigger, which destabilizes the brace and the heavy object falls on the animal. In North America these traps were developed by the Indians and Eskimos. The Indians used logs or rocks and the Eskimos used blocks of ice. **Unattended traps are dangerous.**

Trap Release

Trap Release

Snare Trigger

Trigger Wire

TREE DEADFALL

This trapping method drops a weight from a tree onto the unsuspecting animal. This trap is located on a well used animal path, on a favorite scratch tree, or on a baited tree. The triggering device is usually a trip wire or slip hook device. This trapping device is used for larger animals that use regular paths (deer, badgers). The weight should drop on the neck or back to immobilize the animal. The weight of the stone or log, the height it is placed above the ground, and the triggering device will depend upon the animal you want to catch.

DANGERS OF RABBIT FEVER

The *Tularemia* germ can be fatal if it gets into an open scratch or wound. Wear gloves when cleaning a wild rabbit or work a heavy soap lather into your skin *before* opening the body. The soap film will protect your skin. Thoroughly wash your hands when finished. Do not hunt slow sluggish rabbits. Wait 2 or 3 weeks *after a heavy frost* before hunting for rabbit. *Cook all rabbits until well done.* The rabbit fever germ can be destroyed by intensive heat. Be very careful when trapping as you will not know the health of the rabbit.

Bait

4

3

Bait

1

2

Sequence of Figure 4 Trigger Action
1 Bait stick moved.
2 Bait stick disengaged from notch.
3 Angle stick loses its support.
4 Rock falls.

FIGURE 4 DEADFALL

This is the classic form of the Dead Fall Trap. One of the simplest methods of trapping. The rock, heavy plank, log or ice blocks is braced as in the illustrations. This method can catch animals from the size of a mouse to a bear the weight of the deadfall being the limiting factor.

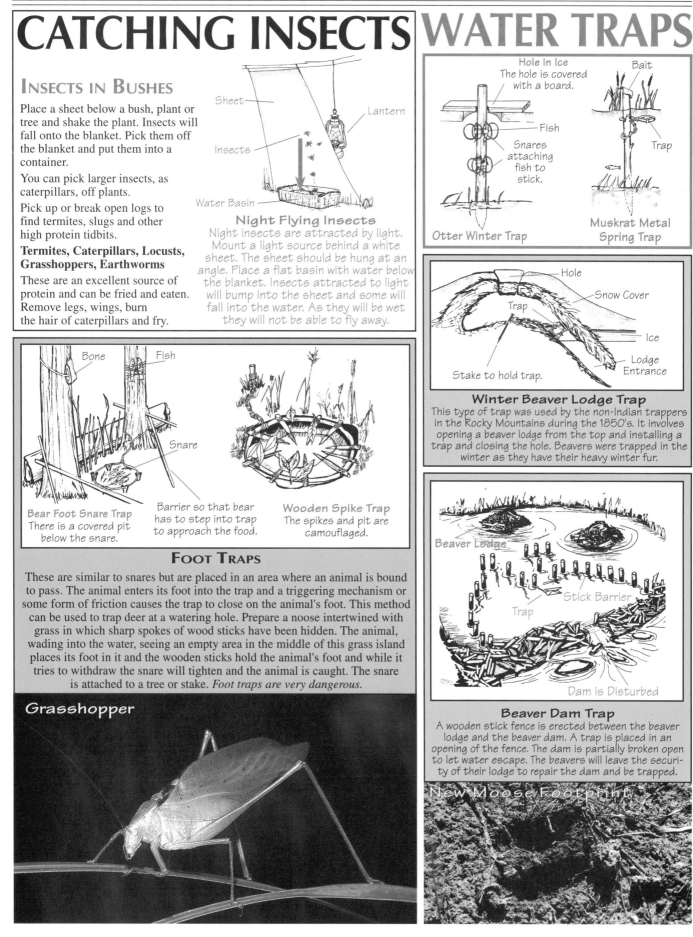

CATCHING INSECTS

INSECTS IN BUSHES

Place a sheet below a bush, plant or tree and shake the plant. Insects will fall onto the blanket. Pick them off the blanket and put them into a container.

You can pick larger insects, as caterpillars, off plants.

Pick up or break open logs to find termites, slugs and other high protein tidbits.

Termites, Caterpillars, Locusts, Grasshoppers, Earthworms

These are an excellent source of protein and can be fried and eaten. Remove legs, wings, burn the hair of caterpillars and fry.

Night Flying Insects
Night insects are attracted by light. Mount a light source behind a white sheet. The sheet should be hung at an angle. Place a flat basin with water below the blanket. Insects attracted to light will bump into the sheet and some will fall into the water. As they will be wet they will not be able to fly away.

Bear Foot Snare Trap
There is a covered pit below the snare.

Barrier so that bear has to step into trap to approach the food.

Wooden Spike Trap
The spikes and pit are camouflaged.

FOOT TRAPS
These are similar to snares but are placed in an area where an animal is bound to pass. The animal enters its foot into the trap and a triggering mechanism or some form of friction causes the trap to close on the animal's foot. This method can be used to trap deer at a watering hole. Prepare a noose intertwined with grass in which sharp spokes of wood sticks have been hidden. The animal, wading into the water, seeing an empty area in the middle of this grass island places its foot in it and the wooden sticks hold the animal's foot and while it tries to withdraw the snare will tighten and the animal is caught. The snare is attached to a tree or stake. *Foot traps are very dangerous.*

Grasshopper

WATER TRAPS

Hole in Ice
The hole is covered with a board.

Fish

Snares attaching fish to stick.

Otter Winter Trap

Bait

Trap

Muskrat Metal Spring Trap

Hole

Snow Cover

Trap

Ice

Lodge Entrance

Stake to hold trap.

Winter Beaver Lodge Trap
This type of trap was used by the non-Indian trappers in the Rocky Mountains during the 1850's. It involves opening a beaver lodge from the top and installing a trap and closing the hole. Beavers were trapped in the winter as they have their heavy winter fur.

Beaver Lodge

Stick Barrier

Trap

Dam is Disturbed

Beaver Dam Trap
A wooden stick fence is erected between the beaver lodge and the beaver dam. A trap is placed in an opening of the fence. The dam is partially broken open to let water escape. The beavers will leave the security of their lodge to repair the dam and be trapped.

New Moose Footprint

163

TIME TO FISH

The best time varies for each species and the environment the species lives in. In general fish feed just before dawn and just after dusk; before a storm as a cold front approaches; and at night when the moon is full or waning. Rising fish and jumping minnows may also be signs of feeding fish.

WHERE TO FIND FISH

The place depends on the type of water available and the time of day.

Birds gathering around a school of fish.

Dorsal fin of a large fish.

During the Day: In fast running streams *in the heat* of the day, try deep pools that lie below the riffles. On lakes in the heat of the summer, fish deep because fish seek the coolness of deeper water.

Large fish in trunk of tree.

Fish hiding between logs.

During the Evening or Early Morning: Float the bait over the riffle, aiming for submerged logs, undercut banks, and overhanging bushes. On lakes fish the edges as fish are more apt to feed in shallow water.

In the Spring and Late Fall: On a lake fishing is more productive on the edge in shallow water because fish are either bedding or seeking warmer water. You can locate the beds of some species of fish by their strong, distinctively "fishy" odor.

Fish at stream's entry into lake. The stream's water has more oxygen and is cool.

Large predator fish in the shallows on moonlit nights.

Large fish hunting small fish below lily pads.

Fish gathering near cool water from underground stream.

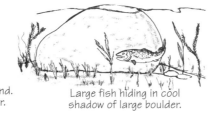

Fish gathering on leeward side of island. The wind can blow insects into water.

Large fish hiding in cool shadow of large boulder.

FISHING SPOTS

FISHING CHAPTER 15

Egyptian Fishing

Fish are probably the most difficult water food to catch. If you have no previous fishing experience it may take hours or even days before you are successful. Fishing is possible with very crude equipment. Hooks can be improvised out of pins, bone, plant thorns, or hardwood. Line can be made by twisting bark or cloth fibers. With patience and trial and error you will find the right location, correct bait and the best time of day.

Large Fish Chasing Small Fish

Crab Left on Shore After the Receding Tide

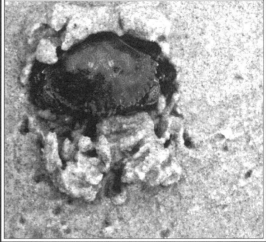

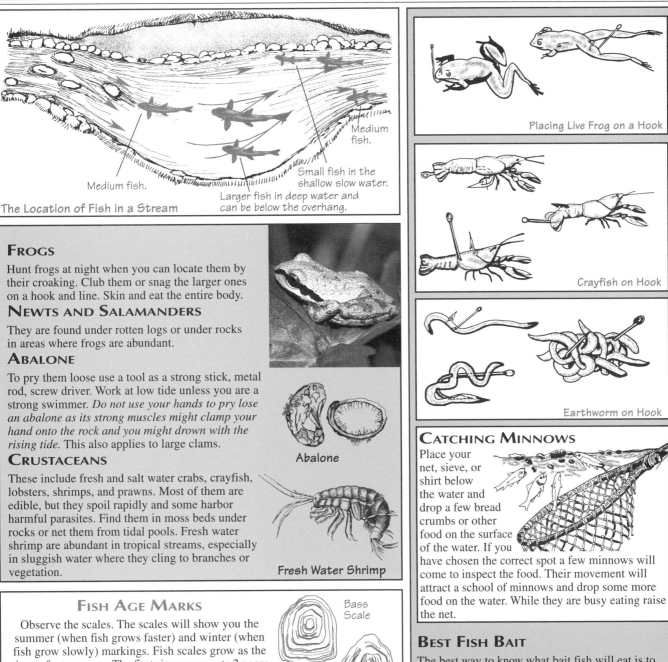

The Location of Fish in a Stream

Medium fish.

Medium fish.

Small fish in the shallow slow water.

Larger fish in deep water and can be below the overhang.

Placing Live Frog on a Hook

Crayfish on Hook

Earthworm on Hook

FROGS

Hunt frogs at night when you can locate them by their croaking. Club them or snag the larger ones on a hook and line. Skin and eat the entire body.

NEWTS AND SALAMANDERS

They are found under rotten logs or under rocks in areas where frogs are abundant.

ABALONE

To pry them loose use a tool as a strong stick, metal rod, screw driver. Work at low tide unless you are a strong swimmer. *Do not use your hands to pry lose an abalone as its strong muscles might clamp your hand onto the rock and you might drown with the rising tide.* This also applies to large clams.

Abalone

CRUSTACEANS

These include fresh and salt water crabs, crayfish, lobsters, shrimps, and prawns. Most of them are edible, but they spoil rapidly and some harbor harmful parasites. Find them in moss beds under rocks or net them from tidal pools. Fresh water shrimp are abundant in tropical streams, especially in sluggish water where they cling to branches or vegetation.

Fresh Water Shrimp

CATCHING MINNOWS

Place your net, sieve, or shirt below the water and drop a few bread crumbs or other food on the surface of the water. If you have chosen the correct spot a few minnows will come to inspect the food. Their movement will attract a school of minnows and drop some more food on the water. While they are busy eating raise the net.

BEST FISH BAIT

The best way to know what bait fish will eat is to look at what is floating on the surface of the water and what items attract the curiosity of the fish.

After you have caught your first fish, examine the stomach and intestines and you will see what they are biting. Could be: worms, minnows, fish eggs, crayfish, wood grubs or insects. You can use the intestines as bait for a larger fish.

Finding Bait in a Rotten Log

Rotten logs are an excellent source of bait for fishing. Look for a log that is on moist soil and roll it over to find worms, grubs, and larvae. You can then break open the log and find more tidbits of bait. Some of these insects might even add protein to your diet in case of an emergency.

FISH AGE MARKS

Observe the scales. The scales will show you the summer (when fish grows faster) and winter (when fish grow slowly) markings. Fish scales grow as the rings of a tree grow. The first ring represents 2 years of growth in the fry stage. Each additional summer (wide line) and winter (dark narrow line) indicate the age of the fish.

Bass Scale

Salmon Scale

BAIT FROM NATIVE WATERS

In general fish bite bait taken from their native water. Look for crabs, fish eggs, and minnows and on the banks for worms and insects. Inspect the stomach of a hooked fish to see what it has been eating and try to duplicate this food. Use the intestines and eyes of a caught fish for bait. If worms are used completely cover the hook. With minnows, pass the hook through the body of the fish under its backbone in the rear of the dorsal fin. Be sure you do not sever the minnow's backbone because you want it to keep active.

B A I T

FISH HOOKS

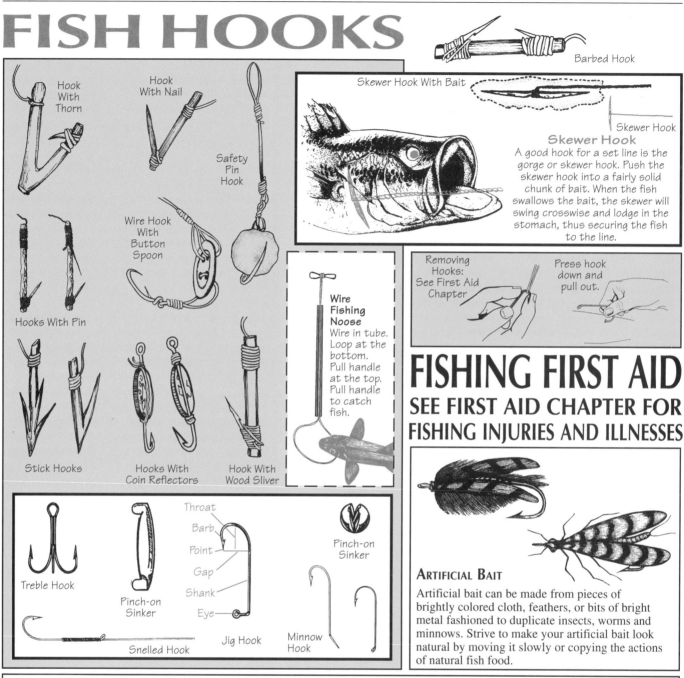

Barbed Hook

Skewer Hook With Bait

Skewer Hook

Skewer Hook
A good hook for a set line is the gorge or skewer hook. Push the skewer hook into a fairly solid chunk of bait. When the fish swallows the bait, the skewer will swing crosswise and lodge in the stomach, thus securing the fish to the line.

Hook With Thorn

Hook With Nail

Safety Pin Hook

Wire Hook With Button Spoon

Hooks With Pin

Stick Hooks

Hooks With Coin Reflectors

Hook With Wood Sliver

Wire Fishing Noose
Wire in tube. Loop at the bottom. Pull handle at the top. Pull handle to catch fish.

Removing Hooks: See First Aid Chapter

Press hook down and pull out.

FISHING FIRST AID
SEE FIRST AID CHAPTER FOR FISHING INJURIES AND ILLNESSES

Treble Hook

Pinch-on Sinker

Throat
Barb
Point
Gap
Shank
Eye

Pinch-on Sinker

Snelled Hook

Jig Hook

Minnow Hook

ARTIFICIAL BAIT
Artificial bait can be made from pieces of brightly colored cloth, feathers, or bits of bright metal fashioned to duplicate insects, worms and minnows. Strive to make your artificial bait look natural by moving it slowly or copying the actions of natural fish food.

CATCHING WORMS
Worms are the most tempting tidbit for fish including trout, bass, perch, eels, suckers, and bullheads. Collect them at night on a lawn, after a rainfall, or watering of the lawn. Use a flashlight and upon seeing a worm grasp it close to the end near the burrow and pull. The worm might look slow but he can return to his burrow in a flash. Store worms in a tin can on a bed of powdered peat moss covered with wet sphagnum moss. This should keep a worm for several days. Do not store the tin in the sun or in a closed car, or you will have some sorry looking cooked worms!

CRAYFISH
These are available in most of temperate North America. They look like a grayish green lobster but are all tail and from 3 - 6 inches (8-15cm) long. Look for them in waters from a few inches to a few feet (meter) deep. They are especially easy to catch in small ponds or backwash. You can catch them by grabbing them, in shallow water, by their back to avoid their claws. In deeper waters they can be caught (or they crawl into) a baited net or shirt.

BAIT

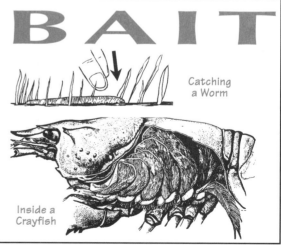

Catching a Worm

Inside a Crayfish

FISHING

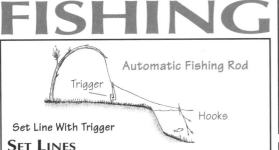

Automatic Fishing Rod

Trigger

Hooks

Set Line With Trigger

SET LINES

Tie *several* hooks onto a line. Bait them and fasten the line to a low-hanging branch that will bend when a fish is hooked. Permanently keep the set line in the water checking it periodically to remove fish and re-bait the hooks. A good hook for a set line is the gorge or skewer hook. Push the skewer hook into a fairly solid chunk of bait. When the fish swallows the bait, the skewer will swing crosswise and lodge in the stomach thus securing the fish to the line.

JIGGING

Jigging requires a wood pole, a hook, a piece of shiny metal shaped like a fishing spoon, a strip of white meat, pork rind or fish intestine, and a piece of short line about 10 inches (25 cm) long. Attach the hook just *below* the spoon on the end of the short line, and tie the line to the end of the pole. Submerge the hook just below the surface of the water near the edge of a lily pad or bed of weeds. From time to time slap the water with the tip of the pole to attract larger fish to the bait. This effective at night when the moon is out or when using a flashlight or lantern

Jigging is a term also used for a fishing method in which an unbaited hook or hooks are moved up and down on the water in a school of fish to catch a fish by hooking a part of its body. This method is used to catch carp and suckers. This unbaited method is illegal in some areas as it lets many injured fish escape.

BARE-HANDED FISHING

This takes patience but can be very successful. This method is effective in small streams with undercut banks or in shallow ponds left by receding flood waters.

- Place your hands in the water and allow them to reach water temperature. Slowly reach under a river bank, keeping your hands close to the bottom. Slowly move your hands until you touch a fish. Work your hands gently along its belly until you reach its gills. Grasp the fish firmly just behind its gills otherwise it might slip away.

- In faster water where there are boulders, feel into the nooks and crannies and you will possibly find trout and other fish that cannot escape. Do not do this in the ocean because you might be bitten by a moray eel.

Moray Eel

MUDDYING THE WATER

Small isolated pools caused by the receding waters of flooded streams are often abundant in fish. Muddy the bottom of the puddle by stamping or using a stick. Fish will seek clear water and rise to the surface. Catch and throw them onto the shore with your hands. You can catch the fish with your hands when the cloud gradually obscures the eyes of the fish.

DRUGGING FISH

This fish catching method to be used only in survival situations.

It involves drugging fish in a pond or slow flowing water. You can use the root of the soap plant (*chlorogalum pomdeidianum*), seeds of the southern buckeye (*aesculus pavia*), and leaves and stalks of fishweed or mullein (*croton setigerus*).

Crush any of the above and drop them into the pool. The fish will momentarily be drugged and float to the surface where you can catch them. The fish can be cleaned and eaten. This method was used by American Indian tribes.

FISH POISON

Collect pieces of coral and sea shells. Burn the coral and sea shells to obtain lime which is a fish poison.

Troll for fish below vegetation.

TROLLING FOR FISH

Use a shiny object, such as a spoon blade, with a hook fastened to the end. Paddle slowly on a log or boat, creating as little disturbance as possible. Let out a lot of line so the troll is far from the boat. The darting about of the flashy spoon will attract some fish. You can also troll by attaching your line to a piece of driftwood. Attach the driftwood to a line and let it drift with the current. Place a floater on the line to see if a fish has bitten.

ICE FISHING

In the winter fish can be caught by fishing through a hole in the ice. Keep the hole open by covering it with brush and piling loose snow over the cover.

Fish in the winter tend to gather in deep pools. Cut the ice holes over the deepest part of the lake. Place a baited rig at several holes. The flag moving to an upright position will signal a catch.

The pole should be 3 feel long with a line long enough to reach the bottom. Make a small spoon-shaped spinner from a piece of bright metal. Attach a hook to the line with the spinner just above the hook. When fishing move the rod in an up and down motion in such a way that the bright metal object will vibrate.

Try to fish close to where the shelf near the shore drops off to lake bottom, at the edge of the reeds, or close to a projecting rock formation.

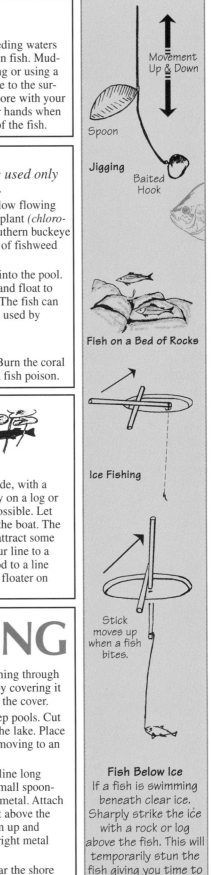

Movement Up & Down

Spoon

Jigging

Baited Hook

Fish on a Bed of Rocks

Ice Fishing

Stick moves up when a fish bites.

Fish Below Ice
If a fish is swimming beneath clear ice. Sharply strike the ice with a rock or log above the fish. This will temporarily stun the fish giving you time to cut a hole and remove the fish.

TRAPPING FISH

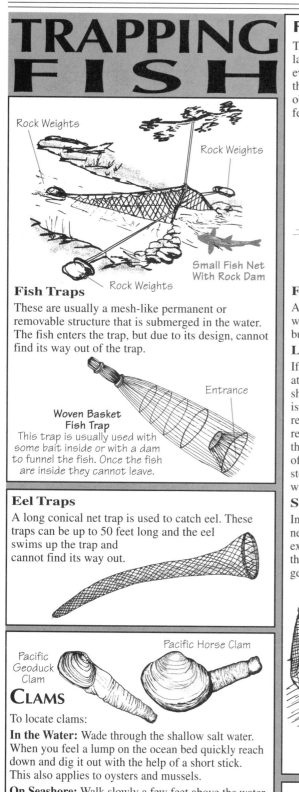

Rock Weights

Rock Weights

Rock Weights

Small Fish Net
With Rock Dam

Fish Traps

These are usually a mesh-like permanent or removable structure that is submerged in the water. The fish enters the trap, but due to its design, cannot find its way out of the trap.

Entrance

**Woven Basket
Fish Trap**
This trap is usually used with some bait inside or with a dam to funnel the fish. Once the fish are inside they cannot leave.

Eel Traps

A long conical net trap is used to catch eel. These traps can be up to 50 feet long and the eel swims up the trap and cannot find its way out.

Pacific Horse Clam

Pacific
Geoduck
Clam

CLAMS

To locate clams:

In the Water: Wade through the shallow salt water. When you feel a lump on the ocean bed quickly reach down and dig it out with the help of a short stick. This also applies to oysters and mussels.

On Seashore: Walk slowly a few feet above the water-line and hit the ground with a piece of driftwood. If you see small air holes these are from clams trying to reach the water. Place yourself between the water and the bubbles and start digging real fast because this clam is in a hurry and they are fast.

A *healthy clam* will close its shell very tightly. If you see that the shell is not tightly closed when you tap the clam throw it away. Do not eat clams that are found in inhabited and industrial estuaries or sea shores.

FISH TRAPS OR WEIRS

Traps can be used to catch fish especially those moving in schools. In lakes or large streams, fish approach the banks and shallows in the morning and evening. Sea fish traveling in large schools regularly approach the shore with the incoming tide, often moving parallel to the shore and circumventing obstructions in the water. Sea fish schools can be located by watching the feeding water birds.

Current

Top View

Fish

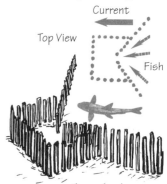

Tidal Shore Weir Traps

Fish Trap

A basic fish trap is an enclosure with a blind opening where two fence-like walls extend out like a funnel from the entrance. The effort you put into building a trap depends upon the length of time you plan to stay in one spot.

Location for Natural Barrier Traps

If you are on a tidal sea, pick a trap location at high tide and build it at low tide. On rocky shores use natural rock pools. On coral islands use natural pools on the surface of reefs by blocking the openings as the tide recedes. On sandy shores, use sand bars and the ditches they enclose. Fish in the lee of offshore sandbars. Build your trap as a low stone wall extending out into the water forming an angle with the shore.

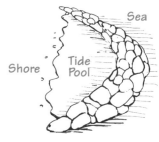

Sea

Shore

Tide
Pool

Rocks

Stream Traps

In small, shallow streams, make your fish trap with stakes, rocks, logs, fish net, earth, or branches set in the stream bottom so that the stream is blocked except for a small narrow opening into a stone or brush pen. Wade in and herd the fish into your trap. Dam the shallow area. Catch or club them when they get into the shallow water.

NETTING

The edges and tributaries of lakes and streams are usually abundant with fish too small to hook or spear but large enough to net. Make a circular frame with a forked sapling. Tie your T-shirt or mosquito netting to the frame. Scoop upstream around rocks or in pools with this improvised net.

MOLLUSKS

These include fresh and salt water invertebrates such as snails, clams, mussels, bivalves, periwinkles, chitons, and sea urchins. Most members of this group are edible; however, be sure that you have a fresh mollusk and that you boil it. Do not eat it raw as you might introduce parasites into your body. To find them in fresh water look in the shallows, especially in water with a sandy or muddy bottom. Near the sea, wait for low tide and check in tidal pools or on and in the sand.

Fresh Water Mussel

SPEARING FISH

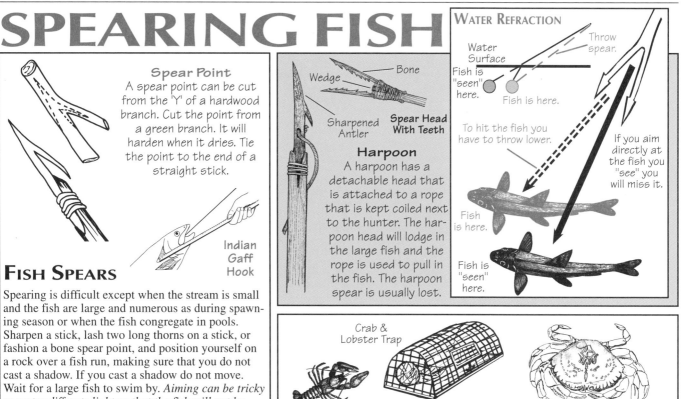

Spear Point

A spear point can be cut from the 'Y' of a hardwood branch. Cut the point from a green branch. It will harden when it dries. Tie the point to the end of a straight stick.

Indian Gaff Hook

FISH SPEARS

Spearing is difficult except when the stream is small and the fish are large and numerous as during spawning season or when the fish congregate in pools. Sharpen a stick, lash two long thorns on a stick, or fashion a bone spear point, and position yourself on a rock over a fish run, making sure that you do not cast a shadow. If you cast a shadow do not move. Wait for a large fish to swim by. *Aiming can be tricky as water diffracts light so that the fish will not be where you think it is. The fish will be closer to you, so you have to aim low. To learn how to judge the fish's position point your spear at a rock on the bed of the stream and push, without throwing, the spear into the water to touch the rock. You will not touch the rock because of diffraction but you will see the angle of your error.*

Hardwood Sapling Spear

Cut a straight young hardwood sapling just below a branch. The spear can be five feet long and about 3/4 (2 cm) of an inch thick. Remove all branches except the first branch. The first branch and the stick should be trimmed into a barbed spear head. Tie a leather thong or twine to the end of the stick to help you retrieve the stick. This spear can be used for fish or frogs.

Bamboo Spear

A dry bamboo pole an inch thick and 5 feet (1.5 m) long can be used to make a effective spear. Cut two spear points opposite to each other on the heavier end of the bamboo stick. This point should be between the natural divisions in the bamboo. A bamboo spear can be very sharp because the point is cut in the direction of the grain and the wood is dry. This spear can be used for fish, frogs and small animals.

INDIAN GAFF HOOK

Made in the same way as the fish spear except that the sharpened branch is longer and sharpened at the end.

FISHING TORCH

The Ojibway fished at night, in a boat or from the shore, while carrying a torch above the water.

To make a torch, a stick, about 9 feet (2.7 m) long, was split at one end. A piece of tightly folded birch bark, soaked in some oil, was placed between the split of the stick and lit. Fish drift towards the light and can be speared or netted.

Harpoon

A harpoon has a detachable head that is attached to a rope that is kept coiled next to the hunter. The harpoon head will lodge in the large fish and the rope is used to pull in the fish. The harpoon spear is usually lost.

Spear Head With Teeth

WATER REFRACTION

Crab and Lobster Traps

These traps are baited with smaller crabs or fish. Crabs and lobsters usually live on rocky beds near to the coast. To get at the bait the lobster or crab enters by tunnels at the ends of the trap. The bait might be enclosed in a protective cage so that it will be available to catch numerous lobsters in the same trap.

FISHING FIRST AID

FISH POISONING (*Erysipeloid*)

This disease is more common during warmer months. It is a skin disease that usually occurs on the hands and forearms. It is caused by the skin being punctured by fins of fish, sharp bones, or fish hooks and the residue of fish slime or rotten fish enters these openings. A small red spot at the point of entry indicates the start of an infection. It will spread to adjacent areas. The infection will gradually become clear at the center with a reddish-purple color at the spreading margins. The affected parts will swell, itch, and have a burning sensation. First aid can be started with frequent hot bathing of the affected areas. *See a doctor for complete treatment.*

FISHERMAN'S CONJUNCTIVITIS

Fisherman's conjunctivitis is a severe inflammatory condition of the eyes. It is caused by contact with the juices of marine animal growth that look like suet. These growths can be crushed and release juice which can accidentally enter the eye. This causes a very acute and painful inflammation of the conjunctiva or thin covering of the eye. *Wash the slime off fish when they are caught and wash hands after handling caught fish. See a doctor for treatment.*

SALT WATER BOILS

Is very common with deep water fishermen. It is a collection of small boils around the wrists, back of the hands or forearms and occasionally around the neck. These are the areas that get rubbed by cracked, sodden and dirty oilskin jackets, and by the residue brought up from the sea bed. The friction causes minute cracks in the skin which become infected by organisms present in fish slime. Cleanliness will lessen the risk of infection from the slime. The condition if neglected becomes very painful and disabling. *Keep your clothing clean especially at the abrasion points. See a doctor for treatment.*

See First Aid Chapter for more details on fish injuries.

DANGERS IN THE TROPICS

Bare Feet

Coral reefs, dead or alive, can severely cut your feet.

Slide Feet When Walking

Slide your feet along muddy or sandy bottoms. This will help you to avoid *stepping on* sting rays or spined fish. A misplaced step on a stingray, pinning down its body, will give it leverage to throw up its tail and stab you with its stinging spine. The broken off spine (because of the barbs) can only be removed by cutting it out.

Sponges and Sea Urchins

They can slip fine needles of lime or silica into your skin where they will break off and fester. Do not dig them out but use lime juice or other citric acid to dissolve them.

Camouflaged Stone Fish

Well camouflaged stone fish with thirteen poisoned spines can be stepped on with bare feet or light running shoes. The poison can cause great agony and death. This poison should be treated as a snakebite.

Hands

Do not probe in dark holes or around rocks as your fingers can look like supper.

Blue Shark

Cone Snails

These have poison teeth that can bite (as well as long, slender pointed terebra snails). Cone shells have smooth, colorful mottled shells with elongated, narrow openings. They live under rocks, in crevices of coral reefs, and along rocky shores of protected bays. They are shy and active at night. They have a long mouth and a snout which is used to jab or inject their teeth. These teeth are actually tiny hypodermic needles, with a tiny poison gland on the back end of each. The sting is swift and produces acute pain, swelling, paralysis, blindness, and possible death in four hours. Avoid handling all cone shells.

Big Conchs

Handle with caution as they have razor-sharp trap doors which might suddenly jab out puncturing your skin.

Sharks, Barracudas, and Moray Eel

When crossing deeper portions of a reef, check the reef edge shadows for sharks, barracudas, and moray eels.

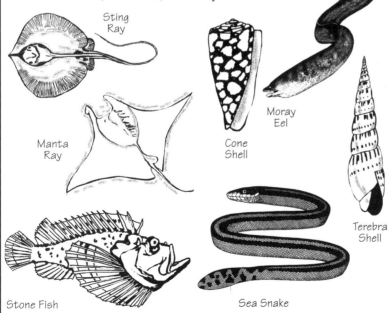

Sting Ray

Manta Ray

Moray Eel

Cone Shell

Terebra Shell

Stone Fish

Sea Snake

FISHING IN TROPIC WATERS

Warm tropical waters and special circumstances in temperate waters can trigger problems that make certain fish inedible.

The US Air Force Survival Manual indicates:

- Fish can be *edible* or *inedible* and this can vary from area to area due to their diet or special seasonal characteristics.
- Cooking will *not* eradicate the poison.
- Barracudas: Large fish can cause serious digestive illness. Barracudas under three feet can be eaten with safety.
- Oilfish: Tasty, white flaky flesh but *very poisonous*.
- Great sea eels: Avoid them.
- Never eat eggs or entrails of tropical fish.
- *Avoid* all fish with round or box like bodies with hard, shell-like skins covered with bony plates or spines. They can have parrot-like mouths, small gill openings, belly fins which are small or absent. They are named after their shape: puffer fish, file fish, globe fish, trigger fish, trunk fish.

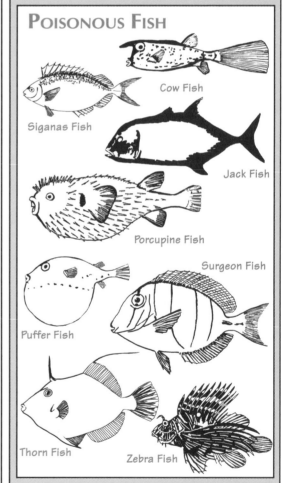

POISONOUS FISH

Cow Fish

Siganas Fish

Jack Fish

Porcupine Fish

Surgeon Fish

Puffer Fish

Thorn Fish

Zebra Fish

POISONOUS FISH
SEE FIRST AID CHAPTER
FOR MORE INFORMATION

CHOPPING A TREE

- Ax should be sharp, well-balanced and the correct size for you and the job being done.
- Secure footing. Build a level platform if you are cutting a very large tree.
- Your clothing should not obstruct your movement.
- Swing with short, smooth strokes as this will keep you on target.
- The most efficient cut is at a 45° angle. This cut will cut 5 times deeper than a perpendicular cut. It will easily eject the wood chips.
- Check the direction of lean of the tree and heavy branches. Establish in which direction it will have a tendency to fall. A well placed notch might give you some control of the direction of fall.
- Before starting make sure that you have planned an escape route. Check for other trees and branches that might be affected by your cutting or the falling tree. Watch for dead branches that might be dislodged and fall. Do not forget hornet's or wasp's nests

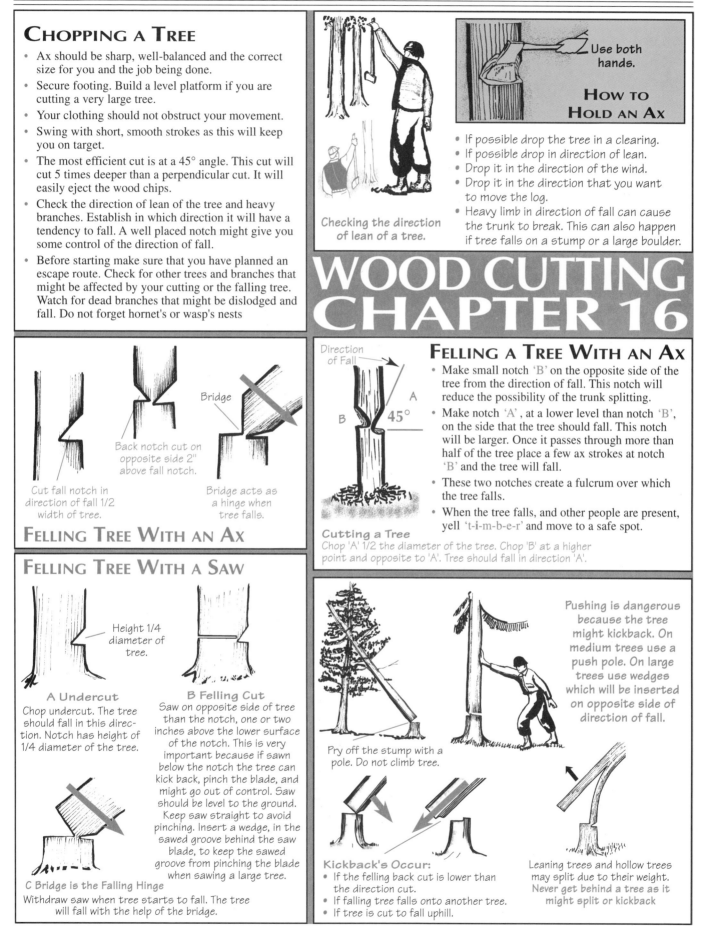

Checking the direction of lean of a tree.

Use both hands.

HOW TO HOLD AN AX

- If possible drop the tree in a clearing.
- If possible drop in direction of lean.
- Drop it in the direction of the wind.
- Drop it in the direction that you want to move the log.
- Heavy limb in direction of fall can cause the trunk to break. This can also happen if tree falls on a stump or a large boulder.

WOOD CUTTING CHAPTER 16

FELLING A TREE WITH AN AX

- Make small notch 'B' on the opposite side of the tree from the direction of fall. This notch will reduce the possibility of the trunk splitting.
- Make notch 'A', at a lower level than notch 'B', on the side that the tree should fall. This notch will be larger. Once it passes through more than half of the tree place a few ax strokes at notch 'B' and the tree will fall.
- These two notches create a fulcrum over which the tree falls.
- When the tree falls, and other people are present, yell 't-i-m-b-e-r' and move to a safe spot.

Direction of Fall

45°

Cutting a Tree
Chop 'A' 1/2 the diameter of the tree. Chop 'B' at a higher point and opposite to 'A'. Tree should fall in direction 'A'.

Bridge

Back notch cut on opposite side 2" above fall notch.

Cut fall notch in direction of fall 1/2 width of tree.

Bridge acts as a hinge when tree falls.

FELLING TREE WITH AN AX

FELLING TREE WITH A SAW

Height 1/4 diameter of tree.

A Undercut
Chop undercut. The tree should fall in this direction. Notch has height of 1/4 diameter of the tree.

B Felling Cut
Saw on opposite side of tree than the notch, one or two inches above the lower surface of the notch. This is very important because if sawn below the notch the tree can kick back, pinch the blade, and might go out of control. Saw should be level to the ground. Keep saw straight to avoid pinching. Insert a wedge, in the sawed groove behind the saw blade, to keep the sawed groove from pinching the blade when sawing a large tree.

C Bridge is the Falling Hinge
Withdraw saw when tree starts to fall. The tree will fall with the help of the bridge.

Pry off the stump with a pole. Do not climb tree.

Kickback's Occur:
- If the felling back cut is lower than the direction cut.
- If falling tree falls onto another tree.
- If tree is cut to fall uphill.

Pushing is dangerous because the tree might kickback. On medium trees use a push pole. On large trees use wedges which will be inserted on opposite side of direction of fall.

Leaning trees and hollow trees may split due to their weight. Never get behind a tree as it might split or kickback

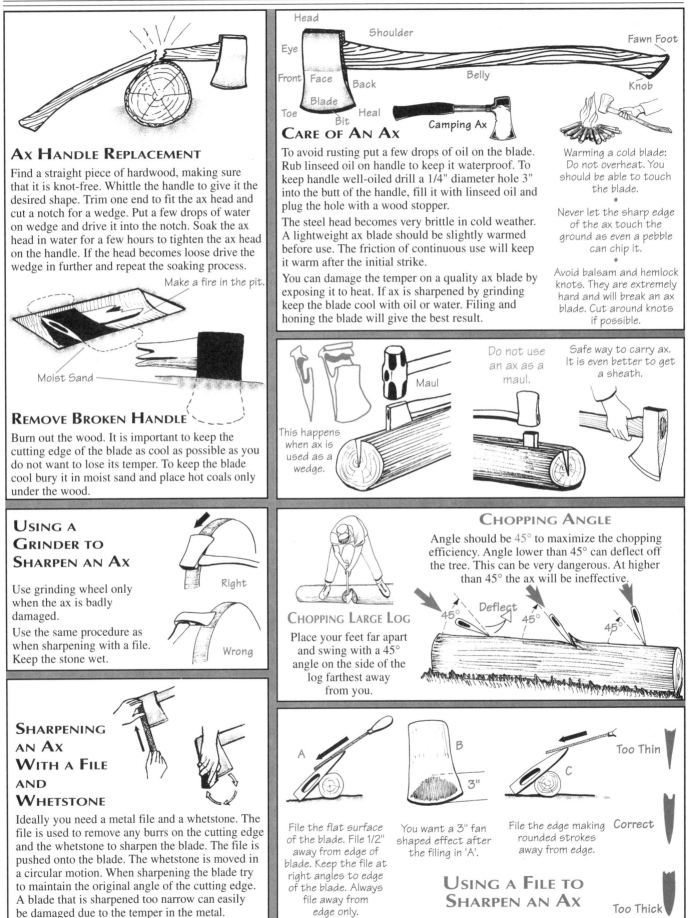

AX HANDLE REPLACEMENT

Find a straight piece of hardwood, making sure that it is knot-free. Whittle the handle to give it the desired shape. Trim one end to fit the ax head and cut a notch for a wedge. Put a few drops of water on wedge and drive it into the notch. Soak the ax head in water for a few hours to tighten the ax head on the handle. If the head becomes loose drive the wedge in further and repeat the soaking process.

Make a fire in the pit.

Moist Sand

REMOVE BROKEN HANDLE

Burn out the wood. It is important to keep the cutting edge of the blade as cool as possible as you do not want to lose its temper. To keep the blade cool bury it in moist sand and place hot coals only under the wood.

USING A GRINDER TO SHARPEN AN AX

Use grinding wheel only when the ax is badly damaged.

Use the same procedure as when sharpening with a file. Keep the stone wet.

Right

Wrong

SHARPENING AN AX WITH A FILE AND WHETSTONE

Ideally you need a metal file and a whetstone. The file is used to remove any burrs on the cutting edge and the whetstone to sharpen the blade. The file is pushed onto the blade. The whetstone is moved in a circular motion. When sharpening the blade try to maintain the original angle of the cutting edge. A blade that is sharpened too narrow can easily be damaged due to the temper in the metal.

Head
Shoulder
Fawn Foot
Eye
Front   Face
Back
Belly
Knob
Toe
Blade
Bit   Heal
Camping Ax

CARE OF AN AX

To avoid rusting put a few drops of oil on the blade. Rub linseed oil on handle to keep it waterproof. To keep handle well-oiled drill a 1/4" diameter hole 3" into the butt of the handle, fill it with linseed oil and plug the hole with a wood stopper.

The steel head becomes very brittle in cold weather. A lightweight ax blade should be slightly warmed before use. The friction of continuous use will keep it warm after the initial strike.

You can damage the temper on a quality ax blade by exposing it to heat. If ax is sharpened by grinding keep the blade cool with oil or water. Filing and honing the blade will give the best result.

Warming a cold blade: Do not overheat. You should be able to touch the blade.

Never let the sharp edge of the ax touch the ground as even a pebble can chip it.

Avoid balsam and hemlock knots. They are extremely hard and will break an ax blade. Cut around knots if possible.

This happens when ax is used as a wedge.

Maul

Do not use an ax as a maul.

Safe way to carry ax. It is even better to get a sheath.

CHOPPING ANGLE

Angle should be 45° to maximize the chopping efficiency. Angle lower than 45° can deflect off the tree. This can be very dangerous. At higher than 45° the ax will be ineffective.

CHOPPING LARGE LOG

Place your feet far apart and swing with a 45° angle on the side of the log farthest away from you.

45°   Deflect   45°   45°

A

B

3"

C

File the flat surface of the blade. File 1/2" away from edge of blade. Keep the file at right angles to edge of the blade. Always file away from edge only.

You want a 3" fan shaped effect after the filing in 'A'.

File the edge making rounded strokes away from edge.

USING A FILE TO SHARPEN AN AX

Too Thin

Correct

Too Thick

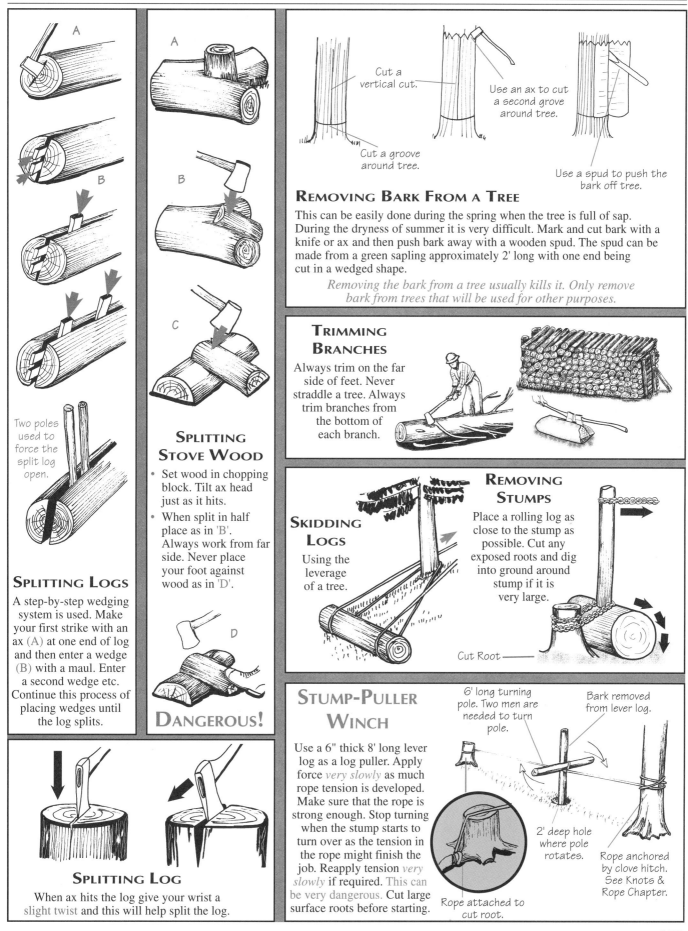

Cut a vertical cut.

Use an ax to cut a second grove around tree.

Cut a groove around tree.

Use a spud to push the bark off tree.

REMOVING BARK FROM A TREE

This can be easily done during the spring when the tree is full of sap. During the dryness of summer it is very difficult. Mark and cut bark with a knife or ax and then push bark away with a wooden spud. The spud can be made from a green sapling approximately 2' long with one end being cut in a wedged shape.

Removing the bark from a tree usually kills it. Only remove bark from trees that will be used for other purposes.

TRIMMING BRANCHES

Always trim on the far side of feet. Never straddle a tree. Always trim branches from the bottom of each branch.

SKIDDING LOGS

Using the leverage of a tree.

REMOVING STUMPS

Place a rolling log as close to the stump as possible. Cut any exposed roots and dig into ground around stump if it is very large.

Cut Root

STUMP-PULLER WINCH

Use a 6" thick 8' long lever log as a log puller. Apply force *very slowly* as much rope tension is developed. Make sure that the rope is strong enough. Stop turning when the stump starts to turn over as the tension in the rope might finish the job. Reapply tension *very slowly* if required. This can be very dangerous. Cut large surface roots before starting.

6' long turning pole. Two men are needed to turn pole.

Bark removed from lever log.

2' deep hole where pole rotates.

Rope anchored by clove hitch. See Knots & Rope Chapter.

Rope attached to cut root.

A

B

Two poles used to force the split log open.

SPLITTING LOGS

A step-by-step wedging system is used. Make your first strike with an ax (A) at one end of log and then enter a wedge (B) with a maul. Enter a second wedge etc. Continue this process of placing wedges until the log splits.

A

B

C

SPLITTING STOVE WOOD

• Set wood in chopping block. Tilt ax head just as it hits.
• When split in half place as in 'B'. Always work from far side. Never place your foot against wood as in 'D'.

D

DANGEROUS!

SPLITTING LOG

When ax hits the log give your wrist a slight twist and this will help split the log.

SURVIVAL SAW

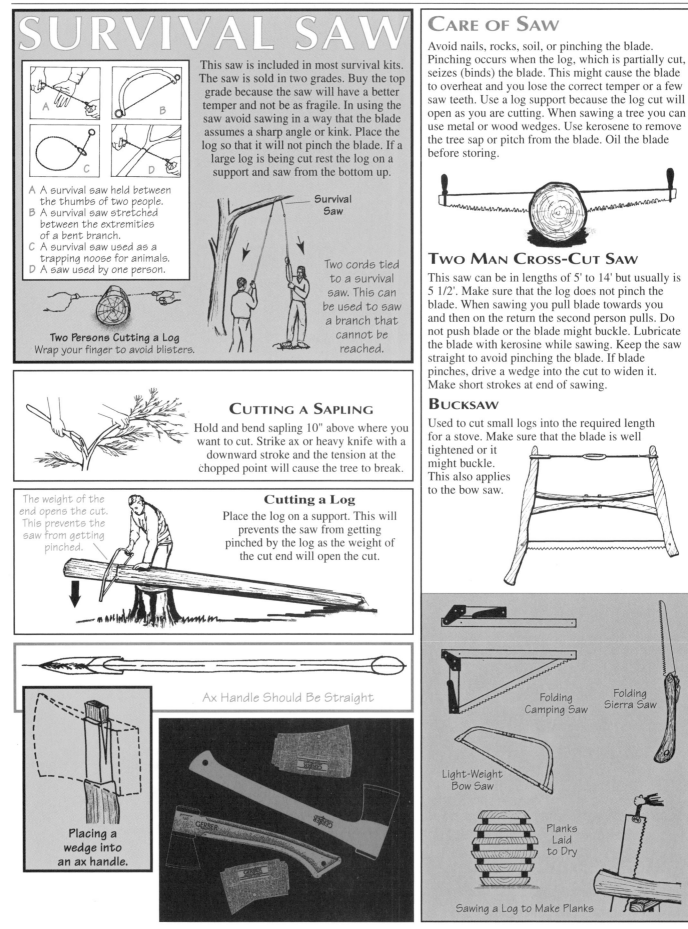

A A survival saw held between the thumbs of two people.
B A survival saw stretched between the extremities of a bent branch.
C A survival saw used as a trapping noose for animals.
D A saw used by one person.

Two Persons Cutting a Log
Wrap your finger to avoid blisters.

This saw is included in most survival kits. The saw is sold in two grades. Buy the top grade because the saw will have a better temper and not be as fragile. In using the saw avoid sawing in a way that the blade assumes a sharp angle or kink. Place the log so that it will not pinch the blade. If a large log is being cut rest the log on a support and saw from the bottom up.

Survival Saw

Two cords tied to a survival saw. This can be used to saw a branch that cannot be reached.

CUTTING A SAPLING

Hold and bend sapling 10" above where you want to cut. Strike ax or heavy knife with a downward stroke and the tension at the chopped point will cause the tree to break.

Cutting a Log

Place the log on a support. This will prevents the saw from getting pinched by the log as the weight of the cut end will open the cut.

The weight of the end opens the cut. This prevents the saw from getting pinched.

Ax Handle Should Be Straight

Placing a wedge into an ax handle.

CARE OF SAW

Avoid nails, rocks, soil, or pinching the blade. Pinching occurs when the log, which is partially cut, seizes (binds) the blade. This might cause the blade to overheat and you lose the correct temper or a few saw teeth. Use a log support because the log cut will open as you are cutting. When sawing a tree you can use metal or wood wedges. Use kerosene to remove the tree sap or pitch from the blade. Oil the blade before storing.

TWO MAN CROSS-CUT SAW

This saw can be in lengths of 5' to 14' but usually is 5 1/2'. Make sure that the log does not pinch the blade. When sawing you pull blade towards you and then on the return the second person pulls. Do not push blade or the blade might buckle. Lubricate the blade with kerosine while sawing. Keep the saw straight to avoid pinching the blade. If blade pinches, drive a wedge into the cut to widen it. Make short strokes at end of sawing.

BUCKSAW

Used to cut small logs into the required length for a stove. Make sure that the blade is well tightened or it might buckle. This also applies to the bow saw.

Folding Camping Saw

Folding Sierra Saw

Light-Weight Bow Saw

Planks Laid to Dry

Sawing a Log to Make Planks

GEOGRAPHIC COORDINATES

LOCATING A PLACE ON EARTH

By drawing a set of east-west rings around the globe (parallel to the equator), and a set of north-south rings crossing the equator at right angles to the equator and converging at the poles, a network of reference lines is formed from which any point on the earth's surface can be located.

Parallel of Latitude

The angular distance of a point north or south of the equator is known as its *latitude*. The rings around the earth *parallel to the equator* are called parallels of latitude or simply parallels.

Meridians of Longitude

A second set of rings around the globe at right angles to lines of latitude and passing through the poles are known as *meridians of longitude* or simply meridians. One meridian is designated as the *Prime Meridian* (it is the 0° meridian) and it passes through Greenwich, England. The distance east or west of the prime meridian to a point is known as its *longitude*.

Geographic Coordinates

Geographic coordinates are expressed in angular measurement.

Each circle is divided into 360°, each degree into 60 minutes, and each minute into 60 seconds.

Latitude: Starting with 0° at the Equator, the parallels of latitude are numbered to 90° both north and south. The extremities are the North Pole at 90° North latitude and the South Pole at 90° South latitude. Latitude can have the same numerical value north or south of the equator, so the direction N or S must always be given.

Longitude: Starting with 0° at the Prime Meridian, longitude is measured both East and West around the world. Lines east of the prime meridian are numbered to 180° and identified as East longitude; lines west of the prime meridian are numbered to 180° and identified as West longitude. The direction E or W must always be given. The line directly opposite the prime meridian, 180°, may be referred to as either east or west longitude.

All places on earth have a unique latitude and longitude which are represented as
Latitude 32°15'00"N, Longitude 84°50'00"W.

Angular Distance on the Surface of the Earth

1° (degree) of latitude:

Is approximately 111 kilometers (69 miles).

1' (second) of latitude:

Is equal to approximately 30 meters (100 feet).

1° (degree) of longitude:

At the equator is also approximately 111 kilometers (69 miles).

1° (degree) of longitude:

At the poles is zero as all longitudes *meet* at the poles.

Use degrees to express direction and location.
One degree (°) = 60 minutes (')
One minute (') = 60 seconds (")

COMPASS & MAPS CHAPTER 17

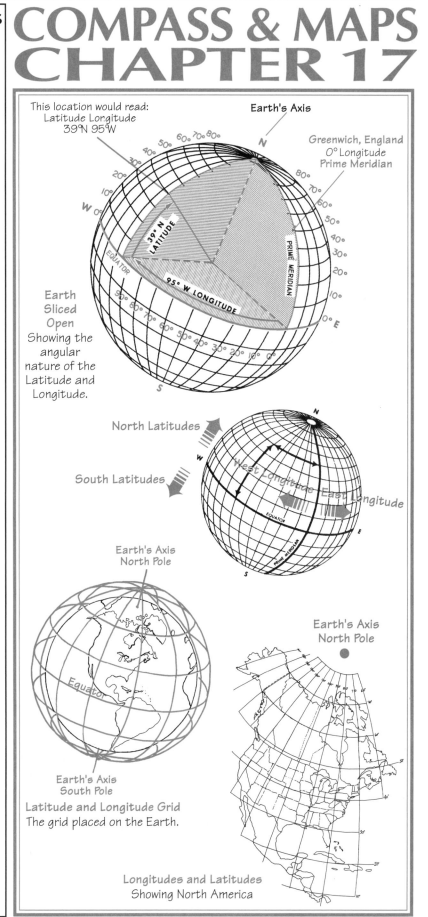

This location would read:
Latitude Longitude
39°N 95°W

Earth's Axis

Greenwich, England
0° Longitude
Prime Meridian

Earth Sliced Open
Showing the angular nature of the Latitude and Longitude.

39° N LATITUDE

95° W LONGITUDE

PRIME MERIDIAN

EQUATOR

North Latitudes

South Latitudes

West Longitude   East Longitude

EQUATOR

PRIME MERIDIAN

Earth's Axis
North Pole

Earth's Axis
South Pole

Latitude and Longitude Grid
The grid placed on the Earth.

Earth's Axis
North Pole

Longitudes and Latitudes
Showing North America

MAGNETIC NORTH POLE

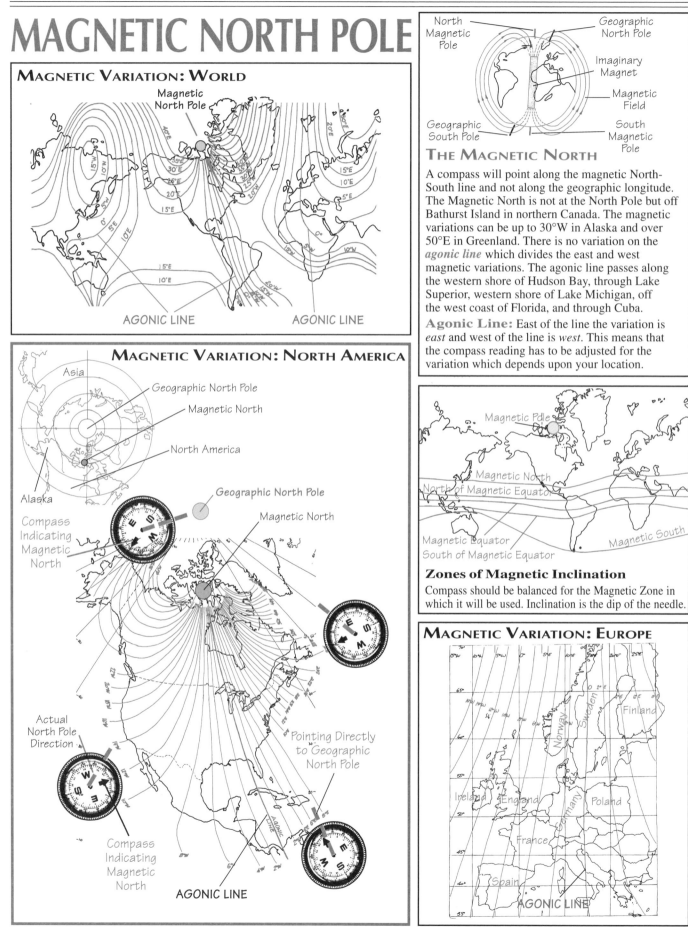

MAGNETIC VARIATION: WORLD

Magnetic North Pole

AGONIC LINE   AGONIC LINE

THE MAGNETIC NORTH

North Magnetic Pole
Geographic North Pole
Imaginary Magnet
Magnetic Field
South Magnetic Pole
Geographic South Pole

A compass will point along the magnetic North-South line and not along the geographic longitude. The Magnetic North is not at the North Pole but off Bathurst Island in northern Canada. The magnetic variations can be up to 30°W in Alaska and over 50°E in Greenland. There is no variation on the *agonic line* which divides the east and west magnetic variations. The agonic line passes along the western shore of Hudson Bay, through Lake Superior, western shore of Lake Michigan, off the west coast of Florida, and through Cuba.

Agonic Line: East of the line the variation is *east* and west of the line is *west*. This means that the compass reading has to be adjusted for the variation which depends upon your location.

MAGNETIC VARIATION: NORTH AMERICA

Asia
Geographic North Pole
Magnetic North
North America
Alaska

Compass Indicating Magnetic North
Geographic North Pole
Magnetic North

Actual North Pole Direction

Pointing Directly to Geographic North Pole

Compass Indicating Magnetic North

AGONIC LINE

Magnetic Pole
Magnetic North
North of Magnetic Equator
Magnetic Equator
South of Magnetic Equator
Magnetic South

Zones of Magnetic Inclination

Compass should be balanced for the Magnetic Zone in which it will be used. Inclination is the dip of the needle.

MAGNETIC VARIATION: EUROPE

Norway
Sweden
Finland
Ireland
England
Poland
Germany
France
Spain

AGONIC LINE

COMPASS READING

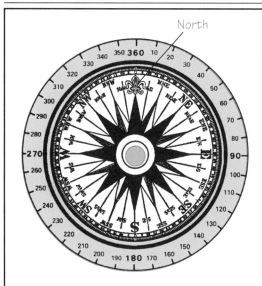

North

THE COMPASS ROSE

This is the traditional design of a compass dial.

The outside scale is graduated in 360 degrees (°). The cardinal points or directions, which are 90° apart, are North, South, East, and West.

For ease of use the compass is divided into quadrants: northeast (NE), 0°-90°; southeast (SE), 90°-180°; southwest (SW), 180°-270°; northwest (NW), 270°-360°. The use of quadrants is important as they are the first indicator of your direction of travel. Knowing the quadrant helps you avoid the potential 180° error. If the compass points in the 45° (NE quadrant) direction but the map indicates the southwest direction (SW quadrant) you will know that you are facing 180° in the *wrong direction*.

The classical compass has more subdivisions of the compass rose that are not frequently used as we now usually position ourselves in degrees (°).

HANDLING A COMPASS

When getting a new compass check:

- That the dial does not stick.
- Sighting wire on lensatic compass is not bent.
- Glass and crystal parts are not broken.
- Numbers on the dial are legible.
- Check for accuracy along a known line of direction.
- Discard a compass with more than a 3°+/- variation
- When travelling make sure that the rear sight is totally folded down as this will lock the floating dial and prevent vibration.

EFFECTS OF METAL AND ELECTRICITY

Magnetic metals and electrical sources can affect the performance of a compass.

Metal Object	Distance	
High-tension power lines	180 ft.	55 m
Truck, Car	32.8 ft.	10 m
Telephone wires, barbed wire	32.8 ft.	10 m
Machine gun, Electric drill	6.6 ft.	2 m
Steel helmet, Shovel	1.6 ft.	1/2 m

METHODS OF EXPRESSING DIRECTION

Directions are expressed in everyday life, as right, left, and straight ahead; but the question arises, "to the right of what?"

Angular Measure

Directions are expressed as units of angular measure the most common being the unit of angular measure of degrees with its subdivisions of minutes and seconds.

Base Lines

To measure anything there must always be a starting point or zero measurement. The most common zero point is the magnetic north when working with the compass, or the true north when on a map.

True North

True north is a line from any position on the earth's surface to the north pole. All lines of longitude are true north lines. True north is usually symbolized by a star on a compass or map.

Magnetic North

Magnetic North points in the direction to the North Magnetic Pole, as indicated by the north-seeking needle of a magnetic compass. Magnetic north is usually symbolized by a half an arrowhead.

AZIMUTH AND BACK AZIMUTH

Azimuth

An azimuth is defined as a horizontal angle, measured in a clockwise manner from a north base line.

When using an azimuth, the point from which the azimuth originates is imagined to be the center of the azimuth circle. Azimuths take their name from the base line from which they have been measured; true azimuths from the true north and magnetic azimuths from the magnetic north. Therefore, any one given direction can be expressed in two different ways: a magnetic azimuth if measured by a compass, or a true azimuth if measured from a meridian of longitude on a map.

Back Azimuth

A back azimuth is the reverse direction of an azimuth. It is comparable to doing an "about face." To obtain a back azimuth from an azimuth, add 180° if the azimuth is 180° or less, or subtract 180° if the azimuth is 180° or more. The back azimuth of 180° may be stated as either 0° or 360°.

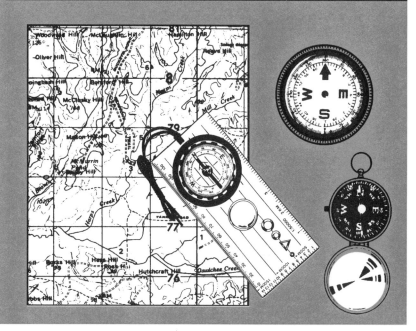

COMPASS

The magnetic compass is the most commonly used and simplest instrument for measuring directions and angles outdoors.

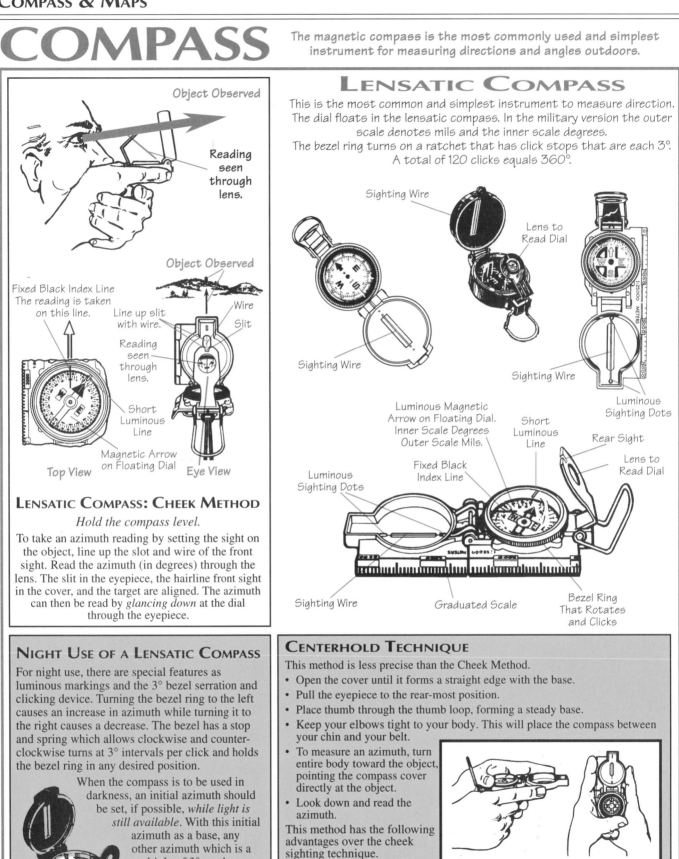

Object Observed

Reading seen through lens.

Fixed Black Index Line
The reading is taken on this line.

Object Observed

Line up slit with wire.

Wire

Slit

Reading seen through lens.

Short Luminous Line

Magnetic Arrow on Floating Dial

Top View

Eye View

LENSATIC COMPASS

This is the most common and simplest instrument to measure direction. The dial floats in the lensatic compass. In the military version the outer scale denotes mils and the inner scale degrees.
The bezel ring turns on a ratchet that has click stops that are each 3°. A total of 120 clicks equals 360°.

Sighting Wire

Lens to Read Dial

Sighting Wire

Sighting Wire

Luminous Sighting Dots

Luminous Magnetic Arrow on Floating Dial. Inner Scale Degrees Outer Scale Mils.

Short Luminous Line

Rear Sight

Lens to Read Dial

Luminous Sighting Dots

Fixed Black Index Line

Sighting Wire

Graduated Scale

Bezel Ring That Rotates and Clicks

LENSATIC COMPASS: CHEEK METHOD

Hold the compass level.

To take an azimuth reading by setting the sight on the object, line up the slot and wire of the front sight. Read the azimuth (in degrees) through the lens. The slit in the eyepiece, the hairline front sight in the cover, and the target are aligned. The azimuth can then be read by *glancing down* at the dial through the eyepiece.

NIGHT USE OF A LENSATIC COMPASS

For night use, there are special features as luminous markings and the 3° bezel serration and clicking device. Turning the bezel ring to the left causes an increase in azimuth while turning it to the right causes a decrease. The bezel has a stop and spring which allows clockwise and counter-clockwise turns at 3° intervals per click and holds the bezel ring in any desired position.

When the compass is to be used in darkness, an initial azimuth should be set, if possible, *while light is still available*. With this initial azimuth as a base, any other azimuth which is a multiple of 3° can be established through use of the clicking feature of the bezel.

CENTERHOLD TECHNIQUE

This method is less precise than the Cheek Method.
- Open the cover until it forms a straight edge with the base.
- Pull the eyepiece to the rear-most position.
- Place thumb through the thumb loop, forming a steady base.
- Keep your elbows tight to your body. This will place the compass between your chin and your belt.
- To measure an azimuth, turn entire body toward the object, pointing the compass cover directly at the object.
- Look down and read the azimuth.

This method has the following advantages over the cheek sighting technique.
- It is faster and easier to use.
- Can be used under all weather conditions or difficult terrain.
- Can be used without putting down the backpack.
- Can be used without removing glasses.

USING A COMPASS ON A MAP

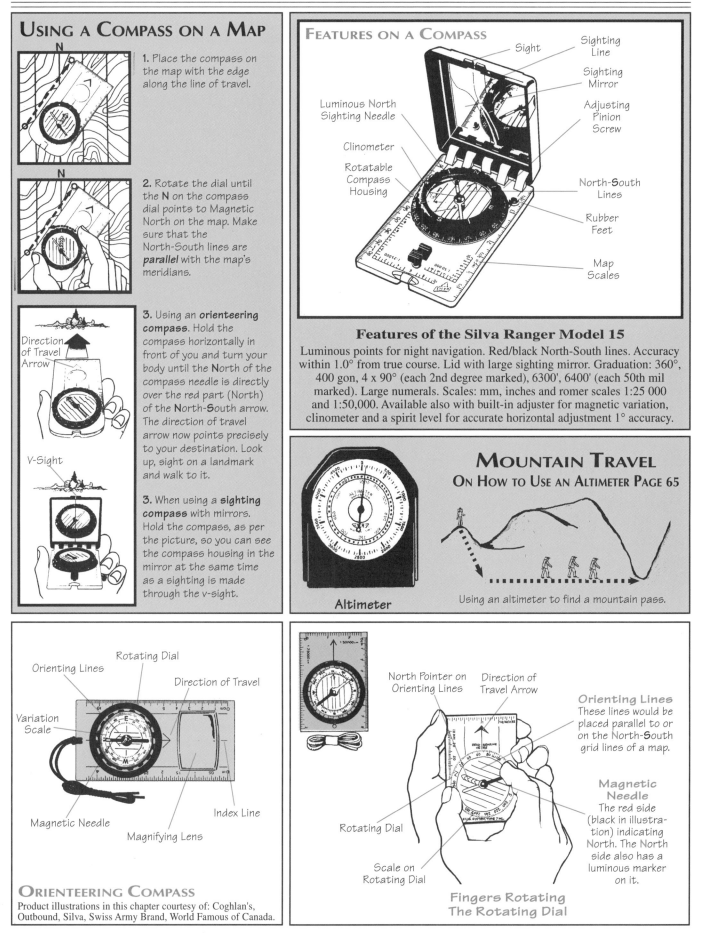

1. Place the compass on the map with the edge along the line of travel.

2. Rotate the dial until the **N** on the compass dial points to Magnetic North on the map. Make sure that the North-South lines are *parallel* with the map's meridians.

3. Using an **orienteering compass**. Hold the compass horizontally in front of you and turn your body until the North of the compass needle is directly over the red part (North) of the North-South arrow. The direction of travel arrow now points precisely to your destination. Look up, sight on a landmark and walk to it.

Direction of Travel Arrow

V-Sight

3. When using a **sighting compass** with mirrors. Hold the compass, as per the picture, so you can see the compass housing in the mirror at the same time as a sighting is made through the v-sight.

FEATURES ON A COMPASS

Sight
Sighting Line
Sighting Mirror
Adjusting Pinion Screw
Luminous North Sighting Needle
Clinometer
Rotatable Compass Housing
North-South Lines
Rubber Feet
Map Scales

Features of the Silva Ranger Model 15

Luminous points for night navigation. Red/black North-South lines. Accuracy within 1.0° from true course. Lid with large sighting mirror. Graduation: 360°, 400 gon, 4 x 90° (each 2nd degree marked), 6300', 6400' (each 50th mil marked). Large numerals. Scales: mm, inches and romer scales 1:25 000 and 1:50,000. Available also with built-in adjuster for magnetic variation, clinometer and a spirit level for accurate horizontal adjustment 1° accuracy.

MOUNTAIN TRAVEL
ON HOW TO USE AN ALTIMETER PAGE 65

Altimeter

Using an altimeter to find a mountain pass.

ORIENTEERING COMPASS

Orienting Lines
Rotating Dial
Direction of Travel
Variation Scale
Magnetic Needle
Magnifying Lens
Index Line

Product illustrations in this chapter courtesy of: Coghlan's, Outbound, Silva, Swiss Army Brand, World Famous of Canada.

North Pointer on Orienting Lines
Direction of Travel Arrow

Rotating Dial
Scale on Rotating Dial

Orienting Lines
These lines would be placed parallel to or on the North-South grid lines of a map.

Magnetic Needle
The red side (black in illustration) indicating North. The North side also has a luminous marker on it.

Fingers Rotating The Rotating Dial

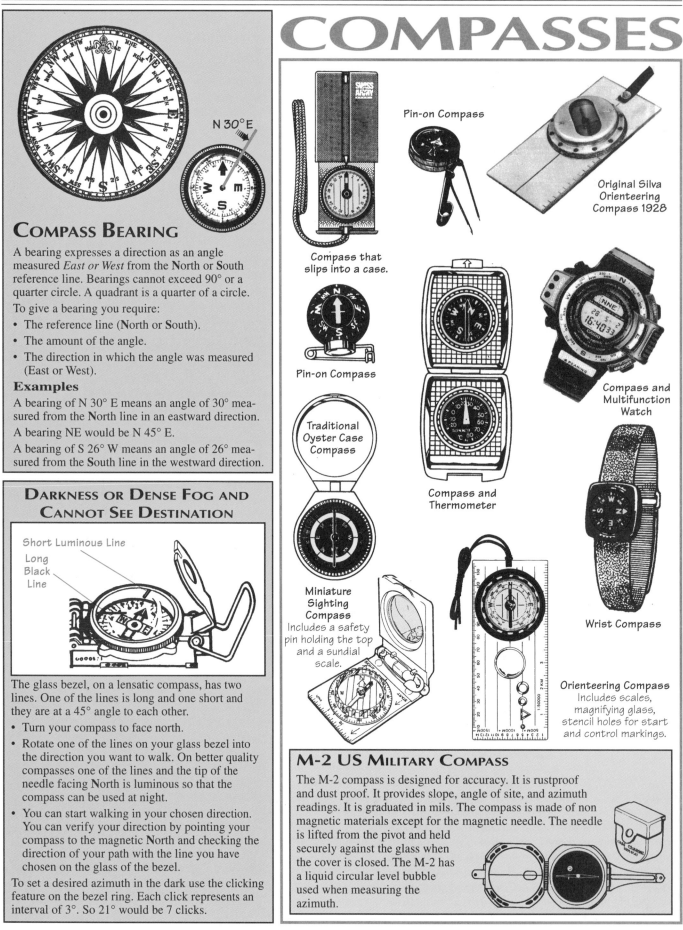

COMPASSES

COMPASS BEARING

A bearing expresses a direction as an angle measured *East or West* from the **N**orth or **S**outh reference line. Bearings cannot exceed 90° or a quarter circle. A quadrant is a quarter of a circle.

To give a bearing you require:

- The reference line (**N**orth or **S**outh).
- The amount of the angle.
- The direction in which the angle was measured (**E**ast or **W**est).

Examples

A bearing of N 30° E means an angle of 30° measured from the **N**orth line in an eastward direction.

A bearing NE would be N 45° E.

A bearing of S 26° W means an angle of 26° measured from the **S**outh line in the westward direction.

N 30° E

DARKNESS OR DENSE FOG AND CANNOT SEE DESTINATION

Short Luminous Line
Long Black Line

The glass bezel, on a lensatic compass, has two lines. One of the lines is long and one short and they are at a 45° angle to each other.

- Turn your compass to face north.
- Rotate one of the lines on your glass bezel into the direction you want to walk. On better quality compasses one of the lines and the tip of the needle facing **N**orth is luminous so that the compass can be used at night.
- You can start walking in your chosen direction. You can verify your direction by pointing your compass to the magnetic **N**orth and checking the direction of your path with the line you have chosen on the glass of the bezel.

To set a desired azimuth in the dark use the clicking feature on the bezel ring. Each click represents an interval of 3°. So 21° would be 7 clicks.

Pin-on Compass

Original Silva Orienteering Compass 1928

Compass that slips into a case.

Pin-on Compass

Traditional Oyster Case Compass

Compass and Thermometer

Compass and Multifunction Watch

Wrist Compass

Miniature Sighting Compass
Includes a safety pin holding the top and a sundial scale.

Orienteering Compass
Includes scales, magnifying glass, stencil holes for start and control markings.

M-2 US MILITARY COMPASS

The M-2 compass is designed for accuracy. It is rustproof and dust proof. It provides slope, angle of site, and azimuth readings. It is graduated in mils. The compass is made of non magnetic materials except for the magnetic needle. The needle is lifted from the pivot and held securely against the glass when the cover is closed. The M-2 has a liquid circular level bubble used when measuring the azimuth.

GLOBAL POSITIONING SYSTEMS (GPS)

These are the latest positioning devices for wilderness or water travel. They eliminate some of the tedious functions of a compass. These functions are finding your location by using triangulation and bearing position relative to features on a topographic map, after which you have to calculate your path by more back bearing readings.

The GPS device is a mini computer into which you can enter position data on your route which will assist you in retracing your steps or finding a destination.

The GPS device will, upon pushing the location button, give you your location per latitude and longitude within 328 feet (99.9 m). The device uses signals from the 24 NAVSTAR satellites (used to guide missiles for the US military).

To obtain your position the GPS has to receive signals from at least three orbiting satellites. The accuracy of the GPS device is limited as the signals transmitted for public GPS's have reduced accuracy due to military considerations. They are battery powered and have limited use when obstructed by mountain peaks and in deep valleys. They can not be used indoors. An example of a GPS is the "SILVA GPS Compass"

Take a position
reading of your car.   Hike

Before leaving the location of your car enter MY CAR into your GPS. This will register the location of your car in the memory of the GPS. You can start your hike. That evening you can camp and enter your camp site's location as LOCATION 1. The next day you can leave your camp and continue hiking. That evening you want to return to your camp site so you enter LOCATION 1 into your GPS and an arrow will appear on the LCD to give you the direction of your camp site. The next day you want to return to your car so you enter MY CAR and the GPS will guide you back to the car. The Silva GPS can retain 79 place locations.

To return ask for location of
car and Silva GPS will give you
the bearing of the car and the
direction to follow.   At your car.

FEATURES OF THE SILVA GPS COMPASS

Silva GPS Compass is a hand held GPS navigator with a built-in electronic compass sensor. With the magnetic sensor, the Silva GPS Compass shows you in which direction to travel.

The GPS compass will give range and bearing from a reference position. This feature enables you to navigate on any map, even if the Latitude / Longitude or grid system is now shown on the map.

It will tell you the range and bearing to your destination. The built-in compass will guide you in the right direction and indicate this by *distinct arrows* on the LCD display. The compass can also be used when the GPS receiver is turned off.

* Battery life: 5 hours of continuous use.
* Batteries: 6 AA, 6 AA Ni-Cd, or 12V plug in.
* Waterproof and floats.
* Memory: 79 name place locations.
* Date and time.
* Indicates with how many satellites the bearing has been calculated. This gives you the possible accuracy of the reading.
* Altitude indication in feet or meters.
* Displacement speed indications (miles/h, km/h, knots).
* Estimate of arrival time at predetermined destination point.
* Route direction compass.
* Automatic local magnetic compass deviation correction.

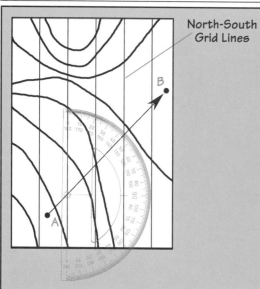

North-South Grid Lines

USING A PROTRACTOR

There are different types. The model shown is a half circle. They all divide the circle into units of angular measurement, and each has a scale around the outer edge and an index mark. A full circle has 360° and a half circle has 180° (as shown).

When using a protractor on a map the base line is always oriented parallel to the North-South grid line.

To determine the grid azimuth

1. Draw a line connecting point A and point B.
2. Place the index of the protractor at a point where the line A-B crosses a vertical (North-South) grid line.
3. Keeping the index of the protractor at the intersection point align the index line (the 0°- 180° line) of the protractor on the vertical grid line (North-South).
4. Read the value of the angle from the scale. This is the grid azimuth from point A to point B. Note that this reading is based on the grid North **not** the magnetic north.

VARIATION DIAGRAM

- A variation diagram is placed on most large-scale maps to enable the user to orient the map properly. The diagram shows the interrelationship of *magnetic north, grid north, and true north.* On medium-scale maps variation information is shown by a note in the map margin.

- Variation is the angular difference between true north and either magnetic or grid north. There are two variations, a magnetic declination and a grid declination.

- The variation diagram contains three prongs representing magnetic north, grid north, and true north.

Grid North

GN

Magnetic North

True North

TRAVELING WITH A COMPASS

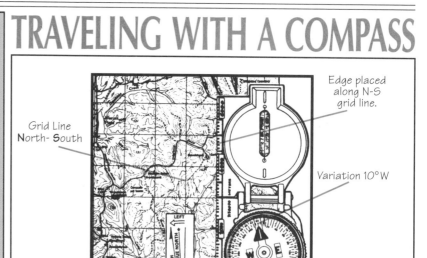

Grid Line North-South

Edge placed along N-S grid line.

Variation 10°W

Variation 10°W

ORIENTING MAP WITH A COMPASS

Place the map on a flat surface. Place the compass edge along the grid line on the map. Rotate the map and compass so that the map's North matches the magnetic north of the compass. The compass needle will indicate north. Specialized maps will show the magnetic north and magnetic variation from the true north. Adjust the grid north on the map to compensate for the magnetic variation.

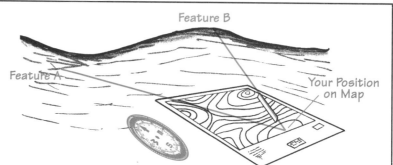

Feature B

Feature A

Your Position on Map

FIND POSITION ON MAP WITH A COMPASS

Take two magnetic azimuth bearings (readings) on two prominent features that are visible on the terrain and on the map. Orient your map in the same position as the features on the terrain. Take the angle reading of feature A. Take a reading of feature B. Draw a line from feature A and from feature B with the readings that you have obtained. The point where the lines intersect is your present location.

True North
A line or longitude that points to the Geographic North Pole. The North Pole is usually represented with a star.
Magnetic North Pole
The direction of the North Magnetic Pole, as indicated by the north seeking needle of a compass. Usually indicated by a line ending by a half arrow.
Magnetic Variation
The angular difference between the true north and the magnetic north.
Magnetic Pole
A compass, being a magnet, points to the magnetic north which is not at the same location as the Geographic North Pole.

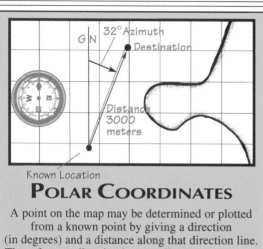

POLAR COORDINATES

A point on the map may be determined or plotted from a known point by giving a direction (in degrees) and a distance along that direction line. The reference direction is normally expressed as an azimuth and the distance in any convenient unit of measurement such as meters or yards. Polar coordinates are useful in the field because magnetic azimuth can be determined from the compass and the distance can be estimated.

DELIBERATE OFFSET OR INTENTIONAL ERROR

If you want to reach a spot which is located on a road, river bank, coast, or mountain range (base line), you might want to make an *intentional error* in your calculation of direction that will eliminate the need to decide "is it to the left or right?" when you get to the base line.

Make your calculation as to the direction to take to reach the exact spot, whether by your compass, distant landmark, map, etc. Then choose a point to the left or right of your objective. Navigate to this chosen point. Upon reaching the base line you know that you have made an intentional error to the left or to the right. If you have made a left "error", then upon reaching the base line, turn right and you will walk towards your true destination.

The error point chosen should be further from the destination if the destination is at a greater distance.

RELOCATE A FISHING SPOT ON A LAKE

Choose two prominent features; in this case a large tree and a boat dock. You will have to take cross bearings. First point the compass, with the direction of travel or wire on lensatic compass, towards the tree. Then rotate the compass until the north indicator points north. You will read 300°. Now point the compass towards the boat dock and obtain a reading of 30°.

So 300° to the tree and 30° to the boat dock.

To find your spot next time; go towards the general area set your compass at 300°, the reading of the tree, and continue towards the tree until the pointer points at the tree. This is one (tree line) of your coordinate lines for your fishing sight. Now look across the lake or behind the tree as a reference point for your "tree line". Then set your compass at 30° and point in the direction of the dock. If the pointer does not point at the dock move up or down your "tree line" until you are at the right place.

Establish bearing before descending into the hollow as you will not be able to see the tree on the hill when you are in the woods.

Cannot see tree on hill.

STAYING ON COURSE WHEN DESTINATION IS NOT ALWAYS VISIBLE

If the path to a location is not always visible because of woods or hollows then a compass can be used to give you the direction.

- At a point when the destination can be seen use your compass to establish the bearing of your path. To establish the bearing point the *Direction of Travel Arrow* at the destination.
- Turn the *rotating dial* so that the N on the rotating dial is lined up with the *North end* (the luminous end) of the magnetic compass needle.
- Read the bearing at the *Direction of Travel Arrow* line. This is the bearing of the destination. If you do not turn the rotating dial while you are traveling use the *Direction of Travel Arrow* to indicate your direction when you can not see the destination; otherwise remember the reading.
- Check your reading whenever the destination can be seen.

The magnetic deviation does not have to be taken into consideration as all the readings are based upon the magnetic north.

Orientation
Before leaving your camp try to remember the point of departure and what you can see from this point:
large trees, hills, mountains, roads, direction of sun, predominant wind, and in which direction does the water flow?

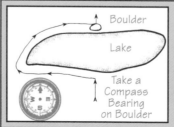

BYPASS OBSTACLE USING A COMPASS

You have approached a lake. Look at the other side and find a distinct feature, in this case the boulder; take a sighting on the boulder. The same method as *Staying on Course When Destination Not Always Visible*. Walk around the lake to the boulder; take a sighting from the boulder and continue on your route.

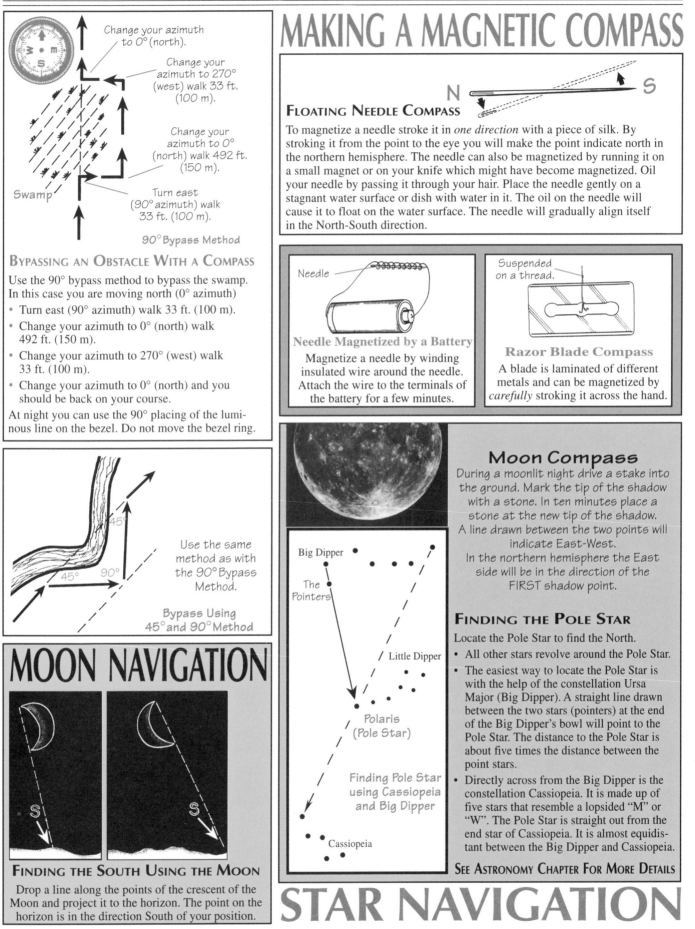

Change your azimuth to 0° (north).

Change your azimuth to 270° (west) walk 33 ft. (100 m).

Change your azimuth to 0° (north) walk 492 ft. (150 m).

Turn east (90° azimuth) walk 33 ft. (100 m).

Swamp

90° Bypass Method

BYPASSING AN OBSTACLE WITH A COMPASS

Use the 90° bypass method to bypass the swamp. In this case you are moving north (0° azimuth)

- Turn east (90° azimuth) walk 33 ft. (100 m).
- Change your azimuth to 0° (north) walk 492 ft. (150 m).
- Change your azimuth to 270° (west) walk 33 ft. (100 m).
- Change your azimuth to 0° (north) and you should be back on your course.

At night you can use the 90° placing of the luminous line on the bezel. Do not move the bezel ring.

Use the same method as with the 90° Bypass Method.

Bypass Using 45° and 90° Method

MOON NAVIGATION

FINDING THE SOUTH USING THE MOON

Drop a line along the points of the crescent of the Moon and project it to the horizon. The point on the horizon is in the direction South of your position.

MAKING A MAGNETIC COMPASS

N　　S

FLOATING NEEDLE COMPASS

To magnetize a needle stroke it in *one direction* with a piece of silk. By stroking it from the point to the eye you will make the point indicate north in the northern hemisphere. The needle can also be magnetized by running it on a small magnet or on your knife which might have become magnetized. Oil your needle by passing it through your hair. Place the needle gently on a stagnant water surface or dish with water in it. The oil on the needle will cause it to float on the water surface. The needle will gradually align itself in the North-South direction.

Needle

Needle Magnetized by a Battery

Magnetize a needle by winding insulated wire around the needle. Attach the wire to the terminals of the battery for a few minutes.

Suspended on a thread.

Razor Blade Compass

A blade is laminated of different metals and can be magnetized by *carefully* stroking it across the hand.

Moon Compass

During a moonlit night drive a stake into the ground. Mark the tip of the shadow with a stone. In ten minutes place a stone at the new tip of the shadow. A line drawn between the two points will indicate East-West. In the northern hemisphere the East side will be in the direction of the FIRST shadow point.

FINDING THE POLE STAR

Locate the Pole Star to find the North.

- All other stars revolve around the Pole Star.
- The easiest way to locate the Pole Star is with the help of the constellation Ursa Major (Big Dipper). A straight line drawn between the two stars (pointers) at the end of the Big Dipper's bowl will point to the Pole Star. The distance to the Pole Star is about five times the distance between the point stars.
- Directly across from the Big Dipper is the constellation Cassiopeia. It is made up of five stars that resemble a lopsided "M" or "W". The Pole Star is straight out from the end star of Cassiopeia. It is almost equidistant between the Big Dipper and Cassiopeia.

Big Dipper

The Pointers

Little Dipper

Polaris (Pole Star)

Finding Pole Star using Cassiopeia and Big Dipper

Cassiopeia

SEE ASTRONOMY CHAPTER FOR MORE DETAILS

STAR NAVIGATION

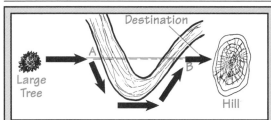

BYPASS METHOD USING NO COMPASS

This method requires two distinctive features that can be seen from each side of the obstacle. In this example there is a large tree behind you and a hill, *in the distance*, in front of you. At position A look at the tree behind you; turn 180°, and see the hill in front of you. Walk around the bend in the river until you reach a point where you will be between the hill and the tree. At this point B you will be on course and proceed towards the distant hill.
Your destination is before you reach the hill.

STEERING MARKS

Steering marks are well-defined objects in the direction of travel.

Steering Marks by Day

Objects such as lone trees, hills, and shapes on the horizon. A cloud formation or wind direction may be used if checked periodically by compass.

Steering Marks by Night

Stars are usually the single source of steering marks at night. It is important to find Polaris (the Pole Star) because of the rotation of the earth the positions of *other stars are continually changing*. Polaris is fixed in the sky and is less than 1° off true north, but above latitude 70° it is too high in the sky to be useful. A star near the north horizon serves for about a half hour. When moving south, azimuth checks should be made every 15 minutes to be safe. When traveling east or west, the difficulty of staying on azimuth is caused more by the likelihood of the star climbing too high in the sky or losing itself behind the western horizon than it is by the star changing direction angle. In all the above cases, it is necessary to change to another guide star.

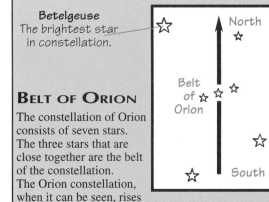

Betelgeuse
The brightest star in constellation.

North

BELT OF ORION

The constellation of Orion consists of seven stars. The three stars that are close together are the belt of the constellation. The Orion constellation, when it can be seen, rises on the horizon *due East* and sets *due West*. At the Equator it will pass directly overhead, in the southern latitudes north of directly overhead, and in the north latitude south of directly overhead.

TRAVELING WITH NO COMPASS

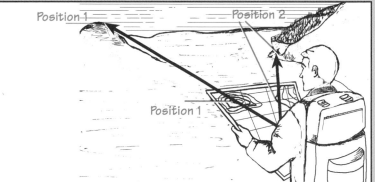

LOCATE POSITION ON A MAP WITHOUT A COMPASS

- Go to a high point or climb a tree to see the surrounding area.
- Look for prominent features such as rivers, hills, valleys, cliffs, swamps, forests, ridge areas, or linear features such as roads, railroads, fence lines, power lines, etc.
- Find direction to place the map relative to your position and the surroundings.
- Find *two* prominent features and compare their relative location to each other and to you. Additional features will help you to be more precise or confirm your first estimate.
- Make sure that you have not aligned the map in reverse. A third feature would help you correct this potential error. Direction can also be verified by noting the position of the sun and the time of the day.
- From these observations you can *approximate* your position on the map.
- With the approximate position you can now use the map to establish a route while always keeping your prominent features as reference points.

LOCATE POSITION ON A MAP WITHOUT A COMPASS (MORE PRECISE)

This method is similar to the above.

- Orient the map on a flat surface using the above method.
- Choose *at least* two distant features and mark them on the map.
- Place a straightedge (rule, edge of pad, etc.) on the map placing the edge on one of the feature marks that you have marked on the map. Align the straightedge with the distant feature and its mark on the map. Draw a line away from the feature mark on the map.
- Repeat the above with your second feature.
- The *intersection point* of the lines you have drawn is your location. You can determine your grid coordinates from your map grid.

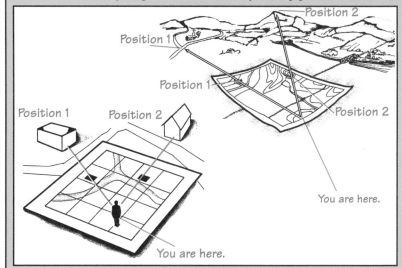

FINDING NORTH WITH THE SUN

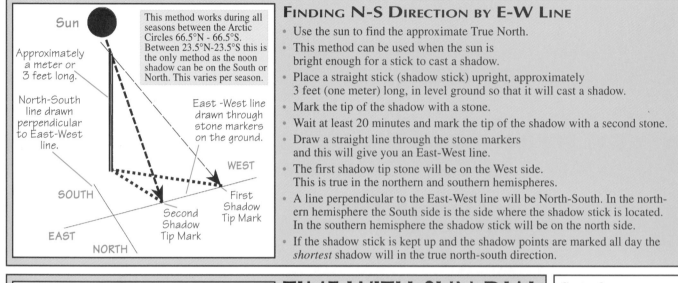

FINDING N-S DIRECTION BY E-W LINE

- Use the sun to find the approximate True North.
- This method can be used when the sun is bright enough for a stick to cast a shadow.
- Place a straight stick (shadow stick) upright, approximately 3 feet (one meter) long, in level ground so that it will cast a shadow.
- Mark the tip of the shadow with a stone.
- Wait at least 20 minutes and mark the tip of the shadow with a second stone.
- Draw a straight line through the stone markers and this will give you an East-West line.
- The first shadow tip stone will be on the West side. This is true in the northern and southern hemispheres.
- A line perpendicular to the East-West line will be North-South. In the northern hemisphere the South side is the side where the shadow stick is located. In the southern hemisphere the shadow stick will be on the north side.
- If the shadow stick is kept up and the shadow points are marked all day the *shortest* shadow will in the true north-south direction.

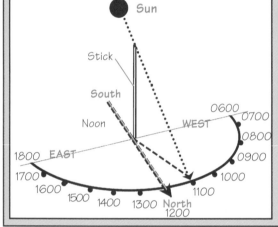

TIME WITH SUN DIAL

Use the East-West line as found above. Place a shadow stick *vertically* at intersection of North-South line.

- The WEST side will be 0600 hours and the EAST side will be 1800 hours.
- The North-South line will indicate 1200 hours on the NORTH side. In the southern hemisphere it will be 1200 hours on the SOUTH side.
- Divide the arc into equal segments and this sun dial will give you the *approximate* time. The season is an important factor in the accuracy of the dial but it is fairly accurate around noon (1200).

Placing Stone

Marking East-West Line

N-S BY THE EQUAL SHADOW METHOD

- Place a stick *vertically* in flat sandy ground. This stick should be placed *before* noon and should cast a shadow at least a foot long.
- Place a stone or peg at the shadow tip.
- Draw an arc the radius of the shadow with the stick as the center.
- The sun's shadow becomes shorter at noon and then starts to get longer and it will cross the drawn arc.
- Mark the spot where the shadow crosses the arc.
- Draw a line straight line through the marks and this is the East-West line.
- Draw a line perpendicular to the line and it will indicate North-South.

This method is more accurate than the East-West Line method as it is used when the sun's shadow passes through noon. The disadvantage is that you have to wait to find your direction through the noon period.

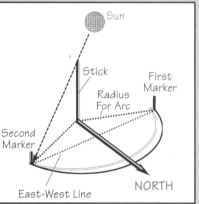

FINDING N-S DIRECTION BY E-W LINE

Sun

6 Fingers Represent One Hour

Hours to Sunset
Each finger represents 2.5° and the sun moves 15° per hour. That is 2.5°, one finger, represents 10 minutes.

DIRECTION WITH WATCH

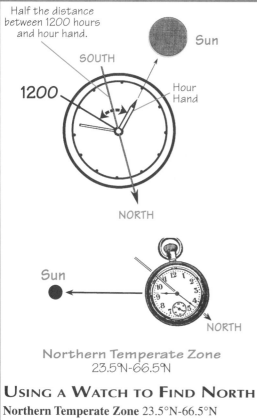

Half the distance between 1200 hours and hour hand.

SOUTH

1200

Sun

Hour Hand

NORTH

Sun ← NORTH

Northern Temperate Zone
23.5°N-66.5°N

USING A WATCH TO FIND NORTH

Northern Temperate Zone 23.5°N-66.5°N
- Point hour hand towards sun.
- The South is half way between the hour hand and 1200 hours (Noon). North is in the opposite direction.
  If watch is on Day Light Savings Time use 1300 hours instead of 1200 hours.

Southern Temperate Zone 23.5°N-66.5°N
- Point 1200 hours at sun.
- The North is half way between the 1200 hours on watch and the hour hand.
  If watch is on Day Light Savings Time use 1300 hours instead of 1200 hours.

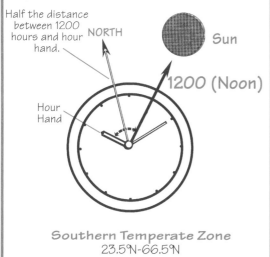

Half the distance between 1200 hours and hour hand.

NORTH

Sun

1200 (Noon)

Hour Hand

Southern Temperate Zone
23.5°N-66.5°N

NAVIGATION WITH THE HELP OF NATURE

DIRECTION FROM TREES AND PLANTS

Each species of tree has its own distinct profile or silhouette. The wind and sun will affect a tree's normal profile and this is a clue to establish the North-South direction. *See Tree Chapter for more illustrations.*

WIND EFFECTS ON TREES

- Trees can be windswept so sharing the direction of the dominant wind.
- Knowing the direction of the dominant wind, you can find the cardinal points by looking at a windswept tree.
- Wind can retard tree growth by damaging or desiccating young shoots on the windward side (the side *from* which the wind blows) of a tree.
- A tree used to determine the direction has to be in an exposed location and not sheltered by hills, trees, or buildings. Examine several trees in the vicinity. Make sure that these trees have not been pruned.

SUN EFFECTS ON TREES

While the wind effect usually retards the growth of trees, the sun enhances the growth of the leaves and branches.

- In the northern hemisphere, the arc of the sun is on the south side of the tree. The growth is more luxuriant on the south side. This is most evident on black and white poplars, beech, oak, plane tree, horse chestnut, Norway maple, and the black locust tree. These trees also show a *slight declination* towards the south. Make sure that these trees *are sheltered* from the predominant wind.
- Branches on the south of a tree are more horizontal and those on the north more vertical as if they were looking for the sun. Trees such as spruce, firs, and pyramid poplars remain straight.
- Flowering plumes of reeds grow away from the sun.
- Moss and lichen will grow on the side with the most shade. Still more important is where the moisture is retained the longest. In North America, as a general rule, there is less evaporation in the north and northeast sides of trees and rocks. Moss will have a brownish hue when growing in more sunlight and be greener or grayish-green in more shaded and humid spots.
- In the northern hemisphere, deciduous trees usually grow on the southern slope of a hill and evergreens are on the northern slope.
- In the Rocky mountains, the limber pines will be on the southern slope and the Engelmann spruce on the northern.
- The barrel cactus *(Ferocactus)* has a permanent lean to the south.
- In the northern temperate climate, flowers and plants have a tendency to face south or east.
- The pilot weed *(Silphium Lacinatum)* grows with its leaves pointing north-south when it is growing in the sunlight.

DIRECTION FROM THE WIND

**Winds are named for the directions from which they blow:
i.e. North wind from the North.**

Each area has a predominant wind that dominates a season or all seasons.

The *dominant wind* is nearly always the same as the prevailing wind which blows the longest or most violently from a given direction. The dominant wind will affect the growth of trees, direction of snow drifts, or direction of tall grass.

- The prevailing wind in all regions has its own characteristics as velocity, temperature, and humidity. It might vary with the seasons.
- On the ocean, the prevailing wind has its own characteristics and also its own accompaniment of clouds.

DIRECTION OF DOMINANT WIND

Temperate Regions: The wind usually *blows from the West*.
(both in the Northern and Southern hemispheres)

Tropics: Winds are between northeast and southeast.

Equator: Usually from the east.

Northern Hemisphere: Northerly wind is usually colder than a southerly wind.

SPECIAL EFFECTS OF THE WIND

Desert Winds: Are dry and might carry dust.

Winds From Ocean: Are moisture laden and might bring clouds and rain.

Polar Regions: Wind temperature, if warmer than the surroundings, will indicate the direction of water. A sudden drop in temperature, without change in direction, might indicate the presence of an iceberg.

On Land: A person can use the prevailing wind to find his direction and to keep moving in a straight line. The wind should keep blowing onto the same part of the body. Watch for any change in temperature, humidity and strength as this will indicate a shift in the wind direction.

In Forests: Watch the direction of the movement of clouds, especially the high clouds which are usually blown by the prevailing wind.

Look at the tips of tall trees to see the direction of the wind.

ANIMALS AND INSECTS

- Spider webs are not made against the wind. A broken and recently remade web might indicate that the current wind is not the prevailing wind.
- Most animals, birds and insects build their homes in protected areas out of the wind.
- In the high northern latitudes the east side of hills are more sheltered and one finds mice burrowing under dead logs, woodpecker nests, and open-nesting birds. This indicates the east, southeast or south directions.

Predominant Wind Direction
A solitary tree in an exposed area will adapt to the prevailing wind especially in temperate climates. In the winter the prevailing winds will blow hard snow and ice pellets on the tree and break or sand off the young growth on the windward side. Tree branches get longer on the leeward side.

SNOW FORMS AND DIRECTION

The Polar regions have much in common with hot sand deserts.

- Snow dunes have the same shapes and properties of sand dunes but they are smaller and less stable.
- The most common snow dunes are similar to the longitudinal sand dune which is parallel to the prevailing wind. The *"sastrugi"* are a few inches high to three feet high and are always found close together. They are used for navigation on cloudy days. They are very useful near the magnetic pole where compasses do not work. Dig through newly fallen snow to see the direction of the sastrugi.
- The prevailing wind can polish compacted snow and ice.
- Erosion by frost is more evident on the southern slopes as there is more cooling at night and heating by day.
- On the southern slopes, the heat of the sun will leave "melted shadows" of trees, shrubs and stones in the accumulated snow. This is especially true in the spring.
- The direction of the wind is very important as a warm strong wind can melt snow faster than the sun. This can be misleading when trying to determine your direction.

SEA ICE AND NAVIGATION

Bay ice, which is smooth, low and flat can give you an indication as to the distance from a bay. If the pieces of ice are close together like a jigsaw puzzle you are not far from land. If the edges of the ice are sharp and fresh this will indicate a closeness to shore. If the edges are rounded and the pieces far apart, this indicates that the shore is at some distance.

ANTHILL SIGNPOSTS

Some southern ants build their anthills on slopes facing southeast. This is to maximize the anthill's exposure to the rising sun in the fall and winter. When they build their mounds near trees or rocks they are found on the south or southeast side.

In the western part of the United States the harvester ant *(Pogonomyrmes occidentalis),* the mound-building ant, builds the only entrance to the mound on the bottom of the southeastern side. The nest of the silver ant *(Formica argentata)* is oriented the same way in the Long Mountain areas of the State of Colorado.

DIRECTION ON GLACIERS

Boulder   Sun

Glaciers with large boulders at the surface form "glacier tables". These large rocks will protect the ice under them from melting and the rocks will gradually protrude above the surface of the ice. The boulder will gradually sit on a pedestal of ice. These pedestals can indicate the south because they usually tilt towards the south as the greatest amount of melting occurs on this side due to the sun's radiation. After a while, the boulder slips off and its original pedestal melts and the sun begins this process over again on the boulder's new position

REFLECTIONS IN THE SKY

Clouds can reflect certain features of the land surface.

- On land near an ice covered sea the clouds can reflect open water as there is less light reflected off dark water that the white frozen area. This reflection is a dark spot on the underside of the clouds. The dark spot does not indicate the size of the open water because a small area can affect a large area of cloud. This might happen as open water in the Arctic will give off a vapor and this will affect the reflected light around the open area and increase the dark spot area. This is known as a "water sky".
- An ice flow or iceberg can be seen by an "ice blink" which can be seen as a noticeable patch of brightness in a gray sky. A small area of ice can show a large "ice blink".
- On land, clouds can show the light "pollution" of a city. A city which would be below the observable horizon can be seen at 30-50 miles (48-80 km).
- In the Arctic or snow mountain country, the whole anatomy of the land surface can be reflected in a high overcast sky. You will be able to see snow fields, open water areas, naked rock areas, new ice (blue green will show as gray patches), patches of vegetation or the plants called "pink snow" might reflect pinkish. These contrasting areas will reflect on the lower sides of the clouds.
- In vegetation-covered areas, ice patches and small snow fields will reflect steel-blue on the under surface of the clouds.
- In a cloudless desert there is a "desert blink", a shimmering caused by heat reflection. An oasis can produce a desert blink because of a lower reflecting power due to the vegetation.
- In the Sahara desert a camel rider is 10 feet (3 m) from the ground and the oasis is usually in depressions and may be surrounded by hills up to one thousand feet (305 m) high. The rider can see a special kind of haze produced by the sun's heat upon the green palmed oasis.

EFFECTS OF SUN AND WIND

- Erosion by frost is more evident on the south slope as there is more cooling at night and heating by day.
- In the warmer hemisphere, the northern inclines of hills are smoother due to erosion.
- On the southern slopes, the heat of the sun will leave "melted shadows" of trees, shrubs and stones in the accumulated snow - especially in the spring.
- Note that the direction of the wind is very important as a warm strong wind can melt snow faster than the sun.

DIRECTION BY ODORS

SENSE OF SMELL

The sense of smell is useful in finding the direction.

- The Polynesians carried pigs on their 100 ft. (30 m) catamarans because pigs have a highly developed sense of smell and would get excited upon smelling land.
- The smell of the sea breeze can help give the direction of the land.
- New smells are easier to distinguish at sea than on land as the smell of salt is more constant.
- In the desert, any odor indicates human inhabitation. The best times are early morning and in the evening when the wind direction is predictable.
- Scent is nearly always stronger near the ground if a ground object is emitting the smell.

USE OF EARS TO FIND THE DIRECTION

Eskimos of Greenland use the sound of the male snow-bunting nesting area as a guide in the fog. Each male bird has a distinctive song and the Eskimos know the song of the snow-bunting at the head of their fjord. During a fog they will turn at this song and head home.

- When walking rotate your head to "scan" for sounds. You will hear your environment - a brook, stream, highway traffic, wind down the valley, or heavy surf.
- In a fog or at night, in hilly country, a shout or whistle will echo from the hills. Sound takes 5 seconds to travel a mile (1.6 km), you can determine your relative position by ear. This is used on ships during fogs. They use bells, gunshots, siren blasts or shouting. Each second between a blast and the returning echo means a distance of about 560 feet (170 m) from the reflecting surface.
- Boaters can also listen to the sound of nesting seabirds, or the surf. When the sound of the breakers disappears, that indicates the presence of an inlet or harbor. *See the Water Travel Chapter for more information.*

SIGNS USED BY THE NORTH AMERICAN INDIANS

- Tips of some trees point south as they are attracted by the sun.
- Bark on some trees is more dull and dark on the northern side.
- Tree rings formed in the trunk of a tree are thicker on the side that faces north than those that face south.
- If a log is struck on the ground on the south side of a hill the ground has a hollow ring. On the north side the ground sounds heavy as it is not as dry as the south side.

DIRECTIONS FROM HILLS AND RIVERS

By looking at maps one can see an orderly arrangement of mountain ranges and rivers that originate in the mountains. Rivers only meander on flat plains.

Horseback in North East

In the area of New Brunswick, Nova Scotia to Maine and New Hampshire one finds a group of low ridges (horsebacks) that run nearly parallel to the Appalachian chain (northeasterly southeastern direction). They are like ripples on water and are between fifteen and fifty feet high. On the southern side, the slopes are gradual. In the northerly side, they are steeper. Many lakes and ponds occur between the horsebacks. These areas were affected by glaciers.

The Rocky Mountains and the Pre-Cambrian Shield around Hudson's Bay are other examples. The ends of the crescent on oxbow lakes or ponds always point towards the river that formed them.

STRAIGHT LINE WALKING

"Shortest distance is a straight line between two points"

In open, treeless country:

- Pick a distant landmark and walk towards it or orient by it.
- Find two landmarks *ahead* of you and line them up. Or find two prominent points *behind* you and line them up.
- If only one landmark is available, place a second one yourself (e.g. a flag on a stick which you can use then line up with a distant hill and walk forward). You could even make small fires along your path to help you maintain direction in the day and night. This would be useful on a flat surface such as a plain or desert.
- In the dark or a fog, shouts or a penetrating whistle can be used to keep direction. A distant noise can be the destination.

Indian File

A group of travelers in a landmarkless area can become landmarks themselves. The line of travelers should be spaced so that the last individual is far enough back so he can watch the leader and the line. He should line up the leader with the people in the line. When he sees the leader deviate he can signal him to fall in line. This method can be used during snow storms (the group should be rope-linked). A dog team and sled which has a length of 50 feet (15 m) can be aligned to a distant landmark or with a definite angle to the direction of the snowdrifts (these are formed by the predominant winds).

PACE COUNT

A pace is the length of your natural step and is approximately 30" (76 cm). If you will be using this method you should determine your pace. Walk a pre-measured distance while maintaining your normal pace and count your footsteps. Divide the distance in inches or meters by the number of steps. If you have stopped growing this is your pace for life.

Pace distance can change because of:

Slopes

Pace gets longer on a down slope and shortens on the upgrade. If you normally pace 120 paces per 100 meters (328 feet) on a slope the number of paces can increase to 130, an 8.3% increase.

Winds

Head wind will shorten pace, a tail wind will increase the pace.

Surface

A rough surface of sand, mud, gravel, will shorten the pace.

Elements

Snow, rain, or ice cause the pace to shorten.

Clothing

Excess clothing and boots with poor traction tend to shorten the pace.

Visibility

Reduced visibility will shorten your pace because you do not feel secure. Your pace will also shorten if you are stalking or trying to be secretive.

DEAD RECKONING

Dead Reckoning

Dead reckoning is the process by which one's present location is determined by plotting the course and distance from the last known location.

With a Map

One's starting location and destination are known and if a map is available, are plotted, along with any known intermediate features along the route. These intermediate features, if clearly recognizable on the ground, serve as invaluable checkpoints. It is a matter of knowing one's position at all times through association of map features with the ground features.

With No Map

For many centuries, mariners have used dead reckoning to navigate their ships when they are out of sight of land or during bad weather, and it is just as applicable to navigation on land.

If a map is not available, the plotting is done on a blank sheet of paper. A scale is selected such that the entire route will fit on one sheet. A north direction is clearly established. The starting point and destination are then plotted in accurate relationship to each other. The route of travel usually consists of several courses, with an azimuth established at the starting point for the first course to be followed. Distance measurement begins with the departure and continues through the first course until a change in direction is made. A new azimuth is established for the second course and the distance is measured until a second change of direction is made, and so on. Records of all data are kept and all positions are plotted.

PACING DISTANCE

A pace is approximately 30 inches. To measure distance, you count the number of paces in a given course and convert to the map unit. Paces are counted in hundreds, and the hundreds can be kept track of in many ways: count on your fingers, place small objects such as pebbles into an empty pocket, or tie knots in a string. It is important that each person who uses dead reckoning navigation establish the length of his average page.

In the field, an average pace must be adjusted because of the following conditions:

Slopes: The pace lengthens on a downgrade and shortens on the upgrade.

Winds: A head wind shortens the pace while a tail wind increases it.

Surfaces: Sand, gravel, mud, and similar surface materials tend to shorten the pace.

Elements: Snow, rain, or ice cause the pace to be reduced in length.

Clothing: Excess weight of clothing shortens the pace while the type of shoes affects the pace length.

Fatigue: Tiredness affects the length of the pace.

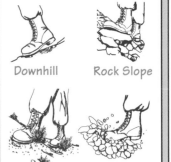

Downhill   Rock Slope

Grassy Slope   Rock Surface

STRAIGHT LINE DEVIATION

- We all have a *dominant eye*. If you point at something, at a distance, with both eyes open, you will see that the finger has been aligned by only one eye.
- Wrong balance of items in a backpack or pack incorrectly adjusted.
- Person tends to "edge away" from an obstacle such as the wind, rain, slope of a hill, snow, dust storm or strong sun in the face.
- The individual might tend to always pass an obstacle on the "right" side and this will gradually veer him off course. This has been shown in Swiss studies on mountain travel. *See Summer Hiking Chapter.*

FACTORS TO CONSIDER IN RANGE ESTIMATION

Distance is underestimated when starting and overestimated at the end of the trip.

Factors	Under Estimation	Over Estimation
Clear Outline and Detail	Clear outline and most of object exposed.	Only part can be seen, object is small in relationship to surroundings.
		The color of the object blends with the background.
Nature of Terrain	When looking across a depression mostly hidden from view.	When looking across a depression that is totally visible.
Position of Observer	When looking downward from high ground.	
	When looking down a straight open road or along a railroad.	When vision is narrowly confined, as in streets, draws, or forest trails.
	When looking over uniform surfaces like water, snow, desert, or grain fields.	When looking from low ground toward high ground.
		Looking over undulating ground.
Light and Atmosphere	In bright light or when the sun is shining from behind the observer.	In poor light, such as at dawn or dusk, in rain, snow, fog, or when the sun is in the observer's eyes.
	When the object is in sharp contrast with the background or is silhouetted because of its size, shape, or color.	When object blends into the background or terrain.
	When seen in the clear air of high altitudes.	

MEASURING DISTANCE BY ESTIMATION

Visualize a distance of 330 ft. (100 m).

Estimate a 330 ft. (100 m) distance and then pace it to see how far off you are. Repeat this procedure until you are not too far off. Double the 330 ft. (100 m) distance to guesstimate to 660 ft. (200 m).

When you want to estimate a distance first estimate 100 m and then multiply this to estimate the total distance. Past 1640 ft. (500 m) estimate the distance of the half way point and double the distance.

Rifle or Cannon Flash Method

This method uses the difference in time between seeing a flash of light (the speed of light can be considered instantaneous over distances of miles or kilometers) and hearing the sound.

When you see the flash start counting the seconds. You can use a stopwatch or a steady count by saying one-thousand-one, one-thousand-two, ...

Multiply the number of seconds by 1085 feet (330 m) to get the approximate distance.

Sound carries better in dry cold air.

ESTIMATING DISTANCE

FINGER METHOD OF JUDGING DISTANCE

This method is based upon the principle that the distance between the eyes is about 1/10 of the distance from the eye to the extended finger.

To know the width or height of a distant object.

- Extend your right arm and hold your forefinger upright and align it with one eye at the end of the object.
- Do not move finger but observe where it is when looking with the other eye.
- Estimate the displacement in feet or meters along the length of the object.
- The distance from the object is 10 times the displacement of the fingers.
- With binoculars measure the distance *between the center of the eyepieces*, when adjusted for your eyes, and multiply this distance by 10. Use this factor as above.

SEE TRAIL BLAZES IN SIGNALING CHAPTER

PACE

- An average person has a pace of 30" (76 cm) and will walk at three miles an hour over flat ground. You might want to calculate your average pace.
- To count the pace, count your right foot pace only and multiply by two when you reach 100 paces.
- To keep track of counted paces put pebbles in one pocket and transfer a pebble to the other pocket at each 100 paces.

JUDGING DISTANCE

50 yds	46 m	Mouth and eyes of a person can be clearly distinguished.
100 yds	91 m	Eyes appear as dots.
200 yds	182 m	General details of clothing can be distinguished.
300 yds	247 m	Faces can be seen.
500 yds	457 m	Colors of clothing can be distinguished.
800 yds	752 m	A person looks like a post.
1 mile	**1.6 km**	**Trunks of large trees can be seen.**
2 1/2 mi	4 km	Chimneys and windows can be distinguished.
6 mi	10 km	Large houses, silos and towers can be recognized.
9 mi	14 km	Average church steeple can be seen.

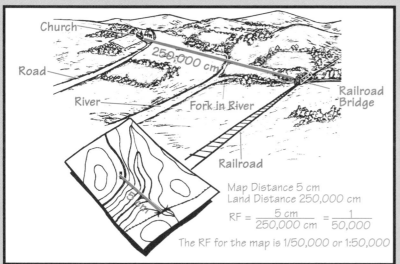

Map Distance 5 cm
Land Distance 250,000 cm

$$RF = \frac{5 \text{ cm}}{250,000 \text{ cm}} = \frac{1}{50,000}$$

The RF for the map is 1/50,000 or 1:50,000

MAP SCALE

All maps represent a portion of the earth's surface. The surface of the earth is represented on a much smaller scale on the map. All maps have a scale which represents the distance on the map to the distance on the ground. The scale of the map permits the determination of ground distance from the map.

The numerical scale of a map expresses the ratio of horizontal distance on the map to the corresponding horizontal distance on the ground. It usually is written as a fraction and is called the *representative fraction (RF)*. It is independent of any unit of measure. An RF of 1/50,000 or 1: 50,000 means that one (1) unit of measure on the map is equal to 50,000 of the same units of measure on the ground.

DIFFERENT MAP SCALES

Small Scale

Maps at scales of 1:600,000 and smaller are used for general military planning and for strategical studies.
The standard small scale is 1: 1,000,000.

Medium Scale

Maps at scales larger than 1: 600,000 but smaller than 1: 75,000.
The standard medium scale is 1: 250,000.

Large Scale

Maps at scales of 1: 75,000 and larger.
The standard large scale is 1: 50,000.

Ground Distance to Map Scale

These are some of the standard scales used on maps:

Map Scale	1 Inch Equals	1 Centimeter Equals
1:5,000	416.67 feet 127.00 meters	164.0 feet 50 meters
1:10,000	833.33 feet 254.00 meters	328.1 feet 100 meters
1:12,500	1,041.66 feet 317.00 meters	410.1 feet 125 meters
1:20,000	1,666.7 feet 508.00 meters	656.2 feet 200 meters
1:25,000	2,083.3 feet 635.00 meters	820.2 feet 250 meters
1:50,000	4,166.7 feet 1,270.0 meters	1640.4 feet 500 meters
1:63,360	5,280.0 feet (mile) 1,609.3 meters	2,078.7 feet 633.6 meters
1:100,000	8,333.3 feet 2,540.0 meters	3,280.8 feet 1,000 meters
1:250,000	20,833 feet 6,350.0 meters	8,202.0 feet 2,500 meters
1:500,000	41,667 feet 12,700 meters	16,404.0 feet 5,000 meters

SCALE 1:24000

1000   0   1000   2000   3000   4000   5000   6000   7000 FEET
1 MILE

1   5   0   1 KILOMETER

Scale 1:50,000

1   ½   0   1   2   3 Statute Miles
1000   500   0   1000   2000   3000   4000 Meters
1000   500   0   1000   2000   3000   4000 Yards
1   ½   0   1   2   3 Nautical Miles

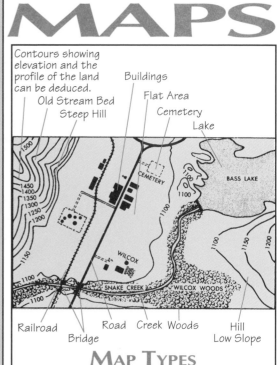

Contours showing elevation and the profile of the land can be deduced.
Old Stream Bed
Steep Hill
Buildings
Flat Area
Cemetery
Lake
BASS LAKE
CEMETERY
WILCOX
SNAKE CREEK
WILCOX WOODS
Railroad
Bridge
Road   Creek   Woods
Hill
Low Slope

MAP TYPES

A map is a graphic representation of a portion of the earth's surface in a uniform and proportional relationship. The proportional relationship is known as the *map scale*. A map will show features that are present on the earth's surface or below the surface. Most maps are made for a specific purpose as: street map, highway map, elevation map (topographic), geology of soil or rock formations below the surface, thermal maps showing the effluence of rivers, etc.

All maps have their own set of symbols by which the features they show are represented.

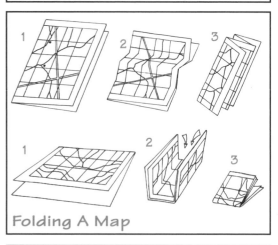

Folding A Map

Cartography

Cartography (map making) is the art and science of expressing known physical features of the earth's surface graphically by maps. A map is a graphic representation, drawn to scale, of a portion of earth's surface as seen from above. Features on the ground are depicted by symbols, lines, colors, and forms.

GROUND DISTANCE

Map Reader Wheel

The ground distance between two points is determined by measuring between the points on the map and multiplying the map measurement by the denominator of the RF.

Straight-Line Ground Distance

To determine a straight-line ground distance between two points on a map, place a straight-edged piece of paper on the map so that the edge of the paper touches both points. Make a tick mark on the edge of the paper at each point. Move the paper down to the graphic scale and read the ground distance between the points.

GROUND DISTANCE ALONG A WINDING ROAD

To measure distance along a winding road, stream or any other curved line, use the straight edge of a piece of paper. Make a tick mark at or near one end of the paper and place it at the point from which the curved line is to be measured. Align the edge of the paper along a straight portion, and make a tick mark on both map and paper at the end of the aligned portion. Keeping both tick marks together, place the point of the pencil on the paper's tick mark to hold it in place. Pivot the paper until another approximately straight portion is aligned and again make a tick mark on both map and paper. Continue in this manner until the measurement is complete. Then place the paper on the graphic scale and read the ground distance.

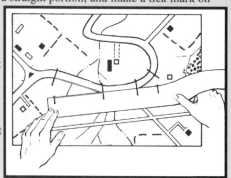

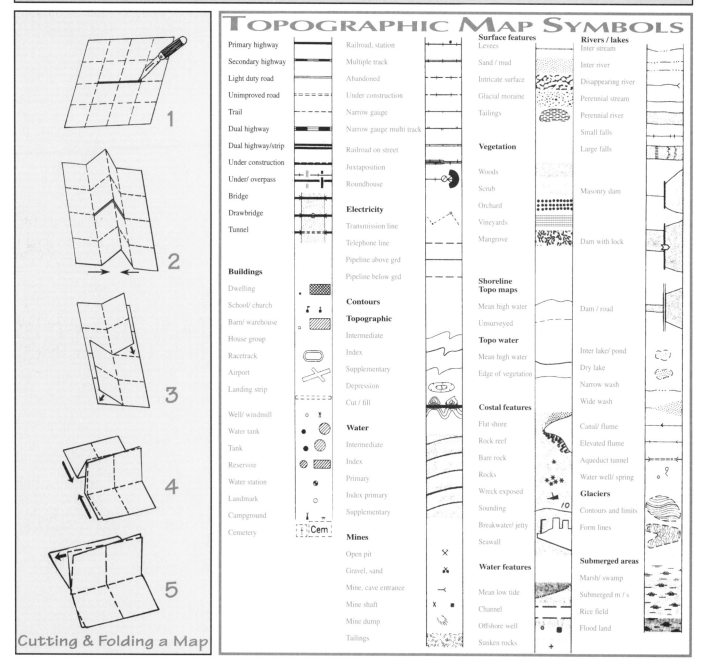

Cutting & Folding a Map

TOPOGRAPHIC MAP SYMBOLS

Primary highway	Railroad, station	**Surface features** Levees	**Rivers / lakes** Inter stream	
Secondary highway	Multiple track	Sand / mud	Inter river	
Light duty road	Abandoned	Intricate surface	Disappearing river	
Unimproved road	Under construction	Glacial moraine	Perennial stream	
Trail	Narrow gauge	Tailings	Perennial river	
Dual highway	Narrow gauge multi track		Small falls	
Dual highway/strip	Railroad on street	**Vegetation**	Large falls	
Under construction	Juxtaposition	Woods		
Under/ overpass	Roundhouse	Scrub	Masonry dam	
Bridge		Orchard		
Drawbridge	**Electricity**	Vineyards		
Tunnel	Transmission line	Mangrove	Dam with lock	
	Telephone line			
	Pipeline above grd	**Shoreline Topo maps**	Dam / road	
Buildings	Pipeline below grd	Mean high water		
Dwelling		Unsurveyed		
School/ church	**Contours**	**Topo water**	Inter lake/ pond	
Barn/ warehouse	**Topographic**	Mean high water	Dry lake	
House group	Intermediate	Edge of vegetation	Narrow wash	
Racetrack	Index		Wide wash	
Airport	Supplementary	**Costal features**		
Landing strip	Depression	Flat shore	Canal/ flume	
	Cut / fill	Rock reef	Elevated flume	
Well/ windmill		Bare rock	Aqueduct tunnel	
Water tank	**Water**	Rocks	Water well/ spring	
Tank	Intermediate	Wreck exposed	**Glaciers**	
Reservoir	Index	Sounding	Contours and limits	
Water station	Primary	Breakwater/ jetty	Form lines	
Landmark	Index primary	Seawall		
Campground	Supplementary		**Submerged areas**	
Cemetery		**Water features**	Marsh/ swamp	
	Mines		Submerged m / s	
	Open pit	Mean low tide	Rice field	
	Gravel, sand	Channel	Flood land	
	Mine, cave entrance	Offshore well		
	Mine shaft	Sunken rocks		
	Mine dump			
	Tailings			

TOPOGRAPHIC MAPS

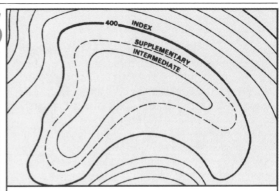

Topographic maps portray terrain and land forms in a measurable form, as well as the horizontal positions of the features represented. The vertical positions, or relief, are normally represented by contours. On maps showing relief, the elevations and contours are measured from mean sea level.

A knowledge of map symbols, grids, scale, and distance gives enough information to identify two points, locate them, measure between them, and determine how long it would take to travel between them. What happens if there is a 300 foot cliff between the two points? The map user reading a topographic map recognizes various landforms and irregularities of the earth's surface and will determine the elevation and relative differences in height of the terrain features.

Datum plane: This is a reference from which vertical measurements are taken. The datum plane for most maps is the *average sea level*.

Elevation: This is defined as the height (vertical distance) of an object above or below a datum plane.

Relief: Relief is the representation of the shape and height of landforms.

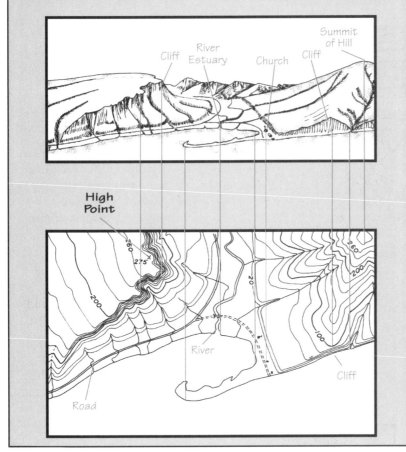

CONTOUR LINES

There are several ways of indicating elevation and relief on maps. The most common way is by *contour lines*. A contour line is a line representing an imaginary line on the ground along which all points are at the same elevation.

Contour lines indicate a vertical distance above or below a datum plane. Starting at sea level, normally the *zero contour*, each contour line represents an elevation above sea level.

The vertical distance between adjacent contour lines is known as the *contour interval* and the amount of the contour interval is given in the marginal information on the map.

• The contour lines are usually printed in brown.

Index Contour: Every fifth contour line is drawn with a heavier line and called index contours. The elevation is indicated on these lines.

Intermediate Contours: The contour lines falling *between* index contours are called intermediate contours. They are drawn with a finer line than the index contours and usually do not have their elevations marked.

USING CONTOUR LINES

• Find the contour interval of the map from the marginal information.
• Find the numbered contour line (or other given elevation) nearest the point for which the elevation is being sought.
• Determine the direction of the slope from the numbered contour line to the point.
• Counting the number of contour lines that must be crossed to go from the numbered line to the desired point and noting the direction - up or down. *The number of lines crossed multiplied by the contour interval is the distance above or below the starting value.*
• To estimate the elevation of the top of an unmarked hill, add half the contour interval to the elevation of the highest contour line around the hill.
• To estimate the elevation of the bottom of a depression, subtract half the contour interval from the value of the lowest contour around the depression.

COLORS USED ON A MILITARY MAP

Black: Indicates cultural (man-made) features (buildings, roads).

Reddish-Brown: Red and brown are combined to identify cultural features, all relief features, and elevation, such as contour lines on red-light readable maps.

Blue: Hydrography or water features such as lakes, swamps, rivers, and drainage.

Green: Vegetation with military significance, such as woods, orchards, and vineyards.

Red: Classifies cultural features, such as populated areas, main roads, and boundaries on older maps.

Other: Shows special information. These are indicated as marginal information.

Summit of Hill   1

Valley   2

To the south lies a valley. The valley slopes downward from east to west; note that the U of the contour line points to the east, indicating higher ground in that direction and lower ground to the west. Another look at the valley shows high ground to the north and south of the valley.

Ridge   3

There are four prominent ridges. A ridge is on each end of the ridge line and two ridges extend south from the ridge line. All of the ridges have lower ground in three directions and higher ground in one direction.

Saddle   4

The saddles have lower ground in two directions and higher ground in the opposite two directions. The contour lines of each saddle form half an hourglass shape. Because of the difference in size of the higher ground on the two opposite sides of a saddle, a full hourglass shape of a saddle may not be apparent.

Ridge Line

Depression   5

Just east of the valley is a depression. Looking from the bottom of the depression, there is higher ground in all directions.

Draws   6

Between the ridges and spurs are draws. They, like valleys, have higher ground in three directions and lower ground in one direction. Their contour line U's and V's point toward higher ground.

Spurs   7

There are several spurs extending generally south from the ridge line. They, like ridges, have lower ground in three directions and higher ground in one direction. Their contour line U's point away from higher ground.

Cliff   8

Three contour lines on the north side of the center hill are touching or almost touching. They have ticks indicating a vertical or nearly vertical slope or a cliff.

Cut 9   Fill 10

The road cutting through the eastern ridge depicts cuts and fills. The breaks in the contour lines indicate cuts, and the ticks pointing away from the road bed on each side of the road indicate fills.

INTERPRETATION OF TERRAIN FEATURES SHOWN BY CONTOUR LINES

A terrain feature does not stand alone but is interrelated with its adjoining features.

These maps show a top view of the terrain.

They depict elevation by the use of contour lines. Contour lines are the graphic symbols that tie all the features together and tell their story.

TOPOGRAPHIC MAP SYMBOLS AND COLORS

The purpose of a map is to permit one to visualize an area of the earth's surface with pertinent features properly positioned. The map maker uses symbols to represent the natural and man-made features of the earth's surface.

Topographic Symbols

Topographic symbols are usually printed in different colors to facilitate the identification of features on the map. Each color identifies a class of features. The colors vary with different types of maps, but on a standard large-scale topographic map, the colors and features are:

Black: The majority of cultural or man-made features.

Blue: Water features such as lakes, rivers, and swamps.

Green: Vegetation such as woods and orchards.

Brown: Relief features such as contour lines.

Red: Main roads, built-up areas, and special features.

In the process of making a map, everything must be reduced from its actual size on the ground to the size at which it appears on the map. This requires, for purposes of clarity, that some of the symbols be exaggerated. They are positioned, however, in such a manner *that the center of the symbol remains in its true location.* An exception to this would be the position of a feature adjacent to a major road. If the width of the road has been exaggerated, then the feature is moved from its true position to preserve its relation to the road.

Ridge Line

Running east to west across the complex land mass is a ridge line. A ridge line is a line of high ground, usually with changes in elevation along its top and low ground on all sides. The changes in elevation are the three hilltops and two saddles along the ridge line. From the top of each hill, there is lower ground in all directions.

U's

The closed ends of the U's formed by the contour lines point away from higher ground.

WATER CREATED FEATURES

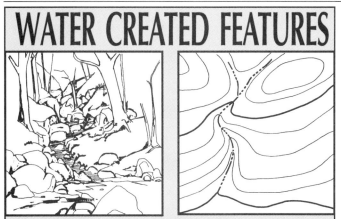

Draw: A draw is a miniature valley that with time might develop into a valley. The contour lines look similar to a valley. There are usually many boulders on the stream bed of a draw.

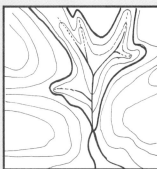

Valley: A valley is usually created by erosion by a river or stream. A valley has rising slopes on two sides, a slight incline at the head of the water source (or where the water source was) and a decline to where the water flows. To find valleys on the map look for V shaped or U shaped contour lines. The water flows or flowed from the closed end of the V or U.

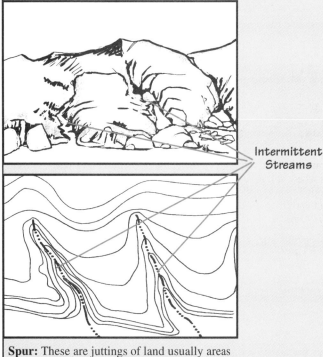

Intermittent Streams

Spur: These are juttings of land usually areas between parallel valleys formed by streams or rivers. They usually will form off a ridge line. Spurs usually are in the shape of U's or V's.

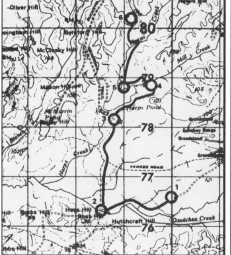

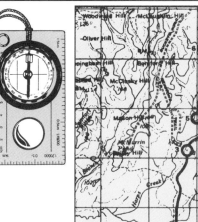

Marked Orienteering Map With Station Locations

The object of orienteering is to locate control points by using a map and compass to navigate through the woods. It is a competitive sport in that teams try to complete the preestablished course as fast as possible. A course can be 10 kilometers long.

Each orienteer is given a topographic map and a compass with the various control points of the circuit circled. Each control point has a flag marker and a distinctive punch which is used to mark the score card. Competitive orienteering involves running from checkpoint to checkpoint.

ORIENTEERING

CARE OF MAPS

Maps should be correctly folded.

Maps should be folded to make them small enough to be carried and still be available for use without having to unfold them entirely. After a map has been folded it should be placed in a folder for protection. This will prevent the corners and edges of the map from wearing out and tearing easily when opened.

Waterproofing Maps

Most maps are printed on paper and require protection from water, mud, and tearing. Whenever possible, a map should be carried in a waterproof packet to prolong its life. A liquid coating is available to protect paper maps. Some hiking trails have maps printed on non tearable waterproof plastic sheets.

Marking a Map

If it is necessary to mark a map, use light lines so that they may be erased without smearing or smudging. If the margins of the map must be trimmed note any marginal information which may be needed, such as grid data, and magnetic declination data.

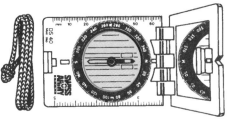

TYPES OF SLOPES

The following examples show how contour lines represent different types of slopes.

Gentle Slope: The contour lines are wide apart and evenly spaced.

Steep Uniform Slope: The contour lines are close together and evenly spaced. The closer the contour lines the steeper the slope. When the lines are on top of each other this represents a cliff.

Convex Slope: The contour lines spacing is wide at the top and close at the bottom. Note that the road has been cut into the slope and this creates the flat area on the slope.

Concave Slope: The contour lines are closely spaced at the top of the hill, the middle has a relatively wider spacing, and the bottom is even wider. In the illustration the contour lines near the road are closer as the road might have been cut into or filled on the slope.

Hill: A hill is shown by relatively concentric contour lines. The highest area on the hill is shown by the smallest closed circle. The highest elevation can be shown by an "X" and a numeric height.

Cut and Fill: Cut and fill are man-made and are used when laying train tracks, making roads, terracing or building on slopes. The cut is where soil is removed from high ground. A fill is where soil is added to low land. The contour line extends along the length of the cut and fill with tick marks indicating a cut or fill. Cuts and fills are only shown if they are 10 feet or higher.

Cliffs: Cliffs can be shown as in A where all contour lines merge or as in B where the lines merge and tick marks show the fall-off side of the cliff. These ticks are similar to the marks in a depression.

MAJOR TERRAIN FEATURES

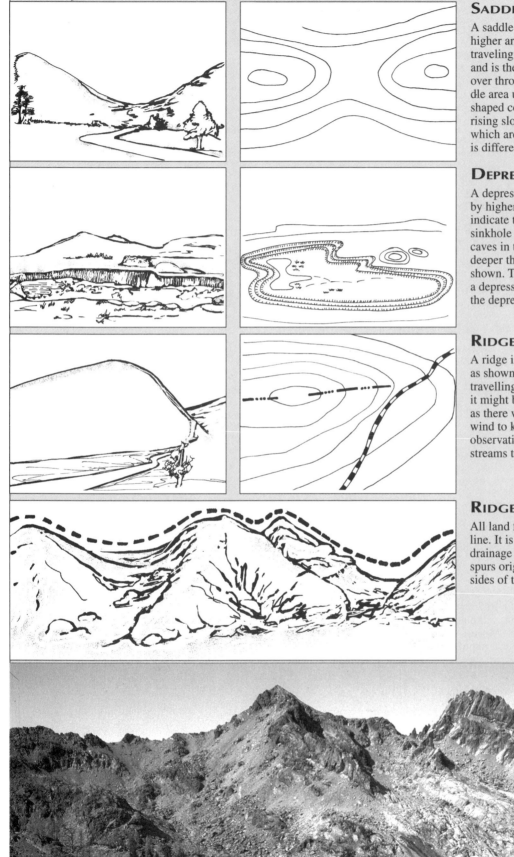

SADDLE

A saddle is a low area between two higher areas. A saddle is important in traveling overland as it represents a pass and is the least difficult route to pass over through a high area or ridge. A saddle area usually looks like a figure-eight shaped contour area. A saddle has two rising slopes and two declining slopes which are opposite each other. This is different from a valley.

DEPRESSION

A depression is a low area surrounded by higher ground. A depression might indicate the presence of water. A sinkhole in limestone might indicate caves in the area. Depressions that are deeper then a contour interval will be shown. Ticks on the contour line indicate a depression and they will slope into the depression.

RIDGE

A ridge is a sloping line of high ground as shown in the illustration. When travelling on foot in a temperate climate it might be easier to travel on the ridge as there will be less undergrowth, more wind to keep insects away, better observation, less of a slope to climb, no streams to cross, and no valleys to cross.

RIDGE LINE

All land features originate from a ridge line. It is the dividing line between drainage basins. Valleys, draws, and spurs originate in the slopes of the sides of the ridge line.

CHOICE OF BINOCULARS

Field of View

This is the angle of view or the area you will see through the binoculars at 1,000 yards. The recommended range is 300 to 450 feet across. This is important when viewing fast moving objects because if the angle (feet across) is too small the object will be hard to find and easily leave the field of view.

Eye Relief

This is the distance that the eye should be from the viewing lens to properly see the image. Most binoculars are made to have correct relief for normal eyes. Eyeglass wearers require a longer eye relief of an average of 16-20 mm. Many binoculars are now made with rubber eye cups that fold down to accommodate eyeglasses. This places the eyes at the correct distance.

Near Focus

Near focus is the closest distance to which a pair of binoculars will focus (provide a sharp image). For watching birds you will require a near focus of 15 feet or closer to allow close-up viewing.

Fit and Feel

How do the binoculars fit to your face and eyes? Do they have an eye space adjustment to accommodate the distance between your eyes? How well or comfortably can they be held? Do they feel stable in your hands? These are factors in your choice of binoculars.

Chemical Coatings

These are applied to lenses to reduce light scattering which will give an impression of higher contrast and improved sharpness.

Manufacturers designation of "coated" means at least one surface of the lens is coated. "Multi-coated" indicates that all air-to-glass surfaces have received more than one coating.

Armor Shielding or Coating

This provides a better grip, might be waterproofed, and reduces wear and tear. This coating increases the weight.

Eyeglass Wearers

You will need a "long eye relief" of 16-20 mm. If you have this you can look through your binoculars without removing your glasses. Modern binoculars have a rubber cap on each eye ring which can be folded back to accommodate glasses.

Auto Focus Binoculars

These binoculars use averages to establish a focus and usually are not as bright because they use a large "f number". Photography buffs would understand this and also "depth of field". Avoid this "special" feature of some models of binoculars.

Zoom Binoculars

These binoculars work in a similar fashion as zoom lenses for cameras. In general it is difficult enough for the manufacturer to align the lens without including the zoom feature. Each barrel has to be aligned and focused for all distances and magnifications. These binoculars are more sensitive to abuse. Avoid them if you want a half-decent optic.

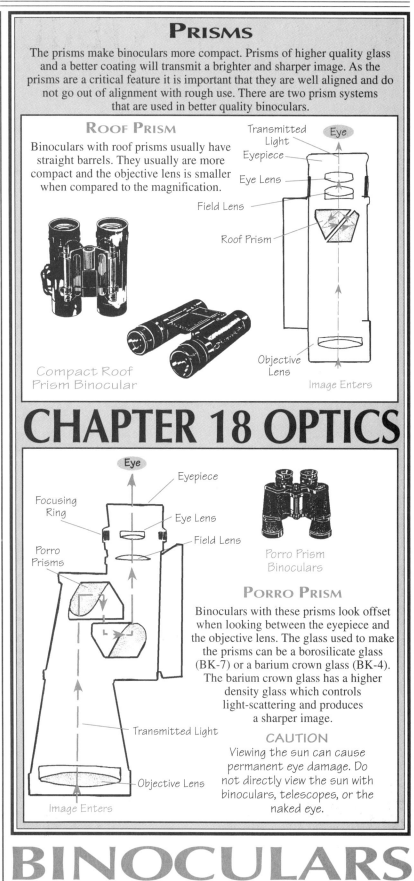

PRISMS

The prisms make binoculars more compact. Prisms of higher quality glass and a better coating will transmit a brighter and sharper image. As the prisms are a critical feature it is important that they are well aligned and do not go out of alignment with rough use. There are two prism systems that are used in better quality binoculars.

ROOF PRISM

Binoculars with roof prisms usually have straight barrels. They usually are more compact and the objective lens is smaller when compared to the magnification.

Compact Roof Prism Binocular

Transmitted Light
Eye
Eyepiece
Eye Lens
Field Lens
Roof Prism
Objective Lens
Image Enters

CHAPTER 18 OPTICS

Eye
Eyepiece
Focusing Ring
Eye Lens
Field Lens
Porro Prisms
Porro Prism Binoculars
Transmitted Light
Objective Lens
Image Enters

PORRO PRISM

Binoculars with these prisms look offset when looking between the eyepiece and the objective lens. The glass used to make the prisms can be a borosilicate glass (BK-7) or a barium crown glass (BK-4). The barium crown glass has a higher density glass which controls light-scattering and produces a sharper image.

CAUTION

Viewing the sun can cause permanent eye damage. Do not directly view the sun with binoculars, telescopes, or the naked eye.

BINOCULARS TELESCOPES

TESTING OF OPTICS AND ALIGNMENT

Focus Test

Focus on a distant object. Remove your eyes from the binoculars, wait a minute, cover one lens (do not refocus) look at the same object. Do the same with your second eye. If your eye is not immediately in focus when you look through the eyepiece the optics are of bad quality and your eye is compensating for the lens errors. Do not buy these binoculars or others of the same brand.

Alignment Test

After the binoculars have been adjusted for your eyes, focus, *with both eyes*, on a distant object e.g. a flagpole. Look through the binoculars and both eyes should, in your mind, merge this flagpole as one. If they do not coincide the alignment is off. Try this while holding the binoculars at 45° and vertically. If this problem occurs at any angle try another pair of binoculars (even the same brand).

Pincushion and Forms of Astigmatism

When the binoculars have been adjusted for your vision you can check for distortion produced by the binoculars.

Go outside and look at a tall building with long parallel vertical lines. Focus on the lines. Do they stay parallel and vertical? You will see a slight divergence which will vary from binocular to binocular but will nearly be eliminated on very expensive binoculars. Choose a pair that you can live with.

Flare

Look at a shiny surface or a burning light bulb. Are there many reflections? Can you see past the light bulb or is it all "burnt out". The amount of flare that a pair of binoculars can eliminate depends upon the quality of the binoculars. Choose what you can accept depending upon your use. For night vision you would want less flare.

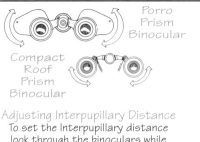

MAGNIFICATION AND ANGLE OF VIEW

Magnification

Binoculars and monoculars are described by two numbers: Magnification x front (objective) lens diameter (in mm). Example 7 x 50.

Magnification (Power): The number of times the object looked at is enlarged. The larger the number the greater the magnification. A magnification of greater than 10 is not practical without a tripod, as your hand would shake. Usual magnifications will read **6** x 30, **7** x 35, **7** x 50, **10** x 50. In the 7 x 50 the image would appear 7 x closer or 7 x larger than to the naked eye.

Lens (Objective) Size: This is the diameter of the front lens. The larger the front lens the more light is admitted and the image will be brighter. This is important in choosing a pair of binoculars because at dusk or in a forest the larger lens size will be more important than the power. Usual lens size will read 6 x **30**, 7 x **35**, 7 x **50**, 10 x **50**. The larger the objective lens the wider the *field of view*. This means that you will be able to see more of the landscape at one time. This is important if you are watching an active sport or wildlife which might fly out of view. *See Field of View page 199.*

TO CHOOSE A PAIR OF BINOCULARS

Testing the Binoculars for Sharpness
Focus the binoculars at a point source of light. By moving the binoculars the point should remain in sharp focus to at least 2/3 the way to the edge of the viewing area.

CHOICE OF BINOCULARS

	7 x 25	7 x 35	7 x 50	8 x 25	8 x 40	10 x 25	10 x 50	16 x 50
General Use		x	x		x			
Sports		x			x			N.R.
Bird watching/Nature		x	x		x			N.R.
Hunting			x	x			N.R.	
Travel	x			x		x		N.R.
Hiking	x			x		x		N.R.
Boating (Waterproof)			x	x				N.R.
Astronomy	N.R.		x	N.R.	N.R.	N.R.	x	x

TO FOCUS BINOCULARS

- Close your right eye and sight an object with your left eye. Focus the binocular by rotating the *center focus wheel* until the image in the left eye is sharp and clear.

- Now close your left eye. Rotate the *right eyepiece* until the object sighted is sharp and clear. Note the setting on the diopter scale on the right eyepiece. This will be the adjustment for your eyes. Both sides of the binoculars are now in focus and you only use the center focus wheel to focus them.

VIEWING WITH GLASSES

Fold down the rubber rim on the binoculars if you are wearing eyeglasses while using the binoculars.

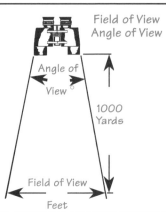

Porro Prism Binocular

Compact Roof Prism Binocular

Adjusting Interpupillary Distance
To set the Interpupillary distance look through the binoculars while grasping them and gradually bending until you see one circle of view. If they do not merge the binoculars are the wrong size or the prisms are out of alignment.

Field of View
Angle of View

Angle of View

1000 Yards

Field of View

Feet

ASTRONOMY

BINOCULARS AND THE SKY

Binoculars are ideal for a beginner stargazer. They are more compact, easier to use, have a wider angle of vision and are less expensive than a telescope.

For star watching the objective lens of a binocular should be as large as possible as it gathers more starlight. If the binoculars are too large they will be heavy and difficult to hold. In general the ideal binocular for astronomy is the 7 x 50. If the binoculars are of a larger magnification you will need a special clamp and tripod to keep it stable.

Binoculars

6 to 8 power can be hand held.
12 to 18 power should be mounted on a tripod.

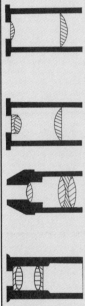

Huygens Eyepiece
Works well with long focus refractors, but image distortion by spherical aberration occurs with short focal ratios. As it does not used cemented lenses it is recommended for solar projection.

Kellner Eyepiece
An all purpose eyepiece.

Orthoscopic Eyepiece
All purpose lens well suited for short focal length telescopes. It gives a high quality image and good eye relief.

Plossl Eyepiece
A high quality image over a wide field of view with good eye relief. Works well on a telescope with a short focal length.

EQUATORIAL TELESCOPE MOUNT

Is a telescope mount which rotates about the polar axis and the declination axis. The advantage of an equatorial mount is that it only has to be moved around the polar axis to compensate for the Earth's rotation. A Second type of mounting system is the *Altazimuth* mount which allows you to move the telescope up and down (altitude) and to the left and right (azimuth) to help you keep track celestial bodies.

Polar Axis

Declination Axis

TELESCOPES

In buying a telescope the most important factor is the aperture (the diameter of the lens or mirror). The larger the aperture the more light can be gathered and the brighter the object viewed.

REFRACTING TELESCOPE

This is the type of telescope invented by Galileo. It is a tube with an objective lens that collects the light, and an eyepiece which can be changed to have different powers. These telescopes are fairly inexpensive in small sizes and are of good value for a beginner. In the case of telescopes bigger is usually better because they accumulate more light and can be of higher magnification. Refractors have a good resolution of fine line detail especially when used for planetary observation. It is physically more stable than the reflector.

Objective Lens

Refracting Telescope

Eyepiece

REFLECTING TELESCOPE

This telescope uses a concave mirror as the main optical element (primary mirror). The mirror, which acts as a lens, is at the bottom of the tube. The light goes down the tube to the primary mirror, is focused, and reflected back to a mirror which reflects into the eyepiece. Sir Isaac Newton used this type of telescope in 1668.

The advantage of this type of telescope is that the image is captured and focused in a relatively short tube. These telescopes are lighter, easier to mount, and stabilize than a refractor. Reflecting telescopes are more sensitive to misalignment than the refracting telescope.

A catadioptric telescope, is a hybrid, with mirrors and lenses that achieves the widest aperture for the shortest possible barrel.

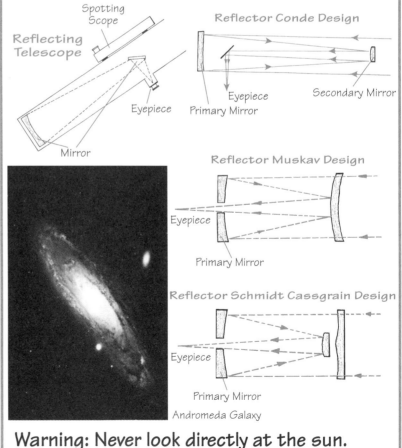

Spotting Scope

Reflecting Telescope

Mirror

Eyepiece

Reflector Conde Design

Eyepiece

Primary Mirror

Secondary Mirror

Reflector Muskav Design

Eyepiece

Primary Mirror

Reflector Schmidt Cassgrain Design

Eyepiece

Primary Mirror

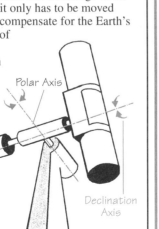

Andromeda Galaxy

Warning: Never look directly at the sun.

ADDITIONAL FEATURES FOR TELESCOPES

Eyepieces

Eyepieces are interchangeable on telescopes so you can increase or decrease the magnification.

Camera Adapters

The telescope can be used for astrophotography or, if low-powered, for distant nature photography.

Filters

These help increase contrast or enhance astrophotography.

Image-Erecting Prisms

These are for terrestrial viewing as these prisms will make the image right-side up.

Equatorial Mount

This mount inclines the axis of the celestial sphere. You will only have to move the telescope in one direction to follow a star.

Barlow Lenses

These expand the performance of the eyepieces.

Spotting Scopes

As the name indicates this is a sight on a high powered telescope. It is of lower magnification and helps you position your telescope on a star or object. If an erecting prism is placed on a spotting scope it can be used to watch birds or animals.

MOON PHASES

Best watching time is between the moon's last quarter and the first quarter. Three hours after sunset so that the sky is dark enough to see the low intensity stars.

You can see the phases of the moon on a calendar.

No Moon: Excellent for viewing the stars as there is no light from the moon.

First Quarter Moon: Is seen in the afternoon and evening. It will have gone down by midnight.

Full Moon: Difficult to see the stars as the sky is filled with glare.

Last Quarter Moon: Comes up after midnight and can be seen until noon.

SKY WATCHING

Star Identification

With time and using a sky chart you can learn the approximate shape and location of 20 constellations and 10 to 15 of the brightest starts. The Sky Chart in this book is an excellent start.

Stars and Star Groupings

- Study the constellations. Look for Ursa Major and Minor, Cassiopeia, Draco, and Cepheus (these are the circumpolar constellations and are visible all night and rotate around the Pole Star (Polaris)). Constellations are grouping of stars which have been given legendary or historical significance. These groups have been joined together with lines, outlining a figure or symbol, so that you can find them in the sky.
- Look for the Big Dipper in Ursa Major (the Great Bear). From the Big Dipper look at the pointer stars Dubhe and Merak to find the North Star (Polaris).
- Polaris is the star closest to the true north (*Note: the Pole Star was not always the Pole Star due to the movement of the earth. During time of the Egyptian pyramid building the pole star was Thuban in Draco*).
- Look for the constellations of the Zodiac: Aries, Taurus, Gemini, Cancer, Leo, Virgo, Libra, Scorpio, Sagittarius, Capricorn, Aquarius, and Pisces.
- Look at the inside of the Milky Way galaxy. The earth is part of it.
- Look for the five planets that you can see without a telescope, Mercury, Venus, Mars, Jupiter, and Saturn. Unlike the stars, the planets wander through the sky just like earth. The planets are seen because they *reflect* the light from the sun. Mercury and Venus, which are closer to the sun than earth, are seen as the evening or morning stars.
- Meteor showers can be seen with the best coming out of the Perseid constellation in August.
- Stars have colors examples are: Igel, blue white. Capella, yellow white. Anthers, red.

Star Magnitude

The brightness of stars are categorized into magnitudes.

- The brightest are of 0 or 1st magnitude.
- The ones barely visible to the naked eye are of the 6th magnitude.

Some stars have variable magnitudes.

Northern Lights (Auroras)

These lights can be seen in the northern latitudes. They are like moving curtains and can be whitish, yellow, green, pinkish. One theory is that they are caused by the sunlight hitting space gases at very high altitude. They have a neon light type reaction to the light. These Auroras usually occur a few days after the development of large sun spots.

Milky Way Galaxy

Our sun, all the planets around our sun (including the planet Earth) are a part of the Milky Way galaxy. Galaxies are islands or clusters of many millions of stars in the universe. The milky way is only one of these galaxies. All galaxies rotate about their centers. When you see the Milky Way in the sky it looks like a spiraling band of stars but actually we are in the Milky Way looking down the long axis of our galaxy.

UT UNIVERSAL TIME

This time standard is used in astronomy and shortwave radio transmission. UT is the time at 0° longitude (Greenwich, England) and is divided into 24 time zones around the world. To convert North American Time zones into UT.

EST (Eastern Standard Time winter) subtract 5 hours.

EDT (Eastern Daylight Time summer) subtract 4 hours.

PST (Pacific Standard Time winter) subtract 8 hours.

AST (Atlantic Standard Time winter) subtract 4 hours.

PST (Prairie Standard Time winter) subtract 6 hours.

MST (Mountain Standard Time winter) subtract 7 hours.

DIRECTION OF THE EARTH'S ROTATION

Venus NASA

You will notice that at the edge of the sky chart there is a rotation arrow. This arrows shows the stars come up (in the east) and going down in the west. Actually the stars are fixed and it is the earth *rotating 15° per hour* that give you the impression of the stars moving. This movement occurs around the Pole Star (Polaris).

Our sky map shows the stars for 9:00 PM and if you are watching the stars at 10:00 PM (*one hour* after the 9:00 PM chart time) the stars will have "moved" 15° in the direction of the arrow.

Movement of Earth in its Orbit

This illustration shows how the Big Dipper will appear from earth at different times of the year. This displacement is due to the movement of earth in its orbit around the sun. The sky charts show the same phenomenon for the sky.

January 1
October 1
☆ Polaris
April 1
Big Dipper
July 1

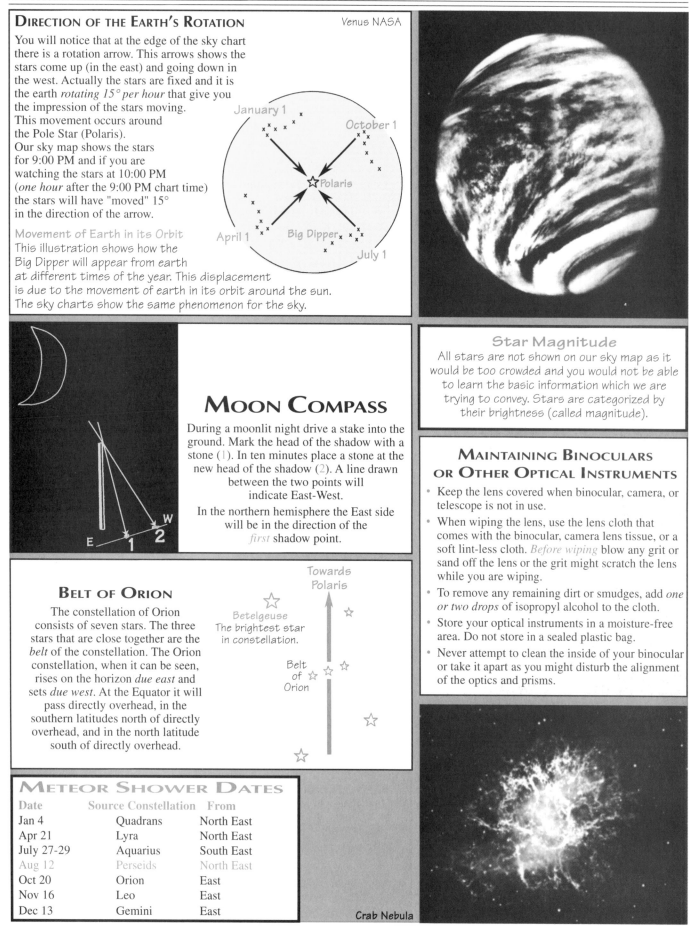

MOON COMPASS

During a moonlit night drive a stake into the ground. Mark the head of the shadow with a stone (1). In ten minutes place a stone at the new head of the shadow (2). A line drawn between the two points will indicate East-West.

In the northern hemisphere the East side will be in the direction of the *first* shadow point.

W
E 1 2

Star Magnitude

All stars are not shown on our sky map as it would be too crowded and you would not be able to learn the basic information which we are trying to convey. Stars are categorized by their brightness (called magnitude).

MAINTAINING BINOCULARS OR OTHER OPTICAL INSTRUMENTS

- Keep the lens covered when binocular, camera, or telescope is not in use.
- When wiping the lens, use the lens cloth that comes with the binocular, camera lens tissue, or a soft lint-less cloth. *Before wiping* blow any grit or sand off the lens or the grit might scratch the lens while you are wiping.
- To remove any remaining dirt or smudges, add *one or two drops* of isopropyl alcohol to the cloth.
- Store your optical instruments in a moisture-free area. Do not store in a sealed plastic bag.
- Never attempt to clean the inside of your binocular or take it apart as you might disturb the alignment of the optics and prisms.

BELT OF ORION

The constellation of Orion consists of seven stars. The three stars that are close together are the *belt* of the constellation. The Orion constellation, when it can be seen, rises on the horizon *due east* and sets *due west*. At the Equator it will pass directly overhead, in the southern latitudes north of directly overhead, and in the north latitude south of directly overhead.

Towards Polaris

☆ Betelgeuse
The brightest star in constellation.

Belt
of
Orion

METEOR SHOWER DATES

Date	Source Constellation	From
Jan 4	Quadrans	North East
Apr 21	Lyra	North East
July 27-29	Aquarius	South East
Aug 12	Perseids	North East
Oct 20	Orion	East
Nov 16	Leo	East
Dec 13	Gemini	East

Crab Nebula

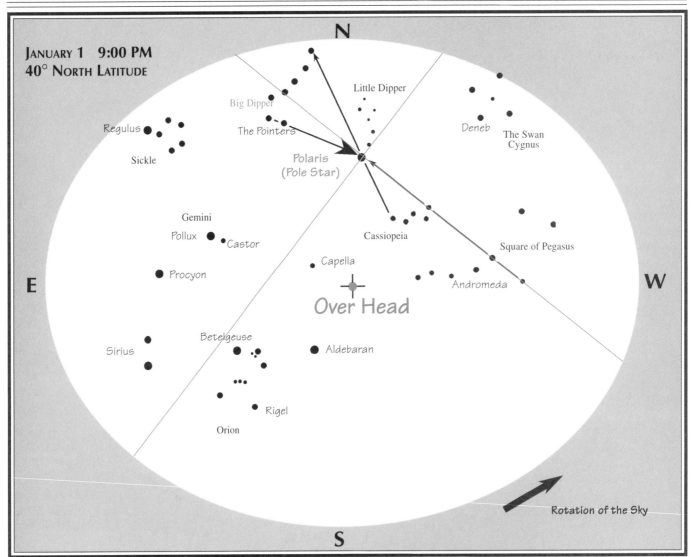

JANUARY 1   9:00 PM
40° NORTH LATITUDE

N

Big Dipper

The Pointers

Little Dipper

Deneb

The Swan
Cygnus

Regulus

Sickle

Polaris
(Pole Star)

Cassiopeia

Square of Pegasus

Gemini

Pollux   Castor

Capella

Andromeda

E

Procyon

Over Head

W

Sirius

Betelgeuse

Aldebaran

Rigel

Orion

Rotation of the Sky

S

WHAT IS A SKY CHART?

This is a map of the sky above your head at a certain time and place (Latitude). The map is round because when you look up the horizon is all around you and forms a near circle.

Latitude

Our sky maps are for 40° North Latitude and can be used for most of the Northern Hemisphere (United States, Southern Canada and Europe).

If you are in Northern Canada or Alaska then stars on the southern edge of our sky maps will disappear but additional stars will be seen to the North. At the North Pole the Polaris star will be at the middle of the sky (above your head) and you will see *all* of the Northern Hemisphere sky. If you are further south you will see more of the southern sky and the Polaris star will be closer to the Northern edge of the sky chart.

NAVIGATION
BY THE STARS

To read the sky chart, in the dark, use a flash light with a red filter so that your eyes will not have to readjust to the dark sky.

Locate the north by using a compass or by finding the Big Dipper and following "The Pointers" to find Polaris (North Star). Place the chart *above* your head with the "N" on the chart pointing North.

You will have noticed that the East and West printed on the sky map are on the opposite side of the East and West of an Earth map. The reason for this is that when the sky chart is *held above your head* the East and West markings will be the same as the terrestrial (earth) East and West.

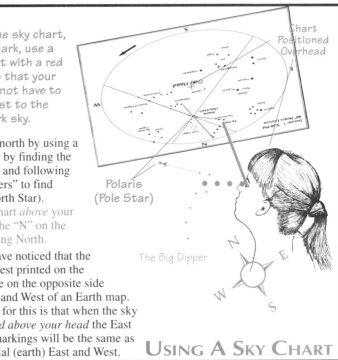

Chart Positioned Overhead

Polaris
(Pole Star)

The Big Dipper

USING A SKY CHART

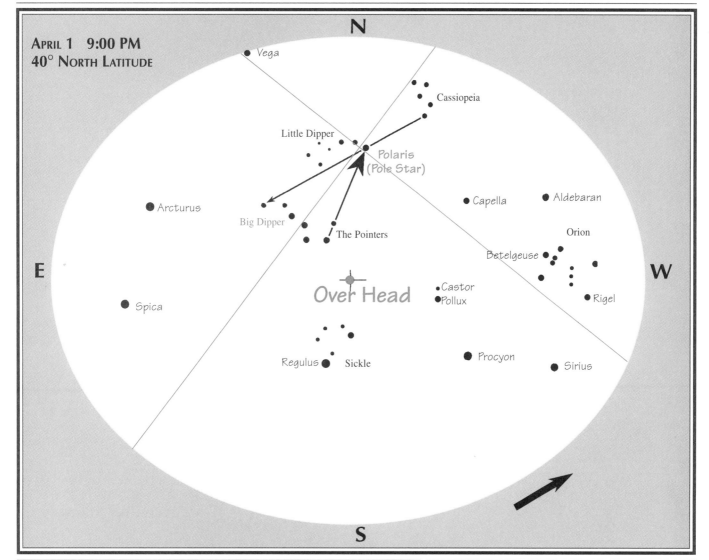

APRIL 1   9:00 PM
40° NORTH LATITUDE

N

Vega

Cassiopeia

Little Dipper

Polaris
(Pole Star)

Arcturus

Capella   Aldebaran

Big Dipper

Orion

The Pointers

Betelgeuse

E   W

Over Head   Castor
Pollux   Rigel

Spica

Regulus   Sickle   Procyon

Sirius

S

SOUTHERN CROSS

Polaris is not visible in the Southern Hemisphere and the Southern Cross is the most distinctive constellation.

An imaginary line drawn through the long axis of the Southern Cross or *True Cross* points toward the South Pole.

The True Cross should not be confused with the False Cross a larger cross nearby known as the False Cross. In the False Cross the stars are more widely spaced, is less bright and *has a star in the center*. The False Cross has five *stars* while the True Cross has only *four* stars. The stars on the southern and eastern arms are among the brightest stars in the heavens. Those on the northern and western arms, white bright, are smaller.

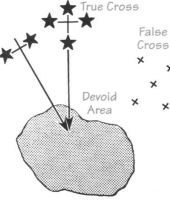

True Cross

False Cross

Devoid Area

• When the lines are projected from the True Cross and between the two very bright stars east of the True Cross the intersection point is in an area *devoid* of any stars and very dark known as the *Dark Pocket*.

• First extend an imaginary line along the long axis of the True Cross to the south. Join the two bright stars to the east of the True Cross with an imaginary line. Bisect this line with one at right angles. Where the two lines intersect is the South Pole. This *South Pole Point* can be used to estimate the latitude in the same way as with the North Pole Star.

FINDING THE NORTH

Upon finding the *Big Dipper* project a line through Merak and Dubhe (*The Pointers*) *and* you will intersect Polaris which indicates the North.

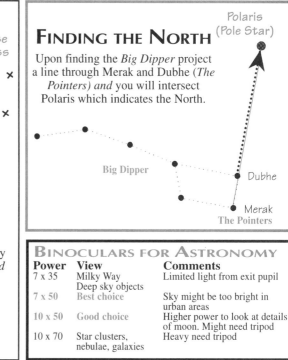

Polaris
(Pole Star)

Big Dipper

Dubhe

Merak
The Pointers

BINOCULARS FOR ASTRONOMY

Power	View	Comments
7 x 35	Milky Way Deep sky objects	Limited light from exit pupil
7 x 50	Best choice	Sky might be too bright in urban areas
10 x 50	Good choice	Higher power to look at details of moon. Might need tripod
10 x 70	Star clusters, nebulae, galaxies	Heavy need tripod

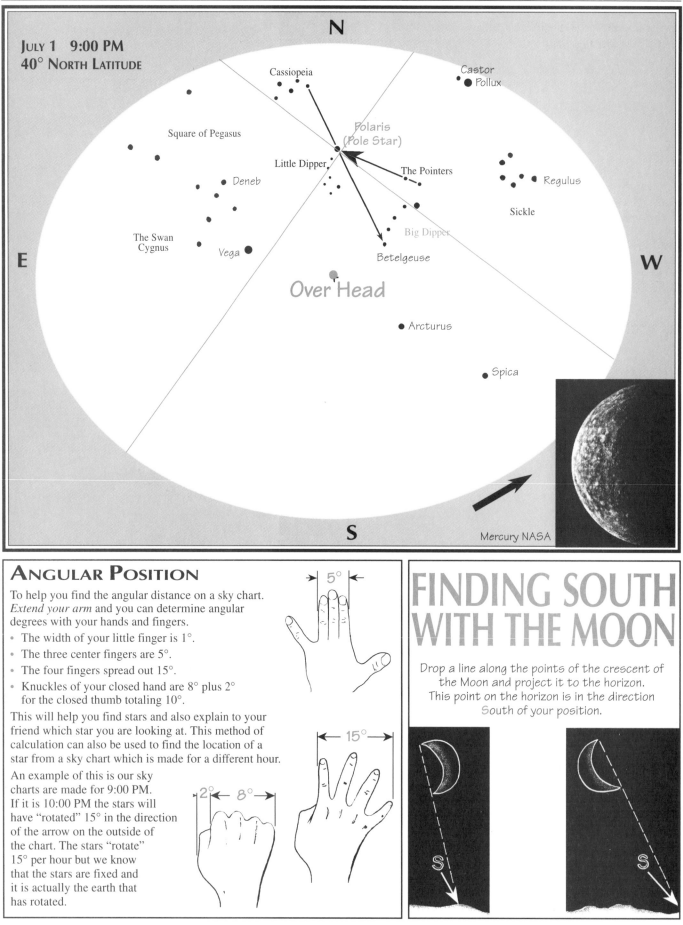

JULY 1   9:00 PM
40° NORTH LATITUDE

N

Cassiopeia

Castor
Pollux

Square of Pegasus

Polaris
(Pole Star)

Little Dipper

The Pointers

Regulus

Deneb

Sickle

E

The Swan
Cygnus

Vega

Big Dipper

W

Betelgeuse

Over Head

Arcturus

Spica

S

Mercury NASA

ANGULAR POSITION

To help you find the angular distance on a sky chart. *Extend your arm* and you can determine angular degrees with your hands and fingers.

- The width of your little finger is 1°.
- The three center fingers are 5°.
- The four fingers spread out 15°.
- Knuckles of your closed hand are 8° plus 2° for the closed thumb totaling 10°.

This will help you find stars and also explain to your friend which star you are looking at. This method of calculation can also be used to find the location of a star from a sky chart which is made for a different hour.

An example of this is our sky charts are made for 9:00 PM. If it is 10:00 PM the stars will have "rotated" 15° in the direction of the arrow on the outside of the chart. The stars "rotate" 15° per hour but we know that the stars are fixed and it is actually the earth that has rotated.

5°

15°

2°   8°

FINDING SOUTH WITH THE MOON

Drop a line along the points of the crescent of the Moon and project it to the horizon. This point on the horizon is in the direction South of your position.

S

S

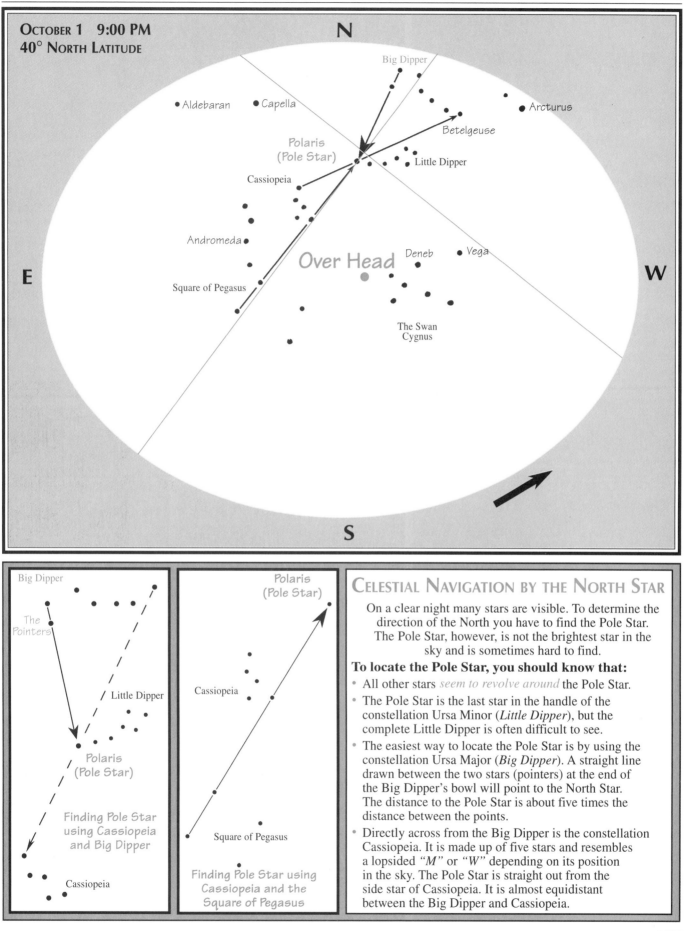

October 1 9:00 PM
40° North Latitude

N

Big Dipper

Aldebaran • • Capella • Arcturus

Betelgeuse

Polaris
(Pole Star)

Little Dipper

Cassiopeia

Andromeda

Over Head

Deneb • Vega

Square of Pegasus

The Swan
Cygnus

E   W

S

CELESTIAL NAVIGATION BY THE NORTH STAR

On a clear night many stars are visible. To determine the direction of the North you have to find the Pole Star. The Pole Star, however, is not the brightest star in the sky and is sometimes hard to find.

To locate the Pole Star, you should know that:

- All other stars *seem to revolve around* the Pole Star.
- The Pole Star is the last star in the handle of the constellation Ursa Minor (*Little Dipper*), but the complete Little Dipper is often difficult to see.
- The easiest way to locate the Pole Star is by using the constellation Ursa Major (*Big Dipper*). A straight line drawn between the two stars (pointers) at the end of the Big Dipper's bowl will point to the North Star. The distance to the Pole Star is about five times the distance between the points.
- Directly across from the Big Dipper is the constellation Cassiopeia. It is made up of five stars and resembles a lopsided "M" or "W" depending on its position in the sky. The Pole Star is straight out from the side star of Cassiopeia. It is almost equidistant between the Big Dipper and Cassiopeia.

Big Dipper

The Pointers

Little Dipper

Polaris
(Pole Star)

Finding Pole Star
using Cassiopeia
and Big Dipper

Cassiopeia

Polaris
(Pole Star)

Cassiopeia

Square of Pegasus

Finding Pole Star using
Cassiopeia and the
Square of Pegasus

PHOTOGRAPHY CHAPTER 19

Moose antler that shows gnawing marks.

CAMERA AND FILM

To Store Camera and Film

Use a compact cooler to store the camera and preserve color film. This cooler will float if your canoe capsizes, and will not attract any special attention from thieves.

Pictures of Animals

Photograph animals from inside a parked car as they will be frightened if you get out. Set up a blind for long time observation.

For Close-up Pictures

Use your standard 50mm lens on a reflex camera (SLR) and screw a close up lens onto the camera lens. Close-up lenses are available in 1, 2, and 3 diopter powers and can be mounted one, two or three at a time to produce up to 6 diopter magnification. The advantage of close-up lenses is that they do not lose any light as would occur when using a macro lens. These lenses, and a tripod, will be your best investment in macro nature photography.

Film Types

All films have a speed. This is the amount of light required to produce a latent image on its surface. The speed is measured in IS0 (formerly ASA) and might read ISO 100 or ISO 400 etc. This number shows that ISO 400 film requires less light than ISO 100 film to produce an image on the film. That means that ISO 400 film is faster and would be used in lower light conditions. A "fast" film produces more grainy photographs or slides and the speed might be too fast for your camera, especially in high light situations as snow scenes. An ideal all around film for most cameras would be ISO 400. You can buy color slide film, color print film and black and white film.

Ideal Camera

The ideal camera is one that you will use and not keep stored in a box or be so scared to use that it is always packed in 3 waterproof bags. A "one-shot" throw away camera might be for you or a professional SLR 35mm with a complement of lenses and filters. A professional photographer will usually have a beat up camera that is always at hand, even in the rain.

To Photograph Animals

In most cases you will require a telephoto lens and much patience. Most of the 'professional' photos you see in books are taken under tightly controlled situations in zoos, animal farms, etc. When traveling through the bush you will run into animals but in most cases you are both surprised and the animal runs while you fumble for your camera. To get some good pictures you would set up a camouflaged hiding spot in an area where you are sure a certain can animal will pass. This would be done by studying the tracks, finding a watering hole, checking the direction of the wind, using lures (*See Trapping*), etc.

Cameras in Cold Weather

Keep your camera as close to your body as possible. You can remove the batteries from your camera and keep them in an inside pocket. This might not be a total solution as the oils in the mechanism of the camera have become less viscous and effect your shutter speeds.

ROADKILL PHOTOGRAPHY

Paul's rules of roadkill photography are:
- Do not touch the victim.
- Photo should be taken at *in situ*.
- The photographer should not disturb the passing traffic *nor get killed**!

* *These photos are taken at your own risk.*

Wasp Nest
This photo was taken at night. A flashlight was shone on the nest. The nest was lightly tapped with a stick. In a few seconds the wasps started to emerge and where photographed with a flash. The results were one photo and three wasp sting bites.

PIONEER WEATHER INDICATORS

- Many acorns, bad weather.
- Thick corn husk, bad weather.
- Think onion skins, light winter.
- Squirrels have heavy coat, bad winter.
- Field mice enter houses early then there will be a bad winter.
- Cows lying in field indicates rain.
- Bees staying near their hive indicates rain.
- Flies are more active before the rain.
- Geese fly low before the arrival of bad weather.
- Fish bite better before a rainfall.
- Campfire smoke stays near the ground before a storm and rises upon improving weather.
- Alders and cottonwood show the bottoms of their leaves before bad weather.
- Birds and bats fly at a lower level as the insects they eat stay closer to the ground before bad weather.
- Fish swim near the surface when rain is expected.
- At high temperature fish will stay in cooler, deeper water and will not bite.
- Spiders spin long webs on hot dry days but when wet weather is coming, the webs will be short or none at all.
- Woodpeckers will call before rain falls.
- Screeching owls announces rain.
- Rabbits will be out at unusual times before a storm.
- Toads and frogs moving towards water means rain.
- Dew on grass indicates there will be no rain as the dew (moisture) deposited out of the air onto the colder vegetation.
- Ring(s) around the moon means rain (the ring is due to high ice clouds). With the barometer falling at the same time the probability of being correct is 75%.
- Soft billowing cumulus clouds in the afternoon forecast fair weather (if they grow to cumulus nimbus in the late afternoon they indicate a fast and heavy rainstorm).
- Kelp: This seaweed is very sensitive to humidity. When the weather is fine it will be all shriveled up but if the humidity increases, and rain is coming, it will swell and feel damp. This seaweed has been used for centuries along the seashore to be a forecaster of the weather. Weather plays an important role in fishing villages as when the fishermen go to sea they can easily risk their lives if a storm blows up.

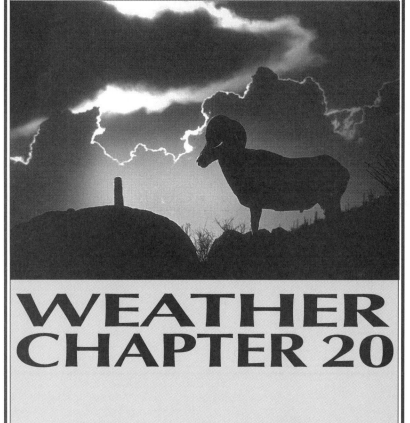

WEATHER CHAPTER 20

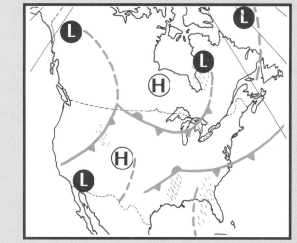

This chapter explains weather with the great outdoors in mind. In the wilderness you can see the horizon all around you, you see the movement of the different cloud formations, and you will gradually recognize cloud patterns, wind, animal movements, trees, insects which precede certain weather conditions. In the city you just see wisps of clouds between buildings and even then they might be hidden by the smog.

The origins of our weather are highlighted with illustrations and numerous photographs. These will help you "see" the weather around you.

LOCAL WEATHER

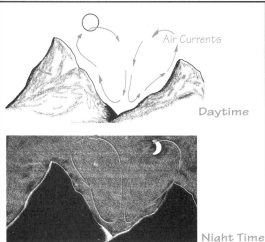

Daytime

Night Time

VALLEY BREEZE

In hilly areas the air flows up the slope in the daytime and down slopes at night. This happens because in the day the tops of the hills become warmer causing the air in the valley to rise. Hills cool off faster than the surrounding area at night and heavy cold air flows into the valleys.

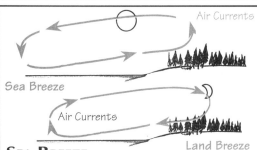

SEA BREEZE

Occurs in the daytime because air on the sea is cooler and heavier than the air on the land. The air on the land will rise and be replaced by the cooler air from the sea.

LAND BREEZE

At night the land cools off faster than the water. The warmer air on the water rises and the heavier cool air from the land flows onto the sea to replace the hot air that has risen. The land breeze is less intense than the sea breeze.

BANNER CLOUDS

Similar to Mountain Clouds but they occur over islands at sea. These clouds are also called standing clouds as they remain over the island. The cloud will dissipate once it has passed over the island but a new cloud is always forming. This special cloud is used by mariners to find land and is discussed in the *Water Travel Chapter*.

HIGH MOUNTAIN CLOUDS

These clouds are formed by the wind blowing across water and rising when moving over mountains. The humidity in the air condenses and forms mountain clouds. The loss of temperature is approximately 5 1/2°F (3°C) per 1000 feet (304 m). Rain has fallen on the windward side and the wind pushes over the hill and upon descending the slope the air will warm up and the relative humidity will become very dry as it has lost its humidity on the windward side. This phenomenon causes the Chinook of the North America plains, the Santa Ana of Southern California.

Chinook Cloud Strato Cumulus

TRAVELING STORMS IN MOUNTAINS

The most severe storms involve strong winds and heavy precipitation, are the result of widespread atmospheric disturbances which generally travel in an easterly direction.

Traveling storms result from the interaction of cold and warm air. The center of the storm is a moving low pressure area where cyclonic winds are generally the strongest. Extending from this storm center is a warm front which marks the advancing thrust of warm air, and the cold front which precedes the onrushing cold and gusty winds. The sequence of weather events, with the approach and passing of a traveling storm depends on the stage of the storm's development, and whether the location of its path is to the north or south of a given mountain area. Generally, scattered cirrus clouds merge into a continuous sheet which thickens and lowers gradually until it becomes altostratus. At high levels, this cloud layer appears to settle. Lower down, a Stratus deck may form overhead. A storm passing to the north may bring warm temperatures with southerly winds and partial clearing for a while before colder air with

Warm Front Arriving

Cold Air

thundershowers or squally conditions moves in from the northwest. However, local cloudiness often obscures frontal passages in the mountains. The storm may go so far to the north that only the cold front phenomena of heavy clouds, squalls, thundershowers, and colder weather are experienced. The same storm passing to the south would be accompanied by a gradual wind shift from northeasterly to northwesterly, with a steady temperature fall and continuous precipitation. After colder weather moves in, the clearing at high altitudes is usually slower than the onset of cloudiness, and storm conditions may last several days longer than in the lowlands.

MOUNTAIN WEATHER

Storm Clouds in Mountains

BAD WEATHER IN MOUNTAIN AREAS

Most of the bad weather experienced in mountain regions is a result of;

- **Local storms** in the form of thunderstorms with or without showers.
- **Traveling storms** which may be accompanied by radical and severe weather changes over a broad area. Usually, each type of storm may be identified by the clouds associated with it.
- **Seasonal moisture-bearing winds** of the monsoon type which bring consistently bad weather to some mountain ranges for weeks at a time.

Characteristics of Mountain Weather

Mountain weather is erratic. Hurricane force winds and gentle breezes may occur just short distances apart. The weather in exposed places contrast sharply with the weather in sheltered areas. Weather changes in a single day can be so variable that in the same locality one may experience hot sun and cool shade, high winds and calm, gusts of rain or snow, and then perhaps intense sunlight again. This variability results from the life cycle of a local storm or from the movement of traveling storms. In addition, the effects of storms are modified by the following local influences:

- Variation in altitude.
- Differences in exposure to the sun and to prevailing winds.
- Distortion of storm movements and the normal winds by irregular mountain topography. These local influences dominate summer storms.

Desert Mountain Storm

CLOUDINESS AND PRECIPITATION IN MOUNTAIN AREAS

Cloudiness and precipitation increase with height until a zone of maximum precipitation is reached; above this zone they decrease. Maximum cloudiness and precipitation occurs near the 5900 feet (1800 m) elevation in middle latitudes and at lower levels as the Poles are approached. Usually a dense forest marks the zone of maximum rainfall.

Slopes facing the prevailing wind are cloudier, foggier, and receive heavier precipitation than those protected from the wind, especially when large bodies of water lie to the windward side. However, at night and in winter, valleys are likely to be colder and foggier than higher slopes. Heads of valleys often have more clouds and precipitation than adjacent ridges and the valley floor.

Fog in Mountains

On windward slopes, persistent fog, as well as cloudiness and precipitation, frequently can last for days. They are caused by the local barrier effect of the mountain on prevailing winds. Any cloud bank appears as a fog from within. Fog limits visibility and causes whiteout conditions.

MOUNTAIN WEATHER INDICATORS

Approaching Traveling Storms

- A thin veil of cirrus clouds spreads over the sky, thickening and lowering until altostratus clouds are formed. The same trend is shown at night when a halo forms around the moon and then darkens until only the glow of the moon is visible. When there is no moon, cirrus clouds only dim the stars while altostratus clouds hide them completely.
- Low clouds which have been persistent on lower slopes begin to rise at the time upper clouds appear.
- Various layers of clouds move in at different heights and become more abundant.
- Lens-shaped clouds accompanying strong winds lose their streamlined shape and other cloud types appear in increasing amounts.
- A change in the direction of the wind is accompanied by a rapid rise in temperature not caused by solar radiation. This may also indicate a warm damp period.
- A light green haze is observed shortly after sunrise in mountain regions above timberline.

Local Disturbances

Indications of local thunderstorm showers, or squally weather are:

- An increase in size and rapid thickening of scattered cumulus clouds during the afternoon.
- The approach of a line of large cumulus or cumulonimbus clouds with an advance guard of altocumulus clouds. At night, increasing lightning windward of the prevailing wind gives the same warning.
- Massive cumulus clouds hanging over a ridge or summit at night or in the daytime.

Strong Winds

Indications of strong winds seen at a distance may be:

- Plumes of blowing snow from the crests of ridges and peaks or ragged shreds of cloud moving rapidly.
- Persistent lens-shaped clouds, or a band of clouds, over high peaks and ridges or downwind from them.
- A turbulent and ragged banner cloud which hangs to the lee side of a peak.

Fair Weather

Fair weather may be associated with:

- A cloudless sky and shallow fog or layers of smoke or haze at valley bottoms in the early morning; or from a vantage point of high elevation, a cloudless sky that is quite blue down to the horizon or down to where a level haze layer forms a secondary horizon.
- Conditions under which small cumulus clouds appearing in the forenoon do not increase, but decrease or vanish during the day.
- Clear skies, except for a low cloud deck which does not rise or thicken during the day.

During Precipitation

When there is precipitation and the sky cannot be seen:

- Very small snowflakes or ice crystals indicate that the clouds above are thin and there is fair weather at high altitudes.
- A steady fall of snowflakes or raindrops indicates that the precipitation has begun at high levels and that bad weather is likely to be encountered on ridges and peaks.

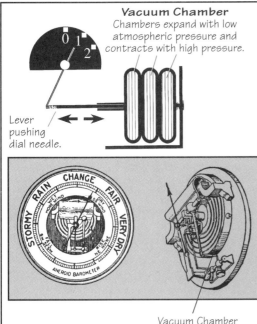

Vacuum Chamber
Chambers expand with low atmospheric pressure and contracts with high pressure.

Lever pushing dial needle.

ANEROID BAROMETER

Vacuum Chamber

BAROMETRIC PRESSURE

BAROMETER

The barometer was invented by Torricelli (1608-1647) a pupil of Galileo. He said that we live submerged in the bottom of an ocean of air which, by experiment, undoubtedly has weight and is the most dense near the surface of the earth. This led to mercury barometers being developed to measure air pressure and make rudimentary projections of weather.

ANEROID BAROMETER

Is a barometer which contains no liquid. It has a small metal container from which most of the air has been removed. The rise and fall of the atmospheric pressure causes the metal container to contract and expand. The surface movement is amplified and transmitted by gears to a pointer that indicates the pressure in millibars or inches. Aneroid barometers are not as accurate as mercury barometers but can be adjusted by a set screw and an elevation indicator.

BAROMETRIC PRESSURE

At sea level, the air pressure is 14 pounds per square inch. This is equal to the weight of a column of mercury, 29.92 inches or 760 mm of height. Barometers indicate the air pressure in inches or millibars of mercury. Weather stations use the unit millibars and 29.92 inches of mercury is equal to 1,013.2 millibars. Each 3.4 millibars of fluctuation is equal to 1/10 of an inch of mercury.

WEATHER PREDICTING WITH A BAROMETER

Pressure measured as a scale of inches of mercury.

Barometric Pressure (in)*	Movement	Wind Direction	Weather Forecast
29.80 or less	rapid fall	N to E	"Nor'easter" gale due in hours. Snow or heavy rain continuing.
29.80 or less	rapid fall	E to S	Severe storm due in hours, then clearing.
29.80 or less	rapid rise	Moving to W	Storm ending, clearing and colder
30.00 or less	rapid fall	NE to SE	Rain with high winds, then clearing within 35 hours.
30.00 or less	slow fall	NE to SE	Rain continuing.
30.00 or less	slow rise	SW to S	Clearing within hours, followed by long term fair weather.
30.10 or more	rapid fall	NE to E	Rain or snow in 12 to 14 hours.
30.10 or more	slow fall	NE to E	Rain in 2 to 4 days or in winter snow within 24 hours.
30.10-30.20	rapid fall	NE to SE	Rain in 12 hours with wind.
30.10-30.20	rapid fall	SE to S	Rain in 12 hours with wind.
30.10-30.20	slow fall	SE to S	Rain in 24 hours.
30.10-30.20	rapid rise	NW to SW	Fair with rain in 48 hours.
30.10-30.20	steady	NW to SW	Fair for 24 to 48 hours.
30.20 or more	slow fall	NW to SW	Fair and warmer for 48 hours.
30.20 or more	steady	NW to SW	Fair weather.

*reduced to sea level.

Weather Forecasting
The use of the portable aneroid barometer, thermometer, and hygrometer can be of great assistance in making local weather forecasts.

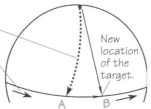

CORIOLIS EFFECT

Trajectory of the bullet relative to the earth.

Rotation of Earth

New location of the target.

A   B

The earth rotates and the atmosphere which moves with the earth is affected by this rotation. The movement of an object relative to a rotating surface is called the Coriolis Effect.

An example is in the diagram. The Coriolis Effect causes the large movements of air which will bring tomorrow's weather.

If a gun is shot at a target on the equator 'A'. While the bullet is in flight the earth keeps on rotating and the bullet will hit 'A' but by this time the target will have rotated to 'B'.

DIRECTION OF STORMS

Low: The wind blowing at your face the Low will be to your right. This is the direction of the upcoming storm.

High: The wind blowing from *behind* you in the northern hemisphere. Rotate your body by 45° right. The high pressure area will be to your right and low pressure area to your left.

AIR MASSES

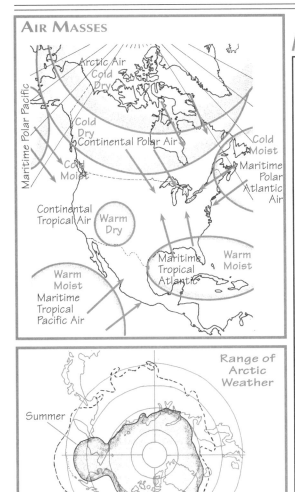

Range of Arctic Weather

Summer

Winter

AIR MASSES OF NORTH AMERICA

AIR MASSES

This is the movement of large bodies of air, in the atmosphere, which cause the changes in our weather. In North America we have seven air masses that are continually pushing each other for predominance in their area of action.

Arctic

Very cold and dry air. It is too cold to retain much humidity. This air mass occupies the northern parts of Alaska and northern Canada. It creates the cold winters in Canada with temperatures down to -60° F (-50° C) and with a very high windchill factor caused by the blowing wind.

Continental Polar (cP)

This cold air mass can penetrate into the United States especially in the winter when it will stay for a week at a time. This mass develops the snow storms off the Great Lakes.

Maritime Polar Pacific (mP)

This air comes from Siberia and collects moisture over the Pacific. The moisture is dropped, because of the mountains, as rain or snow over the Pacific Coast west of the Rocky Mountains right down to California.

Maritime Polar Atlantic

This comes from the Northern Atlantic Ocean and brings devastating snow storms to Newfoundland and Nova Scotia. In the early summer it brings the banks of fog over the Grand Banks and the "east wind" of New England.

Maritime Tropical Atlantic (mT)

This air mass originates in the Gulf of Mexico and adjacent Atlantic Ocean. It is hot and moving north over the ocean makes it is very humid. It causes steady showers that can reach southern Canada and up to the Rocky Mountains. The heavy snowfalls, in the winter, in Nova Scotia and along the United States Atlantic coast are caused by this air mass when it meets the Arctic air.

Maritime Tropical Pacific (mT)

This mass originates in the equatorial Pacific. It causes the heavy rainfalls in California and the southwestern states.

Continental Tropic (cT)

This is the very dry air originating in the desert southwest of the United States. This air is very hot and causes the drought conditions across the plains.

MAJOR NORTH AMERICAN AIR MASSES

Air mass	Typical Weather	Origin
Marine Tropical	Cloudy with rain or drizzle. Fog.	Pacific high on west coast.
Marine Polar (Marine Arctic)	Showers and bright periods. Good visibility.	Polar high.
Returning Marine Polar	Cool but fair, good visibility.	Same as Marine Polar but changed by ocean passage.
Continental Polar	Intense cold can also have cloudy sky in winter.	North Canadian (Arctic) high.
Continental Tropic	Very warm and usually cloudless.	Southern USA.

CLASSIFICATION OF CLOUDS

	High Clouds	Middle Clouds	Low Clouds	Vertical Clouds
Group	16,500 feet to 45,000 feet 5-13 km	6,500 feet to 25,000 feet 2-8 km	surface fog to 6,500 feet 0-2 km	1,600 feet and up 488 m
Cloud Type	Cirrus (Cu) Cirrostratus (Cist) Cirrocumulus (Cicu)	Altostratus (Ast) Altocumulus (Acu) Altocumulus (Acu)	Stratus (St) Nimbostratus (Nbst) Stratocumulus (Stcu)	Cumulus (Cu) Heavy Cumulus Cumulonimbus (Cunb)

MOVEMENT OF AIR MASSES

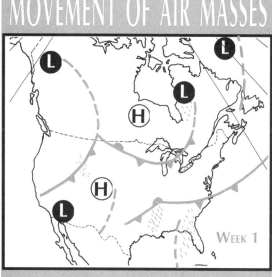

WEEK 1

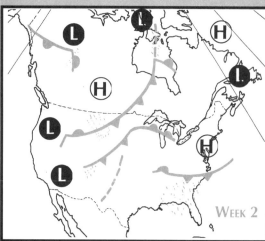

WEEK 2

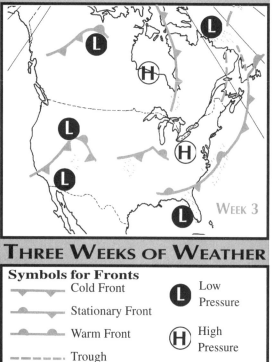

WEEK 3

THREE WEEKS OF WEATHER

Symbols for Fronts

▽▽ Cold Front	**L** Low Pressure
⌒⌒ Stationary Front	
⌒⌒ Warm Front	**H** High Pressure
- - - - Trough	

TYPES OF WEATHER FRONTS

Cold Front

Cold air is denser and heavier than warm air. The warm air is pushed upward.

Warm Front

A warm front is warm air moving towards a cold air mass. It will squeeze the cold air mass away from the area at the surface. This occurs when the warm air mass is *stronger* than the cold air front.

Stationary Front

This occurs when two touching air masses do not move.

Occluded Front

Occurs when a cold front rapidly overtakes a warm front and meets another cold or cool front. This causes the warm air to be lifted or 'pinched' by the two cooler fronts. There are three types of occluded fronts:

Cold Occluded: Precipitation falls close to and behind the front

Warm Occluded: Produces precipitation ahead of the front

Neutral: Precipitation falls along the front line

MOVEMENT OF FRONTS

Fronts can move 30 to 50 miles per hour (48-80 km/h).

Frontal Slope

Cold air mass displacing a warm mass

The cold air mass slides *under* the warm mass which is pushed *upward*. The cold air mass has a downward slope.

Warm mass displacing a cold mass

The slope is upward when the warmer air pushes on a colder air mass.

Two major air masses in North America

• Polar

• Tropical

Forecasting the Weather

Clouds can give us visible signs of upcoming weather as they show the change of wind patterns, amount of humidity in the atmosphere, and arrival of cold or warm fronts.

FORECASTING THE WEATHER WITH WARM AND COLD FRONTS

Advancing Warm Front

	Before Arrival	During Passage	After Passage
Pressure	Falls steadily.	Fall stops.	Little or no change.
Wind	Backs and increases.	Veer and decreases.	Remains steady in direction.
Temperature	Slow rise.	Rise continues.	Little change.
Cloud	Cirrus well ahead, then lower cloud.	Low cloud, mainly nimbus.	Higher clouds, Stratus or stratocumulus.
Weather	Continuous rain or snow as front is approached.	Rain or snow stops.	Fair, with some drizzle or intermittent showers.
Visibility	Good before the rain	Poor	Poor (mist or fog rising from the wet ground).

Advancing Cold Front

	Before Arrival	During Passage	After Passage
Pressure	Falls	Rises rapidly.	Rises slowly.
Wind	Backs and increases, becoming squally.	Sudden veer, often with heavy squall.	Backs a little, then steady and veers in later squalls.
Temperature	Fairly steady	Sudden fall.	Little change.
Cloud	Patchy, then continuous; heavy towering cloud near front.	Low dense cloud.	Cloud lifts rapidly.
Weather	Rain and perhaps thunder.	Heavy rain, perhaps thunder and hail.	Heavy rain for short period, fine with occasional showers.
Visibility	Poor	Poor	Good

ADVANCING COLD FRONT

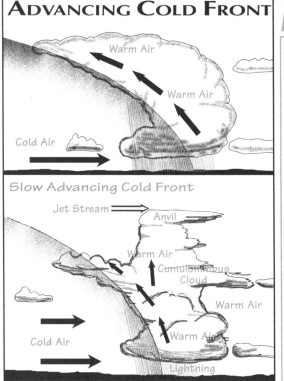

Warm Air

Warm Air

Cold Air

Slow Advancing Cold Front

Jet Stream

Anvil

Warm Air

Cumulonimbus Cloud

Warm Air

Cold Air

Warm Air

Lightning

Rapidly Advancing Cold Front

WEATHER AT COLD FRONT

Cold air is heavier than warm air so the advancing cold air wedges *under* the warm air. This lifting of the warm air causes it to cool and if there is a high humidity content, precipitation. The weather that can be expected from this encounter depends upon the speed of the cold front and the moisture content of the warm air. *The cold front will only affect a the narrow line of encounter with the warm air causing brief heavy precipitation ranging from showers, squalls, to thundershowers.*

Rapidly Advancing Cold Front: If the cold front arrives very fast the angle of the wedge is usually steeper therefore rapidly raising the warm air and causing thunderstorms and violent winds.

Slowly Advancing Cold Front: The slow advance will result in a lower angled wedge causing the warm air not to raise as fast and the resulting rain will not be as severe but might last longer.

MOVING AIR MASSES

ADVANCING WARM FRONT

WEATHER AT A WARM FRONT

Warm air is lighter than cold air so that when a warm front advances it will run *onto* the cold air and the wedge will be in the opposite direction than that of a cold front. Warm fronts contain more water vapor than cold air. Warm frontal changes are usually less abrupt than cold front changes. *A warm front overrunning (rising over the cooler air) will bring clouds that thicken and gradually come lower. There will be steady precipitation.* Warm fronts at one time will affect thousands of square miles of land. Cold fronts will *only* have dramatic effects on the line of encounter with the warm area. A sudden shift (a veer) of the wind will occur with the arrival of a warm front. The wind changing from cold to warm air. The change of the wind with the arrival of a cold front is more gradual.

Moist and Stable Warm Front Overrunning Cold Air

A warm front rolling over a retreating cold mass of air. The warm air rising will cause precipitation and where some warm air mixes with the cold air clouds will form in the cold air.

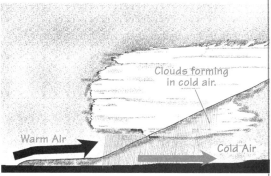

Clouds forming in cold air.

Warm Air

Cold Air

Moist and Stable Warm Front Overrunning Cold Air

Moist and Unstable Warm Front Overrunning Cold Air

The warm front being unstable will cause cumulonimbus clouds to form with very heavy precipitation under the cloud. The rain from the cumulonimbus cloud can be heavy and brief at a specific location but the rain from the front will last for some time.

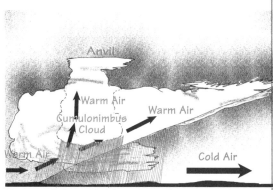

Anvil

Warm Air

Warm Air

Cumulonimbus Cloud

Warm Air

Cold Air

Moist and Unstable Warm Front Overrunning Cold Air

CLOUDS THAT PREDICT RAIN

Cloud Type	Form of Precipitation
Stratus and Stratocumulus	Drizzle, freezing drizzle, snow grains
Thick Altostratus and Nimbostratus	Snow (continuous), rain (continuous)
Thick Altostratus and Stratocumulus	Snow (intermittent), rain (intermittent)
Altocumulus, Heavy Cumulus, Cumulonimbus	Snow showers, rain showers
Cumulonimbus	Snow pellets and/or hail, showers of ice pellets
Any cloud that will give rain,	Hail
(Non-showery precipitation in the form of hail is usually the result of the rain drops freezing)	
No Cloud Necessary	Ice prisms deposits at night on cold surfaces

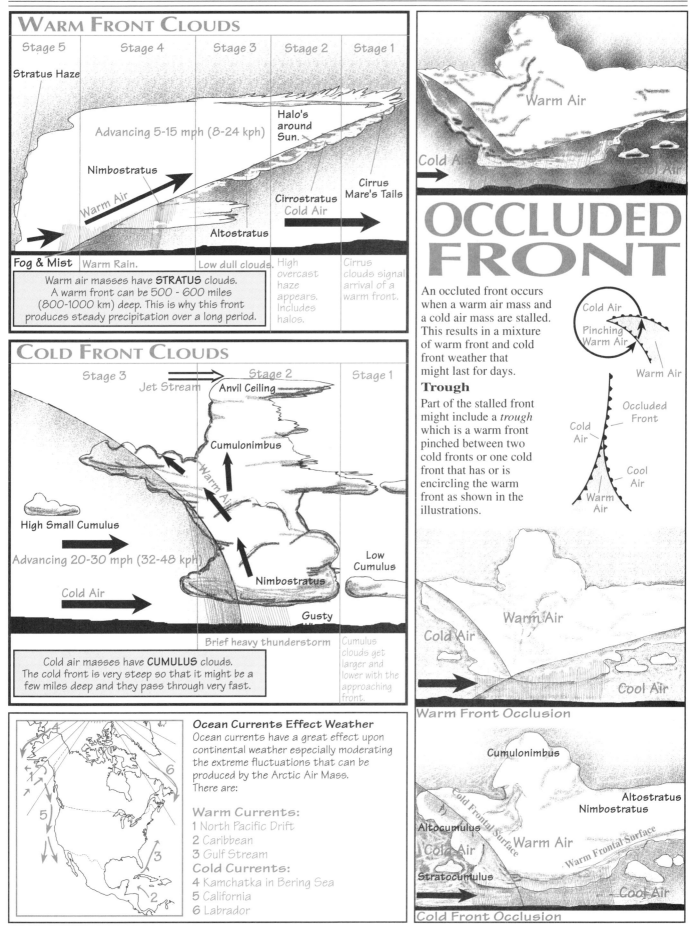

WARM FRONT CLOUDS

Stage 5	Stage 4	Stage 3	Stage 2	Stage 1

Stratus Haze

Advancing 5-15 mph (8-24 kph)

Nimbostratus

Warm Air

Halo's around Sun.

Cirrostratus

Cold Air

Cirrus Mare's Tails

Altostratus

Fog & Mist	Warm Rain.	Low dull clouds.	High overcast haze appears. Includes halos.	Cirrus clouds signal arrival of a warm front.

Warm air masses have **STRATUS** clouds.
A warm front can be 500 - 600 miles
(800-1000 km) deep. This is why this front
produces steady precipitation over a long period.

COLD FRONT CLOUDS

Stage 3	Stage 2	Stage 1

Jet Stream

Anvil Ceiling

Cumulonimbus

Warm Air

High Small Cumulus

Advancing 20-30 mph (32-48 kph)

Cold Air

Nimbostratus

Low Cumulus

Gusty

	Brief heavy thunderstorm	Cumulus clouds get larger and lower with the approaching front.

Cold air masses have **CUMULUS** clouds.
The cold front is very steep so that it might be a
few miles deep and they pass through very fast.

Ocean Currents Effect Weather
Ocean currents have a great effect upon
continental weather especially moderating
the extreme fluctuations that can be
produced by the Arctic Air Mass.
There are:

Warm Currents:
1 North Pacific Drift
2 Caribbean
3 Gulf Stream
Cold Currents:
4 Kamchatka in Bering Sea
5 California
6 Labrador

OCCLUDED FRONT

An occluted front occurs
when a warm air mass and
a cold air mass are stalled.
This results in a mixture
of warm front and cold
front weather that
might last for days.

Trough

Part of the stalled front
might include a *trough*
which is a warm front
pinched between two
cold fronts or one cold
front that has or is
encircling the warm
front as shown in the
illustrations.

Warm Air

Cold Air

Cold Air

Pinching Warm Air

Warm Air

Occluded Front

Cool Air

Warm Air

Warm Air

Cold Air

Cool Air

Warm Front Occlusion

Cumulonimbus

Altostratus
Nimbostratus

Altocumulus

Cold Frontal Surface

Warm Air

Warm Frontal Surface

Cold Air

Stratocumulus

Cool Air

Cold Front Occlusion

Cumulonimbus anvil above clouds. Photograph taken from an airplane.

Cirrus

Cirrocumulus

Cirrostratus

Stratocumulus

Cumulus

Anvil Formation

Cirrus
8000

Cirrocumulus
7000

6000

Cirrostratus
5000

Altocumulus
4000

Stratocumulus
3000

2000

Cumulonimbus

Cumulus
1000

500

0 Meters

Cumulonimbus Forming

Cumulus with Altocumulus in the background.

CLOUD TYPES

HIGH CLOUDS 16,500 - 45,000 FT (5-13 KM)

Cirrus (Ci)

Composed of: Ice particles or crystals.

Shape: Slightly dense veil from which narrow bands of tenuous filaments emerge which produce hooks and banner like forms.

Nickname: "Mares' Tails"

These clouds are traveling at 100 mph (160 km/h).

Weather Prediction: There is a strong cyclonic weather system upwind and there might be strong winds within the next 8-15 hours especially at sea in the winter. Temperature will become cooler and if windy it can become bitter in winter.

Cirrus

Cirrocumulus (Cc)

Composed of: Small ice crystals super cooled water or mixture of both.

Shape: High sheets of white balls or puffs with distinct outlines having a rippled regular appearance.

Nickname: "Mackerel Sky"

They can be confused with altocumulus which are at a lower elevation.

Cirrocumulus

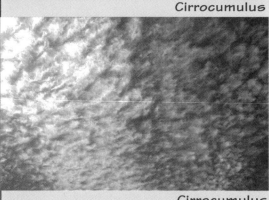

Cirrocumulus

Cirrostratus

Cirrostratus

Cirrostratus (Cs)

Composed of: Ice crystals

Shape: High, thin, whitish, smooth and transparent. Can be seen by the halos they form around the sun or moon. These halos are caused by the reflection of light in ice crystals.

CLOUDS AND WEATHER

High Altitude

(Cirrus, Cirrostratus, Cirrocumulus)

Cloud: High Cirrus

Indicates:	Fair weather.
Followed by:	Cirrostratus.
Indicates:	Rain within 18 to 36 hours.

Cloud: Lower Cirrus known as mare's hair

Indicates:	Bad weather.
Followed by:	Cirrostratus.
Indicates:	80% chance of rain next 24 hours.
Followed by:	Altostratus.
Indicates:	Rain or snow in 6 to 12 hours.

Cloud: Cirrocumulus

Indicates:	Fair weather.

Middle Altitude Clouds

(Altostratus and Altocumulus)

Cloud: Cirrus or Cirrostratus

Then:	Altostratus.
Indicates:	90% rain in 6 to 12 hours.

Cloud: Altostratus (low)

Followed by:	Towering Cumulus.
Indicates:	Rain.

Low Altitude

(Stratocumulus, Stratus, Nimbostratus)

Cloud: Stratocumulus

Indicates:	In winter short rain or snow.

Cloud: Stratocumulus

Indicates:	Clearing in evening and cooler.

Cloud: Stratus

Indicates:	Drizzle.

Cloud: Nimbostratus

Indicates:	Long steady snow or rain.

Towering Cloud

Cloud: Cumulus (warm weather)

Indicates:	High possibility of forming of cumulonimbus clouds.
Weather:	Heavy thunder showers.

MIDDLE CLOUDS 6,500 - 25,000 FT (2-8 KM)

Altocumulus (Ac)

Composed of: Small water droplets that can be super cooled.

Shape: They are *level* heap clouds that can be in a checkerboard pattern of white and gray layers seldom covering the whole sky. They can be lenticular (lens-shaped) and castellanus (looking like small towers) and floccus (chaotic clouds of thunder skies).

Nickname: "Mackerel Sky" (see Cirrocumulus)

Altostratus (As)

Composed of: Super cooled water droplets and ice crystals.

Shape: Gray or bluish cloud cover, thin and smooth that might blanket the whole sky. They look dark and opaque when the sun or moon tries to shine through.

Nickname: "A watery sun".

Weather: Can produce a *light continuous* precipitation.

Nimbostratus (Ns)

Composed of: Suspended water droplets (which are sometimes super cooled) and by falling raindrops or snow flakes.

Shape: Dark gray in color and cover a large area across the sky. They are very thick and blot out the sun. A lower layer of clouds can form below them called 'facto cumulus' clouds. These clouds are formed by the heavy precipitation of Nimbostratus.

Weather: These clouds are not always seen due to the continuous precipitation they produce. Nimbostratus rarely produce lightning, thunder, or hail. They can be confused as a thick altostratus.

Cumulus with Altocumulus behind.

Altostratus

Nimbostratus

LOW CLOUDS 0-6,500 FT (0-2 KM)

Stratocumulus (Sc)

Composed of: Small water droplets, sometimes including large ones, soft hail and rarely snow flakes.

Shape: Gray or whitish and are rounded heap rolls broken or covering the sky.

Weather: These clouds usually indicate that there is no change in weather. Wind is normally light to moderate and can gradually shift direction.

Stratus (St)

Composed of: Minute water droplets and if temperatures are low ice crystals.

Shape: Gray with a uniform structureless base. A low hanging cloud that covers coasts or hills. Stratus clouds are similar to altostratus, but much lower.

Weather: Precipitation is not usually associated with this cloud as it comes into existence by the lifting of lower layers of a fog bank. This may happen in a fog layer in which the bottom portion has evaporated, or where up-slope winds are blowing. These up-slope winds will cause the humidity in the air to condense forming stratus clouds. This often occurs as standing or banner clouds over islands in the ocean. Another form is called the 'stratus fractus' which brings unpleasant weather.

Strato-cumulus and rain

Strato-cumulus

Stratus

TOWERING CLOUDS

Cumulus (Cu)

Composed of: Close packed, small water droplets usually super cooled. Larger droplets usually fall from the base of the cumulus cloud as rain. Ice crystals can form in the upper parts of a large cumulus cloud.

Shape: The cumulus clouds are formed by the vertical movement of air currents. They are dense in appearance and have a clearly defined outline (with the exception of the cumulus-strato cumulus combination). These clouds form over land in the afternoon and over water at night.

Cumulonimbus (Cb)

Composed of: In upper portion of ice crystals and super cooled water droplets.

Shape: This is a billowing cloud of great height rising up to the high cloud range. The upper portion of this cloud is frequently classed as a cirrus variety because of their great height.

The high portion nearly always assumes a distinctive *anvil shape* which is caused by the strong horizontal winds (jet stream) that flatten the towering rounded heads.

This cloud causes lightening, thunder and often torrential rain and hail.

Weather: These clouds are summer clouds producing violent thunderstorms and possibly tornadoes.

Cumulus that can build up into a cumulonimbus in the late afternoon

Anvil Head

Cumulus

Anvil Head on Cumulonimbus Above Clouds US Weather Service

Cumulonimbus With falling Rain

CUMULONIMBUS CLOUD BUILD-UP

This sequence of photographs was taken in the afternoon in a time lapse of 20 minutes. The rapid growth of a cumulonimbus cloud can be seen with the beginning of the anvil head.

Cumulonimbus Clouds From Below

BEAUFORT SCALE

Sir Francis Beaufort (1774-1857)
Developed the Beaufort Wind Scale.

BEAUFORT SEA WIND SCALE

Beaufort Scale	Descriptive Term	Speed mph	Appearance of the Sea
0	Calm	-	Like a mirror (no ripples).
1	Light air	1-3	Ripples with the appearance of scales; no foam crests.
2	Light breeze	4-7	Small wavelets; crests of glassy appearance, no breaking waves.
3	Gentle breeze	8-12	Large wavelets; crests begin to break; scattered whitecaps.
4	Moderate breeze	13-18	Small waves that are becoming longer; numerous whitecaps.
5	Fresh breeze	19-24	Moderate waves, longer form; many whitecaps; some spray.
6	Strong breeze	25-31	Large waves beginning to form; whitecaps everywhere; more spray.
7	Near gale	32-38	Sea forms heaps. White foam from breaking waves begins to be blown in streaks.
8	Gale	39-46	Moderately high waves of greater length; edges of crests begin to break into spin drift; foam is blown in well-marked streaks.
9	Strong gale	47-54	High waves; dense streaks of foam and sea begins to roll; spray may affect visibility.
10	Storm	55-63	Very high waves with overhanging crests; foam is blown in dense white streaks, sea appears white; rolling of the sea becomes heavy; visibility reduced.
11	Violent storm	64-72	Exceptionally high waves (small and medium-sized ships might temporarily lost to view in the troughs of the waves); the sea is covered with white patches of foam; everywhere the edges of the wave crests are blown into froth; visibility further reduced.
12	Hurricane	73-82	The air is filled with foam and spray; sea completely white with driving spray; visibility greatly reduced.

BEAUFORT LAND WIND SCALE

Speed mph	Beaufort Scale	Air Movement	Indicators
0-1	0	Calm	Smoke and steam rises vertically.
2-3	1	Light air	Wind affects direction of smoke but not waves.
4-7	2	Slight breeze	You feel wind on face, leaves rustle, fresh snow swirls in eddies.
8-12	3	Gentle breeze	Leaves and twigs move continuously. Flags fly.
13-18	4	Moderate breeze	Small branches move continuously, dust and snow stirs.
19-24	5	Fresh breeze	Small deciduous trees sway, tents flap.
25-31	6	Strong breeze	Large branches wave, whitecaps on most waves. Difficult to use umbrella
32-38	7	Moderate gale	Whole large trees sway. Difficult to walk.
39-46	8	Fresh gale	Twigs break off trees, you lean into the wind in order to walk.
47-54	9	Strong gale	Whole branches break off, high waves. Slight damage to roofs.
55-63	10	Full gale	Poorly rooted trees topple, branches fly.
64-75	11	Storm	Extensive wind damage of all types can occur.
75+	12	Hurricane	Devastation.

TABLE OF RELATIVE HUMIDITY

System for measuring the moisture content of air.

Difference Between Wet-bulb	Temperature of Air, Dry-Bulb Thermometer and Dry-Bulb Readings							
	30°F	40°F	50°F	60°F	70°F	80°F	90°F	100°F
1	90	92	93	94	95	96	96	97
2	79	84	87	89	90	92	92	93
3	68	76	80	84	86	87	88	90
4	58	68	74	78	81	83	85	86
6	38	52	61	68	72	75	78	80
8	18	37	49	58	64	68	71	71
10		22	37	48	55	61	65	68
12		8	26	39	48	54	59	62
14			16	30	40	47	53	57
16			5	21	33	41	47	51
18				13	26	35	41	47
20				5	19	29	36	42
22					12	23	32	37
24					6	18	26	33

Dry Bulb

Wet Bulb

WINDS

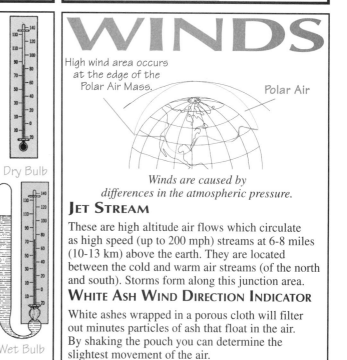

High wind area occurs at the edge of the Polar Air Mass.

Polar Air

Winds are caused by differences in the atmospheric pressure.

JET STREAM

These are high altitude air flows which circulate as high speed (up to 200 mph) streams at 6-8 miles (10-13 km) above the earth. They are located between the cold and warm air streams (of the north and south). Storms form along this junction area.

WHITE ASH WIND DIRECTION INDICATOR

White ashes wrapped in a porous cloth will filter out minutes particles of ash that float in the air. By shaking the pouch you can determine the slightest movement of the air.

HURRICANES & TORNADOES

Tornadoes frequently happen in conjunction with cold front thunderstorms. Before a tornado arrives the air become a very still and very turbulent clouds form.

TORNADOES (TWISTERS)

Tornadoes are considered as the most vicious type of storm and their life span is a few minutes or even seconds. They are common in the Great Plains region of North America. Tornadoes have a very low barometric pressure at their center. This causes buildings to explode because of the higher inside pressure.

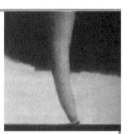

Windows and doors in tornado areas should be left slightly ajar on the lee side of buildings so that the internal pressure has time to equalize with the outside pressure so as to avoid the possible explosive force of the pressure differential.

The winds of a tornado are very strong and blowing in a counter clockwise direction of up to 500 miles (800 km) per hour. These winds cause a terrifying roar. Tornadoes over water are called water spouts.

Dark clump of cloud hanging down can be start of next tornado.

Lightning

Funnel 2000 Feet (600 m) High

Path about 275 Feet (83 m) Wide

Emergency measures when a tornado seems imminent:

• Seek shelter in a brick or cement building.

• Tornadoes usually travel in a S-W to N-E direction. The corner of a basement that will be first reached by a twister should be used for shelter. Any debris will be carried away from the people in the basement. Cover yourself with a mattress for protection from falling objects.

Hurricane's Eye

Direction of the Wind

HURRICANES

Hurricanes originate over tropical ocean areas and they usually are accompanied by torrential rain, giant waves and high tides. The winds blow counterclockwise around a calm area called the "eye". Wind velocity is over 74 mph (119 km/h) and the maximum speed is between 100 to 150 mph (160-240 km/h). Some powerful hurricanes can have speeds up to 300 mph (500 kph). A hurricane can travel several thousand miles before dissipating. The life span being a few hours to a month. Hurricanes usually occur between June and November. There are approximately 80 hurricanes per year in the world and they kill 15,000 people. Most North American hurricanes develop in the tropic Atlantic within 20° of the equator.

Early Indicators:

• Wind blows from an unusual direction.

• Appearance of high cirrus clouds also known as "mare's tails".

• On the sea there will be high waves and swells from an abnormal direction. These swells might give a few days of warning.

• Wave frequency will change from a 4-6 second cycle to a 10-12 second cycle.

• Barometer will drop for 12 hours or less *before* the storm.

If you receive a hurricane warning:

• Evacuate low lying areas that might be flooded by torrential rains.

• Board up windows *but leave some partly open on the leeward side* of the winds to let the atmospheric pressure equalize.

• Store any loose items as tools, trash cans, lawnmowers, etc.

• Assemble a supply of emergency food, drinking water in closed plastic bottles, batteries for radios and lights, candles, and a first aid kit. Also know where you can obtain a hydraulic jack in case there are fallen timbers.

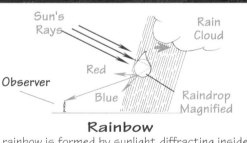

Sun's Rays

Rain Cloud

Red

Observer

Blue

Raindrop Magnified

Rainbow

A rainbow is formed by sunlight diffracting inside individual raindrops. This usually happens when a summer storm rapidly passes through an area and then the sun reemerges. The upper side of a rainbow is red and the lower side is blue-violet. Raindrops only have a diameter of 0.05 inch.

THUNDERSTORM

TYPES OF THUNDERSTORMS

Warm Front Thunderstorm

Usually takes place when warm moist air overruns a retreating mass of cold air. The warm air becomes very unstable.

Cold Front Thunderstorm

This occurs in the warm air near the frontal zone where cold air is pushing against the warmer air. This type of storm usually occurs in the afternoon, in the summer, and is more violent than a warm front thunderstorm.

Air Mass Thunderstorms

These storms are formed *within* a warm moist air mass and are scattered over a large area.

Convective Thunderstorm

In temperate zone during the summer months. They develop over land and water during the afternoon hours when cool, moist air from the water is heated as it travels towards the warmer land surfaces. They can form over the water at night as cool land air moves out over the warmer water, then rises to form clouds. Convective thunderstorms usually start as cumulus clouds which are fed by rising currents of warm air to become large menacing thunderheads.

Orographic Thunderstorm

This occurs when unstable air is forced upwards by an obstacle as a mountain barrier. These storms can form quickly and spread over a large area. They can stay stationary on the windward side, and rumble for hours. These storms are a major threat to mountain climbers. *See Mountain Travel.*

Nocturnal Thunderstorms

These occur late at night or in the early morning usually at the end of spring and in the summer. They are common on the Central Plains from the Mississippi westward.

THUNDERSTORMS

The presence of a thunderstorm is shown by a thick column(s) of dark, fleecy cumulus clouds that rise to the height of twenty thousand feet or more. You will see:

- Wisps of cloud that swirl both up and down. These show the powerful wind currents that are present.
- A flattened top of the cloud projects horizontally, in one direction, in the shape of a blacksmith's **anvil**. This flattened top occurs because the top of this massive cloud is being moved by the jet stream.

Although individual thunderstorms are normally local in nature and usually are of short duration, they can be part of a large weather system. In the alpine zone above timberline, thunderstorms may be accompanied by freezing precipitation and sudden squally winds. Ridges and peaks become focal points of concentrated electrical activity which is highly dangerous.

Thunderstorms occurring at night or in the early morning are associated with *major changes* in the weather conditions, which often results in a long period of foul weather before clearing on high mountain summits. Thunderstorms occurring at these times may also be part of a general storm front and are followed by a prolonged period of cool, dry weather.

Local Thunderstorms

Local thunderstorms develop from rising air columns resulting from the intense heating by the sun of a relatively small area. They occur most frequently in the middle or late afternoon. Scattered fair weather clouds (cumulus) often appear harmless, but when they continue to grow larger and reach a vertical depth of several thousand feet they may rapidly turn into thunderstorms.

Hail

Hail is only found in thunderstorm conditions. It consists of opaque pellets of ice that can reach the size of tennis balls. Hail storms are most frequent and violent in spring and early summer.
A local thunderstorm may drop a million tons of water as rain and hail in half an hour.

LIGHTNING

There is not definitive answer as to why an electrical charge is accumulated in cumulonimbus clouds. One theory is that as the raindrops fall they produce a positive charge (+) at the top of the cloud and a negative charge (-) at the bottom of the cloud.

Lightning flashes between the upper and lower layers of the cloud and also between the lower layer and the ground.

LIGHTNING BACKGROUNDER

- Lightning flashes can reach 50,000°F (27,760°C) Five times hotter than the sun.
- Thunder is the concussion produced by the sudden local expansion of the air, caused by the high heat of the electrical spark.
- A lightning flash lasts 1/1000 of a second.
- Trees can be blown up by a lightning strike. Heat of the lightning strike generates steam in the tree and the steam pressure causes it to blow up.
- A lightning bolt can be several miles long and travels up to 60,000 miles (100,000 km) per second.
- Lightning strikes earth several thousand times every minute.
- Aircraft are hit by lightning with no visible effect.
- There are more than 15 million thunderstorms a year around the world. In Florida and New Orleans, there are around 70 storms a year. Florida can have 13 lightning strikes per square kilometer per year.

LIGHTNING KILLS

During a lightning storm you can be killed by:

- The direct impact of a lightning bolt from above.
- Be electrocuted by being adjacent to an item that is struck.
- Be killed or injured by being on the current path.

Cloud to Cloud Lightning

Can be dangerous to hang gliders or glider pilots.

Cloud to Ground Lightning

Are fatal 30% of time if struck by a bolt.

Ground to Cloud Lightning

This is extremely hot as you are close to the source, the ground. If you are in its path (in effect at the origin of the strike) you're cooked!! *Nearly always fatal.*

US Weather Service

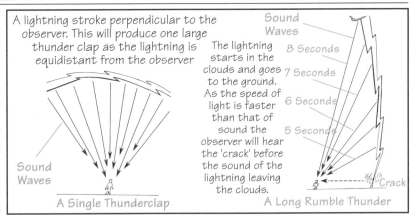

A lightning stroke perpendicular to the observer. This will produce one large thunder clap as the lightning is equidistant from the observer

Sound Waves

A Single Thunderclap

Sound Waves

8 Seconds

7 Seconds

6 Seconds

5 Seconds

The lightning starts in the clouds and goes to the ground. As the speed of light is faster than that of sound the observer will hear the 'crack' before the sound of the lightning leaving the clouds.

Crack

A Long Rumble Thunder

TYPES OF LIGHTNING

Three Types of Lightning

- Cloud to cloud.
- Cloud to ground (down stroke).
- Ground to cloud (upstroke).

Forked Lightning

Lightning bolts that have numerous leaders. These leaders can shoot between the clouds with some hitting the ground.

Single Streak Lightning

The most common form of lightning. It can flash between clouds or hit the ground.

St-Elmo's Fire

Is the flickering discharge or glow on the yardarms of sailing ships, the wind shields of aircraft or tall buildings. This might show an area of electrical differential.

Heat Lightning

Illuminates the lower sky at night. Not a form of lightning but regular lightning flashes that might be active below the horizon.

Ball Lightning

Is very rare and its origin is not known. The electrical charge seems to float in the air, move and all of a sudden explode.

Cold Front Advance

A cold front advances 20 miles (33 km) per hour, faster during the winter months. This is the speed of approach of possible thunderstorms and lightning as cold fronts, in the summer, are the major source lightning.

THINGS TO WATCH FOR BEFORE AND DURING A STORM

- A thunder storm can arrive very fast and lightning can strike in *front* of the storm.
- A lightning bolt can be 4 or 5 miles long.
- Calculate the speed of the approaching storm by the time between the flash and the thunderclap.
- Make sure that you are not the prominent high point in the area (in a field, on a beach, in the water), that you are not next to a prominent high point (next to an isolated tree, steeple, flagpole).
- Avoid being in a boat, on a lake, during a storm. Ground boat.
- Make sure that you are not in a location where the electric current from the ground would pass through you. Examples are: in small, humid caves, on the ledge of a mountain or in a small mountain canyon, as your body might act as a conductor for the current that wants to pass across the canyon.
- Damp area as a damp cave or ledge below a high point.
- Canyons are dangerous because there can be a flash flood caused by a storm. Because of the thunder you will not be able to hear the noise of the water descending the canyon.
- Walk fast but do not run as your rapid movement can cause air currents that might attract an electrical strike.
- Avoid a humid hollow in which there is lichen growing as it would be a good conductor.
- If in the open, crouch very low and try to insulate yourself from the ground by standing on a backpack (with no metal), raincoat, jacket, sleeping bag. The importance of this insulation is that the ground charge cannot rise through your body to attempt to reach the lightning discharge.
- Keep your hands off the ground especially if it is humid.
- Stay away from any metal as tent poles, metal backpack frames, metal walking poles, etc. You might even abandon these items, in a flat field, as they might create a better potential impact point than yourself.
- Do not lean against a stone wall as it might be a conductor.
- Make sure that the storm has completely passed and that you do not attract the last lightning strike.
- If hiding next to a wall, stay 2 to 3 meters from the wall and the wall should be 5 to 6 times your height. Make sure that this wall is not the most prominent location on a flat field.
- Do not group together during a storm. A flash of lightning killed 504 sheep that had huddled together during a storm.

The barometric pressure will drop rapidly before an approaching storm.

GROUND SHOCK (STEP VOLTAGE)

Is the fusion of electrical voltage through the ground. Ground shock is where ground electrical currents try to joint up with a lightening strike. It will be strongest near where lightning has hit.

To protect against ground shock *lie on a dry surface or place some dry insulation between you and the ground*. This insulation can be sleeping bags, bed roll, clothing - *but no metal*. A 4" (10 cm) thick dry insulation should be enough.

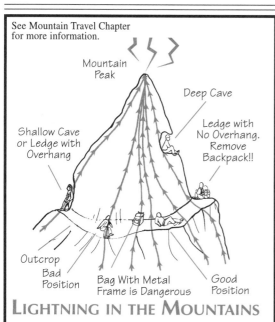

See Mountain Travel Chapter for more information.

Mountain Peak

Deep Cave

Ledge with No Overhang. Remove Backpack!!

Shallow Cave or Ledge with Overhang

Outcrop Bad Position

Bag With Metal Frame is Dangerous

Good Position

LIGHTNING IN THE MOUNTAINS

The electrical conduit lines shown in the illustration show the ground charges (+) that rise through the mountain and where and how they meet the lightning charge (-). These lines of conduit have certain characteristics but we can not predetermine the exact paths.

Mountain Peak

Very hazardous as it is the highest point and would normally be the shortest route for a lightning bolt strike.

Outcrop

Lightning sometimes strikes at a large outcrop. This might be partially explained by the equipotential lines that have built up. On the outcrop the person should lie on a dry cover *perpendicular* to the direction of the equipotential line. Keep all pieces of metal *away* from the body.

Ledge with No Overhang

Fairly secure but do not lean against the wall. Stay crouched, preferably on a dry spot, as a sleeping bag or dry clothing.

Shallow Cave or Ledge with Overhang

Very dangerous as your body might become the conduit for the ground electrical charge to cross the air space. Do not lean against the wall.

Deep Cave

Can be safe but stay crouched, avoid the walls and entrance. *See comments as with a shallow cave.*

How Far Is The Lightning Storm?

To calculate your distance from the lightning. Count how many seconds there are between the flash and the thunder and divide this by 5 and you will have the distance in miles.

By counting a few times you will know if the storm is approaching and at what speed.

Lightning takes 5 seconds to travel a mile (3 seconds per kilometer).

The probability of lightning striking are the highest where the equipotential lines are the closest together and the closest to the negative charge of the lower clouds.

ELECTRICAL EQUIPOTENTIAL LINES

See Mountain Travel Chapter for more information.

All objects during a storm have electrical force lines around them. The lines of equal force (similar to contour lines on a map) are called electrical equipotential lines. The major electrical equipotential lines are between the storm cloud and the land profile. The probability of lightning striking are the highest where the equipotential lines are the closest together and the closest to the negative charge of the lower clouds. At a certain point the insulation offered by the air breaks down and lightning strikes.

To Recognize Electrical Equipotential Critical Areas

- Watch for hair standing on end. This is the (+) charge of the ground trying to reach the (-) charge of the lower clouds.
- There can be a bluish halo around objects (St-Elmo's Fire).
- There can be a high frequency "zinging" sound.

These signs might indicate an imminent lightning strike.

LIGHTNING AND MOUNTAINEERING

Statistically lightning is not one of the major hazards of mountaineering. Casualties and near casualties are reported making it a matter of concern. Mountain climbers often find themselves on prominent peaks and exposed ridges, which are particularly subject to lightning.

There are two reasons for this:

- Ridges help produce the vertical updrafts and the rain cloud conditions which generate lightning.
- Prominences serve to trigger lightning activity.

The weather in the mountains can change rapidly especially in the afternoons when most storms occur. Watch for changes in the wind, cloud movement, animals and insects becoming excited (bees might make noise in their hives).

Sometimes, the storm arrives so fast that you can see the cumulus clouds become cumulonimbus clouds in front of your eyes and engulf the mountain. The air bristles with energy and there might be unusual odors.

Lightning might strike before the actual storm arrives.

There are, however, precautionary measures that can be taken by the climber. The most obvious way of avoiding lightning in the mountains is not to be on exposed peaks or ridges, or in an unprotected flat area during an electrical storm. Do not climb if a storm is predicted. Avoid being under prominent or isolated trees. If you are caught in an exposed place, and you have some time before the storm reaches you, you should get as far down the mountain and away from the exposed ridges as you can. Especially avoid ridges that dominate the skyline. If stuck in the middle of a ridge it is better than being at the end of a ridge.

If lightning seems imminent or is striking nearby, at once seek a place that will protect you from direct strikes and from ground currents. A flat shelf, a slope, or a slightly raised place dominated by a nearby high point would give protection from lightning. If there is a choice select a spot on dry, clean rock in preference to damp or lichen covered rock. A scree slope would be very good. If on a slope tie yourself down. If lightning hits you will be in severe shock and you might fall. The main thing to remember when caught in an electrical storm is to quickly take precautions.

ROPE MAKING MATERIAL

Yucca Cord

The Indians of the Southwest make cord from the yucca plant. They boil the leaves and chew them to extract the tough, threadlike fibers. These fibers are used for cordage.

NYLON

Nylon is the material of choice as it has the maximum breaking strength to the least weight. It resists most chemicals, rot, mildew, abrasion, and has minimum loss of strength upon exposure to sunlight. Nylon has elasticity, depending upon construction, and will stretch approximately 10% at normal working loads and up to 40% to 70% at breaking loads. Nylon is used as a *dynamic rope* in mountain climbing as it will absorb the energy of a fall. It is easier to tie a knot in nylon than stiff polypropylene. Three strand nylon has a more bumpy surface which makes knots more stable.

POLYESTER

Has a low elasticity and is used as a *static rope* in mountain climbing. Used both for repelling and rescue work. Polyester has a slightly lower breaking point than nylon. When new, polyester is the least inclined to slip when making a knot.

POLYPROPYLENE

Floats on water and does not absorb water so it will not freeze in the winter. Only has 2/3 the strength of an equivalent nylon rope. It is sensitive to ultraviolet rays which cause it to degenerate and it can lose 50% of its strength at 150°F (65°C).

HEMP

Hemp was the traditional rope of choice. It is a natural fiber but on a per weight per strength basis the synthetic ropes are a better buy. It should be kept humid as it loses its strength when dry. The best current use for hemp ropes is as a fire rope because it is easier to grasp due of its rough texture.

MAKING CORDAGE FROM NETTLE

Collect the stalks of nettle, preferably in the fall and winter when they are dry. If they are wet, dry them in the sun or over a fire. Crush the stalk with a round smooth rock to expose the pith (sponge like substance) at the center. Break the pith into small sections by bending the nettle stalk and peel out the pith with your fingers. You will now have a long strip of fibers that are rubbed between your hands or slowly pulled while rotating, over a round smooth piece of wood. The fiber strip will become soft and pliable.

To make a long piece of cordage braid several of these strips together. Nettle grows up to seven feet high.

Storage of Rope

Store rope in a dry, cool, clean, well ventilated area and away from sunlight and extreme heat. Examine the rope for frays and powdery internal fibers. Do not store it wet or with acids or alkaline.

Qualities of a Good Knot

Should be easy to tie.
Should not jam or be hard to untie.
Should not slip when under tension.

Rope Safety

Knots weaken rope and the reef knot (or square knot) is the most destructive. Avoid sharp bends in a rope and if using a pulley, use the largest pulley possible. If rope is under tension and has a risk of breaking, hang a blanket, heavy coat, or rug, on the rope to absorb the tensile energy if the rope snaps.

After and before usage, inspect your rope for damage so that you will avoid any surprises. Have the right rope for the job. The safe static load of a rope is usually 10 to 20% of the breaking strength.

ROPE & KNOTS CHAPTER 21

ROPE TERMINOLOGY

Bight: Rope doubled over and usually is between the end and the standing part.

Clockwise: Placing the rope from left to right around a fixed object (counter clockwise is the opposite).

Cow's Tail: Rope end that is frayed or unraveling.

End: Either extremity of the rope. Usually one end is worked with to tie a knot.

Eye: Loop usually at the end of a rope.

Grommet: Ring made of metal, stitched, or rope. Used to attach a tarpaulin, etc.

Hawser: Thick rope over 6" in circumference. Rope can be specified in diameter or circumference - sailors use circumference.

Hitch: Method to attach ropes together or to attach a rope to a fixed object. (e.g. horse hitch)

Knot: Tying the rope onto itself by using a loop. Knot in a rope will reduce its carrying strength.

Lash: Tie down or attach objects together so that they will not move.

Loop: Rope that is curved and usually an end will be passed through.

Messenger: Light rope that is used to pull a heavier rope. This is usually used to pull a heavier rope onto a ship.

Overhand loop: End brought over the standing part.

Painter: Short rope used to tie a small boat to a mooring post.

Rope: Cord over one inch in circumference.

Round Turn: Rope looped twice around a fixed object.

Seize: Use cord to tie two rope ends together.

Snugged: To tighten.

Splice: Join two rope ends together by interweaving the unraveled end strands. This is different than "Seizing"

Standing Part: Part of the rope that is not actually being used in tying the knot.

Toggle: Piece of smooth hard wood that is pushed into a knot to either tighten the knot or used to undo a knot.

Turn: Rope looped once around a fixed object.

Underhand Loop: End brought under the standing part.

Whip: Winding of cord around the end of a rope to stop the rope from fraying.

STOPPER KNOTS

Knots used to make a knot at the end of a rope.

Overhand Knot (Thumb Knot)

Stopper knot at the end of a rope, to stop a rope from passing through a hole or end knot to stop a cord from fraying.

Figure of Eight Knot

Stopper knot which is larger than the Overhand Knot.

Overhand Knot

Figure 8 Knot

BINDING KNOTS

Knots used to tie packages or bandages.

Square Knot (Reef Knot)

Very reliable and serves many purposes. It ties and unties very easily. It is used to tie bandages. It can be used to join two ropes of the *same size*. This knot will not slip or jam. When tying be careful that you do not tie a granny knot. A granny knot slips and jams.

Granny Knot

This knot is unstable under tension as it might slip. It is a miss-tied square knot. (Note: A granny knot *will not lie flat* when it is pulled tight).

Bow Knot (Shoelace Knot)

Name is obvious. It is useful as it is easy to tie. The rope has to remain *under tension* to keep this knot stable.

Square Knot

Ends of bandage fall in the **same direction** as the bandage

Granny Knot

Ends of bandage in a Granny Knot **do not lie** in the direction of the bandage.

Do Not Use the Granny Knot To Tie Bandages

LOOP KNOTS

Knots used to fasten a rope to something.

Bowline Knot 'King of Knots'

Very stable from untieing and can be used for different sized ropes. The bowline is used to form a loop which *will not slip*.

Overhand Loop

To make a loop in the middle of a rope. Both ends of the rope are still unused.

Honda Knot

One of the oldest knots that was used on bowstrings by primitive people. Some variants can be made by whipping an end with cord.

Harness Knot (Fisherman's Loop)

To put a loop in the middle of a rope. This is handy when several people are pulling on a rope.

Running Bowline

A Bowline Knot made into a noose.

Bowline

Running Bowline

Overhand Loop

Harness Knot

Honda Knot

Honda

BENDS USED TO JOIN ROPES

Sheet Bend (Weaver's Knot)

Join two ropes of *unequal size*. Can also be used for ropes of equal size.

Slippery Sheet Bend

Tie two ropes together that might have to be detached rapidly. Use when tying up the flaps on a tent when expecting a storm.

Heaving Line Bend

To joint two ropes of different sizes. This knot will hold without seizing.

Carrick Bend

Is very bulky but one of the strongest bends especially if it is whipped.

Sheet Bend

Double Sheet Bend

Carrick

Splice

Join two ropes together with their unraveled strands. The joint can be very smooth if well done.

Eye Splice

Where a permanent sized eye is required as in mooring boats.

Short Splice

Eye Splice

1   2   3   4

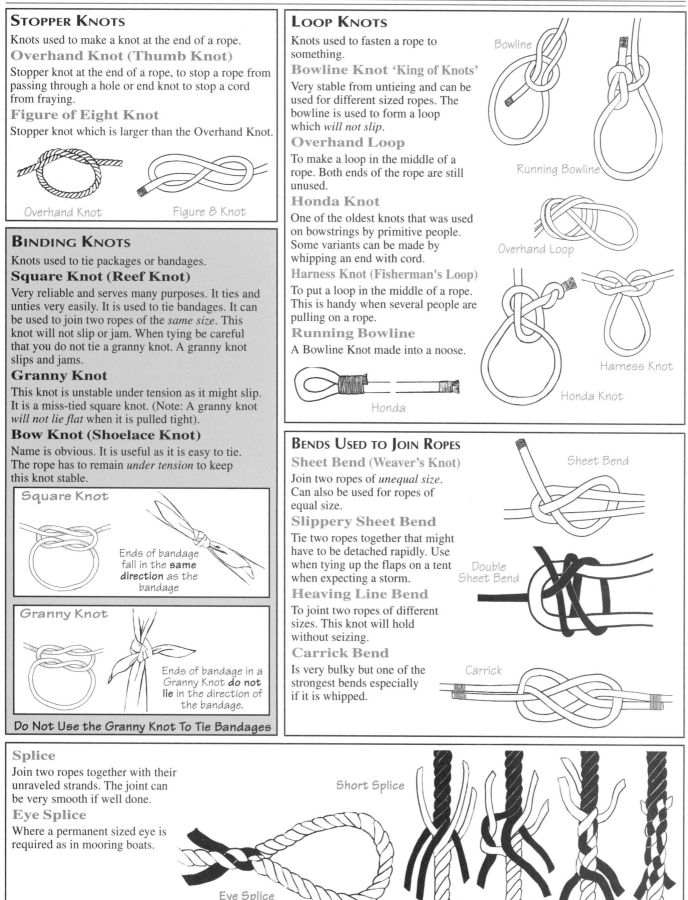

HITCH TO ATTACH A ROPE TO SOMETHING

Half Hitch

Easy to tie but not secure as it might slip without the end being seized.

Two Half Hitch

More secure than the half hitch but seize the end. This knot is used to moor boats to posts or rings.

Round Turn (Two Half Hitch)

To moor a boat. The advantage over the two half hitch is that the additional turn around the pole will lessen the wear on the rope. You should seize the end.

Canoe Hitch (Slipped Half Hitch)

Easy knot to tie and untie especially if fingers are cold or oily.

Figure 8 Hitch

If the post to which the rope is hitched is of a small diameter this hitch is better than the Half Hitch.

Clove Hitch

Holds well, nearly non slipping. Best used on a vertical pole. Leave the end part long if you fear slippage. This is a great knot for tying down a tent or attaching a hammock. It can be used to secure the middle of a rope without using the ends.

Cow Hitch (Lanyard Hitch)

Attach an animal to a post or horizontal bar. To attach an object which has a looped rope on it. Hitch a horse onto a post where the rope can be passed over the post end. To attach baggage hang tags.

Timber Hitch

Easily tied and will not undo if the rope is not under tension.

Sheepshank

Knot to shorten rope. It can also act to strengthen rope at a specific location.

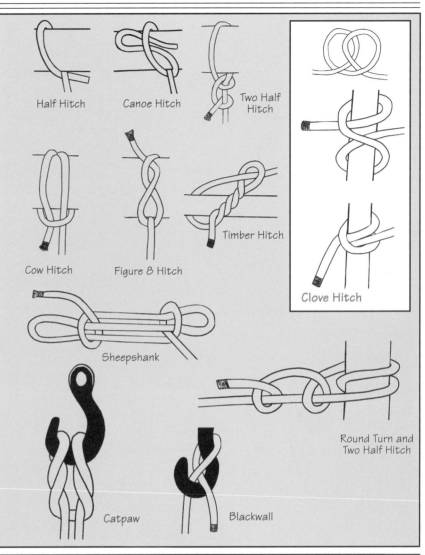

Half Hitch   Canoe Hitch   Two Half Hitch

Cow Hitch   Figure 8 Hitch   Timber Hitch

Clove Hitch

Sheepshank

Catpaw   Blackwall

Round Turn and Two Half Hitch

SPECIAL KNOTS

Taut Line Hitch

For tent line hitches as it will only slide one way. It is better than the clove hitch on slippery poles.

Fisherman's Figure of Eight Knot

To attach fish hooks. Hooks will hang in the same direction as the line. As Figure 8 Knot.

Fisherman's Knot (Smooth Knot)

To attach nylon leaders.

Square Lashing

To attach two poles at right angles to each other. This form of attaching poles can be very rigid if using rawhide or rope that shrinks when it dries.

Prusik Knot

Used by climbers to climb a vertical rope.

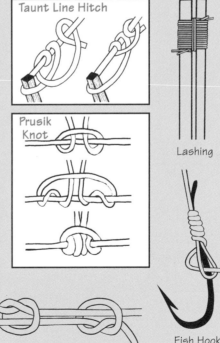

Taunt Line Hitch

Prusik Knot

Lashing

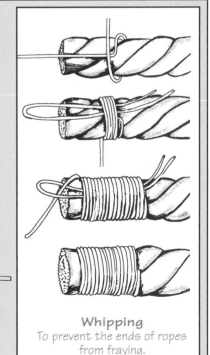

Whipping
To prevent the ends of ropes from fraying.

Fisherman's Bend

Fisherman's Knot

Fish Hook Knot

INDIAN SIGN LANGUAGE

Indians, to communicate with different tribes developed a common sign language. Some examples of this non vocal method of communications are shown.

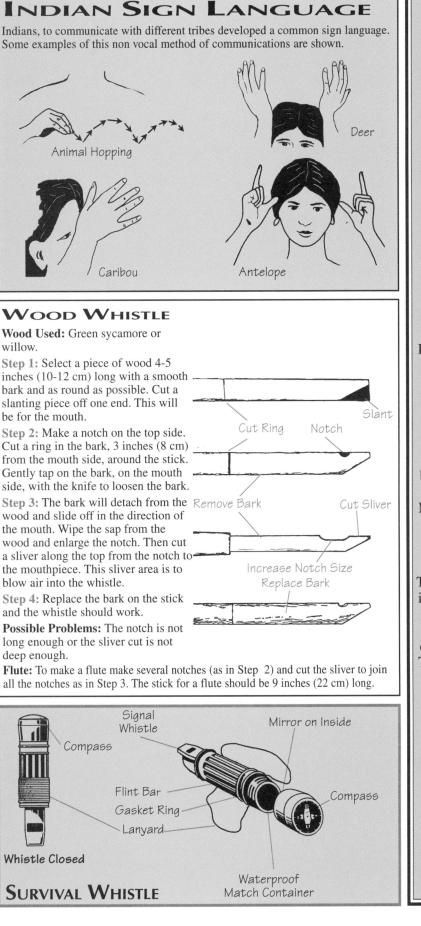

Animal Hopping

Deer

Caribou

Antelope

WOOD WHISTLE

Wood Used: Green sycamore or willow.

Step 1: Select a piece of wood 4-5 inches (10-12 cm) long with a smooth bark and as round as possible. Cut a slanting piece off one end. This will be for the mouth.

Step 2: Make a notch on the top side. Cut a ring in the bark, 3 inches (8 cm) from the mouth side, around the stick. Gently tap on the bark, on the mouth side, with the knife to loosen the bark.

Step 3: The bark will detach from the wood and slide off in the direction of the mouth. Wipe the sap from the wood and enlarge the notch. Then cut a sliver along the top from the notch to the mouthpiece. This sliver area is to blow air into the whistle.

Step 4: Replace the bark on the stick and the whistle should work.

Possible Problems: The notch is not long enough or the sliver cut is not deep enough.

Flute: To make a flute make several notches (as in Step 2) and cut the sliver to join all the notches as in Step 3. The stick for a flute should be 9 inches (22 cm) long.

Slant · Cut Ring · Notch · Remove Bark · Cut Sliver · Increase Notch Size · Replace Bark

Compass · Signal Whistle · Mirror on Inside · Flint Bar · Gasket Ring · Lanyard · Compass · Whistle Closed · Waterproof Match Container

SURVIVAL WHISTLE

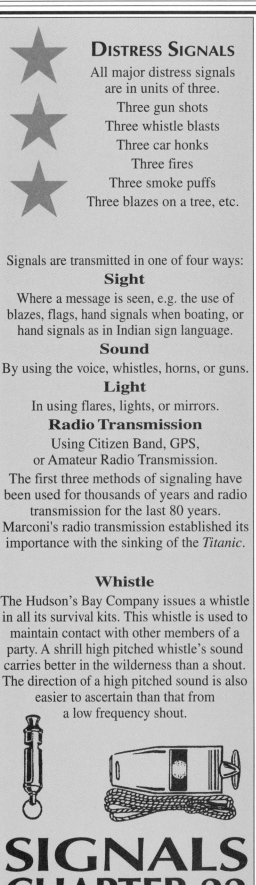

DISTRESS SIGNALS

All major distress signals are in units of three.
Three gun shots
Three whistle blasts
Three car honks
Three fires
Three smoke puffs
Three blazes on a tree, etc.

Signals are transmitted in one of four ways:

Sight
Where a message is seen, e.g. the use of blazes, flags, hand signals when boating, or hand signals as in Indian sign language.

Sound
By using the voice, whistles, horns, or guns.

Light
In using flares, lights, or mirrors.

Radio Transmission
Using Citizen Band, GPS, or Amateur Radio Transmission.

The first three methods of signaling have been used for thousands of years and radio transmission for the last 80 years. Marconi's radio transmission established its importance with the sinking of the *Titanic*.

Whistle
The Hudson's Bay Company issues a whistle in all its survival kits. This whistle is used to maintain contact with other members of a party. A shrill high pitched whistle's sound carries better in the wilderness than a shout. The direction of a high pitched sound is also easier to ascertain than that from a low frequency shout.

SIGNALS CHAPTER 22

BLAZES

	On Trail	Turn Right	Turn Left	Important Warning
Grass				
Rocks				
Tree				
Branch				

Camp Here	Council Meeting	Good News	Lost, Help!
Smoke			

Camp to Right	Trap to Left	Trap to Right	Surveyor's Line

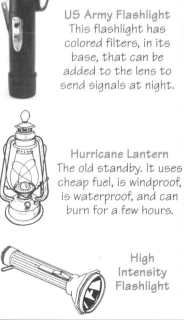

US Army Flashlight
This flashlight has colored filters, in its base, that can be added to the lens to send signals at night.

Hurricane Lantern
The old standby. It uses cheap fuel, is windproof, is waterproof, and can burn for a few hours.

High Intensity Flashlight

VELOCITY OF SOUND

In quiet open air

Temperature	Velocity	1 Mile
F°	*Ft./Sec*	*Seconds*
-30°	1030	5.13
-20°	1040	5.08
-10°	1050	5.03
-0°	1060	4.98
10°	1070	4.93
20°	1080	4.88
32°	1092	4.83
40°	1100	4.80
50°	1110	4.78
60°	1120	4.73
70°	1130	4.68
80°	1140	4.63
90°	1150	4.59
100°	1160	4.55
110°	1170	4.51
120°	1180	4.47

The velocity of sound can be used to determine distance. If a rifle shot flash is seen on a distant hill the distance can be calculated by counting the number of seconds it takes the sound of the shot to be heard.

MARKING BLAZES

On a thin barked tree, a blaze is made by a single downward stroke, the ax being held almost parallel to the trunk. Do not swing too hard as you might injure yourself.

The blaze stays at the *original height* above the ground. To check the age of the blaze chop a billet of the wood, adjacent to the blaze and containing the mark and count the annular rings that have grown from the bottom of the scar outwards. There will be one annular growth per year. Blazes on the bark of chestnut, tulip poplar, young white oak, many locusts, and some other trees *are not permanent* because these trees shed their bark.

FOLLOWING A BLAZED TRAIL

Most trails are spotted (marked) coming and going so that they can be seen from both directions of travel. Professional woodsmen usually mark a blaze on the trail side of the tree and only mark one blaze per tree.

Make sure that you are following a blaze and not an abrasion on a tree caused by a falling branch or gnawed by an animal such as a moose, beaver or bear. Man-made blazes will usually have a mechanical feature such as a straight cut. When there is not much light you might have to check a blaze by touching it.

If a path seems to have stopped (if you see no more blazes) mark your spot and return to the last blaze and check to see that it is a valid blaze, if yes, try to line yourself in the direction of the path. It is possible that a tree with the next blaze has fallen. If you feel unsure of yourself and it is late in the day pitch camp and proceed in the light of day.

Old blazes on spruce or pine trees are the easiest to follow because the resin deposits of the oozing sap leaves a very noticeable and durable mark. Blazes are made at breast height. When a blazed line turns abruptly, so that you might miss the turn, a long slash is made on the side of the tree facing the new direction. If it snows the blowing snow might be stuck to the tree and make them hard to find.

Where Does a Blazed Trail Lead?

- **Hiking Trail:** The blazes and the trail have a point of origin and have a destination. The trail might circle back to the point of origin or merge with the main trail.

- **Trapper's Line:** Trail leads from one stream to another, the blazes would usually not be too visible, the trail meanders, every eight to ten miles there is bound to be a small shelter that will contain some supplies.

Camp to Left

- **Woodcutter's Line:** This would mark the easiest route toward some select timber and towards a river to float the timber.

- **Surveyor's Line:** This blazed trail would be nearly absolutely straight. When it reaches a cliff or swamp there would be right angle turns. The blazes would be well placed and usually cut square.

RADIO SIGNALS

SHORT-WAVE RADIO

Portable shortwave (SW) radios are important tools in times of emergency. There are seven distinct SW radio bands. Broadcasters usually use the same frequencies but they may change if another station affects its transmission or prevailing atmospheric conditions make transmission difficult.

The 13, 16 and 19 meter bands are vulnerable to atmospheric disruption. The 31 and 41 meter bands are the most popular. Broadcasters will transmit simultaneously on different wavelengths to limit any local interference.

To Buy a Radio

For a beginner, buy an inexpensive portable with sufficient features to satisfy your future needs.

Best Choice

Frequency Range: have entire range of 1.6 to 30 megahertz, but you only need the 6 to 16 megahertz range as these include the most popular bands of 19, 25, 31 and 41 meters.

Tuning: old method of using a dial has been replaced by a digital frequency readout. This lets you see the actual frequency and you can even enter the selected frequency.

Performance of a SW Radio

Look for:

- **Stability:** measure of the radio to stay tuned to a specific frequency.
- **Sensitivity:** ability to receive weak stations over the inherent noise on radio.
- **Selectivity:** this is the measure of a radio to reject unwanted signals.

Short-Wave Antennas

Best reception is in the country as there is less interference from man-made objects such as neon lights, electrical devices, wires, etc.

Antennas

An antenna comes with the radio which is good for regular listening especially in the mountains.

Active Antenna: These electronically select and amplify the incoming signal. They can significantly increase the reception.

Exterior Wire Antenna: these give the best reception and are inexpensive. They are made of copper wire and are erected as high as possible.

- Strung at right angles to existing telephone or power lines.
- Constructed of insulated wire to reduce corrosion.
- Should be well grounded.
- An apartment dweller can use the bedsprings as an antenna.

Disconnect external antennas during lightning storms and install a lightning arrestor for added protection.

FM ANTENNA

FM antenna to receive distant FM stations:

Full FM Band Range Reception

FM antennas cover the 88 MHz (Megahertz) to 108 MHz wavelengths. For the best reception, use a T-shaped antenna of 300 ohm wire. The most important part of the antenna is the crossbar of the T. To pick up the *full FM band range* the T should be exactly 4 feet 9 inches (1.45 m) long.

FM Antenna for a Specific Selected Frequency

To help in the *reception of an actual station*, divide the frequency of the station in MHz into 468. The result will be the length of the crossbar (T) in feet.

The higher the antenna is placed the better will be the FM reception and the T (crossbar) should be perpendicular to the *line of broadcast from* the FM station that you are trying to optimize. The quality of reception depends upon the power of the broadcasting station, the intervening topography of the land and the direction of the antenna. In mountains and valleys rotate the antenna for optimum reception as the radio waves bounce off elevated areas.

PHONETIC ALPHABET

Phonetic alphabet used in pronouncing letters in radio communications.

Letter	Pronunciation	Letter	Pronunciation
A	**AL** FAH	N	**NO** VEM BER
B	**BRAH** VOH	O	**OSS** CAH
C	**CHAR** LEE	P	**PAH** PAH
D	**DELL** TAH	Q	**KEH** BECK
E	**ECK** OH	R	**ROW** MEOH
F	**FOKS** TROT	S	**SEE** AIR RAH
G	**GOLF**	T	**TANG** GO
H	**HOH** TELL	U	**YOU** NEE FORM
I	**IN** DEEAH	V	**VIK** TAH
J	**JEW** LEE ETT	W	**WISS** KEY
K	**KEY** LOH	X	**ECKS** RAY
L	**LEE** MAH	Y	**YANG** KEY
M	**MIKE**	Z	**ZOO** LOO

Emergency Radio Signals

The best time to send an emergency message is during the international silent periods which occur at 15 minutes before and 15 minutes after each hour Greenwich Time. Obtain the local wavelengths used for this signal before leaving on a trip.

DIPOLE ANTENNA LENGTHS FOR FM RECEPTION

To receive the best reception, in remote areas, of an FM station build a dipole antenna for the exact frequency for that station.

FM Stations (MHz)	Antenna Lengths (Inches)
88	63 3/4
88.5	63 1/2
89	63
89.5	62 3/4
90	**62 1/2**
90.5	62
91	61 3/4
91.5	61 1/2
92	61
92.5	**60 3/4**
93	60 1/2
93.5	60
94	59 3/4
94.5	59 1/2
95	**59**
95.5	58 3/4
96	58 1/2
96.5	58 1/4
97	58
97.5	**57 1/2**
98	57 1/4
98.5	57
99	56 3/4
99.5	56 1/2
100	**56 1/4**
100.5	56
101	55 1/2
101.5	55 1/4
102	55
102.5	**54 3/4**
103	54 1/2
103.5	54 1/4
104	54 1/4
104.5	53 3/4
105	**53 1/2**
105.5	53 1/4
106	53
106.5	52 3/4
107	52 1/2
107.5	**52 1/4**
108	52

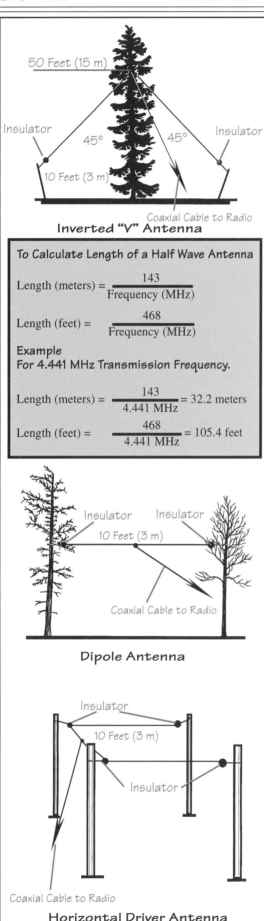

Inverted "V" Antenna

To Calculate Length of a Half Wave Antenna

$$\text{Length (meters)} = \frac{143}{\text{Frequency (MHz)}}$$

$$\text{Length (feet)} = \frac{468}{\text{Frequency (MHz)}}$$

Example
For 4.441 MHz Transmission Frequency.

$$\text{Length (meters)} = \frac{143}{4.441 \text{ MHz}} = 32.2 \text{ meters}$$

$$\text{Length (feet)} = \frac{468}{4.441 \text{ MHz}} = 105.4 \text{ feet}$$

Dipole Antenna

Horizontal Driver Antenna

AMATEUR RADIO TRANSMISSION

You require a license from the Federal Government to transmit on the amateur radio frequencies. When using these frequencies:

- Communications dealing with distress, urgency, or safety have a priority.
- Identify yourself with your call letters.
- Speak clearly.
- Keep your communications as brief as possible.

High Frequency Reception and Transmission

These vary depending upon atmospheric conditions especially during periods of intense solar activities when a "blackout" may occur.

The quality of transmission and reception also depends upon the quality of the transmitter, the antenna, the location, the ground, and the power in a portable battery if one is used.

ANTENNAS

Inverted "V" Antenna

This antenna will radiate effectively in all directions. The inverted "V" antenna is useful when you are unsure of your location or lost and you want to cover a large a radius as possible. This antenna is not very efficient but is easy to install.

- The *middle* of the antenna should be at least 50 feet (15 m) high.
- The *ends* 10 feet (3 m) off the ground at 45° to the vertical supporting structure or tree. Attach an insulator at each end of the antenna. Tie the ends to some suitable support maintaining the 45° angle. The antenna *should not touch* the ground.
- Install the antenna as high as possible, on a hill, and avoid obstructions that will cause interference.
- The distance of transmission depends upon the length of the antenna wire, the height from the ground of the middle support, and the angle from the middle support.
- The length of the antenna, which is a "half wave" antenna, varies with the frequency used and can be calculated as in the example.

Dipole Antenna

This antenna is used by base stations. The antenna is used to transmit in a *definite* direction and the receiving station should have its antenna parallel to the transmitting station.

- The antenna is strung horizontally between two supports at least 10 feet (3 m) above the ground. Insulators should be used at the ends of the antenna.
- The length of the antenna depends upon the frequency used. See the chart provided with your transmitter.

Horizontal Driver Antenna

This antenna is used by base stations. The antenna is used to transmit in a *radius* and can transmit, depending upon the terrain, around 200 miles (300 km). This is useful for expeditions traveling through the wilderness.

- Antenna is square "U" shaped.
- Install horizontally 10 feet (3 m) above the ground.

GROUNDING FOR A TRANSMITTER

Good grounding will improve your radio transmission.

- Dig a hole 3 feet (1 m) deep.
- Place a copper pipe vertically in the hole and cover it with a mixture of salt, fire ash, water and soil. Leave 2 inches (5 cm) of the pipe protruding above the ground.
- Connect to the radio.

Copper Pipe

Grounding

BODY AIRCRAFT SIGNALS

These signals are used by aircraft crew members. Position yourself in a location where you are well contrasted from the background or wear bright clothing. Exaggerate your movements so that they will give the correct message.

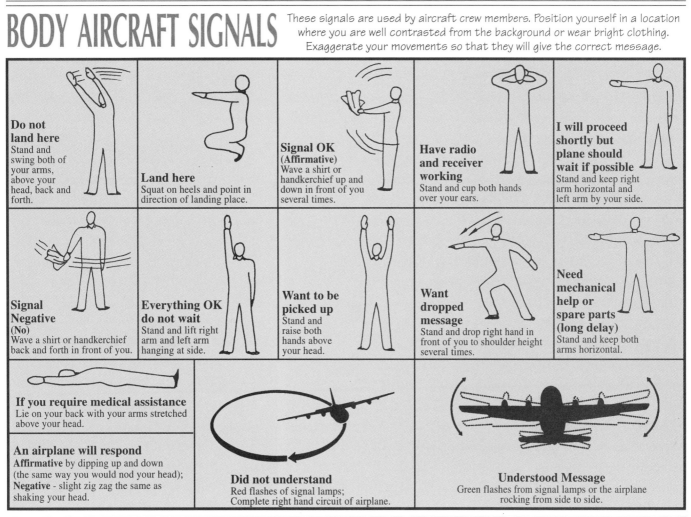

Do not land here
Stand and swing both of your arms, above your head, back and forth.

Land here
Squat on heels and point in direction of landing place.

Signal OK (Affirmative)
Wave a shirt or handkerchief up and down in front of you several times.

Have radio and receiver working
Stand and cup both hands over your ears.

I will proceed shortly but plane should wait if possible
Stand and keep right arm horizontal and left arm by your side.

Signal Negative (No)
Wave a shirt or handkerchief back and forth in front of you.

Everything OK do not wait
Stand and lift right arm and left arm hanging at side.

Want to be picked up
Stand and raise both hands above your head.

Want dropped message
Stand and drop right hand in front of you to shoulder height several times.

Need mechanical help or spare parts (long delay)
Stand and keep both arms horizontal.

If you require medical assistance
Lie on your back with your arms stretched above your head.

An airplane will respond
Affirmative by dipping up and down (the same way you would nod your head); **Negative** - slight zig zag the same as shaking your head.

Did not understand
Red flashes of signal lamps; Complete right hand circuit of airplane.

Understood Message
Green flashes from signal lamps or the airplane rocking from side to side.

These markings are recognized internationally. They can be made on a beach with stones, driftwood, salvage, stamping in the sand, on a snowfield, field with a uniform vegetation growth that can be stamped. The markings should contrast with the background and high contrast shadows should be used.

I Require doctor, serious injuries	**II** Require medical supplies	**X** Unable to proceed	**F** Require food and water	**≋** Require firearms and ammunition	**K** Indicate direction to proceed
↑ Proceeding in this direction	**I)** Will attempt takeoff	**⌐⌐** Aircraft seriously damaged	**△** Probably safe to land here	**LL** All's well	**L** Require fuel and oil
N NO or Negative	**Y** YES or Affirmative	**JL** All's well	**W** Require engineer	**□** Require map and compass	**⫶** Require signal lamp with battery and radio

GROUND TO AIRCRAFT SIGNALS

In the Snow

Walk back and forth on snow to write your message. Position the message north and south to maximize the shadow that will fall in the packed snow area. You can also add evergreen boughs to the trench to increase the contrast.

In a Field or Rocky Area

Lay rock piles, trample grass, strips of cloth. Attempt to maximize the contrast of colors or shadows.

The symbols should be large with the letters or lines 10 feet wide and if possible 40 to 100 feet long. The markings should be deep or high and positioned so that the shadows cast by the sun are the longest.

You could use the simple signal of S O S or build three smoky fires if you can not remember the ground to aircraft codes.

Pointing Arrow

Shows the direction in which you intend to go or have gone.

K: asks the pilot to indicate the direction you should go. The pilot will waggle his wings in confirmation, of your question, and fly in the direction that you should follow.

SEMAPHORE

These are messages sent by flags. They can be seen over a long distance especially if the receiver has a telescope or binoculars and the sender is well contrasted against the background. Semaphore uses two hand flags employed to form characters. The arms holding the flags are placed at an exact position for each letter, a distinct pause is made before the next letter. The arms are moved from one position to the next by the shortest possible motion. Numbers are spelled out to avoid errors. Semaphore is also called "wigwagging". The positioning of the flags for signaling are shown below.

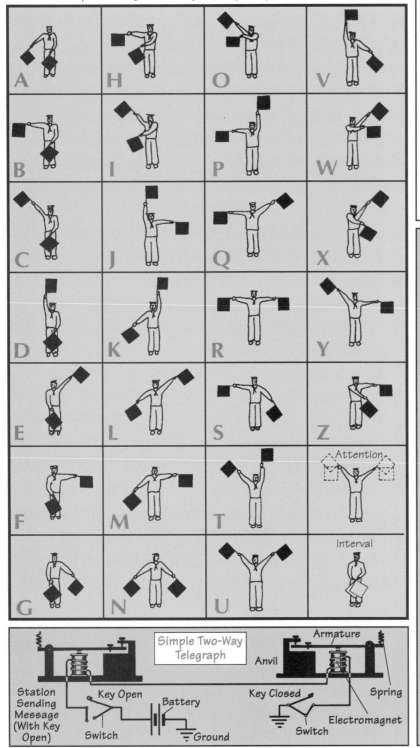

U.S. COAST GUARD SIGNALS

Red light, red rocket, flare

Indicates that you have been seen and assistance will come as soon as possible.

Waving a red flag from shore (during daylight), red light, or red rocket.

Indicates 'Haul away'.

Waving a white flag from shore (during daylight), slowly back and forth or firing a white rocket, white roman candle.

Indicates 'Slack away'.

Waving a red and white flag at the same time (during daylight), or slowly waving a white light and red light, waving a blue light.

Indicates 'Landing in your boat is not possible'.

Beckoning of a man ashore (daylight), or burning two torches close together at night.

Indicates 'Good landing spot'.

To respond from the boat in the daytime

• wave flag, shirt or hand.

To respond from the boat at nighttime

• reply by rocket, gun, blue light or by briefly showing a light over the ship's gunwale and then hiding it.

MORSE CODE

A	•—	S	•••
B	—•••	T	—
C	—•—•	U	••—
D	—••	V	•••—
E	•	W	•——
F	••—•	X	—••—
G	——•	Y	—•——
H	••••	Z	——••
I	••	1	•————
J	•———	2	••———
K	—•—	3	•••——
L	•—••	4	••••—
M	——	5	•••••
N	—•	6	—••••
O	———	7	——•••
P	•——•	8	———••
Q	——•—	9	————•
R	•—•	0	—————

With the Morse alphabet, messages can be sent by day by waving the arms or a flag. If the signaler brings the flag down on his right side he means to send a dot. If he brings it down on his left side, he intends to send a dash. Between each word he brings the flag down in front of him once.

The Morse Code is also used in radio and telegram transmission. The adjacent telegraph illustration shows the assembly of a transmission system. The switch being open or closed determines in which direction the transmission is going.

Simple Two-Way Telegraph

Armature
Anvil
Station Sending Message (With Key Open)
Key Open
Battery
Key Closed
Spring
Electromagnet
Switch
Ground
Switch

HELIOGRAPHY

Heliography is the use of the sun's light to transmit messages. It uses mirrors or polished combat shields as used by the Greeks and Romans. The US Army troops in the 1880's used mirrors to communicate over long distances from mountain range to mountain range in the west. Pocket survival mirrors, which can be aimed, can reflect light and be seen at distances exceeding ten miles.

USE OF DOUBLE FACE SIGNAL MIRROR

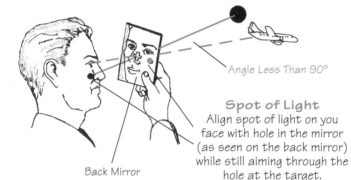

Angle Less Than 90°

Spot of Light
Align spot of light on you face with hole in the mirror (as seen on the back mirror) while still aiming through the hole at the target.

Back Mirror

Angle of Sun to Target is *Less Than* 90°

Hold mirror 3" to 6" (7-14 cm) from the face and sight the target through the hole in the mirror. The sun shines a spot of light through the hole, in the mirror, onto your face. To aim the mirror, at the target, align the reflected spot of light on your face with the hole in the mirror while still aiming your eye, through the hole, at the target. Note that the mirror is coated on the front and back sides so that you can see the spot of light on your face's reflection on the back coating. The front of the mirror will be aiming the reflected light, of the sun, at your target.

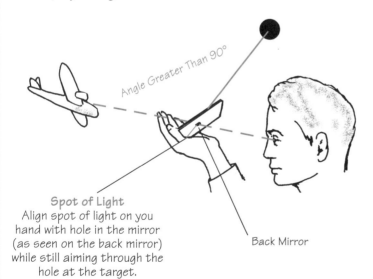

Angle Greater Than 90°

Spot of Light
Align spot of light on you hand with hole in the mirror (as seen on the back mirror) while still aiming through the hole at the target.

Back Mirror

Angle Between Sun and Target is *Greater Than* 90°

Use this method when the target is almost on the horizon and the sun on the opposite horizon (180° degrees apart).

See illustration. Sight the target through hole. The spot of light coming through the hole, in the mirror, will appear on your hand. Move the mirror (while still sighting your target through the hole) *so that the reflection* of the light spot (as seen on the back mirror) coincides with the hole in the center of the mirror and disappears (into the hole).

USE OF SURVIVAL MIRRORS

The flash of light provided by reflected light from a mirror can be seen for many miles limited only by the curvature of the earth or the height of an airplane above the horizon.

The basic strategy, if one is lost, is to sweep the horizon from an elevated point. A sudden flash of light can easily attract a potential rescuer's attention. Survival mirrors have mirror coated faces on both sides and an uncoated spot (hole) in the middle.

Gerber Survival Mirror

Uncoated Spot (hole)

Mirror Coated on Both Sides

This type of mirror is used in the United States Military. It is available at Army/Navy stores and better outdoor stores.
If you *do* not have a double coated mirror you can use a tin can top by punching a hole in the center. Flatten any sharp edges before using.

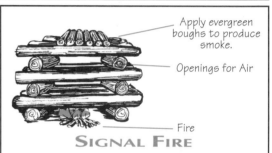

Apply evergreen boughs to produce smoke.

Openings for Air

Fire

SIGNAL FIRE

If you are lost and people are searching for you prepare a signal fire. *The fire should ignite quickly, generate a lot of smoke and at night have a high exposed flame.* The fire wood should be kept dry until lit. To ignite quickly have good tinder, adequate ventilation, wood and branches containing much pitch. To produce a heavy smoke burn green branches, rubber, plastic, and heavy oil. Emergency signals are usually grouped in 3's so if possible have three fires in line. If you have one fire you can use a wet blanket to temporarily cut off the fire to send smoke signals in puffs of three. In the winter drain the engine oil before it congeals.

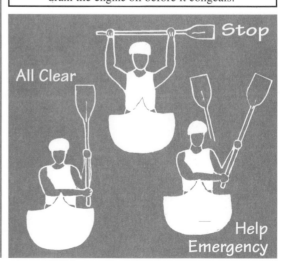

Stop

All Clear

Help Emergency

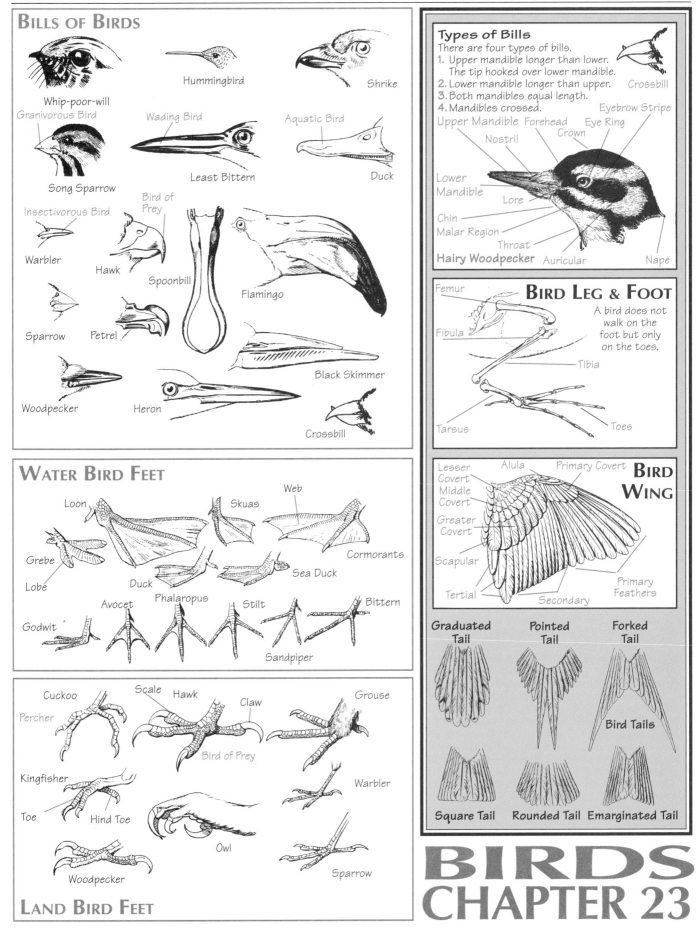

BILLS OF BIRDS

Whip-poor-will

Hummingbird

Shrike

Granivorous Bird

Wading Bird

Aquatic Bird

Song Sparrow

Least Bittern

Duck

Insectivorous Bird

Bird of Prey

Warbler

Hawk

Spoonbill

Flamingo

Sparrow

Petrel

Black Skimmer

Woodpecker

Heron

Crossbill

Types of Bills

There are four types of bills.
1. Upper mandible longer than lower. The tip hooked over lower mandible.
2. Lower mandible longer than upper.
3. Both mandibles equal length.
4. Mandibles crossed.

Crossbill

Upper Mandible   Forehead   Eyebrow Stripe
Nostril   Crown   Eye Ring
Lower Mandible
Lore
Chin
Malar Region
Throat
Hairy Woodpecker   Auricular   Nape

BIRD LEG & FOOT

Femur

A bird does not walk on the foot but only on the toes.

Fibula

Tibia

Tarsus

Toes

BIRD WING

Lesser Covert   Alula   Primary Covert
Middle Covert
Greater Covert
Scapular
Tertial   Secondary   Primary Feathers

WATER BIRD FEET

Loon

Skuas

Web

Grebe

Lobe

Duck

Sea Duck

Cormorants

Godwit

Avocet

Phalaropus

Stilt

Bittern

Sandpiper

Graduated Tail   Pointed Tail   Forked Tail

Bird Tails

Square Tail   Rounded Tail   Emarginated Tail

LAND BIRD FEET

Cuckoo   Scale   Hawk   Claw   Grouse

Percher

Bird of Prey

Kingfisher

Warbler

Toe   Hind Toe

Owl

Woodpecker

Sparrow

BIRDS
CHAPTER 23

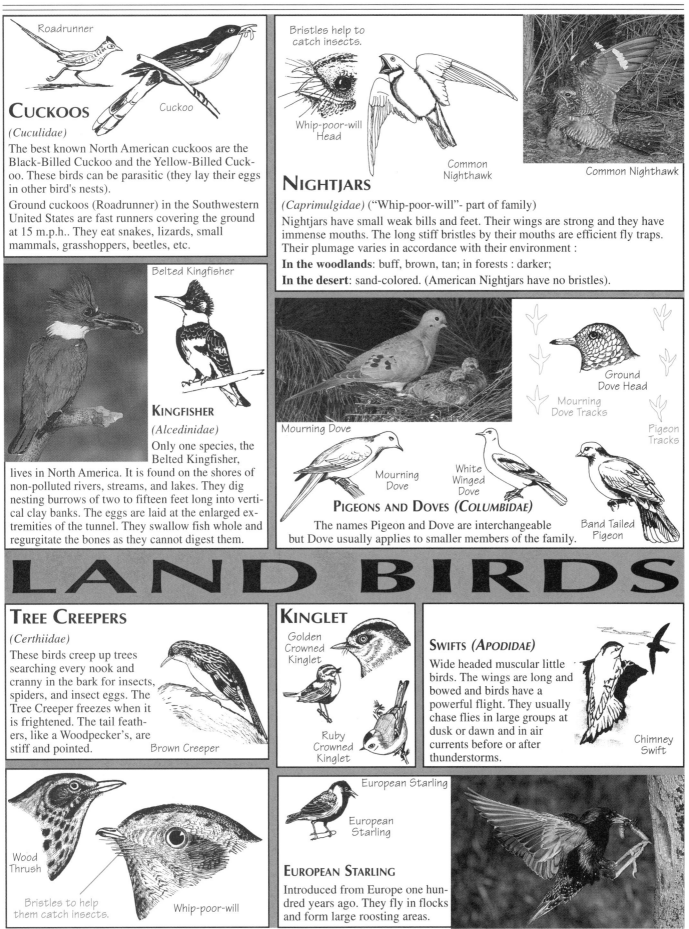

CUCKOOS

(Cuculidae)

The best known North American cuckoos are the Black-Billed Cuckoo and the Yellow-Billed Cuckoo. These birds can be parasitic (they lay their eggs in other bird's nests).

Ground cuckoos (Roadrunner) in the Southwestern United States are fast runners covering the ground at 15 m.p.h.. They eat snakes, lizards, small mammals, grasshoppers, beetles, etc.

Roadrunner

Cuckoo

NIGHTJARS

(Caprimulgidae) ("Whip-poor-will"- part of family)

Nightjars have small weak bills and feet. Their wings are strong and they have immense mouths. The long stiff bristles by their mouths are efficient fly traps. Their plumage varies in accordance with their environment :

In the woodlands: buff, brown, tan; in forests : darker;

In the desert: sand-colored. (American Nightjars have no bristles).

Bristles help to catch insects.

Whip-poor-will Head

Common Nighthawk

Common Nighthawk

KINGFISHER

(Alcedinidae)

Only one species, the Belted Kingfisher, lives in North America. It is found on the shores of non-polluted rivers, streams, and lakes. They dig nesting burrows of two to fifteen feet long into vertical clay banks. The eggs are laid at the enlarged extremities of the tunnel. They swallow fish whole and regurgitate the bones as they cannot digest them.

Belted Kingfisher

Mourning Dove

Ground Dove Head

Mourning Dove Tracks

Pigeon Tracks

Mourning Dove

White Winged Dove

Band Tailed Pigeon

PIGEONS AND DOVES (COLUMBIDAE)

The names Pigeon and Dove are interchangeable but Dove usually applies to smaller members of the family.

LAND BIRDS

TREE CREEPERS

(Certhiidae)

These birds creep up trees searching every nook and cranny in the bark for insects, spiders, and insect eggs. The Tree Creeper freezes when it is frightened. The tail feathers, like a Woodpecker's, are stiff and pointed.

Brown Creeper

KINGLET

Golden Crowned Kinglet

Ruby Crowned Kinglet

SWIFTS (APODIDAE)

Wide headed muscular little birds. The wings are long and bowed and birds have a powerful flight. They usually chase flies in large groups at dusk or dawn and in air currents before or after thunderstorms.

Chimney Swift

Wood Thrush

Bristles to help them catch insects.

Whip-poor-will

European Starling

European Starling

EUROPEAN STARLING

Introduced from Europe one hundred years ago. They fly in flocks and form large roosting areas.

Grouse

GROUSE (TETRAONIDAE)

All Grouse have a mat of feathers on their nostrils, a skin comb above the eyes, and have feathers on their legs (includes ptarmigans).

PTARMIGAN & GROUSE

Sharp Tailed Grouse

Ptarmigan (Winter)

Ptarmigan Tracks

Summer

Winter

Ruffed Grouse

VIREOS AND GREENLETS (VIREONIDAE)

These birds are 4" to 6" long and most are gray-green with slate or yellow areas, but not brightly colored. They sing a lot even during the heat of midday when most birds are quiet.

Birds are: Philadelphia Vireo, Red-Eyed Vireo.

Greenlets are in the tropics.

Shrike Vireos: three types having strong colors.

Philadelphia Vireo

Warbling Vireo

White Eyed Vireo

AMERICAN QUAILS

Gambel's Quail jumping from an Ocotillo

(Phasianidae - Odontophorinae)

Quail have legs that are not feathered *(grouse are feathered)* and the nostrils are shielded by a naked scale *(not with a dense mat of small feathers)*.

Bob White Quail

Gambel's Quail

Mountain Quail Head

Gambel's Quail's Head

Gambel's Quail

Ruby Throated Hummingbird

Ruby Throated Hummingbird

HUMMINGBIRDS

(Trochilidae)

They can be recognized by their small size, bright colors, and the humming sound of their flight. They can fly backwards, forwards, and hover. Like the woodpecker, they have extensible tongues used to extract nectar and small insects from deep-throated blossoms.

TYRANT FLYCATCHERS

Flycatcher

Most are small, greenish-olive birds with short, rounded chests.

Eastern Kingbird

Phoebe Flycatcher

Wood Pewee Flycatcher

Say's Phoebe Flycatcher

Yellow Belied Flycatcher

Say's Phoebe Flycatcher

Eastern Kingbird

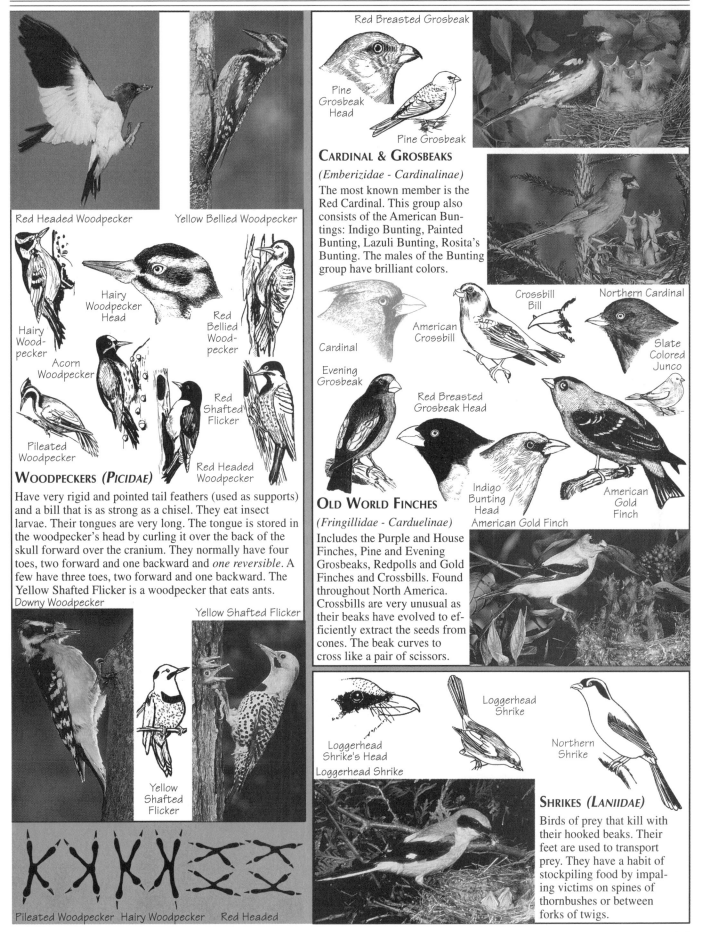

Red Headed Woodpecker

Yellow Bellied Woodpecker

Hairy Woodpecker Head

Red Bellied Woodpecker

Hairy Woodpecker

Acorn Woodpecker

Red Shafted Flicker

Pileated Woodpecker

Red Headed Woodpecker

WOODPECKERS (*PICIDAE*)

Have very rigid and pointed tail feathers (used as supports) and a bill that is as strong as a chisel. They eat insect larvae. Their tongues are very long. The tongue is stored in the woodpecker's head by curling it over the back of the skull forward over the cranium. They normally have four toes, two forward and one backward and *one reversible*. A few have three toes, two forward and one backward. The Yellow Shafted Flicker is a woodpecker that eats ants.
Downy Woodpecker

Yellow Shafted Flicker

Yellow Shafted Flicker

Pileated Woodpecker   Hairy Woodpecker   Red Headed

Red Breasted Grosbeak

Pine Grosbeak Head

Pine Grosbeak

CARDINAL & GROSBEAKS

(Emberizidae - Cardinalinae)
The most known member is the Red Cardinal. This group also consists of the American Buntings: Indigo Bunting, Painted Bunting, Lazuli Bunting, Rosita's Bunting. The males of the Bunting group have brilliant colors.

Cardinal

Evening Grosbeak

American Crossbill

Crossbill Bill

Northern Cardinal

Slate Colored Junco

Red Breasted Grosbeak Head

Indigo Bunting Head

American Gold Finch

American Gold Finch

OLD WORLD FINCHES

(Fringillidae - Carduelinae)
Includes the Purple and House Finches, Pine and Evening Grosbeaks, Redpolls and Gold Finches and Crossbills. Found throughout North America. Crossbills are very unusual as their beaks have evolved to efficiently extract the seeds from cones. The beak curves to cross like a pair of scissors.

Loggerhead Shrike's Head
Loggerhead Shrike

Loggerhead Shrike

Northern Shrike

SHRIKES (*LANIIDAE*)

Birds of prey that kill with their hooked beaks. Their feet are used to transport prey. They have a habit of stockpiling food by impaling victims on spines of thornbushes or between forks of twigs.

239

Field Sparrow

Chipping Sparrow

Meadow Lark Tracks

Henslow's Sparrow

Clay Colored Sparrow

Song Sparrow

English Sparrow

SPARROWS

Pine Woods Sparrow

Vesper Sparrow

Sharp Tailed Sparrow

Swamp Sparrow

Savannah Sparrow

Chipping Sparrow

Fox Sparrow

Field Sparrow

Sea Side Sparrow

Lincoln's Sparrow

White Throated Sparrow

BUNTINGS (EMBERIZIDAE - EMBERIZINAE)

Most are the size of Sparrows.

Many members are called Song Sparrow, White-Throated Sparrow, Fox Sparrow...

The bill is used to crush seeds but it can also delicately pick up insects.

Savannah Sparrow

White Throated Sparrow

Meadow Lark

Eastern Meadow Lark

Red Winged Blackbird

Red Winged Blackbird Head

Horned Lark

Horned Lark Tracks

Horned Lark Head

Rusty Blackbird

Bobolink

Cowbird

Boattailed Grackle

Baltimore Oriole

Yellow Headed Blackbird

Bobolink

ICTERIDS (ICTERIDAE)

This family is very diverse and includes the Meadowlark, Baltimore Oriole, Grackle, Cowbird, Bobolink, Red-Winged Blackbird, Military Blackbird...

They are strong birds from 6 to 21 inches long. Bills are hard, conical, and pointed. Feet are large and strong. They are noisy and showy. The male bows, bringing his head below the level of the perch and raising his tail to the vertical and beyond.

Pinon Jay

Blue Jay

Blue Jay

Common Crow

Canada Jay

Black Billed Magpie

Clark's Nutcracker

Common Raven

Grey Jay

Grey Jay

Brown Thrasher

Mockingbird

Gray Catbird

Catbird

MOCKINGBIRDS & THRASHERS
(Mimidae)

The Mockingbird is known for its *excellent imitation of the songs of other birds*. The Northern Mockingbird even copies the sound of sewing machines and cats' mews. Thrashers are similar to Mockingbirds.

White Breasted Nuthatch

Red Breasted Nuthatch

Red Breasted Nuthatch

CROWS & JAYS (CORVIDAE)

These birds have succeeded to coexist with man and are considered as the most intelligent of birds. They will eat anything.

Two distinct families:

Corvinae - Crows, Ravens, Nutcrackers, Choughs.

All of the thirty birds of this group are black, black with gray cape and belly, or black with white cape and belly. The big, all-black Northern Raven is the largest.

Garrulinae - Jays, Magpies, Tree Pies.

The Jays have undergone a change of color and other features (long tails, crests and habit). They are more specialized ecologically. The majority of the Jays of North America are blue or partly blue (e.g. Stellar's Jay). The exceptions of the Blue Jays are the Gray Jay or Whisky Jay of the northern evergreen forests, Brown Jay of Mexico, and the Green Jay of Southern Texas.

NUTHATCHES (SITTIDAE)

They eat nuts. To break the shells they wedge the nut into cracks of tree bark and hammer, on the nuts, with their chisel-like bill. They hang upside down and go down a tree (this is exclusive to Nuthatches). On its way down it looks for insects. At the bottom of a tree it flies to the top of the next tree and proceeds down.

Bohemian Waxwing Head

Bohemian Waxwing

Cedar Waxwing

WAXWINGS
(Bombycillidae)

The common species in North America are the Cedar Waxwing and the Bohemian Waxwing. These birds have fine upstanding crests, robber's face masks and bright yellow tips on the tail feathers.

Cactus Wren

Barn Swallow

Bank Swallow

Bank Swallow

Cliff Swallow

Purple Marlin

SWALLOWS (*HIRUNDINIDAE*)

Swallows have adapted to living in the surroundings of man.

Barn and Cliff Swallows live in overhanging eaves.

Rough Winged Swallows and soft earth burrowing swallows live in the cut banks for railways and highways.

Tree Swallows live in the hollows of fence posts.

Violet-Green Swallows of the Pacific Coast still prefer natural cliffs.

We see swallows flying high before storms as the air currents are lifting the insects to higher altitudes.

Barn Swallow

Tree Swallow

Tree Swallow

SWALLOWS AND MARTINS

Marsh Wren

House Wren

Bewick's Wren

Winter Wren

Carolina Wren

Short Billed Wren

Long Billed Wren

Chestnut Backed Chickadee

Black Capped Chickadee

Black Capped Chickadee

Black Capped Chickadee

Tufted Titmouse

Tufted Titmouse

TITMICE & CHICKADEES (*PARIDAE*)

The best known is the Black-Capped Chickadee. It visits the urban areas in winter. The Boreal Chickadee is found in the northern forests of Canada.

WRENS
(*Troglodytidae*)

House Wren

There are sixty species of Wrens in the Americas. The American Wrens have adjusted to all kinds of environments from marshes and grassy flat lands to deserts.

Eastern Bluebird

Veery

Wood Thrush

Hermit Thrush

Gray-Cheeked Thrush

Bluebird

Hermit Thrush

American Robin

Townsend Solitaire

Perching Bird

Hermit Thrush

THRUSHES (*TURDIDAE*)

The best known birds of this group are the American Robin and the Bluebird.

Other Thrushes are: Forest Thrushes, Hermit Thrushes, Swainson's Thrush, Gray-Cheeked Thrush...

They are related to the old-world Nightingale.

American Robin

American Goldfinch

Purple Finch

Tufted Titmouse

Louisiana Tanager

TANAGERS

(Emberizidae-Thraupinae)
The Scarlet, Winter, Summer and Hepatic Tanagers live in North America. They are seven or eight inches long.

WILD TURKEY

Wild Turkey

PHEASANT

Pheasant Tracks

Pheasant

243

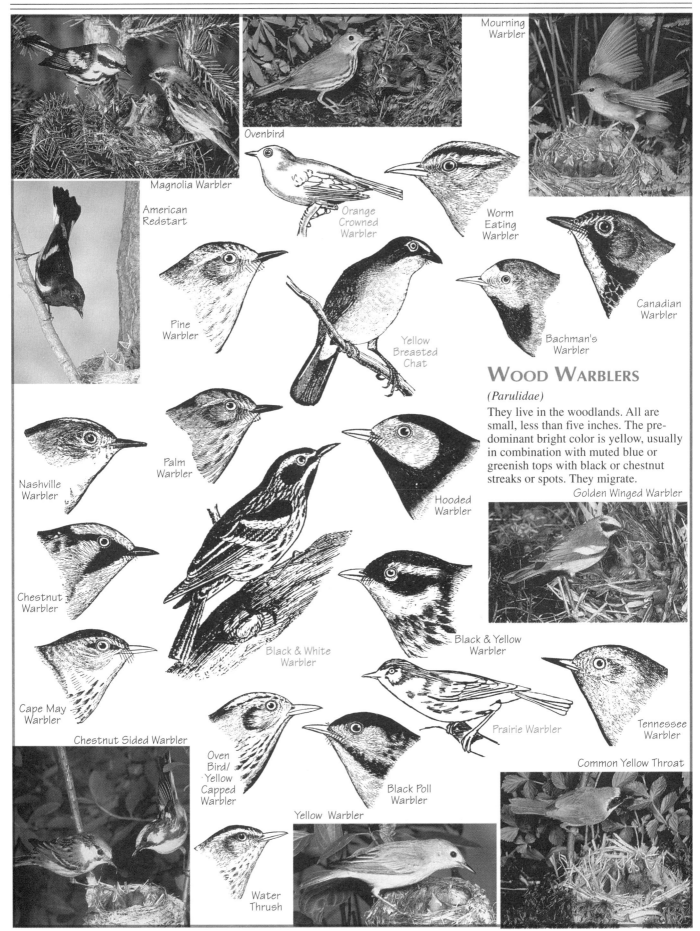

Mourning Warbler

Ovenbird

Magnolia Warbler

American Redstart

Orange Crowned Warbler

Worm Eating Warbler

Canadian Warbler

Pine Warbler

Yellow Breasted Chat

Bachman's Warbler

Nashville Warbler

Palm Warbler

WOOD WARBLERS

(Parulidae)

They live in the woodlands. All are small, less than five inches. The predominant bright color is yellow, usually in combination with muted blue or greenish tops with black or chestnut streaks or spots. They migrate.

Hooded Warbler

Golden Winged Warbler

Chestnut Warbler

Black & White Warbler

Black & Yellow Warbler

Cape May Warbler

Prairie Warbler

Tennessee Warbler

Chestnut Sided Warbler

Oven Bird/ Yellow Capped Warbler

Black Poll Warbler

Common Yellow Throat

Yellow Warbler

Water Thrush

Summer

Winter

Ptarmigan (Winter)

Ptarmigan Tracks

Hairy
Woodpecker

Red Headed
Woodpecker

LAND BIRD TRACKS

English
Sparrow

Horned Lark

Mourning Dove

Pheasant
Tracks

Perching
Bird Tracks

Horned
Lark
Tracks

Meadow
Lark
Tracks

Mourning
Dove Tracks

Pigeon
Tracks

Pheasant

ALBATROSS
This oceangoing bird needs the wind to stay aloft as it glides through the sky.

WATER BIRDS

CRANES

Crane
Tracks

Crane in flight. Note that the neck is straight. See the flight neck of the heron.

Crowned Crane

Whopping
Crane Head

Lesser Sandhill Crane

CRANES (GRUIDAE)
The Whooping Crane and the Sandhill Crane are the only cranes in North America. They stand over five feet tall. The Whooping Crane is nearly extinct.

Wattled
Cranes

Whooping
Crane

Coots

Coot Mudhen

Coot Head

Coot Foot

These are large duck-like birds with long toes with membranous lobes. Bill is extended up the forehead.

Rails

Virginia Rail

Virginia Rail Head

Rail Tracks

Virginia Rail Foot & Track

They have very flat bodies adapted so that they can slip between close-growing reeds and grasses.

Gallinule Head & Foot

Common Gallinule

Loons (Gaviidae)

LOONS

They are excellent swimmers and can swim long distances under water. They can change their specific gravity (with grebes) so they can sink into the water without diving. Because of the construction of their feet they can hardly walk on land. Loons have to take a long taxiing run to get airborne. It is a northern bird. It has a very special melancholic cry.

Feet are not made for walking.

Loon Tracks

Common Loon

Red Throated Loon

Common Loon

Storks (Ciconiidae)

STORKS

The American Wood Stork is the only native stork of North America. It has a bare head. It feeds in shallow water and coastal areas. It eats fish, crabs, insects and frogs.

Black Necked Stork

Wood Stork

Painted Storks

Wood Stork

GREBES

Horned Grebe Heads
Male (R)
Female (L)

Horned Grebe

Pied-Billed Grebe

Western Grebe

Grebes (Podicepedidae)

These birds resemble Loons but their toes are *not connected by webs*. Their toes have a lump of skin that extends when the foot is on the propulsive push and then folds back on the return stroke. These birds live on prairie lakes.

Pied-Billed Grebe Tracks

Horned Grebe

FLAMINGO & IBIS

Glossy Ibis Bill

Flamingo Track

Wood Ibis Head

FLAMINGOS *(PHOENICOPTORIDAE)*

They eat mollusks, shrimps, worms, insects, algae and other foods found in the water.

American Flamingo

American Flamingo

Ibis

IBISES & SPOONBILLS

(Thresiciornithidae)

They are similar to storks but their bills are soft and leathery rather than hard and horny. The family has two groups:

Ibis - has long, thin, down curved bills.

Spoonbill - has a spoon-shaped bill.

Roseate Spoonbill

BITTERN

BITTERNS *(BOTAURINAE)*

Marsh inhabiting heron-like birds. They are heavier and less graceful than heron. The least bittern is only 13" long.

American Bittern

American Bittern

Bittern Beak

American Bittern

Least Bittern

Least Bittern

Least Bittern

EGRET

Egret Track

EGRET

The Egrets are white and live around the Gulf of Mexico and are sometimes seen in southern Canada. They eat small fish , crawfish, insects, and frogs.

Great Egret in Flight

Little White Egret

American Egret

Snowy Egret

Snowy Egret

HERONS (*ARDEIDAE*)

Herons can be distinguished in flight by their head being folded back onto their body. The Heron impales its prey on its bill. Herons vary in size from the Blue Heron (5 feet) to the Least Bittern (1 foot).

Louisiana Heron

Heron in flight. (Notice bent neck.)

Little Blue Heron

Great Blue Heron

Little Green Heron

Great Blue Heron

Yellow Crowned Night Heron

Great Blue Heron

Great Blue Heron Track

Black Crowned Night Heron

Black Crowned Night Heron

Pond Heron

Great White Heron

Northern Phalarope Track

Goose Track

Killdeer Tracks

Pied-Billed Grebe Tracks

Duck Track and Foot

Loon Tracks

Flamingo Tracks

Crane Tracks

Goose Leg

Pelican Track

Green Heron

Little Green Heron Tracks

Little Blue Heron

Virginia Rail Tracks

248

Hooded Merganser

Red Breasted Merganser

Common Merganser

Merganser Foot

American Mergansers in Flight

Merganser bill is narrow when compared to duck's bill.

Black Duck

Velvet Scooter

Eider

Duck bill is flat when compared to merganser's bill.

Eider

Labrador/ Pied Duck

Common Scooter

Duck Track

Common + Stellar's Eider

Mallard Duck

Surface feeding duck foot.

Great Scaup

American Green Winged Teal

MERGANSERS, DUCKS, GEESE, & SWANS (ANATIDAE)

This family has the majority of larger waterfowl in North America. They are swimming birds with four toes and only two webs. To eat they strain the water through their bills.

Ducks: Have a rapid wing beat.

Geese: Have larger wings and a slower powerful wing beat.

The difference between Duck and Mergansers is that ducks have flattened bills and Mergansers have narrow bills. Teals are the smallest of ducks.

SWAN

Swan Flying: Note that the neck is straight and that the legs barely extend past the tail.

Whistling Swan Bill

Mute swan taking off on ice

SWANS (CYGNINAE)

Swans are all white and fly with their necks extended forward (like the crane). But they do not have the long protruding legs of the cranes.

Blue Goose

Atlantic Brant Goose

Snow Geese in Flight

Goose Leg

GEESE (ANSERINAC)

Geese are similar to ducks but are larger, have flattened bodies and longer legs. They have a strong low frequency flight.

White Fronted Goose

Canada Goose landing on water

Brant Goose

Greater Snow Goose

Emperor Goose

Barnacle Goose

Canada Goose

Barnacle Goose

Canada Goose

Canada Geese on Ice

WHY CERTAIN MIGRATING BIRDS FLY IN A "V" FORMATION

The lead bird flaps its wings and disturbs the air leaving a wind eddy behind it. Heavy birds (as geese) take advantage of these eddies by flying in a "V" formation. This gives additional support from the wake of the bird immediately ahead. Quite often you see a "V" reforming and the leader of the group changing position to take a rest.

PELICAN

White Pelican

PELICAN (PELECANIDAE)

Pelicans can hold from a gallon to three gallons of food and water in their bills.

Barnacle Goose

Migrating Snow and Blue Geese

250

AUK, MURRES & PUFFINS (*ALICIDAE*)

Alicidae - are three-toed, web-footed sea-birds. The hind toe is missing. All the birds of this family are short-tailed, short-legged, small-winged, and have large heads. (These birds are not like the southern hemisphere penguins). The difference in these birds can be seen by their bills. They all walk badly but fly well.

The Great Auk did not fly and this lead to its extinction.

AUK, MURRES, PUFFIN, GUILLEMOT

Common Puffin

Murres

Atlantic Puffin

Razor-Billed Auk

Black Guillemot

GUILLEMOT

Are similar to Murres but smaller.

Black Guillemot

Pigeon Guillemot

PUFFIN (*FRATERCULINAE*)

Puffins are stocky saltwater birds that are superb swimmers. It is distinguished by its highly colored and exaggerated bill.

AUK

The Razor-Billed Auk looks similar to the Murre but has a very large bill.

Skua & Jaeger Beak

Gull Beak

Tern Beak

Gannet

Cormorant Beak

Cormorant Foot

Skua

Gannet

CORMORANTS

(*Phalacrocoracides*)

They are birds of the sea-coast and large lakes. They live all over the world except in the Arctic regions. They dive into the water from a swimming position. Their feathers are not water proof so they have to dry in the sun after each feeding trip.

Fulmar

Great Cormorant

Fulmar

FULMARS

Large bird of gull-like colors. Note that they have tube like nostrils on the top of their beak.

GANNETS (*SULIDAE*)

These birds have bare faces which have distinctive colors: green, pink, red, gray, slate, blue-black, orange-yellow, etc. They plunge into the water after fish and are strictly marine birds.

Jaeger

Jaeger Foot

JAEGERS & SKUA

(*Stercorariidae*)

They have webbed toes with sharp curved talons and long beaks with hooked tips. Jaegers breed in the Arctic and during the winter wander the sea. They sometimes travel as far as the Great Lakes. They both hunt for food (other birds or fish) or scavenge food from other birds.

Black Necked Stilt

Black Necked Stilt Tracks

Black Necked Stilt

Avocet

American Avocet Tracks

Avocet

AVOCETS & STILTS (*RECURVIROSTRIDAE*)

Avocets: Avocets are swimmers and waders. Their toes are fully webbed. They sweep their bill through the water to catch the smell of aquatic animal life.

Stilts: Beak is long and straight with a slight up curve, tapering to a sharp point.

Black Tern

TERNS

When compared to gulls they are lighter and smaller in build, have a more graceful agile form of flight, constantly diving from the wing. They point their *bill towards the water.*

Common Tern Tracks

Roseate Tern

Arctic Tern

Royal Tern

Arctic Tern

Skua & Jaeger Beak

Gull Beak

Tern Beak

Gull

Tern

Gull and Tern Heads

GULLS & TERNS (*LARIDAE*)

These birds are long-winged swimmers and they can be differentiated from the Skua or Jaeger by the shape and construction of their beaks.

Common Tern

Tern sees fish.

Tern dives into water.

Tern with fish.

TERN FISHING

Little Least Tern

Roseate Tern

Cabot's Tern

Herring Gull

GULLS

Gulls look similar to Terns but they have a more robust build, are not as acrobatic in flight, and fly with their bills in the *same direction as their bodies.*

Gull Tracks

Gull Bill

Franklin Gull

Bonaparte's Gull

Laughing Gull

Heermann's Gull

Kittiwake Gull

California Gull

Common Gull

Herring Gull

Great Black Backed Gull

Red-Billed Gull

PHALAROPES

(Phalaropodidae)

These small birds are similar to sandpipers but more delicate in appearance.

Shorebird looking for food in beach sand.

Wilson Phalarope Male (R) Female (L)

Rednecked Northern Phalarope

Ruddy Turnstone

Turnstone Head

Turnstone

Killdeer Tracks

Killdeer

When a predator approaches a Killdeer's nest the adult feigns injury. The predator seeing an easy catch will follow the "injured" Killdeer and be distracted from the nest.

Turnstone Beak

PLOVERS, TURNSTONES & SURFBIRDS

Ringed Plover

Golden Plover in Flight

Snowy Plover

Plover Foot

Snowy Plover

Lapwing

PLOVERS, TURNSTONES & SURFBIRDS

(Charadriidae) These birds are waders.

Turnstones: Their bill has an upward turn. They turn over stones on the shore and eat the uncovered invertebrates.

Plovers: They are well camouflaged and run along the beach. They have *dry* sand colored backs. They are great actors - to lead predators away from their nests they pretend to be crippled and an easy catch, until the predator is out of the nesting area, and then they fly away.

The **Ringed Plover** has a *wet* sand colored back.

Lapwings: Larger member of the Plover family.

WATER TURKEY

Water Turkey

(Anhingidae)

Are found in warmer regions. They swim and catch fish under water by spearing them with their bill.

Measuring A Bird

Wing: From bend of wing A to end of longest feather B.
Tail: Tip of longest feather C to where it enters body D.
Tarsus: From *front* of leg E to *root* of the middle toe F.
Bill: Tip of bill G to longest distance where bill (upper mandible) joins the skin of forehead H.

OYSTERCATCHER

Oystercatcher

(Haematopodidae)

This bird is a master at opening oysters and extracting the meat. It detachs barnacles and limpets from rocks. The feet only have three toes. These birds have red irises.

253

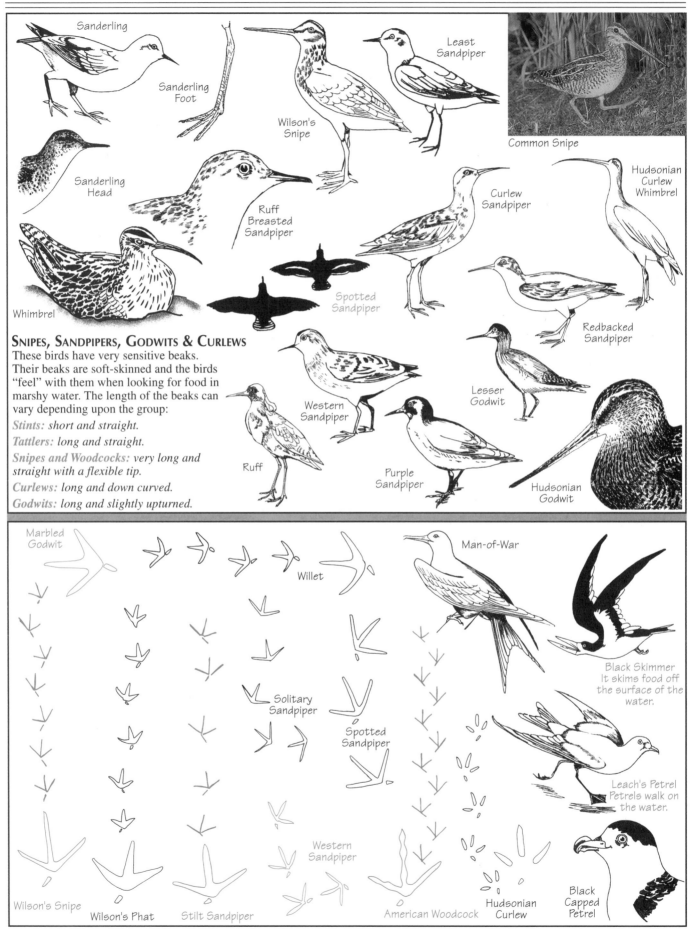

BIRDS

Sanderling
Sanderling Foot
Wilson's Snipe
Least Sandpiper
Common Snipe

Sanderling Head
Ruff Breasted Sandpiper
Curlew Sandpiper
Hudsonian Curlew Whimbrel

Whimbrel
Spotted Sandpiper
Redbacked Sandpiper

SNIPES, SANDPIPERS, GODWITS & CURLEWS

These birds have very sensitive beaks. Their beaks are soft-skinned and the birds "feel" with them when looking for food in marshy water. The length of the beaks can vary depending upon the group:

Stints: short and straight.

Tattlers: long and straight.

Snipes and Woodcocks: very long and straight with a flexible tip.

Curlews: long and down curved.

Godwits: long and slightly upturned.

Western Sandpiper
Ruff
Purple Sandpiper
Lesser Godwit
Hudsonian Godwit

Marbled Godwit
Willet
Man-of-War

Solitary Sandpiper
Spotted Sandpiper

Black Skimmer
It skims food off the surface of the water.

Leach's Petrel
Petrels walk on the water.

Western Sandpiper

Wilson's Snipe
Wilson's Phat
Stilt Sandpiper
American Woodcock
Hudsonian Curlew
Black Capped Petrel

254

Wide wings for hours of gliding and silent descent on prey.

Sharp curved beak to hook onto flesh and pull it apart.

Eyes positioned to look forward to focus on prey.

Sharp claws to catch prey.

BIRDS OF PREY

Osprey

OSPREY (PANDIONIDAE)

The Osprey is found all over temperate North America. They are fishers and plunge from great heights onto their unsuspecting food near the surface of the water. They build large stick nests.

OSPREY

Saw-Whet Owl

Hawk Owl

White Tailed Kite

Turkey Vulture

Sharp beak to tear the flesh of the prey.

Turkey Vulture

"Fingers" at the tips of the wings help birds of prey glide and silently swoop down on prey.

VULTURES (CATHARTIDAE)

There are three North American Vultures: Turkey Vulture, Black Vulture, California Condor. Vultures see their food and do not smell it.

Turkey Vulture

Black Vulture

VULTURE

Prairie Falcon

Gyrfalcon

FALCONS (FALCONIDAE)

They chase living prey as birds in flight, mice, and squirrels.

FALCONS

255

Rough Legged Hawk

Juvenile Soft Shinned Hawk

Marsh Hawk

Swallow Tailed Hawk

Swainson's Hawk

Hawk in Flight

Red-Tailed Hawk

Sparrow Hawk

Pigeon Hawk

Juvenile Goshawk

Rough-Legged Hawk Claw

Goshawk

Red Tailed Falcon Talon Marks

Marsh Hawk

HAWKS

Bald Eagle

Eagle Claw

Bald Eagle

Golden Eagle

Bald Eagle

Gold Eagle Foot

Golden Eagle

Bald Eagle

EAGLES

White Tailed Sea Eagle

OWLS

Screech
Owl

Great
Horned
Owl

Owl

Bared
Owl

Great
Gray
Owl

Snowy
Owl

Barn
Owl

Sharp
Shinned
Owl

Richardson's
Owl

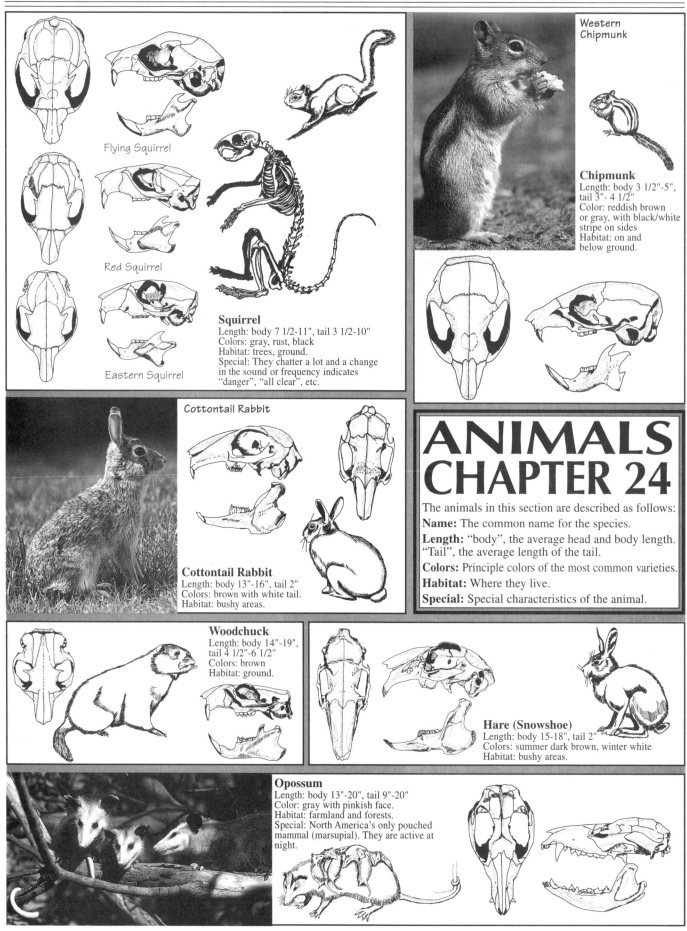

Flying Squirrel

Red Squirrel

Eastern Squirrel

Squirrel
Length: body 7 1/2-11", tail 3 1/2-10"
Colors: gray, rust, black
Habitat: trees, ground.
Special: They chatter a lot and a change in the sound or frequency indicates "danger", "all clear", etc.

Western Chipmunk

Chipmunk
Length: body 3 1/2"-5", tail 3"- 4 1/2"
Color: reddish brown or gray, with black/white stripe on sides
Habitat: on and below ground.

Cottontail Rabbit

Cottontail Rabbit
Length: body 13"-16", tail 2"
Colors: brown with white tail.
Habitat: bushy areas.

ANIMALS
CHAPTER 24

The animals in this section are described as follows:
Name: The common name for the species.
Length: "body", the average head and body length. "Tail", the average length of the tail.
Colors: Principle colors of the most common varieties.
Habitat: Where they live.
Special: Special characteristics of the animal.

Woodchuck
Length: body 14"-19", tail 4 1/2"-6 1/2"
Colors: brown
Habitat: ground.

Hare (Snowshoe)
Length: body 15-18", tail 2"
Colors: summer dark brown, winter white
Habitat: bushy areas.

Opossum
Length: body 13"-20", tail 9"-20"
Color: gray with pinkish face.
Habitat: farmland and forests.
Special: North America's only pouched mammal (marsupial). They are active at night.

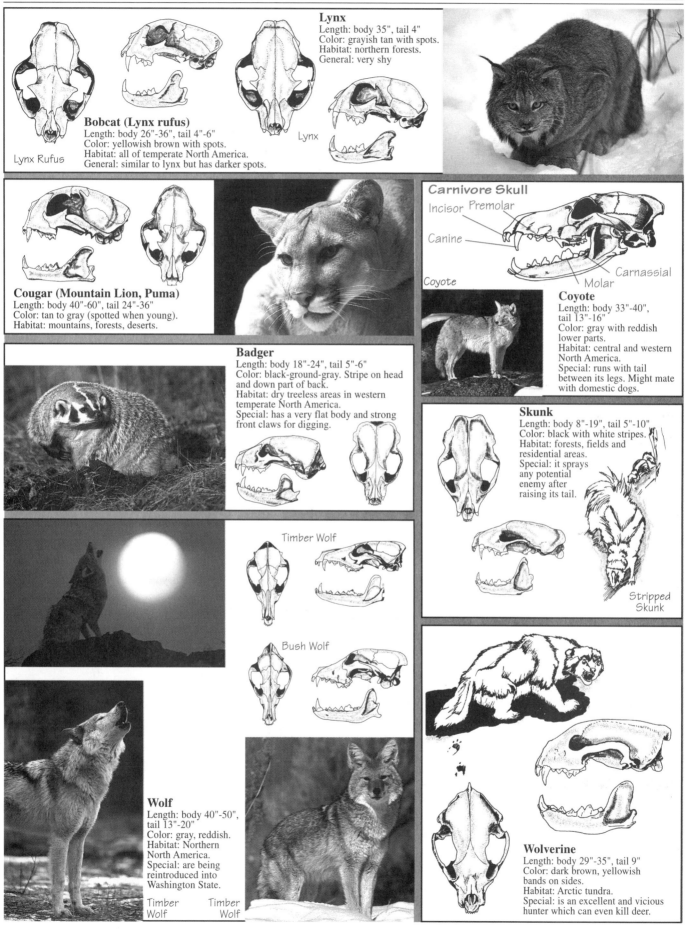

Lynx
Length: body 35", tail 4"
Color: grayish tan with spots.
Habitat: northern forests.
General: very shy

Bobcat (Lynx rufus)
Length: body 26"-36", tail 4"-6"
Color: yellowish brown with spots.
Habitat: all of temperate North America.
General: similar to lynx but has darker spots.

Lynx Rufus

Lynx

Cougar (Mountain Lion, Puma)
Length: body 40"-60", tail 24"-36"
Color: tan to gray (spotted when young).
Habitat: mountains, forests, deserts.

Carnivore Skull
Incisor Premolar
Canine
Coyote
Carnassial
Molar

Coyote
Length: body 33"-40",
tail 13"-16"
Color: gray with reddish
lower parts.
Habitat: central and western
North America.
Special: runs with tail
between its legs. Might mate
with domestic dogs.

Badger
Length: body 18"-24", tail 5"-6"
Color: black-ground-gray. Stripe on head
and down part of back.
Habitat: dry treeless areas in western
temperate North America.
Special: has a very flat body and strong
front claws for digging.

Skunk
Length: body 8"-19", tail 5"-10"
Color: black with white stripes.
Habitat: forests, fields and
residential areas.
Special: it sprays
any potential
enemy after
raising its tail.

Stripped
Skunk

Timber Wolf

Bush Wolf

Wolf
Length: body 40"-50",
tail 13"-20"
Color: gray, reddish.
Habitat: Northern
North America.
Special: are being
reintroduced into
Washington State.

Timber
Wolf

Timber
Wolf

Wolverine
Length: body 29"-35", tail 9"
Color: dark brown, yellowish
bands on sides.
Habitat: Arctic tundra.
Special: is an excellent and vicious
hunter which can even kill deer.

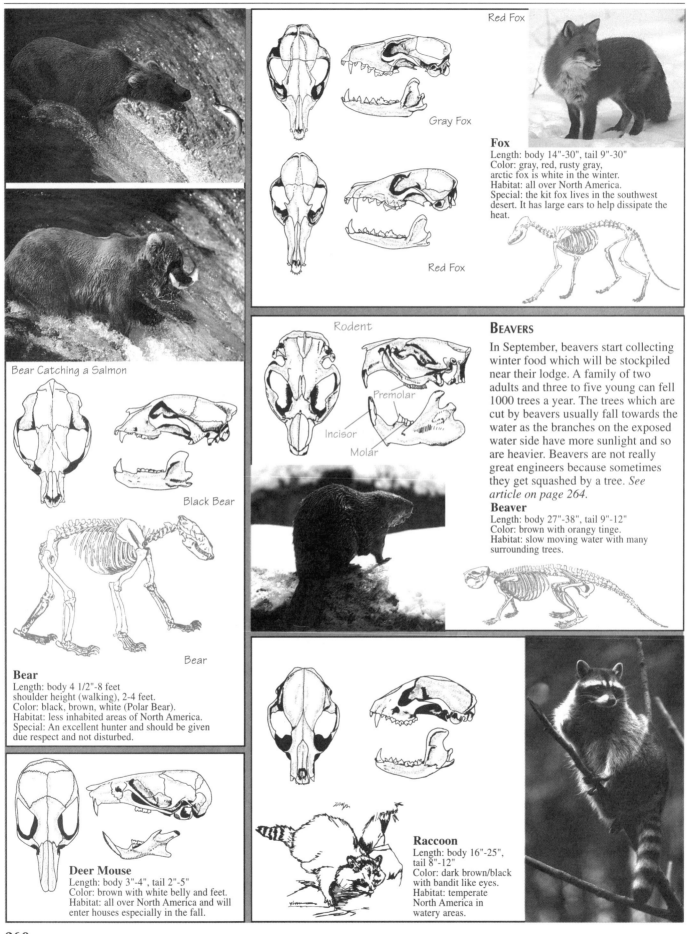

Red Fox

Gray Fox

Red Fox

Fox
Length: body 14"-30", tail 9"-30"
Color: gray, red, rusty gray,
arctic fox is white in the winter.
Habitat: all over North America.
Special: the kit fox lives in the southwest
desert. It has large ears to help dissipate the
heat.

Bear Catching a Salmon

Black Bear

Bear

Bear
Length: body 4 1/2"-8 feet
shoulder height (walking), 2-4 feet.
Color: black, brown, white (Polar Bear).
Habitat: less inhabited areas of North America.
Special: An excellent hunter and should be given
due respect and not disturbed.

Rodent

Premolar

Incisor

Molar

BEAVERS

In September, beavers start collecting
winter food which will be stockpiled
near their lodge. A family of two
adults and three to five young can fell
1000 trees a year. The trees which are
cut by beavers usually fall towards the
water as the branches on the exposed
water side have more sunlight and so
are heavier. Beavers are not really
great engineers because sometimes
they get squashed by a tree. *See
article on page 264.*

Beaver
Length: body 27"-38", tail 9"-12"
Color: brown with orangy tinge.
Habitat: slow moving water with many
surrounding trees.

Deer Mouse
Length: body 3"-4", tail 2"-5"
Color: brown with white belly and feet.
Habitat: all over North America and will
enter houses especially in the fall.

Raccoon
Length: body 16"-25",
tail 8"-12"
Color: dark brown/black
with bandit like eyes.
Habitat: temperate
North America in
watery areas.

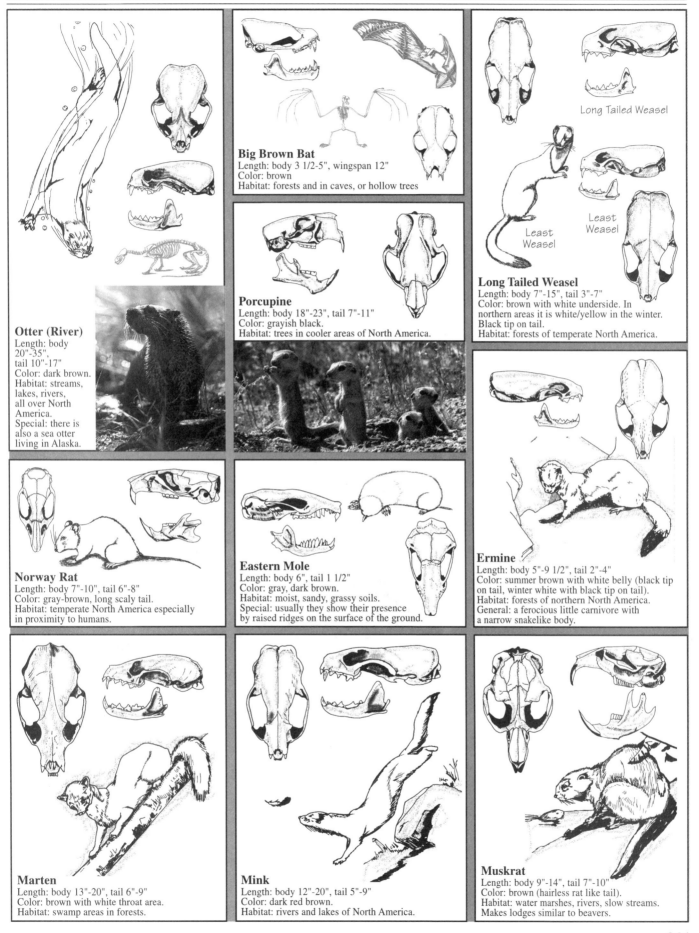

Big Brown Bat
Length: body 3 1/2-5", wingspan 12"
Color: brown
Habitat: forests and in caves, or hollow trees

Long Tailed Weasel

Least Weasel

Least Weasel

Long Tailed Weasel
Length: body 7"-15", tail 3"-7"
Color: brown with white underside. In northern areas it is white/yellow in the winter. Black tip on tail.
Habitat: forests of temperate North America.

Porcupine
Length: body 18"-23", tail 7"-11"
Color: grayish black.
Habitat: trees in cooler areas of North America.

Otter (River)
Length: body 20"-35", tail 10"-17"
Color: dark brown.
Habitat: streams, lakes, rivers, all over North America.
Special: there is also a sea otter living in Alaska.

Norway Rat
Length: body 7"-10", tail 6"-8"
Color: gray-brown, long scaly tail.
Habitat: temperate North America especially in proximity to humans.

Eastern Mole
Length: body 6", tail 1 1/2"
Color: gray, dark brown.
Habitat: moist, sandy, grassy soils.
Special: usually they show their presence by raised ridges on the surface of the ground.

Ermine
Length: body 5"-9 1/2", tail 2"-4"
Color: summer brown with white belly (black tip on tail, winter white with black tip on tail).
Habitat: forests of northern North America.
General: a ferocious little carnivore with a narrow snakelike body.

Marten
Length: body 13"-20", tail 6"-9"
Color: brown with white throat area.
Habitat: swamp areas in forests.

Mink
Length: body 12"-20", tail 5"-9"
Color: dark red brown.
Habitat: rivers and lakes of North America.

Muskrat
Length: body 9"-14", tail 7"-10"
Color: brown (hairless rat like tail).
Habitat: water marshes, rivers, slow streams.
Makes lodges similar to beavers.

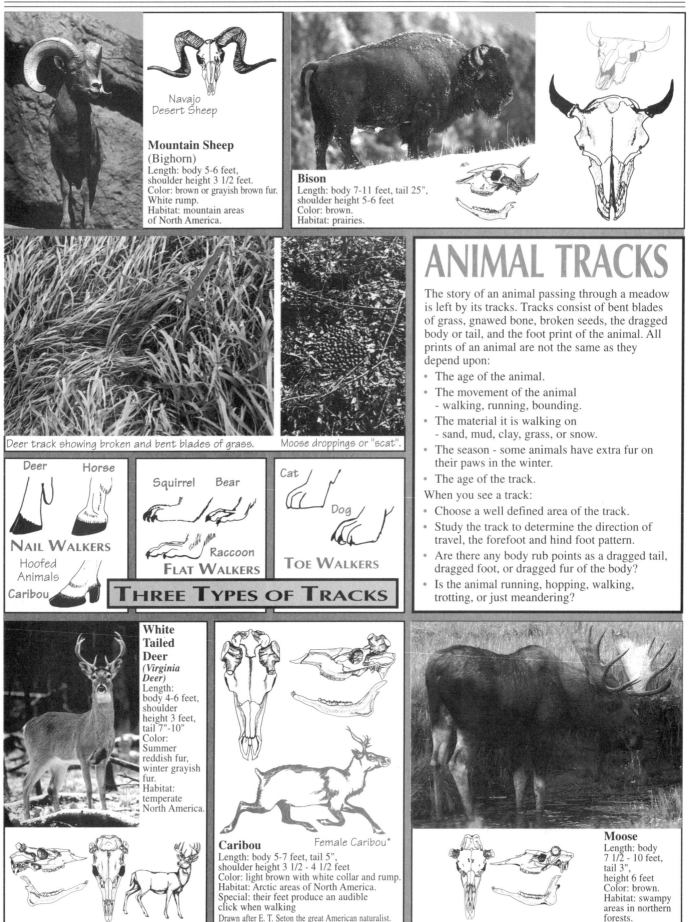

Mountain Sheep
(Bighorn)
Length: body 5-6 feet,
shoulder height 3 1/2 feet.
Color: brown or grayish brown fur.
White rump.
Habitat: mountain areas
of North America.

Navajo
Desert Sheep

Bison
Length: body 7-11 feet, tail 25",
shoulder height 5-6 feet
Color: brown.
Habitat: prairies.

Deer track showing broken and bent blades of grass.

Moose droppings or "scat".

Deer   Horse

NAIL WALKERS
Hoofed
Animals
Caribou

Squirrel   Bear

Raccoon
FLAT WALKERS

Cat

Dog

TOE WALKERS

THREE TYPES OF TRACKS

ANIMAL TRACKS

The story of an animal passing through a meadow is left by its tracks. Tracks consist of bent blades of grass, gnawed bone, broken seeds, the dragged body or tail, and the foot print of the animal. All prints of an animal are not the same as they depend upon:

- The age of the animal.
- The movement of the animal
  - walking, running, bounding.
- The material it is walking on
  - sand, mud, clay, grass, or snow.
- The season - some animals have extra fur on their paws in the winter.
- The age of the track.

When you see a track:

- Choose a well defined area of the track.
- Study the track to determine the direction of travel, the forefoot and hind foot pattern.
- Are there any body rub points as a dragged tail, dragged foot, or dragged fur of the body?
- Is the animal running, hopping, walking, trotting, or just meandering?

White Tailed Deer
(*Virginia Deer*)
Length:
body 4-6 feet,
shoulder
height 3 feet,
tail 7"-10"
Color:
Summer
reddish fur,
winter grayish
fur.
Habitat:
temperate
North America.

Caribou
Length: body 5-7 feet, tail 5",
shoulder height 3 1/2 - 4 1/2 feet
Color: light brown with white collar and rump.
Habitat: Arctic areas of North America.
Special: their feet produce an audible
click when walking
Drawn after E. T. Seton the great American naturalist.

Female Caribou*

Moose
Length: body
7 1/2 - 10 feet,
tail 3",
height 6 feet
Color: brown.
Habitat: swampy
areas in northern
forests.

TRACKS OF A RUNNING ANIMAL

This illustration shows a running dog and the foot contact made with the ground. Observe that the paws touch the ground in a definite sequence. All animals have a different stride for walking, trotting, stalking, running, and just meandering. The track will also vary for each animal, sex of animal, age, and its physical condition.

AGE OF TRACK

Tracks made by animals "age" by the action of weather and other tracks being made over them. A track is made by the pressure of the weight of the animal on the ground and this pressure usually breaks the surface exposing humid soil or a lower layer of snow. As soon as a track is made the weather will start acting (aging) on the track. If frost crystals have formed on the track after a cold night, the track was made before the frost. If there is no frost, the track is recent. A fresh track in snow will have a crisp curl with snow particles kicked in the direction of movement. A track is old when evaporation or blown snow have dulled the crispness. Aging happens in a few hours as the sun dries the dew, frost, or humidity from a dirt track and the edges start to crumble.

Floor of Track
Wall of Track

Direction
New Track of Hoofed Animal

SUN ACTION

Sun
New Track
Sun will rapidly dry this side.
Dry sand falling off side.
Erosion and shrinkage. Faster than shadow side.
Old Track
Debris and track becomes shallow.

WIND ACTION

Wind
Wind will rapidly dry this side.
New Track
Wind deposit of sand.
Erosion and shrinkage. Faster than lee side.

Looking For Tracks

Tracks are found on undisturbed sand, dusty roads, riverbeds, snow, and grass in areas where animals travel for water or food.

Spray

Moose Track on Crusty Snow with Snow Spray

Moose Track on Stones and Humid Sand

Animal "Highway" in the Winter Forest

COTTONTAIL MAKING TRACKS

Rabbit starts a leap with its hind legs leaving the ground.

In the air the rabbit's legs will reposition themselves to prepare to land and start the next leap.

Front legs will first make contact with the ground. When looking at the tracks you will see that the front leg's print will be behind the hind leg's print.

The hind legs touch the ground and the next bound starts.

A cluster is called a 'set'.

Straddle the width of a track.

A 'leap' is the distance between the toe and heal of two following sets.

Front   Hind

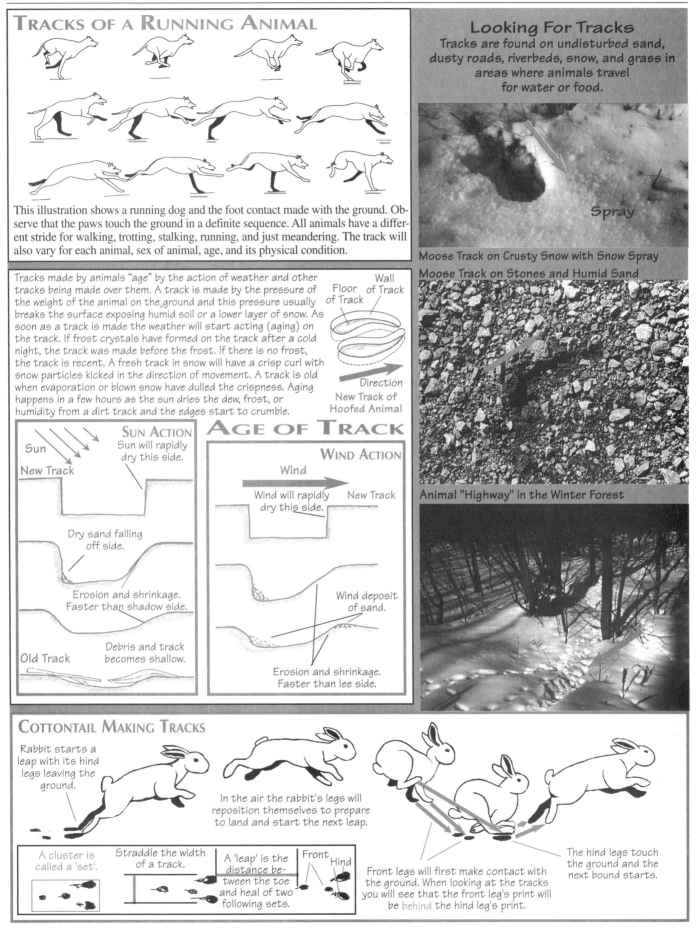

EVIDENCE OF ANIMALS

Porcupine

Print: L" x W"
Fore: 1³/4 x 1¹/4
Hind: 2¹/4 x 1¹/2

A porcupine has a "toes in" walk because it is a tree climber where he has to "hang on". The hole in the stream bank is the entrance to a porcupine

Ermine following mouse.

Deer Mouse Track

An ermine following a deer mouse. As there was fresh fallen snow the mouse paddled across the snow surface. The ermine bounded along the sides of the escaping mouse. The mouse got caught as at a point in the mouse's track disappeared and the ermine's track was deeper. This sequence was photographed next to the cottage while writing this book. The ermine 'Gaspar' lived in the basement of the house for the winter.

Mouse entering into fresh snow for shelter.

Dog track in mud that is drying (see crack).

Beavers are considered as being great engineers but a tree fell on the head of this "worker".

Beaver lodge built in a hidden part of a stream. There are floating logs cut by the beavers in the water in front of the lodge. These logs are for food and are sunk to supply food for the winter.

Print: L" x W"
Fore: 3 x 3
Hind: 5 x 4¹/2

Beaver Hind Foot

BEAVER

From the tracks you can see that the beaver is not made for walking. Its whole body drags. The feet are crossed. The beaver is built for swimming as shown from its webbed hind feet and its powerful tail.

Hind foot webbed for swimming.

Front foot has fingers to manipulate pieces of wood and mud when dam-building.

Beavers will cut trees along streams where they build their houses and dams. The trees usually fall towards the stream bank because trees have a heavier growth on the exposed sunny side.

Line made from the body and fur dragging.

264

BADGER

Fore Foot

The front feet have large claws because the badger is an animal that digs for its food.

Front

Badger Trotting

Hind

Badger Walking

Print: L" x W"
Fore: 2¹/₂ x 2
Hind: 2¹/₈ x 2

SUN, WIND, AND RAIN EFFECT ON A TRACK

Weather	Surface	Impact on Track
Sun	Sand	Rapidly dry track and cause sides to fall.
	Snow	Melt snow, enlarge hole, and obliterate details.
	Rock	Wet footprint will dry it in a few minutes.
Rain	Sand	Wash out track.
	Snow	Obliterate track.
	Rock	No track will be made.
Wind	Sand	Dry track and cause sides to fall. Leave sand and other debris deposits in cavity.
	Snow	Drift snow across the track.
	Rock	Wet footprint will dry it in a few minutes.

GROUND SURFACE AND QUALITY OF TRACK

Surface	Track
Dry sand	Walls rapidly collapse and there are not many details.
Very wet sand	Track fills with water and mud and disappears.
Dry sand surface	Ideal track when the surface is dry but humid below.
When Humid Below Surface Then:	
Humid sand	Good track. Track size will *increase* upon drying.
Humid clay	Can dry and preserve the track.
Humid snow	Good track.
Crusty snow	Track breaks crust but details lost in dry snow below.
Grass field	Track will be twisted and broken grass.

Black Bear Front Claw

Front Paw

Hind Paw

Print: L" x W"
Fore: 4¹/₂ x 4
Hind: 7 x 3¹/₂

Front Paw

Hind Paw

Black Bear Walking

Black Bear

Brown Bear Front Claw

Hind Paw

Front Paw

Brown Bear

Grizzly Bear Front Claw

Print: L" x W"
Fore: 5¹/₂ x 5¹/₂
Hind: 10 x 5⁵/₈

Hind Paw

Front Paw

Grizzly Bear

Front Paw   **Hind Paw**

Hind Paw

Front Paw

Polar Bear

Front Hoof

Hind Hoof

Print: L" x W"
Fore: 5 x 5
Hind: 5 x 5

Buffalo

Cat claw in normal retracted position.

Claw — Middle Phalanx

Tendon

Proximal Phalanx

Ligament keeps the claw raised. The cat has to make its claw tendon lower the claw.

Ligament

Tendon

Print: L" x W"
Fore: 1¹/₂ x 1¹/₂
Hind: 1³/₈ x 1³/₈

Front   Hind

Cat Walking

Domestic Cat

Hind

Front

Print: L" x W"
Fore: ¹/₂ x ¹/₂
Hind: 1 x ³/₄

Chipmunk

Fore   Ocelot

Hind

Ocelot

Trotting

Stalking

Print: L" x W"
Fore: 3 x 3¹/₂
Hind: 3 x 3

Cougar

Domestic Dog

Fore

Hind

Hind   Fore

Print: L" x W"
Fore: 2³/₄ x 2¹/₄
Hind: 2³/₄ x 2

Coyote

Wild Cat

Fore

Hind

Print: L" x W"
Fore: 4³/₄ x 4³/₈
Hind: 4¹/₂ x 4

Wolf

Arctic Fox

Fore   Fore

Hind   Hind

Fore

Hind

Print: L" x W"
Fore: 2¹/₄ x 2¹/₈
Hind: 2¹/₈ x 1⁷/₈

Arctic Fox Jumping on a Mouse

Red Fox
Print: L" x W"
Fore: 2³/₈ x 2
Hind: 2¹/₈ x 2

Grey Fox
Print: L" x W"
Fore: 1³/₄ x 1³/₈
Hind: 2¹/₂ x 2

Desert Fox

Fore

Hind

Right Fore   Claw

Digital Pad

Right Hind

Red Fox

Palmar Pad

Dew Claw

Red Fox

Kit Fox

Fore

Hind

Print: L" x W"
Fore: 1¹/₂ x 1³/₈
Hind: 1¹/₂ x 1¹/₄

Kit Fox

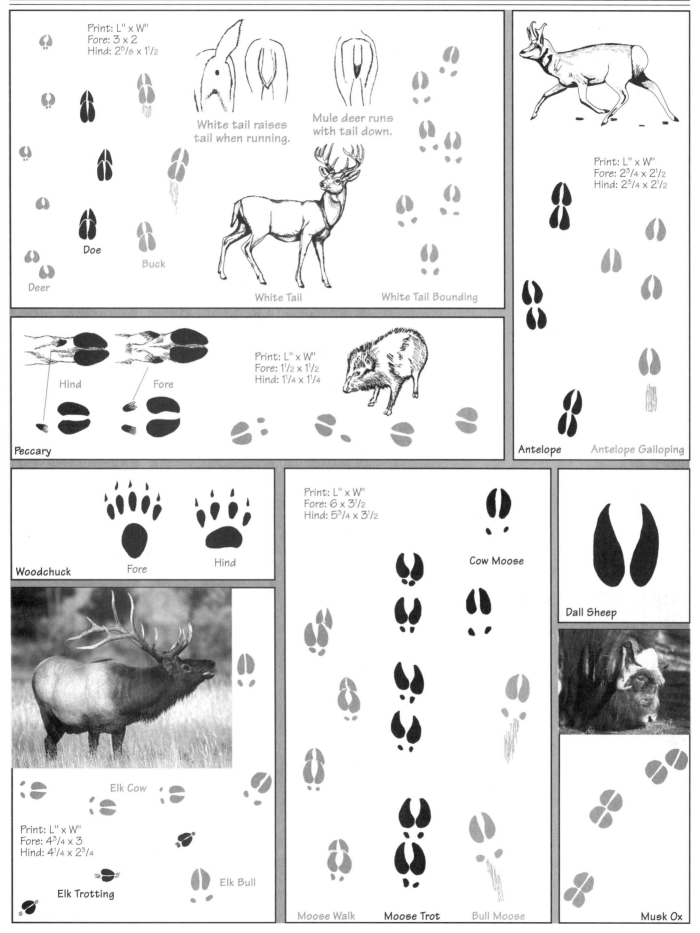

Print: L" x W"
Fore: 3 x 2
Hind: $2^5/8$ x $1^1/2$

White tail raises tail when running.

Mule deer runs with tail down.

Doe

Buck

Deer

White Tail

White Tail Bounding

Print: L" x W"
Fore: $2^3/4$ x $2^1/2$
Hind: $2^3/4$ x $2^1/2$

Antelope

Antelope Galloping

Hind

Fore

Print: L" x W"
Fore: $1^1/2$ x $1^1/2$
Hind: $1^1/4$ x $1^1/4$

Peccary

Woodchuck

Fore

Hind

Print: L" x W"
Fore: 6 x $3^1/2$
Hind: $5^3/4$ x $3^1/2$

Cow Moose

Dall Sheep

Elk Cow

Print: L" x W"
Fore: $4^3/4$ x 3
Hind: $4^1/4$ x $2^3/4$

Elk Trotting

Elk Bull

Moose Walk

Moose Trot

Bull Moose

Musk Ox

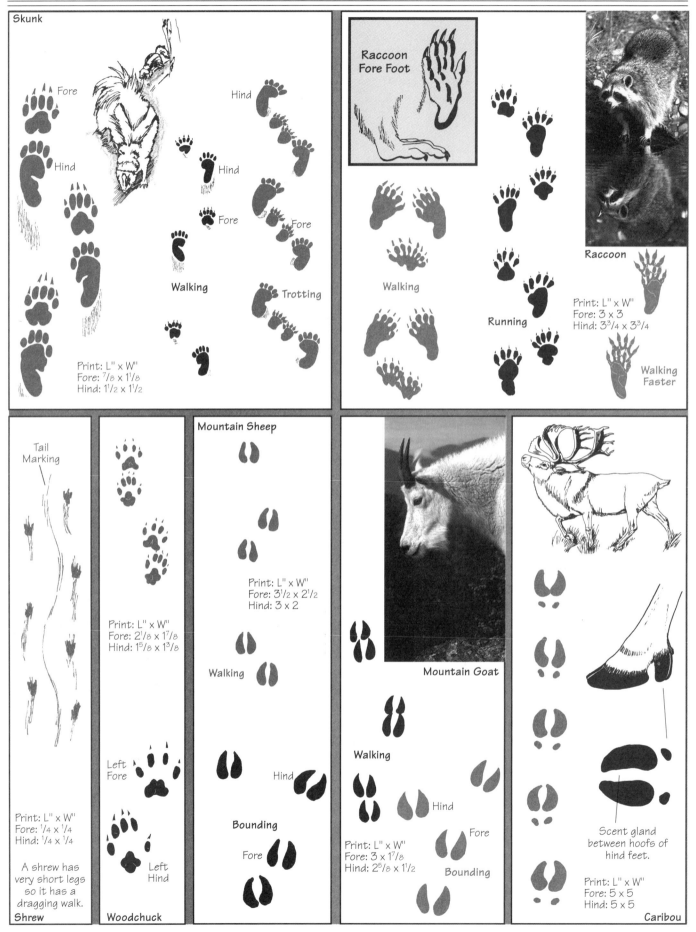

Skunk

Fore

Hind

Hind

Fore

Hind

Fore

Walking

Trotting

Print: L" x W"
Fore: $^7/_8$ x $1^1/_8$
Hind: $1^1/_2$ x $1^1/_2$

Raccoon
Fore Foot

Walking

Running

Raccoon

Print: L" x W"
Fore: 3 x 3
Hind: $3^3/_4$ x $3^3/_4$

Walking
Faster

Tail
Marking

Print: L" x W"
Fore: $^1/_4$ x $^1/_4$
Hind: $^1/_4$ x $^1/_4$

A shrew has
very short legs
so it has a
dragging walk.

Shrew

Print: L" x W"
Fore: $2^1/_8$ x $1^7/_8$
Hind: $1^5/_8$ x $1^3/_8$

Left
Fore

Left
Hind

Woodchuck

Mountain Sheep

Print: L" x W"
Fore: $3^1/_2$ x $2^1/_2$
Hind: 3 x 2

Walking

Hind

Bounding

Fore

Mountain Goat

Walking

Hind

Fore

Print: L" x W"
Fore: 3 x $1^7/_8$
Hind: $2^5/_8$ x $1^1/_2$

Bounding

Scent gland
between hoofs of
hind feet.

Print: L" x W"
Fore: 5 x 5
Hind: 5 x 5

Caribou

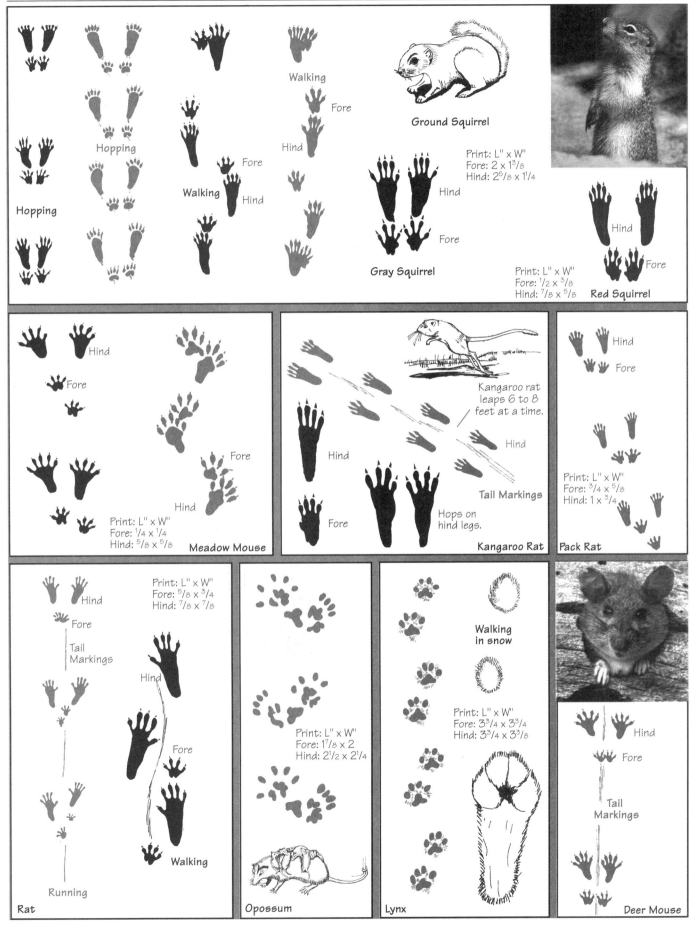

Hopping

Hopping

Walking

Hopping

Walking

Walking

Fore

Hind

Fore

Hind

Ground Squirrel

Print: L" x W"
Fore: 2 x 1³/₈
Hind: 2⁵/₈ x 1¹/₄

Hind

Fore

Gray Squirrel

Print: L" x W"
Fore: ¹/₂ x ³/₈
Hind: ⁷/₈ x ⁵/₈

Hind

Fore

Red Squirrel

Hind

Fore

Fore

Hind

Print: L" x W"
Fore: ¹/₄ x ¹/₄
Hind: ⁵/₈ x ⁵/₈

Meadow Mouse

Hind

Fore

Kangaroo rat
leaps 6 to 8
feet at a time.

Hind

Tail Markings

Hops on
hind legs.

Kangaroo Rat

Hind

Fore

Print: L" x W"
Fore: ³/₄ x ⁵/₈
Hind: 1 x ³/₄

Pack Rat

Hind

Fore

Tail
Markings

Hind

Fore

Print: L" x W"
Fore: ⁵/₈ x ³/₄
Hind: ⁷/₈ x ⁷/₈

Walking

Running

Rat

Print: L" x W"
Fore: 1⁷/₈ x 2
Hind: 2¹/₂ x 2¹/₄

Opossum

Walking
in snow

Print: L" x W"
Fore: 3³/₄ x 3³/₄
Hind: 3³/₄ x 3³/₈

Lynx

Hind

Fore

Tail
Markings

Deer Mouse

269

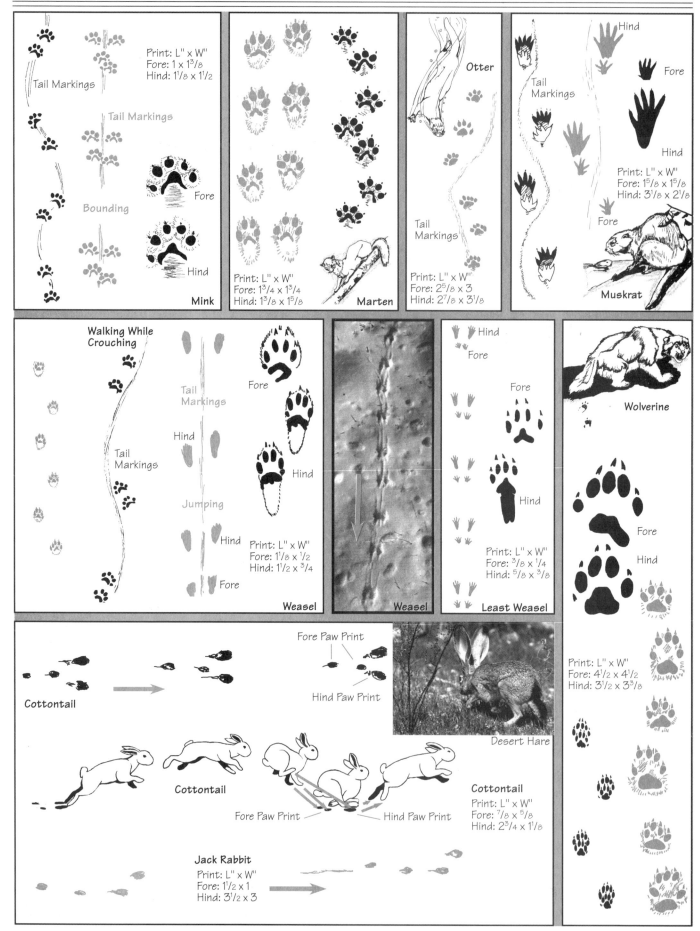

Mink

Print: L" x W"
Fore: 1 x 1³/₈
Hind: 1¹/₈ x 1¹/₂

Tail Markings

Tail Markings

Bounding

Fore

Hind

Marten

Print: L" x W"
Fore: 1³/₄ x 1³/₄
Hind: 1³/₈ x 1⁵/₈

Otter

Tail Markings

Tail Markings

Print: L" x W"
Fore: 2⁵/₈ x 3
Hind: 2⁷/₈ x 3¹/₈

Muskrat

Hind

Fore

Hind

Tail Markings

Print: L" x W"
Fore: 1⁵/₈ x 1⁵/₈
Hind: 3¹/₈ x 2¹/₈

Fore

Weasel

Walking While Crouching

Tail Markings

Fore

Hind

Tail Markings

Jumping

Hind

Fore

Print: L" x W"
Fore: 1¹/₈ x ¹/₂
Hind: 1¹/₂ x ³/₄

Weasel

Least Weasel

Hind

Fore

Fore

Hind

Print: L" x W"
Fore: ³/₈ x ¹/₄
Hind: ⁵/₈ x ³/₈

Wolverine

Fore

Hind

Print: L" x W"
Fore: 4¹/₂ x 4¹/₂
Hind: 3¹/₂ x 3³/₈

Fore Paw Print

Hind Paw Print

Cottontail

Cottontail

Fore Paw Print

Hind Paw Print

Desert Hare

Cottontail

Print: L" x W"
Fore: ⁷/₈ x ⁵/₈
Hind: 2³/₄ x 1¹/₈

Jack Rabbit

Print: L" x W"
Fore: 1¹/₂ x 1
Hind: 3¹/₂ x 3

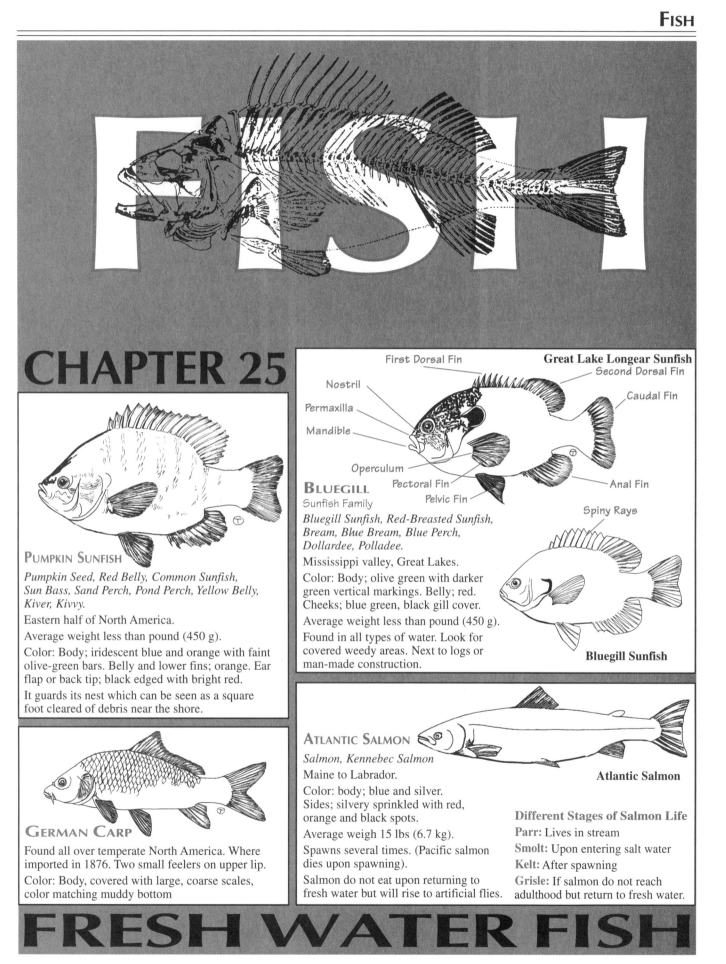

CHAPTER 25

PUMPKIN SUNFISH

Pumpkin Seed, Red Belly, Common Sunfish, Sun Bass, Sand Perch, Pond Perch, Yellow Belly, Kiver, Kivvy.

Eastern half of North America.

Average weight less than pound (450 g).

Color: Body; iridescent blue and orange with faint olive-green bars. Belly and lower fins; orange. Ear flap or back tip; black edged with bright red.

It guards its nest which can be seen as a square foot cleared of debris near the shore.

GERMAN CARP

Found all over temperate North America. Where imported in 1876. Two small feelers on upper lip.

Color: Body, covered with large, coarse scales, color matching muddy bottom

Great Lake Longear Sunfish

First Dorsal Fin
Second Dorsal Fin
Nostril
Caudal Fin
Permaxilla
Mandible
Operculum
Pectoral Fin
Anal Fin
Pelvic Fin

BLUEGILL
Sunfish Family

Bluegill Sunfish, Red-Breasted Sunfish, Bream, Blue Bream, Blue Perch, Dollardee, Polladee.

Mississippi valley, Great Lakes.

Color: Body; olive green with darker green vertical markings. Belly; red. Cheeks; blue green, black gill cover.

Average weight less than pound (450 g).

Found in all types of water. Look for covered weedy areas. Next to logs or man-made construction.

Spiny Rays

Bluegill Sunfish

ATLANTIC SALMON

Salmon, Kennebec Salmon

Maine to Labrador.

Color: body; blue and silver. Sides; silvery sprinkled with red, orange and black spots.

Average weigh 15 lbs (6.7 kg).

Spawns several times. (Pacific salmon dies upon spawning).

Salmon do not eat upon returning to fresh water but will rise to artificial flies.

Atlantic Salmon

Different Stages of Salmon Life

Parr: Lives in stream

Smolt: Upon entering salt water

Kelt: After spawning

Grisle: If salmon do not reach adulthood but return to fresh water.

FRESH WATER FISH

Brown Trout

Golden Trout

Rainbow Trout

TROUT

Lake Trout

Speckled Trout / Brook Trout

Cutthroat Trout

BROWN TROUT

English Brown Trout, Dutchmen.

All over temperate North America. This fish was imported in 1883.

Color: Body; brownish with large scales. Back; almost black. Belly; almost white. Fins; bottom have white edges. Sides; red and black spots surrounded with lighter rings.

Average weight one pound (450 g).

Feed from the surface at night. They are in warmer waters than Speckled (Brook) Trout.

GOLDEN TROUT

Roosevelt Trout, Golden, Volcano Creek Trout

Native of cold waters of high Sierra Nevada Mountains and have been introduced to other mountain systems.

Color: Body; golden yellow. Side; red stripe with dark splotches. Dorsal fin, tail; red markings. Pectoral fins, lower half of gill plates; red. Lower fins; tipped red.

Average weight one pound (450 g).

Found at elevations over 10,000 feet (3000 m).

RAINBOW TROUT

Rainbow, California Trout, Pacific Trout, Steelhead Trout, Salmon, Hardhead, Salmon Trout.

Lives all over North America including Mexico.

Average weight two pounds (900 g).

Lake Rainbow Trout characteristics: Body and fins are spotted with black. Broad horizontal red or purplish-red band running the full length of body. Lower fins edged with white. Roof of mouth has zigzag rows of teeth.

If they enter the ocean they will change coloration and become silvery and be considered a sea-run trout and called Steelheads.

LAKE TROUT

Salmon Trout, Mackinaw Trout, Great Lakes Trout, Laker, Togue, Gray Trout.

Cold water fish found in Northern States, Canada and Alaska.

Color: Body; gray with yellowish spots.

Average weight five pounds (2.2 kg).

Has teeth on base of tongue and roof of mouth. In the summer only found in deep water. In the Spring and Fall they can be caught in shallow water.

SPECKLED TROUT

Brook Trout, Red Trout, Native Trout,

Natives of cold water streams mainly in Eastern North America.

Color: Body; depends upon type of water and food eaten, usually back is black mottled with lighter tones. Sides; red or pink spots. Belly; almost white. Lower fins; red with white edges.

Likes deep cold water. Look for deep shade and other cover. They look scaleless but have minute scales embedded in the skin.

CUTTHROAT TROUT

Colorado River Trout, Black-spotted Trout, Rocky Mountain Trout, Blueback, Red-throated Trout.

Western fish native to waters in the Rocky Mountains from California to Alaska.

Color: Body; yellowish with black spots. Under lower jaw; bright red marking.

Average weight of 2 lbs (990 g).

They live in the sea and ascend rivers to spawn. In the Spring they are in the estuaries and have a light blue or green back. When they ascend a stream they will change colors to having sides that are rosy pink and black spots will appear.

Northern Smallmouth Bass

Smallmouth Bass

Black Bass, River Bass, Tiger Bass, Jumper, Oswego Bass, Green Bass.

Require clear cold water and are found all over North America excepting a few states on the Gulf of Mexico. Average Weight: 2 lbs (900 g).

Color: Body; bronze green with light gray or yellowish belly. Back: darker with vertical descending markings.

See Largemouth characteristics. Smallmouth also has scales on the base of dorsal fin. There are none on those of the largemouth.

Will eat anything. In lakes look for rock formations and in streams for shallow water or deep pools.

Northern Largemouth Bass

Largemouth Bass

Black bass, Bigmouth Bass, Marsh Bass, Chub, Stra Bass, Bayou Bass, Green Bass, Mossback, Slough Bass, Oswego Bass.

Found all over North America.

Average weight: 2-3 lbs (900-1,400 g).

Color: Greenish bronze with darkness depending upon water.

To differentiate from Smallmouth Bass: mouth on Largemouth extends *past* area below the eye and fins on back are *separated*.

Morning and evening enter shallow water. During hot hours they enter deep water holes.

BASS

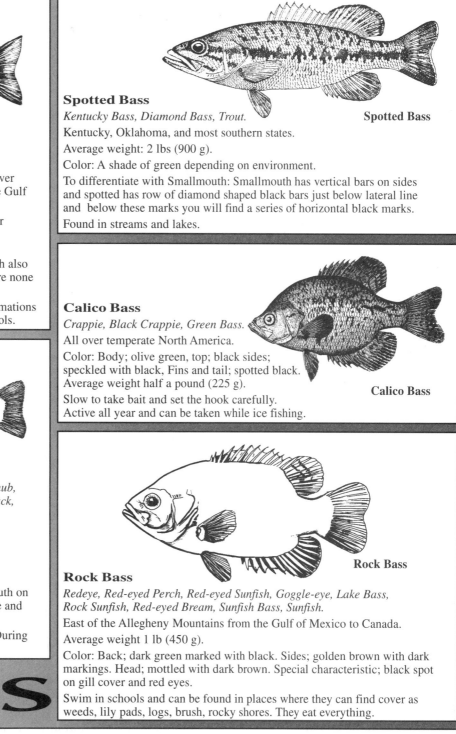

Spotted Bass

Kentucky Bass, Diamond Bass, Trout.   **Spotted Bass**

Kentucky, Oklahoma, and most southern states.

Average weight: 2 lbs (900 g).

Color: A shade of green depending on environment.

To differentiate with Smallmouth: Smallmouth has vertical bars on sides and spotted has row of diamond shaped black bars just below lateral line and below these marks you will find a series of horizontal black marks.

Found in streams and lakes.

Calico Bass

Crappie, Black Crappie, Green Bass.

All over temperate North America.

Color: Body; olive green, top; black sides; speckled with black, Fins and tail; spotted black. Average weight half a pound (225 g).

Calico Bass

Slow to take bait and set the hook carefully. Active all year and can be taken while ice fishing.

Rock Bass

Redeye, Red-eyed Perch, Red-eyed Sunfish, Goggle-eye, Lake Bass, Rock Sunfish, Red-eyed Bream, Sunfish Bass, Sunfish.

Rock Bass

East of the Allegheny Mountains from the Gulf of Mexico to Canada.

Average weight 1 lb (450 g).

Color: Back; dark green marked with black. Sides; golden brown with dark markings. Head; mottled with dark brown. Special characteristic; black spot on gill cover and red eyes.

Swim in schools and can be found in places where they can find cover as weeds, lily pads, logs, brush, rocky shores. They eat everything.

White Bass

Stripped Bass

White Bass

Related to the Stripped Bass.

Silver Bass, Silversides, Gray Bass, Stripped Bass, Stripped Lake Bass, Barfish.

Mississippi Valley, Great Lakes, deep lakes as far south as Texas, up to eastern Canada.

Average weight: 1-5 pounds (450- 2,200 g).

Body: Silvery with darker horizontal stripes.

Feed at night in large schools.

Walleyed Pike

Pike Perch, Walleye, Blue Pike, Yellow Pickerel, Dore, Glasseye, River Trout, Yellow Pike, Golden Pike, Jack Salmon.

In lakes and rivers east of the Mississippi from the Gulf of Mexico to Canada.

Average weight 3-4 pounds (1.4-1.8 kg).

Color: brassy brown color, flecked with yellow, marked with dark brown bars. Eyes; are filmy with milky appearance.

Have two *separate* dorsal fins. Feed at night. Stay in deep water during the day preferring clear water, with clean gravel or rock bottoms.

Northern Pike

American Pike, Common Pike, Great Lakes Pike, Jackfish, Snake, Pickerel, Lake Pike, Great Pike.

In northern lakes of America, Europe, Asia, British Isles.

Average weight: 5 lbs (2.2 kg).

Color: top; blue green or gray green. Sides; lighter with white belly. Have yellowish horizontal spots on sides. Fins; dark spots. Cheeks; covered with scales.

Have sharp teeth that curve backwards in mouth. They remain in shallow water all summer and will strike at anything that swims.

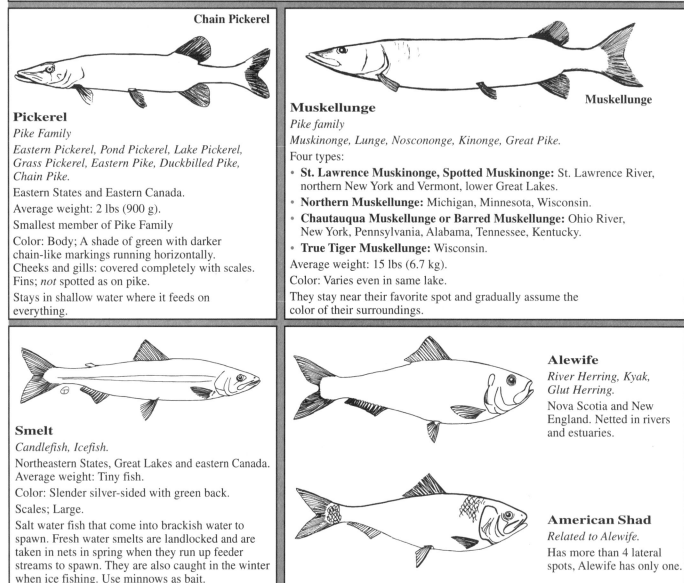

Chain Pickerel

Pickerel

Pike Family

Eastern Pickerel, Pond Pickerel, Lake Pickerel, Grass Pickerel, Eastern Pike, Duckbilled Pike, Chain Pike.

Eastern States and Eastern Canada.

Average weight: 2 lbs (900 g).

Smallest member of Pike Family

Color: Body; A shade of green with darker chain-like markings running horizontally. Cheeks and gills: covered completely with scales. Fins; *not* spotted as on pike.

Stays in shallow water where it feeds on everything.

Muskellunge

Muskellunge

Pike family

Muskinonge, Lunge, Noscononge, Kinonge, Great Pike.

Four types:

- **St. Lawrence Muskinonge, Spotted Muskinonge:** St. Lawrence River, northern New York and Vermont, lower Great Lakes.
- **Northern Muskellunge:** Michigan, Minnesota, Wisconsin.
- **Chautauqua Muskellunge or Barred Muskellunge:** Ohio River, New York, Pennsylvania, Alabama, Tennessee, Kentucky.
- **True Tiger Muskellunge:** Wisconsin.

Average weight: 15 lbs (6.7 kg).

Color: Varies even in same lake.

They stay near their favorite spot and gradually assume the color of their surroundings.

Smelt

Candlefish, Icefish.

Northeastern States, Great Lakes and eastern Canada.
Average weight: Tiny fish.

Color: Slender silver-sided with green back.

Scales; Large.

Salt water fish that come into brackish water to spawn. Fresh water smelts are landlocked and are taken in nets in spring when they run up feeder streams to spawn. They are also caught in the winter when ice fishing. Use minnows as bait.

Alewife

River Herring, Kyak, Glut Herring.

Nova Scotia and New England. Netted in rivers and estuaries.

American Shad

Related to Alewife.

Has more than 4 lateral spots, Alewife has only one.

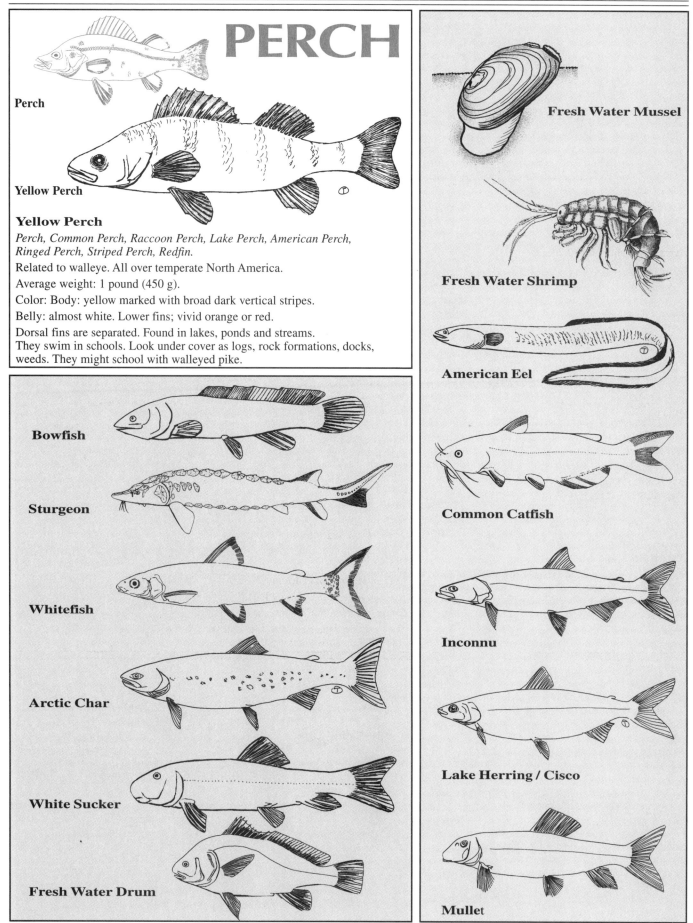

PERCH

Perch

Yellow Perch

Yellow Perch

Perch, Common Perch, Raccoon Perch, Lake Perch, American Perch, Ringed Perch, Striped Perch, Redfin.

Related to walleye. All over temperate North America.

Average weight: 1 pound (450 g).

Color: Body: yellow marked with broad dark vertical stripes.

Belly: almost white. Lower fins; vivid orange or red.

Dorsal fins are separated. Found in lakes, ponds and streams. They swim in schools. Look under cover as logs, rock formations, docks, weeds. They might school with walleyed pike.

Bowfish

Sturgeon

Whitefish

Arctic Char

White Sucker

Fresh Water Drum

Fresh Water Mussel

Fresh Water Shrimp

American Eel

Common Catfish

Inconnu

Lake Herring / Cisco

Mullet

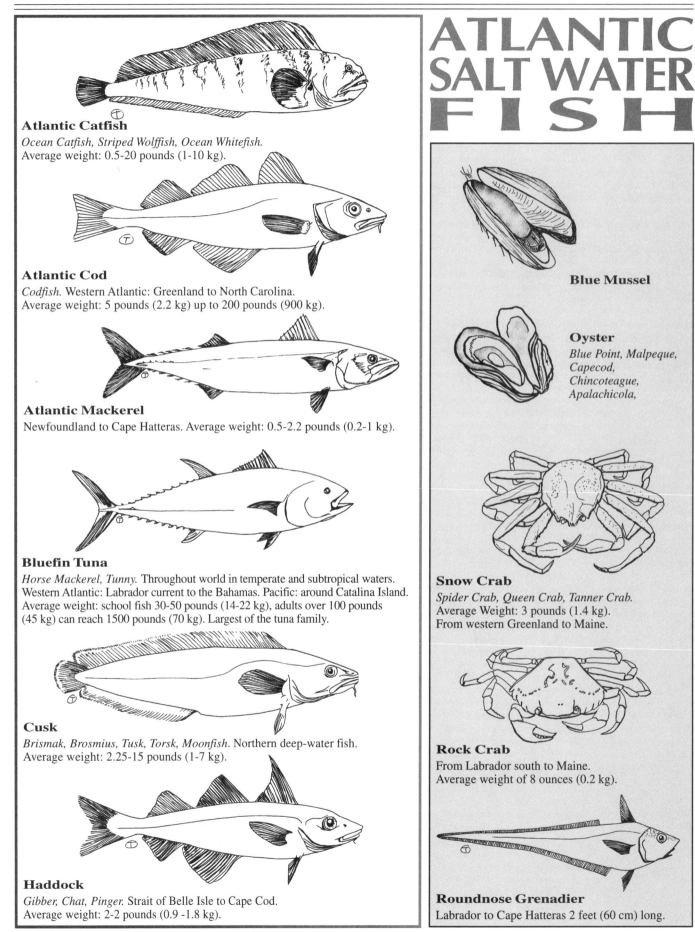

ATLANTIC SALT WATER FISH

Atlantic Catfish

Ocean Catfish, Striped Wolffish, Ocean Whitefish.
Average weight: 0.5-20 pounds (1-10 kg).

Atlantic Cod

Codfish. Western Atlantic: Greenland to North Carolina.
Average weight: 5 pounds (2.2 kg) up to 200 pounds (900 kg).

Atlantic Mackerel

Newfoundland to Cape Hatteras. Average weight: 0.5-2.2 pounds (0.2-1 kg).

Bluefin Tuna

Horse Mackerel, Tunny. Throughout world in temperate and subtropical waters.
Western Atlantic: Labrador current to the Bahamas. Pacific: around Catalina Island.
Average weight: school fish 30-50 pounds (14-22 kg), adults over 100 pounds
(45 kg) can reach 1500 pounds (70 kg). Largest of the tuna family.

Cusk

Brismak, Brosmius, Tusk, Torsk, Moonfish. Northern deep-water fish.
Average weight: 2.25-15 pounds (1-7 kg).

Haddock

Gibber, Chat, Pinger. Strait of Belle Isle to Cape Cod.
Average weight: 2-2 pounds (0.9 -1.8 kg).

Blue Mussel

Oyster
*Blue Point, Malpeque,
Capecod,
Chincoteague,
Apalachicola,*

Snow Crab

Spider Crab, Queen Crab, Tanner Crab.
Average Weight: 3 pounds (1.4 kg).
From western Greenland to Maine.

Rock Crab

From Labrador south to Maine.
Average weight of 8 ounces (0.2 kg).

Roundnose Grenadier

Labrador to Cape Hatteras 2 feet (60 cm) long.

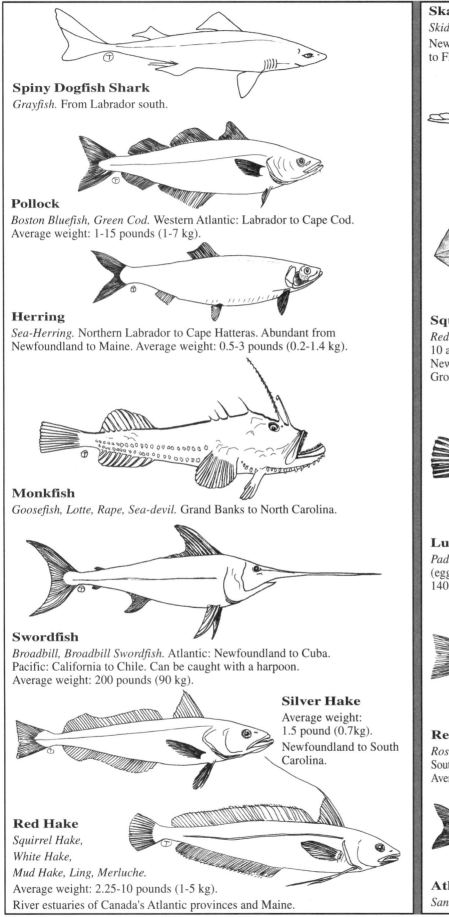

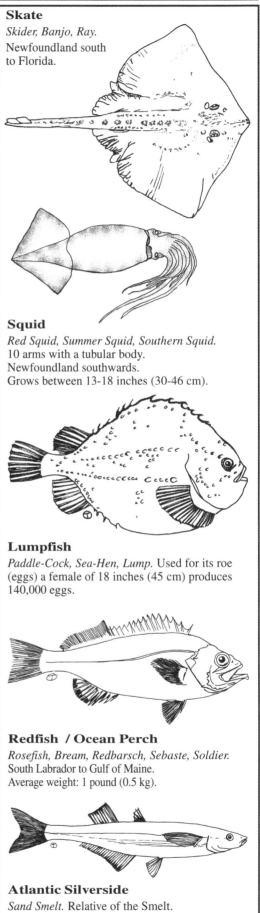

Spiny Dogfish Shark
Grayfish. From Labrador south.

Pollock
Boston Bluefish, Green Cod. Western Atlantic: Labrador to Cape Cod.
Average weight: 1-15 pounds (1-7 kg).

Herring
Sea-Herring. Northern Labrador to Cape Hatteras. Abundant from
Newfoundland to Maine. Average weight: 0.5-3 pounds (0.2-1.4 kg).

Monkfish
Goosefish, Lotte, Rape, Sea-devil. Grand Banks to North Carolina.

Swordfish
Broadbill, Broadbill Swordfish. Atlantic: Newfoundland to Cuba.
Pacific: California to Chile. Can be caught with a harpoon.
Average weight: 200 pounds (90 kg).

Silver Hake
Average weight:
1.5 pound (0.7kg).
Newfoundland to South
Carolina.

Red Hake
Squirrel Hake,
White Hake,
Mud Hake, Ling, Merluche.
Average weight: 2.25-10 pounds (1-5 kg).
River estuaries of Canada's Atlantic provinces and Maine.

Skate
Skider, Banjo, Ray.
Newfoundland south
to Florida.

Squid
Red Squid, Summer Squid, Southern Squid.
10 arms with a tubular body.
Newfoundland southwards.
Grows between 13-18 inches (30-46 cm).

Lumpfish
Paddle-Cock, Sea-Hen, Lump. Used for its roe
(eggs) a female of 18 inches (45 cm) produces
140,000 eggs.

Redfish / Ocean Perch
Rosefish, Bream, Redbarsch, Sebaste, Soldier.
South Labrador to Gulf of Maine.
Average weight: 1 pound (0.5 kg).

Atlantic Silverside
Sand Smelt. Relative of the Smelt.

277

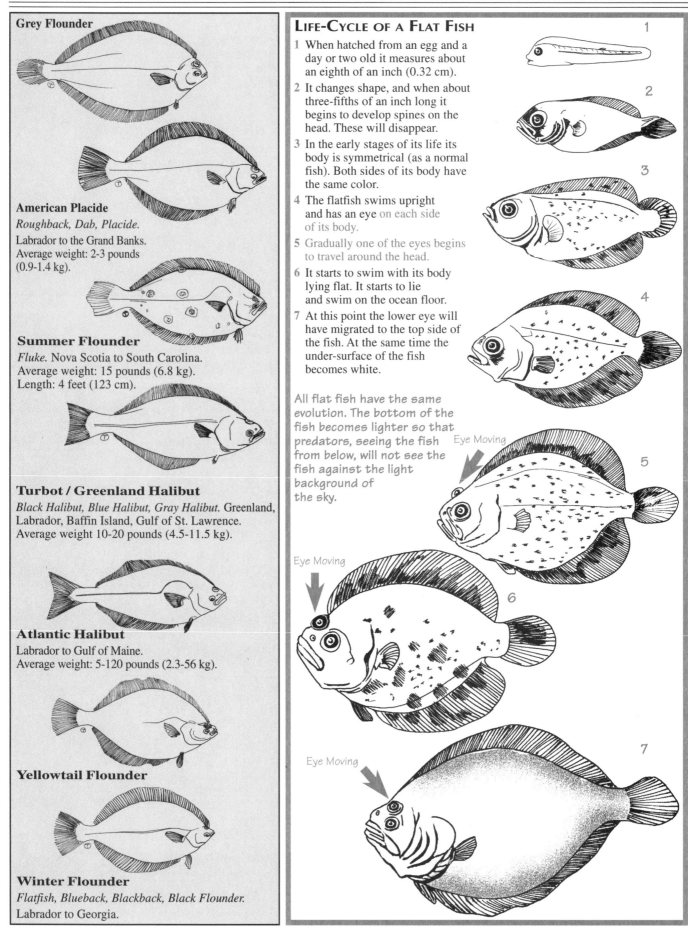

Grey Flounder

American Placide

Roughback, Dab, Placide.
Labrador to the Grand Banks.
Average weight: 2-3 pounds
(0.9-1.4 kg).

Summer Flounder

Fluke. Nova Scotia to South Carolina.
Average weight: 15 pounds (6.8 kg).
Length: 4 feet (123 cm).

Turbot / Greenland Halibut

Black Halibut, Blue Halibut, Gray Halibut. Greenland,
Labrador, Baffin Island, Gulf of St. Lawrence.
Average weight 10-20 pounds (4.5-11.5 kg).

Atlantic Halibut

Labrador to Gulf of Maine.
Average weight: 5-120 pounds (2.3-56 kg).

Yellowtail Flounder

Winter Flounder

Flatfish, Blueback, Blackback, Black Flounder.
Labrador to Georgia.

LIFE-CYCLE OF A FLAT FISH

1 When hatched from an egg and a day or two old it measures about an eighth of an inch (0.32 cm).

2 It changes shape, and when about three-fifths of an inch long it begins to develop spines on the head. These will disappear.

3 In the early stages of its life its body is symmetrical (as a normal fish). Both sides of its body have the same color.

4 The flatfish swims upright and has an eye on each side of its body.

5 Gradually one of the eyes begins to travel around the head.

6 It starts to swim with its body lying flat. It starts to lie and swim on the ocean floor.

7 At this point the lower eye will have migrated to the top side of the fish. At the same time the under-surface of the fish becomes white.

All flat fish have the same evolution. The bottom of the fish becomes lighter so that predators, seeing the fish from below, will not see the fish against the light background of the sky.

Eye Moving

Eye Moving

Eye Moving

PACIFIC
SALT WATER
FISH

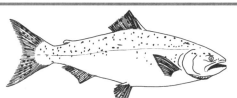

Spring Salmon

Chinook Salmon, King Salmon, Chub Salmon. Spawns in Pacific Coast rivers and streams. Weight: 10-50 pounds (4.5-22.5 kg). Fishing season from March to October. Fattest of all Pacific Salmon. Flesh is large, flaked and rich in oil.

Sockeye Salmon

Pacific Salmon. Average weight: 5 pounds (2.2 kg). Spawning in Pacific from June to September. Fat fish, firm flesh of small flake and deep orange or red coloration.

Pink Salmon

Weight: 3-5 pounds (1.4-2.2 kg). Spawns in Pacific rivers and streams from July to September. Firm flesh, fine texture and small flake.

SALMON

Coho Salmon

Jack Salmon, Medium Red Salmon. Weight: 4-10 pounds (1.8-4.5 kg). Spawns mid-June to November. Fat fish, fine textured flesh, pink or red.

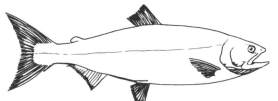

Chum Salmon

Keta Salmon, Dog Salmon, Qualler, Calico Salmon, Fall Salmon. Similar to Sockeye but has slimmer "waist" above tail. Spawns in Pacific rivers and streams in October and November. Flesh pale to light pink.

Chinook Salmon

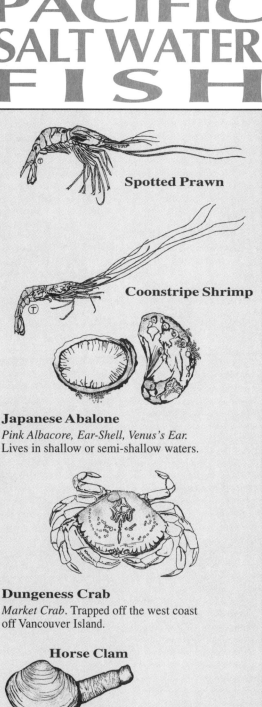

Spotted Prawn

Coonstripe Shrimp

Japanese Abalone

Pink Albacore, Ear-Shell, Venus's Ear. Lives in shallow or semi-shallow waters.

Dungeness Crab

Market Crab. Trapped off the west coast off Vancouver Island.

Horse Clam

Geoduck Clam

Weight: 3-10 pounds (1.4-4.5 kg). Caught in the intertide area. Great for cutlets and chowders.

Pacific Oyster

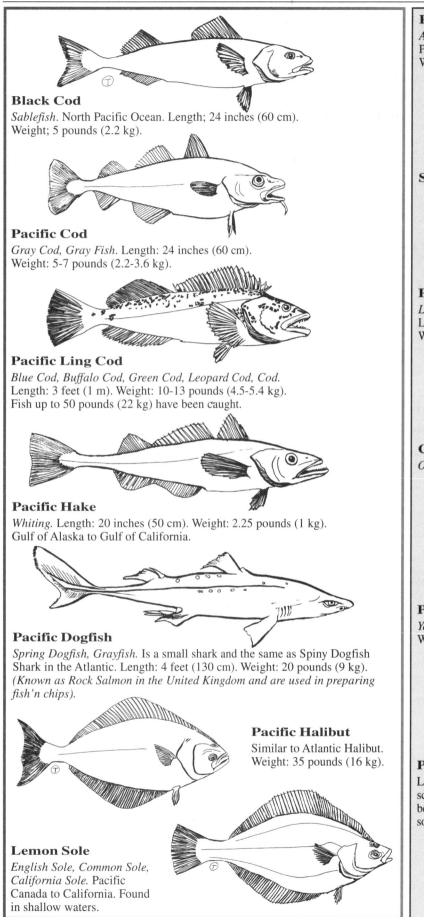

Black Cod

Sablefish. North Pacific Ocean. Length; 24 inches (60 cm).
Weight; 5 pounds (2.2 kg).

Pacific Cod

Gray Cod, Gray Fish. Length: 24 inches (60 cm).
Weight: 5-7 pounds (2.2-3.6 kg).

Pacific Ling Cod

Blue Cod, Buffalo Cod, Green Cod, Leopard Cod, Cod.
Length: 3 feet (1 m). Weight: 10-13 pounds (4.5-5.4 kg).
Fish up to 50 pounds (22 kg) have been caught.

Pacific Hake

Whiting. Length: 20 inches (50 cm). Weight: 2.25 pounds (1 kg).
Gulf of Alaska to Gulf of California.

Pacific Dogfish

Spring Dogfish, Grayfish. Is a small shark and the same as Spiny Dogfish
Shark in the Atlantic. Length: 4 feet (130 cm). Weight: 20 pounds (9 kg).
*(Known as Rock Salmon in the United Kingdom and are used in preparing
fish'n chips)*.

Pacific Halibut

Similar to Atlantic Halibut.
Weight: 35 pounds (16 kg).

Lemon Sole

*English Sole, Common Sole,
California Sole*. Pacific
Canada to California. Found
in shallow waters.

Pacific Pollock

Alaska Pollock, Bigeye Pollock. Northern Canadian
Pacific Coast and Alaska Coast.
Weight; 1.5-2 pounds (680-900 g).

Silvergrey Rockfish

Pacific Ocean Perch

Longjaw Rockfish.
Length: 20 inches (50 cm).
Weight: 1-3 pounds (0.5-1.4 kg).

Canary Rockfish

Orange Rockfish. Length: 30 inches (76 cm).

Pacific Red Snapper

Yellow-eye Rockfish. Length: 38 inches (1 m).
Weight: 2.25-5 pounds (2- 3 kg).

Pacific Herring

Length: 6 inches (15 cm). Alaska south. Swims in large
schools but spawns in shallow bays close to shore. Can
be caught with a fill net. In spring they are an excellent
source of roe.

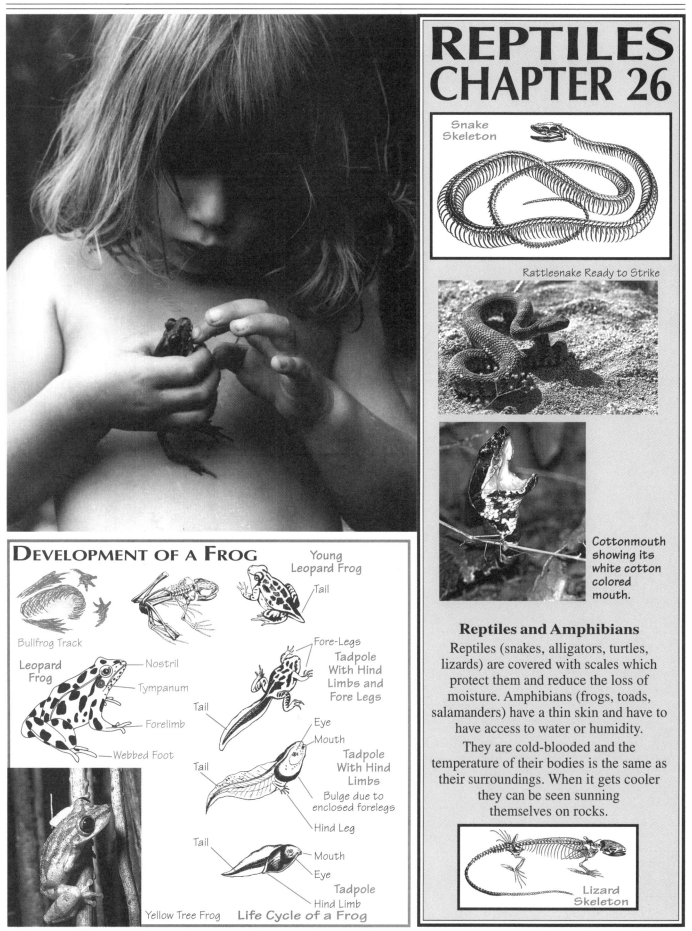

REPTILES CHAPTER 26

Snake Skeleton

Rattlesnake Ready to Strike

Cottonmouth showing its white cotton colored mouth.

Reptiles and Amphibians

Reptiles (snakes, alligators, turtles, lizards) are covered with scales which protect them and reduce the loss of moisture. Amphibians (frogs, toads, salamanders) have a thin skin and have to have access to water or humidity.

They are cold-blooded and the temperature of their bodies is the same as their surroundings. When it gets cooler they can be seen sunning themselves on rocks.

Lizard Skeleton

DEVELOPMENT OF A FROG

Young Leopard Frog

Tail

Bullfrog Track

Leopard Frog

Nostril

Tympanum

Forelimb

Webbed Foot

Fore-Legs

Tadpole With Hind Limbs and Fore Legs

Tail

Eye

Mouth

Tail

Tadpole With Hind Limbs

Bulge due to enclosed forelegs

Hind Leg

Tail

Mouth

Eye

Tadpole

Hind Limb

Yellow Tree Frog   **Life Cycle of a Frog**

AVOIDING RATTLESNAKES BITES

- Do not lift stones, logs or other possible hiding places before moving the object with a stick or a properly protected foot (with a heavy high boot).
- Do not gather firewood during the dark. When picking it up follow the same precautions as above.
- Do not reach into holes in the ground, trees or cacti even if a bird has just flown into it.
- Remember that rattlesnakes are usually in the shade on hot days and due to their camouflage colors are hard to detect.
- Be very observant when walking along a path and even more when walking through low bushes.
- Rattlers can be found in trees, bushes and they can swim.
- Rattlers are found at altitudes up to 11,000 feet (3,300 m) in the southwest and up to 14,500 feet (94,400 m) in Mexico.
- Always watch the ground even if you are photographing game birds in the sky.
- If you are walking single file and the leader has passed a point it does not mean that there are no snakes on the path. He might just have disturbed it and it might bite a person further down the line.
- If mountaineering, do not reach above your head for a hand hold. Avoid placing your hands in or near a crevice into which you cannot see.
- Avoid walking below rock ledges.
- A snake might enter your boat while you are traveling. Do not panic, he only wants to rest. Remove him with your paddle.
- When you hear the rattle, do not move, until you see the snake as you might walk into its range. If you back away make sure that you do not back into another snake.
- Do not step over logs step on them, so that you can see what is lurking on the other side, and only then step down.
- Look around your seating area before you sit down.
- Rattlers usually only attack moving objects.
- Pitch your tent in a clearing and make sure that a rattler will not crawl into your boots, clothing or backpack. Do not camp near rock piles or deep brush.
- Do not play with dead rattlesnakes as the head has been known to bite 1/2 an hour after it was removed from the body. Bury the head.

Protective Clothing Against Rattlers

- Protect your feet and legs by wearing heavy boots or thick puttees (see page 30). The material should be impenetrable and should rise up to the knee.
- Wear your pants over your boots as the loose pant legs will provide added protection.
- If you rock climb wear heavy gauntlet-type gloves.

SNAKE BITE KIT

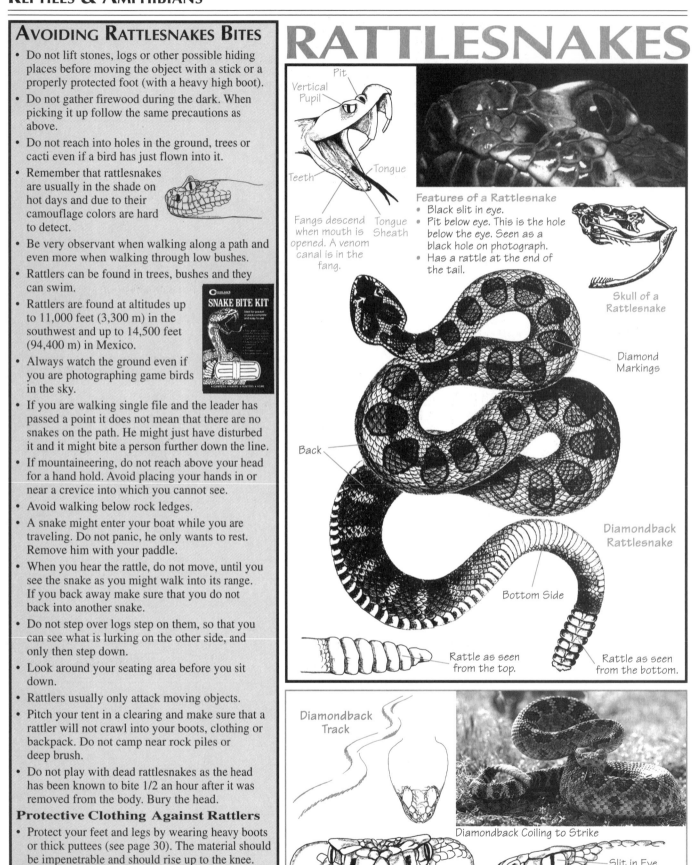

RATTLESNAKES

Vertical Pupil — Pit

Teeth — Tongue

Fangs descend when mouth is opened. A venom canal is in the fang. — Tongue Sheath

Features of a Rattlesnake
- Black slit in eye.
- Pit below eye. This is the hole below the eye. Seen as a black hole on photograph.
- Has a rattle at the end of the tail.

Skull of a Rattlesnake

Diamond Markings

Back

Diamondback Rattlesnake

Bottom Side

Rattle as seen from the top.

Rattle as seen from the bottom.

Diamondback Track

Diamondback Coiling to Strike

Slit in Eye

Pit

Diamondback Head

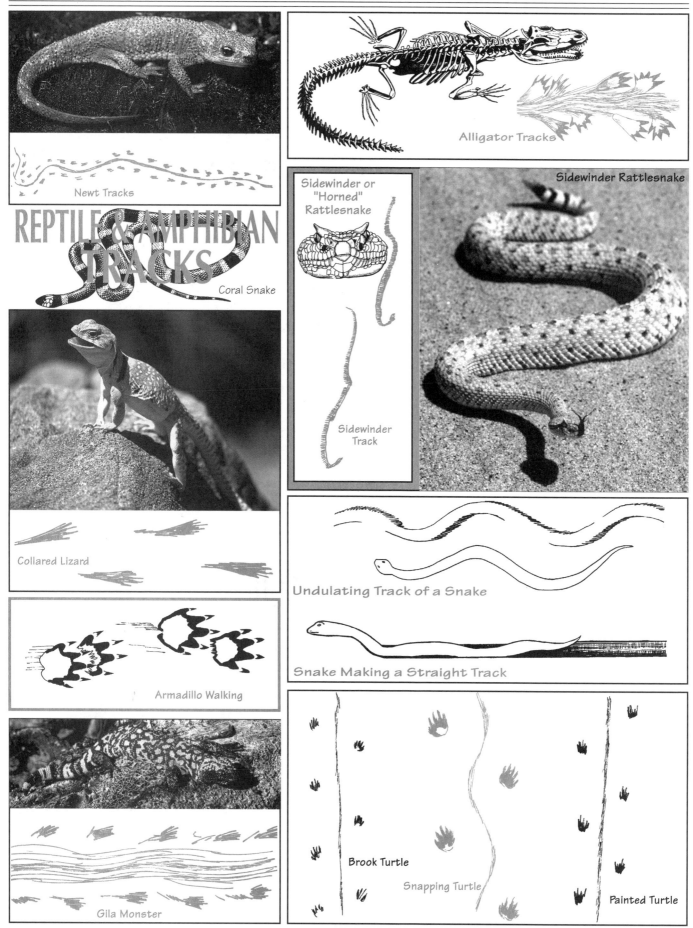

Newt Tracks

Alligator Tracks

REPTILE & AMPHIBIAN TRACKS

Coral Snake

Sidewinder or "Horned" Rattlesnake

Sidewinder Rattlesnake

Sidewinder Track

Collared Lizard

Undulating Track of a Snake

Armadillo Walking

Snake Making a Straight Track

Gila Monster

Brook Turtle

Snapping Turtle

Painted Turtle

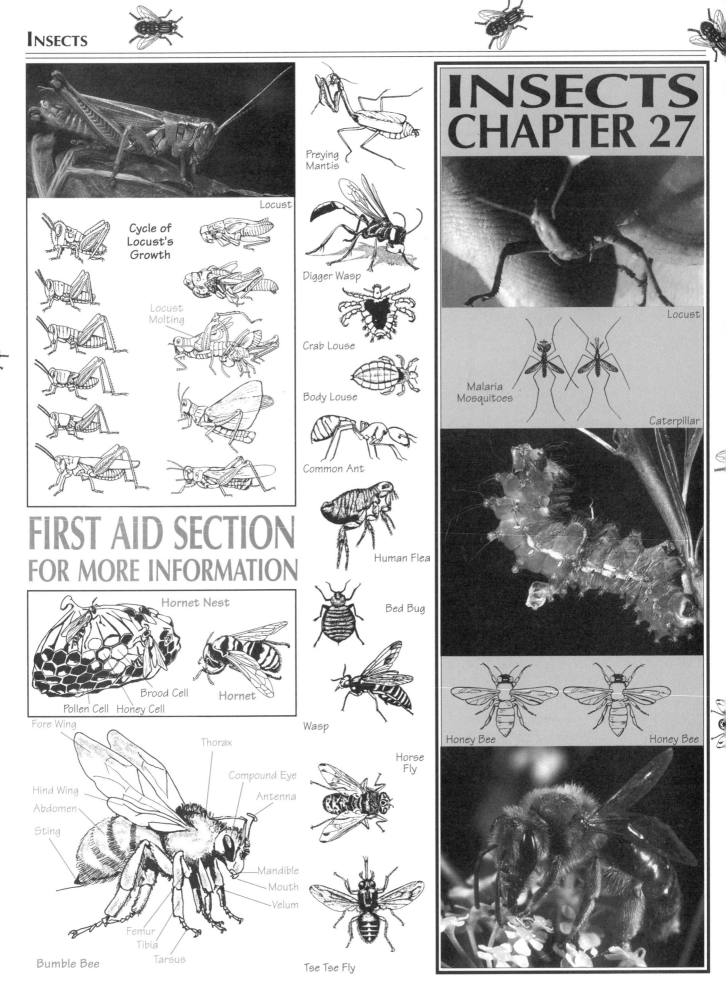

Locust

Cycle of Locust's Growth

Locust Molting

FIRST AID SECTION
FOR MORE INFORMATION

Hornet Nest

Brood Cell

Hornet

Pollen Cell   Honey Cell

Fore Wing

Thorax

Compound Eye

Antenna

Hind Wing

Abdomen

Sting

Mandible

Mouth

Velum

Femur

Tibia

Tarsus

Bumble Bee

Preying Mantis

Digger Wasp

Crab Louse

Body Louse

Common Ant

Human Flea

Bed Bug

Wasp

Horse Fly

Tse Tse Fly

INSECTS
CHAPTER 27

Locust

Malaria Mosquitoes

Caterpillar

Honey Bee

Honey Bee

Insects and Insect-Borne Diseases

Common insects such as flies, mosquitoes, lice, ticks, and mites carry many of our most serious diseases such as typhoid fever, dysentery, malaria, brain fever, and yellow fever. Every possible means should be used to avoid the contamination of food by flies and bites of mosquitoes and other insects. If you have no screening, bed net, insecticides, or repellents it is difficult to keep insects away.

- Protect food and beverages from flies and other vermin.
- Cover the body to reduce exposure to mosquitoes, especially after dark.
- When available take a suppressive drug to prevent malaria.
- Keep free of lice.
- Promptly remove ticks.

Citronella Candle

Insect Cover

US Army Insect Bar

See First Aid Section for more information.

Insect Hammock

COGHLAN'S
CLEAR LOTION
INSECT REPELLENT
Formulated for Outdoor Families
ACTIVE INGREDIENTS PERCENT

CONTENTS 2 FL OZ   60 ml

CAUTION
KEEP OUT OF REACH OF CHILDREN

Insect Repellant

Mosquito Coil

STING-EZE

KILLER BEES

The threat of killer bees ("African bees") has been greatly exaggerated but they have arrived in the United States. African bees are more aggressive than the European bees.

The European honey bee is less aggressive as they live in well protected hollow trees and other cavities. They do not have to protect their nests so they do not have to be aggressive and sting as frequently to protect their home.

African bees come from arid regions, making nests in the open on tree branches and in holes in the ground, their nests are vulnerable to attack and they have to fight any potential predator. For this reason they are *easily provoked* and *highly defensive*. The alarm scent from one worker might trigger the defensive action of hundreds or thousands of fellow bees. African bees respond more quickly, stay agitated longer, and chase enemies further than European bees. The sting of a single African bee is no more dangerous than the one that of other honey bees but the massive attack of hundreds of bees and hundreds of stings can prove fatal.

African honey bees do not store large amounts of honey and they use more cells to raise their young. This causes the hive population to grow very rapidly and the bees swarm more frequently. *Absconding* is when all bees in a hive permanently leave due to some major disturbance. African honey bees have a tendency to abandon their nests.

African honey bees escaped from a research area in Brazil in 1957 and reached the southern United States in 1990.

The African bees overwhelm European bees and even steal their honey. African drones mated with European bees and the following generations retain their aggressive characteristics. African bees being referred to as "Killer Bees" give a false impression because they only sting to defend their hive or swarm. *Stinging incidents involving many bees is not common.*

Identification

African bees look like other honey bees but they are slightly smaller, weigh less, and have shorter stingers and forewings. They are more nervous in their hives and fly farther and in a more zig zag pattern than European bees.

Precautions

- People can coexist with the African honey bee by learning about the bee's behavior and being alert to their presence.
- The main danger is in encountering a wild colony that might be swarming.
- Watch for potential nesting areas: stone walls, underground holes, bird houses, discarded tires, empty flower pots, etc.
- If under attack leave as quickly as possible (release any attached animals). Enter a car or building. If no shelter is available run behind bushes, trees, fence or other obstacle that blocks the bees' line of vision.
- If you have numerous stings see a doctor *as soon as possible* especially if you feel dizzy and have difficulty breathing.

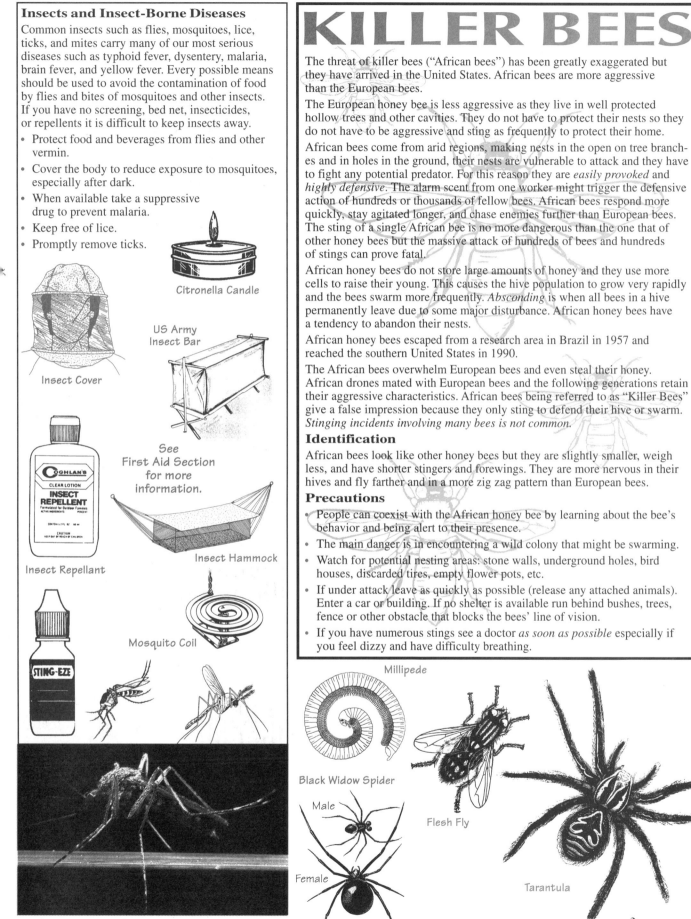

Millipede

Black Widow Spider

Male

Female

Flesh Fly

Tarantula

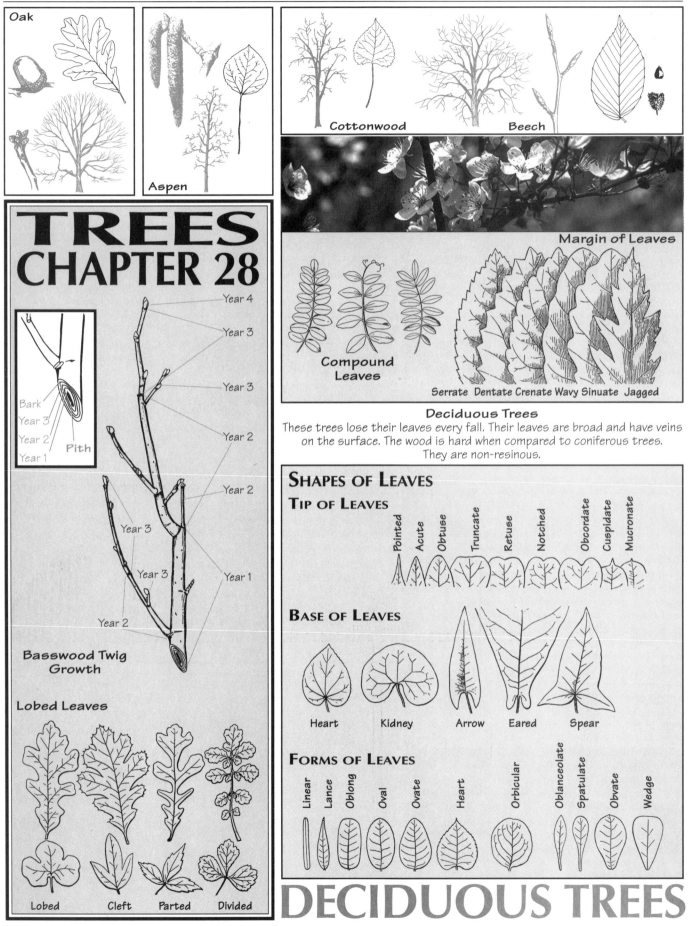

Oak

Aspen

Cottonwood

Beech

TREES
CHAPTER 28

Bark
Year 3
Year 2
Year 1
Pith

Year 4
Year 3
Year 3
Year 2
Year 2
Year 2
Year 3
Year 3
Year 1

Basswood Twig Growth

Lobed Leaves

Lobed   Cleft   Parted   Divided

Margin of Leaves

Compound Leaves

Serrate Dentate Crenate Wavy Sinuate Jagged

Deciduous Trees
These trees lose their leaves every fall. Their leaves are broad and have veins on the surface. The wood is hard when compared to coniferous trees. They are non-resinous.

SHAPES OF LEAVES
TIP OF LEAVES

Pointed Acute Obtuse Truncate Retuse Notched Obcordate Cuspidate Mucronate

BASE OF LEAVES

Heart   Kidney   Arrow   Eared   Spear

FORMS OF LEAVES

Linear Lance Oblong Oval Ovate Heart Orbicular Oblanceolate Spatulate Obvate Wedge

DECIDUOUS TREES

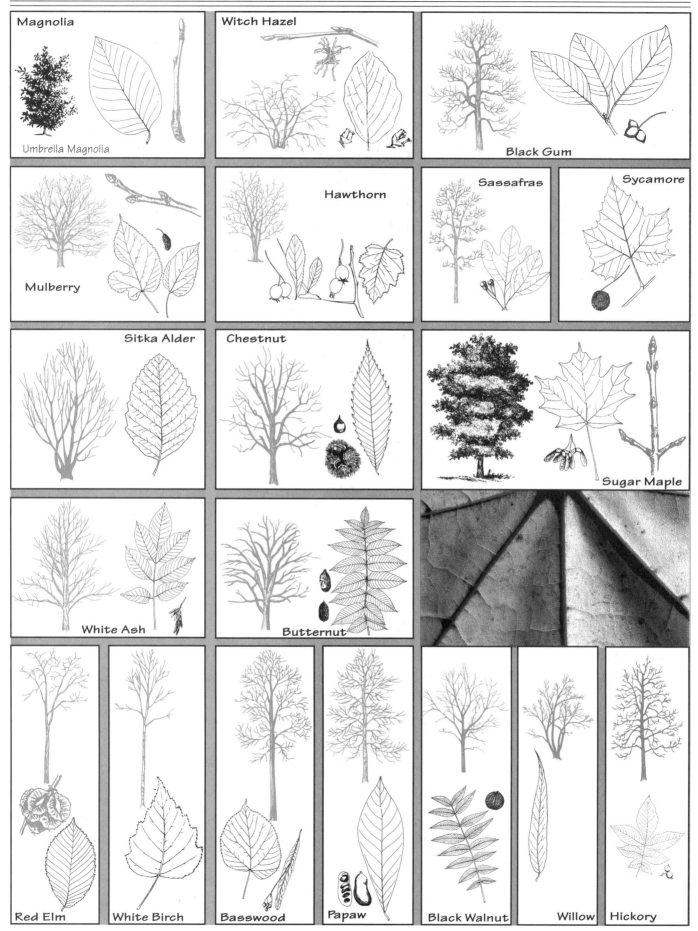

Magnolia

Umbrella Magnolia

Witch Hazel

Black Gum

Mulberry

Hawthorn

Sassafras

Sycamore

Sitka Alder

Chestnut

Sugar Maple

White Ash

Butternut

Red Elm

White Birch

Basswood

Papaw

Black Walnut

Willow

Hickory

CONIFER TREES

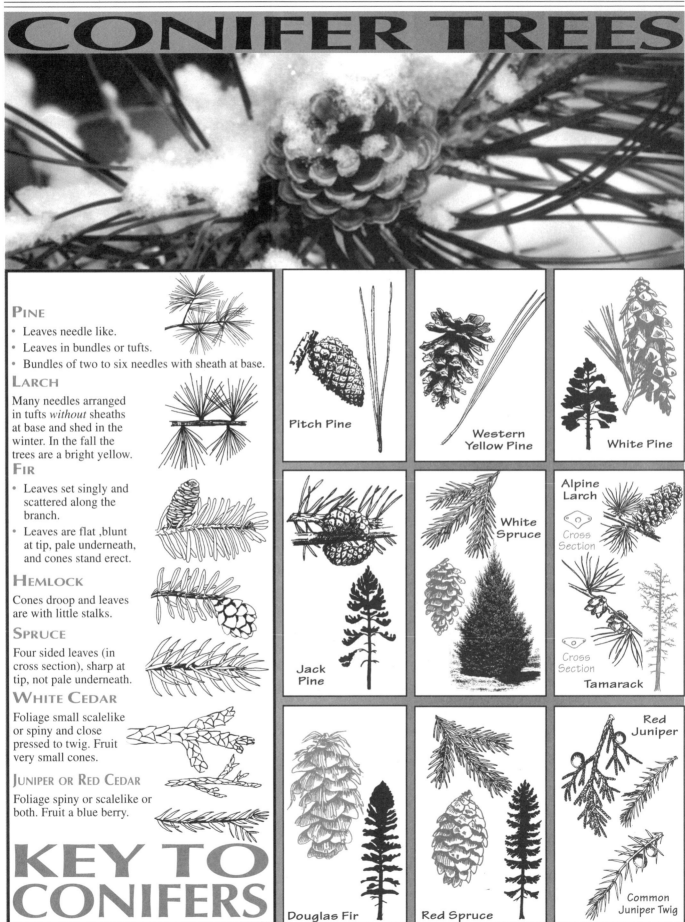

PINE

- Leaves needle like.
- Leaves in bundles or tufts.
- Bundles of two to six needles with sheath at base.

LARCH

Many needles arranged in tufts *without* sheaths at base and shed in the winter. In the fall the trees are a bright yellow.

FIR

- Leaves set singly and scattered along the branch.
- Leaves are flat ,blunt at tip, pale underneath, and cones stand erect.

HEMLOCK

Cones droop and leaves are with little stalks.

SPRUCE

Four sided leaves (in cross section), sharp at tip, not pale underneath.

WHITE CEDAR

Foliage small scalelike or spiny and close pressed to twig. Fruit very small cones.

JUNIPER OR RED CEDAR

Foliage spiny or scalelike or both. Fruit a blue berry.

KEY TO CONIFERS

Pitch Pine

Western Yellow Pine

White Pine

Jack Pine

White Spruce

Alpine Larch

Cross Section

Cross Section

Tamarack

Douglas Fir

Red Spruce

Red Juniper

Common Juniper Twig

Black Spruce

Sitka Spruce

Norway Spruce

Western Hemlock

Eastern White Cedar

Spruce or Fir?
Take a needle between your fingers and roll it:
Spruces will spin as needles are nearly round.
Firs have a flat cross-section and will slide.

Hemlock Fir

Hemlock

Red Pine

Yew

Western Yew

Western Larch

Cross Section

Balsam Fir

Height of a Tree
Move away from the tree looking through your legs until you can see the top of the tree. Measure your pace back to the tree and this is the height of the tree. This works because the angle when looking through your legs is 45°.

45°

Age of Pine Tree
Evergreens as spruce and pine indicate their age by the number of whorls (branch levels) of their branches.

Age of a Tree
The age can be determined by the number of tree rings in the trunk (trees normally only have one ring per year).

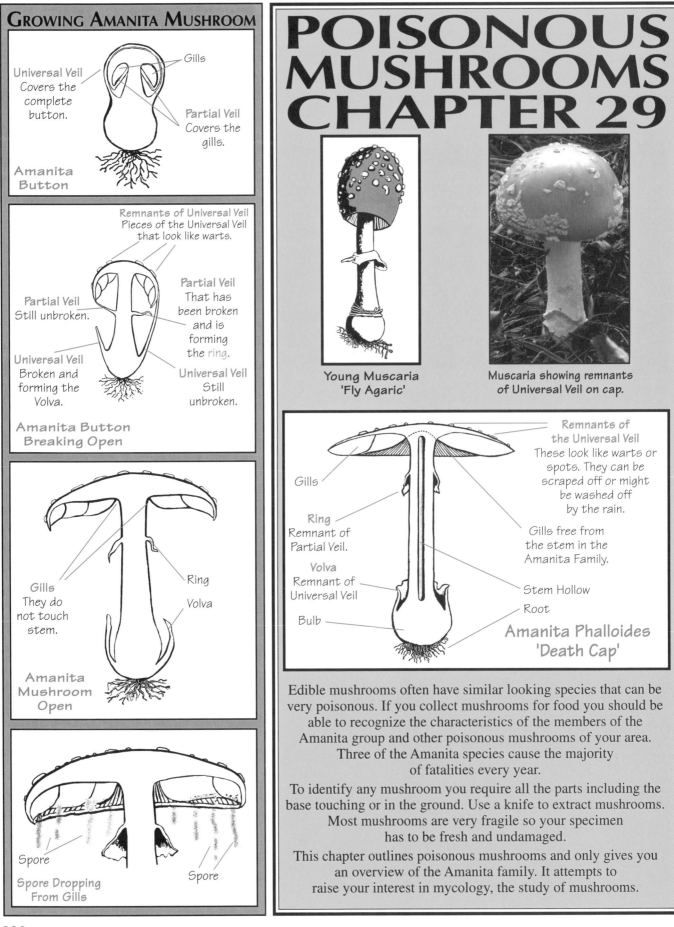

GROWING AMANITA MUSHROOM

Gills

Universal Veil
Covers the
complete
button.

Partial Veil
Covers the
gills.

Amanita
Button

Remnants of Universal Veil
Pieces of the Universal Veil
that look like warts.

Partial Veil
Still unbroken.

Partial Veil
That has
been broken
and is
forming
the ring.

Universal Veil
Broken and
forming the
Volva.

Universal Veil
Still
unbroken.

Amanita Button
Breaking Open

Gills
They do
not touch
stem.

Ring

Volva

Amanita
Mushroom
Open

Spore

Spore

Spore Dropping
From Gills

POISONOUS MUSHROOMS CHAPTER 29

Young Muscaria
'Fly Agaric'

Muscaria showing remnants
of Universal Veil on cap.

Gills

Ring
Remnant of
Partial Veil.

Volva
Remnant of
Universal Veil

Bulb

Remnants of
the Universal Veil
These look like warts or
spots. They can be
scraped off or might
be washed off
by the rain.

Gills free from
the stem in the
Amanita Family.

Stem Hollow

Root

Amanita Phalloides
'Death Cap'

Edible mushrooms often have similar looking species that can be very poisonous. If you collect mushrooms for food you should be able to recognize the characteristics of the members of the Amanita group and other poisonous mushrooms of your area. Three of the Amanita species cause the majority of fatalities every year.

To identify any mushroom you require all the parts including the base touching or in the ground. Use a knife to extract mushrooms. Most mushrooms are very fragile so your specimen has to be fresh and undamaged.

This chapter outlines poisonous mushrooms and only gives you an overview of the Amanita family. It attempts to raise your interest in mycology, the study of mushrooms.

POISONOUS AMANITA MUSHROOMS

AMANITA PHALLOIDES

Death Cap

Color: Cap greenish-olive to yellowish.

Cap: 2-6 inches (5-15 cm)

Stem: Lighter color than cap

Volva: Large

Gills: White

Flesh: White

MOST POISONOUS

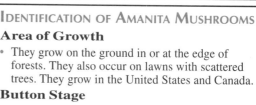

Remnants of Universal Veil

Gills

Ring

Volva or Cup

AMANITA VIROSA

Destroying Angel, Angel of Death

Color: Completely pure white.

Cap: More conical. 2-8 inch (5-20 cm)

Stem: Scaly

Volva: Large

Gills: White

Smell: Sweet pungent odor.

DEADLY POISON

Northeastern states and eastern Canada. Also in the Pacific Northwest.

Gills

Ring falling as a skirt.

Volva or Cup

AMANITA PANTHERINA

Panther Cap

Color: Cap brownish with pure white specks which can wash off.

Cap: 2-4 inches (5-10 cm)

Stem: White and thick.

Gills: White

Veil: Pure White

Gills: White

VERY POISONOUS

Causes coma-like sleep and delirium.

Remnants of Universal Veil: White

Gills

Ring

Volva or Cup

AMANITA MUSCARIA

Fly Agaric

Color: Cap red with white spots. The spots can wash off in the rain.

Cap: 3-10 inches (7.5-25 cm)

Stem: White with rings of white to yellow warts at the base.

Gills: White

POISONOUS

There is also a yellow form in eastern America found under pine trees. The red variety is found under pine and birch trees in the west.

Ring falling as a skirt.

Volva

Amanita Family

This family has some of the most deadly mushrooms in the world.
The poison attacks the liver and kidneys. The physical reaction usually occurs after 24 hours and the symptoms are stomach pain, diarrhea, vomiting.
Once the symptoms are present the damage usually is done.
There is no antidote. Not all Amanita are poisonous but an error in identification makes it a high risk to eat any of them.

IDENTIFICATION OF AMANITA MUSHROOMS

Area of Growth

- They grow on the ground in or at the edge of forests. They also occur on lawns with scattered trees. They grow in the United States and Canada.

Button Stage

- The universal veil completely covers the button.
- The universal veil and a partial veil is visible when the button is split lengthwise.
- The universal veil can break in different ways so that the resulting pattern can vary.

Opened Stage

- The veils break when the button expands. Spots or flattened membrane from the outer veil will remain on the cap. *The veil can easily break off.*
- A cuplike volva from the veil fragments remains at the base. Some of the cups on the volva are not open but might be a series of ridges. The volva might remain in the ground when the mushroom is removed. The volva can wither away with age and remnants can be found around the stem base. *The cuplike volva is a distinguishing characteristic of the Amanita family.*

Volva is in ground and hard to see.

- The inner veil will break and remains as a *ring* or skirt on the stem below the cap. This ring can be poorly formed and may be hard to see or not be there. *The ring is a distinguishing characteristic of the Amanita family.*
- *Always check for the cuplike base and ring.*

Other Features

- Amanita mushrooms are beautiful.
- Gills are pure white or cream colored.
- Gills do not touch or just touch stem and are of unequal length.
- Stem separates cleanly and easily from cap.
- Spore is white.

Muscaria with remnants of Universal Veil on cap.

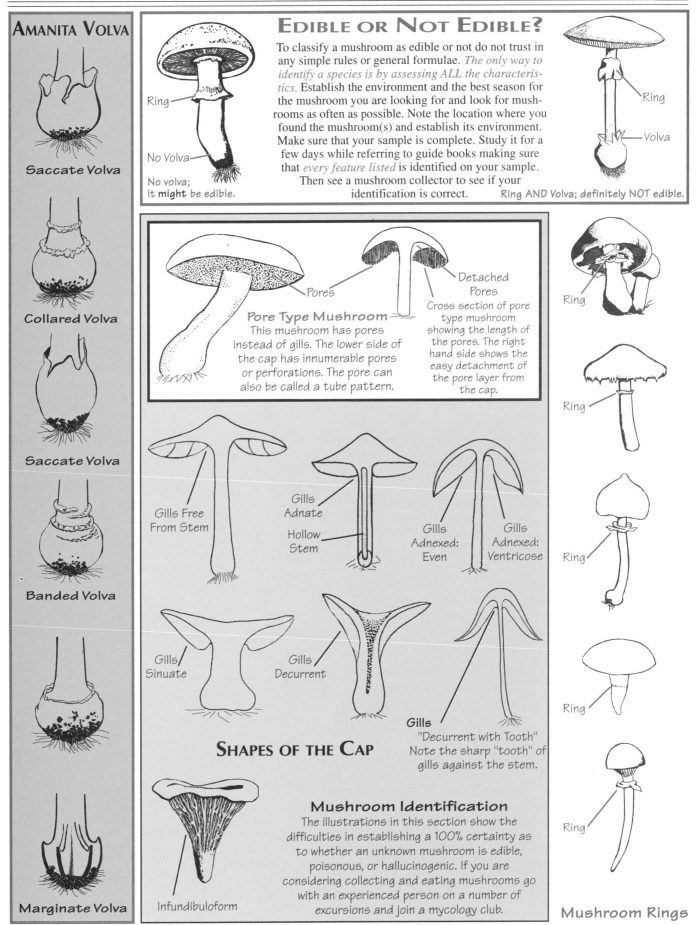

AMANITA VOLVA

Saccate Volva

Collared Volva

Saccate Volva

Banded Volva

Marginate Volva

EDIBLE OR NOT EDIBLE?

To classify a mushroom as edible or not do not trust in any simple rules or general formulae. *The only way to identify a species is by assessing ALL the characteristics.* Establish the environment and the best season for the mushroom you are looking for and look for mushrooms as often as possible. Note the location where you found the mushroom(s) and establish its environment. Make sure that your sample is complete. Study it for a few days while referring to guide books making sure that *every feature listed* is identified on your sample. Then see a mushroom collector to see if your identification is correct.

Ring

No Volva

No volva;
it **might** be edible.

Ring

Volva

Ring AND Volva; definitely NOT edible.

Pores

Detached Pores

Pore Type Mushroom
This mushroom has pores instead of gills. The lower side of the cap has innumerable pores or perforations. The pore can also be called a tube pattern.

Cross section of pore type mushroom showing the length of the pores. The right hand side shows the easy detachment of the pore layer from the cap.

Gills Free From Stem

Gills Adnate

Hollow Stem

Gills Adnexed: Even

Gills Adnexed: Ventricose

Gills Sinuate

Gills Decurrent

SHAPES OF THE CAP

Gills "Decurrent with Tooth" Note the sharp "tooth" of gills against the stem.

Mushroom Identification
The illustrations in this section show the difficulties in establishing a 100% certainty as to whether an unknown mushroom is edible, poisonous, or hallucinogenic. If you are considering collecting and eating mushrooms go with an experienced person on a number of excursions and join a mycology club.

Infundibuloform

Ring

Ring

Ring

Ring

Ring

Mushroom Rings

This chapter gives you information on the location and traditional use of a selection of 94 edible North American plants. Take every opportunity to see the plants in their natural habitat. Eating plants provides you with energy and calorie-giving carbohydrates. *All parts of a plant are not necessarily edible.* The parts of a plant are:

Roots and Underground Parts
Tubers: They are found below the ground and are cooked or roasted. Example is the potato.
Roots and Rootstock: Roots are rich in starch, are usually several feet long, and are not swollen like tubers. Rootstock are underground stems which can be several inches thick, short, and pointed. Examples are bulrush roots and stems, water plantain, and cattail.
Bulbs: All bulbs are high in starch content and, with the exception of the wild onion, are more palatable if they are cooked. Examples are the wild onion, and wild tulip.

Shoots and Stems
Edible shoots grow very similarly to asparagus. Most are better when parboiled for 10 minutes, the water drained off, and reboiled until tender. Example is bamboo and ferns.

Nuts
Nuts are among the most nutritious of all plant foods and contain valuable protein. Examples are walnut, hazelnut, chestnut, and acorn.

Leaves
Leaves can be eaten raw or cooked. Do not cook them too long as the vitamins will be destroyed. Leaves can also be dried to make tea. Examples are water lettuce, dock, sorrel, chicory, arctic willow, and rhubarb.

Seeds and Grain
The seeds of all cereals and most grasses are rich in oils and plant protein. Grains can be stored and ground into flour. Examples are rice, corn, and sunflowers.

Fruit
There are many edible fruits from berries, grapes, figs, to apples.

Bark
The inner bark, the layer next to the wood, can be eaten raw, cooked or dried and ground into a flour.

The popular names of the plants may vary so use the scientific name as a reference.

EDIBLE PLANTS CHAPTER 30

Plants were an important ingredient of the Indian diet. They used over 250 species of wild fruit to round off their diet. Indians migrated and established summer settlements around the different harvesting seasons of plants and berries.

TABLE OF MEDICINAL PLANTS AND USAGE

Plant	Action	Indication
Alfalfa	Source of vit. A,C,E,K and minerals such as calcium, potassium, phosphorus and iron	To prevent a avitaminoses of vit. A,C,E,K.
Artichoke	Helps bile evacuation, diuretic	Liver disorders
Balm	Antispasmodic, sedative	Depressive states
Bearberry	Diuretic	Cystitis
Black Radish	Helps bile evacuation	Galibladder disorder
Boldo	Liver stimulant	Liver pains
Burdock	Diuretic	Skin eruptions, rheumatism
Cascara Sagrada	Mild laxative	Constipation
Chamomile	Sedative	Acidity, heartburns
Dandelion	Helps bile evacuation, diuretic	Constipation, muscular rheumatism
Devil's Claw	Anti-inflammatory	Arthritis, rheumatism
Fennel	Carminative	Flatulence
Flowering Oat	Antidepressant	Melancholy, depression
Ginseng	Reputed as being an aphrodisiac	Neuralgia
Hop	Sedative	Insomnia
Lindenbark	Diuretic	Digestive disorders
Mountain Grape	Helps bile evacuation	Helps bile secretion
Nettle	Anti-hemorrhagic, known to have hypo-glycemic properties	Skin eruptions, infantile eczema
Passion Herb	Sedative, antispasmodic	Insomnia, hysteria
Patience	Mild laxative	Constipation, chronic skin disease
Primrose	Mild diuretic, sedative	Insomnia, hysteria
Sage	Astringent, antiseptic	Pharyngitis, gingivitis
Sarsaparilla	Anti-rheumatism	Skin problems, rheumatism
Senna	Laxative	Constipation
Walnut Tree Bark	Laxative	Constipation
Willow	Anti-inflammatory, antiseptic	Flu and respiratory catarrh
Valerian	Sedative	Insomnia, migraine

British Herbal Medicine Association, BRITISH HERBAL PHARMACOPOEIA, 1983 Jii Stodola and Jan Volák, THE ILLUSTRATED ENCYCLOPEDIA OF HERBS, 1992

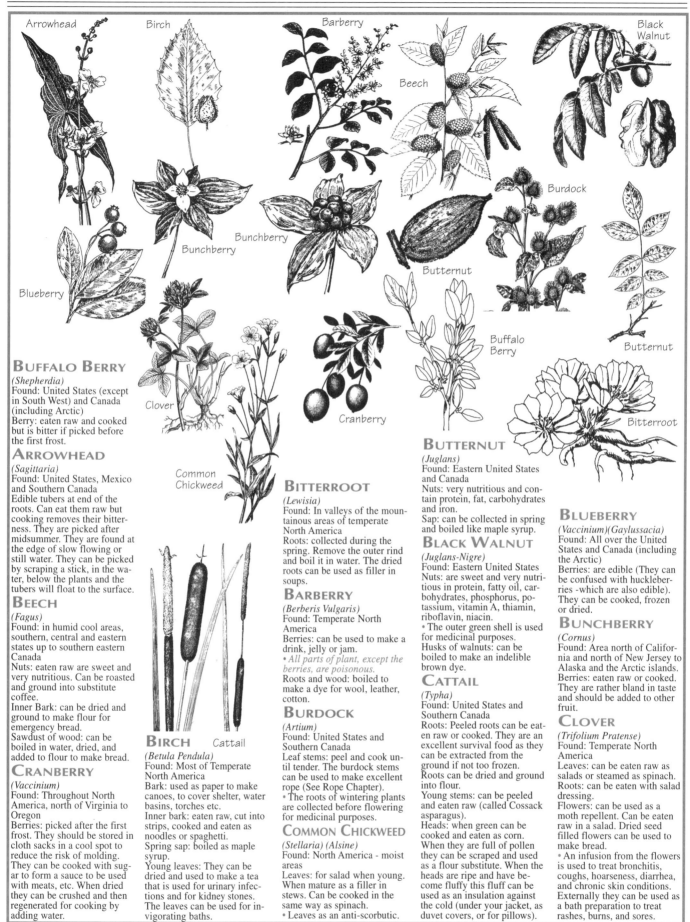

Arrowhead
Birch
Barberry
Beech
Black Walnut
Burdock
Bunchberry
Bunchberry
Butternut
Blueberry
Buffalo Berry
Butternut
Clover
Cranberry
Common Chickweed
Bitterroot
Birch   Cattail

BUFFALO BERRY

(Shepherdia)
Found: United States (except in South West) and Canada (including Arctic)
Berry: eaten raw and cooked but is bitter if picked before the first frost.

ARROWHEAD

(Sagittaria)
Found: United States, Mexico and Southern Canada
Edible tubers at end of the roots. Can eat them raw but cooking removes their bitterness. They are picked after midsummer. They are found at the edge of slow flowing or still water. They can be picked by scraping a stick, in the water, below the plants and the tubers will float to the surface.

BEECH

(Fagus)
Found: in humid cool areas, southern, central and eastern states up to southern eastern Canada
Nuts: eaten raw are sweet and very nutritious. Can be roasted and ground into substitute coffee.
Inner Bark: can be dried and ground to make flour for emergency bread.
Sawdust of wood: can be boiled in water, dried, and added to flour to make bread.

CRANBERRY

(Vaccinium)
Found: Throughout North America, north of Virginia to Oregon
Berries: picked after the first frost. They should be stored in cloth sacks in a cool spot to reduce the risk of molding. They can be cooked with sugar to form a sauce to be used with meats, etc. When dried they can be crushed and then regenerated for cooking by adding water.

BIRCH

(Betula Pendula)
Found: Most of Temperate North America
Bark: used as paper to make canoes, to cover shelter, water basins, torches etc.
Inner bark: eaten raw, cut into strips, cooked and eaten as noodles or spaghetti.
Spring sap: boiled as maple syrup.
Young leaves: They can be dried and used to make a tea that is used for urinary infections and for kidney stones. The leaves can be used for invigorating baths.

BITTERROOT

(Lewisia)
Found: In valleys of the mountainous areas of temperate North America
Roots: collected during the spring. Remove the outer rind and boil it in water. The dried roots can be used as filler in soups.

BARBERRY

(Berberis Vulgaris)
Found: Temperate North America
Berries: can be used to make a drink, jelly or jam.
• *All parts of plant, except the berries, are poisonous.*
Roots and wood: boiled to make a dye for wool, leather, cotton.

BURDOCK

(Artium)
Found: United States and Southern Canada
Leaf stems: peel and cook until tender. The burdock stems can be used to make excellent rope (See Rope Chapter).
• The roots of wintering plants are collected before flowering for medicinal purposes.

COMMON CHICKWEED

(Stellaria) (Alsine)
Found: North America - moist areas
Leaves: for salad when young. When mature as a filler in stews. Can be cooked in the same way as spinach.
• Leaves as an anti-scorbutic.

BUTTERNUT

(Juglans)
Found: Eastern United States and Canada
Nuts: very nutritious and contain protein, fat, carbohydrates and iron.
Sap: can be collected in spring and boiled like maple syrup.

BLACK WALNUT

(Juglans-Nigre)
Found: Eastern United States
Nuts: are sweet and very nutritious in protein, fatty oil, carbohydrates, phosphorus, potassium, vitamin A, thiamin, riboflavin, niacin.
• The outer green shell is used for medicinal purposes.
Husks of walnuts: can be boiled to make an indelible brown dye.

CATTAIL

(Typha)
Found: United States and Southern Canada
Roots: Peeled roots can be eaten raw or cooked. They are an excellent survival food as they can be extracted from the ground if not too frozen.
Roots can be dried and ground into flour.
Young stems: can be peeled and eaten raw (called Cossack asparagus).
Heads: when green can be cooked and eaten as corn. When they are full of pollen they can be scraped and used as a flour substitute. When the heads are ripe and have become fluffy this fluff can be used as an insulation against the cold (under your jacket, as duvet covers, or for pillows).

BLUEBERRY

(Vaccinium) (Gaylussacia)
Found: All over the United States and Canada (including the Arctic)
Berries: are edible (They can be confused with huckleberries -which are also edible). They can be cooked, frozen or dried.

BUNCHBERRY

(Cornus)
Found: Area north of California and north of New Jersey to Alaska and the Arctic islands.
Berries: eaten raw or cooked. They are rather bland in taste and should be added to other fruit.

CLOVER

(Trifolium Pratense)
Found: Temperate North America
Leaves: can be eaten raw as salads or steamed as spinach.
Roots: can be eaten with salad dressing.
Flowers: can be used as a moth repellent. Can be eaten raw in a salad. Dried seed filled flowers can be used to make bread.
• An infusion from the flowers is used to treat bronchitis, coughs, hoarseness, diarrhea, and chronic skin conditions. Externally they can be used as a bath preparation to treat rashes, burns, and sores.

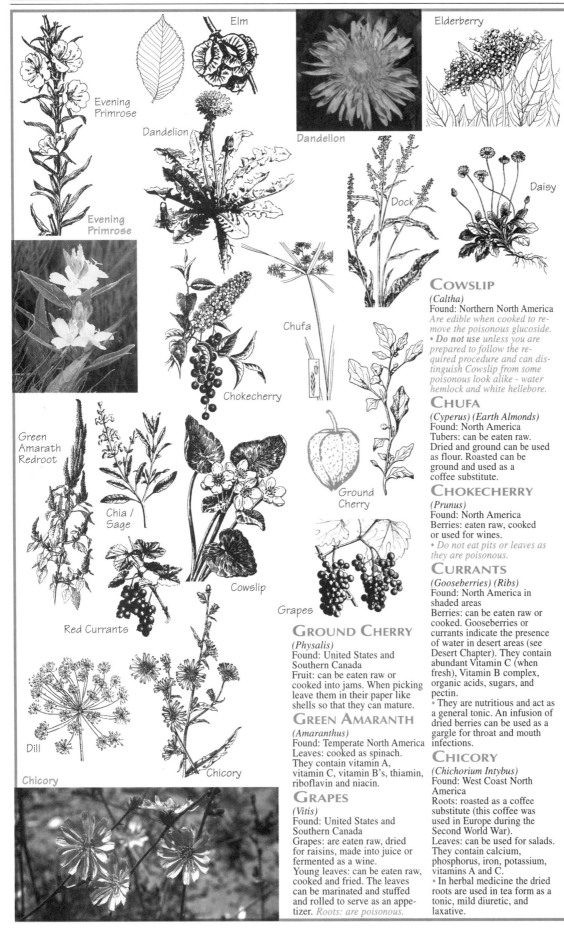

Evening Primrose

Elm

Dandelion

Evening Primrose

Dandelion

Dock

Elderberry

Daisy

Chufa

Green Amarath Redroot

Chokecherry

Chia / Sage

Ground Cherry

Cowslip

Red Currants

Grapes

Dill

Chicory

Chicory

COWSLIP

(Caltha)
Found: Northern North America
Are edible when cooked to remove the poisonous glucoside.
• *Do not use unless you are prepared to follow the required procedure and can distinguish Cowslip from some poisonous look alike - water hemlock and white hellebore.*

CHUFA

(Cyperus) (Earth Almonds)
Found: North America
Tubers: can be eaten raw. Dried and ground can be used as flour. Roasted can be ground and used as a coffee substitute.

CHOKECHERRY

(Prunus)
Found: North America
Berries: eaten raw, cooked or used for wines.
• *Do not eat pits or leaves as they are poisonous.*

CURRANTS

(Gooseberries) (Ribs)
Found: North America in shaded areas
Berries: can be eaten raw or cooked. Gooseberries or currants indicate the presence of water in desert areas (see Desert Chapter). They contain abundant Vitamin C (when fresh), Vitamin B complex, organic acids, sugars, and pectin.
• They are nutritious and act as a general tonic. An infusion of dried berries can be used as a gargle for throat and mouth infections.

CHICORY

(Chichorium Intybus)
Found: West Coast North America
Roots: roasted as a coffee substitute (this coffee was used in Europe during the Second World War).
Leaves: can be used for salads. They contain calcium, phosphorus, iron, potassium, vitamins A and C.
• In herbal medicine the dried roots are used in tea form as a tonic, mild diuretic, and laxative.

GROUND CHERRY

(Physalis)
Found: United States and Southern Canada
Fruit: can be eaten raw or cooked into jams. When picking leave them in their paper like shells so that they can mature.

GREEN AMARANTH

(Amaranthus)
Found: Temperate North America
Leaves: cooked as spinach. They contain vitamin A, vitamin C, vitamin B's, thiamin, riboflavin and niacin.

GRAPES

(Vitis)
Found: United States and Southern Canada
Grapes: are eaten raw, dried for raisins, made into juice or fermented as a wine.
Young leaves: can be eaten raw, cooked and fried. The leaves can be marinated and stuffed and rolled to serve as an appetizer. *Roots: are poisonous.*

DOCK

(Rumex)
Found: North America
Greens: can be eaten like spinach (raw, cooked, pureed). Tastes like lemon.
Seeds: can be dried and ground into flour.
The plant is very rich in vitamin C, vitamin A and potassium.

ELDERBERRY

(Sambucus)
Found: United States and Canada
Berries: berries should be dried and cooked as they are very bitter. They are used as an ingredient in mixed fruit jams.
• The Indians used the berries as a tasty additive in pemmican. The berries can be blue, red, amber, black.

EVENING PRIMROSE

(Oenothera)
Found: United States and Temperate Canada. Usually found on well drained sandy slopes.
Roots: they are tasty only before the plant blooms in the first year. The nutty tasting roots are peeled and boiled. They can be dried and stored. They can be used in stews.

DAISY

(Bellis Perennis)
Found: North America
Young leaves: eaten raw as a salad
Flower: can be dried to make tea.

ELM

(Ulmus)
Found: Temperate North America
The yellow inner bark can be used for medicinal purposes.

DANDELION

(Taraxacum Officinale)
Found: North America
Root: can be boiled in salt water and eaten. They can be roasted and ground to make a coffee substitute.
• An infusion made of dried roots will stimulate the appetite and aid digestion.
Flowers and buds: eaten as a salad. They can be used to make an excellent wine.
Stems and young leaves: eaten as a salad.
Plants contain vitamin A, calcium, sodium, potassium, ascorbic acid, riboflavin.

DILL

(Anethum Graveolens)
Found: North America where it has escaped from gardens.
Flowering stems: used in cooking or flavoring preserved food.

CHIA-SAGE

(Salvia)
Found: South Western United States
Seeds: can be ground into flour. Can be eaten dry or drink mixture of seeds and water. Seeds are very nutritious.

Jack- in-the-Pulpit

Hazelnut

(Corylus Avellana)
Found: North America
Nut: the nut can be eaten raw
or mixed into salads, etc. Do
not pack them in plastic bags
as they have to breath during
storage. They contain up to
60% fatty oils, plus proteins,
sugars, and vitamins.
Leaf: as a tea it has diuretic
properties. Externally has
been used in a bath to treat
slow healing wounds.

Hickory

(Carya)
Found: North America -
different trees of this family
live in different areas of
North America
Hickory nuts (this includes
the Pecan): these nuts are
very nutritious and can be
eaten raw or added to other
dishes (pecan pie).
Liquor: made by pounding the
whole nut (including shells)
until it is a powder. Add water.
Let ferment until you have a
thick milky colored oily liquid. Try it you might like it!

Iceland Moss

(Cetraria Islandica)
Found: Northern United
States up to Alaska and
Northern Canada
It is a lichen and not a moss
Moss: this is an edible lichen
that is a multifaceted food.
To prepare the Iceland Moss
it should be soaked in two
changes of water and then
dried. The soaking removes
the bitter tasting organic acid.
After drying crush the lichen
into a powder. This powder
can be stored in a dry dark
location and used as required.
When gently boiled and
cooked it makes a nutritious
jelly.
• It is used in folk medicine
for its nutritive properties and
for treating chest ailments.
• The Indians mixed the powder with water or milk and
lightly heated it to produce a
porridge like substance. You
can mix the powder with flour
to bake bread. The powder can
be added to soups or stews.
• An excellent and easily
obtainable survival food

Highbush Cranberry

(Viburnum)
Found: United States and Canada
Berries: are a very important
survival food in the winter as
they remain frozen on the
branches. These berries can be
eaten off the branch or cooked
and eaten as a compote. They
are very rich in vitamin C.

Horseradish

(Armoracia)
Found: North America
Leaves: cooked, steamed or
baked in salty water and served
as spinach with oil or butter.
Roots: grate the roots and add
lemon to produce horseradish
which you can use to season
bland food (usually cooked
meats). The roots are nutritious
and contain calcium, phosphorous, iron, potassium and
ascorbic acid.
• Horseradish roots can be
cooked, the liquid cooled and
drinking small quantities at a
time, will help bowel
movements. *Do not use large
doses as it may irritate the
digestive track.*

Hackberry

(Celtis)
Found: North America
Berries: can be eaten raw.
Pits: the white kernels in the
pits can be eaten and taste like
dates. The dried pits can be
ground and used as flavoring
on wild game.

Hawthorn

(Crataegus Laevigata)
Found: United States and
Southern Canada
Fruit: looks like tiny apples.
Colors can be reddish, yellow,
black or bluish. They can be
eaten fresh or dried to be
ground and mixed with pemmican. The fruit makes excellent
jams and jellies. The fruit
contains flavonoid glycosides,
organic acids, tannins, an
essential oil, Vitamin C, B
complex, and pectin.

Live-Forever

(Sedum)
Found: North America
Young leaves: as a salad.
Leaves: cooked in a stew.
Tubers: can be added to salads.

Lamb's Quarter

(Chenopodium)
Found: North America
on former farmlands
Leaves: can be eaten
as a spinach.
Seeds: dried and ground
for flour or can be cooked
in water as a porridge.
Very nutritious containing
calcium, vitamin A, thiamin,
riboflavin, and niacin.

Kinnikinic

(Arctostaphylos)
Found: Northern Region
of North America
Berries: eaten raw or cooked.
Young leaves: tea made to
cleanse the kidneys.
Leaves: cure and dry, cut
up and use as a tobacco.

Knotweed

(Polygonum)
Found: United States and
Canada
Roots: are tubers that can
be roasted or boiled.
Young shoots: cooked in
boiling salted water and
seasoned as asparagus.
Long shoots: peel and cook.

Jack-in-the-Pulpit

(Arisaema)
Found: Eastern North America
from Florida to the Canadian
Maritime provinces
Roots: it is very important to
remove the acridness by
drying the fresh roots. It might
take a month to dry naturally.
When dry the roots can be
eaten like chips. If the roots
are pulverized the powder can
be added to wheat flour.

Jerusalem Artichoke

(Helianthus)
Found: United States and
Central Canada - grows in
damp but not wet areas
Tubers: should be dug after
first frost. By removing the
skin you can eat the tubers
raw. To cook them simmer
them in water and remove
the skin. Serve the same
way as potatoes.

Groundnut

(Apios)
Found: Florida, New Mexico
to Southern Canada
Tubers on roots: look like
potatoes and can be eaten raw
or cooked. When cooked they
should be eaten hot for the
best flavor. The tubers are
found just below the surface
and a stick can be used to
probe and remove them.
Seeds: are in bean like pods
and can be cooked in salty
water, as peas.

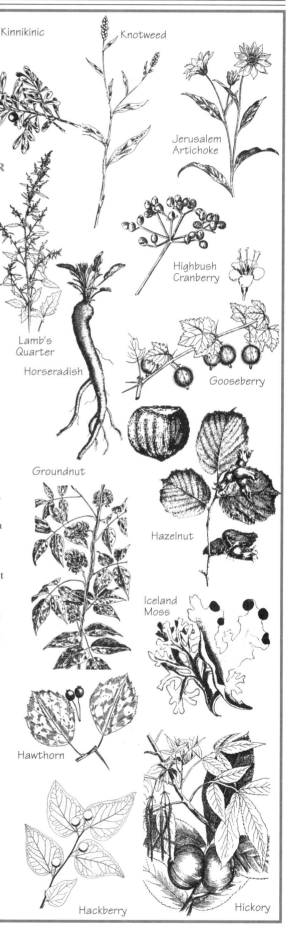

Live Forever

Kinnikinic

Knotweed

Jerusalem
Artichoke

Lamb's
Quarter

Horseradish

Highbush
Cranberry

Gooseberry

Groundnut

Hazelnut

Iceland
Moss

Hawthorn

Hackberry

Hickory

MILKWEED

(Asclepias)
Found: United States and
Southern Canada
Young sprouts: when up to
7" long are cooked and
eaten as asparagus.
Young leaves and young
flower buds: can be boiled
or steamed.
To remove the bitter milky
sap bring the plant to a boil
in water twice and discard
the water each time.

MINT

(Mentha)
Found: United States and
Southern Canada
Leaves: eaten as a salad.
Fresh mint tea - leaves should
be added to hot water and steep
overnight. Do not boil leaves
as they will lose the aromatic
oil and vitamin A and C.
Young leaves: they should
be picked on a dry morning,
dried and stored in a sealed
jar. They makes excellent tea.

NEW JERSEY TEA

(Ceanothus)
Found: Eastern North America
Southern Canada to Florida
Young leaves: green or dried
for tea. The leaves are caffeine
free. The best tea is made
from dry leaves.

MOUNTAIN ASH

(Sorbus)
Found: United States and Canada. The tree prefers wet soil.
Berries: can be eaten fresh or
dried and ground into flour.
They can also be cooked as
jams and marmalades. They
can make an excellent
bittersweet wine.

LETTUCE SAXIFRAGE

(Saxi Frage)
Found: North America
Young leaves: for salads.
Leaves: cooked as a soup. or
in a frying pan, with bacon,
as a substitute for eggs.

LABRADOR TEA

(Ledum)
Found: Northern United States
and Canada. Mainly in wet areas.
Leaves: dry and use for tea.

KENTUCKY COFFEE TREE

(Gymnocladus)
Found: United States, New
York State to Oklahoma
Seeds: roasted and ground for
a coffee substitute. Can be
roasted and eaten like nuts.

JUNIPER

(Juniperus)
Found: North America
Berries: can be eaten raw. Can
be dried and ground to use as a
tasty flour additive. They can
be roasted and ground to make
a coffee substitute.
• *Do not eat too many berries
as they are a diuretic and
might irritate your kidneys.*
Twigs: use berry-less twigs to
make juniper tea. If you want
a high concentration of vitamin
C steep the tea overnight.

MUSTARD

(Brassica)
Found: United States and
Southern Canada
Seeds: as a spice for salads,
seasoning, soups, stews.
Can be used to prepare table
mustard (crush seeds, add
vinegar or white wine to make
paste. You can also add
paprika, pepper, garlic).
Flowers: cook and eat as
broccoli. They are very
rich in vitamin A.
Leaves: cook as spinach.
Leaves contain large quantities
of calcium, phosphorous, iron,
potassium, vitamin A, thiamin,
riboflavin, niacin, vitamin C.

MULBERRY

(Morus)
Found: United States and
Southern Ontario
Berries: can be eaten
raw or prepared for juice.
Young twigs: can be
eaten raw or cooked.

MAPLE

(Acer)
Found: North America
Seeds: remove covering and
can be eaten raw or cooked.
Can be dried and stored.
Young leaves: these are rich
in sugar and can be eaten
raw, in a salad, or cooked
and added to stews.
Sap: make syrup and sugar.
Inner bark: eaten raw or
cooked after being cut into
spaghetti like strips.
To make maple syrup
Cut a 'V' into a tree and
drill a 2" deep hole and insert
a spout. Hammer a nail above
the 'V' and hang the pail from
this nail.

MAY APPLE

(Podophyllum)
Found: Quebec, Ontario
to Florida
Fruit: eaten raw, as a juice
or an uncooked jam.
• *Roots, stems, leaves are
poisonous.*

MOUNTAIN SORREL

(Oxyria)
Found: In North America at
higher elevations, in the
southern areas, and at lower
levels in the Arctic.
Young leaves: in sandwiches.
Leaves: chewed raw as a thirst
quencher and can be used in
salads or cooked as spinach.
Older leaves: can be used to
give body to soup.
• This plant is very rich
in vitamin C.

PRICKLY PEAR CACTUS

(Opuntia)
Found: United States
Fruit: slice in half and scoop
out the meaty interior.
Seeds: can be dried and
ground into flour.
• Stems: can press a watery
liquid from stems. This can
be used in survival situations.

NETTLES

(Urtica)
Found: North America
Young leaves: can be boiled
or steamed and eaten as a
spinach. They are very rich
in protein.
• *In survival situations you
can eat nettle leaves and they
will be a cornerstone of your
diet. You could even be imagi-
native and cook nettles with
some exotic foods such as
insects and slugs.*

Mountain Sorrel

New
Jersey
Tea

May Apple

Sugar Maple

White
Mulberry

Spearmint

Mustard

Labrador
Tea

Milkweed

Lettuce
Saxifrage

Mountain Ash

Juniper Nettles

Nettles

Kentucky
Coffee Tree

Prickly
Pear
Cactus

Prickly Pear Cactus

POPLAR

(Populus)
Found: North America
Inner bark: in the spring it can be eaten raw or cooked as spaghetti. Can be dried and ground into flour.

PURSLANE

(Portulaca)
Found: United States and Southern Canada
Leaves: can be eaten raw, in salads, cooked (as spinach) or conserved by marinating.
Seeds: dried and ground into flour. Contains: vitamin A, vitamin C and riboflavin.

ROSE

(Rosa)
Found: North America
Flowers: eaten raw after bitter white base has been removed. Tea can be made from flowers.
Leaves: for tea
Hips: (these are the developed flowers which form seed pods) Hips produce an excellent tea "Rosehip tea" and can also be eaten raw. Hips contain: Vitamin C (up to 1%), carotene, Vitamin B complex, sugars, pectin, tannins, malic and citric acids. The tea has tonic, astringent, mild diuretic, and mild laxative effects.
Seeds: can be ground into flour. They are an excellent source of vitamin 'C'.
When making tea - First boil water and then add tea making ingredients and let it steep at least 15 minutes. If you boil tea you will lose much of the vitamin C content.

PLANTAIN

(Plantago)
Found: United States and Canada
Young leaves: eaten raw.
Leaves: can be cooked as spinach or pureed. They can be dried for tea.
• Very rich in vitamin A and C and have a high mineral content. Do not over cook as the nutritive components would be destroyed.
• A thickened syrup made from leaves, sweetened with honey, can be used as a cough syrup for children.
• Crushed fresh leaves can be applied externally to swellings, bruises and inflamed wounds.

PASTURE BRAKE

(Pteridium)
Found: North America
Young ferns are called "fiddle heads": can be eaten raw or steamed.
• *Do not eat too many raw because the thiaminate enzyme, which is destroyed by cooking, will eliminate vitamin B from your body.*

PAPAW

(Asimina)
Found: United States to Southern Ontario
Fruit: raw or cooked has a very special taste which one has to get used to. It is an excellent source of nutrients. The fruit can be gathered green and ripened in the sun.

PINE

(Pinus)
Found: North America
Young needles: can be chewed and have nutritional value.
Spring inner bark: can be eaten raw or cooked. To cook cut the bark lengthwise into strips and cook like spaghetti. Can be dried and ground into flour and used to bake bread.

PARTRIDGE BERRY

(Mitchella)
Found: Eastern Atlantic Coast
Berry: These berries stay on the plants all winter, so are an excellent survival food. They are usually found in pine forests.

RUM CHERRY

(Prunus)
Found: Canadian Maritime Provinces to Mexico in moist fertile soil.
Cherry: eaten raw or cooked, used to make a liquor.

PIN CHERRY

(Prunus)
Found: Southern Canada to South Dakota
Cherry: eaten raw or cooked as a jelly. Eating raw cherries will quench your thirst and they are nutritional.

RASPBERRY & BLACKBERRY

(Rubus Idaeus + Fruticosus)
Found: Northern areas of United States and in Canada and is found further south at higher cooler elevations
Berries: raw and cooked, have a high content of vitamin C (when fresh), pectin, organic acids, and sugars. They can be used to make liquors.
Young twigs: peeled and eaten raw.
• Blackberry leaf tea is used to cure colds, flu, and coughs.
• Raspberry leaf tea is used to treat diarrhea and stomach disorders. It can also be used as a mouthwash and gargle.

POKEWEED

(Phytolacca)
Found: South Eastern United States
Young sprouts: cook them in salted water and strain.
• *Roots: are poisonous.*
• *Grown stalks: are narcotic and poisonous (they have a purple sheen).*

PRICKLY LETTUCE

(Lactuca)
Found: United States and Southern Canada
Young leaves: salad
Leaves: cook to remove the prickly texture on the leaves. Parboil to remove bitter flavor but this will reduce their nutritional value.

ORACH

(Atriplex)
Found: United States and Southern Canada grows along the coast in wet marshlands
Leaves: as a salad or steamed as a spinach.
Seeds: eaten raw or dried and ground into a flour.

OAK ACORN

(Querus)
Found: USA and Southern Canada
Acorns are one of the major foods of the forest and all are edible. Some are bitter and you can remove the bitterness by boiling the shelled acorns in water until the water become yellow. (This yellow liquid, can be further boiled, to increase its concentration to use it to dye cotton, wool or leather.) Slowly dry the acorns in a cast iron frying pan or in a stove. Dried acorns can be eaten whole or ground into a flour and baked. Roast and grind acorns and use them as a coffee substitute. If the ground acorns are mixed with cocoa and sugar it makes a beverage that will stop diarrhea and act as a general tonic.
• To remove the bitterness from acorns the Indians would bury them in a muddy swamp and retrieve them the following year.
• Crushed fresh oak leaves will promote the healing of wounds.

Rose
Pine (Jack Pine)
Partridge Berry
Purlane
Rum Cherry
Poplar: Lombardy
Papaw
Orach
Blackberry
Raspberry
Pokeweed
Pasture Brake
Oak Acorn
Prickly Lettuce
Plantain

Spring Beauty

Serviceberry

Sumac

Wild Lettuce

Silverweed

Wintergreen

Sassafras

Spring Beauty

Toothwort

Spice Bush

Salsify

Wild Strawberry

Sunflower

Shepherd's Purse

Sweet Flag

Sow Thistle

Wintergreen

WILD STRAWBERRY

(Fragaria Vesca)
Found: North America
Berries: raw or cooked. They contain iron, potassium, sulfur, calcium, sodium, and citric acid.
Leaves: have a bitter taste and can be dried for tea. They have astringent, diuretic and tonic properties.
• Young leaves: put fresh leaves into boiling water and let steep for night to have a vitamin C rich drink (do not boil the leaves).
Stems and stalks: eaten in a salad or steamed as spinach.

SALSIFY

(Tragopogon)
Found: Northern United States and Southern Canada
Roots (from short plants): clean and cook with two changes of fresh water.
Young leaves and stems: are edible when cooked.
• Indian gum: the Indians used the sap excretions of the Salsify plant as a chewing gum that would alleviate indigestion.

SASSAFRAS

(Sassafras)
Found: Southern Ontario to Florida and Texas
Young roots: for tea
• Roots: for tea but remove the rough bark before using. Do not drink too much of this tea as it has a narcotic effect.
Leaves: dried leaves can be added to soup.
Young stems and leaves: dried and ground to produce the sassafras spice. Twigs: chewed as a filler when you are hungry.

SUNFLOWER

(Helianthus)
Found: North America
Seeds: eaten raw, roasted or crushed. When crushed they are boiled in water and the oil is skimmed off the water.
• High energy food: To make seed loafs they can be crushed and mixed with fat, oil, or honey and this mixture can be eaten as a meal.
• To break the shells of large quantities of seeds at one time roll the seeds with a rolling pin. Pour the seeds and shells into a pail full of water. Agitate the water until the seeds settle to the bottom and skim the shell husks off the top. Dry the seeds.

SWEET FLAG

(Acorus Calamus)
Found: United States and Southern Canada in wetlands
Leaves, flowers and stems: can be eaten raw in the springtime.
Roots: dry and grind them. Use the powder as a natural insecticide. Is used in herbalism as a stomachic and carminative. It is also used in perfumes

SPICE BUSH

(Benzoin)
Found: United States
Young leaves, twigs and bark: for tea and can also be dried and ground to replace allspice.
Young bark: can be chewed to activate the saliva glands.

SHEPHERD'S PURSE

(Capsella)
Found: United States and Canada
Young leaves: raw in salads
Leaves: cooked in stews as a filler. Seeds: dried and ground into flour.

SOW THISTLE

(Sonchus)
Found: United States and temperate Canada
Young plant: eaten in salads
Older plants: for stews. The older plants might be bitter so you can lightly cook them twice discarding the first batch of water. Do not overcook as they will lose their nutritive properties.

WILD LETTUCE

(Lactuca)
Found: United States and Southern Canada
Leaves: used in stews, small plants can be eaten raw.

WINTERGREEN

(Gaultheria)
Found: St. Lawrence, Great Lake Waterway and the Mississippi
Leaves: as a tea. Berries: eaten frozen off the plant all winter.

SPRING BEAUTY

(Claytonia)
Found: North America
Young leaves: eaten raw for their vitamins and in salads.
Roots (tubers): are like small potatoes and are cooked in salt water like potatoes. They grow a few inches below the surface and can be dug up with a stout stick having a wedge like point. Do not remove the skin as it is very nutritious.

SILVERWEED

(Potentilla)
Found: Arctic region south to New Jersey and the Mexican border. Damp soil around a source of water.
Roots: boiled or roasted. The roots can be boiled to make a strong reddish dye.
Leaves: tea can be made from fresh leaves to relieve diarrhea. This is an important survival food.

SUMAC

(Rhus)
Found: United States and Southern Canada
• Berries: to make "Indian lemonade' crush berries and steep until the liquid is well colored. Strain to remove fine hairs of plant. This is an excellent source of vitamin A.

SERVICEBERRY

(Amelanchier)
Found: North America.
In damp and open areas
Berry: edible raw or cooked and are used in pies.
• Dried berries are ground to be used in pemmican (*see Cooking Chapter*).

TOOTHWORT

(Dentaria)
Found: Central and Eastern areas. Roots: grated they can be used to add flavor to salads. Prepare as a mustard.

WILD PLUM

(Prunus)
Found: United States and Southern Canada
Fruit: eaten raw or cooked as a jam, jelly, or to make a liquor.
• To make a heavy jam remove pits and cook slowly in a bit of water while adding a small quantity of sugar. Let the liquids evaporate while stirring. This will give you a heavy jam.

WILD GINGER

(Asarum)
Found: Southern Canada to California and North Carolina
Root: collected in the spring and can be sliced to be used in cooking. The roots can be dried and ground to use as a spice.

WILD ONION

(Allium)
Found: North America
Onions: mild ones can be eaten raw. Cooked with wild fowl eggs. To keep their high vitamin A content do not overcook them.
• Wild onions have high sulfur-containing compounds that are excellent antiseptics. They also contain essential oils, sugars, vitamins and minerals. They can be used to treat infections of the respiratory passages (coughs, bronchitis, and colds). Fresh crushed onions can be applied to insect bites and boils. The bulbs are not effective when dried.

WILD RICE

(Zizania)
Found: North America but mainly in the Northern States from the Great Lakes to Maine.
Grain (seeds): the grain can be picked at the end of the summer. Wash the rice in cold water before using.

WILD GARLIC

(Allium Sativum)
Found: forests in temperate North America
Bulb: can be added to food for flavoring or eaten raw. Garlic can be applied to insect bites and boils. Eating garlic is said to keep colds away,
• To cleanse breath of garlic smell: chew basil leaf, mint, parsley, or thyme.

WILLOW

(Salix)
Found: North America
Young Leaves: can be raw survival food.
• Young shoots: that are found in the Arctic tundra can be peeled and eaten raw. Inner bark: eaten raw, cooked as strips to make a "spaghetti" or dried and ground into flour.

WILD APPLE

(Malus) (Pyrus)
Found: United States and Southern Canada
Fruit eaten raw or cooked.

SLIPPERY ELM

(Ulmus)
Found: Gulf of Mexico to South Eastern Canada
• Inner bark: cut into small pieces, pour boiling water onto them, cover and allow to steep until cool. Add lemon and sugar or honey and drink. This is medication for coughs due to colds.
• Can be used for dysentery and bronchitis.
• Powdered inner bark mixed with hot water to make a paste is used as a poultice for inflammation.

WINTERCRESS

(Barbarea)
Found: North America along the waterways
Leaves: can be eaten raw or cooked. To remove the bitterness in older leaves boil twice.
Buds: steam like spinach but not too much as they will disintegrate into a mush.

WATERCRESS

(Nasturtium Officinale)
Found: North America floating on water
Leaves: eaten raw or steamed like spinach.
Stems, flowers, pods: Presoak in water in which you have placed a water purifier tablet. Boil to remove any additional water contaminants.
• *Watercress should be eaten in limited quantities as large doses may cause inflammation of the mucosa of the bladder and gastrointestinal tract.*

Wild Ginger

Willow

Watercress

Slippery Elm

Wild Plum

Wild Onion

Wild Garlic

Wild Ginger

Wild Apple

Wintercress

Wild Rice

PLANT FOOD FROM THE SEA

IRISH MOSS

(Chondrus)
Found: Eastern Shores of North America
• This seaweed was the universal food of the seagoing people of North America and Iceland, Ireland, Norway, etc.
To eat, it should be soaked in fresh water to remove the salty taste. It can be dried and stored in a slab-like form. Boil it in fresh water and it will become tender and can be eaten in a stew or soup.
• Irish moss has especially high nutritive values in fat, fiber, ash, calcium, phosphorus, iron, sodium and potassium. It is helpful for diarrhea.

LAVER

(Porphyra)
Found: on coasts
Blades: eaten raw or dried. When partially dried, cut into small pieces and continue drying. Store in a sealed container in a cool dry dark location. Use in soups and fish stews. It keeps indefinitely due to its high salt content.

DULSE

(Rhodymenia)
Found: Pacific and Atlantic coasts of North America.
Leaves: can be dried in the sun and used in soap. They are very nutritious, containing calcium, fat, phosphorus, sodium, potassium. They can be chewed raw. You can let them partially dry, and then heat them, in a frying pan or over a fire, to get a more consistent food to chew.

KELP

(Nereocystis)
Found: Atlantic and Pacific Coast
Algae: small pieces can be eaten as picked. Let them dry for better flavor.
Giant Ribbon Kelp can be found along the shoreline after a storm: it is washed, peeled and used as a relish (the same as green cucumber relish).
Hollow bulbs: can be peeled, cooked and pickled.

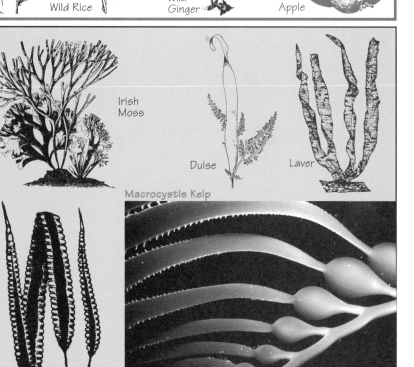

Irish Moss

Dulse

Laver

Macrocystis Kelp

Kelp

CONTENTS OF FIRST AID CHAPTER

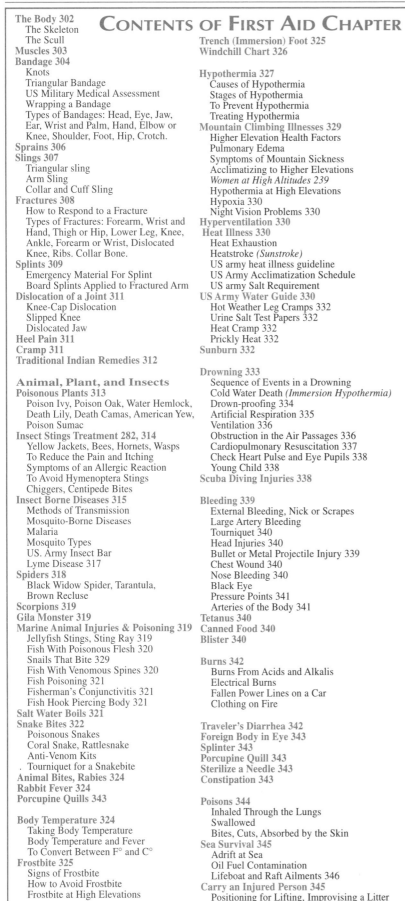

FIRST AID CHAPTER 31

Nervous System

NOTICE

The First Aid information in this book can not, and does not, give all details of First Aid treatment. Only a doctor can give a correct assessment of the accident, the variables of the victim's condition, past medical history, etc. Consult a doctor before attempting any of the methods outlined in this section.

The First Aid Chapter has been included in this book to let the reader appreciate the potential hazards that might occur if not vigilant in the wilderness.

First Aid treatment in an emergency can occur under many different conditions and circumstances.

On the spot treatment for an injury depends upon the injury itself, the knowledge and training of people present, the medical materials available, the environment, the correct diagnosis of the problem, the ability to work under possible panic conditions, etc.

This section should motivate a reader to enlist in a first aid training course.

The author and publisher disclaim all liability with the use of this information

THE BODY

The skeleton, which gives the body its shape and keeps us upright, has 206 bones. These bones are connected by joints.
Some bones do not move relative to the adjacent bones (fixed joint) while others have freely moveable joints that have great dexterity.

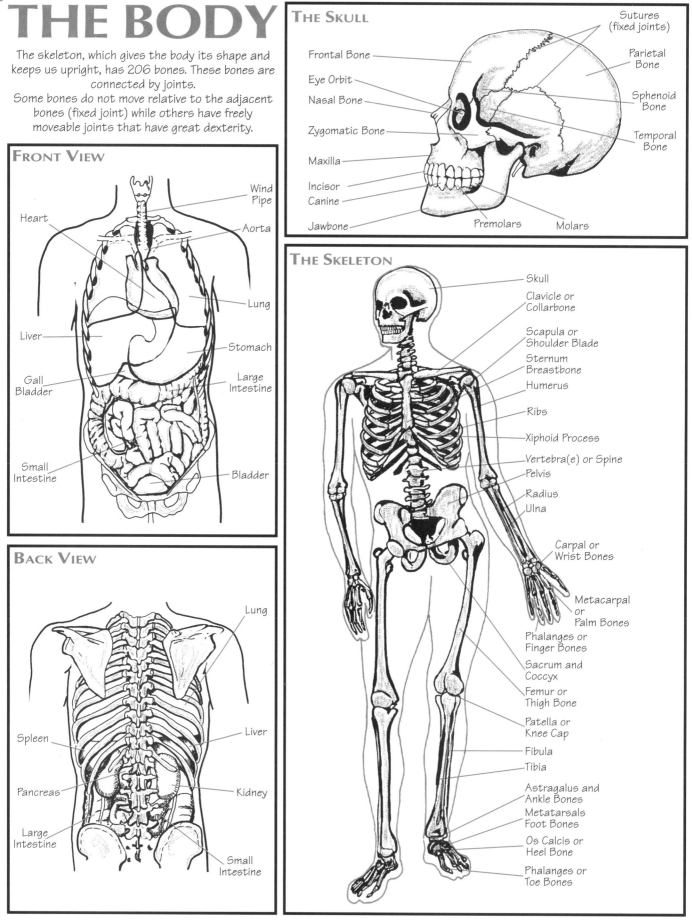

THE SKULL

Frontal Bone
Eye Orbit
Nasal Bone
Zygomatic Bone
Maxilla
Incisor
Canine
Jawbone
Sutures (fixed joints)
Parietal Bone
Sphenoid Bone
Temporal Bone
Premolars
Molars

FRONT VIEW

Heart
Liver
Gall Bladder
Small Intestine
Wind Pipe
Aorta
Lung
Stomach
Large Intestine
Bladder

BACK VIEW

Spleen
Pancreas
Large Intestine
Lung
Liver
Kidney
Small Intestine

THE SKELETON

Skull
Clavicle or Collarbone
Scapula or Shoulder Blade
Sternum Breastbone
Humerus
Ribs
Xiphoid Process
Vertebra(e) or Spine
Pelvis
Radius
Ulna
Carpal or Wrist Bones
Metacarpal or Palm Bones
Phalanges or Finger Bones
Sacrum and Coccyx
Femur or Thigh Bone
Patella or Knee Cap
Fibula
Tibia
Astragalus and Ankle Bones
Metatarsals Foot Bones
Os Calcis or Heel Bone
Phalanges or Toe Bones

MUSCLES

Muscles produce the movements of the body. Muscles are made up of parallel interlocking fibers that are from a few millimeters to 30 cm long. Most of the muscles are attached to a tendon or skin. The body has over 600 muscles.

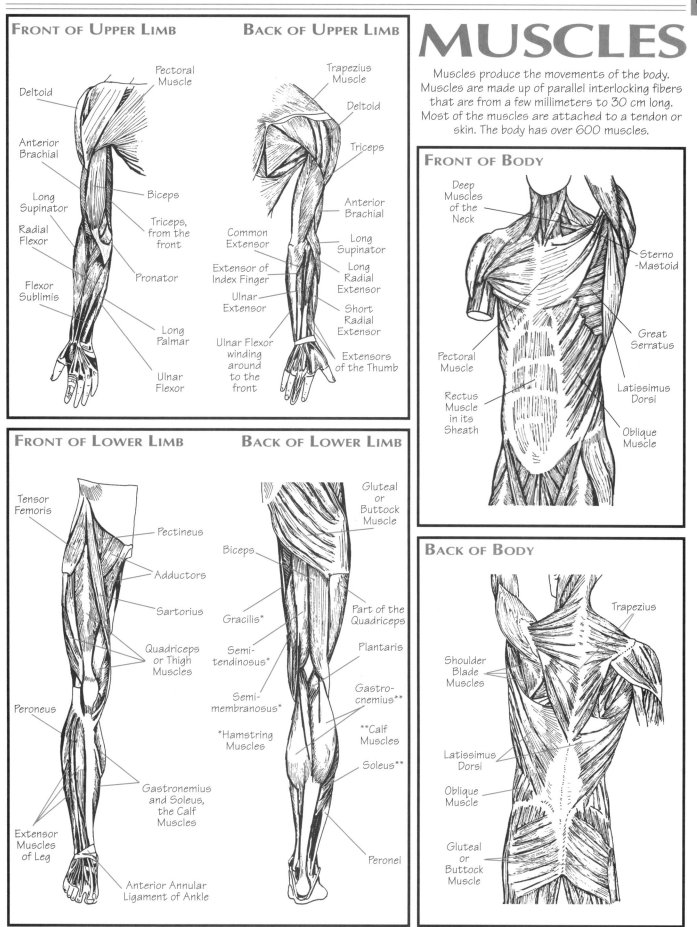

FRONT OF UPPER LIMB

- Deltoid
- Pectoral Muscle
- Anterior Brachial
- Long Supinator
- Biceps
- Radial Flexor
- Triceps, from the front
- Flexor Sublimis
- Pronator
- Long Palmar
- Ulnar Flexor

BACK OF UPPER LIMB

- Trapezius Muscle
- Deltoid
- Triceps
- Anterior Brachial
- Common Extensor
- Long Supinator
- Extensor of Index Finger
- Long Radial Extensor
- Ulnar Extensor
- Short Radial Extensor
- Ulnar Flexor winding around to the front
- Extensors of the Thumb

FRONT OF BODY

- Deep Muscles of the Neck
- Sterno-Mastoid
- Pectoral Muscle
- Great Serratus
- Rectus Muscle in its Sheath
- Latissimus Dorsi
- Oblique Muscle

FRONT OF LOWER LIMB

- Tensor Femoris
- Pectineus
- Adductors
- Sartorius
- Quadriceps or Thigh Muscles
- Peroneus
- Gastronemius and Soleus, the Calf Muscles
- Extensor Muscles of Leg
- Anterior Annular Ligament of Ankle

BACK OF LOWER LIMB

- Gluteal or Buttock Muscle
- Biceps
- Gracilis*
- Part of the Quadriceps
- Semi-tendinosus*
- Plantaris
- Semi-membranosus*
- Gastro-cnemius**
- *Hamstring Muscles
- **Calf Muscles
- Soleus**
- Peronei

BACK OF BODY

- Trapezius
- Shoulder Blade Muscles
- Latissimus Dorsi
- Oblique Muscle
- Gluteal or Buttock Muscle

303

Splint Tie

When securing a splint a narrow bandage can be folded double and passed around the limb and splint. Then *one* end is inserted through the loop forming a double bandage and it is tied, with a reef knot, to the free end.

One end of bandage passed through loop.

Both ends of the bandage are passed through the loop.

The same as the Splint Tie but *both* ends of the bandage are passed, in *opposite* directions, through the loop and then knotted with a reef knot on the outside.

Ends tied with a reef knot.

See Chapter on Knots.

THE FEMUR

Spongy Tissue

Marrow

Compact or Dense Tissue

The femur or the big leg bone is hollow. The hollow is filled with marrow.

Upper Arm Bone (Humerus)

Ulna

Radius

Wrist Bones

Palm Bones

Finger Bones

The Palm Upwards

Palm of Hand Turned Downwards

TRIANGULAR SLING

1

2

Place the base of the bandage under the hand.

Injured Shoulder

3

Reef Knot

Pinned

Sling raises and rests the hand. It can be used for a fractured collar bone or to rest the arm or hand. Place the victim's forearm across the chest with the fingers point towards the shoulder. The palm resting on the breast bone.

Method of Wrapping a Bandage

On finishing, wrap the remaining bandage around the head.

Wrap one bandage horizontally and the second goes back and forth over the head.

KNOTS

Knots Used to Attach Bandages

Wrapping a Bandage
The thumb holds down the bandage which is then folded over to adapt to the curvature of the limb.

Do not use the Granny Knot to tie bandages.

Granny Knot

Ends of bandage in a Granny Knot do not lie in the direction of the bandage.

GRANNY KNOT

The Granny Knot is very similar to the Reef Knot *but should not be used as it has a tendency to slip and unravel.* When a bandage is tied with a Granny knot it will look untidy with the ends being perpendicular to the direction of the bandage.

Reef Knot

Reef Knot Used to Tie Bandage
Note the difference from a Granny Knot. The ends will point in the same direction as the bandage.

REEF KNOT (SQUARE KNOT)

To securely tie the ends of a bandage a reef knot should be used. The knot should be placed where it will not cause any discomfort to the injured person or a pad should be placed between the knot and the body. The tieing of a reef Knot can be confused with a Granny Knot. *Note that the Granny Knot is not stable and has a tendency to slip so should not be used.*

Half Fold Used For Slings

Upper Layer Fastening Bandage or for Restricted Areas

Fold Used to Cover Large Areas and as a first Bandage

Narrow Fold Used For Tying and Tourniquets

TRIANGULAR BANDAGE

This is the most useful format for a first aid bandage. The ends should always be tied with a reef knot. The illustration shows how to fold this format to give you different widths.

US MILITARY PROCEDURE OF ASSESSING EMERGENCY MEDICAL TREATMENT

Primary Survey of the Patient

a. Talk to the patient to determine the extent of injuries and the level of consciousness.

b. Check the patient's pulse, preferably the carotid. *See page 341.*

c. Check the patient's breathing.

- Look for a rise and fall of the chest.

- Listen for the escape of air from the patient's mouth or nose by placing your ear next to the patient's mouth and nose.

- Feel the exchange of air at the mouth or nose with your ear at the same time as you are listening for the air exchange.

d. Look the patient over quickly and carefully to determine if there is any arterial bleeding to be controlled or other life threatening injuries to be taken care of immediately. *See page 341.*

Caution: A quick, but complete check of the immediate area should be made to remove or reduce hazards to your life and the patient's life such as live electrical wires that are exposed, spilled gas, fire, etc.

Note: This examination should be performed by a person with the required medical training. Life threatening problems that are found in the primary survey are treated first and then the secondary survey is conducted.

Problem: A patient with an unknown injury under field conditions.

To perform primary and secondary patient surveys by examining (look, listen, and feel) the patient to determine probable injury or illness.

Secondary Survey of the Patient

Caution: Care must be taken so that injuries are not aggravated.

a. Examine the scalp. Part the hair to look and feel for:

- Bleeding

- Fractures

b. Examine the facial area. Look for obvious injuries as well as blood and/or cerebrospinal fluid at ears and/or nose.

c. Examine the neck for obvious injuries as well as for possible internal injuries such as a cervical fracture.

d. Examine the chest for injuries.

- Look for abnormal movement, color and appearance on one side of the body, face, limb etc. that does not appear on the other as well as bleeding.

- Feel the area for abnormal movement.

e. Examine the abdominal region for spasms, tenderness, bleeding, rigidity, and protruding organs.

f. Examine the pelvic region for fractures and bleeding.

g. Examine the extremities for fractures, dislocations, paralysis, loss of feeling, pain, and/or bleeding.

h. Examine the buttocks for fractures and bleeding.

Caution: Before rolling the patient over, check to make sure there are no spinal injuries.

Treatment may range from treating life-threatening conditions to observation. It is possible (and a part of medical practice) for one person to survey a patient and another person to follow up with the actual treatment.

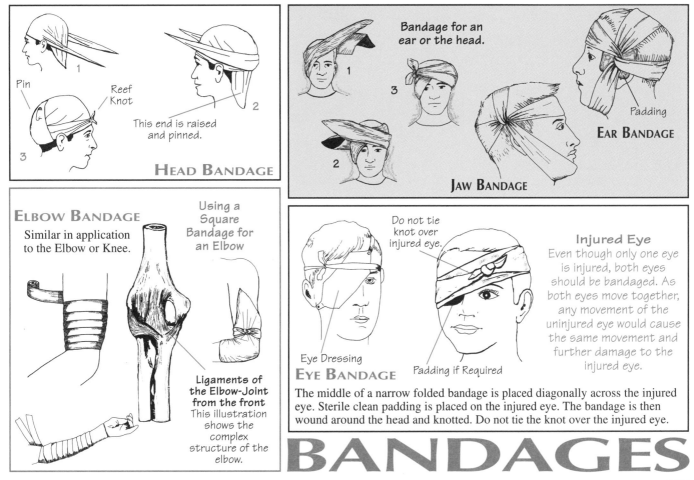

Pin · **Reef Knot** · This end is raised and pinned.

HEAD BANDAGE

Bandage for an ear or the head.

JAW BANDAGE

Padding

EAR BANDAGE

ELBOW BANDAGE

Similar in application to the Elbow or Knee.

Using a Square Bandage for an Elbow

Ligaments of the Elbow-Joint from the front
This illustration shows the complex structure of the elbow.

Do not tie knot over injured eye.

Eye Dressing

EYE BANDAGE

Padding if Required

Injured Eye

Even though only one eye is injured, both eyes should be bandaged. As both eyes move together, any movement of the uninjured eye would cause the same movement and further damage to the injured eye.

The middle of a narrow folded bandage is placed diagonally across the injured eye. Sterile clean padding is placed on the injured eye. The bandage is then wound around the head and knotted. Do not tie the knot over the injured eye.

BANDAGES

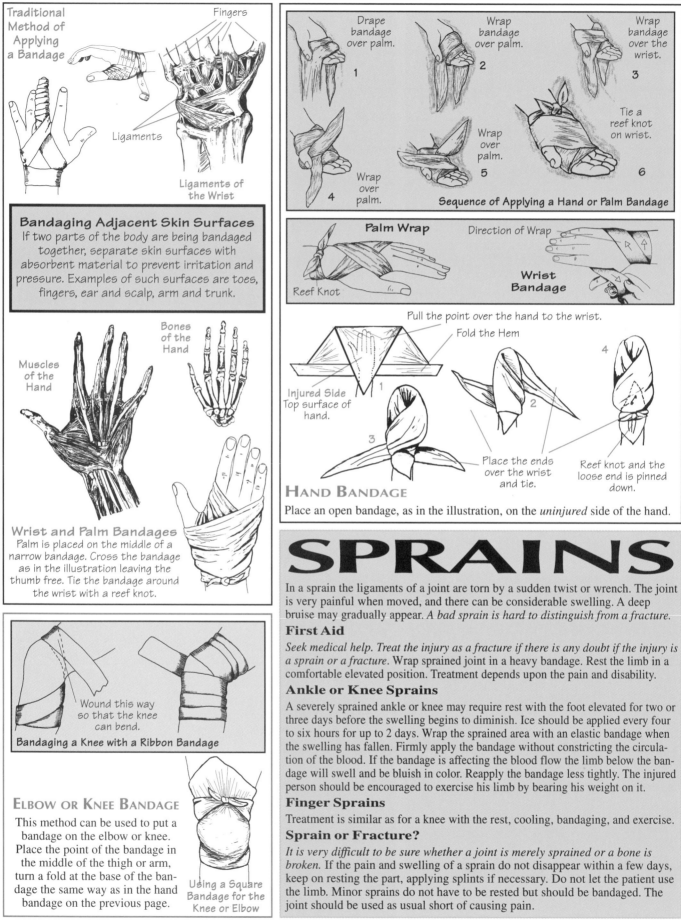

Traditional Method of Applying a Bandage

Fingers

Ligaments

Ligaments of the Wrist

Bandaging Adjacent Skin Surfaces

If two parts of the body are being bandaged together, separate skin surfaces with absorbent material to prevent irritation and pressure. Examples of such surfaces are toes, fingers, ear and scalp, arm and trunk.

Muscles of the Hand

Bones of the Hand

Wrist and Palm Bandages

Palm is placed on the middle of a narrow bandage. Cross the bandage as in the illustration leaving the thumb free. Tie the bandage around the wrist with a reef knot.

Wound this way so that the knee can bend.

Bandaging a Knee with a Ribbon Bandage

ELBOW OR KNEE BANDAGE

This method can be used to put a bandage on the elbow or knee. Place the point of the bandage in the middle of the thigh or arm, turn a fold at the base of the bandage the same way as in the hand bandage on the previous page.

Using a Square Bandage for the Knee or Elbow

Drape bandage over palm. 1

Wrap bandage over palm. 2

Wrap bandage over the wrist. 3

Wrap over palm. 4

Wrap over palm. 5

Tie a reef knot on wrist. 6

Sequence of Applying a Hand or Palm Bandage

Palm Wrap

Direction of Wrap

Reef Knot

Wrist Bandage

Pull the point over the hand to the wrist.

Fold the Hem

Injured Side Top surface of hand. 1

2

3

4

Place the ends over the wrist and tie.

Reef knot and the loose end is pinned down.

HAND BANDAGE

Place an open bandage, as in the illustration, on the *uninjured* side of the hand.

SPRAINS

In a sprain the ligaments of a joint are torn by a sudden twist or wrench. The joint is very painful when moved, and there can be considerable swelling. A deep bruise may gradually appear. *A bad sprain is hard to distinguish from a fracture.*

First Aid

Seek medical help. Treat the injury as a fracture if there is any doubt if the injury is a sprain or a fracture. Wrap sprained joint in a heavy bandage. Rest the limb in a comfortable elevated position. Treatment depends upon the pain and disability.

Ankle or Knee Sprains

A severely sprained ankle or knee may require rest with the foot elevated for two or three days before the swelling begins to diminish. Ice should be applied every four to six hours for up to 2 days. Wrap the sprained area with an elastic bandage when the swelling has fallen. Firmly apply the bandage without constricting the circulation of the blood. If the bandage is affecting the blood flow the limb below the bandage will swell and be bluish in color. Reapply the bandage less tightly. The injured person should be encouraged to exercise his limb by bearing his weight on it.

Finger Sprains

Treatment is similar as for a knee with the rest, cooling, bandaging, and exercise.

Sprain or Fracture?

It is very difficult to be sure whether a joint is merely sprained or a bone is broken. If the pain and swelling of a sprain do not disappear within a few days, keep on resting the part, applying splints if necessary. Do not let the patient use the limb. Minor sprains do not have to be rested but should be bandaged. The joint should be used as usual short of causing pain.

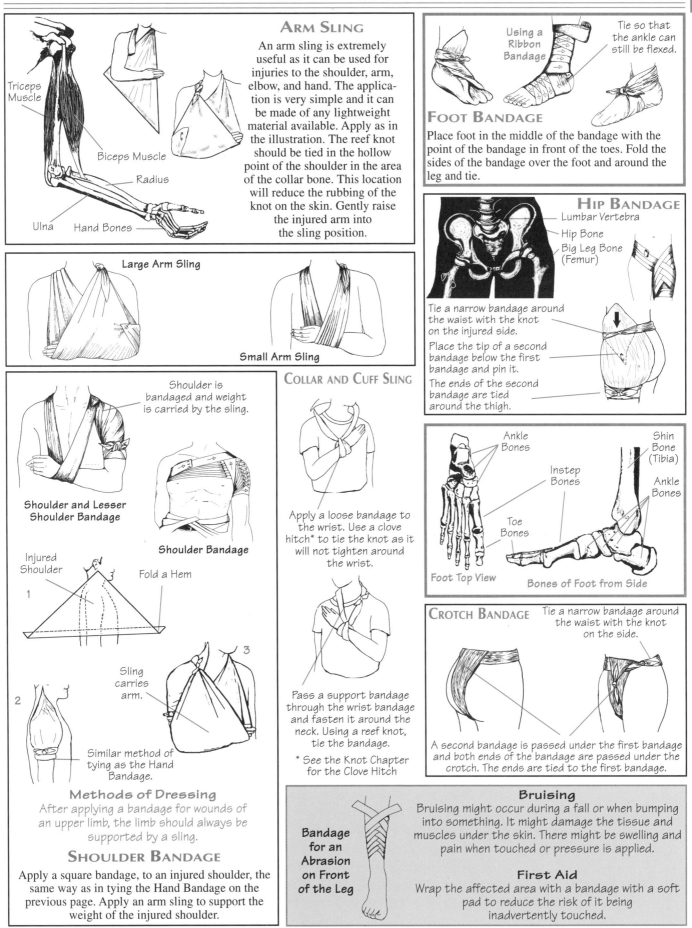

ARM SLING

An arm sling is extremely useful as it can be used for injuries to the shoulder, arm, elbow, and hand. The application is very simple and it can be made of any lightweight material available. Apply as in the illustration. The reef knot should be tied in the hollow point of the shoulder in the area of the collar bone. This location will reduce the rubbing of the knot on the skin. Gently raise the injured arm into the sling position.

Triceps Muscle
Biceps Muscle
Radius
Ulna
Hand Bones

Large Arm Sling

Small Arm Sling

Shoulder is bandaged and weight is carried by the sling.

Shoulder and Lesser Shoulder Bandage

Shoulder Bandage

Injured Shoulder
Fold a Hem
1
2
3
Sling carries arm.
Similar method of tying as the Hand Bandage.

Methods of Dressing
After applying a bandage for wounds of an upper limb, the limb should always be supported by a sling.

SHOULDER BANDAGE
Apply a square bandage, to an injured shoulder, the same way as in tying the Hand Bandage on the previous page. Apply an arm sling to support the weight of the injured shoulder.

COLLAR AND CUFF SLING

Apply a loose bandage to the wrist. Use a clove hitch* to tie the knot as it will not tighten around the wrist.

Pass a support bandage through the wrist bandage and fasten it around the neck. Using a reef knot, tie the bandage.

* See the Knot Chapter for the Clove Hitch

Bandage for an Abrasion on Front of the Leg

Using a Ribbon Bandage
Tie so that the ankle can still be flexed.

FOOT BANDAGE
Place foot in the middle of the bandage with the point of the bandage in front of the toes. Fold the sides of the bandage over the foot and around the leg and tie.

HIP BANDAGE
Lumbar Vertebra
Hip Bone
Big Leg Bone (Femur)

Tie a narrow bandage around the waist with the knot on the injured side.

Place the tip of a second bandage below the first bandage and pin it.

The ends of the second bandage are tied around the thigh.

Ankle Bones
Shin Bone (Tibia)
Instep Bones
Ankle Bones
Toe Bones

Foot Top View
Bones of Foot from Side

CROTCH BANDAGE
Tie a narrow bandage around the waist with the knot on the side.

A second bandage is passed under the first bandage and both ends of the bandage are passed under the crotch. The ends are tied to the first bandage.

Bruising
Bruising might occur during a fall or when bumping into something. It might damage the tissue and muscles under the skin. There might be swelling and pain when touched or pressure is applied.

First Aid
Wrap the affected area with a bandage with a soft pad to reduce the risk of it being inadvertently touched.

FRACTURES

Fractures (broken bones) can cause total disability or death. Usually they can be treated so that there is complete recovery. Recovery usually depends upon the first aid received before moving the victim. The basic splinting principle is to immobilize the joints above and below any fracture.

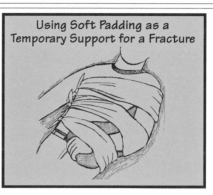

Using Soft Padding as a Temporary Support for a Fracture

Signs of a Broken Bone
- Swelling.
- Pain.
- Difficulty in moving injured part.
- Broken bone might protrude through skin.
- Misalignment or deformity of the injured part.
- There can be internal injuries.

Do not move injured person unless in a dangerous location.

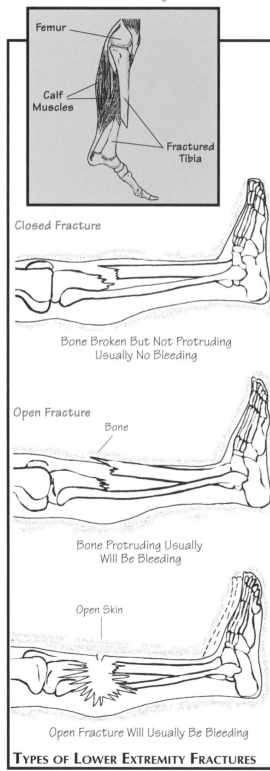

Femur

Calf Muscles

Fractured Tibia

Closed Fracture

Bone Broken But Not Protruding Usually No Bleeding

Open Fracture

Bone

Bone Protruding Usually Will Be Bleeding

Open Skin

Open Fracture Will Usually Be Bleeding

TYPES OF LOWER EXTREMITY FRACTURES

TYPES OF FRACTURES

Closed Fracture

A closed fracture is a break in the bone without a break in the overlying skin. In a closed fracture there may be tissue damage beneath the skin. *Even though an injury may be a dislocation or sprain, it should be considered as a closed fracture for purposes of applying first aid.*

Open Fracture

An open fracture is a break in the bone as well as in the overlying skin. The broken bone may have come through the skin. An open fracture can be contaminated and is subject to infection.

Signs and Symptoms of a Fracture

A fracture is easily recognized when the bone is protruding through the skin, the body part is in an unnatural position, or the chest wall is caved in. Other indications of a fracture are tenderness or pain when light pressure is applied to the injured part and swelling as well as discoloration of the skin at the site of the injury. A deep, sharp pain when the victim attempts to move the part is also a sign of a fracture. Do not, however encourage the victim to move a part in order to identify a fracture as movement of the part would cause further damage to surrounding tissue and promote shock. *If you are not sure whether or not a bone is fractured, treat the injury as a fracture.*

Purpose of Immobilizing a Fracture

A body part which contains a fracture must be immobilized to prevent the razor-sharp edges of the bone from moving and cutting tissue, muscle, blood vessels, and nerves. Furthermore, immobilization greatly reduces pain and helps to prevent or control shock. In a closed fracture, immobilization keeps bone fragments from causing an open wound which could become contaminated and possibly infected. Immobilization is accomplished by splinting.

Rules for Splinting

If the fracture is open, first stop the bleeding, then apply a dressing and bandage as you would for any other wound.

- Apply the proven principle *"Splint them where they lie"*. This means to splint the fractured part *before any movement* is attempted and without any change in the position of the fractured part. If a bone is in an unnatural position or a joint is bent, do not try to straighten it. If a joint is not bent, do not try to bend it.
- Collect appropriate splinting material and padding for the body area involved.
- Apply a splint so that the joint *above the fracture and the joint below the fracture are immobilized.*
- Use padding between the injured part and the splint to prevent undue pressure and further injury to tissue, blood vessels, and nerves. This is especially important at the crotch, in the armpit, and in places where the splint comes in contact with bony parts such as the elbow, wrist, fingers, knee, and ankle joint.
- Bind the splint with bandages at *several points above and below* the fracture, but do not bind so tightly to interfere the flow of the blood. At least two binding points above and two below. No bandage should be applied across the fracture. Tie bandages that the knot is against the splint, and tie them with a square knot (reef knot).
- Use a sling to support a splinted arm which is bent at the elbow, a fractured elbow which is bent, a sprained arm, and an arm with a painful wound.

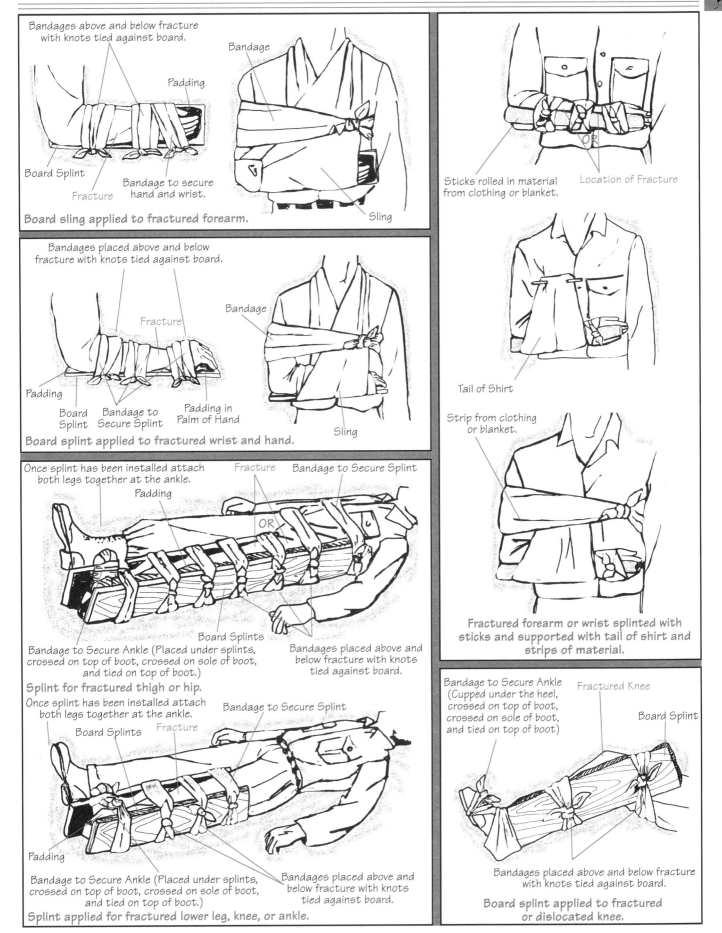

Bandages above and below fracture with knots tied against board.

Padding

Board Splint

Fracture

Bandage to secure hand and wrist.

Bandage

Sling

Board sling applied to fractured forearm.

Bandages placed above and below fracture with knots tied against board.

Fracture

Bandage

Padding

Board Splint

Bandage to Secure Splint

Padding in Palm of Hand

Sling

Board splint applied to fractured wrist and hand.

Once splint has been installed attach both legs together at the ankle.

Fracture

Bandage to Secure Splint

Padding

Board Splints

Bandage to Secure Ankle (Placed under splints, crossed on top of boot, crossed on sole of boot, and tied on top of boot.)

Bandages placed above and below fracture with knots tied against board.

Splint for fractured thigh or hip.

Once splint has been installed attach both legs together at the ankle.

Bandage to Secure Splint

Board Splints

Fracture

Padding

Bandage to Secure Ankle (Placed under splints, crossed on top of boot, crossed on sole of boot, and tied on top of boot.)

Bandages placed above and below fracture with knots tied against board.

Splint applied for fractured lower leg, knee, or ankle.

Sticks rolled in material from clothing or blanket.

Location of Fracture

OR

Tail of Shirt

Strip from clothing or blanket.

Fractured forearm or wrist splinted with sticks and supported with tail of shirt and strips of material.

Bandage to Secure Ankle (Cupped under the heel, crossed on top of boot, crossed on sole of boot, and tied on top of boot)

Fractured Knee

Board Splint

Bandages placed above and below fracture with knots tied against board.

Board splint applied to fractured or dislocated knee.

309

SPLINTS

First aid splints are not used to "set" fractures but to relieve pain by giving rest to the injured limb and to prevent the broken bone from piercing the skin.

By splinting you will avoid additional damage to the bone, muscles, arteries, veins, or nerves.

If no splints are available use an uninjured part of the body as a temporary support.
Use an uninjured leg for the leg or the chest for the injured arm.

The skin should be well protected by padding. Tight string, cord, wire, etc., can cause serious damage to the skin if it presses or rubs. Knots, in particular, should never be in direct contact with the bare skin.

MATERIAL TO MAKE AN EMERGENCY SPLINT

If the required material is not available the following can be used.

Cover Blankets	Drapes, curtains, clothing, or rugs.
Padding	Bed sheets, rags, leafy vegetation, soft clothing, bandages, and moss.
Bandages	Belt, tie, scarf, tape, large handkerchief, strips of shirt or light pants, stockings. Narrow material such as wire or cord *should not be used* to secure a splint in place.
Splints	Suitable-sized pieces of wood, rolled cardboard, rugs, rolled newspapers, sticks, or broom handles.
Wound Dressing	Any clean material such as handkerchiefs, strips of shirt, curtains or bed sheets. Place the cleanliest absorbent material closest to the wound especially if there is an open fracture.
Slings	Slings may be improvised by using the tail of a coat or shirt, belts, and pieces torn from such items as clothing and blankets. The triangular bandage is ideal.

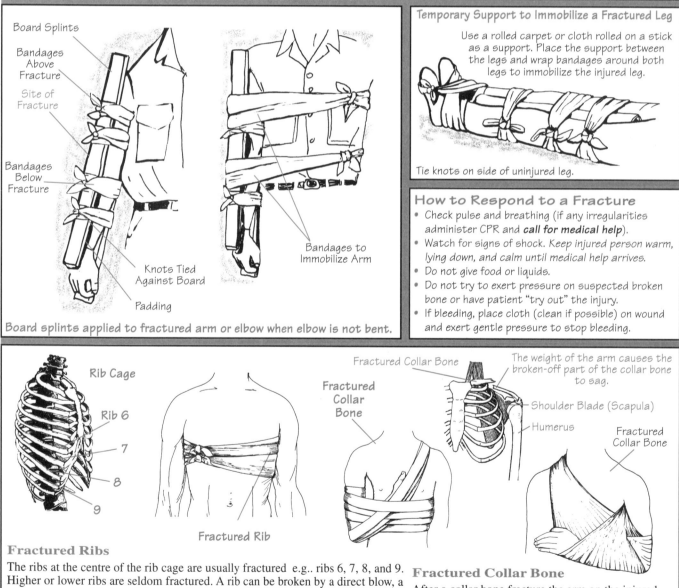

Board Splints
Bandages Above Fracture
Site of Fracture
Bandages Below Fracture
Knots Tied Against Board
Padding
Bandages to Immobilize Arm

Board splints applied to fractured arm or elbow when elbow is not bent.

Temporary Support to Immobilize a Fractured Leg

Use a rolled carpet or cloth rolled on a stick as a support. Place the support between the legs and wrap bandages around both legs to immobilize the injured leg.

Tie knots on side of uninjured leg.

How to Respond to a Fracture

- Check pulse and breathing (if any irregularities administer CPR and **call for medical help**).
- Watch for signs of shock. Keep injured person warm, lying down, and calm until medical help arrives.
- Do not give food or liquids.
- Do not try to exert pressure on suspected broken bone or have patient "try out" the injury.
- If bleeding, place cloth (clean if possible) on wound and exert gentle pressure to stop bleeding.

Rib Cage
Rib 6
7
8
9
Fractured Rib

Fractured Collar Bone
Fractured Collar Bone
The weight of the arm causes the broken-off part of the collar bone to sag.
Shoulder Blade (Scapula)
Humerus
Fractured Collar Bone

Fractured Ribs

The ribs at the centre of the rib cage are usually fractured e.g.. ribs 6, 7, 8, and 9. Higher or lower ribs are seldom fractured. A rib can be broken by a direct blow, a squeeze or a crush injury. A broken rib is very painful. *The danger with a broken or fractured rib is the possible injury to the lungs.*

Some fracture articles & illustrations based on EFMB Study Guide, Department of Military Medicine, US Army

Fractured Collar Bone

After a collar bone fracture the arm on the injured side is partially helpless and the injured person will support it at the elbow with his hand. He will also incline his head towards the injured side.

DISLOCATION OF A JOINT

A dislocation is an injury to a joint in which bones making the joint have slipped or moved out of their usual position relative to one another. A dislocation is very painful. The joint will not be able to be moved and will be "stuck" in an abnormal position. Sometimes it may prove difficult to ascertain if it is a dislocation or a fracture in the area of the joint. It is possible that both have occurred.

First Aid

- Generally, do not attempt to replace the bones. Keep the injured part as found or place it in a less painful position.

- Treat the injury as a fracture by making a well-padded splint.

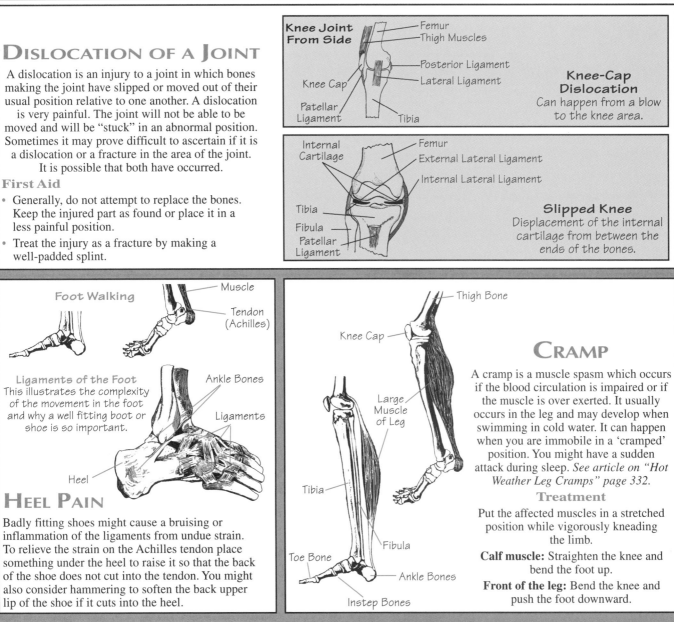

Knee Joint From Side
Femur
Thigh Muscles
Posterior Ligament
Lateral Ligament
Knee Cap
Patellar Ligament
Tibia

Knee-Cap Dislocation
Can happen from a blow to the knee area.

Internal Cartilage
Femur
External Lateral Ligament
Internal Lateral Ligament
Tibia
Fibula
Patellar Ligament

Slipped Knee
Displacement of the internal cartilage from between the ends of the bones.

Foot Walking
Muscle
Tendon (Achilles)

Ligaments of the Foot
This illustrates the complexity of the movement in the foot and why a well fitting boot or shoe is so important.
Ankle Bones
Ligaments
Heel

HEEL PAIN

Badly fitting shoes might cause a bruising or inflammation of the ligaments from undue strain. To relieve the strain on the Achilles tendon place something under the heel to raise it so that the back of the shoe does not cut into the tendon. You might also consider hammering to soften the back upper lip of the shoe if it cuts into the heel.

Thigh Bone
Knee Cap
Large Muscle of Leg
Tibia
Fibula
Toe Bone
Ankle Bones
Instep Bones

CRAMP

A cramp is a muscle spasm which occurs if the blood circulation is impaired or if the muscle is over exerted. It usually occurs in the leg and may develop when swimming in cold water. It can happen when you are immobile in a 'cramped' position. You might have a sudden attack during sleep. *See article on "Hot Weather Leg Cramps" page 332.*

Treatment

Put the affected muscles in a stretched position while vigorously kneading the limb.

Calf muscle: Straighten the knee and bend the foot up.

Front of the leg: Bend the knee and push the foot downward.

DISLOCATED JAW

Usually caused by a big yawn. The jaw freezes in a forward position, and cannot move. *Make sure there is no broken bone.*

Try to replace the bone:

- Wind a piece of handkerchief around each of your thumbs. This will serve as padding.

- The person should be sitting and facing you. Remove any dentures. Press steadily downwards while moving your *protected thumbs* along the teeth of the lower jaw as far back into the mouth as possible. While pressing downwards with your thumbs slightly raise the chin with your palms and the jaw will suddenly fall back in place.

- *Keep thumbs were well protected.*

- The person should not to try to open his mouth wide as a dislocation will almost certainly reoccur.

Take a First Aid course before rock climbing in a cave.

TRADITIONAL REMEDIES

Juniper

Sassafras

Slippery Elm

Yucca Cactus

Yucca Plant Indian Shampoo

The Indians of the Southwest use the yucca plant roots to make shampoo. To extract the "shampoo", the roots are crushed with a stone and soaked for a few minutes and then stirred into a soapy lather. The root fragments are removed and the remaining liquid is the shampoo. Your hair will be soft and lustrous.

Gourd Soap

To produce soap the Southwest Tesuque Pueblo people use the Missouri gourd (mock orange). This gourd is a brilliant yellow-orange. You can recognize this plant by the large leaves which can spread over 2.5 feet (0.75m). It grows in areas with rocky soils. The crushed leaves give off a garlic-like odor. To make soap use the pith and roots of the plant.

Tooth Filling

The Southwest Indians used the gum of the juniper tree to fill decayed teeth.

Hair Growth Tonic

The Indians of New Mexico used the apache plume plant to help hair growth. They would soak the leaves until they became soft, strain the liquid and wash the hair and scalp with the liquid.

Indian Sting Medication

The Eastern Indians used the crushed leaves and stems of the jewelweed as a medicine for stings, mosquito bites and poison ivy. This plant, the orange-flowered jewelweed or spotted touch-me-not *(impatiens biflora)* grows in wet areas, along streams, ponds, springs and swamps. It has orange flowers.

Witch Hazel Bark: Skin Inflammation

The brewed bark was used by the Senecas as an eye wash or for skin inflammation.

Balsam Gum: Cuts and Wounds

The gum of the balsam tree was used on cuts and wounds. This gum soothed the cuts and covered them to keep out foreign substances.

Nosebleeds

Use powdered, dry witch hazel leaves.

Sore Throat

A sore throat astringent can be made by using the inner bark of the hemlock tree. Boil a pound of bark in a gallon of water until a quart remains and gargle with some of this liquid.

Indian Talcum Powder

The yellow spores of club moss *(lycopodium)* can be powdered on tender skin. Finely ground corn meal can also be used as talcum powder.

Inner Bark of the Slippery Elm: Poultice

Dry and grind this bark and mix with hot water to form a paste. This can be used for diarrhea, dysentery, and urinary trouble. It can also be used as a poultice.

Witch Hazel Leaves: Bruises

Dry and use as an astringent in the treatment of external bruises and inflammation.

Chills and Fever Medicine

Sip a strong tea made from the twigs of the spice bush. Spice bush *(lindera benzoin)* grows in eastern North America.

Sassafras Bark and Root: Constipation

A pound of sassafras bark and root was boiled in a gallon of water until only a pint remained. A tablespoon of this liquid used three times a day was a remedy for constipation.

Cough Remedies

A pound of chopped slippery-elm bark or sap of the cherry birch in a gallon of water was boiled down into a syrup which was used to help your cough. A teaspoon would be used every hour.

Soak a pound of bark from the black cherry tree *(prunus serotina)* for six hours in a gallon of water. Boil down to a pint and take one tablespoon three or four times a day.

Spice Bush

Sassafras

Witch Hazel

Hemlock

POISONOUS PLANTS

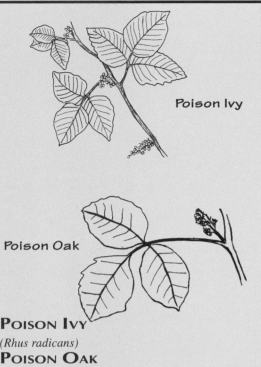

Poison Ivy

Poison Oak

POISON IVY

(Rhus radicans)

POISON OAK

(Rhus toxicodendron)

Location: North America, Bermuda and the Bahamas

Found: Nearly everywhere but mostly along fences and stone walls.

Description: Poison Ivy is a vine that can be found high on trees. Fruit is gray and *does not* have a hairy surface. Leaves are slightly lobed.

• Poison Oak is usually a shrub but can climb trees. Leaves are lobed and resemble oak leaves. Fruit *is* hairy.

• Poison Ivy and Poison Oak: leaves alternate, composed of three leaflets borne on a long stem. Leaves are dark, waxy green above and light, more fuzzy beneath. *Fruit stays on plant all winter and spring.*

Caution: Over half the population is allergic to Poison Ivy and Poison Oak. The urushiol oil in Poison Ivy and Poison Oak cause the red rash. Can poison *on contact* and the poison can be carried by smoke if plants are burned. Poison causes inflammation, spreading blisters and scabs 4 to 24 hours after contact. May cause temporary blindness. *Wash all items that were in contact with the plants.*

Treatment: Wash several times with warm water and soap. To stop the itching use calamine lotion which cools the skin and distracts your skin from the itching sensation. Calamine lotion leaves a dry crust on the skin which absorbs the oozing liquid. Apply three or four times a day and stop applying when oozing stops. *See the doctor.*

Traditional Treatment:

• Jewelweed ("impatiens or touch-me-not"): Slit stem and put juice on rash.

• Leaf of black nightshade plant (NOT deadly nightshade): Crush plant and mix with milk or cream and apply to rash.

• Milkweed plant: Smear the white milky latex on the rash.

Water Hemlock

Death Camas

Poison Sumac

WATER HEMLOCK

(Cicuta Maculata)

Location: Throughout North America.

Found: In swampy areas.

Description: Has toothed leaves and a yellow sap when stem is cut.

Caution: All parts of this plant are poisonous.

Poison Hemlock is similar but has lacy leaves and white flowers. It grows in open areas throughout North America.

DEATH LILY, DEATH CAMAS

(Zygadenus Venenosus)

Location: Western North America.

Found: A spring and summer plant in fields. Individual plants or in large groups.

Description: Death Lily leaves are grasslike, long, narrow, and bent, so much resembling the leaves of grass that they are not recognized. Flowers are numerous, small, about 1/4" in diameter, six petals, yellowish or greenish white, some having a green heart shaped structure in them.

Caution: All of the plant is poisonous with the seeds being more toxic.

POISON SUMAC

(Rhus Vernix)

Location: Maine to Florida, west to Minnesota, Missouri and Louisiana.

Found: Only in wet, acidy soil swamps

Description: Poison Sumac tree or shrub grows to height of 25 ft. Trunk diameter to 6 ft, coarse and gray bark. Leaves alternate. Fruit gray, globular, smooth, 1/6" in diameter. *Stays on plant all winter.*

Caution: Whole plant very poisonous. Leaves have a brilliant color therefore attracting amateur collectors. As the plant is tall, it usually affects the face and head (poison ivy usually the feet and legs).

POISONOUS MUSHROOMS

Angel of Death

Fly Agaric

Fly Agaric

Angel of Death

Panther Cap

See Poisonous Mushroom Chapter

INSECT STINGS

YELLOW JACKETS, BEES, HORNETS, WASPS

(Hymenoptera)

• These insects inject venom under the skin.

• The sting produces a few minutes of fierce burning, followed by redness and itching at the point of the sting. A welt may form and subside in 3 or 4 hours. Should be normal within 24 hours.

Honey bee: Stings only once as the barbed stinger *will stay embedded* in the skin. Remove the stinger as soon as possible as the venom sac will continue to pump for two to three minutes driving the venom deeper into the skin. The best way to remove the stinger is to scrape it out with a fingernail as this will avoid squeezing the venom sac.

Bumble bees, wasps, hornets and yellow jackets: have smooth stingers and so *can sting numerous times*. If a yellow jacket is squashed and the venom sac is broken, the chemical scent given off will attract other yellow jackets so don't stick around!

Treatment

A victim stung in the mouth or throat should be given ice to suck and immediately sent to a hospital, as rapid swelling may occur; this may obstruct breathing.

• Wash the sting area with water and soap.

• If stinger and venom sac remains in the wound scrape them out with your fingernail or knife blade. Wash the sting area again.

To Reduce the Pain and Itching

• Sprinkle some meat tenderizer on some gauze and apply to the sting for 30 minutes. Instead of tenderizer you can use ice, cold compresses, calamine or other soothing lotions.

• Apply an alkaline lotion such as a strong solution of sodium bicarbonate (baking soda). 1 tablespoonful to 1 pint of water.

• Itching may also be relieved by applying a mixture of baking soda and ammonia (a few drops of household cleaning ammonia).

• Wash the sting area with soap and water.

• Wash with an antiseptic (to relieve pain).

• Apply ice pack or ice cubes.

• Rub an Aspirin tablet on wet sting area (do not use if allergic to aspirin).

• Dab household ammonia on spot.

• Apply mud to sting area and cover with bandage. Keep in place until dry.

Symptoms of an Allergic Reaction

If there is an allergic reaction to a sting see a doctor immediately.

Some symptoms are:

• Labored breathing, difficulties in swallowing, constricted chest, abdominal pain, nausea, state of confusion, vomiting, weakness, blurriness, rapid fall of blood pressure, collapse, incontinence, unconsciousness.

To Avoid Hymenoptera Stings

• Destroy all nests around houses or do not camp in their proximity. Watch for old stumps and holes in the ground.

• Avoid scented soaps, lotions, shampoo, perfumes, avoid floral prints and bright colors. Basically do not look or smell like a flower.

• When camping keep food covered until served and pack leftovers. Keep the garbage disposal area far from the camp. Avoid eating melons as they attract *Hymenoptera*.

• Do not act aggressively with insects. Be calm or slowly back away. Do not try to swat it.

• Consume vitamin B (thiamin), on days of potential insect activity. The smell of the vitamin secreted through the skin might keep them away.

• Wear light colored clothing - white, grey, or khaki.

Hornet

See Insect Chapter for article on Killer Bees

Honey Bee

Bumble Bee

Wasp

Black Fly

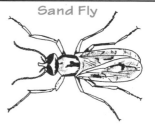

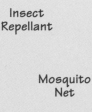

Insect
Repellant

Mosquito
Net

REDUCE EXPOSURE TO BITING INSECTS

- Stay away from breeding areas. Usually slow flowing or stagnant bodies of water.
- Avoid areas with high grass or dense vegetation.

Insure that you

- Have a good bed net.
- Your immunizations are current.
- Laundry and bathing facilities are available.
- Shirt is buttoned.
- Sleeves are rolled down.
- Pants tucked inside boots.
- Bathe or shower regularly.
- Have clean clothing.
- Use insect repellant.
- Take malaria pills if prescribed.

Preventing Skin Infections

Bathe frequently. If showers or baths are not available, wash the following with a wash cloth every daily.

- Your genital area.
- Your armpits.
- Your feet and between toes.
- Other areas where you sweat or that become wet such as: between thighs or (for females) under the breasts.

Sting-Eze
Helps Reduce
the Pain of an
Insect Sting

Keep the Skin Dry

- Use foot powder on your feet, especially if you have had previous fungal infections on the feet.
- Use talcum powder in areas where wetness is a problem, such as: between the thighs or (for females) under the breasts.

Wear Proper Clothing

- Wear loose fitting clothing as this allows for better ventilation. Tight fitting clothing reduces blood circulation and ventilation.
- Do not wear nylon or silk undergarments; cotton undergarments are more absorbent and allow the skin to dry.

For Females

- Wash your genital area each day.
- Do not use perfumed soaps or feminine deodorants in the field as they cause irritation and attract insects.
- Do not douche unless directed by a doctor.
- Drink extra fluids, even when it is not hot.

Some individuals do not drink enough fluid and tend to hold their urine due to the lack of privacy. Urinary tract infections are one of the most frequent medical problems females face in the field. Drinking extra fluids will help prevent these infections.

Insect articles partially based on EFMB Study Guide, Department of Military Medicine, US Army

---

 Mosquito   Sand Fly

INSECT-BORNE DISEASES

The term insects in this book refers to mosquitoes, flies, fleas, lice ticks, mites, chiggers spiders, and scorpions which are properly called arthropod.

Insects affect the health of human beings:

- By transmitting disease.
- By injecting venom.
- By invading living tissue.
- By annoyance.

Tsetse Fly

The principal insect-borne diseases include some of the most common and most serious epidemics of mankind such as malaria, plague, yellow fever, and the typhus fevers. They are most common in the tropics but may occur in most parts of the world.

PRINCIPAL INSECT-BORNE DISEASES

Conenose Bug

Black Fly

Human Flea

Disease	Insect
Dengue fever	Mosquito
Encephalitis (sleeping sickness)	Mosquito
Filariasis (elephantiasis)	Mosquito
Malaria	Mosquito
Yellow fever	Mosquito
Typhus fever (epidemic)	Body louse
Rocky Mountain spotted fever	Tick
Bubonic plague	Flea
Typhus fever (Murine)	Flea
Scrub typhus	Larval mite (chigger)
Leishmanissis	Sand fly (*Phlebotomus*)
Sand fly fever or Phlebotomus fever	Sand fly (*Phlebotomus*)
Onchocerciassis	Black fly (buffalo gnat)
Chagas' disease	Conenosed bug (kissing bug)

Methods of Transmission

Disease agents are transmitted by insects in two general ways;

- **Mechanical Transmission:** Is when the disease organisms are picked up on the body or the legs of the insect and are then deposited on food, drink or open sores. An example of this method is the transfer of typhoid or dysentery organisms from fecal matter.
- **Biological Transmission:** Is when the insect becomes infected with an organism by biting a diseased human or animal. The organism develops in the body of the insect which later is transmitted to a susceptible individual by a bite. This occurs in the case of malaria or less commonly by contamination of chafed skin with the body juices or feces of the carrier, as in the case of louse-borne typhus. Certain species of bees, wasps, scorpions and spiders inject poisons which can produce symptoms of varying severity.

Insect Annoyance

When gnats, mosquitoes, flies and other pests become sufficiently numerous they can affect the health *and morale* of a person.

Control Measures

Control measures are directed primarily toward the source of infection (human beings and animals) and toward the transmitting insect. The sources of infection are controlled through personal hygiene, surveillance, isolation, quarantine, and treatment. The transmitting insects are controlled through the practice of sanitation. Individual protective measures and chemical measures.

MOSQUITOES

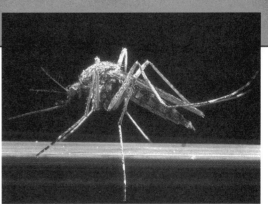

Aedes Mosquito

MOSQUITO-BORNE DISEASES AND THEIR CONTROL

Mosquitoes are found all over the world. In the tropics and subtropics they breed throughout the year. In the sub-Arctic regions they appear in tremendous numbers during the brief summer season. Most of the disease-carrying mosquitoes are found in milder climates and in the tropics. Different types of mosquitoes transmit different diseases. The three most common types of mosquitoes which transmit disease are *Anopheles*, *Aedes*, and *Culex*. Each of these types consist of many species.

Mosquito-Borne Diseases

There are many diseases transmitted by mosquitoes. Some of the more important ones are malaria, yellow fever, dengue fever, encephalitis, and filariasis. Of these diseases, *malaria is the greatest threat in normal travel*. It is important to know that antimosquito measures is the major weapon against this group of diseases. Drugs are available for the suppression and cure of malaria and a vaccine for the prevention of yellow fever. Overuse of drugs have made some insect-borne diseases immune to their use.

Malaria

Malaria is rare in the United States but it is common in most tropical, subtropical, and semitropical areas of the world. Malaria is caused by a microscopic parasite carried by the *Anopheles* mosquito. This parasite destroys the blood cells and causes chills, fever, weakness, and anemia. *Unless the disease is treated promptly and properly, it may cause death from damage to the brain.* The only sure way of preventing malaria is to avoid the bites of infected mosquitoes.

Top View Malaria Mosquito
(Anopheles)

MOSQUITO TYPES

Anopheles

Anopheles mosquitoes primarily bite during the period from dusk to dawn. They may bite during the daylight hours in an area which is heavily shaded or in a dark room. Normally, most species will breed in any collection of water and some species breed only in tree holes. The larvae lie parallel to the surface of the water. The adults usually rest and feed with the body at an angle of 45° to the surface.

Aedes

Aedes mosquitoes bite in daylight. They breed in fresh, stagnant, or brackish water. *Aedes aegypti,* one of the most important disease transmitters, breed almost entirely in old tires, cans, and other similar manufactured containers. The adults rest and feed with their body parallel to the surface.

Culez

Culez mosquitoes. Depending upon the species may bite at any time of day or night. They are commonly found in fresh or stagnant water in and about buildings as well as swamps, ditches, street gutters, and other water containing areas. The common house mosquitoes found in the United States are members of this group. The adults rest and feed parallel to the surface as the *Aedes*.

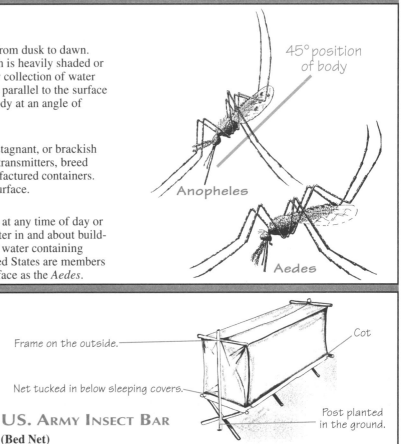

45° position of body

Anopheles

Aedes

Mosquitoes

- Wet clothing is preferred over dry.
- Clothing with perspiration is more attractive than wet clothing.
- Mosquitoes appear to prefer the color blue.

Protection Against Biting Insects

If you do not have any insect repellent.
  You might want to try:
- Smoking up the camp - insects do not like smoke.
- Mud plaster: Plaster mud on exposed surfaces of skin during travel. This will hurt, when the mud dries, if the mud is applied too thick.
- Birch bark: Place thin sheets of bark below thin socks and below T-shirts etc.
- Install your tent in a windy area so that pests get blown away.

Frame on the outside.

Net tucked in below sleeping covers.

Cot

Post planted in the ground.

US. ARMY INSECT BAR
(Bed Net)

An insect bar should be used in all malaria areas. You must take care not to come in contact with the net as insects can bite through it.

There are places in the tropics where 20% of the US troops have become ill with malaria as the result of being exposed to mosquitoes for one night without the protection of an insect bar.

LYME DISEASE

Lime disease is a newly identified disease that is transmitted by deer ticks that are about the size of this period. These ticks are found on deer, birds, rodents, mice and other small animals.

Location: Northeastern coastal area, upper Midwest and Pacific coast.

Season: Usually late spring and early summer.

Avoiding Ticks

• Wear long-sleeved shirts fastened at wrist.

• Wear long pants tucked into socks, with laced shoes.

• Wear light-colored fabric to see ticks.

• Walk on cleared trails and not through grass.

• Use insect repellent with DEET and/or permethrin. Follow instructions in the use of these and other repellents. *See Hiking with Kids Article page 13.*

• Avoid contact with wild animals and birds (including bird's nests) in tick endemic areas.

If bitten by a tick

First, kill tick by covering it with nail polish, vegetable oil or petroleum jelly. The oil prevents the tick from breathing and it will release its hold immediately. If it does not come off leave the oil on for half an hour and use a pair of tweezers to remove it by pinching as close to the skin as possible, pulling gently. *Make sure that all parts have been removed.* Wash the area with water and soap. Keep the tick to show to a doctor.

Symptoms of Lyme Disease

• Rash at location of bite. The rash has a red circle with a light center forming around bite.

• Flu-like symptoms.

• Possible local paralysis, skin sensations, hearing loss, insomnia.

• Painful joints and other arthritic complications.

See a doctor as soon as possible.

CHIGGERS

Chiggers are found in low damp places covered with vegetation such as woods, tall grass, and weeds. The larva of chiggers attach themselves to the body by sticking their mouths into the follicle (hole through which hair grow) of hair. They inject enzymes and feed upon human cells. After several hours you will feel intense itching and small red welts will appear. To remove the chiggers lather several times with soap. Place a cold pack on affected area to relieve stinging feeling.

ALLERGY TO BEE, WASP, & ANT STINGS

Five per cent of people are allergic to the venom of the bee, wasp or ant. A person who is allergic to bee stings should carry a "bee sting kit" which can be used after being stung. A bee can sting only once but wasps, hornets, ants can sting or bite repeatedly. Common Ant

CENTIPEDE BITES

Are very painful, but seldom dangerous. The poisonous Giant Desert Centipede is 6 inches long with jaws that can inflict a painful bite. The poison enters the broken skin from poison glands at the base of the centipede's jaws. The centipede has 42 legs and there are claws at the end of these legs that are used for climbing, These claws might cut small openings in the skin which might get infected.

Centipede

First Aid

Treated in the same way as snake bites. The tourniquet should be completely removed after 20 minutes.

Bumble Bee

FLEA

These small wingless insects can be extremely dangerous. In some areas they can transmit the plague to man after feeding on plague-ridden rodents.

Human Flea

Honey Bee

SPIDERS

The female Black Widow has a red or yellow hourglass marking on the underside of the abdomen.

Black Widow Male

Black Widow Female

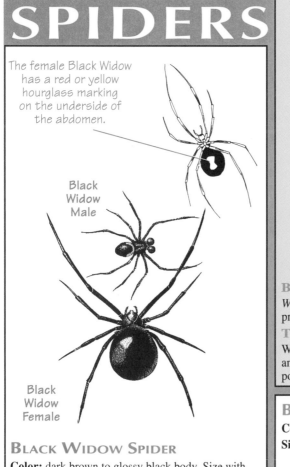

BLACK WIDOW SPIDER

Color: dark brown to glossy black body, Size with legs extended: 1" wide 1 1/2" long (2.54 x 3.81 cm).

Female is poisonous: Has a red or yellow hourglass marking on the underside of the abdomen. The male does not have this marking.

Habitat: Outdoors in sheds, outhouses, under stones, logs, in hollow stumps, and sometimes indoors in dark corners of garages, rock walls, barns or wood piles.

Reaction to Bite

• Local redness occurs, with two tiny red spots.
• There is an immediate sharp pain which may go away.
• The venom's effect will occur in about 30 minutes.
• Heavy perspiration, dizziness, nausea, and vomiting.
• Abdominal muscles will become rigid. The victim can writhe in agony.
• Great pain in limbs and there will be difficulty in talking and breathing.
• Death might be caused, in 5% of cases, from breathing paralysis.

Action

• *See a doctor immediately, serum will be needed.*

While Traveling to See a Doctor

• Keep the victim calm and apply an antiseptic to sting area.
• Place an ice pack around the bite area to slow the spread of the venom.

Color: Dark, Size: 6-7" (15-18 cm) toe to toe.

Habitat: Found in the southwest of the United States and the Tropics. The tropical variety is poisonous.

Bite

Will not bite unless teased. Bite produces a small pin prick sensation.

Treatment

Wash with warm water and soap and apply an antiseptic to prevent a possible secondary infection.

TARANTULA

BROWN RECLUSE SPIDER

Color: Light yellow to dark brown body

Size: Oval shape, 1/8 to 1/4 inch (0.3-0.6 cm) long 1/4" wide (0.6 cm), eight legs and a distinctive fiddle shaped mark on its back

Habitat: Southern and Midwestern United States. Lives in dark places: Trash piles, attics, closets, dresser drawers.

Reaction to Bite

• Sting is almost painless.
• In 2 to 8 hours pain will occur followed by blisters, swelling or ulceration.
• In some cases rash, nausea, jaundice, chills, fever, cramps or joint pain.

Action

If quick medical action is not taken weak adults or children have been known to die.

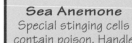

Sea Anemone

Special stinging cells contain poison. Handle with gloves. If stung wash wound with alcohol or ammonia. Recovery might take from minutes to hours.

SCORPIONS

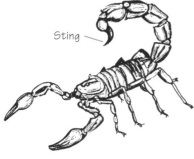

Sting

Scorpions live in all of temperate North America. The only poisonous scorpions (Centraviodes) live in the Southwest.

Size: 2 1/4 to 4" (6-10 cm) long.

Color of poisonous type: Solid straw yellow or yellow with irregular black stripes on their backs.

Habitat: By day they stay out of the heat in humid areas, under stones, bark, boards, outhouse floors, or burrow in the sand. At night they roam around and can enter under doors into houses. To avoid scorpions do not put your hands in areas you cannot see, watch where you sit and shake your clothing and boots before you put them on. Be careful at night when scorpions are out and about. It is not easy to identify a scorpion bite as the victim usually does not see what has stung him. *They sting by thrusting their tail over their head.*

Non-Poisonous Sting

- A nonpoisonous sting: Usually causes swelling and discoloration and is painful.

Poisonous Sting

- Poisonous stings do not change the appearance of the area around the sting.
- The area only becomes very sensitive.
- The poison will usually cause the victim to have facial contortions and an increased flow of saliva.
- A fever of 104° F (40°C) will develop, the tongue will become sluggish and there will be increasing intense convulsions, which may be fatal.

Action

Keep victim quiet, call a doctor *immediately* and apply a tourniquet between the sting area and the heart. Do not give a painkiller as this will increase the toxicity of the venom.

JELLYFISH STINGS

To Remove Attached Tentacles

Do not use bare hands. Wrap hands in a towel or plastic sheet and whip away attached tentacles. Apply sand and seawater and scrape off with a knife or piece of wood.

Treatment

- Apply baking soda as a paste on jellyfish stings.
- Apply vinegar for man-of-war stings.
- Relieve itchy area with antihistamines.
- Take a pain reliever if pain persists.
- Make sure that your tetanus shot is up to date.

JELLYFISH & PORTUGUESE MAN-OF-WAR

Jellyfish toxins are injected by the tentacles. These toxins are used to catch fish and other food. Upon brushing your skin their stinging cells pierce your skin and release the poison. Avoid touching a jellyfish but if you come in contact with the tentacles:

- Do not move the affected area as the muscle action will increase the amount of toxin that enters the bloodstream.
- Rinse with salt water (not fresh water) immediately, neutralize the poison with alcohol, vinegar, ammonia or meat tenderizer.
- The toxin reacts very rapidly and immediate attention should be given. The victim's physical condition and age might be a factor causing a critical reaction.
- Remove all tentacles that are attached to the skin.

GILA MONSTER

This is one of the two most venomous lizards in the world. It is the only poisonous lizard in North America. The monster will not bite you unless it is handled. It is very rare so it should not be killed or disturbed. It lives in the Southwest.

STING RAY

(Dasyatis Centrouta)

The Sting Ray is found from Maine to Cape Hateris with 30 relatives extending its range throughout the warmer salt waters of the world.

Venom from the tail spine can be fatal to man or it can cause a dangerous wound by breaking off.

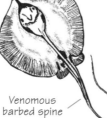

Venomous barbed spine in tail.

Manta Ray

The Devilfish of the sea with a "wingspan" of up to 15 feet (4.5 m) and weighing up to 300 pounds (136 kg).

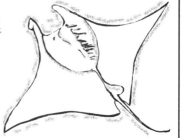

Manta Ray as seen on the surface.

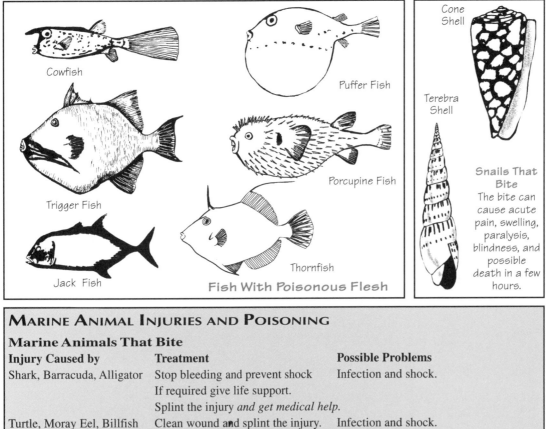

Cowfish

Puffer Fish

Trigger Fish

Porcupine Fish

Jack Fish

Thornfish

Fish With Poisonous Flesh

Cone Shell

Terebra Shell

Snails That Bite
The bite can cause acute pain, swelling, paralysis, blindness, and possible death in a few hours.

Fish Bites
Poisonous fish, and other aquatic animals exist in most tropical waters.
Their venom may be conveyed to man either by bites, stings, or scrapes.

First Aid
A strong solution of sodium bicarbonate should be applied (1 tablespoonful (15 ml) to 1 pint (625 ml) of water). Shock may occur.
Get medical help.

MARINE ANIMAL INJURIES AND POISONING

Marine Animals That Bite

Injury Caused by	Treatment	Possible Problems
Shark, Barracuda, Alligator	Stop bleeding and prevent shock If required give life support. Splint the injury *and get medical help.*	Infection and shock.
Turtle, Moray Eel, Billfish	Clean wound and splint the injury.	Infection and shock.

Marine Animals That Puncture Skin With Spines

Injury Caused by	Treatment	Possible Problems
Cone Shell**, Spiny Fish* Terebra Shell**, Stingrays, Urchins	Neutralize with hot water, do not scald victim.	Allergic reactions: collapse, infections, tetanus, granuloma formation.

*Toad Fish, Stone Fish, Oyster fish, Zebra Fish, Catfish, Weeverfish, Scorpion Fish, Stargazer, Stonecat.

**These shells have venom apparatus avoid contact with soft parts.

Marine Animals That Puncture the Skin With Stings on Tentacles

Injury Caused by	Treatment	Possible Problems
Portuguese man-of-war*, Jellyfish*, Anemones* *Handle with gloves.	Wash with ammonia or alcohol. Dry affected skin with talcum powder and remove the embedded stings.	Allergic reactions, respiratory arrest, stomach cramps, dizziness, numbness, infections.

Marine Animals That Have Poisonous Flesh

Meat Eaten	Treatment	Possible Reaction
Puffer fish, Oil Fish, Porcupine Fish, Cowfish, Thornfish, or Trigger Fish Shark Liver	Give basic life support and prevent self-injury from convulsions. *Get medical attention as soon as possible.*	Allergic reactions, asthmatic reactions, paresthesia, numbness, temperature reversal phenomena, respiratory arrest and circulatory collapse.

Miscellanies Marine Life Injuries

Marine Life	Injury	Treatment	Possible Reaction
Electric fish*	Shocks	Electric shock is temporary.	Shock may cause a panic reaction.
Marine parasites	Skin rashes	Usually clear up with time.	
Corals	Abrasions on body	Treat abrasions.	Infections are possible if not well cleaned.
*Electric Eels are the most common.			
Sea Snakes	Possibly fatal bite.	Apply a tourniquet.	Pain may occur from 20 min to hours. *Get medical attention.*

MARINE ANIMAL INJURIES
MARINE ANIMAL INJURIES
MARINE ANIMAL INJURIES

FISHERMAN'S CONJUNCTIVITIS (PINK EYE)

Fisherman's conjunctivitis is a severe inflammatory condition of the eyes. It is caused by contact with the juices of marine animal growth that look like dumplings. These growths when crushed release the juice which may accidentally enter the eye. This juice in the eye causes a very acute and painful inflammation of the conjunctiva or thin covering of the eye. Avoid rubbing your eyes when handling fish.

See a doctor for treatment.

Monk Fish

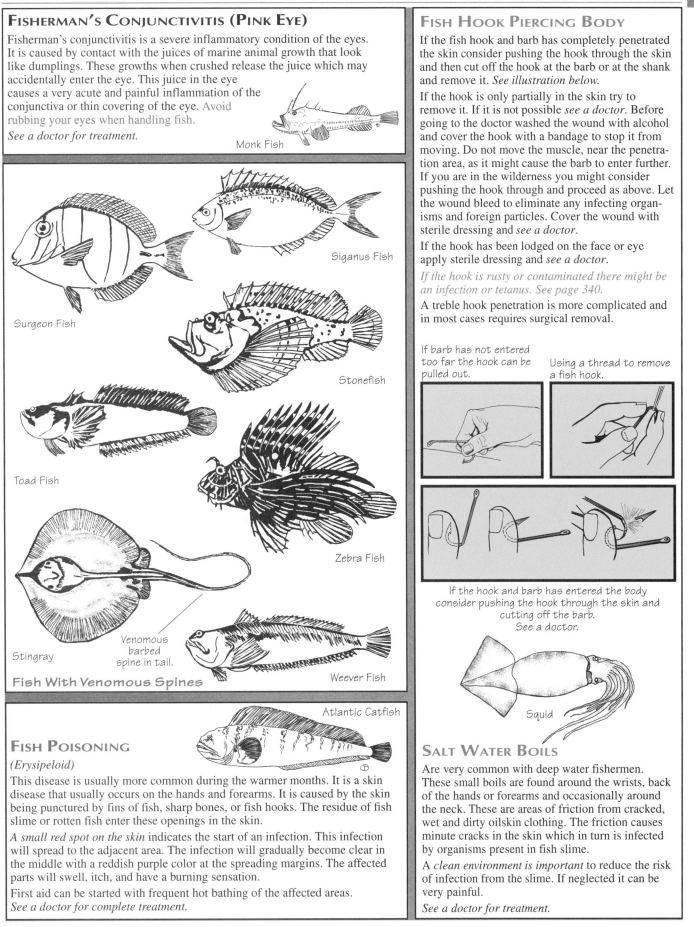

Surgeon Fish

Siganus Fish

Stonefish

Toad Fish

Zebra Fish

Stingray

Venomous barbed spine in tail.

Weever Fish

Fish With Venomous Spines

Atlantic Catfish

FISH POISONING

(Erysipeloid)

This disease is usually more common during the warmer months. It is a skin disease that usually occurs on the hands and forearms. It is caused by the skin being punctured by fins of fish, sharp bones, or fish hooks. The residue of fish slime or rotten fish enter these openings in the skin.

A small red spot on the skin indicates the start of an infection. This infection will spread to the adjacent area. The infection will gradually become clear in the middle with a reddish purple color at the spreading margins. The affected parts will swell, itch, and have a burning sensation.

First aid can be started with frequent hot bathing of the affected areas. *See a doctor for complete treatment.*

FISH HOOK PIERCING BODY

If the fish hook and barb has completely penetrated the skin consider pushing the hook through the skin and then cut off the hook at the barb or at the shank and remove it. *See illustration below.*

If the hook is only partially in the skin try to remove it. If it is not possible *see a doctor.* Before going to the doctor washed the wound with alcohol and cover the hook with a bandage to stop it from moving. Do not move the muscle, near the penetration area, as it might cause the barb to enter further. If you are in the wilderness you might consider pushing the hook through and proceed as above. Let the wound bleed to eliminate any infecting organisms and foreign particles. Cover the wound with sterile dressing and *see a doctor.*

If the hook has been lodged on the face or eye apply sterile dressing and *see a doctor.*

If the hook is rusty or contaminated there might be an infection or tetanus. See page 340.

A treble hook penetration is more complicated and in most cases requires surgical removal.

If barb has not entered too far the hook can be pulled out.

Using a thread to remove a fish hook.

If the hook and barb has entered the body consider pushing the hook through the skin and cutting off the barb. See a doctor.

Squid

SALT WATER BOILS

Are very common with deep water fishermen. These small boils are found around the wrists, back of the hands or forearms and occasionally around the neck. These are areas of friction from cracked, wet and dirty oilskin clothing. The friction causes minute cracks in the skin which in turn is infected by organisms present in fish slime.

A clean environment is important to reduce the risk of infection from the slime. If neglected it can be very painful.

See a doctor for treatment.

SNAKE BITES

There are approximately 50,000 snake bites in the United States annually. 7,000 of these are caused by poisonous snakes with approximately 15 fatalities per year.

POISONOUS SNAKES

North America has two families of poisonous snakes.

Pit Viper Family

Rattlesnakes, copperheads, cottonmouth moccasins. These snakes are identified by the *indented pit between the eye and nostril* on each side of the triangular head. The pit is a heat sensing organ that allows the snake to strike a warm target even in the dark. The *pupil of the eye is vertical and slit-like.* The fangs are normally up flat against the roof of the mouth. When striking the snake opens its mouth wide and the fangs are pulled down and penetrate the target. *The venom affects the blood circulation system.*

Cobra Family

Coral Snake: Is part of the cobra family and *its toxic venom affects the nervous system.* This snake has red, yellow, and black rings around the body with a black nose.

Coral Snake

CORAL SNAKE

Remember the ditty:

"Red on yellow will kill a fellow
Red on black, venom will lack"

* This snake is very colorful with bright red, yellow and black bands completely encircling the body.
* *Note that the red band is next to the yellow.* This is important as there are many similar colored snakes but the coral snake is the only one with the red adjacent to the yellow band.
* It is very rare and lives in Florida and the desert of the Southwest. It will only bite when mishandled.
* The coral snake has tiny fangs at the rear of its mouth and injects its venom with its teeth. *A chewing motion is used to inject the venom.* Because of its small mouth, teeth and limited jaw expansion it usually bites on a small extremity such as the foot, hand, or a finger. After the bite you will see tiny punctures or scratch marks.
* The initial symptoms are a slight burning pain and mild local swelling at the wound. After a few minutes additional symptoms will occur: blurring of vision, drooping eyelids, slurred speech, drowsiness, sweating, increased salivation, difficulty in breathing and nausea.

Coral Snake Bite

Take victim to the hospital immediately. Call ahead so that the anti-venom will be available. The first aid treatment for a coral snake's poison is different than that for a rattlesnake.

Action

A coral snake's venom is toxic to the brain and central nervous system
* Calm the victim.
* Flush the area with one or two quarts of water to remove any poison that might be remaining on the surface.
* Apply a tourniquet between the bite and the heart.
* Minimize the movement of the bitten extremity.

SNAKE BITES

The majority of snakes in North America are not poisonous. The main poisonous ones belong to the viper and cobra families.

Sea snakes of the Indian and Pacific Oceans are almost all poisonous.

Harmless snakes have no poisonous fangs and inflict a bite with two roughly parallel rows of small tooth marks.

Front of Head

Harmless
Snake Bite

Poisonous snakes, have two large fangs, and sometimes smaller ones behind. They inflict a bite which have two main punctures (from the fangs) and some small marks.

Fang Marks

Front
of Head

Poisonous
Snake Bite

*A **poisonous snake bite** is painful and a swelling develops around the bite. There can be symptoms of shock, faintness, vomiting and a difficulty in breathing.*

Tourniquet for a Snakebite

Apply a half inch or wider constricting bandage (or handkerchief, bandana, belt, etc.) two to three inches above the bite towards the heart.

The bandage should not be too tight. You should be able to easily insert your finger between the bandage and the skin surface.
Do not cut off the blood circulation (do not apply bandage if bite is on face).

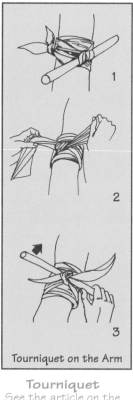

1

2

3

Tourniquet on the Arm

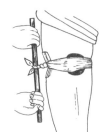

Tourniquet
on the Leg

Tourniquet

See the article on the application of a tourniquet.

Black Slit on Eye — Pit

Fangs that drop down when mouth is opened.

Rattlesnake Striking

Diamondback Rattlesnake

Diamondback Rattlesnake

See Reptile Chapter for more information.

Rattle

SNAKE BITE KIT

Ideal for pocket or pack complete and easy to use

+ CAMPERS + HIKERS + HUNTERS + HOME

RATTLESNAKE ANTI-VENOM KITS

Before using the kit carefully read the instructions and test the victim's skin for any potential allergies. Before going into a possible rattlesnake area read the instructions and make sure that you have all the required emergency material on hand because when, and if, a snake bites there will be a slight panic. Rattlesnake bites are quite rare.

RATTLESNAKES

All rattlesnakes are poisonous. Rattlesnakes inject their venom from their fangs and their poison is a blood-destroying poison (different from the coral snake). Their dens are usually on the south side of rocky areas. The rocks act as a heat collector which keep the cold-blooded snakes warm especially at night. Be careful in shady areas during a hot day as rattlesnakes avoid the heat by hiding behind rocks, below bushes, behind debris, in your clothing or behind your backpack. They travel at night when it is cooler.

To protect against rattlesnakes

- Never put your feet or hands in areas that you cannot see.
- Wear heavy high boots, long loose pants.
- Walk in open areas.
- At night use a flash light.

If You Hear the Rattle

(a rattlesnake *does not* always rattle before striking)

- If you hear a rattle - *freeze.*
- Try to locate the snake by *slowly* moving your head.
- Slowly retreat. When you see the snake, make sure there is *only* one snake. Make no sudden movements.

Sidewinder or "Horned" Rattlesnake

Rattlesnake Strike Range

The striking distance of a rattlesnake *is from half the snake's body length to the length of the snake's body.* The Western Diamondback can strike at its full length from an uncoiled position and can actually leave the ground while striking.

Symptom of Rattlesnake Bite

- Look for the actual fang bite (these are two fangs, one on each side of the mouth).
- Swelling will occur within a few minutes to an hour.
- Bite location will discolor and become painful.
- The victim might go into a state of shock.
- Further symptoms: numbness, breathing problems, nausea, and temporary blindness.

Kill the snake and take the reptile to a hospital for identification as the venom treatment may vary between different snakes.

If Bitten by a Rattlesnake

Take victim to the hospital immediately. Call ahead so that the anti-venom will be available. The first aid treatment for a rattlesnake's poison is different than that for a coral snake .

- Lay the victim in a comfortable position *making sure that the bite location is below the level of the heart.*
- Apply a half inch or wider constricting bandage (or handkerchief, bandanna, belt, etc.) two to three inches above the bite towards the heart. The bandage should not be too tight. You should be able to easily insert your finger between the bandage and the skin surface. Do not cut off the blood circulation (do not apply a constricting bandage if bite is on the face).
- If the swelling spreads, move the bandage 2-3" (5-8 cm) above the swelling towards the heart.
- If professional medical assistance is available within three to four hours drive take the victim to the hospital. *See a doctor.*

If it is Not Possible

1. Sterilize the wound with an antiseptic or soap and water.
2. With a sterilized knife or scalpel make a straight incision between both fang marks and 1/4" (0.6 cm) past each mark. Cut into the skin and fat only (not into muscles, tendons, blood vessels, or nerves). This incision should not be deeper than 1/4" (0.6 cm).
3. Squeeze the blood, liquid, and venom gently from the incision with your fingers for 20 to 30 minutes or *until the victim reaches the hospital.*

Do not use oral suction as your mouth contains bacteria and this could infect the bite incision.

Animal Bites
Immediately wash with water to remove animal saliva then spend 5 to 10 minutes cleansing the wound with water and soap.

ANIMAL BITES

RABIES

(Hydrophobia)

Human symptoms of rabies can appear from 10 days to up to two years after the bite.

Rabies, or hydrophobia, is caused by an organism which enters the blood as the result of a bite by an animal suffering from the disease. Once rabies has developed it is invariably fatal.

A doctor has to be seen and an antirabies treatment has to be followed as soon as possible.

To Identify Animals with Rabies

Types of Rabies

Furious rabies: An animal is vicious and agitated, it then gets paralyzed and dies.

Dumb rabies: Animal looks paralytic.

The most common symptom is when an animal is not following its normal behavior. Some indicators might be: animals losing their fear of humans, animals not following their normal living patterns e.g. bats flying during the daytime.

If you have any indication or fear of infection see a doctor.

Watch for other infections as tetanus, swelling, etc. that might occur after an animal bite.

DOG BITES

- Encourage bleeding for a short time by bathing the bitten area in hot water to with some antiseptic. Apply a clean dressing.
- The dog may be suffering from rabies (*hydrophobia*), and special treatment is necessary. Rabies should be suspected if the dog was acting abnormally, Abnormal activities as irrationally snapping at objects and persons, barking wildly, has its tongue hanging out with quantities of frothy saliva. The dog is often partly paralyzed.

First Aid

- Apply a tourniquet just above the wound, tighten it to make the wound bleed freely which helps to wash out the poison or;
- Hold the wound under a tap of hot running water or bathe it freely for about five minutes. This will stop the blood from coagulating.
- Remove the tourniquet and apply a clean dressing.

The patient should get medical attention as soon as possible for antirabies treatment. Try to keep access to the dog for further testing if required.

DANGERS OF RABBIT FEVER

The *Tularemia* germ can be fatal if it gets into an open scratch or wound. Wear gloves when cleaning a wild rabbit or work a heavy soap lather into your skin *before* opening the body. The soap film will protect your skin. Thoroughly wash your hands when finished. Do not hunt slow sluggish rabbits. Wait 2 or 3 weeks *after a heavy frost* before hunting for rabbit. *Cook all rabbits until well done.* The rabbit fever germ can be destroyed by intensive heat. Be careful when trapping as you will not know the health of the rabbit.

BODY TEMPERATURE

TAKING BODY TEMPERATURE

- The body temperature is taken with a clinical thermometer which is made of a little glass tube with a fine bore containing mercury.
- A body thermometer is usually graduated from 95°F (35°C) to 110°F (43.3°C). Each degree is subdivided into fifths by small lines, and each fifth is equal to 0.2°F.
- The average normal temperature of the body is 98.4° F (36.9°C) indicated by an arrow.
- Shake down the thermometer, below 96°F (35.6°C), each time before using.

Take Body Temperature

- Before taking the temperature shake down the thermometer, below 96°F (35.6°C), each time before using.
- Take the temperature under the tongue with the lips closed, but not between the teeth. It should remain there for at least three minutes.
  Do not take the temperature by the mouth for 20 minutes after drinking a hot beverage.
- Take a reading in the armpit if the patient is restless or unconscious. Keep the thermometer in the *dry* armpit for five minutes. Keep the arm across the patient's chest while taking the temperature.

Body Temperature and Fever

Temperature above 99.4°F (37.4°C) is suspect.

•

Between 100°F (37.8°C) to 102°F (38.9°C), a moderate fever.

•

Above 102°F (38.9°C), a high fever.

Feverish illness temperature does not rise much above 104°F (40°C).

•

Early morning temperature of an adult may be between 96°F (35.6°C) and 98.4°F (36.9°C).

Convert Between F° and C°

Convert F° to C°:
Subtract 32, multiply by 5, and divide by 9

Convert C° to F°:
Multiply by 9, divide by 5, and add 32

	F°	C°
Fatal	110°	43.3°
(usually)	109°	42.8°
	108°	42.2°
Dangerous	107°	41.7°
Fever	106°	41.1°
High	105°	40.6°
Fever	104°	40.0°
	103°	39.4°
Moderate	102°	38.9°
Fever	101°	38.3°
	100°	37.8°
Healthy	99°	37.2°
	98°	36.7°
	97°	36.1°
	96°	35.6°
Weakness	95°	35.0°

FROSTBITE

FROSTBITE

Frostbite is a condition in which the skin, and sometimes deeper tissues, actually become frozen. Common areas of frostbite are the nose, cheeks, ears, fingers, and toes. Frostbite is similar to a skin burn.

Signs of Frostbite

The area initially might have a painful pin-prick sensation and then become cold, hard, and numb. The freezing can occur quite suddenly especially if it is windy and the skin exposed.

Splotches of opaque pale and yellowish-white areas appear on the exposed skin. These areas gradually get hard and freeze. If they are not covered and warmed they will spread. Check the extremities as the ears, tips of fingers, nose, toes and cheeks. The defensive measure of the body getting cold is to withdraw blood from its extremities, to keep the vital organs warm, which will let the extremities freeze. *Touch the exposed areas and if there is no feeling immediately enter a warm area or if not possible cover the frozen skin so that it can gradually thaw out.* If traveling alone, check your face in a mirror and watch for white yellow splotches on your skin. Frozen skin remains unchanged until it thaws when it becomes inflamed. The damage depends upon the degree of freezing. Do not touch the frozen area and let it thaw out from the heat within your body. The highest risk of frostbite is when you do not realize the windchill factor is very high so that *the actual temperature is much lower due to the wind.*

How to Avoid Frostbite

Know the temperature, the windchill factor, and wear the correct clothing before going out. Leave no skin exposed. Wear mitts and not gloves, balaclava with a face cover, boots that are well insulated and not too tight. Watch for any discoloration of the skin on yourself and your fellow travelers.

First Aid

See a doctor.

Enter a warm area and take a warm (not hot) bath. If a bath is not possible wrap the victim in a warm blanket and place his hands in his armpits.

- All tight clothing, including boots and socks, should be removed. Clothing frozen onto the body should be thawed by immersion in warm water. *Avoid damaging the frozen skin.*
- Frostbitten parts should be warmed by immersion in warm water (temperature 100°F, 37.8°C). If warm water is not readily available exposure the body to warm air. Do not, expose skin directly to an open fire. *Do not massage frozen area, rub the skin, or apply snow to the skin.*
- Give hot drinks or soup. Do not give any alcohol.
- Do not prick or break blisters. Do not aggressively move the injured extremities or limbs.

TRENCH FOOT

Feet, legs, arms or hands immersed for hours in cold water, wet boots or mud, at temperatures below 50°F (10°C), the nerves, blood vessels, and skin will gradually be damaged. Trench foot injuries can occur at any point on the windchill chart and *is much more likely to occur than frostbite* especially during extended travel in a wet environment. The longer the stay, the colder the temperature, the greater the damage to the tissue. North of latitude 50° the Atlantic and Pacific waters are cold enough to cause injuries in winter and summer months.

Trench Foot is called "Trench Foot" because this condition was a common occurrence during the First World War. Combatants, on both sides of the conflict, lived and fought in wet trenches for months on end.

Cause

Wet/damp feet (socks and boots) for several hours or days with the temperature being below 50°F (10°C).

Signs of Trench Foot

Long immersion in water can be painful. The long term problem is that the body adapts to the pain. The condition getting worse without being noticed or treated. In half an hour the exposed part becomes red and numb and it is difficult to move the toes or fingers. Within three hours the limb is slightly swollen. The swelling will increase especially if the limb is hanging down. If the immersion ends and the limbs can be warmed and dried this initial damage will quickly disappear. If the exposure to humidity and cold lasts several days swelling of ankles, wrists, and feet will occur. There will also be blisters or dark patches and the skin will crack.

First Aid

Remove clothing and keep the victim warm and dry. *Get medical help.*

WINDCHILL

WINDCHILL FACTORS AT DIFFERENT TEMPERATURES AND WIND SPEEDS

Wind speeds greater than 64 KPH or 40 MPH have little additional effect.

Temperature in Still Air °C / °F

Wind Speed KPH/MPH	0°C/32°F	-5°C/25°F	-10°C/15°F	-15°C/5°F	-20°C/-5°F	-25°C/-15°F	-30°C/-20°F	-35°C/-30°F	-40°C/-40°F	-45°C/-50°F	-50°C/-60°F
8 / 5	-2C/25F	-7C/20F	-12C/10F	-17C/0F	-23C/-25F	-28C/-20F	-33C/-25F	-38C/-35F	-44C/-45F	-49C/-55F	-54C/-70F
16 / 10	-8C/15F	-14C/10F	-20C/0F	-26C/-15F	-32C/-30F	-38C/-40F	-44C/-45F	-51C/-60F	-57C/-70F	-63C/-80F	-69C/-95F
24 / 15	-11C/10F	-18C/0F	-25C/-10F	-32C/-25F	-38C/-40F	-45C/-50F	-52C/-60F	-58C/-70F	-65C/-85F	-72C/-100F	-78C/-110F
32 / 20	-14C/5F	-21C/0F	-28C/-15F	-36C/-30F	-42C/-45F	-49C/-60F	-57C/-65F	-64C/-80F	-71C/-95F	-78C/-110F	-85C/-120F
40 / 25	-16C/0F	-23C/-5F	-31C/-15F	-38C/-35F	-46C/-50F	-53C/-65F	-61C/-71F	-68C/-90F	-76C/-105F	-83C/-120F	-90C/-135F
48 / 30	-17C/0F	-25C/-10F	-33C/-20F	-41C/-40F	-48C/-55F	-56C/-70F	-63C/-80F	-72C/-95F	-78C/-110F	-86C/-125F	-94C/-140F
56 / 35	-18C/-5F	-26C/-10F	-34C/-25F	-42C/-40F	-49C/-60F	-57C/-75F	-65C/-80F	-73C/-100F	-81C/-115F	-88C/-130F	-97C/-145F
64 / 40	-19C/-5F	-27C/-15F	-35C/-30F	-43C/-45F	-51C/-60F	-59C/-75F	-66C/-85F	-74C/-100F	-82C/-115F	-91C/-130F	-98C/-148F
72 / 45	-19C/-5F	-28C/-17F	-36C/-30F	-43C/-45F	-52C/-60F	-59C/-75F	-67C/-85F	-75C/-100F	-83C/-115F	-91C/-130F	-99C/-150F
80 / 50	-20C/-7F	-28C/-17F	-36C/-30F	-44C/-45F	-52C/-60F	-60C/-75F	-69C/-85F	-76C/-100F	-84C/-115F	-92C/-130F	-100C/-150F

LITTLE DANGER IF PROPERLY DRESSED

CONSIDERABLE DANGER FLESH MAY FREEZE WITHIN ONE MINUTE

VERY GREAT DANGER FLESH MAY FREEZE WITHIN 30 SECONDS

Windchill Index
The windchill index gives the equivalent temperature of the cooling power of wind on exposed flesh.
Any dry clothing (mittens, scarves, masks or material) which reduces wind exposure will help protect the covered area.

WINDCHILL

Windchill is the effective temperature of the surroundings upon your bare skin. The temperature decreases with an increase of the wind speed as the wind accelerates the dissipation of warmth from your skin.

Windchill Factor

- To obtain the windchill factor take the actual temperature of your surroundings (in °C or °F).
- Estimate the speed of the wind by looking at the characteristics outlined on the Beaufort Wind Scale. *See Weather Chapter.*

TO READ THE WINDCHILL CHART

Look at the column headed with your actual "Temperature in Still Air (°C /°F)" and look at the horizontal line with your "Wind Speed KPH/MPH".

The intersection of the column and line will indicate your *"windchill factor"*. For example, with a wind speed of 24 kph/15 mph and the *"temperature in still air"* of -10°C/15°F, the windchill factor temperature is -25°C/-10°F.

WINDCHILL AND WINTER TRAVEL

30°F (-1°C) and below

Alert group to the potential for cold injuries.

25°F (-4°C) and below

Check that group has sufficiently warm winter clothing. Provide warm-up tents or areas and hot beverages.

0°F (-18°C) and below

Inspect the group for cold injuries. Discourage smoking.

-13°F (-25°C) and below

Initiate the buddy system by having members of the group check each other for cold injuries.

-25°F (-33°C) and below

Plan to curtail all but essential travel or outdoor activity especially in wind exposed areas.

HYPOTHERMIA

CAUSES OF HYPOTHERMIA

A person weakened by lack of food, has a low energy level, is not well dressed, or does not have a strong will to live is a prospect for hypothermia. The major conditions are:

- Cold (even temperatures between 32°F-50°F (0°C-10°C)).
- Wind.
- Being wet or in very high humidity.

Optimum Body Temperature

Human body temperature is nearly 98°F (37°C) and any major deviation up or down can cause problems.

The uncovered body will start to shiver at approximately 95°F (35°C). Shivering is an automatic body reaction to cold that is intended to move the muscles to produce more heat.

When a body gets cold there is an automatic defense mechanism that reduces the flow of blood to the extremities (toes, fingers, etc.) and tries to heat the vital life sustaining body organs - heart, lungs, brain.

Hypothermia is the drop of the vital core temperature of the body. This condition is a major threat to life. 85% of wilderness deaths are caused by hypothermia.

Body Nutrition

Food is our source of fuel to keep our bodies warm.

Carbohydrates - e.g. sugar, are instant sources of energy as they are quickly burned by the body. Consuming small amounts at regular intervals will provide energy for the outdoors.

Proteins and Fat - burn more slowly but are required by the body and protein is important for its staying power.

PRODUCTION OF HEAT BY THE BODY

You should have no problem with hypothermia if your body can continue to produce sufficient heat to complement the heat loss the cold. If the heat loss exceeds heat production you are a candidate for hypothermia.

Body Heat Production

The body combines fuel (food that you have eaten) with oxygen to produce heat. There are three types of body heating:

- **Basal Heat Production**

  This is the basic production of heat for a sedentary person. This heat production is partly controlled by the thyroid gland and cannot respond very fast to an emergency, e.g. heat loss, thus leading to hypothermia.

- **Thermoregulatory (Shivering)**

  This form of heat production, *which is involuntary*, responds to a drop in body temperature. This response is in the form of shivering which can increase the heat production by up to three times the basal rate. Heat production by shivering is not very productive. It can be stopped by putting on more clothing or getting out of the cold.

- **Exercise**

  A well planned activity in a survival situation can be very productive.

  • Hiking uphill with a load can increase heat production up to six times the basal rate. Hiking is very productive in producing body heat. This activity, performed by a healthy adult, might be sustained for an hour or two and *is recommended if you know where you are and how far away the shelter is.*

  If you are not sure of your location or destination it might be better to use your energy to develop heat by building a shelter and fire which will last the night.

  • Heavy exertion, where you can produce heat up to ten times the basal rate, can be maintained for 10 minutes by a healthy adult. This should only be done if you are 100% sure of your destination and a proper shelter can be reached in that time. Make sure that your clothing is well ventilated to release humidity. *At the end of this heavy exertion, if you are not in a warm dry shelter, fatigue and humid clothing can lead to hypothermia.*

BODY HEAT LOSS

By understanding heat loss we can learn how to prevent or avoid hypothermia. Body heat is lost by *Radiation, Conduction, and Convection.*

Radiation

The major form of heat loss which is the direct transfer of heat from our body by heat waves to the air. To reduce this transfer we wear clothing and protect ourselves in shelters such as tents or snow trenches.

The head has many blood vessels to heat and feed the brain. If uncovered, at 40°F (4°C), up to 50% of the body's heat loss is through the head. At 5°F (-15°C) the loss is 75%. If there is a high windchill factor the heat loss is higher and much more rapid.
For this reason a hat should be warn to keep the body warm.

Conduction

Conduction is caused by the transfer of heat to an adjacent colder medium. This medium can be the adjacent air, the cold seat you are sitting on, etc. To reduce conduction wear clothing with many pores or air pockets e.g. wool or down fill. Solids such as ice, metal, snow and cold water against bare skin are very high conductors of heat and cause high and rapid heat loss.

Cold water heat loss is the most dramatic because water will wet clothing, filling the insulating air pockets, and this will accelerate heat loss from the body.

Clothing can get wet from the outside but if the clothing does not breath, absorb or transmit humidity from the body you will soon get clammy and wet especially if you are exerting yourself. For this reason many people recommend natural fibers such as wool and cotton as they have many pores and a higher wicking factor to absorb humidity.

Convection

Is the removal of heat from the body by the motion of the surrounding air. This is a minor factor if there is no wind but with wind the exposed skin will be affected by the windchill factor.

Windchill factor at 0°C / 32°F.

Temperature lowered to	Wind Speed
-2°C/ 25°F	5 mph (8 km/h)
-11°C/10°F	15 mph (24 km/h)
-19°C/-5F	40 mph (64 km/h)

For this reason windproof breathable clothing should be warn over the porous insulation on your body. If your clothing is wet windchill can be fatal.

Clothing

Wet clothing loses heat by conduction and evaporation. If your clothing is totally waterproof (rubber or dense nylon) water, humidity or water vapor from the body cannot escape and you will soon become humid and cold.

Respiration

Warm air is exhaled with your breath. Limit heat loss by breathing through your nose. This is especially true at high elevations where, to obtain more oxygen, there is more frequent and labored breathing.

STAGES OF HYPOTHERMIA

SHIVERING

This is the first indication that there is a small drop in the core temperature of the body and that heat loss from the body exceeds heat production. Shivering will start at a core temperature just below 98.6°. This is the first sign of a mild hypothermia and the person will start to be in a withdrawn state. *This is a warning that heat loss should be reduced.*

If your core temperature is 91°F-95°F (33°C-35°C) you will have:

- Intense shivering. Trembling hands.
- Difficulty in speaking, memory lapse, become forgetful, lack concentration, cannot think logically, and becomes indecisive.
- Exhaustion and drowsiness.
- Loss of coordination, stumbling, falling, and inability to use hands.

Accidents from the lack of coordination can occur. You might have an accident on the trail, not be able to build a shelter, put up your tent or unroll your sleeping bag. *These are early stages of hypothermia and hopefully you have a partner who will recognize these symptoms and prepare a shelter, build a fire and give you some carbohydrates.*

TENSE MUSCULAR RIGIDITY

This is the second stage in hypothermia when the core temperature drops to 86°-91°F (30°-33°C) and shivering decreases but your muscles become tense and rigid. Your thinking will be impaired, you cannot speak but you can still walk. *The fact that you have stopped shivering should tell you that your core temperature is still falling.* At 90°F (32°C) or lower the heart beat can fall to three or four beats a minute. With increased hypothermia the healthy beat will disappear and ventricular fibrillation will occur. The person should be treated in a clinic even if he looks dead as the heartbeat can be extremely low and breathing undetectable.

BODY'S GRADUAL FAILURE

Below 86°F (30°C), depending upon your personal physical condition, the body chemistry begins to change and major problems can occur:

- Pulse and respiration slows down.
- May fall into a coma.
- Behavior becomes uncoordinated and irrational and can evolve into lethargy, e.g. a person sitting down to die of heat loss. *You will require assistance to stop the continued falling of the core temperature.*

UNCONSCIOUSNESS

The core temperature below 80°F (27°C) will result in a deep unconsciousness.

- Reflexes will be dramatically reduced. Breathing is difficult
- Heartbeat will be erratic and the pulse weaker.
- Cardiac arrhythmias may be noted.

If you are warmed up at this stage your core temperature will continue falling and nothing can be done in a wilderness survival situation.

DEATH

Around 78°F (25°C) the respiratory and cardiovascular systems fail. This is followed by pulmonary edema and ventricular fibrillation and then cardiac standstill.

TO PREVENT HYPOTHERMIA

- stay dry
- avoid cold
- get rest
- avoid wind
- eat well
- stay active

Have warm dry clothing available. Natural insulation might be available in the wilderness.

Travel with an emergency space blanket.

Do not be strong-headed and attempt to complete a challenging excursion.

Turn back, seek shelter, avoid hypothermia.

Find shelter and heat when you still have enough energy left. Build your shelter when your mind is still lucid. *Avoid perspiring.*

TREATING HYPOTHERMIA

- Get the victim out of adverse weather into a shelter that is dry and not in the wind. If the victim is in the water get him out as soon as possible.
- Replace wet clothing with dry clothing or put him in a dry sleeping bag. You might even consider joining the victim in the sleeping bag.
- Give the victim some warm liquid or soup. This will help increase the core temperature from the inside. A more rapid way to heat the inside of the body is to have victim inhale steam from boiling water as it will heat the heart and lungs. *Make sure that he is not too close to the source of the steam as he might be scalded and damage the lungs and airway.*
- Do not give alcohol as it will open the blood vessels near the skin which will dissipate heat and less heat will be available for the key body organs.
- *Get medical help.*

328

MOUNTAIN CLIMBING ILLNESSES

HIGHER ELEVATION HEALTH FACTORS

- Air is colder.
- Air is thinner so there is less oxygen.
- Weather is more severe and can change rapidly.
- Above 14000 feet (4100 meters) our metabolism lacks oxygen to process and use fatty foods. Climbers can get bloated as they cannot digest fatty foods.
- Diet has to be changed to more carbohydrates (sugar, rice, wheat) and proteins (meat and dairy products).
- Air is dry. Sweating and deep breathing will rapidly dehydrate the body.

Medical Problems of Mountain Climbing

At 7000-8000 feet (2000-2350 meters) mountain sickness can develop in *some* travelers.

At 12000+ feet (3500+ meters) everyone can develop mountain sickness. *See Pulmonary Endema.*

Symptoms of Mountain Sickness

- General sense of weakness and lack of energy.
- Tiredness even when not exerting.
- Nausea and headaches.

Symptoms of Lack of Oxygen

- Lips and fingertips have a bluish cast.
- Face has a lack of color and looks greyish.

If Symptoms are Present

- Do not eat heavily as your system will require more oxygen to digest the food.
- Do not smoke.
- Do not drink alcohol.

Acclimatizing to Higher Elevations

Acclimatization requires the body to change by increasing the blood's capacity to absorb oxygen and the lungs to become more efficient. People have different acclimatization rates from 10 days to 5 or 6 weeks.

High Altitude Pulmonary Edema

Symptoms are similar as those of pneumonia. It is the accumulation of fluids in the lungs that reduces the their breathing capacity. Death can result from suffocation or heart failure.

Pulmonary edema usually occurs above 9000 feet (2700 meters) but it varies from person to person. It depends upon the individual's capacity to become acclimatized to the elevation.

PULMONARY EDEMA (HAPE)

SYMPTOMS OF PULMONARY EDEMA

If susceptible, the symptoms occur 12 to 36 hours after arrival at a high elevation. Usually above 7000 feet (2000 m). This is one of the reasons mountain climbers travel in stages to higher elevations.

THE FIRST INDICATIONS

- Weakness, tiredness
- Nausea
- Loss of appetite
- Develop a shortness of breath without exertion
- Constricted feeling around the chest

SECOND STAGE

Dry hacking cough develops becoming more frequent and deeper.

THIRD STAGE

- Cough brings up a frothy liquid which might be pink with blood.
- Blood pulse and respiration may increase and become rapid.
- Lack of oxygen will be indicated by the lips and fingertips turning blue.

FINAL STAGE

- Victim feels that he is drowning (which he is as their lungs are filling with liquid).
- Bubbling sound occurs in the chest as the lung fluid gurgles with each breath.
- Death will occur if no prompt action is taken.

TREATMENT FOR PULMONARY ENDEMA

While the victim is still mobile he should be brought to a lower elevation. Even a descent of 2000 feet (600 meters) might restore normal breathing. Victim should not be allowed to continue the climb even if his condition improves or all signs disappear. *Every case should get medical attention.*

WOMEN AT HIGH ALTITUDES

Women have a different physiology than men so that at higher altitudes they will have different reactions.

- Less suffering from pulmonary edema (HAPE).
- Women can experience swelling of the extremities in their premenstrual stage.
- The lack of ideal washing facilities will lead you to procrastinate on long trips and this can cause vaginal and urinary tract infections. To avoid or limit this possibility change your underwear every day and wear loose fitting cotton pants to maximize ventilation. Drink large quantities of cranberry juice to limit urinary tract infections.

See your doctor before going on a long trip especially in a humid warm climate.

HYPOXIA

Hypoxia occurs when there is a lack of oxygen. This occurs at high elevations.

Symptoms are:
- Breathing rate increases.
- Dizziness.
- Warm sweating sensation.
- Sleepiness.
- Skin, fingernails, and lips turning blue.
- Reduced field of vision. (Angle of vision)
- Problems of judgment and behavior. (Logic)
- Loss of consciousness.

Individuals who are not in good physical shape are more susceptible to be affected by hypoxia.

NIGHT VISION PROBLEMS AT HIGH ELEVATION

At 5000 feet (1500 m) vision might become blurred, angle of vision is reduced, and night vision might be reduced. At 8000 feet (2400 m) night vision might be reduced by 25%. This does not occur during the day time.
With increased elevation and reduced oxygen other symptoms will occur.
Treat by increasing the supply of oxygen.

MOUNTAIN CLIMBING PROBLEMS

Hypothermia at High Elevations
High elevations have all the ingredients for hypothermia as being cold, wet, and windy.
Low energy reserves due to the exertion involved in climbing and the probability of not eating properly will also be possible contributing factors.

HYPERVENTILATION

Hyperventilation is excessive ventilation of the lungs from breathing too rapidly and too deeply. This results in the excessive loss of carbon dioxide from the body.

Excess ventilation can be caused by anxiety or possible fear of the unknown which can occur if lost.

The symptoms are:
- Dizziness and nausea. Shortness of breath.
- Muscle spasms and tingling of the fingers and toes.
- Body feels hot. Increase of the heart rate. Vision becomes blurred. Fainting and lose consciousness.

Help person to slow rapid breathing by giving reassurance and explaining why his fears are unfounded. Have him breath into a bag to increase the level of carbon dioxide in his system.

US ARMY HEAT ILLNESS GUIDELINE

An individual who has already had a heat stroke or severe case of heat exhaustion is more likely to fall sick again than one who has not suffered from these illnesses. An individual who has already been affected should be subsequently exposed to potential heat stress with caution.

Symptoms to distinguish between salt depletion and water depletion:

Symptoms	Salt Depletion	Water Depletion
Duration of symptoms	3-5 days	1 day
Thirst	seldom	prominent
Fatigue	prominent	seldom
Cramps	prominent	none
Vomiting	prominent	none
Weakness	progressive	acute

US ARMY WATER REQUIREMENT GUIDELINES

Activity	Typical Duties	Quarts Per Person Per Day	
		Less than 105°F (41°C)	More than 105°F (41°C)
Light	Desk work, Radio operating, Guard duty.	6	10
Moderate	Route march on level ground.	7	11
Heavy	Forced marches, Route march with heavy loads, Digging in.	9	13

US ARMY SALT GUIDELINES

Addition of table salt to produce a 0.1% salt solution:

Table Salt	Amount of Water
1/4 spoon (6 ml)	1 quart canteen (1.25 L)
1 1/3 level mess kit spoons	5 gallon can (19 L)
9 level mess kit spoons (3/10 lb)	36 gallon bag (136 L)
1 LB (450 g)	100 gallon tank (379 L)
1 level canteen cup	250 gallons (946 L)

HEAT ILLNESSES

Illness	Cause	Symptoms	First Aid
Heat Exhaustion	Excessive loss of water and salt	*Cool moist skin, profuse sweating.* Headache, dizziness, vomiting, weakness, rapid pulse and breathing. May be a slight rise in temperature.	Heat cramps are promptly relieved by replacing the salt lost from body. Place individual in cool outer clothing. Give water slowly in the form of 0.1% saline solution. If cramps are very severe individual should be sent to a hospital.
Heat Cramps	Excessive loss of salt from body	Severe cramps in limbs, back and/or abdomen, following exposure to heat. Body temperature remains normal.	Move patient to cool shaded place. Remove outer clothing. Elevate feet and either move legs up and down or massage legs. Give all water that can be drunk in form of 0.1% saline solution.
Heat Stroke	Collapse of body cooling mechanism	*Hot dry skin.* Headache, mental confusion, and bizarre behavior, dizziness, weakness and rapid breathing and pulse. H High temperature (106°F or more). May be unconscious.	*Medical emergency. Seek medical aid immediately.* Lower the patient's body temperature as rapidly as possible. This is the most important objective in the treatment of heat stroke. Move individual to shaded area. Remove clothing. Sprinkle or bathe patient with cool water and fan to increase cooling effect. Massage trunk, arms, and legs. If evacuating to hospital continue treatment on the way.

HEATSTROKE
HEAT EXHAUSTION

HEAT ILLNESS

Heatstroke, Heat Exhaustion & Heat Cramps

- These are caused by the surrounding heat especially when humid.

  Heatstroke and heat exhaustion are mainly due to the excessive loss of fluid and salt from continuous sweating or overexertion in a hot climate. **This fluid and salt must be continually replaced.**

- Heat illness can be expected when the *wet bulb temperature* is above 90°F (32.2°C), or the *dry bulb temperature* is above 110°F (43.3°C)*.

- With much exertion the body can loose up to 2 quarts of fluids per hour in hot and humid environments.

Heat Illnesses

- Heatstroke (sunstroke).
- Heat Exhaustion.   *See Weather Chapter.
- Heat Cramps.

You should be able to recognize the symptoms and treatment and how to avoid these heat illnesses.

You might save a life.

HEAT EXHAUSTION

Excessive sweating in hot climates causes dehydration (loss of body fluids) and loss of salt. The use of alcohol, vomiting, diarrhea, or other loss of body fluids will increase a persons exposure to heat exhaustion.

The loss of salt and water unbalances the body fluids which results in a series of symptoms called heat exhaustion.

It is usually caused by extreme physical exertion in hot and humid areas to which a person lacks acclimatization. *Its effect accumulates over a prolonged period if the physical activities are maintained.*

Symptoms

Thirst, listlessness, loss of appetite, ashen skin, dizziness, cool clammy sweating skin, nausea and vomiting and mild muscular heat cramps. Concentration is difficult. The heart may race with the pulse at 100 beats per minute. The temperature may be below normal or slightly raised. Fainting may occur the victim might even become unconscious. *Prickly Heat* (see article) is also a form of heat exhaustion. *Get medical help.*

Treatment

Keep patient in a cool well ventilated area. Loosen and wet the clothing. Administer water to which a level teaspoonful of table salt (or 8 salt tablets) per pint has been added. Have the person rest for at least 24 hours while still drinking a saline solution. Add salt to light food.

HEATSTROKE (SUNSTROKE)

Heatstroke can occur after a few hours of exposure to intense heat, but usually after a few days or weeks of exposure as in a heat wave or holiday in the tropics. People from temperate climates who have not had a chance to acclimatize are at a higher risk of being affected. The problem of heat is increased when combined with strenuous activities.

Heatstroke is caused by the failure of the brain in regulating the heat mechanism of the body which will cause a cessation of sweating (cooling).

- The initial symptoms are a feeling of weakness, nausea and headache (symptoms which are typical of heat exhaustion). Its appearance is usually sudden.
- *Onset is very rapid.*
- *Immediate attention is required as a heatstroke is dangerous to life.*

A heatstroke is characterized by:

- The skin being dry, flushed and burning *and sweating will stop.*
- Person appears feverish. Lack of coordination.
- Nausea and vomiting.
- Have a headache.
- Restlessness and mental confusion.

This may lead to:

- Respiration rate will rise.
- The pulse rate is high even up to 160.
- Twitching and cramps of the muscles will occur.
- Body temperature can be between 105°-110°F (40.5°-43.3°C).

US Army Acclimatization Schedule

Hours of work that may be performed in a minimum period of acclimatization.

Day	Less than 105°F (41°C)		More than 105°F (41°C)	
	AM	PM	AM	PM
1	1 hr	1 hr	1 hr	1 hr
2	1.5	1.5	1.5	1.5
3	2	2	2	2
4	3	3	2.5	2.5
5	regular duty		3	3
6	regular duty		regular duty	

- Delirium, collapse, convulsions, and coma will lead to death.

The patient's temperature will be at 105°F (40.5°C) and can go to 110°F (43.3°C) before death occurs. Medical attention is required if the initial stages of heatstroke are suspected.

TREATMENT OF HEATSTROKE

Immediately Cool the Patient

Cooling the patient is the very important in treating a heatstroke and should be carried out immediately.

Continually watch the fall of the temperature as prolonged exposure to cold might cause hypothermia. *Reduce the temperature of the patient to below 100°F (37.8°C) as soon as possible.*

Move patient to a cool place and strip naked. Cover with a wet sheet and massage vigorously with a cold cloth and ice cubes. If you have a fan direct its airflow over the wet sheets. The fan increases the cooling by evaporation. If available, immerse the patient in a tub of ice cold water.

At 100°F (37.8°C) natural body sweating usually resumes. Keep the patient in a cool spot and watch for symptoms of hypothermia. Continually take the temperature and *if it begins to rise resume the cooling treatment.*

Urgently get medical help.

Replace Lost Body Fluid and Salt

- Have patient drink a saline water mixture of a teaspoon of table salt (or 8 salt tablets) per pint of water. The patient can also drink water or fruit juices.
- In general the patient should have at least 8 pints of saline or other fluid in 24 hours.
- The patient, upon recovering, should be covered with a light *dry* blanket and kept in a cool spot for a week. Make sure that he drinks sufficient water. *Watch for any signs of a relapse.*

PRECAUTIONS AGAINST HEAT ILLNESS

- Avoid heavy exertion if not acclimatized to the heat or humidity.

- Eat fruits and vegetables to have an additional source of salt.

- Increase the movement of the air as it helps the natural cooling system of the body. Wear light colored loose fitting cotton clothing.

- Increase water consumption to at least 8 pints (5 L) per day. Drink small quantities of water at frequent intervals to avoid an increase in sweating.

- Increase salt intake. Use 2 salt tablets with a quart of water, four times daily. If table salt is used take a level teaspoonful (5 ml) dissolved in a quart of water every morning and evening. Add extra salt to the food. Extra salt will reduce fatigue and listlessness common to hot and humid climates. *Use the Urine Test outlined on this page to check for salt deficiency.*

- Avoid exposure to the sun during the hottest part of the day. Wear a wide-brimmed hat. From time to time douse the head with cold water. Do not remove your shirt as it helps to retain the sweat that cools your body. Keep your body covered at all times.

- Noon meals should be light. Eat the more substantial meals in the evening. Avoid caffeine (coke, tea and coffee).

- If working take frequent rests and drink a lot of fluids. Avoid alcohol.

- Bathe frequently as clean skin helps sweating. Do not use too much skin cream as it clogs the pores. Keep your clothing clean and dry to avoid fungal infection.

- If you have any of the symptoms of Heat Illness *get medical help.*

PRICKLY HEAT

Occurs when it is hot with high humidity. It is a rash of tiny red pimples which is extremely itchy and irritating.

It affects any part of the body but most common in areas where tight fitting clothing does not let the body breath and sweat and humidity build up. *This impairs the sweat glands and they do not function properly.* Prickly heat might occur on the forehead below a cap, on the back below a backpack, or below a pant waistline. If the area is not washed and dried a minor rash can develop into septic spots or boils. If very humid it can occur on areas exposed to the sun such as the forearms and hands. There might be some of the symptoms of heat illness.

Treatment

Try to avoid the rash by taking frequent showers. Clothing worn should be light, loose, porous and *washed* frequently. Place a cotton towel between your nylon backpack and your back when traveling on hot humid days. When stopping on a hike let the humid clothing dry in the sun. This will reduce the possibility of fungal growth.

If you have a rash bathe frequently every day in cold water, dry well, and put on clean clothing (preferably clean loose cotton garments).

During showers avoid the use of soap or rubbing the affected parts. After a shower pat the affected area dry and apply some calamine which will dry to a fine powder. *Avoid creams that will clog pores.*

SUNBURN

- For minor burns, apply cold cream, talcum powder or mineral oil to relieve the pain.

- If badly burned and blistered apply cold compresses of water, whole milk, or a saline solution. An effective saline solution would be one teaspoon of salt to a pint of cool water.

  A severe sunburn should be treated by a doctor to avoid infection.

Prevention

- Keep the body covered. Especially if your skin is very sensitive and has not previously been exposed to the sun.

- The body should be gradually exposed to the sun. Initially at 15 minute intervals per day (including cloudy days). Increase the exposure 5 to 10 minutes a day until it is less sensitive. *Cloudy days can cause sunburns.*

- Apply a high rated sunscreen but to minimize any risk of skin cancer keep your body covered and wear a wide brimmed hat.

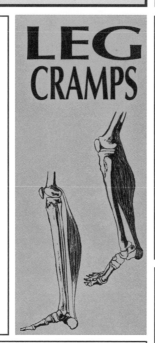

LEG CRAMPS

HEAT CRAMP

Heat cramps are caused by the loss of salt when there is excessive sweating. The lack of salt will affect the muscles of the abdomen and limbs giving severe and painful cramps. There may be vomiting. Cramps may be a side affect of heat exhaustion.

Treatment

The victim should lie down. If there are abdominal cramps apply a hot water bottle and massage the cramped muscles. Give the victim saline water of a 1/4 teaspoon of salt in a quart of water. The victim should rest for at least 12 hours before resuming any strenuous activities. In the victim continues the activities causing the sweating he should increase his water and salt intake to reduce the risk of cramps. *See the article on Hot Weather Leg Cramps.*

URINE SALT TEST PAPERS

To test for excessive salt loss place a salt test paper in a urine sample or pass urine on to it and watch for the color change.

If *normal* the color becomes bright yellow.

If salt is *immediately required* the paper will take a long time to change, be incomplete or not change at all.

The paper is light sensitive and should be stored in the dark. If unexposed it is brick red, when exposed to light it becomes harder and the color becomes like chocolate and then slate colored. The paper is sensitive to the salty sweat on the hands, which might cause it to change, *handle with care.*

HOT WEATHER LEG CRAMPS

Loss of potassium, sodium, and salt might cause leg cramps in hot weather. This loss causes cramps that are spasmodic painful contractions of muscles, usually in the leg. To reduce the probability of these cramps eat well balanced meals rich in potassium and sodium. Foods to eat are eggs, liver, chicken, milk, citrus fruits, bananas and dark green leafy vegetables. The victim of an attack should rest in a cool area and drink a saline solution or lemonade. *Avoid cramps by warming up before any strenuous activity.* During an attach stretch out the muscle while massaging *above* the painful area to increase the flow of blood.

DROWNING

Drowning

Drowning is caused by the airway to the lungs being clogged with water, and death usually results from the lack of oxygen.
The victim will usually have water in his stomach.

COLD WATER DEATH *(Immersion Hypothermia)*

Drowning can be caused by water in the lungs or by *immersion hypothermia* which is the same as hypothermia on land. In cold water the unprotected body chills rapidly and as its temperature falls the victim becomes numb, unconscious, and slides below the water. *See Hypothermia as outlined on page 328.* The exposed body in water below 20°C (68°F) cannot maintain its normal functions and the pulse slows, breathing and, heartbeat is erratic and death follows. Clothing reduces heat loss. Wet clothing does not retain the insulation loft of dry clothing but it reduces the water's convection currents on the body. Clothed and not moving in the water will help reduce heat loss. Swimming and movement increases heat loss. If the victim is not recovered in a short time he will succumb to hypothermia. Cold water death can occur when falling through the ice.

Treatment

Rewarm the victim in a hot bath or remove all the wet clothing, dry the body, and wrap it in a warm blanket. Offer some hot drinks. Artificial resuscitation might be required.
"Drowning victims" might be revived by rewarming.

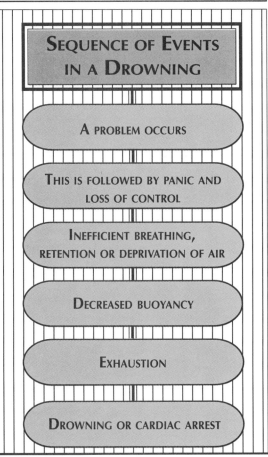

SEQUENCE OF EVENTS IN A DROWNING

- A PROBLEM OCCURS
- THIS IS FOLLOWED BY PANIC AND LOSS OF CONTROL
- INEFFICIENT BREATHING, RETENTION OR DEPRIVATION OF AIR
- DECREASED BUOYANCY
- EXHAUSTION
- DROWNING OR CARDIAC ARREST

Cold Water Death

Water in May, June and July is still cold. Body temperature, in the water, might drop 6°- 8°F which affects rational thinking. Studies indicate that if a person remains immobile in the water his probability of rescue is increased 30%. Swimming increases the loss of core heat by 35% to 50% as opposed to remaining still.

Drown-Proofing

This method of bobbing up and down in the water should only be used in warm water as it increases the loss of heat especially from the head. At 50°F (10°C) the survival time is doubled by staying immobile rather that swimming.

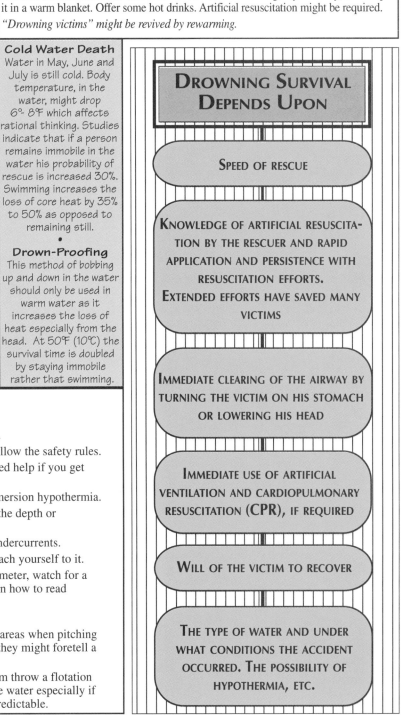

DROWNING SURVIVAL DEPENDS UPON

- SPEED OF RESCUE
- KNOWLEDGE OF ARTIFICIAL RESUSCITATION BY THE RESCUER AND RAPID APPLICATION AND PERSISTENCE WITH RESUSCITATION EFFORTS. EXTENDED EFFORTS HAVE SAVED MANY VICTIMS
- IMMEDIATE CLEARING OF THE AIRWAY BY TURNING THE VICTIM ON HIS STOMACH OR LOWERING HIS HEAD
- IMMEDIATE USE OF ARTIFICIAL VENTILATION AND CARDIOPULMONARY RESUSCITATION (CPR), IF REQUIRED
- WILL OF THE VICTIM TO RECOVER
- THE TYPE OF WATER AND UNDER WHAT CONDITIONS THE ACCIDENT OCCURRED. THE POSSIBILITY OF HYPOTHERMIA, ETC.

TO AVOID DROWNING

- Respect the "power" of water.
- Learn to swim and understand the water environment.
- Do not swim alone or without a life guard present. Follow the safety rules.
- If swimming underwater tell a friend as you might need help if you get tangled in debris, blackout or have cramps.
- Beware of cold water as it might cause cramps or immersion hypothermia.
- Watch where you dive especially if you do not know the depth or what debris is at the bottom.
- Watch for strong currents, waves, rapids, tides, and undercurrents.
- Stay with a capsized boat or debris and if possible attach yourself to it.
- Avoid storms, listen to weather forecasts, have a barometer, watch for a change in the direction of the wind or waves, and learn how to read the clouds for major changes in weather.
- Be careful when fording streams.
- Watch for flash floods on dry riverbeds and high tide areas when pitching camp for the night. Listen for any unusual sounds as they might foretell a flash flood from a distant storm.
- When attempting to rescue a potential drowning victim throw a flotation device, rope, or extend a stick. Avoid jumping into the water especially if you are a weak swimmer or water conditions are unpredictable.

DROWN PROOFING

FLOAT STROKE

Every camper or boat traveler should know and have practiced drown proofing. Swimming in a pool is quite different from choppy lake water where a hundred feet can feel like a major challenge. Be prepared psychologically to face the unknown element of open water.

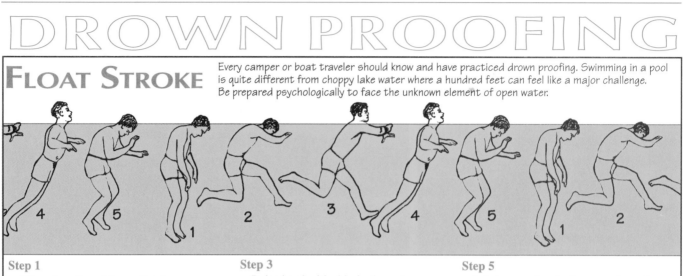

Step 1
- Take a breath and immediately
- Lay your head forward with chin on chest.
- Relax body with hands dangling
- Rest with back of your head protruding above the water.

Step 2
- Before air is needed *gradually* cross arms in front of head.
- Smoothly raise one knee toward chest while extending foot forward. At the same time extending the second foot behind you (Scissor movement). Remain vertical.

Step 3
- Raise head with chin in the water.
- Exhale though the nose *while raising* the head.

Step 4
- Complete exhaling.
- Open mouth to inhale while ge*ntly* sweeping palms *outward* and stepping downwards in the water, bringing legs together. This helps keep mouth above the water while inhaling. A complete air change is not required.

Step 5
- Inhale completed, close mouth, and drop head forward toward the knees.
- Relax, and repeat Step 1.

All movements should be smooth.

Problems That Might Occur:
Sink a few feet below surface:
Arms have not been dropped after head returned into water.
Chest feels tight under the water:
Remaining under water between breaths too long or not exhaling enough.
Little water entering mouth, spurt it out under water between pursed lips.

SWIMMING STROKE

A person who is relaxed, has lungs filled with air, and no food in the stomach will float on the water. If you do not panic you can not sink. Men will usually float vertically and women with a slight forward angle due their heavier hips. You require some movement, as illustrated, as the tip of your head will only protrude above the water when floating and you will not be able to breath.

Step 1
- Inhale and sink vertically.
- As head sinks, push down gently with your hands to stop any tendency to sink too deep.

Step 2
- Tilt head to a facedown position.
- Raise hands to forehead.
- Open-scissor legs raising the rear foot as high as possible.
- This movement will swing body into a horizontal position.

Step 3
- Gradually raise arms, with hands together, forward toward the surface.
- When arms are fully extended make a scissors kick with legs.

Step 4
- While feet come together after kicking *slowly* sweep arms outward and back reaching the thighs.

Step 5
- While floating forward and upward, keep hands extended to the thighs.
- All the while exhaling through the nose through Steps 5, 6, and 7.

Step 6
- To breath return to the vertical position by raising the back, bringing both knees toward chest, and lifting hands toward the head.

Source: Joseph P. Blank, "Nobody Needs to Drown " Everywoman's Family Circle, June 1960

Step 7
- To reach the vertical extend a leg in front while bringing the second foreword. At the same time raise arms in front of head with the forearms together and palms facing out.

Step 8
- Prepare to inhale.
- Open-scissor legs to propel body upward.
- Start raising head. Only raise head when body is vertical.

Step 9
- Open mouth to inhale while gently sweeping palms outward and stepping downwards in the water. This is done to help keep the mouth above the water while inhaling. Do not overexert yourself as a complete air change is not required.

ARTIFICIAL RESPIRATION

Artificial respiration is a procedure to help air enter into the victim's lungs when natural breathing has been reduced or totally stopped.
To perform artificial respiration the airway has to be kept open and a rhythmic method of providing air has to be maintained to restore the victim's breathing

ARTIFICIAL RESPIRATION

A victim who cannot breathe naturally or has stopped breathing should receive artificial respiration as soon as possible.

Continuously perform artificial respiration until you are sure that the victim can be assumed to be dead. The brain requires oxygen and that if deprived of oxygen *for more than four minutes*, irreversible damage can occur.
Artificial respiration is used to immediately oxygenate the blood.

Natural breathing can be interrupted by:

* Drowning.
* Suffocation from choking on food, vomit, or object in the airway.
* Pressure on the windpipe that may have been caused by a sporting accident or strangulation.
* Pressure on the chest from running into someone or something while skiing, skating, snowmobile, hitting the steering wheel during an accident, etc.
* Poisons or poisonous gases as carbon dioxide or monoxide.
* Shock or electric shock.

OPENING THE AIRWAY BY THE HEAD TILT MANEUVER

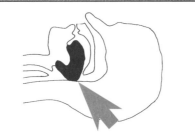

When the victim is laid flat on the ground the tongue might block the airway (pharynx).

Position of Victim
The victim should be lying face up on a flat hard horizontal surface.

•

First Check the Airway
If there are no signs of breathing check to see what is blocking the air passage. The airway may be blocked by the victim's tongue or by foreign matter in the mouth or throat.

•

Gurgling or Noise
Gurgling or noisy breathing indicates the need to clear the throat of fluid or debris.

•

Breathing
Check for breathing by placing your ear one inch from the mouth or nose and listen for the movement of air.
You might also be able to feel or see some movement in the victim's chest or abdomen.

•

Vomiting
When the victim vomits during resuscitation turn him onto his side and clear out his mouth before proceeding.

•

Restoring Breathing
If the victim's breathing is not adequate after the airway has been opened, artificial ventilation should be started.
Your exhaled air is approximately 16% oxygen which is sufficient to sustain the victim's life.

Jaw-Thrust Maneuver

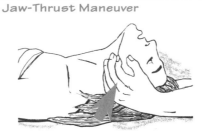

Tilt victim's head back as far as possible. Sometimes the victim might start breathing spontaneously.

Neck raised forehead tilted backwards and tongue moves to open the airway.

Head Tilt- Neck Lift Maneuver

The best way to tilt the head backwards is by placing a hand on the victim's forehead and pressing down as far as possible with the palm. The second hand can be used to apply a neck lift or chin lift.

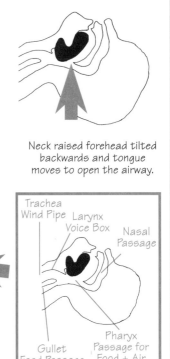

Trachea
Wind Pipe   Larynx
Voice Box   Nasal
Passage

Gullet   Pharyx
Food Passage   Passage for
Food + Air

Head Tilt-Jaw Lift Maneuver

One of these maneuvers usually works to free the airway. If not, pull the jaw forward (this can be done quite forcefully) while pushing on the forehead. Do not press on the soft tissue below the chin as it might obstruct the airway.

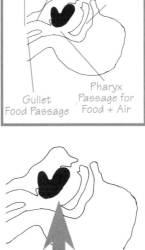

Pull the jaw and pushing the forehead will assure the opening of the airway.

VENTILATION

Delay of a few seconds may prove fatal.

If in doubt as to the condition of the victim start *mouth-to-mouth* (or *mouth-to-nose*) respiration immediately.

Advantages of *mouth-to-mouth* (or *mouth-to-nose*):

• This gives the largest volume of air to the lungs and maximizes the oxygenation of the blood.

• You can see the amount of ventilation by watching the up and down movement of the chest.

• It requires little strength to apply and can be sustained for a long time.

When these methods are used, air has to be blown to inflate the lungs. The head should be well positioned to limit the obstruction of the tongue. You might have to blow hard to blow past any debris that might be in the windpipe.

Often it will be found that as soon as the air passage is clear and the lungs have been inflated, the victim will gasp and start to breathe spontaneously.

Obstruction in the Air Passages

If Mouth-to-Mouth or Mouth-to-Nose methods fail, check for any obstruction in the mouth or throat.

If a foreign body or other obstruction is found, remove it (turning the head to one side if necessary), then restart resuscitation.

If you feel the obstruction is in the windpipe turn the victim onto his side and strike three or four sharp blows between the shoulders. Check, with your fingers, to see if any debris has been displaced into the throat. If so, remove it and start resuscitation again.

Watching the Victim's Chest Deflate

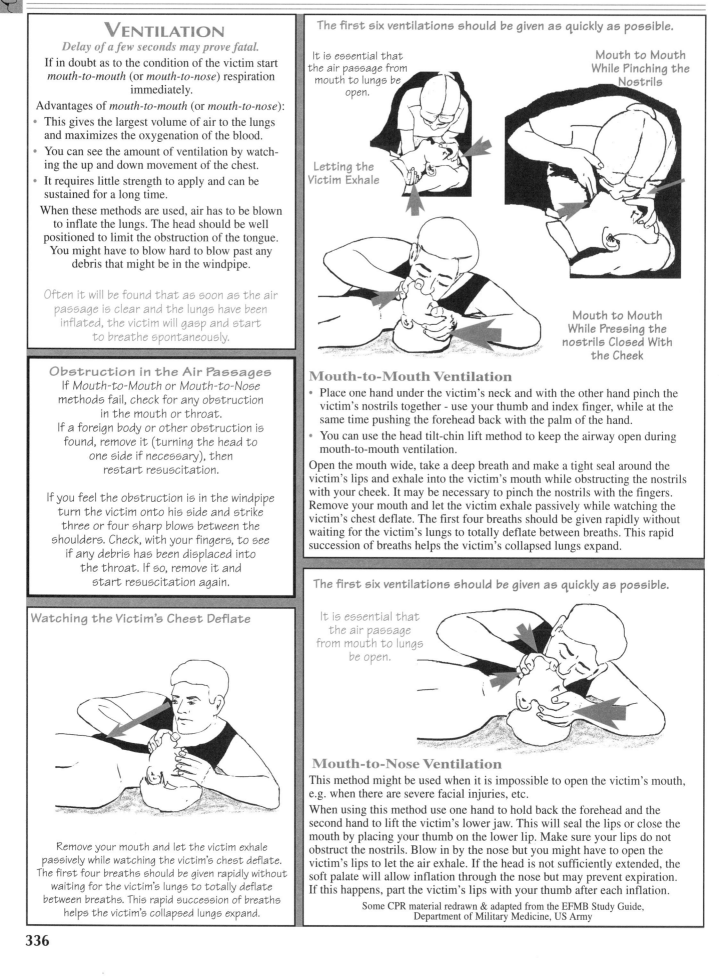

The first six ventilations should be given as quickly as possible.

It is essential that the air passage from mouth to lungs be open.

Letting the Victim Exhale

Mouth to Mouth While Pinching the Nostrils

Mouth to Mouth While Pressing the nostrils Closed With the Cheek

Remove your mouth and let the victim exhale passively while watching the victim's chest deflate. The first four breaths should be given rapidly without waiting for the victim's lungs to totally deflate between breaths. This rapid succession of breaths helps the victim's collapsed lungs expand.

Mouth-to-Mouth Ventilation

• Place one hand under the victim's neck and with the other hand pinch the victim's nostrils together - use your thumb and index finger, while at the same time pushing the forehead back with the palm of the hand.

• You can use the head tilt-chin lift method to keep the airway open during mouth-to-mouth ventilation.

Open the mouth wide, take a deep breath and make a tight seal around the victim's lips and exhale into the victim's mouth while obstructing the nostrils with your cheek. It may be necessary to pinch the nostrils with the fingers. Remove your mouth and let the victim exhale passively while watching the victim's chest deflate. The first four breaths should be given rapidly without waiting for the victim's lungs to totally deflate between breaths. This rapid succession of breaths helps the victim's collapsed lungs expand.

The first six ventilations should be given as quickly as possible.

It is essential that the air passage from mouth to lungs be open.

Mouth-to-Nose Ventilation

This method might be used when it is impossible to open the victim's mouth, e.g. when there are severe facial injuries, etc.

When using this method use one hand to hold back the forehead and the second hand to lift the victim's lower jaw. This will seal the lips or close the mouth by placing your thumb on the lower lip. Make sure your lips do not obstruct the nostrils. Blow in by the nose but you might have to open the victim's lips to let the air exhale. If the head is not sufficiently extended, the soft palate will allow inflation through the nose but may prevent expiration. If this happens, part the victim's lips with your thumb after each inflation.

Some CPR material redrawn & adapted from the EFMB Study Guide, Department of Military Medicine, US Army

CPR... CARDIOPULMONARY RESUSCITATION

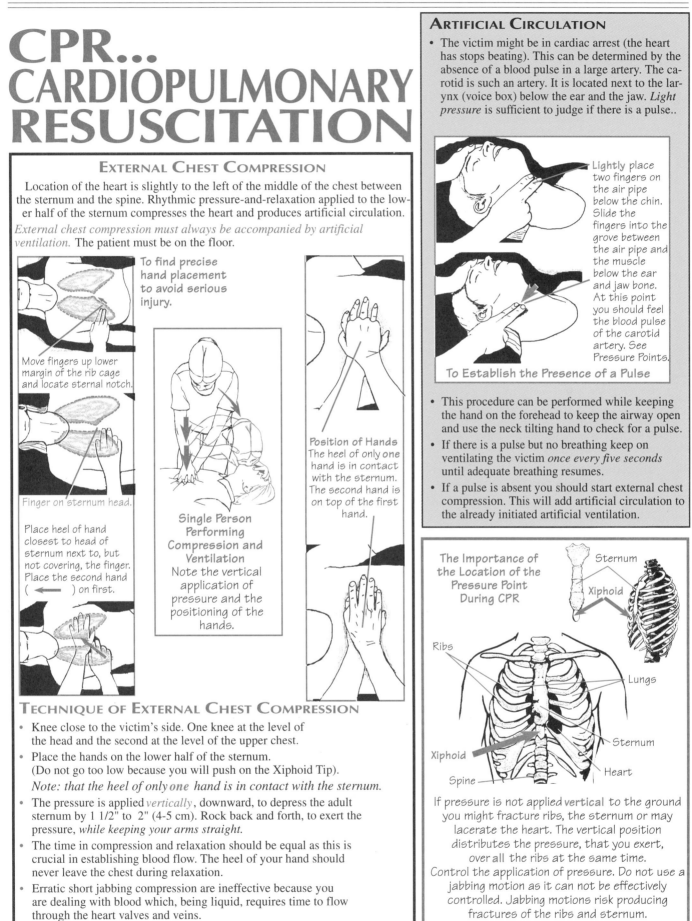

EXTERNAL CHEST COMPRESSION

Location of the heart is slightly to the left of the middle of the chest between the sternum and the spine. Rhythmic pressure-and-relaxation applied to the lower half of the sternum compresses the heart and produces artificial circulation.

External chest compression must always be accompanied by artificial ventilation. The patient must be on the floor.

To find precise hand placement to avoid serious injury.

Move fingers up lower margin of the rib cage and locate sternal notch.

Finger on sternum head.

Place heel of hand closest to head of sternum next to, but not covering, the finger. Place the second hand (←) on first.

Single Person Performing Compression and Ventilation
Note the vertical application of pressure and the positioning of the hands.

Position of Hands
The heel of only **one** hand is in contact with the sternum. The second hand is on top of the first hand.

TECHNIQUE OF EXTERNAL CHEST COMPRESSION

- Knee close to the victim's side. One knee at the level of the head and the second at the level of the upper chest.
- Place the hands on the lower half of the sternum.
  (Do not go too low because you will push on the Xiphoid Tip).
  Note: that the heel of only one hand is in contact with the sternum.
- The pressure is applied *vertically*, downward, to depress the adult sternum by 1 1/2" to 2" (4-5 cm). Rock back and forth, to exert the pressure, *while keeping your arms straight.*
- The time in compression and relaxation should be equal as this is crucial in establishing blood flow. The heel of your hand should never leave the chest during relaxation.
- Erratic short jabbing compression are ineffective because you are dealing with blood which, being liquid, requires time to flow through the heart valves and veins.

ARTIFICIAL CIRCULATION

- The victim might be in cardiac arrest (the heart has stops beating). This can be determined by the absence of a blood pulse in a large artery. The carotid is such an artery. It is located next to the larynx (voice box) below the ear and the jaw. *Light pressure* is sufficient to judge if there is a pulse..

Lightly place two fingers on the air pipe below the chin. Slide the fingers into the grove between the air pipe and the muscle below the ear and jaw bone. At this point you should feel the blood pulse of the carotid artery. See Pressure Points.

To Establish the Presence of a Pulse

- This procedure can be performed while keeping the hand on the forehead to keep the airway open and use the neck tilting hand to check for a pulse.
- If there is a pulse but no breathing keep on ventilating the victim *once every five seconds* until adequate breathing resumes.
- If a pulse is absent you should start external chest compression. This will add artificial circulation to the already initiated artificial ventilation.

The Importance of the Location of the Pressure Point During CPR

Sternum
Xiphoid
Ribs
Lungs
Sternum
Xiphoid
Heart
Spine

If pressure is not applied **vertical** to the ground you might fracture ribs, the sternum or may lacerate the heart. The vertical position distributes the pressure, that you exert, over **all** the ribs at the same time.
Control the application of pressure. Do not use a jabbing motion as it can not be effectively controlled. Jabbing motions risk producing fractures of the ribs and sternum.

Two People Working Together

When two people are reviving someone then the compression rate should be 60 per minute with a breath given every 5 compressions. This system is more efficient than one person as ventilation can proceed without any pause in compression.

Check Heart Pulse

Check the heart pulse every few minutes.

Do not interrupt CPR for more than five seconds for any reason. It is still important to get your victim to a hospital.

Dilated Pupil   **Pupil That Constricts to Light**

CHECK EYE PUPIL

To verify the effectiveness of your CPR check the pupils of the eyes from time to time.

- Pupils that *constrict when exposed to light* indicate adequate oxygenation and blood flow to the brain.
- Pupils that *remain dilated and do not react to light* indicate that serious brain damage may be imminent or may have occurred. Dilated pupils, but still reacting, are a less ominous sign.

Dislodging a Foreign Object From the Respiratory Track of a Young Child

The young child can be laid prone with the head downwards over the knee and given three or four sharp slaps between the shoulders to dislodge the foreign body. If the child is light enough you can hold the child up by the legs and then slap three or four times between the shoulders.

SINGLE PERSON PERFORMING COMPRESSION AND VENTILATION

External chest compression must always be accompanied by artificial ventilation.

A single person giving compression should maintain a rate of 80 compressions per minute to achieve 60 compressions per minute (as you are inflating at intervals). After 15 compressions you should deliver two inflations.

The 15 compressions are delivered in 10 to 11 seconds followed by two full rapid ventilations (with minimal exhalation time) delivered in four to five seconds. Using this technique 60 cardiac compressions can be provided per minute.

DESCENT INJURIES

These injuries usually are compression problems by which the normal air-containing structures in the body (lungs and inner ear) cannot readily adapt in response to the outside pressure. They cannot equalize the pressure because the nose or throat passages may be blocked by the ventilating gear or the individual may be holding his breath. This will cause a sharp pain and the diver usually stops diving to equalize the pressure.

In a severe situation the tympanic (eardrum) membrane might rupture. The water entering the inner ear will unbalance the diver. *The diver should be taken to a hospital immediately.*

Bottom Problems

These are related to the length and depth of the dive. These problems are rare with sport diving equipment but might occur with deep-sea diving equipment.

ASCENT INJURIES

Two problems might occur.

1. Air Embolism

This problem can occur at all depths especially if the diver holds his breath *during a rapid ascent*, not exhaling adequately, or airway obstruction. The water pressure on the chest is rapidly reduced and the air within the lungs rapidly expands. Too rapid an expansion can force air through the alveoli of the lungs into adjacent blood vessels. This air will travel as emboli to the heart and systemic circulation to the brain. *These bubbles act as plugs depriving body tissue of their normal supply of blood and oxygen.* Brain damage is possible. To avoid this problem the diver should ascend slowly while exhaling adequately. The symptoms are a pain in the chest under the breast bone and a swollen neck. *Consult a physician and take the victim to a recompression chamber.*

2. Decompression Sickness (The Bends)

Is caused by nitrogen gas coming out of solution, forming bubbles, and plugging the small blood vessels of the body. Rapid ascent and inadequate decompression for the dissolution of excessive nitrogen to be removed from tissue and blood. Symptoms are localized pain where nitrogen bubbles have formed, usually in the arm or leg. Others: respiratory difficulties, and neurological problems. *Consult a physician and take the victim to a recompression chamber. Consult a diving book for a complete overview.*

SCUBA DIVING

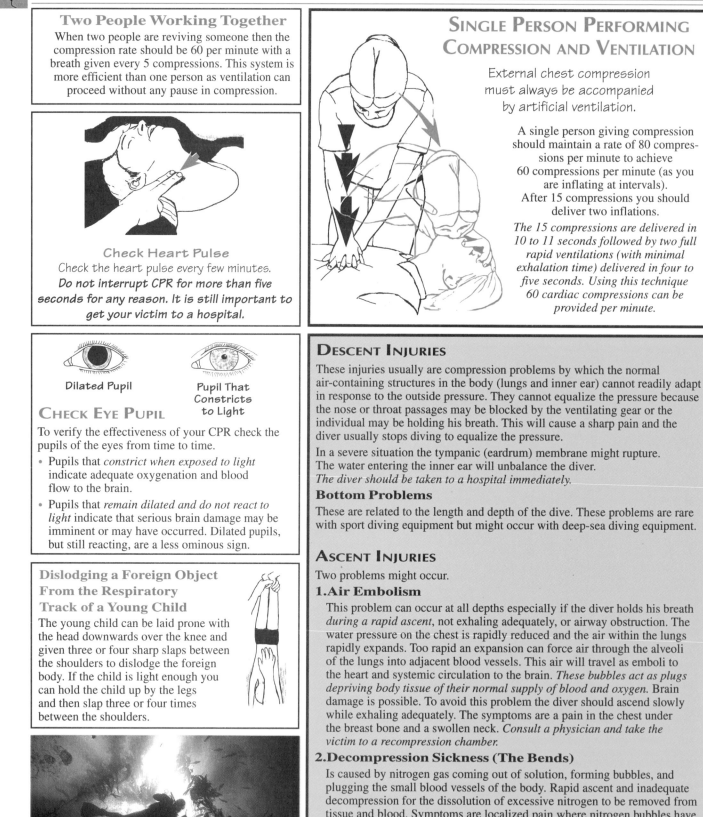

BLEEDING

Nick or Scrapes

The gentle ooze which occurs when you slightly cut your finger or nick yourself shaving is known as *capillary bleeding*. It stops by itself or upon the application of a small dressing and is of no consequence but should be kept clean to avoid infection.

Common Bleeding

Is a welling up of the blood from the depths of the wound in a slow steady stream. The blood comes from numerous blood vessels, except large arteries, of all sizes that have been severed. *Usually it is not dangerous but it may look alarming. It can be controlled by a firm dressing. See adjacent article.*

Large Artery Bleeding

If a large artery is damaged, bleeding may be severe. The blood spurts from the wound in a pulsating stream and several pints may be lost in a few minutes. *This is the type of bleeding which can endanger life, but is fairly rare. See Pressure Points page 341.*

Severe Arterial Bleeding

Immediately apply direct pressure with the thumbs and fingers over that part of the wound from which the blood is coming. Continue pressure, while a suitable pad and bandage is being found, will help to reduce the flow of blood pending the application of a pad and firm bandaging. *On the very rare occasion when these measures fail, and it is obvious that the wound is continuing to bleed, a tourniquet should be applied. See article on Tourniquets page 340.*

Effects of Severe Bleeding

When bleeding is severe, or moderate and continuous, the whole body is affected. The presence of internal bleeding can be assumed by observing symptoms, as indicated below, without any blood being visible.

Symptoms of Severe Bleeding

The immediate effect is shock. With additional bleeding the shock gradually becomes worse and eventually the patient becomes very restless, aimlessly moving his arms and legs. Breathing becomes hurried and labored, with sighing or gasping for air. Check the pulse every 15 minutes to judge the amount of bleeding. If the pulse rate continues to increase this indicates continued bleeding.

Bleeding from Artery
It sprays and is bright red.

Capillary
A slow steady oozing.

Flow from Vein
Steady dark red or reddish-blue flow.

Intensity of blood flow from a wound depends upon the source of the blood.

FIRST AID FOR COMMON BLEEDING

The following is an outline of first aid *but medical attention should be obtained immediately.*

- If bleeding is from the *area of the mouth* the victim should be laid on his side or sit with his head tilted forwards, so that the blood does not drain into his mouth or nose and choke him.
- Lay the victim down and raise the bleeding area or limb (as long as it is not fractured) above the level of the heart. This might slow or stop the flow of the blood.
- The victim with a wound on one side of his body should be laid with the wound on the upper side.
- Remove the clothing from the spot that is bleeding. Stop the bleeding by applying a sterilized dressing or clean padding *large enough to cover* the wound. Firmly apply a bandage over the dressing. *The bandage should not be too tight as the area of the wound area will swell during the next few hours.*
- With *severe bleeding*, the bandage must *initially be tight*. Once the bleeding subsides cut through the layers of the original bandage (without disturbing the wound) and apply a new loose bandage *over the original.*
- If blood soaks and seeps through the original bandage *do not remove the original bandage* but place a larger dressing *over* the original. Apply the new bandage *on a larger area* over new dressing but apply it *more firmly* than the first bandage. More layers might be required.
- Immobilize the injured part with a sling and splints if necessary.
- Victim might be in shock if the wound is severe and there has been loss of blood.

Heart

BULLET OR METAL PROJECTILE INJURY

Wounds caused by a bullet or metal fragment may have an exit wound which is usually larger than the entry wound. The projectile on passing through the body might have broken a bone, cut an artery or damaged a vital organ. The projectile might hit a bone and deflect into the body, causing internal damage, making it difficult to remove the fragment. *See a doctor.*

FIRST AID FOR WOUNDS

If no qualified person is present see a doctor.

- Never wash the wound. Except in a case of a dog bite (page 324) also see article on acid burns (page 342).
- Never try to remove metal fragments or pieces of glass unless they are superficial and can be easily lifted out.
- Never put antiseptic into the wound.
- Never touch the wound with your fingers.
- Remove any superficial fragments of metal or glass only with gauze or a dressing covering your finger and thumb, or with sterilized forceps if readily available.
- Never leave the wound exposed to the air.

CONTROLLING EXTERNAL BLEEDING

Pressure Over Wound

Direct pressure can be applied with the fingers or hand or by using a bandage that is wound fairly tightly. This tight winding should be only temporary, to reduce the flow of the blood, and then should be cut (to reduce the pressure) bot *not removed* as the wound will be disturbed. Place a new bandage *over* first.

Pressure on a Major Artery

Pressure is applied on a major artery leading to the wound. This will slow the rate of flow of the blood but medical assistance will be required to close the cut. *See Pressure Point page 341.*

Apply a Tourniquet

A tourniquet is rarely necessary and can cause harm to injured extremities. *See Tourniquet page 340.*

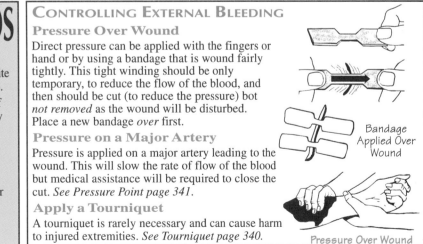

Bandage Applied Over Wound

Pressure Over Wound

TOURNIQUET (CONSTRICTIVE BANDAGE)

Note: Tourniquets are rarely required and should only be used in extreme cases as:

a. *Three successive dressings and firm bandages have been applied and the bleeding has not stopped.*

b. *A location where a firm bandage cannot be applied or for special wounds. An example of a special wound would be an open bone fracture.*
See Pressure Point page 341.

c. *When a limb has been amputated.*

You can use a bandage, a large folded handkerchief, strip of strong cloth, a belt, a piece of rope or rubber tubing. It is applied between the wound and the heart. It can be placed around the upper arm or thigh, tight enough to compress the main artery and control the bleeding. The following must be observed:

Rule 1. A tourniquet should be just tight enough to control the bleeding. If too tight it may damage the nerves and tissue in the limb and may cause unnecessary pain. *A finger should be able to pass between the bandage and the skin.*

Rule 2. A tourniquet must be *loosened after 15 minutes* as permanent damage and gangrene of the limb, may result. If additional bleeding occurs retighten the bandage for an additional 15 minutes. Gradually loosen the tourniquet to see if bleeding has stopped or what *minimal pressure* is required. If bleeding has stopped, then loosen the tourniquet but keep it in place so that it can be reapplied.

Rule 3. Do not cover a tourniquet with clothing, bandage or splint as it might be forgotten. Keep the limb cool and exposed. A blanket can be placed on the victim.

To tighten tourniquet.

To keep tourniquet in place.

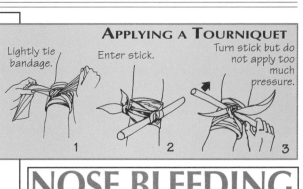

APPLYING A TOURNIQUET

Lightly tie bandage. — 1

Enter stick. — 2

Turn stick but do not apply too much pressure. — 3

NOSE BLEEDING

Bleeding is common after a blow to the nose or if you have a head cold and are continually blowing your nose. It is rarely dangerous.

Treatment: Keep your head up and sit upright, preferably in a cool spot or in a draft. Do not breath through the nose but use the mouth. The nose can be pinched below the nose bone until the bleeding stops. *Avoid blowing your nose.*

BLACK EYE

A "black eye" occurs when the eye area has been bruised. The white of the eye might be partially red from a broken blood vessel. The eyelid and surrounding area may swell so that the eye cannot be opened. This condition will clear with time.

Treatment: As the black eye is a bruise there are no preventive measures. To reduce the pain and the swelling use an ice compress held in place with a bandage. Remove the compress after six hours or you might cause a minor local trench foot like condition. *See Trench Foot article.*

Make sure that your anti-tetanus shot is up to date especially if you live in the country.

The incubation period is usually 2 to 8 days and sometimes up to 3 weeks. Tetanus (Lock-Jaw) is a disease that enters the body through a wound or scratch. The germ, a microbe that is usually found in soil fertilized with manure, is common in nature. Tetanus is characterized by painful muscular contractions and spasms starting in the jaw and neck muscles and soon spreads to the back and upper body. Muscular spasms become more frequent with the victim having a sardonic grin during an attack. If untreated exhaustion, heart failure, and death might occur or the spasms become less frequent and the victim recovers. The mortality rate is high. *Get medical help immediately.*

CANNED FOOD

Examine all tin cans that have been stored. If storing tin cans, date them and consume the oldest first.

The ends of untainted tin cans are usually concave or flat. When you press the end and it moves in and out this means that the can has lost its vacuum and should be thrown away. When a tin is opened and the contents has an abnormal color and/or an unusual odor do not consume the contents. When the ends bulge out (convex) *suspect a problem of decomposition. Do not eat.*

TREATING A BLISTER

If a blister is in a non abrasive area let it gradually disappear. If you are hiking and a large blister forms in an area where it will break.

- Clean blister area with soap and water.
- Puncture edge of blister with a sterilized needle. *Sterilization page 343.*
- Press liquid out through the puncture point by gradually pressing the fluid towards the puncture point.
- Apply a sterile gauze pad and adhesive.
- Replace the gauze pad if it gets wet from the blister liquids.

HEAD INJURIES

Head injuries should not be ignored.

Swelling after a Bump

Apply an ice pack to reduce swelling and find the reason for the swelling. *See a doctor.*

Bleeding Scalp Wound

Much blood goes to the head to maintain the brain so that head wounds bleed profusely. Raise the head and shoulders to slow the bleeding and place a sterile dressing over the wound. When bleeding has slowed wrap a bandage around the head to keep the bandage in place. Strands of hair can be tied together to act as a suture. *See Pressure Points page 341. See a doctor.*

CHEST WOUND

Superficial Wound: If minor can be treated as a regular wound.

Deep Wound: A deep wound might be *penetrating the lungs and require specialized immediate first aid. A lung penetrating wound will produce the sound of air coming from the lungs.* The victim will be in a state of shock and find breathing very difficult. Try to prevent the air from passing through the wound. *See a doctor immediately.*

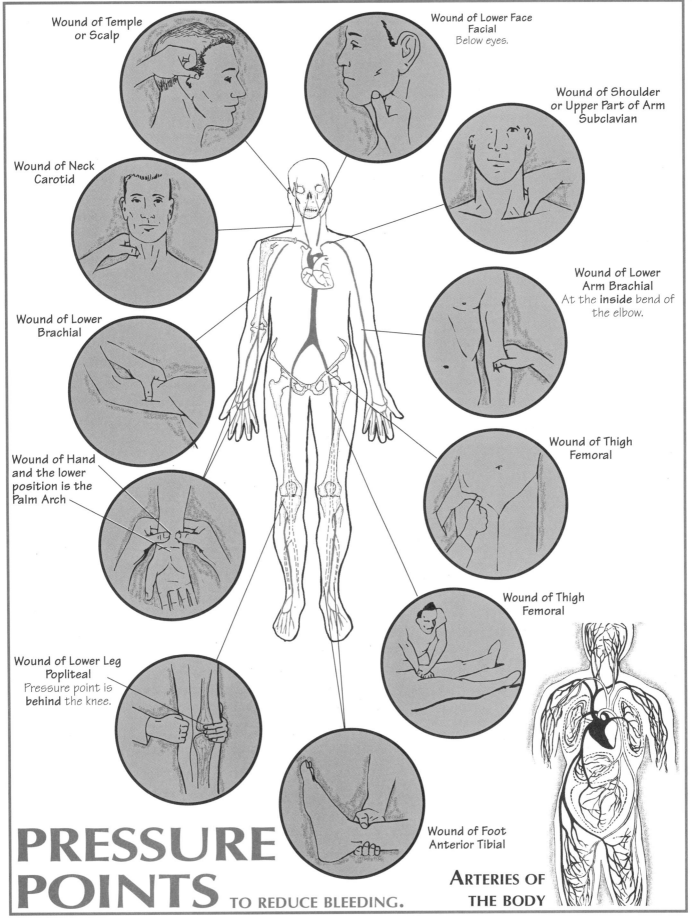

Wound of Temple
or Scalp

Wound of Lower Face
Facial
Below eyes.

Wound of Shoulder
or Upper Part of Arm
Subclavian

Wound of Neck
Carotid

Wound of Lower
Arm Brachial
At the **inside** bend of
the elbow.

Wound of Lower
Brachial

Wound of Hand
and the lower
position is the
Palm Arch

Wound of Thigh
Femoral

Wound of Thigh
Femoral

Wound of Lower Leg
Popliteal
Pressure point is
behind the knee.

Wound of Foot
Anterior Tibial

PRESSURE
POINTS TO REDUCE BLEEDING.

**ARTERIES OF
THE BODY**

BURNS

Scalds of the Mouth and Throat
If some ice is available, give the victim several pieces to suck on or drinks of ice cold water. Get medical attention.

TREATMENT OF BURNS

See a doctor. This article is an outline.

- Minimize the effects of the shock by giving fluids, about half a cup at a time as more might cause vomiting.
- A burn is considered to be an open wound and infection should be prevented. To prevent infection apply sterile dressing to cover the burned area before the victim is moved.
- Do not attempt to pull off any clothing that may be stuck. Use scissors to cut it away, but leave the pieces that are stuck.
- Try not to touch the surface of a burn with your fingers.
- Do not break or prick blisters.
- Reassure the patient, and treat with extreme gentleness.

BURNS FROM ACIDS AND ALKALIS

Acids or Alkalis can cause a severe burn:

- Immediately flood the affected area with water even without removing the clothing. The water should be flushed gently not to affect the damaged skin.
- Keep on flushing with water while removing the contaminated clothing.
- Continue washing injury with water.
- *Get medical attention.*

Acid burns: wash with a one tablespoonful to one pint of water solution of sodium bicarbonate.

Alkali burns: wash with a solution of one unit of vinegar to six units of water.

When camping the most probable cause of a burn would be acid from a car battery or from cooking fluids. See Eye Cleaning & Poison articles.

CLOTHING ON FIRE

- Do not allow the victim to run around as this will provide additional oxygen for the flames.
- Lie the victim down on the ground immediately *with the flames on the upper side.*
- Pour water on the victim and thoroughly soak the clothing. *Do not do this if the victim is saturated with gasoline, oil or paraffin.*
- If water is not available smother the flames with a blanket, rug, coat, etc. Wrap it around the victim to smother the flames, pressing the material against the body, to limit the access of air.
- Do all you can to prevent the victim's face and hands from being burned and take care of your own.
- When the flames have been put out, *get medical attention. A qualified person should give treatment for shock. See Forest Fire Chapter.*

ELECTRICAL BURNS

Electrical burns do not look too serious but a large area of tissue under a small skin wound can have been destroyed.

Electrical burns usually leave *two spots* on the body, one where the current enters and one where the current exits. Both spots should be covered with a dry, sterile dressing and the victim should be *taken to the hospital immediately*. Electrical burns can occur when power lines fall, from lightning, home wiring, etc.

FALLEN POWER LINES

Power lines by themselves are not dangerous as long as the object touching them is *not* grounded. You can see birds sitting on power lines and not getting a shock. If something touches a "hot" power line *and at the same time* is standing on the wet ground he **is** "grounded", the circuit is completed and the electricity will flow through the person giving him an electric shock.

- Do not touch electrical equipment while standing on wet ground. Do not remove the third prong (ground) on a plug. Make sure that the "ground" in a wall receptacle is active.
- Be careful when digging in an area where there are buried power lines as a metal shovel might cut through the insulation and produce an electric shock.
- Be careful when cutting a live wire as the flash from the ends of the wire, when it flips free or because of the wire cutters, may cause severe burns.

FALLEN POWER LINES ON A CAR

If a power line has fallen across a car *assume* that the line is live. The rubber tires of the car form a satisfactory insulation between the fallen wire and the ground. The people in the car are safe as long as they do not touch the metal frame of the car and the ground - *at the same time*. By touching the ground and car at the same time a person would *bypass* the insulation of the car's tires. The person should stay in the car if help is on its way. If the car is on fire, in a dangerous location, or if no help is on the way then the occupants can jump clear of the car making sure that they are *not touching the car and the ground at the same time.*

TRAVELER'S DIARRHEA

The most common cause is the Escherichia coli bacteria. This bacteria is in your digestive tract and helps your intestines in the digestion process. Foreign strains of the bacteria can give you diarrhea by producing a toxin that prevents your intestines from absorbing the water ingested in the form of fluid and food. This will cause runny stools and you might feel nausea, possibly have cramps and a slight fever. Drink a lot of water as it will help you *avoid dehydration.*

How to Avoid Traveler's Diarrhea

- When traveling in underdeveloped areas avoid uncooked vegetables, salads, fruits that cannot peel, under cooked meat, raw shellfish and ice cubes made from local water.
- Dishes and cutlery have to be cleaned with purified water.
- Drink carbonated water that has been sealed in bottles or cans.
- *See Finding Water and Summer Hiking Chapters* on the purification of water.
- Drink acidic drinks like orange juice and colas as these will reduce the bacteria count.

If you have any medical side effects (e.g. red or black stools, fever, abdominal bloating, vomiting) immediately see a doctor. A severe diarrhea can cause excessive fluid and salt loss. This can lead to dehydration, electrolyte imbalance, shock , and possible death.

Natural Remedies if you have no alternatives:

Clay: Type of clay containing kaolin can be eaten. It is found on river banks.

Ash: Brew ash from a fire or burned, pulverized bone fragments into a tea.

Tannic acid: Use a tea with tannic acid as it will stop muscular contractions of the intestines. Brew a tea of acorns, the bark of oak trees or other hardwoods.

Blackberry root: Boil as a tea. *See Edible Plant Chapter.*

Plantain: Make into a tea as the leaves are strongly astringent.

Apple peels: Cook the peels and drink the liquid.

Blueberries: Five or six blueberries will cure diarrhea. If you eat too many blueberries you will become constipated.

FOREIGN BODY IN EYE

Sand, dust, bits of wood can be blown or rubbed into your eye. There is a danger that the particle might scratch the surface or become embedded in the eye. *Do not rub the eye.*

The following procedure should be done by a qualified person.

- Wash your hands and inspect the eye.
- If the object is below the lower lid: Pull down the lower eyelid and ask the patient to look up. If a foreign body can be seen, gently brush it with a corner of a piece of clean linen or paper tissue, towards the inner angle of the eye and then out of the eye. Do not use dry cotton as it might leave some particles behind.
- If the object is below the upper lid see the adjacent box.
- If particle can not be found by the above procedures shine a light at different angles to check the cornea. If you see the particle wash the eye with clean water. *Do not touch eye.* If the particle does not come off it might be embedded in the cornea. Should all attempts fail, keep the eyes* covered, with a dry dressing, and *obtain medical assistance as soon as possible. (*both eyes move when looking)*

Gently grasp the lashes of the upper lid...

OBJECT BELOW THE UPPER EYE LID

This procedure should be done by a qualified person.

With the patient looking down, gently grasp the lashes of the upper lid and pull the lid forward so that tears or to wash out the particle.

If this does not help pull the upper lid forward, push the lower lid under it, and the lashes of the lower lid brushing the under surface of the upper lid, may dislodge the particle. Try this once or twice. Have the patient blow his nose, this sometimes shifts the foreign body to where it can be seen and removed.

— Match stick with a cotton tip.

If this has not removed the foreign body, place the patient on a seat. Ask the patient to look down. Place a dull stick, match stick, narrow spoon handle or similar object horizontally on top of the upper lid. Take the upper eyelashes with the finger and thumb of your other hand and pull them upwards over the match. This turns the upper lid inside out, and you should hold it in this position while you remove the foreign body. Gently replace the lid in position by pulling down on the eye lashes.

WASHING THE EYE

If a chemical enters the eye flush the eye immediately with large quantities of water. Keep flushing for at least twenty minutes especially if it is an alkali in the eye. Place a soft bandage over the eye and *see a doctor immediately.*

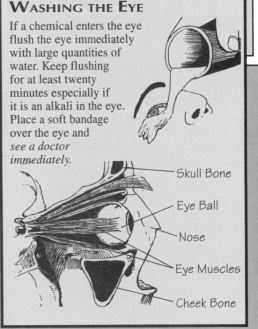

- Skull Bone
- Eye Ball
- Nose
- Eye Muscles
- Cheek Bone

TO REMOVE A SPLINTER

- Wash your hands and area around the splinter with soap and water.
- Sterilize a needle and tweezers. *To sterilize boil in water for 10 minutes or heat until red over a gas flame, match, or electric burner. Remove the black carbon deposit with sterile gauze.*
- Slide the needle under the splinter to raise it, and remove it with the tweezers.
- Wash the area.
- If the skin is infected do not remove the splinter but see a doctor.
- If the splinter is very deep see a doctor.

If a doctor is not available and the splinter has infected the area, soak in warm water until the infection drains. The splinter surfaces and is easy to remove.

To Sterilize a Needle
To sterilize a needle boil it in water for 10 minutes or heat until red over a gas flame, match, or electric burner. Remove the black carbon deposit with sterile gauze.

To Treat Scrapes
After a scrape occurs: Remove all splinters and foreign objects using clean tweezers. Wash the wound with warm water and soap. Cover the wound with sterile dressing. If an infection occurs see a doctor.

PORCUPINE QUILLS

These quills can become embedded in your skin. As with a fish hook the quills are barbed and can only travel one way. If a quill is left in the body, with muscle action, it can migrate through the host part and reemerge on the other side. If a vital organ is on its route this travel through the body can be fatal. To remove quills pull them out, as close to the skin as possible, with a pair of pliers.

Pull them out straight without wiggling back and forth so that the tip is not broken off.

Quill is hollow.

Microscopic barbs are on dark part of the quill.

Constipation is the difficulty in passage or irregularity of the bowel movement. Side affects can include stomach discomfort, headache, loss of appetite, discomfort and listlessness.

A change of diet or environment might result in temporary irregularity. It can be caused by an irregular life-style. It might indicate the onset of appendicitis if there is abdominal pain or fever. *See a doctor.*

Treatment

- Porridge, bread, fruit, or vegetables gives bulk to the stool. Find a vegetable or fruit that might help you establish a regular stool, possibly carrots, prunes etc.
- See the chapter on *Edible Plants* for more ideas.
- Drinking a cup hot water might help.
- Avoid the regular use of purgative as they will lose their effectiveness.
- If the constipation is not relieved by these measures, then it may be necessary to use a soap and water enema. *See a doctor.*

CONSTIPATION

POISONS

Treatment must be prompt as time is vital. This Section on Poisons is an outline as to possible treatment. Additional complications such as severe shock, requirement of artificial respiration, etc. might be present. A qualified individual should be involved in any action. *Get medical help.*

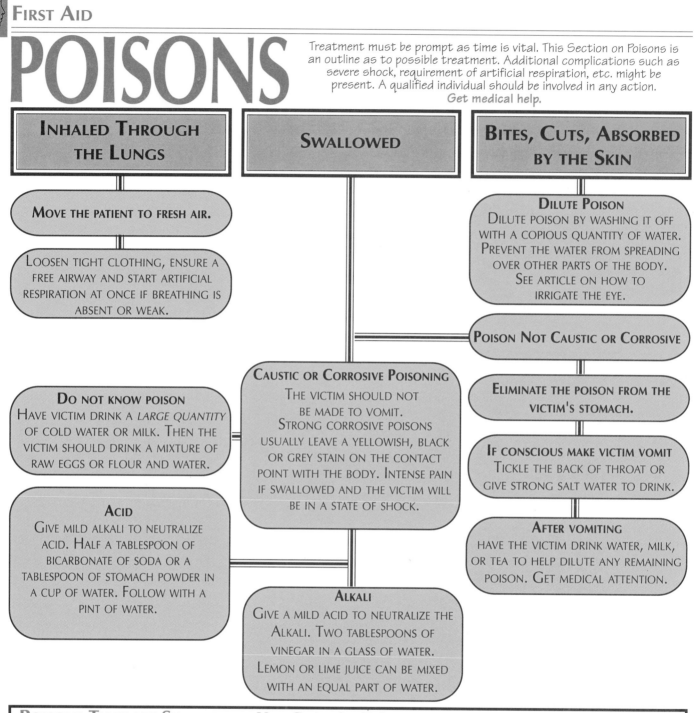

INHALED THROUGH THE LUNGS

MOVE THE PATIENT TO FRESH AIR.

LOOSEN TIGHT CLOTHING, ENSURE A FREE AIRWAY AND START ARTIFICIAL RESPIRATION AT ONCE IF BREATHING IS ABSENT OR WEAK.

DO NOT KNOW POISON
HAVE VICTIM DRINK A *LARGE QUANTITY* OF COLD WATER OR MILK. THEN THE VICTIM SHOULD DRINK A MIXTURE OF RAW EGGS OR FLOUR AND WATER.

ACID
GIVE MILD ALKALI TO NEUTRALIZE ACID. HALF A TABLESPOON OF BICARBONATE OF SODA OR A TABLESPOON OF STOMACH POWDER IN A CUP OF WATER. FOLLOW WITH A PINT OF WATER.

SWALLOWED

CAUSTIC OR CORROSIVE POISONING
THE VICTIM SHOULD NOT BE MADE TO VOMIT. STRONG CORROSIVE POISONS USUALLY LEAVE A YELLOWISH, BLACK OR GREY STAIN ON THE CONTACT POINT WITH THE BODY. INTENSE PAIN IF SWALLOWED AND THE VICTIM WILL BE IN A STATE OF SHOCK.

ALKALI
GIVE A MILD ACID TO NEUTRALIZE THE ALKALI. TWO TABLESPOONS OF VINEGAR IN A GLASS OF WATER. LEMON OR LIME JUICE CAN BE MIXED WITH AN EQUAL PART OF WATER.

BITES, CUTS, ABSORBED BY THE SKIN

DILUTE POISON
DILUTE POISON BY WASHING IT OFF WITH A COPIOUS QUANTITY OF WATER. PREVENT THE WATER FROM SPREADING OVER OTHER PARTS OF THE BODY. SEE ARTICLE ON HOW TO IRRIGATE THE EYE.

POISON NOT CAUSTIC OR CORROSIVE

ELIMINATE THE POISON FROM THE VICTIM'S STOMACH.

IF CONSCIOUS MAKE VICTIM VOMIT
TICKLE THE BACK OF THROAT OR GIVE STRONG SALT WATER TO DRINK.

AFTER VOMITING
HAVE THE VICTIM DRINK WATER, MILK, OR TEA TO HELP DILUTE ANY REMAINING POISON. GET MEDICAL ATTENTION.

POISONS THAT ARE SWALLOWED

These affect the digestive track and will cause vomiting, abdominal pain, and diarrhea. These poisons can be poisonous berries, contaminated food, poisonous mushrooms, etc..

Some swallowed poisons might have a delayed reaction as they will only act after they have been absorbed by the blood and then affect the nervous system. Some of these poisons can be sedative tablets, excessive alcohol, and cyanide.

Treatment

Get medical help. The following is only an outline.

Prompt treatment is essential. Find the source of the poison. If the victim is conscious he might indicate the source. If unconscious, there might be some telltale signs: a bottle, partially eaten food, etc. which might indicate the source of poisoning. *Telephone hospital poison unit for help.*

Non-Corrosive Poisons

It is essential to immediately get the poison out of the victim's stomach. *This should not be done with corrosive poisons.*

Encourage Vomiting: If conscious tickle the back of the throat with the fingers. A mixture of two tablespoonfuls of salt in a glassful of warm water can induce vomiting.

After vomiting have the victim drink water, milk, or tea to help dilute any remaining poison. *Get medical attention.*

Corrosive Poisons

The victim should not be made to vomit.

Strong corrosive poisons usually leave a yellowish, black or grey stain on the contact point with the body. If it has been swallowed the pain will be intense and the victim will be in a state of shock.

For corrosive poisons:

Do not know poison: Have victim drink a *large quantity* of cold water or milk. Then the victim should drink a mixture of raw eggs or flour and water.

Acid: Give the victim a mild alkali to neutralize the acid. This mild alkali can be half a tablespoon of bicarbonate of soda in a cup of water or a tablespoonful of stomach powder in a cup of water. Follow this with a pint of water.

Alkali: Give the victim a mild acid to neutralize the Alkali. This can be two tablespoons of vinegar in a glass of water. Lemon or lime juice can be mixed with an equal part of water.

LITTERS

Chair Used as a Litter

The patient can be attached to a chair with a belt. The carrier at the head position should first tilt the chair back. The carrier at the leg position can bend his knees, keeping his body straight, and then pick up the legs of the chair.

Positioning Victim for Lifting

The first step in manual carries is to position the victim who is to be lifted. If victim is conscious, tell him how he is being positioned and transported. This will reduce his fear of movement and gain his cooperation. It may be necessary to roll the victim onto his abdomen or his back depending upon the position in which he is lying and a particular method of carry to be used.

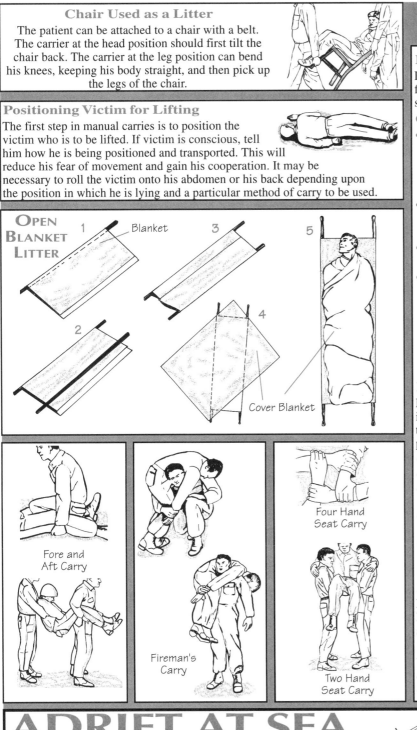

OPEN BLANKET LITTER

1 Blanket
2
3
4 Cover Blanket
5

Fore and Aft Carry

Fireman's Carry

Four Hand Seat Carry

Two Hand Seat Carry

Litter

Litter bearers are ordinarily grouped into squads of four for carrying patients. The fatigue of long carries should be shared by the group of at least four people.

General Rules for Litter Bearers

- In moving a patient, the litter bearers must make every movement deliberately and as gently as possible. The command *STEADY* should be used to prevent undue haste and other irregular movements.
- The rear bearers should watch the movements of the front bearers and time their movements with them to insure easy and steady progress.
- The litter should be kept as level as possible at all times even when crossing obstacles such as ditches.
- As a general rule, *the patient should be carried on the litter feet first except when going uphill or upstairs when the head should be forward.* If the patient has a fracture of the lower extremity (or for any reason beneficial to the patient), he should be carried uphill or upstairs feet foremost and downhill or downstairs head foremost to prevent the weight of the body from pressing upon the injured part.

Improvising a Litter

Many objects and materials may be used to make improvised litters in an emergency. The usual way to make a litter is with a blanket, shelter tent, or poncho and poles about 7 feet (2 m) long.

Open Blanket Method

- The blanket is spread on the ground.
- One pole is laid across the center of the blanket which is then folded over it.
- The second pole is placed across the center of the new fold.
- The blanket is folded over the second pole as over the first.
- The free end of the blanket is attached.

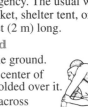

Jacket Method

Fold two or three shirts or field jackets so that the lining is on the outside. Button them up with the sleeves inside. Pass a pole through each sleeve.

Flat Surface Method

Use any flat-surfaced object of suitable size, such as cots, window shutters, doors, benches, ladders, boards, or poles tied together. Pad the litter if possible.

ADRIFT AT SEA

Adrift for a Short Time

People adrift in lifeboats or rafts need warmth, cover from the sun and ocean spray, dry clothing, water, and some food. If survivors had been immersed for a short time in relatively warm water they should be given a warm bath and dry clothing.

Adrift for Many Days

If survivors experienced a shortage of food and water, they will be weak, demoralized, and at some stage of hypothermia if exposed to the elements. Treat for hypothermia if required (see page 327). Give them warm drinks which they should not drink too fast as they might vomit. Food in the form of soup and bread should be given sparingly. Any food should be easy to digest.

Fuel Oil Contamination

Swallowing fuel oil and salt water might produce vomiting and coughing from oil and water in the stomach and lungs. Eyes might be sore form the oil and salt water mixture. These problems will usually clear up. To clean the skin take a bath with a mild soap. Treat the eyes by applying some soft wax to the eyelids. Drink some warm milk with honey or sweet tea to help soothe the stomach. *Get medical attention especially if there are wounds.*

345

SEA SURVIVAL

LIFEBOAT AND RAFT AILMENTS

Ailments can develop because of exposure to saltwater, wind, sun, heat and cold, and shortage of water.

Salt Water Problems

Cracking skin: Skin gets covered with a fine layer of salt from salt water spray. To reduce this problem cover your skin with suntan lotion or soft paraffin wax. If exposed to direct sunlight do not use skin oils as baby oil or butter as you might get a severe sunburn.

Salt water boils: Prolonged salt water spray exposure might lead to salt water boils. Do not squeeze or prick them. Do not remove excess liquid from boils that burst. Bad looking boils should be covered with a dressing.

Lack of Drinking Water

Dry mouth: A common problem which can be relieved by rinsing your mouth with drinking water. You can suck a button or a piece of metal such as a coin. You can chew gum or grease the inside of the mouth with butter or fat.

Urination problems: Urination will be dark and possibly thick as not much water is being consumed. If there is difficulty in passing urine dangle your hand in the sea. This might be of some help.

Sun and Wind Exposure

Cracked and parched lips: These should be smeared with soft paraffin.

Cracked skin: Due to dryness from exposure to the sun and wind. Can be helped by rubbing soft paraffin wax on the skin.

Eye inflammation: Caused by sunburn, wind, fuel oil contamination, or sun glare. Apply soft paraffin wax to the upper and lower eyelids. Make some emergency slit sunglasses. *See Eskimo sunglasses.* These sunglasses will dramatically reduce the intensity of the sun's glare, the salt spray settling in the sensitive eye area, and reduce the drying action of the wind. Bandage eyes if painful and bloodshot.

Motion Sickness

Seasickness:

- A slight feeling of listlessness with a headache.
- A dry mouth.
- Sense of nausea in the stomach.
- Repeated vomiting due to the continual motion of a small boat. It might also have been caused by having swallowed oil or salt water. After severe vomiting lie down and keep warm.
- Feeling of wretchedness and mental depression.

Motion sickness is caused by the movement of the liquids in the inner ear that confuse the balance sensory devices producing a loss of balance and gastrointestinal disturbances. A victim should try to drink as much as possible (but not alcohol), and should eat a little at frequent intervals. *See a doctor who can prescribe seasickness tablet and use them before it occurs..*

Other Problems

Constipation: Bowel movements are limited because of the lack of food. Do not use laxatives.

Swollen legs: Swollen legs are common and will clear up after a few days on land.

Other ailments of exposure are Heat exposure, Frostbite, Hypothermia, Trench Foot, etc.

Moving a slightly injured person:

Piggy Back

A simple method of carrying a person is only useful when he is conscious and able to hold onto the carrier with his arms round the carrier's neck.

Two-Hand Seat Carry

The two-hand seat carry is used in carrying a patient for a short distance and to place a patient on a litter

Three Handed Seat

Handy method of carrying a patient. One arm and hand of one of the helpers is left free and can be used either to support an injured leg or as a back support for the patient.

Four Hand Seat Carry

Two men holding each other's wrists form a four hand seat with which to carry a patient. A conscious patient supports himself with his arms around the shoulders of his helpers. This carry is especially useful in transporting the patient with a head or foot injury for a moderate distance or to place him on a litter or vehicle.

Ordinary Man Handling

A patient may be carried by two helpers without a "seat" being formed by their hands. One arm of each helper supports the back and shoulders and their hands hold the patient's thighs. The patient can help to support himself with his hands on the shoulders of the helpers sufficiently firmly in place to prevent movement, but not so tightly as to interfere with the circulation of the blood in the limb.

Two-Man Supporting Carry

Can be used in transporting both conscious and unconscious patients. If a patient is taller than the bearers, it may be necessary for the bearers to lift the legs and let them rest on their forearms.

Two-Man Arms Carry

Useful in carrying a patient for a moderate distance and for placing a patient on a litter. To lessen fatigue, the bearers should carry the patient as high and close to their chests as possible. In extreme emergencies, when there is no time to obtain a litter, this manual carry is the safest one for transporting a patient with a back injury. Two additional bearers should be used to keep the patient's head and legs in alignment with his body.

Fore-and-Aft Carry

The fore-and-aft carry is a useful two-man carry for transporting the patient a long distance. One helper supports the patient under his arms and the other under his knees. The taller of the two bearers should position himself at the head of the patient. By altering this carry so that both bearers face the patient, it is also useful for placing a patient on a litter.

Fireman's Carry

The fireman's carry is one of the easiest ways for one individual to carry another. After the unconscious patient has been properly positioned, he is raised from the ground, supported and placed in the carrying position. *Page 345.*

TO CARRY AN INJURED PERSON

CHAPPED SKIN OR LIPS

Exposure to cold winds, salt water, or washing in cold weather without adequate drying of the skin, will cause cracks on the backs of the hands, the feet, lips, or ears. There is often much irritation and pain.

Treatment
Avoid this problem by using a cream or smearing the skin with soft paraffin and keeping warm. Wear the appropriate clothing to protect the skin.

ACKNOWLEDGMENTS

Author's Acknowledgments

This book is an accumulation of knowledge on camping, wilderness travel, and related information on the outdoors. Many sources were used including material from:

National Oceanic and Atmospheric Administration, Washington. *Weather photographs.*

National Aeronautic and Space Administration, Washington. *Space photographs.*

Environment Canada: *Weather Ways © 1952,* drawings adapted with the permission of the Minister of Supply and Services Canada 1995. *Pages 215, 216.*

Oxford University Press: *R. L. Peterson, The Mammals of Eastern Canada,* © 1966. Adapted illustrations of animals by permission. *Chapter 24.*

Environment Canada: *B. R. Morton, Native Trees of Canada,* © 1917 etc. Drawings adapted or used.

University of California Press: *Lawrence Klauber, Rattlesnakes: Their Habits, Life Histories, and Influence on Mankind. Abridged Edition. Editor: Karen McClung.* © 1982. Pages 282, 323.

I would like to thank Arlene Berg for a sharp eye, Michele Sweeney & Carole St. Denis for keyboarding, Charles Banal for vision, Agnes Paolella for the path, *Metric* Carolina Slowinska, and Mathilde Borsenberger for tickling frogs. Special thanks to Mireille Goulet for her insight and perspective.

Publisher's Acknowledgments

The publisher would like to thank the following companies for the use of illustrations and material from their promotional material:

Company	Products
Camping Gaz	*Camping stoves.*
Casio	*Watches.*
Coghlan's	*Selection of outdoor accessories.*
Eureka!	*Tents.*
G & V Snowshoes	*Snowshoes.*
Gerber	*Knives.*
Katadyn	*Water purifiers.*
Kelty	*Backpacks.*
Leatherman Tool	*Multipurpose tools.*
MAG Instrument	*Flashlights.*
MSR	*Camping stoves. Water purifiers.*
Opinel	*Knives.*
Optimus	*Camping accessories.*
Outbound Products	*Outdoor accessories, tents, and sleeping bags.*
PentaPure	*Water purifiers.*
Petzl	*Head lamps.*
Pur	*Water purifiers.*
Silva Compass	*Compasses.*
SOG	*Multipurpose tools.*
Swiss Army Brand	*Compasses.*
Wenger SA	*Swiss Army knives.*
World Famous Sales of Canada	*Outdoor accessories, tents, snowshoes, and sleeping bags.*

All *Brand Names* and *Trademarks* mentioned in this book belong to their respective companies. We regret if there has been an oversight and a company's name has been omitted from the above list.

INDEX

THE ULTIMATE OUTDOORS BOOK

The author traveling with his Volkswagen "Thing".

o 1　3 4 5　7 8 9
o 1 2 3 4 5 6 7 8 9
o 1 2 3 4 5 6 7 8 9
o 1 2 3 4 5 6 7 8 9
o 1 2 3 4 5 6 7 8 9
o 1 2 3 4 5 6 7 8 9

Photograph: Paul Tawrell
Subject: *Mathilde & Frog.*
Camera: Leica M4, Summicron 90mm f2.
Film: Ilford HP5 developed in Rodinal.